Preface

The Common Good, which Professor Thomas P. Neill contributes to *The Christian Democracy Series*, was designed as a companion volume or sequel to the American history, *Conceived in Liberty*. And such it is, although it also has the character of an independent, self-contained work. If the author presupposes on the part of the student or reader a general knowledge of the history of our country, he nevertheless has thought it wise to provide ample historical background explanation for the various topics that he treats.

His purpose is as clear as his language: to discuss in an expository manner the main political, economic, and social problems which, recurrently but in ever-changing forms and circumstances, confront American civil society and which must be resolved anew by each generation if our free institutions are to be nourished and preserved. Professor Neill has sought to make plain the real nature of these problems and to show fairly the opinions and arguments of those who propose to solve them. But he does not presume to know the solutions. It is enough for him to show how complex and difficult the problems are and how much must be known and understood before even an informed opinion on any one of them can be reached. Intellectual humility, accurate knowledge, willingness to listen to the opinons of others, the spirit of justice—all these are required by one who would think and act wisely. They abound in this book. It is an admirable example of the spirit that must animate us if we are to solve our problems consistently with Christian morality and the best traditions of our country.

ROSS J. S. HOFFMAN
EDITOR-IN-CHIEF, *The Christian Democracy Series*

20692

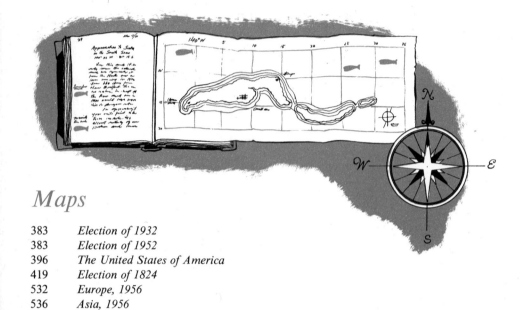

Maps

Charts and pictographs

Debates

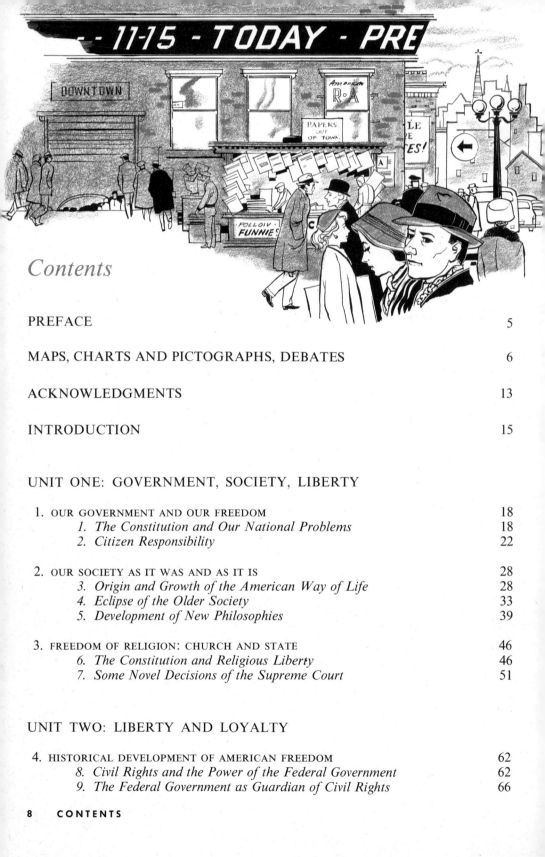

Contents

UNIT SEVEN: GOVERNMENT AND POLITICS

UNIT EIGHT: PROBLEMS OF FEDERAL, STATE, AND LOCAL GOVERNMENT

UNIT NINE: THE SIZE, COST, AND SERVICES OF GOVERNMENT

UNIT TEN: THE FOREIGN POLICY OF THE UNITED STATES

UNIT ELEVEN: FOREIGN TRADE, AID, AND PROCUREMENT

UNIT TWELVE: INTERNATIONAL ORGANIZATION FOR PEACE

Acknowledgments

No one possesses expert knowledge of every problem in American life. At most, one can have an expert scholar's knowledge of some few problems and a literate citizen's knowledge of the others. The worth of any book on national problems therefore depends almost as much on the quality of an author's friends and acquaintances as it does on himself. The author of this text feels himself extremely fortunate in having a group of scholarly, generous friends on whom he called frequently for advice. He has discussed various national problems with scholars, businessmen, and members of the learned professions, and to all of them he is deeply indebted. The author is also indebted in a way that only he can know to the last five Popes for their masterful teaching of Christian truths in many encyclicals and allocutions, and to the host of Catholic scholars who have explained and developed this teaching in Catholic journals.

In addition to these general acknowledgments, the author wishes to acknowledge his particular debt to the following:

Reverend Francis J. Corley, S.J., editor of Social Order, *who placed the resources of his journal and library at the author's disposal, read the manuscript and made innumerable and valuable suggestions, and who was always able to suggest the scholar or the journal helpful in solving a difficult problem.*

Professor John J. O'Brien of St. Louis University, with whom the author discussed problems of education, and who generously read the third unit in manuscript.

Professor Emerson Hynes of St. John's University, Collegeville, Minnesota, long a member of the National Catholic Rural Life Conference and a farmer by background and profession, for his helpful guidance and his critical reading of the chapters on farm problems and natural resources.

Professor Clement Mihanovich of St. Louis University for expert advice on social problems and for supplying the author with literature on these subjects.

Mr. William Herald of the Continental Can Company, a student of business, for long hours of discussion on the problems of free enterprise, and for reading the sixth unit.

Professors Paul G. Steinbicker, Henry J. Schmandt, and Carl Taeusch, all of St. Louis University, specialists in various areas of American government, for their many services and learned advice on matters contained in the last six units of the book.

Reverend John. F. Bannon, S.J., Professor Jasper W. Cross, and Reverend Martin Hasting, S.J., professors of American history at St. Louis University, for helpful suggestions relative to the history of the growth and development of national problems.

The author has been able to treat as wide a variety of problems as he did because he was encouraged to seek the aid and the guidance of all these experts. To them he is deeply grateful.

Writing the original manuscript is only the first part of manufacturing a useful textbook. In putting the material into effective form, the author relied on the experience and the judicious counsel of the following groups and persons:

The priests, sisters, and lay people who teach national problems in high school and who were in the author's seminars while this text was being written.

Reverend Harold McAuliffe, S.J., of Marquette University High School, and the members of the Social Science Division of the Milwaukee Archdiocesan Education Association, with whom the author was privileged to have two long sessions on teaching national problems in the Catholic high school at the Association's semiannual conference in February 1955.

Sister Mary Robert, C.D.P., of Divine Providence Academy in Pittsburgh, and members of the Pittsburgh Diocesan History Honor Society, who invited the author to discuss "American Problems and the Catholic Tradition" with them at their annual public lecture in March 1955.

Sister Mary Consulata, V.H.M., of Visitation Academy, St. Louis, Missouri, for critically reading large portions of the manuscript, for experimenting with it in her classes, and for having a number of her students give it a thorough "test-reading."

Sister Mary Lenore, S.C.L., of Hogan High School, Kansas City, Missouri, for generously providing similar services and for making several helpful basic suggestions.

Sister Mary Timothy, S.S.N.D., of Rosati-Kain High School, St. Louis, Missouri, for discussing various pedagogical problems connected with teaching national problems, and for testing the manuscript in the classroom.

Mr. George Wendell of Mercy High School, University City, Missouri, Mr. James Hartnett of De Andreis High School, St. Louis, Missouri, and Mr. Joseph Funk of DuBourg High School, St. Louis, Missouri, for performing similar services and for making excellent suggestions incorporated in the final revision of the manuscript.

Professor Clement Holland of St. Louis University for supplying word lists and other services to ensure the proper reading level of the text.

Reverend Stanley G. Mathews of Archbishop Stepinac High School, White Plains, New York, for preparing the study aids.

Mrs. Jeanne Posillico Hansen for copy-editing the manuscript and for preparing the index.

Mrs. Alma Reese Cardi for designing the book.

The author also wishes to express his gratitude to Mrs. Sarah White for her excellent typing of the manuscript, frequently at considerable inconvenience to herself. Finally, and most important, my thanks are due to my wife and children for their Christian patience during the period that this book was being written and revised.

Introduction

In the following pages we shall study a series of national problems. Some of these problems affect us personally. Others do not seem to touch us directly, but they obviously do affect some of our neighbors and acquaintances. Still other problems, like those of the immigrant, might seem to be very remote from our immediate interests. But as Americans we all have a direct, immediate interest in the welfare of American society, and we are desirous that justice be done to all classes and all individuals in our country. We all have a personal interest in solving the different problems we shall study in this book.

A study of national problems assumes a number of things. First, it assumes that we live in a free society, that we examine and study our institutions, that we are free to offer constructive criticism and to suggest improvements. Second, it assumes on the part of the student (1) rationality, (2) sincerity, (3) devotion to his country, his Church, his family, and the community in which he lives.

The assumption of rationality means that the student is able to gather information about some problem in order to understand its nature, its complexity, and its connection with other national problems. The author believes that the average high school senior is able to reason about American problems, that he can apply to them sound principles which he has found in his American heritage and in the Catholic tradition.

When we assume rationality on your part we do not assume that you are automatic reasoning-machines. Each of us is influenced in our thinking by our membership in a family, a community, an economic group—in short, by our "social milieu"—and we therefore approach the study of national problems with certain predispositions. Each of us should be aware of this fact and try, as best we can, to keep an open mind about the problems we study. We should admit the possibility of bias on our part, and we should seriously study all sides of a given question. If we do these things, we shall arrive at a fuller understanding of each problem, and our solution will be sounder than it would be if we did not overcome our prejudices.

The author assumes that high school seniors are both capable and desirous of thinking like adults. He believes that the principal difference between yourselves and older people is their wider experience and the wisdom that should result from it. For that reason we have not hesitated to discuss with you serious issues of public business and to refer you to books and articles written for thinking people. The author believes that after eleven years in school a student should be able to handle substantial and difficult material. This may be considered an "act of faith" by the author in the ability and the willingness of high school seniors to think seriously and work studiously at national problems—but it is an act of faith made knowingly as the result of working with typical seniors in high school.

How do we gather material so that we can know what our serious national problems are and how they can be solved? In a limited way, personal experience, observation, and conversation with others will give us some knowledge and some understanding of certain problems. But inevitably we must read, and read widely, to gather in the experience of Americans as a whole. We must consult encyclopedias and yearbooks and other sources of information. And, if we are wise, we shall read what experts on each problem have to say about it.

The perceptive student will soon learn to distinguish between fact and opinion. Frequently it is difficult to separate the two, but the good student will always be alert to distinguish them. And he will learn to evaluate opinion for what it is worth, depending on the qualifications of the person who has formed it.

American students are fortunate in having available a wealth of factual information. Every ten years the Bureau of the Census takes an exhaustive census of the nation. It publishes its accumulated information in many volumes available to you in libraries throughout the country. A digest of this information is published annually in the *Statistical Abstract of the United States.* Here you can find statistical information on the population, on national income, on the volume of exports and imports, and on a thousand other subjects. Also valuable from the factual standpoint are the various yearbooks published by the encyclopedias, the various almanacs, and other books of factual information. From these sources you can obtain most of the data you need to assemble about our national problems.

The reports of presidential or congressional commissions appointed to study various national problems contain both factual information and the considered opinion of the members of the commissions. Typical of these commissions are the President's Commission on Higher Education of 1948 and the famous Hoover Commission on Organization of the Executive Branch of the Government. The government printing office publishes the reports of these commissions, and they are available on request at nominal cost. Another official source of information, of course, is the *Congressional Record*—the official record of proceedings in Congress—in which the good student will find a great deal of information on almost any national problem he is studying.

The competent student will take advantage of work done on national problems by experts who have given more time and experience to each problem than the student can be expected to give. As seniors in high school you should know how to use the *Guide to Periodical Literature* and the corresponding *Guide to Catholic Periodical Literature.* Through these guides you can bring your information up to date on the various national problems you will study in the following pages. *America* and *Commonweal* are Catholic weekly journals that will keep you abreast of current developments. More valuable for thorough analysis of various national problems from the Catholic point of view are *Social Order* and *Catholic Mind.* The former journal is a monthly devoted to the study of just such subjects as we shall discuss in this book. *Catholic Mind* consists of reprints of what its editors consider the best and most important articles and speeches of the month. It is especially valuable for the "documentation" section, in which is published most of the important statements of the Pope. Also valuable are such magazines as *Current History, Time, Newsweek,* and *The United States News and World Report.*

UNIT ONE
Government, Society, Liberty

Chapter 1. Our Government and Our Freedom

1. THE CONSTITUTION AND OUR NATIONAL PROBLEMS

The first seven years of our nation's history as a union of independent states are known as "the critical period." There was danger at that time that the colonies which had won independence from Great Britain would not be able to form a lasting union and become a true nation. Leading citizens from the various states realized how serious the problem had become, so in 1787 they gathered in Philadelphia to discuss ways and means of forming "a more perfect union" of the states.

They meant to form a new federal government that would be strong enough to protect the property and the lives of its citizens. But at the same time they desired to safeguard citizens and property so that government itself could not violate them. They sought to solve that age-old problem of creating a government strong enough to protect its subjects without oppressing them. This is the problem expressed some seventy years later by Lincoln in these classic terms: "It has long been a grave question

whether any government, not too strong for the liberties of its people, can be strong enough to maintain its existence in great emergencies."

The men who met in Philadelphia tried to solve this dilemma by drawing up the American Constitution, perhaps the most remarkable political achievement in the history of the world. It has proved the world's longest-lasting written constitution. And it has succeeded—perhaps beyond its authors' hopes—in keeping a balance between the authority of the government and the freedom of the citizen. Under its protection Americans have prospered in freedom and multiplied.

This has been a remarkable achievement: The Constitution was devised for a country of less than four million people living in an area of less than one million square miles and pursuing a rather simple agricultural and commercial life. Today it is the supreme law over a land of more than 165,000,000 people organized in a highly complex civilization. The City of New York is today twice as populous as was the entire United States when the Constitution was adopted. The cost of maintaining that city's government and

municipal institutions is almost three hundred times as much as the federal government's entire expenditures for 1790. Today eleven cities in the United States have larger populations than had Virginia when it was the most populous and wealthiest state of the original Union.

Our Changing Problems. American population has changed noticeably since the Constitution was adopted. A century ago only 15 per cent of the population lived in cities. Today we are an urban country, a country of cities. Less than 15 per cent of the Americans live on farms, and another 20 per cent live in villages small enough to be called rural. Moreover, most of the people for whom the Constitution was adopted came from the British Isles. They had a similar political

The signing of the Constitution as painted by Howard Chandler Christy shows George Washington presiding in Philadelphia, September 17, 1787. There were some who later tried to have Congress censure the convention for exceeding its authority, but the Constitution was submitted to the states for ratification. (National Archives)

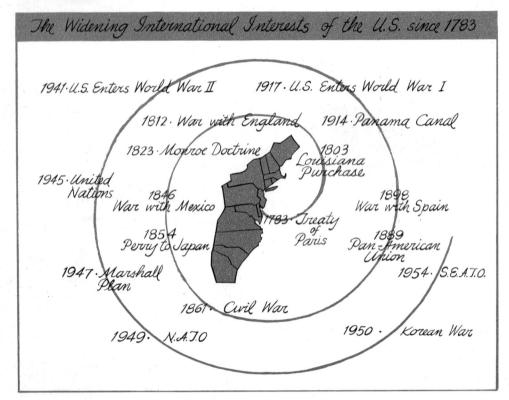

The Widening International Interests of the U.S. since 1783

1941 · U.S. Enters World War II   1917 · U.S. Enters World War I

1812 · War with England   1914 · Panama Canal

1823 · Monroe Doctrine   1803 Louisiana Purchase

1945 · United Nations   1846 War with Mexico   1898 War with Spain

1783 · Treaty of Paris

1854 Perry to Japan   1889 Pan-American Union

1947 · Marshall Plan   1954 · S.E.A.T.O.

1861 · Civil War

1949 · N.A.T.O.   1950 · Korean War

background, were of similar racial stock, and spoke the same language. The people who make up America today have come to our shores from all the countries of Europe, from Africa and neighboring American countries, and in smaller numbers from other parts of the world. They have enriched our land in many ways. But their assimilation, their becoming Americans, was a difficult process that remains one of our national problems today.

But it is not only—or even mainly—in population that America has changed since 1790. A revolution in transportation has brought California closer in point of time to New York than Philadelphia was a century ago. In Washington's time a round trip between Philadelphia and Boston took about three weeks. Many young people travel farther to see a basketball game in the evening and return home the same night than Thomas Jefferson could have traveled in four or

five days. News now travels with the speed of light, whereas in Jefferson's time it traveled on horseback, a few miles an hour.

Means of communication were so slow a century and a half ago that Andrew Jackson fought the Battle of New Orleans fifteen days after we had made the peace with the British that ended the War of 1812. Today the President's voice can be heard and his image seen simultaneously in millions of living rooms everywhere in America.

The Constitution was devised, then, for a small number of people living in a comparatively small corner of the globe. These United States were not then a major power in the world. They could develop their human and natural resources with little fear of interference from the rest of the world. Today America is the wealthiest and one of the largest countries in the world. We are a powerful nation whose interest and responsibility in world affairs have been forced upon it by the condition of the world after two world wars. For the first time in history, moreover, we are exposed to attack from foreign powers that need not land armies on our shores—a fact that creates problems of defense our ancestors never had to solve.

All these changes—in population, in way of life, in transportation and communication, in industry and mechanized culture—have created problems which the authors of the Constitution could never have imagined when they were establishing their more perfect union. How is it, then, that this remarkable document still serves us well? How can it provide solutions for these new problems? How can a legal question involving Jehovah's Witnesses' refusal to salute the flag be covered by a clause in the Constitution? How can it resolve a problem involving labor unions and business management?

This is because the basic problems of political and social life remain essentially the same for men of the Christian heritage wherever and whenever they live together in political society. The object of any such society is to enable men to achieve the good life. Its purpose is to help man live peaceably with his fellow men and to help develop the faculties with which he was endowed by his Creator.

Society must be so organized that man can develop himself as an individual and as a social person. Man is made to live among men. Human beings are formed by nature to live in community and cooperation. The basic problem of government, then, is to enable all its citizens to live in peace and freedom, to develop their faculties, to help one another. Government must therefore have sufficient power to accomplish this task. At the same time, it must be kept from violating the rights of the persons it has the duty to protect. Government must be strong, but not oppressive.

The authors of our Constitution did

The inherent right of the speaker to free speech and of the listeners to peaceable assembly is in evidence in this scene in a small southern town. (Standard Oil Co., N.J.)

exceptionally well in drawing the line between the power of the government and the inviolable rights of the people. They saw clearly what were the basic problems of government. And thus, because the problems remain essentially the same, the same Constitution has remained the supreme law of our land through almost two centuries of astounding changes in the American way of life. Although the basic problems remain the same, their concrete manifestations change. They assume new forms as society creates new institutions. Quartering troops in time of peace, for example, was a violation of property rights in 1789. In our day, property rights are more likely to be violated by excessive regulation of business or by unjust taxes.

The development of big cities has made the problem of men living together assume aspects undreamed of when the Constitution was adopted. Millions of

As thousands gather to watch major-league baseball, the ball park reflects these modern trends: crowded urban living, growing spectator interests, and the rise of professionalism. (New York Yankees)

people living in a few square miles create problems of health and sanitation that are not encountered on the farm or in the village. Freedom of assembly, to cite another instance, might assume dangerous aspects in times of epidemic. Freedom of speech and of movement must be regulated in such fashion as to protect the lives of millions of people huddled close together in a big city. The crowding together in a few square blocks of different national groups—Irish, Italians, Germans, Poles—puts a new face on the problem of men living peacefully together. Tolerance and mutual respect become more pressing problems when people crowd upon each other.

The development of modern industry, again, has modified drastically the basic problem of earning a living. The role of unions and of management in determining wages and hours of work is a problem of critical concern to every laboring man. The conditions of labor must somehow be such as not to degrade and dishonor the person working in the factory. The partial replacement of human labor by machines has made for shorter working days. It has also created the problem

of how to use so much leisure time; for the first time in history working people have faced this problem. The factory system, indeed, has so changed the relationship between worker and employer that their mutual responsibilities and rights must be thought out in terms that men never used a century ago.

Problems of national loyalty, again, are complicated by the strained international situation which has developed since the conclusion of World War II. They are intensified by the development of what is called the secularist mentality, which attempts to solve man's problems without taking God and His laws into consideration. The need for national unity has created new difficulties with respect to freedom of speech and even of religion. These are problems not easily solved.

2. CITIZEN RESPONSIBILITY

The problem of the individual's developing his faculties has taken on a completely different aspect in the last century. One hundred years ago America was still a country of self-reliant people. Through hard work an individual could earn his living, educate himself, and develop his talents for his own and his fellow men's welfare. Today an individual must struggle valiantly to maintain any independence of thought or of action. The means of forming public opinion—radio, television, movies, newspapers, even schools —all tend toward such standardization that they create something like a mass mind. To maintain independence of judgment and resist becoming absorbed in the mass mind is a hard problem facing each individual citizen. In the face of it the young citizen is apt to feel helpless. He is likely to surrender political decisions to the professional politician and to devote all his energy to earning a living and enjoying his leisure time.

This is the most dangerous result that can come about from the complexity of modern life. It is this very attitude that helped dictators gain absolute control over various European peoples before World War II. It is an easy attitude for the young citizen to take. But it is a wrong attitude. It is based on a misconception of his role as a citizen in our American society. Most Americans have consistently taken an active interest in their government and have felt a personal responsibility for its conduct.

Healthy social conditions can be maintained in America and the government can be well conducted only when citizens understand that they have the power to improve the society in which they live. Because there are so many million voters, it is easy for a citizen to evade this responsibility in his own mind. But he is morally responsible for the vote he casts—or does not cast. He also has a duty, as a social person, to influence his fellow citizens according to his own well-formed convictions. In our country each citizen has a share in voting for those who hold government offices, and each also owes obedience to his government.

To take seriously the responsibility of citizenship is an obligation we must fulfill to preserve the decent society our forefathers created for us. If eternal vigilance is the price of liberty, eternal diligence is the price of good government.

A Good Citizen	A Bad Citizen
Considers all points of view	Is intolerant in his attitudes
Exercises his civil rights	Is indifferent to his duties
Has a genuine interest in his community	Is self-centered in his interests

a. To vote for a candidate place "X" in the rectangular space at the left of the name of such candidate.

b. If you tear, soil, deface, or erroneously mark this ballot, return it to the precinct election officers and obtain another ballot.

USE "X" ONLY IN MARKING BALLOT

For Mayor	For Councilman-at-Large
(Vote for not more than one)	*(Vote for not more than three)*
JOHN C. JAWORSKI Democrat	**ROBERT A. EWERS** Republican
JOHN J. PAPPAS Republican	**EARL R. FRANK** Republican
For President of Council *(Vote for not more than one)*	**DAVID E. MOWREY** Republican
STANLEY T. FITZGERALD Republican	**EDWARD F. NOVACK** Democrat
JOHN A. REPKO Democrat	**JAMES S. PAROBEK** Democrat
For Auditor *(Vote for not more than one)*	**JOSEPH PETROSKY** Democrat
JOSEPH J. MITOCK Democrat	**For Member of Council 1st Ward** *(Vote for not more than one)*
PEARL T. TROTTER Republican	**PETER J. DOBROSKY** Democrat
For Treasurer *(Vote for not more than one)*	**WILLIAM A. THOMAS** Republican
MAURICE C. BROWN Democrat	
NELLIE LOVE Republican	
For Solicitor *(Vote for not more than one)*	
EDWARD J. CONLEY Democrat	
JOSEPH C. ZIEBA Republican	

The local ballot tells a story of the "climate of opinion" even before the election. How certain persons are nominated for office is as important a reflection of the interest of the electorate as the vote itself.

Every citizen depends largely on good government for the practical enjoyment of his liberties. Continual interest and participation by all competent citizens, we may add, is the price of the best possible government. Participation in civil society is more than a burden. It is a good and necessary part of human living and development. Moreover, we should remember that the enactment and enforcement of good laws depend upon what we call "the climate of opinion"—the general temper of the people, which is the ultimate ruler of society and government. Each of us plays a part in making up this climate of opinion.

To play an effective role in helping to solve social and political problems, the young citizen must prepare himself in two principal ways. First of all, he must obtain correct standards by which to judge specific measures that will be continually presented to him as a voter and as a citizen of the community in which he lives. Thus he must know the nature of justice, the dignity of the human person, and the rights man possesses *as a man.*

Right reason—which is close to what we usually call good "common sense"—is the faculty of knowing the goodness or badness, the rightness or wrongness of things. It is an intellectual faculty. It does not judge by feeling or self-interest, but objectively, with reverence for truth, respect for tradition, and candid recognition of facts. The second source from which we obtain right standards of judgment are the three proper educational institutions of the home, the church, and the school. Especially in our earlier years do we rely on these authorities rather than on our own reasoning powers. As we grow older we tend to use our minds

Essential to the study of our national problems is an understanding of the fundamental principles necessary to their solution. Students in the Catholic high school have the advantage of being taught Christian principles as a matter of course. (St. Francis Preparatory School, Brooklyn, N. Y.)

more independently, and thus we come to understand the reasons behind the judgments we formerly accepted on authority. From the combination of these agencies and from his own right reason, the ordinarily capable, sincere young citizen will build a set of standards and attitudes by which he can measure the worth of various proposals on which he must pass judgment throughout his life.

In the second place, a good citizen must obtain correct information about any proposal submitted to his judgment. This is sometimes a simple matter, as, for example, whether a community needs and can afford a new school. At other times, however, it is difficult and complicated. Whether a new school should provide a course in manual training or in French, for example, depends on a large number of facts that must be gathered and balanced against each other: the occupational interests of the families that use the school, the facilities the school possesses for shop instruction, the availability of competent teachers, the wishes of the parents on the matter, and a host of other things. Whether a proposed bill to change our immigration law is a good bill depends not only on one's attitude toward immigration but on the bill's effect on our country's foreign relations, on the American labor situation, on the specific proposals as to which groups to admit or exclude, and many other such factors, which must be studied carefully by our national legislators.

Factual information comes from many sources, and it is only by experience that the American citizen learns how to gather it, how to separate the truth from the error, and how to judge the relative importance of each fact. Ordinarily, in a country with freedom of speech and press, one can rely on one's ability to approach close to the truth by reading several well-chosen papers and magazines and by listening to one or more competent radio and television reporters. Ultimately the library and specialized journals will provide the expert information one frequently needs to understand the more complicated social and political problems.

Finally, besides correct standards and the necessary information on which to base his judgments, the good citizen needs something that comes only from himself: the will to act on his information and to exert his influence in order to make justice prevail over injustice, truth over error, wisdom over folly. This will to act is based on the citizen's sense of personal responsibility for his government's conduct and a realization that he can play a part in forming public opinion and influencing public policy. It is only when a dominant portion of Americans are so inclined to act that our society can be healthy and our government assured of backing by an intelligent public opinion.

Conclusion. The problems discussed in the following pages are some of the more serious problems facing Americans today. They cannot be solved easily or perfectly, as a problem in geometry can be solved by one who understands the principles of that science. Indeed, it can be said that these problems are never finally and completely solved. At best we can achieve only a partial and a temporary solution. But this should not discourage us. Ever since the Constitution was adopted, Americans have been solving similar problems. That has been the American way, meeting and solving in some manner each problem as it arose. By working in this fashion our forefathers made and preserved a society that has never been perfect but has always been one in which most men can enjoy a good life, provide for their temporal welfare, and be free to seek the eternal destiny for which they were created. We must continue to find new solutions to the same old problems, new solutions made necessary by the changes always taking place in our society. The solution

Levittown, Pa., a housing development of 70,000, was built in the heart of a critical defense area. Economic planning, community organization, and the co-operation of individuals are essential to keep towns such as this from becoming ghost towns. (Levitt and Sons, Inc.)

of each problem creates new problems which must, in turn, be resolved in some fashion or other.

It is a mistake, then, to believe that we need only apply a few right principles in the correct way to achieve an ideal society. That is the mistake of the idealists who do not understand the effects of original sin. There will be social, economic, and political problems ten years from now, a century from now, and fifty centuries from now, if the world lasts that long. But it is also a mistake to believe we can afford to ignore our problems. The existence of problems and working at their solution are part of life. Moreover, by intelligent work we can solve many problems and make our society better.

The problems with which we are faced today can be understood only in their American setting. For they are not abstract, general problems like those of algebra or geometry. They are social and political problems that have developed out of American history. Because they are peculiar to us as the people inhabit-

ing this land, they can be understood only in the light of our history. Let us therefore quickly retrace a few of the principal lines of the American history you have studied in previous years. Then we can understand the peculiar turn taken in the middle of the twentieth century by the age-old problems of living together peaceably and getting along with other nations.

REVIEW

1. The Constitution and Our National Problems

A. What age-old problem concerning government faced the Founding Fathers at the Constitutional Convention?

B. Our Constitution is a most sagacious document. Giving several reasons, point out the truth of this statement.

C. What is the purpose of society? Why has the Constitution been able to meet the problems of society today as in 1789?

2. Citizen Responsibility

A. Why is it difficult for the individual to maintain independence of thought and action in the present-day world?

B. Why is the individual important in society today? What are his obligations in this regard?

C. Give two ways in which an individual can prepare himself for an effective role in solving current social and political problems. Explain these briefly.

THE CHAPTER IN REVIEW

A. Contrast present-day America with America in 1789 from the political, economic, and social standpoints.

B. A knowledge of the purpose of society is essential to the study of a nation's problems. Why?

C. America needs alert, correctly informed, and interested citizens. Show the contributions of these citizens to society.

SELECTED READINGS

The study of American problems assumes that you can do something about these problems after you have analyzed them. The book by Rev. James Keller, M.M., *You Can Change the World!* (New York: Longmans, Green & Co., Inc., 1948), provocatively shows that you can do something about American problems. Chapter V is especially pertinent. Father Keller's *Government Is Your Business* (Garden City, N.Y.: Doubleday & Company, Inc., 1951), especially Chapter I, also is helpful in showing citizens how to improve their government. The study of American problems reveals differences of opinion among various groups in the country. A practical guide in the etiquette of controversy is James M. O'Neill, *Catholics in Controversy* (New York: The Macmillan Co., 1954).

An understanding of American problems is possible only if one has a basic knowledge of society and man's place among his fellows. Helpful analyses of this subject are: Most Rev. Francis J. Haas, *Man and Society* (New York: Appleton-Century-Crofts, Inc., 1952), Parts I and II; and Eva J. Ross, *Basic Sociology* (Milwaukee: The Bruce Publishing Co., 1953), Part I.

Ethics in government is the concern of the senator from Illinois, Paul H. Douglas, *Ethics in Government* (Cambridge, Mass.: Harvard University Press, 1952); George A. Graham, *Morality in American Politics* (New York: Random House, 1952); and Rev. Francis J. Connell, C.Ss.R., *Morals in Politics and Professions* (Westminster, Md.: The Newman Press, 1946). The Reference Shelf collection of articles on this subject appeared under the editorship of Thomas A. Rousse, *Political Ethics and the Voter* (New York: H. W. Wilson Co., 1952). The Reference Shelf collections are for debaters, and they try to give articles and speeches on both sides of every topic. Catholic pamphlets on this subject are Rev. Francis J. Connell, C.Ss.R., *Morality and Government* (Washington: National Catholic Welfare Conference, 1949), and Rev. John A. O'Brien, *Graft Is Your Business* (St. Louis: The Queen's Work, 1950).

The technique of influencing government is shown in the following: Margaret A. Hickey, "Citizens' Organizations," *Ladies' Home Journal* (July 1948); Joseph A. McLean, *Politics Is What* You *Make It* (Washington: Public Affairs Committee, 1952).

PROJECTS

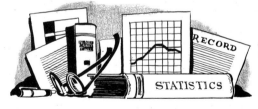

1. To notice the dangers of an indifferent citizenry, examine the voting percentage in the last six presidential elections. What lessons can we learn from these statistics?

2. Show the remarkable elasticity of the Constitution in meeting two current problems: federal flood-control projects, and sports and the interstate commerce clause.

Chapter 2. Our Society As It Was and As It Is

3. ORIGIN AND GROWTH
OF THE AMERICAN WAY OF LIFE

Americans all remember from their history that religion was one of the important motives bringing colonists to our shores. The Pilgrims who landed at Plymouth Rock agreed in their Mayflower Compact that they had undertaken their voyage "for the Glory of God, and Advancement of the Christian Faith." Many Protestants in New England and many Catholics in Maryland braved the hardships of life in the New World so that they could freely worship God according to their consciences. So it was with many of the immigrants in Pennsylvania, Rhode Island, and other colonies.

Public religious affirmations. Religion played an important part in colonial society. Traditions were established in a religious atmosphere, and these traditions played some part in our revolution and in the establishment of our own nation. James Otis voiced the general thought of the Revolutionary age when he observed that supreme power "strictly speaking, belongs alone to God. Parliaments are in all cases to declare what is for the good of

the whole; but it is not the declaration of Parliament that makes it so: there must be in every instance, a higher authority, viz., God." Similarly, the Virginia Bill of Rights, adopted in 1776 by the convention of that state, asserted "that all men are equally entitled to the free exercise of religion, according to the dictates of conscience; and that it is the mutual duty of all to practice Christian forebearance, love, and charity towards each other."

The Declaration of Independence was made that same year with an appeal to "the Supreme Judge of the world for the rectitude of our intentions" and the declaration of "a firm reliance on the protection of Divine Providence." Because there were so many different religious groups in America, no one church was recognized as the official established religion in all thirteen states. But Americans did not expect their new government to be indifferent or hostile to religion. On the contrary, they expected it to foster and protect religion as the basis of a sound society. The important Northwest Ordinance of 1787 included as its third article this admonition: "Religion,

morality, and knowledge, being necessary to good government and the happiness of mankind, schools and the means of education shall be forever encouraged." Religion and morality were to be included with secular learning as part of the school curriculum.

In his famous Farewell Address, George Washington spoke in the American tradition when he warned his fellow Americans: "Of all the dispositions and habits which lead to political prosperity, Religion and Morality are indispensable supports. . . . Whatever may be conceded to the influence of refined education on minds of peculiar structure, reason and experience both forbid us to expect that national morality can prevail in exclusion of religious principle." This was the attitude of the Founding Fathers. They feared, as Thomas Jefferson said, that personal liberties could not "be thought secure, when we have removed their only firm basis, a conviction in the minds of the people that these liberties are the gifts of God." They were convinced of the wisdom of William Penn's succinct statement: "Men must either be governed by God or they must be ruled by tyrants."

From the beginning, then, our nation was a religious nation. The only consti-tutional requirements about religion were that all men be free to worship according to their consciences and that support from the federal government be not given to one religious group in preference to others. No restrictions were made on the practice of religion, save the prohibition against the federal government's prescribing an official, established religion. Our nation continued to be a religious nation throughout the nineteenth century. When that very acute Frenchman, Alexis de Tocqueville, traveled in this country in 1831, he wrote: "There is no country in the world in which the Christian religion retains greater influence over the souls of men than in America."

Fifty years later another visitor, Lord Bryce, reported:

Christianity is in fact understood to be, though not the legally established religion, yet the national religion. So far from thinking their commonwealth Godless, the Americans conceive that the religious character of a government consists in nothing but the religious beliefs of the individual citizens, and the conformity of their conduct to that belief. They deem the general acceptance of Christianity to be one of the main sources of their national prosperity, and their nation as a special object of Divine Favor.

The fact that ours was a Christian nation was simply taken for granted by almost all Americans. The fact revealed itself in many small but significant ways. The House of Representatives, for example, on the very day it passed the First Amendment (which prohibited the government from infringing freedom of religion) also passed this resolution:

That a joint committee of both Houses be directed to wait upon the President of the United States, to request that he would recommend to the people of the United States a day of public thanksgiving and prayer, to be observed by acknowledging, with grateful hearts, the many signal favors of Almighty God, especially by affording them an opportunity to establish a Constitution of government for their safety and happiness.

Again, no one thought it strange that the most widely used textbooks in America—*McGuffey's Readers*—should have been written by a Presbyterian minister and should refer frequently to religion and morality. "In a Christian country," McGuffey wrote, "the man is to be pitied who at this day can honestly object to imbuing the minds of youth with the language and the spirit of the word of God." Many little things testify to this nation's trust in God: mottoes on our coins, prayers opening sessions in Congress and in state legislatures, Thanksgiving as a national holiday, the oath taken on a Bible in the courtroom. These and many other practices were originally established by a religious people.

It is for these reasons that the Catholic bishops of America wrote in 1948:

The essential connection between religion and good citizenship is deep in our American tradition. Those who took the lead in establishing our independence and framing our Constitution were firm and explicit in the conviction that religion and morality are the strong supports of national well-being, that national morality cannot long prevail in the absence of religious principle, and that impartial encouragement of religious influence on its citizens is a proper and practical function of good government.

Life, liberty, and the pursuit of happiness. In American society man has always been regarded as a being of intrinsic worth and dignity. Our government was originally dedicated to the proposition that all men are created free and equal and that they possess certain inalienable rights. Such a belief implies a religious view of man made to the image of God. It assumes that man has a spiritual as well as a physical nature, that he has intelligence and free will. It also assumes that he possesses certain rights by reason of his nature. This means that he obtains these rights from God at the time of his creation. That is why they are natural and inalienable. No government, no group of men can rightfully violate these God-given rights.

The rights we Americans possess to life, liberty, and the pursuit of happiness, therefore, were to be protected by the federal government established in 1789. That, together with promoting our common welfare, was its purpose. The first ten amendments to the Constitution specified certain things the government could *not* do. This was to give additional protection to our natural rights. Thus the Founding Fathers set up what is called a limited government—one that has the right and the power to perform only those tasks specifically given to it by the people. Through the court system and through elections we have the ways and means of holding government to its appointed functions.

Property, family, community. Such limited government, then, was established to serve the welfare of its citizens. It exists for their sake, not they for the government's sake. This concept of the government's proper role in society was easy to maintain in the early period of our history. The symbols of this early period of American history were the home, the church, the school, and the courthouse. They symbolized the important social units of the family, the religious com-

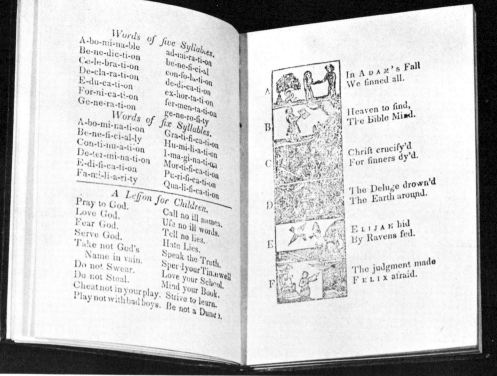

The first schoolbook in America, the New England Primer *(1643), and (below) the famous* History of the United States *by B. Davenport (1831) attest to the moral and religious consciousness of society during the colonial period and early days of our republic. (From* Americana, *courtesy Women's National Book Assn.)*

munity, the neighborhood educational agency, and the civil power. They were all local institutions wherein people participated actively and vigorously. It was in these local institutions that the young citizen grew to maturity.

In the first century of our history the family was respected as the stable unit of social and economic life. The child's religious formation, a good part of his education, and the greater part of his training and discipline continued to be a family function. One reason for the stability of family life was the prevailing Christian concept of the family's importance and its integrity. Another reason was the widespread distribution of property. Through the nineteenth century it was easy for industrious people to acquire land and thus to secure a measure of economic independence. It was not a normal thing for fathers and mothers to

(112)

CHRONOLOGICAL TABLE,

Of remarkable Events, Discoveries, and Inventions, from the Creation of the World, to the year A. D. 1830.

Note.—As Historians differ in regard to many of the events that occurred before the Christian era, it is not necessary that scholars should be required to state the precise date in the table, but merely the events as they occurred between certain periods: see questions at the end of the table.

B. C.
4004 THE Creation of the World, according to the Hebrew text of the Scriptures.
3875 Cain murders Abel.
3017 Enoch translated to Heaven.
2348 The Universal Deluge.
2247 The Building of Babel; the Dispersion of Mankind; and the Confusion of Languages.
2217 Nimrod supposed to have built Babylon, and founded the Babylonish Monarchy; and Assur to have built Nineveh, and founded the Monarchy of Assyria.
2188 Menes (in Scripture Misraim) founds the Monarchy of Egypt.
1996 The Birth of Abram.
1897 Sodom and Gomorrah destroyed by fire from Heaven.
1896 Isaac born.
1836 Jacob and Esau born.
1823 Death of Abraham.
1716 Isaac dies.
1635 Joseph dies in Egypt.
1571 Moses born in Egypt.

have to find jobs away from the family enterprise of farming, pursuing a trade, or conducting a small business. So the family continued to be an economic as well as a social and educational unit far into the nineteenth century.

Our country's economy was relatively simple during the early decades of our existence as a nation. The principal pursuit was agriculture. The farmer in those days tended to be self-sufficient. A self-reliant man, he had to do many things besides tend his crops. He had to build his home and barn, mend his fences, and repair his tools. This self-sufficiency made for a hard life, but it was an independent life. Problems were more often personal than social. And social problems were usually local matters that could be settled fairly easily.

American freedom took root and grew strongly in that kind of society. There was no monopoly of power in any one person or group of persons. No one religion was the official religion. No agency of government possessed unchecked power. In all states, as well as in the national government, the legislative, executive, and judicial branches of government checked one another. Within each state many functions of government were left to counties and villages, while other functions were passed upward to the federal government. And limiting all government was the federal Constitution with its Bill of Rights. Agricultural and commercial interests sometimes helped, sometimes checked each other. Small farmer and large farm owner competed with each other, and each prevented the other from gaining an unfair advantage.

In such a society the individual could retain his respect and his dignity. He could rest them securely in theory on the still accepted religious idea of a man created to the image of God and possessed of certain inalienable rights. He could rest them securely in practice on the possession of productive property and the real freedom to follow the vocation he thought would be most rewarding to him. He could function as a social person through his family, his church, and his local political community.

The American ideal. In this setting there developed something we can call "the American ideal." This ideal is what American life meant to most Americans. It is called the "American dream" by James Truslow Adams, "that dream of a land in which life should be better and richer and fuller for every man, with opportunity for each according to his ability or achievement." In a recent survey of what prominent persons considered the fundamentals of American life, one citizen listed "liberty" as the most important. Another said it was "the dignity of man." Most agreed that the significant aspect of American life was the position it gave the individual and the respect it showed to his person and rights.

This town meeting in Vermont is typical of the community interest that exists in small towns throughout the country. In contrast to the complex government of the larger cities, the town government appeals intimately to the residents who have a strong feeling of personal responsibility for the welfare of their community. (Standard Oil Co., N.J.)

The American ideal included freedom of worship and a genuine tolerance of different religions, but at the same time it recognized God as Creator and man's dependence on Him and His moral law. It included freedom of thought, since without this freedom the dignity of human beings would be a mockery. It included freedom of assembly, of speech, and of the press, because human beings must be able to communicate freely if they are to develop their faculties and help one another attain the good life. It included man's right to the private ownership of property as a necessary means of safeguarding his other rights. It came to include political democracy—which involved intelligent participation in campaigns, study of party platforms, and a concern for the common welfare. Finally, it came to embrace universal education and equality of opportunity so that each man could develop his faculties fully and achieve the position to which his abilities entitled him.

Such an ideal was never completely realized. George Washington had to remind his soldiers, for example, that burning the Pope in effigy, as they planned to do in celebrating Guy Fawkes Day,[1] would be an outrageous insult to the Catholics in his army. Intolerance broke out against Catholics again in the Know-Nothing movement of the 1840s. Churches and convents were burned in the East, and for a time anti-Catholic feeling was strong. The same intolerance against Catholics and immigrants cropped up again in the last decade of the nineteenth century under the guise of the American Protective Association. Again, the revived Ku Klux Klan, strong in the South and Midwest, was a violent form of religious and racial intolerance in the days after World War I.

[1] Guy Fawkes Day was celebrated each November 5 in England and colonial America to commemorate the exposure of the so-called "Gunpowder Plot" of 1605, when Catholic conspirators who were accused of trying to blow up Parliament were seized.

These are examples of what is truly un-American activity. They are contrary to the set of ideals we have described as the American way of life. They are departures from the principles on which our government was founded. Such movements usually lasted for only a short time. They made good Americans feel very much ashamed.

4. ECLIPSE OF THE OLDER SOCIETY

The American ideal has become more difficult to maintain with the passing of each generation in American history. Two interconnected developments in the last century have basically altered American society and changed the American mind. One development is physical: the industrial and technological revolution. The other is mental and spiritual: a new frame of mind and a new attitude toward life. Although these developments are intimately interwoven, let us look at them separately in order to see more clearly how they have created our modern American problems.

The industrial and technological revolution. The industrial revolution was a long process in American history in which machinery was applied to manufacture and farming with revolutionary economic and social effects. The process started slowly in the decades immediately after the Revolution. The needs of the Civil War gave great impetus to large-scale industry. New labor-saving machines were invented for factory and farm. A network of railroads soon covered the nation, enlarging the markets for each product and making available large supplies of raw materials. Waves of immigration and the natural increase of the native population augmented the supply of labor.

Factories became larger. They frequently employed thousands of men. Millions of dollars were invested in each

Hammersmith at Saugus, Mass., was the first ironworks in the United States (1650). Like the modern counterparts, it had its promoters and investors to launch the project and provide capital. The growth of American industry is clearly illustrated by the contrast in these photos of restored Hammersmith (above) and the River Rouge Plant of the Ford Motor Company (below).

company. Profits were divided among the shareholders, many of whom knew little about the business and never saw the factory. Handicraft labor was replaced to a considerable extent by machines, and wherever this change took place the worker tended to become a machine tender or an unskilled worker packing boxes or sweeping floors.

American inventiveness and industry took advantage of the industrial revolution to move our country into first place among the manufacturing nations of the world. Wealth increased tremendously. Although the worker did not secure as large a share of this increase as did the employer and the stockowner, nevertheless he became considerably richer in material goods than he had been before the industrial revolution.

Changes in industry have been even more revolutionary in the twentieth century as a result of what we can call the technological revolution of our age. Developments in the use of electricity, utilization of the ether waves, great improvements in the gas combustion engine, and finally the use of atomic energy have created the world we live in today. Thus in the short space of a century the American has harnessed the mightiest of natural forces to his use—even, if he is not careful and wise, to his destruction.

As a nation we can take pride in our conquest of nature and in harnessing her powers. These accomplishments are, in themselves, good. They have made possible the solution of many of the perennial problems of scarcity, of getting enough to eat, and other such age-old problems as the control of epidemics and plagues. The industrial and technological revolution has made possible a world in which the great masses of mankind can have the leisure and the means for developing their human faculties fully, but at the same time it has created other problems through developments that were almost an inevitable part of the revolution.

The discovery of the formula $E = mc^2$ by Albert Einstein marked the beginning of the atomic age. This photograph, taken in July 1955, shows the lighting of a giant electric bulb at West Milton, N.Y., by atomic power—the free world's first commercial use of the greatest natural force, and a milestone in the new industrial revolution that we are now experiencing. (Wide World Photos)

A nation of cities was one consequence of the movement. Different industries tended to concentrate in certain areas where transportation facilities were good, where raw materials and labor were easily obtained, and where local feeling encouraged large-scale industry. Thus steel plants centered in Pittsburgh and on the southern tip of Lake Michigan. The automobile industry centered around Detroit, the stockyards in Kansas City and Omaha and Chicago, the shoe industry in St. Louis. This concentration of industry in certain localities meant the gathering of thousands of employees in a small area. This, in turn, required hundreds of retail stores, places of entertainment, the development of local transportation systems, an increase of the police force—in short, the growth of a village into a big city.

The American ideals of community life in the local school and church, a close interest in local political activity, a concern with the welfare of one's neighbors—all these have become difficult to maintain in a big city, where most people are nameless strangers to one another. Moreover, as we shall see, the crowding together of hundreds of thousands of people into a small area creates innumerable problems unknown in the early decades of American history.

Concentration of productive property into fewer hands made it more difficult for Americans to maintain their traditional attitude toward human freedom. Liberty has always been closely associated with the ownership of productive property; that is, property which is used to produce wealth of one kind or another. Thus land used for agriculture is productive property, whereas land used as a park or the site of a home is not. Large-scale industry and mechanized farming eliminated many small producers and farmers. Millions of Americans became wage earners. Frequently their wages were enough for a decent kind of life, but they were not sufficient to purchase more than the goods a family consumes from day to day.

We shall see later that large corporations are owned by the stockholders. Stock is usually sold in small shares, and thus ownership of a corporation is spread among thousands of people in the country, many of them small wage earners. But the ownership of small amounts of stock does not give the stockholder control of the business or even an effective voice in its management. A general trend of the industrial revolution, then, has been to divorce millions of people from personal ownership and control of productive property. And we shall see that in such a setting the maintenance of liberty becomes a very difficult problem. Generally a worker let out of his job cannot raise corn and chickens to keep himself alive. He must work at the one job he knows, or go on relief, or starve. The application of the principle of private property in an industrial society is indeed one of the most complicated problems we face today.

Class divisions of a new kind were created by the new industrial system. This is not the simple division of society into the bourgeoisie and the proletariat, as the Communists claim, but a tendency for labor and management to see their interests as opposed to each other's. Such a view is not correct, for, as Pope Pius XII put it, "labor and management, so to speak, eat at the same table." The fact remains, however, that the wage earners had certain problems in common. They formed unions to gain the strength that in our country comes from organization and from numbers. Even earlier in our history the owners of productive property had formed various associations to promote their mutual interests as employers.

Thus a certain degree of division was effected in our industrial society. Management and labor continued to have much in common. Laborers and industrialists went to the same churches, voted in the same voting booths, and frequently enough went to the same places of entertainment. Their children usually attended the same schools. Very often a worker's son became the manager of a plant and so joined the employer group. But in economic matters there was nevertheless this loose division of society into the labor and management classes, with a large number of professional men and small businessmen making up still a third group. Such a division created new problems of an economic and social nature, as we shall see, and made it ever more difficult for agreement to be reached on how to promote the common welfare.

The stability and the integrity of the family deteriorated under the impact of the industrial revolution. In later chap-

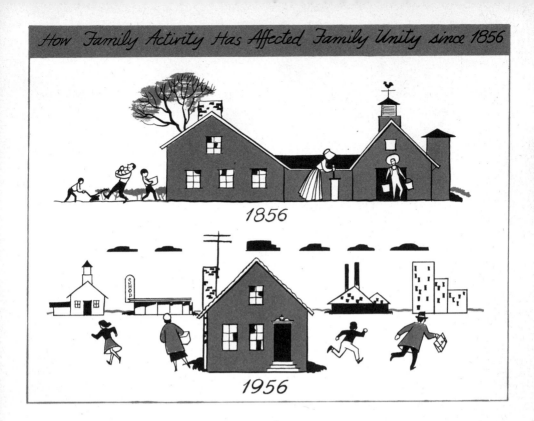

1856

1956

ters we shall study the results of family disintegration. Here let us note that living conditions in the large city made it difficult for parents to maintain the family as the basic social and educational unit. More and more they found it easy, sometimes necessary, to throw the entire burden of education, training, and discipline on the neighborhood school. Entertainment was taken over by the movies, the local youth club, and other outside agencies. Duties and recreation outside the home came to prevent parents and children from spending time together as a family unit. The father was usually a wage earner at some factory, and the family was not interested in his work. Many mothers took jobs to supplement their husbands' earnings, and children frequently found the home an empty place except at night.

Thus the Christian idea of the family grew dim in the newly industrialized American society. Family ties were weakened, and divorce increased sixtyfold in a century. New problems naturally grew out of the deterioration of family life: the care of the aged, juvenile delinquency, the use of leisure time, the education of the children. New agencies had to be created to fulfill *artificially* various functions given up by default in millions of American families.

A society organized on mechanical instead of personal relationships was another development that accompanied the industrial revolution. Large-scale industry—almost of necessity—tends to reduce the human person to a statistic. He is looked upon as a unit in the process of production—along with other units, such as raw material, rent, or advertising. Routine tasks on the assembly line or in the big corporation's office are naturally organized for efficient production, not for fostering the worker's personality or safeguarding his human dignity. The tendency is for man to be identified by a

Assembly-line work is a necessary part of all large-scale industries that are organized for efficient production. The worker is often engaged in non-elevating work of a tedious and routine nature. Management has the responsibility to see that the worker's dignity is respected.

number in the factory, in the union, in the social security system. He is classified and put into an appropriate pigeonhole by welfare agencies. In hospitals he is frequently treated as a "case" or a "type" instead of a unique human person. He often becomes little more than a unit of raw material fed into the great educational mill in those places where mass education has become the usual thing. In political life he becomes an abstraction, a citizen who counts for one vote rather than a person with myriad other social ties.

Managers of large-scale industries are growing aware of this problem and they are seeking ways of respecting human dignity and personality among the mass of workers. The basic problem is how to save the human person from the great industrial machine he has created, how to master the machine to serve the human person. Laws alone cannot solve the problem. Nor can we destroy the machine. A sound Christian view of man must underlie the search for ways and means to protect his dignity in the industrial system.

Centralization and multiplication of government functions were made easy and to some extent necessary by the industrial revolution. Local agencies of government were obviously unable to deal with prob-

lems created by corporations with property holdings throughout the entire country. Railroads and big steel corporations were too big and powerful to be controlled by any one city or state. Moreover, when the means of communication were made widespread and instantaneous, it became possible, and often necessary, for agencies of the central government to regulate them. This development combined with a new attitude that favored turning more and more functions over to the national government. The result was a centralization of governmental power that has put severe strains on the American federal system.

The individual citizen now finds himself standing face to face with a national government that inspects his records, taxes his income, takes part of his salary for insurance, and in various ways provides for his inability to support himself and his family. Such action by the national government is to some extent necessary, but the fact remains that it has altered the composition of our society. From a federation of states, each an organic unit of many social groups, our nation has tended to become a mass of individuals under the direct jurisdiction of the national government. No tyrant has made it so. The developments of the last century have made this trend.

How to preserve our traditional freedoms in the face of an ever-growing state is one of the most pressing problems of our time. It is a problem not easily solved because there is no going back to an agricultural society of the past. We must find a way to keep our heritage of freedom and still accept as much increase of activity by the government as is necessary for national defense and the promotion of the common welfare.

A trend toward what is called cultural monism has been another result of the industrial and technological revolution. This is a trend that has crept into American society quietly. Most Americans have welcomed its coming. Like smoking or drinking, it is a habit that does not seem dangerous until it has a strangling hold on us. Cultural monism is the tendency for all people to think alike, to accept passively the opinions handed to them, to have their minds made up for them by others. It is a tendency to live a passive life rather than an active one. It is an attitude in which a person is afraid to differ from the majority. It is a tendency to resolve conflict by abolishing differences—especially ethnic and religious differences.

This trend has been made possible by recent technological developments in the means of communication. Healthy cultural differences between various parts of the country have tended to disappear as all people see the same movies, hear the same radio programs, read the same syndicated columns in their newspapers, wear clothes styled and manufactured in the same city, and now watch the same television programs. Thus the same agencies tend to think for all Americans. The way we dress, the dishes we select from the menu, the social etiquette we observe, the aesthetic judgments we make, the political opinions we hold are all more and more determined for us by others. The average American tends to accept passively custom-made clothes and custom-tailored opinions. Thought, like houses, is largely prefabricated.

The tendency toward passivity can be seen in such an ordinary thing as the development of American sports through the last century. The trend has been for the great mass of Americans to become passive spectators at professional events. Most boys are content to go to baseball games instead of to play baseball. Even within colleges and high schools the general tendency has been away from intramural sports with widespread competition among many students in favor of semi-professional athletics played by a few and watched by the many. To some extent even spectator reaction to the game has been formalized, with cheering done by a group of selected and uniformed spectators—not cheering spontaneously but according to formula at certain selected times.

The development of cultural monism, we shall see later, involves most important human and political problems. The control of public opinion becomes a dangerous weapon if it falls into the hands of unscrupulous men. For the technological revolution and a culturally passive people combine to offer such men the raw material from which the dictatorial state can be built. Human freedoms are difficult to maintain in an atmosphere of cultural monism, for freedom is an active thing, and one is not really free if he surrenders his judgment to others.

5. THE DEVELOPMENT OF NEW PHILOSOPHIES

During the industrial and technological revolution there developed among millions a new temper of mind which welcomed and justified the trends we have been discussing. Many new currents of thought have modified our American character in the last half century, but for the sake of convenience we can isolate three of the more important trends and discuss them separately.

1. *Secularism* is more a way of thinking than a doctrine. It is a way of thinking which pushes religious considerations out of political and social life. It denies God any role in His creatures' daily life. In 1947 the Catholic bishops of America described secularism as "a view of life that limits itself . . . to the human here and now in exclusion of man's relation to God here and hereafter. Secularism, or the practical exclusion of God from human thinking and living, is at the root of the world's travail today."

Secularism developed slowly as a gradual perversion of the earlier American tendency toward self-reliance and freedom. The challenge of the environment and the promise of success to those who worked hard and relentlessly fostered a tendency toward materialism among Americans from the beginning of our history. Gradually the average American came to confine his religion more and more to attending church services on Sunday and seeing less and less the relation of religion to his daily workaday life.

This development was slow and in some ways insidious. It crept over minds like a blight. The average American did not realize that he was thinking differently from the way his father had thought. But a glance at the panorama of American history reveals how pronounced the change was. In the period after the Civil War we find that Americans had a higher opinion of the successful businessman than they had of the theologian or teacher, a radical departure from prevailing evaluations of earlier times. More and more Americans tended to identify worldly success with virtue, and poverty with vice. Thus William Graham Sumner (1840–1910), although a clergyman and educator, declared: "The weak who constantly arouse the pity of humanitarians and philanthropists are the shiftless, the imprudent, the negligent, the impractical, and the inefficient, or they are the idle, the intemperate, the extravagant, and the vicious."

In time this new secularist spirit, which is contrary to the American tradition, came to permeate many aspects of life. Education, to take one example, was originally conducted in schools of religious foundation; our early colleges all belonged to one religious group or another. Their main purpose was to prepare young men for the ministry in their respective religions. Today most public schools and universities are public institutions from which religion has been excluded.

Religion has been excluded from life by large numbers of people. It has little influence on legislation and not any on the family life of millions of Americans. That is why the American Catholic bishops wrote that secularism "is doing more than anything else to blight our heritage of Christian culture." We have been allowing this trend of secularism, "which breaks with our historical American tradition," the bishops wrote, "to divorce Christian truth from life." That is why the Protestant National Council pleaded that "we should use all legitimate means to prevent our nation from becoming a secular state in the current sense of the term."

Secularism has made the solution of national problems almost impossible. These are problems involving human persons. Unless they are studied as problems involving God's creatures, made to His image and destined to eternal life, then God is excluded from the solution. And any solution excluding the Creator and Supreme Ruler of the world can be neither right nor lasting.

2. *Naturalism* is a theory about human nature that is part of the secularist way of thought. It tries to explain man in purely animal terms. He is seen as the last step in evolution, the most highly developed of the animals but still *only* an animal.

When such a theory of human nature is generally accepted, the solution of our human problems becomes impossible, for naturalism denies man his distinctively human qualities and misconceives the very ends of life. It even strips men of moral responsibility for their actions and denies their duty to obey the laws of God.

To believe that there is no life after death, the naturalists think, will make men happy in this life. "To know clearly and finally," one of them wrote, "that this is our one and only life enables men to focus their minds completely upon the consummation of human happiness here." Such concentration, of course, does not bring happiness, since when man excludes God from his life he can lead only a lowly and ultimately miserable existence. The statement that "all men are created free and equal" becomes a mockery. The Bill of Rights becomes meaningless; human freedom, nonsense. Naturalism, then, wars upon the American way of life.

3. *Pragmatism* is the philosophy that has come to be widely accepted by a great many social and economic theorists who in the twentieth century have had a great influence on the schools and courts of the country. Pragmatism derived from naturalism and the doctrine of evolution; its exponents regard man as a clever animal forever in a state of evolving change, and therefore they recognize no fixed and abiding norms of human nature. From this view, truth is what the clever animal discovers to be practical as he manipulates his biological environment. He has an idea and experiments with it; if it "works," it is true. "Truth," wrote William James, greatest of pragmatist philosophers, "happens to an idea. It *becomes* true, is *made* true by events: its verity *is* in fact an event, a process: the process namely of its verifying itself, its veri-fication." It naturally follows that truth, so conceived, can be unmade by events; what works today may not work tomorrow, and hence today's "truths" become tomorrow's myths.

With the pragmatist, as with the ancient sophists of decadent Greece, truth

What Pragmatism Does to Truth

is not the measure of the mind, but the mind is the measure of truth. In other words, truth does not go into the mind of man, but comes out of it, and there is no truth but that which originates in the mind. Pragmatists are absorbed by facts and events and are not interested in principles. They do not recognize law as anything but man-made contrivance to fit particular moments and situations; to them there is no law for man deriving from his Creator. Hence they have no permanent standards of morality, these being always in a state of flux or change. Nothing is either right or wrong until man makes it so, and then it may not long remain so. Hence pragmatists have little or no reverence for historic American institutions and ways of life, and they look for wisdom rather in experimentation than from the close and careful study of an unchanging human nature. Pragmatism, therefore, can have a recklessly destructive influence on American rights and liberties.

Thus pragmatism, naturalism, and secularism all go against the principles on which American government was founded and on which it operated so successfully for more than a century. They deny the dignity and worth of the human person our government was established to defend. They deny the existence of our inalienable rights. They make it difficult for us to maintain our human freedom. A society built on these new theories would be bound to destroy freedom. For these theories rob the human person of his distinctively human qualities, which are recognized as his because he was created to the image and likeness of God.

Actually, these theories or philosophies are not new. The ancient classical pagan world experimented with all of them, and they proved inimical to human nature and human happiness. They have come back upon the minds of men exactly to the extent that men have lost hold on Christian truth.

There is a great deal of secularism, naturalism, and pragmatism in the spirit and activity of what is called *liberalism.* That is a word of many meanings. Historically it was first used in Spain in the early nineteenth century as a name for a political movement inspired by the ideals of the French Revolution. Later it had various meanings. As a philosophy affirming that man could find full happiness by being liberated from all religious and political

The Spiritual Vision of Man
Time and Eternity

The Pragmatist Vision of Man
Time and No Eternity

Catholic newspapers and magazines have gained wide recognition for their clarity in the presentation of the affairs of the world. Catholic journals of opinion are counter-agents of the press that practically excludes God from human activity. (Catholic Press Assn.)

authority, liberalism was condemned by the Church. In the second half of the nineteenth century the word was appropriated by a political party in England which aimed at the reform of government and the enlargement of political, civil, and economic liberty. Its leaders were Christian men who perpetuated a good deal of the older politics of the Whigs in their liberalism, which of course incurred no condemnation by the Church. On the other hand, liberalism was used in England to designate the doctrine of English economists who opposed governmental control of economic activity. Their slogan was *laissez-faire* ("let things alone"), and they advocated absolute freedom for the businessman to follow his self-interest. They believed that economic laws would set fair prices, give each man what he deserved, and promote the greatest possible well-being of society. Liberals, such as Herbert Spencer (1820–1903), insisted that the state should do nothing but keep the peace. They condemned all forms of social legislation and regulation of business as unwarranted interference with "the natural order of things." They believed that each man should be left entirely on his own and that public relief was immoral and degrading.

Toward the end of the nineteenth century liberalism took on a new meaning. It referred to the program and doctrine of those who advocated social legislation: minimum-wage laws, unemployment insurance, old-age pensions, and the like. This reversal of doctrine came about because liberals no longer feared the government as an oppressor of men's liberties. They believed that big business was the new oppressor, and they desired the government to protect the "little man" by regulating business in the interest of society as a whole. This new meaning of liberalism came to be generally accepted in America by the time of the New Deal. By this time liberalism gave the government a large regulative function over economic life and also a paternalistic function in protecting the "little man."

In this country, however, many people use the term "liberalism" loosely in contradistinction to "conservatism." For them liberalism means a willingness to reject old institutions in favor of new ones, a predisposition to experiment with various reforms, a tendency to disparage the past and look optimistically toward the future. In this loose sense of the term, perhaps half the people in America are liberal. The word is more carefully used, however, to refer to those programs that give the federal government a larger role in economic and social life. Liberals favor social reform by increased governmental regulation and direction of economic life. Liberals today generally advocate what is called by many "the welfare state."

Catholic opposition to liberalism rarely concentrates on the social or political programs espoused by liberals—although for various reasons such programs may be criticized. The point of controversy with Catholics is rather the naturalistic view of man that many liberals hold and the pragmatist, secularist philosophy they embrace. Such liberals believe that man is perfectly good, deny original sin, and think that man can build a perfect society here on earth. They exclude from consideration religious truths. They concentrate exclusively on the materialistic aspect of life, and they consider the production and consumption of material wealth the main objects of society.

This kind of liberalism has done much to bring about the current state of affairs that calls upon government to perform hundreds of functions formerly taken care of by individuals or private societies. For such liberalism "freed" the individual from customary restraints, from moral and religious authority, and from social responsibility. The result was that many people were left without protections and without status in life. They turned, naturally enough, to the government both to protect them and to provide for them. Thus liberalism, so understood, played a major role in the tendency to move toward a welfare state.

As a political term, the word *liberalism* was rarely used in the United States until the twentieth century. We have never had a liberal party in our national life, although in New York State in recent years there has been a small political sect calling itself the Liberal Party. When leading Democratic and Republican politicians declare themselves to be "liberal" (as they often do) they usually mean no more than that they are in favor of liberty.

Liberalism has meant so many different things that one could say that liberalism *is* what liberalism *does*.

Conclusion. Our basic problem, then, is to preserve the largest amount of human freedom possible in this modern technological world. All our other problems cluster around this central one: how to hold the loyalty of all citizens without demanding conformity to an imposed pattern of thought; how to preserve true freedom of speech and assembly and conscience without exposing ourselves to those who would destroy these very things; how to alleviate suffering and distress among the unfortunate without making them wards of the state; how to

give government agencies power to perform their functions efficiently and still leave the citizen free.

REVIEW

3. Origin and Growth of the American Way of Life
A. Cite two public affirmations of the importance of religion in colonial life.

B. What was the extent of the religious reference in the Northwest Ordinance of 1787?

C. George Washington made important references to the matter of religion and politics in his Farewell Address. What were they?

D. Life, liberty, pursuit of happiness, property, family, community—all these have a religious meaning for us. Point out this meaning in each of the above.

E. "The American Ideal" is a phrase often used. Of what does it consist? Give several examples in our history when this ideal was violated.

4. Eclipse of the Older Society
A. What is meant by the industrial and technological revolutions? How did they affect American industry?

B. List some of the technological changes of the twentieth century in America.

C. How were the family unit and the individual's dignity threatened by the developments of the industrial and technological revolutions?

D. The government has entered into many new fields of activity since 1932. Give several examples and point out the danger to the individual in each case.

E. What is cultural monism? Why is it dangerous?

5. Development of New Philosophies
A. Define secularism. Why is it harmful? Show how this influences man's outlook both on life and education.

B. Define naturalism and show how it is contrary to Christian truth.

C. Illustrate the dangers and consequences of pragmatism to society.

D. Liberalism has some elements of each of

the previously mentioned philosophies. Why is it hard to define? Give its proper meaning.

THE CHAPTER IN REVIEW

A. Our country has had many religious traditions. Illustrate these from three important documents issued before 1800.

B. The industrial and technological revolutions have affected this country in many ways. Show how they have changed America physically, politically, economically, socially, and culturally.

C. Secularism and naturalism are present-day evils. Contrast these two philosophies with Christian teachings.

D. Point out how pragmatism and liberalism threaten the moral fabric of America in the twentieth century.

SELECTED READINGS

A quick review of American history is indispensable for understanding American problems in their historical setting. The American history text in this Christian Democracy Series will serve this purpose excellently: Marshall Smelser and Harry Kirwin, *Conceived in Liberty* (New York: Doubleday & Company, Inc., 1955).

Constitutional developments are handled well and in readable fashion by Howard L. McBain, *The Living Constitution* (New York: The Macmillan Co., 1942). This same subject is also covered by Alfred H. Kelly and Winifred A. Harbison, *The American Constitution: Its Origins and Development* (New York: W. W. Norton & Company, Inc., 1948), and by Carl B. Swisher, *American Constitutional Development* (Boston: Houghton Mifflin Co., 1943).

Two excellent treatments of the decline of American political philosophy are: Ross J. S. Hoffman, *The Spirit of Politics and the Future of Freedom* (Milwaukee: The Bruce Publishing Co., 1951), and Walter Lippmann, *The Public Philosophy* (Boston: Little, Brown, & Co., 1955).

Economic change can be followed satisfactorily in F. A. Shannon, *America's Economic Growth* (New York: The Macmillan Co., 1939). The urban movement is well treated, though only for a limited time (1878–1898) by Arthur M. Schlesinger, *The Rise of the City* (New York: The Macmillan Co., 1933). The same author's *New Viewpoints in American History* (New York: The Macmillan Co., 1937) has helpful essays on such subjects as feminism in American history. Also helpful is Harvey Wish, *Society and Thought in America* (New York: Longmans, Green & Co., Inc. 1952). This two-volume work contains chapters on such subjects as "The Urban Impact on Family Life," "The New Immigration," and "The Urban Impact on Rural Life."

The statements of the American bishops for November 1952 and November 1954 deal with naturalism, pragmatism, and secularism. They are available from the NCWC, Washington, D.C. "Liberalism" is the title of an article in *Social Order* (October, 1954) by Thomas Neill.

PROJECTS

1. To show the religious foundations of education in early America, examine the curriculums of five of our earliest colleges and note their religious beginnings. Secondary sources that can be found in your school or local library contain sufficient information for this report.

2. Find out the effects of the industrial and technological revolutions in your own town or city. Compare the way of life in the period of 1900 with that of the present day.

3. There is a danger that we shall all act alike in so many ways because of the cultural monism which these revolutions brought about. Make a list of current questions—social, recreational, economic, political—and present these to the class. Note how the students are divided in their opinions. Find out how they have formed their views on the questions.

4. Bishop John England was the first American bishop or priest to speak before Congress. It would be profitable to note the occasion and review the topics he dealt with in his speech.

Chapter 3. Freedom of Religion: Church and State

6. THE CONSTITUTION AND RELIGIOUS LIBERTY

The First Amendment to the Constitution states that "Congress shall make no law respecting an establishment of religion, or prohibiting the free exercise thereof." These two clauses seem to have an obvious and a clear meaning. How much is to be included in "free exercise" is a matter of interpretation, since it is obviously not the intent of the amendment to protect all practices that may masquerade under the name of religion. Whether a law has some connection with "an establishment of religion" is also a matter for judicial interpretation. Otherwise there seems little to dispute as regards the meaning of these two clauses.

The First Amendment contains two sets of prohibitions on the federal government in respect to religion. The first prohibits Congress from making any laws that would tend to create a national religion or destroy an established religion in any state. In other words, Congress cannot attack religion or favor one religion over others. The second set of prohibitions forbids Congress to interfere with Americans' worshiping God as their consciences dictate. Until 1947 there was no argument about the meaning of these two clauses. Even those who did not like the arrangement provided by this part of the First Amendment admitted that the words could have no other meaning than the one we have indicated.

Church-state relations in 1789. It is helpful, in order to understand the meaning of the First Amendment, to see what the relations between church and state were when the amendment was adopted. Diversity of churches made it a practical necessity that no one church be established by law and supported by Congress; that is, made an official national religion. Before the Revolution nine colonies had established churches (three Congregational and six Anglican), but some of these had now been disestablished. When the Constitution was adopted five states still had established churches—Massachusetts, Connecticut, New Hampshire, Maryland, and South Carolina. It was not until 1833, when the Congregational Church was disestablished in Massachusetts, that such church-state relations came to an end.

It is necessary to understand what the authors of the First Amendment meant by "an establishment of religion." They meant a religion given preferential status by the government, with a consequent discrimination against other churches. Taxes were collected from *all* the people for the support of the official or established religion. It was a form of consecration of the whole body politic in a particular fashion. Such establishments of religion were a common feature of British and European society in the eighteenth century, and many of them survive today. Many Americans disliked them intensely and feared the creation of one by the new federal government. They desired to maintain complete religious liberty and to have no *national* religious establishment.

Madison's original formulation of the amendment shows this clearly. It was: "The civil rights of none shall be abridged on account of religious belief or worship, nor shall any national religion be established, nor shall the full and equal rights of conscience be in any manner, or on any pretext, infringed." The Pennsylvania legislature's proposed text was: "Congress shall make no law establishing religion, or prohibiting the free exercise thereof, nor shall the rights of conscience

be infringed." Such words, however, could not safeguard the existing *state* establishments of religion from the possibility of attack. Hence the words finally adopted simply prohibited the Congress from legislating on the subject of religious establishments and from abridging religious liberty.

Opposition to an establishment of religion is not opposition to religion. Americans felt at the time the Bill of Rights was written, as Madison put it, that religion was an inalienable right that took precedence over society. "The religion," he wrote, "of every man must be left to the conviction and conscience of every man; and it is the right of every man to exercise it as these may dictate." Since there was diversity of religion nationally, it would have been unwise as well as unjust to have a nationally established church.

The aim of the First Amendment, then, was to keep the national government from establishing any one religion or interfering with the citizen's freedom of worship. It did not aim at erecting a "wall of separation between church and state," as some people allege today; nor did it signify interference with the states' having established churches—if the people of a state wanted it that way. No one could prove it was "unconstitutional" for Massachusetts to maintain an established church until 1833, although many thought it impolitic and unfair to people of other faiths.

The authors of the First Amendment had no intention of denying government aid to all religions on an equal basis. The first Congress, for example, provided for a chaplain's salary in its appropriation for the Army in 1791. Similar appropriations have been made by every Congress in our history. Congress has regularly appropriated money for missionaries and missionary organizations working among the Indians. It has supported religious work in many ways, always treating all religious groups equally.

Congress has not supported religious groups in order to further religion for religion's sake but for the contribution they can make to the general civic welfare. This is an important distinction to remember. Especially in the field of education, private schools and religious groups have received aid from the government. The G.I. Bill after World War II is an example of millions of dollars paid to private religious schools as tuition for students supported by the government.

The First Amendment does not express any attitude toward religion. Nor does it provide for any new arrangement in relations between church and state in America. It contains no prohibition of impartial aid to all religions. It makes no mention of government co-operation with religion or of the place of religion in education. It simply provides that no religious group be favored or established by law in preference to others.

This is the way the First Amendment was interpreted by the Supreme Court until 1947. In a nineteenth-century decision involving certain Virginia statutes concerning church property, Justice Story interpreted the First Amendment in these words:

. . . the free exercise of religion cannot be justly deemed to be restrained by aiding with equal attention the votaries of every sect to perform their own religious duties, or by establishing funds for the support of ministers, for public charities, for the endowment of churches, or for the sepulture of the dead.

Court decisions before 1947. The First Amendment's clauses on religion were seldom invoked before 1947. Only four cases reached the Supreme Court in which the establishment prohibition was invoked. The plaintiff in one case claimed that a hospital owned and operated by nuns could not receive government funds without violating the establishment clause. The Supreme Court ruled that there was no violation of the Constitution in this case. Similarly, it ruled that treaty funds[1] could be used by the government in support of Indian mission schools. In another case, the Court ruled that exempting ministers and other clergymen from the draft was not "an establishment of religion." All these decisions permitted government support of religious organizations, because such support did not concern "an establishment of religion" as that phrase is used in the First Amendment.

In 1878 a case involving the "free exercise" clause of the First Amendment reached the Supreme Court. A certain Mormon named Reynolds, who lived in Utah, then a territory and therefore under federal jurisdiction, claimed that a congressional law prohibiting polygamy (a man's having more than one wife at a time) prevented him from the free exercise of his religion. The Mormon religion then permitted polygamy. The Supreme Court upheld the law and denied Reynolds the right, on the basis of his religion, to practice polygamy. The principle on which the Court acted was that the state had the right to use appropriate measures to secure peace and good order

[1] Treaty funds are sums of money belonging to certain Indian tribes but held for them, as wards, by the federal government.

in society. The prevention of polygamy, the court held, was necessary for the welfare of society and was therefore not a violation of the First Amendment. It is obvious that such a principle must be followed, for otherwise every kind of antisocial practice could be defended in the name of some exotic religious cult or another.

In this country a series of cases came before the Court involving freedom of religion for the sect known as Jehovah's Witnesses. These cases involved freedom of assembly and speech as much as the free exercise of religion, but they were decided as religious rather than civil-rights cases. The Jehovah's Witnesses held that they could distribute literature on the street without obtaining permission from civil authorities, that they could accost people on the street, and play phonograph records on their porches. They claimed the right to ring doorbells as part of their religious propaganda campaign. They further claimed the right to sell religious literature on the street or from house to house without obtaining a peddler's license. The Supreme Court allowed these practices as part of the "free exercise of religion" as long as reasonable police regulations were not violated or disturbance of the peace did not take place. The most important of these cases to come before the Supreme Court were two in which the claims of the state and the inviolability of the citizen's conscience seemed to clash. The facts of the first case (*Minersville School District* v. *Gobitis* in 1940) were as follows: Lilian and William Gobitis were expelled from the public schools of Minersville, Pennsylvania, because they refused to salute the flag as part of the

> *I pledge allegiance to the Flag of the United States of America and to the Republic for which it stands, one Nation under God, indivisible, with Liberty and Justice for all.*

The first version of the Pledge to the Flag was drawn up in 1892. Later the words "of the United States of America" were included; most recently "under God" was added, authorized by an act of Congress, June 14, 1954.

class's daily exercise. The children had been taught by their religion to believe that saluting the flag was forbidden by the Bible.

The Supreme Court upheld the expulsion as constitutional. Justice Frankfurter, in delivering the opinion of the Court, argued that a man's conception of religious duty may be brought into conflict with the secular interests of his fellow men and that "the mere possession of religious convictions which contradict the relevant concerns of a political soci-

ety does not relieve the citizen from the discharge of political responsibilities." The legislature of Pennsylvania had decided that saluting the flag was one means of developing a sense of patriotism in young people. "The precise issue," Justice Frankfurter claimed, "for us to decide is whether the legislatures of the various states and the authorities in a thousand counties and school districts of this country are barred from determining the appropriateness of various means to evoke that unifying sentiment without

An assembly of Jehovah's Witnesses attracted thousands to New York City for a public demonstration of their religious beliefs. Such occasions are evidence of the policy of mutual toleration in the United States among all who differ in religion.

which there can ultimately be no liberties, civil or religious." The decision, in effect, was that political loyalty takes precedence over religious belief when the two conflict.

Three years later (1943) the Supreme Court reversed itself when it asserted that political loyalty is not paramount over religious loyalty. The facts in this second case are almost identical with those in the Gobitis case. Children belonging to the Jehovah's Witnesses sect were expelled from school in West Virginia for refusing to salute the flag. Their case was appealed to the Supreme Court, and in the opinion handed down for the Court, Justice Jackson severely attacked the assumptions made by the Court in the Gobitis case.

The sole issue in this case, Justice Jackson held, was the conflict between political authority and individual rights. After a long review of the facts of the case and a point-by-point refutation of the Court's opinion in the earlier Gobitis case, Jackson concluded: "We think the action of the local authorities in compelling the flag salute and pledge transcends constitutional limitations of their power and invades the sphere of intellect and spirit which it is the purpose of the First Amendment to our Constitution to reserve from all official control."

7. SOME NOVEL DECISIONS OF THE SUPREME COURT

Important cases dealing with the "establishment of religion" clause have been decided by the Supreme Court in the last decade. These decisions offered a new interpretation which leaves the meaning of the First Amendment an open question.

The Everson School Bus Case. A New Jersey law of 1941 authorized the use of public funds to pay the cost of transporting children by bus to parochial as well as public schools. Everson contested the

law on the grounds that it provided taxpayers' money to support Catholic education and that it was therefore a law "concerning an establishment of religion." The Supreme Court rejected this contention and upheld the New Jersey law by a 5–4 decision. Justice Black's majority opinion contained some unusual words:

No tax in any amount, large or small, can be levied to support any religious activities or institutions, whatever they may be called, or whatever form they may adopt to teach or practice religion. Neither a state nor the Federal Government can, openly or secretly, participate in the affairs of any religious organizations or groups and vice versa. In the words of Jefferson, the clause against the establishment of religion by law was intended to erect "a wall of separation between Church and State."

Even more startling were the words of Justice Rutledge:

The Amendment's purpose was not to strike merely at the official establishment of a single sect, creed or religion, outlawing only a formal relation such as had prevailed in England and some of the colonies. Necessarily it was to uproot all such relationships. The object was broader than separating church and state in this narrow sense. It was to create a complete and permanent separation of the spheres of religious activity and Civil authority by comprehensively forbidding every form of public aid or support for religion . . . The prohibition broadly forbids state support, financial or other, of religion in any guise, form or degree. It outlaws all use of public funds for religious purposes.

Let us now recall the language of the First Amendment: "Congress shall make no law respecting an establishment of religion, or prohibiting the free exercise thereof." It is difficult to see how Justice Rutledge could read these views into the two rather simple prohibitions. It is particularly difficult to see how he could do this when he had no precedent for his views.

Why, then, was the New Jersey law upheld? The Court held that, because the

The provision for a Catholic chapel at West Point and for chaplains of all faiths in the armed forces attests to the support that has always been given to religion by the Congresses of the United States.

payments were for a service to the students instead of to the school, aid had not been given to Catholic education. The law was therefore in the nature of public-benefit legislation. Further, the Court held that the law merely extended to students attending Catholic schools the benefits given to those attending public schools. Not to do this would be to discriminate against a group of citizens because of their religion. Similar laws providing state funds for textbooks and hot lunches for children attending private schools had been held constitutional on the grounds that they aided school children rather than religion. Late in 1947 a new state constitution for New Jersey legalized publicly provided school-bus transportation for all children, those attending parochial and private as well as public schools. Nineteen states had similar legislation. It was evident, however, that the New Jersey decision left open the questions as to what extent and in what ways public funds can be used to support parochial or private schools.

The McCollum Case. In 1948 the Supreme Court handed down an 8–1 decision in the McCollum case that seemed to preclude any form of state encouragement to religion. The facts of the case are these: The school board of Champaign,

Illinois, allowed representatives of the Jewish, Protestant, and Catholic religions to conduct classes in religious education in public school buildings during a period when students were released to attend such classes. The period was forty-five minutes a week, and students were released only on written request from their parents. The point at issue was that the public school buildings and time "re-

The motto "In God We Trust" first appeared in 1864 on a two-cent piece. Now a commonplace expression of the people of this country, it was at the suggestion of a Rev. Mr. Watkinson that Lincoln's Secretary of the Treasury, Salmon P. Chase, had this inscription struck on a coin. (The Chase National Bank)

leased" from the regular school day were used for religious instruction. The teachers were not paid by the state, nor was any student forced to take religious instructions. Those not taking religious instructions had a study period.

Mrs. Vashti McCollum took action against the school board on the grounds that their released-time program constituted "an establishment of religion." The Illinois Supreme Court upheld the law under which the school board acted, but the United States Supreme Court reversed the decision and declared the law unconstitutional. The Court's reasoning is summed up in this conclusion: "Here not only are the State's tax-supported public school buildings used for the dissemination of religious doctrine. The State also affords sectarian groups an invaluable aid in that it helps to provide pupils for their religious classes through the use of the State's compulsory school machinery. This is not separation of Church and State."

The decision in the McCollum case appeared to many to make unconstitutional any use of public funds that might in any way support religion. In his dissenting opinion, Justice Reed adverted to the fact that public support—without discrimination against any religion or exclusive support of one sect—is widespread in this country and has always been part of the American tradition. He mentioned specifically such institutions as chaplaincies in the armed forces, religious services at West Point and Annapolis, legislation requiring Sabbath observance, permission for Bible reading in the public schools in many states, and—most important of all —exemption of religious institutions from taxation.

Perhaps the Court realized the likely consequences of its decision. In 1952 it rendered a different decision on the constitutionality of New York City's released-time program. The program in New York City differed from that in Champaign because in New York the religious classes took place outside the school buildings, in classrooms provided by the various religious bodies. Six justices thought this difference sufficient to render the New York City program constitutional. They carefully avoided reversing the McCollum decision, but they prepared the way for its reversal in future cases. In handing down the majority opinion Justice Douglas asserted that, "when the state encourages religious institutions or co-operates with religious authorities by adjusting the schedule of public events to sectarian needs, it follows the best of our traditions." The dissenting opinion continued the newly established tradition of the McCollum decision. It condemned the program for utilizing the state's compulsory public school machinery to further religious education.

The decision in the New York City case suggests that perhaps the Supreme Court may return to the original meaning of the First Amendment: that Congress is to pass no law abridging freedom of religion, nor any law giving one religion a privileged position as against other religions.

Separation of church and state today. Some people wrongly believe that American Catholics are opposed to the system of relations worked out between church and state in the United States. These people believe that separation of church and state, as developed in this country, is a "Protestant arrangement" to which Catholics must be opposed. As a matter of fact, the only established churches in our history were Protestant churches, and they were all disestablished by 1833. American Catholics and Protestants agree on this point: practical necessity, as well as political prudence, dictates a policy of *mutual* toleration among all who differ in religion. There has never been basic criticism of the American arrangement by any authoritative spokes-

Francis Cardinal Spellman presents "Ad Altare Dei" awards to outstanding Catholic Boy Scouts at the annual Boy Scout Week spiritual demonstration. (C.Y.O. Photo by Bill Linge)

man of the Catholic Church in the United States. On the contrary, Catholic leaders have all been warm in their praise of this government's attitude toward religion, and they have derived great advantage from the provisions of the First Amendment.

Establishment of a religion is a political matter. So, too, is separation of church and state. In some countries an alliance of church and state seemed the best arrangement for both the state and the church. These are countries where almost everyone belongs to one religion, as Lutherans in Denmark or Catholics in Spain. Such a situation does not exist in this country, where we have more than two hundred different denominations.

Misunderstanding of the Catholics' position has persisted, however, and it is therefore necessary to restate it from time to time.

The great Pope Leo XIII in 1885 stated the unchanging and unalterable Catholic doctrine:

The Almighty, therefore, has appointed the charge of the human race between two powers, the ecclesiastical and the civil, the one being set over divine, the other over human things. Each in its kind is supreme, each has fixed limits within which it is contained, limits which are defined by the nature and special object of the province of each, so that there is, we may say, an orbit traced out within which the action of each is brought into play by its own native right . . . Whatever, therefore, in human things is of a sacred character, whatever belongs either of its own nature or by reason of the end to which it is referred, to the salvation of our souls, or to the worship of God, is subject to the power and judgment of the Church. Whatever is to be ranged under the civil and political order is rightly subject to the civil authority. Jesus Christ has himself given command that what is Caesar's is to be rendered to Caesar, and that what belongs to God be rendered to God.

This doctrine marks the difference between two spheres of authority but does not set these spheres against each other. Bishops and priests have the duty to obey the just laws of civil society, even as laymen have the duty to obey the laws of the Church. Neither authority should transgress the other, and it is to the interest of both that they should stand in amicable relations. If they clash, it can be only because one or the other has abused its authority. In some countries the line of demarcation between the authority of the state and of the Church has been drawn by treaties known as *concordats* between the government and the Papacy; but in the United States this has never been necessary or even possible, since such a

A public awareness of the need for religion in our lives has been manifest by the popularity of religious programs on radio and television and religious themes in modern literature. More important, of course, is the actual practice of religion and the attendance at church, the object of national campaigns by serious-minded people. (The Advertising Council)

treaty clearly would trangress if not the letter, certainly the spirit and principle of the Constitution. Treaties made pursuant to the Constitution become part of the supreme law of the land, and a concordat with the Church would surely be held to be a "law respecting an establishment of religion."

As long as our Constitution stands with its guarantee of religious liberty, the United States will not have the kind of government that could enter into a concordat with the Pope. As a great Catholic thinker once said, the Church makes concordats with its enemies rather than with its friends. Most concordats have been treaties of peace between Church and state negotiated after a quarrel. Under our institutions such a clash is impossible. This being so, there is no reason why the civil and religious institutions should not co-operate in a friendly way

President Eisenhower attended the Red Mass for Supreme Court Justices, legislators, and lawyers upon the opening of Congress. Pictured with the President is Archbishop Patrick A. O'Boyle of St. Matthew's Cathedral, Washington, D.C.

for common purposes. In a formal statement made after the McCollum decision in 1948 the Catholic bishops of America said:

We feel with deep conviction that for the sake of both good citizenship and religion there should be a reaffirmation of our original American tradition of free co-operation between government and religious bodies—co-operation involving no special privilege to any group and no restriction on the religious liberty of any citizen. We solemnly disclaim any intent or desire to alter this prudent and fair American policy of government in dealing with the delicate problems that have their source in the divided religious allegiance of our citizens.

The original American tradition of which the bishops speak has consistently been followed until recent times. Every Congress in our history provided, in some measure, for the friendly support of religion with special privilege for no one church. Every President has given friendly encouragement to all religions. State governments have consistently used public funds to aid religion or religious education in various ways. Every Supreme Court decision until the McCollum case was consistent with the intent and the wording of the First Amendment as traditionally understood in America. The only official deviation from this interpretation was the opinion handed down in the Everson case and reaffirmed in the opinion and the decision of the McCollum case.

Describe this situation. What was and what was not the aim of the First Amendment in regard to the "establishment of religion"?

B. Before 1947, four decisions on this question were rendered. Give the core of the decisions in each case.

C. Cite some examples of government "aid" to all religions on an equal basis.

7. Some Novel Decisions of the Supreme Court

A. Cite the main facts in the Everson bus case. What novel idea did Justice Black introduce in the majority decision? How did Justice Rutledge go further?

B. Give the salient facts of the McCollum case. Show how the decision would influence future government aid to religion. Point out how the Court seemed to reverse itself in the New York case.

C. What do Protestants and Catholics agree on concerning "separation of church and state" in America? Give the views of Pope Leo XIII on this question. Why does America not need a Concordat?

THE CHAPTER IN REVIEW

A. Show historically the position of religion in government in 1787 before the Constitution was adopted.

B. What did the First Amendment intend to achieve with respect to an establishment of religion? Show how the decisions of the Supreme Court before 1947 backed this view.

C. A new interpretation of the "establishment of religion" has come into being. Describe its dangers and show how and why it is new.

D. Point out how the Supreme Court has accepted this new interpretation. Is there any hope that it will return to the original meaning? Use an important recent case to illustrate your answer.

REVIEW

6. The Constitution and Religious Liberty

A. The situation in 1789 helps to explain the reason for the prohibition respecting the establishment of religion in the First Amendment.

SELECTED READINGS

Basic principles of church-state relations are given in Msgr. John A. Ryan and Rev. Francis J. Boland, C.S.C., *Catholic Principles of Politics* (New York: The Macmillan Co., 1940). More specific treatment is given to this subject by Rev. Jeffrey Keefe, O.F.M., *American Separation of Church and State,* and Rev. Gerald G. Walsh, S.J., *Church and State,* both pamphlets published by the Paulist Press of New York City.

Protestant and other attacks on the Catholic Church as an institution in a democratic society are just about all distilled into the book of Paul Blanshard, *American Freedom and Catholic Power* (Boston: Beacon Press, 1949). This book is excellently refuted in the pamphlet of George H. Dunne, S.J., *Religion and American Democracy* (New York: America Press, 1950). Fuller answers, which also give a good deal of historical information on church-state relations in this country, are the excellent works of James M. O'Neill, *Religion and Education under the Constitution* (New York: Harper & Brothers, 1949); *Catholicism and American Freedoms* (New York: Harper & Brothers, 1952); and *Catholics in Controversy* (New York: The Declan X. McMullen Co., Inc., 1954). *Catholic-Protestant Conflicts in America* is the title of an objective study by John J. Kane (Chicago: Henry Regnery Co., 1955) that explains the symptoms of religious conflict. For the matter of church and state and the First Amendment, *The First Freedom* by Wilfrid Parsons, S.J. (New York: The Declan X. McMullen Company, Inc., 1948), is recommended.

For the novel decisions of the Supreme Court, see Msgr. Joseph H. Brady, *Confusion Twice Confounded,* (South Orange, N.J.: Seton Hall University Press, 1954).

PROJECTS

1. The phrase "separation of church and state" has been used frequently in recent years. Find out how this was used by Thomas Jefferson and report to the class how it has since been misused.

2. To understand the true meaning of the First Amendment in regard to religion, we must know how it was developed before Congress adopted it. Report to the class on this early development. The first few chapters of *The First Freedom,* by Wilfrid Parsons, S.J. (New York: Declan X. McMullen Co., 1948) should prove useful in your research.

3. What are some of the many implications in the words of Justice Rutledge's decision in the Everson case? Draw up a list of benefits that you believe the government (state or local) might offer to students in parochial schools as well as to those in public schools. Present this to the class and ask for opinions of your selections.

PROFILES

GEORGE WASHINGTON

BORN: Westmoreland County, Va., Feb. 22, 1732
EDUCATION: Slight formal schooling; apprentice surveyor and Virginia Militia basic training
MARRIAGE: January 6, 1759, to Martha Dandridge Custis
DIED: Mount Vernon, Va., Dec. 14, 1799

Although he was the son of a rather prosperous plantation owner, Washington's education was scanty, owing to the death of his father in 1743. The lack of formal training was made up by extensive surveying experience, the management of his family's much-diminished fortune, and varied military and political service to the colony of Virginia. During the French and Indian War, Washington, with the rank of colonel, earned prestige as the most successful colonial officer, especially after his work in reducing the French fort at Duquesne in 1758. Fellow Virginians elected him to the House of Burgesses and designated him a representative to both Continental Congresses.

His indignation at British threats to colonists' liberties, together with his established military reputation, led to his assignment as commander of the Continental Army in 1775. He distinguished himself in the military field by forcing the British from Boston, later by extricating the American army from almost certain destruction in New York, and by his brilliant tactical moves that led to final victory at Yorktown. More important, he held his severely strained army together through his own example of fortitude in the face of danger, devotion to duty, and an unblushing, publicly proclaimed faith in God. He demonstrated his loyalty to his troops by insisting on the passage of laws that would compensate them for their Revolutionary service, and by his devotion to the newly formed nation. He refused to establish himself as King, urging his officers to "banish such thoughts" from their minds.

The quiet of Mount Vernon was interrupted when Washington played host to a convention there in 1785 which helped to pave the way for the Constitutional Convention in Philadelphia in 1787. The Founding Fathers chose him as their president at the Constitutional Convention, and the people's faith in him helped secure ratification of the Constitution, under which he was immediately and unanimously chosen as first President. During his eight years in office he established the dignity, prestige, and power of the federal government as the shield of liberty and protector of the general welfare. He placed great value on independent action in foreign affairs, a strong government under constitutional restraints, patriotism rather than partisan politics, and morality and religion as the bases for individual and national strength.

The latest and most complete biography of Washington currently available is by Douglas Southall Freeman, 6 vols. (New York: Charles Scribner's Sons, 1954); special studies include Nettels' *George Washington and American Independence* (Boston: Little, Brown & Co., 1951). For intimate personal glimpses of the general and President, sample *The Diaries of George Washington, 1748–1799,* edited in 4 vols., by John C. Fitzpatrick (Boston: Houghton Mifflin Co., 1925). See also *Conceived in Liberty* (New York: Doubleday & Company, Inc., 1955) pp. 104–133; 159–174.

THOMAS JEFFERSON

BORN: Shadwell, Albemarle County, Va., April 13, 1743
EDUCATED: William and Mary College, 1762; private law studies
DIED: Monticello, Va., July 4, 1826

Jefferson, proprietor of an extensive and valuable plantation and an avid reader who spent up to fifteen hours a day in his studies, became one of the outstanding spokesmen of the revolutionary cause against England. His frequently used motto, "Resistance to tyrants is obedience to God," can be traced in the Declaration of Independence, of which he was the principal author.

In 1776 Jefferson returned to Virginia, where he helped organize the state along true republican lines. He led the movement to disestablish the Anglican Church and abolish primogeniture. Following two critical years as war governor while British armies operated in Virginia, and a second term in Congress, Jefferson served as Minister to France from 1785 to 1789. He returned to serve as Washington's Secretary of State. While in the Cabinet he led in the organization of the Republican party. As leader of the Republican opposition to the Adams government, he drafted the Kentucky Resolutions in 1798, which explained his views of states' rights. Following a bitterly waged presidential campaign, he and Aaron Burr were elected by Republican electors in the only tied vote in an American presidential election. Some Federalist votes in the House of Representatives gave Jefferson the presidency.

As President, Jefferson emphasized simple manners, and economy in government. His foreign policy, aimed at securing freedom of the seas for Americans, led to such developments as the Louisiana Purchase, which was originally intended only to secure access to the Gulf of Mexico; the war with the Tripoli pirates; and the Embargo Act, which tried to utilize the colonial tactic of suspending trade to force recognition of American interests.

After retiring to Monticello, which he had personally designed, Jefferson devoted himself to his plantation, his books, and education in Virginia. His chief accomplishment in these later years was the founding of the University of Virginia. His ideal was a limited government .protecting the liberties of a nation of well-educated, small farmers. Above all, the author of the Declaration of Independence and the Virginia statute for religious freedom emphasized the importance of personal liberty: "The God who gave us life, gave us liberty at the same time."

A fine study of Jefferson's early political party work is presented in Adrienne Koch's *Jefferson and Madison: The Great Collaboration* (New York: Alfred A. Knopf, Inc., 1950). Extracts from his writings which illustrate his ideas are included in *Jeffersonian Principles and Hamiltonian Principles,* edited by James T.

Adams (Boston: Little, Brown & Co., 1932). The complete papers of Jefferson are in the process of being published by Princeton University Press under the general editorship of Julian Parks Boyd.

JAMES MADISON

BORN: Port Conway, Va., March 16, 1751
EDUCATED: College of New Jersey (now Princeton University), class of 1771
DIED: Montpelier, Va., June 28, 1836

Intensive study seriously weakened Madison's health, so that his physical activity was limited for a long period. However, shifting from an early interest in theology, he became a public figure in 1776, when he helped draft the Virginia constitution. He substituted a guarantee of the "free exercise of religion" in the Virginia constitution for a phrase guaranteeing "fullest toleration"—which he construed to indicate that government could control religion. In 1784–1785 he was floor leader in the Virginia House of Delegates in the fight to disestablish the Anglican Church, following Jefferson's lead for the first time.

Madison's chief contributions were made in 1787–1788, as delegate to the Constitutional Convention and co-author of *The Federalist,* which spearheaded the campaign to ratify the new Constitution. Madison prepared and co-delegate Randolph presented the "Virginia Plan," which, after modification by other delegates, became the Constitution; moreover, his personal diary is the chief source of information on the convention. A member of the first Congress, he added to his reputation by urging the passage of the Bill of Rights.

Madison strongly supported Jefferson on financial policy and strict interpretation of the Constitution. In 1798 he wrote the Virginia Resolutions, which denounced the Alien and Sedition Acts and were patterned after Jefferson's Kentucky Resolutions. Later, Jefferson appointed Madison Secretary of State and groomed him as successor to the presidency. In 1809, Madison's wife, the famous Dolly Madison, turned the White House into the nation's social center. However, troubles that Madison had experienced with England while he was Secretary of State developed into the War of 1812. American misfortunes in the war were blamed on the unlucky Madison, whose reputation was damaged by military reversals.

His presidency was marked, however, by the chartering of the Second Bank of the United States and the enactment of a protective tariff law—both measures showing that the Republican Madison was willing to adopt former Federalist policies for the good of the country and to change his mind in the public interest, as he had shown earlier in the Constitutional Convention, when he had earned the unique title of "Father of the Constitution."

Specialized studies of the career of James Madison are made in Irving Brant's *James Madison* 4 vols. (Indianapolis: The Bobbs-Merrill Company, Inc., 1953). For a liberal sampling of Madison's writings, a handy book is *The Complete Madison* by Saul K. Padover (New York: Harper & Brothers, 1953). Of all books connected with Madison, unquestionably the most important is *The Federalist.*

DEBATE

The idea of a debate. If we are to study the national problems of America it must be assumed that we recognize the conflicts in our society and the existence of certain inadequate measures for dealing with the business of everyday living in the United States. We must recognize the presence of some prejudice and ignorance, and the element of human frailty in making permanent and lasting prescriptions for the preservation and betterment of our way of life. In short, we must realize there will always be some problems. It must also be assumed that even right-thinking and well-informed individuals will differ among themselves in proposing the solutions for concrete problems. This, of course, gives us the reason for our debate. It is a good reason if it encourages constructive criticism and leads to sound improvements.

"Light and transient causes" are not the proper matter for debates in a National Problems course, and there is no reason for introducing special pleading, or the notion that variety of opinion is a good thing simply because it is varied. The permanence of the *principles* that are to be found in our American heritage and in the Catholic tradition, and which are explained in this text, should be understood. These form a foundation for our argument; reason and correct procedure form the basis for our judgment-making.

The purpose of the debate. The debate has many purposes: to broaden our knowledge of the topic; to teach us how to distinguish the various kinds of evidence and to give us the experience of weighing each kind; to teach us how to organize our thinking so that we recognize the salient features (and the weaknesses) of our argument, and to see the strength and weakness in the opposing view; to make conclusions from the arguments of both sides; to re-form our opinions and to make judgments; to be better informed and to speak articulately on these important problems from a genuine interest in them.

The aims of the debate. There are three immediate aims of the debates: (1) to gain an understanding of the basic principles involved, so that we see the issues in their own proper domain; (2) to learn the sources of information on current events, where to find them, how to use them, and how to evaluate them; (3) to gain an appreciation of the complexities involved in forming judgments in current affairs.

The procedure for the debate. The rules of conduct for debating may be found in a debater's manual. It should be remembered that the issues that are to be debated in this course are serious and often delicate in their nature. They are, moreover, to be based on principles that are constant, and the exercise of a debate should strengthen these principles. There is, then, a good reason to suggest that our arguments be fair, and not dogmatic when the data do not warrant it. We should strive to convince by argument and not persuade by oratory. We should respect evidence, distinguishing the important from the unimportant, the relevant from the irrelevant.

The debate outline. In the debates for Units Two, Five, and Nine, each side of the question is completely outlined. Included in these debates are the presentation, rebuttal, and conclusion for the affirmative and negative sides. The debate itself is not *written* and the organization of the argument is merely *proposed* and can be re-ordered as the debaters wish. You will see, however, the development that the debate will undergo if this organization is followed. For these debates you will notice immediately that there is no *documentation,* no *evidence* has been offered in support of the general statements, and the rebuttals and conclusions are based on the presentation of the opposing side.

For the other debates in the book less direction has been given and the debater is required to fill in additional arguments and to supply rebuttals and conclusions, in addition to gathering evidence and documentary proof for his arguments.

All of the debates include brief instructions for classroom discussions. For all but one of the debates a bibliography is offered. Other sources, of course, can be found in the Selected Readings following each chapter and from the periodical index and other sources common to most libraries.

Participation in the debate. Your teacher will assign members for each team, alternates, and a chairman—but you are all expected to participate in the debate. In some debates your teacher may not include a rebuttal, preferring to have the debaters support their stand by answering the questions of members in the class. You may not reach a judgment by listening to the debate, although you probably will if you are a debater, but you will be better informed and nearer to an opinion than you were before. All students should review the instructions for class discussion and determine which arguments speak to these points.

DEBATE PROJECTS FOR THIS UNIT

1. Draw up an outline for a debate based on one of the topics discussed in this unit. You can test your ability to recognize an "issue," its causes, its history, and its importance, as well as your ability to organize the major arguments for each side. Use the debates at the end of Units Two, Five, and Nine as your guides.

2. From recent commentaries on a controversial matter, select statements "pro" and "con" and read them to the class. Does the class consider the issue involved worthy of a debate? Is it debatable? Does the class agree that you have chosen quotations of equal weight and authority? What do you think now of your "documentation"?

3. From the Letters to the Editor of your local newspaper, or preferably from a journal of opinion such as *America* or *Commonweal,* select one that deals with a controversial subject. Was the writer fair in his presentation? Was he convincing? What would you include in an answer to his letter? Cite evidence and authorities in support of your view.

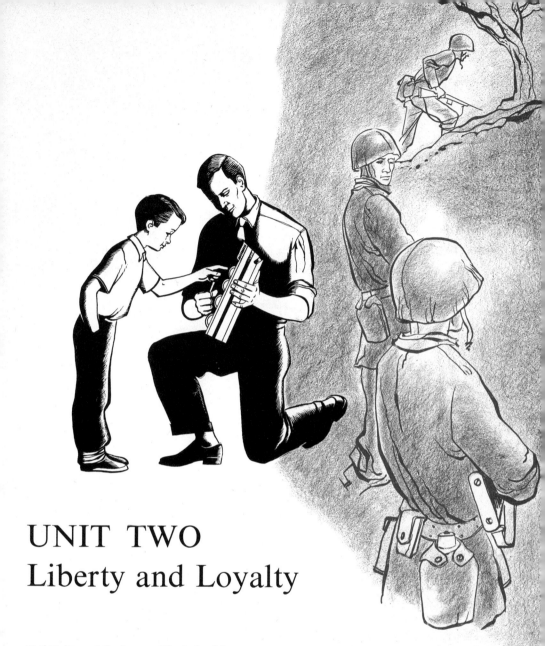

UNIT TWO
Liberty and Loyalty

Chapter 4. The Historical Development of American Freedom

8. CIVIL RIGHTS AND THE POWER OF THE FEDERAL GOVERNMENT

The basic question confronting Americans in the middle of the twentieth century is whether their free society is to survive. We shall see in due course that our free way of life is threatened from abroad. It is also threatened from within. There is always some danger that, while Americans are trying to build defenses against foreign attack, they may unwittingly lose the very freedom they seek to protect. Americans should therefore periodically take inventory of their freedoms, evaluate their importance, and study ways and means of preserving this precious heritage of freedom which has been given to them.

True freedom is not to be confused with the license to do anything that does not violate the freedom of others. A wrong idea of freedom underlies the old saying that one man's freedom to swing his fist ends where another man's nose begins. In the Christian tradition freedom is connected with duty. A man has the

duty to be a good man. He has an obligation to worship God and to respect himself and his fellow men as creatures made to the image and likeness of God. Because a person has these obligations, he has the right to whatever ways and means are necessary to fulfill them. His rights and freedom, then, are related to his duties. They are inalienable and natural because they are from the Creator.

These freedoms have flourished in America. They did not become extreme license on the one hand, nor on the other have they been suppressed arbitrarily in the interest of conformity and security, although they have always been limited by the rights of other persons and by the common welfare. Freedom of speech, for example, has never meant the right to slander a neighbor or to deceive a business associate. Nor has it meant the right to shout "Fire!" in a theater just to see what would happen. With good reason, as we shall see later, it has come to include the right to picket peacefully with placards during a strike. It also includes the right to criticize, in good faith, the

laws of the land and the way in which they are enforced.

Human freedom is basic to the theory of limited government that we subscribe to in this country. For the essence of limited government is the recognition of regions of life that the government cannot arbitrarily restrict or invade. These are specific rights which the people have set beyond governments, but they are limited by the similar rights of others and by the very nature of things. A man who is criminally insane, for example, does not have the same right to freedom of movement in society that the rest of us enjoy. A man subject to sudden fits has no inalienable right to drive a car, because this would jeopardize not only his own safety but other people's right to life.

Bill of Rights. The rights and liberties the American people reserved to themselves when they formed their government are to be found principally in the Bill of Rights of the federal Constitution. They are also to be found in the various state constitutions and in the body of precedents created by judicial decisions in the federal and state courts. No full list of the American citizen's rights can be made. The Ninth Amendment to the federal Constitution states that "the enumeration . . . of certain rights shall not be construed to deny or disparage others retained by the people." But no one knows for sure what these other rights include. Court decisions specify what they are at a given time and under certain conditions. Therefore, the ways in which we may exercise our rights continually undergo modification as conditions change.

It is nevertheless true that our rights remain fundamentally the same throughout our history, since they are inseparable from man's nature, which does not change. It is only the concrete realization of our rights that changes somewhat from time to time. This concrete realization of our rights and freedoms has been accomplished largely through the courts' building up an impressive body of precedents, rules, and doctrines on the subject. It is therefore necessary for us to examine, at least briefly, the historical development of our freedoms.

Historical background of the Bill of Rights. It is well to remember that the American colonists who won their independence from Great Britain in 1781 inherited the rights and freedoms Englishmen had won through centuries of struggle against their king. The right to trial by jury, to subpoena witnesses for one's defense in court, and to be represented by counsel —all stated in the Sixth Amendment—

had been won by Englishmen at the price of long struggle and much bloodshed. The colonists revolted because they believed that their rights were being repeatedly violated by the British Government. It was natural for them to state these rights as specifically as possible and to protect them from invasion by the government they were to create in 1789.

Three states—Virginia, Pennsylvania, and Massachusetts—had adopted constitutions with bills of rights before independence was won. Guarantees were made in these constitutions for free expression of opinion and for freedom of religious worship, and provisions were adopted to prevent abuses in criminal law. Eleven states had adopted constitutions with similar guarantees by the time the federal Constitution was written in 1787. There seemed no reason, then, for the citizens of this new country to fear that the various states would encroach upon their freedom. Nor was there then any reason, in law or logic, to fear that the new federal government would violate their rights. The new government possessed only specified, delegated powers. Lawfully it could do nothing not specifically delegated to it in the Constitution. However, Americans had a great deal of experience to show them that governments could find legal pretexts to do many dangerous and arbitrary acts. Hence there was strong conviction that a list of rights and freedoms should be written in the Constitution.

As we know from American history, the necessary number of states ratified the Constitution only after an understanding was reached that such amendments would be adopted. Alexander Hamilton had argued that a bill of rights was unnecessary and that it might prove a dangerous thing by weakening the doctrine of specified, delegated powers. To enumerate things the federal government could *not* do might imply that it could do everything else. Nevertheless, ten amendments were adopted and took effect in 1791. These constitute our Bill of Rights. Another amendment was proposed to make the Bill of Rights apply to the states. It read: "No State shall infringe the equal rights of conscience, nor the freedom of speech or of the press, nor the right of trial by jury in criminal cases." This proposed amendment passed the House, but it was defeated in the Senate, where it was regarded as an invasion of the rights of the states.

The Bill of Rights, then, was originally meant to apply only to the federal government. It was believed that the various states in their constitutions had already set up sufficient protections for their citizens' rights and freedoms. It was further felt that the federal government should not encroach upon the sovereignty of the states by limiting their powers in the federal Constitution. The Founding Fathers apparently did not conceive that the federal government might in time undertake the task of protecting American citizens from their state and local governments.

Summary statement of the guaranteed rights. The basic list of rights and freedoms found in the federal Constitution is repeated—sometimes in considerably more detail and with many additions—in almost every state constitution. For our purposes, however, it will suffice to list briefly the provisions in the Constitution and its Bill of Rights.

Confusing License with Liberty Violates the Rights of Others

Section 9 of the first article of the Constitution safeguards certain civil rights from violation by the federal government, and Section 10 of the same article protects the same rights from encroachment by the states. In these two sections guarantee is made that the writ of *habeas corpus* cannot be suspended except in time of rebellion or invasion, when public safety would require it. A writ of *habeas corpus* works in this way: Any person held on suspicion of committing a crime may request an immediate hearing in court to determine whether there are adequate grounds for his detention. The writ is issued by the court to the officer holding the suspect in custody. The officer is ordered to bring the prisoner into court. If it is found that he is being held contrary to law, he is given his freedom. Otherwise he is held for trial, with or without bail, depending on the circumstances.

Neither the federal government nor any state is allowed to pass a bill of attainder or an *ex post facto* law. A bill of attainder is a law that punishes an individual or a group of people. Parliament had used this device for punishing people simply by passing a bill "attainting" a person of crime without judicial trial or the hearing of evidence. The Supreme Court has defined an *ex post facto* law as (1) one which "makes an action done before the passing of the law, and which was innocent when done, criminal, and punishes such action"; or (2) one which "aggravates a crime, or makes it greater than it was when committed"; or (3) one which "changes the punishment, and inflicts a greater punishment than the law annexed to the crime when committed"; or (4) one which "alters the legal rules of evidence and requires less, or different, testimony than the law required at the time of the commission of the offense, in order to convict the offender."

Section 2 of Article III guarantees that those accused of criminal offenses against

Although the American press has never been as restricted as this artist's conception, newspaper societies are quick to challenge any act that threatens their freedom. (Kuekes in the Cleveland Plain Dealer—*Wide World)*

federal law shall enjoy the right of trial by jury, and Section 3 of the same article defines treason and sets limits to the method of conviction and the extent of punishment for the crime. Citizens' rights are protected against the states in two other parts of the original Constitution. Section 10 of Article I forbids the states to pass any laws that would impair the obligation of contracts. Section 2 of Article IV guarantees that "the citizens of each State shall be entitled to all privileges and immunities of citizens in the several States."

These are only scattered clauses in the Constitution which refer to civil rights. It is the first ten amendments which constitute our Bill of Rights. The First Amendment guarantees freedom of religion, speech, press, assembly, and the right to petition the government for redress of grievances. The second asserts the people's right to keep and bear arms. The third safeguards citizens from having soldiers quartered in their homes without their permission. The next five amendments protect citizens from unreasonable search, from excessive punishment or bail, and from various abuses that might arise in the courts. The Ninth Amendment states that "the enumeration in the Constitution of certain rights shall not be construed to deny or disparage others retained by the people." The tenth reserves to the states or to the people all powers not explicitly given to the federal government. In addition to the statement of certain specific rights, then, there is a general limitation of the federal government to its delegated powers and a retention by the people of a reservoir of unspecified rights—presumably to be made specific as occasion demands.

9. THE FEDERAL GOVERNMENT AS GUARDIAN OF CIVIL RIGHTS

Before the Civil War the federal government had passed no laws which were declared by the courts to have infringed the freedoms of its citizens. Until that time only two acts of Congress had been declared unconstitutional, and neither of these involved the Bill of Rights. Early court decisions in 1833 and 1845 held that the Constitution and its first ten amendments did not apply to the states. **New constitutional powers.** The Civil War created a new problem. During the war, you will remember from American history, President Lincoln freed the slaves. When the war was over this emancipation was applied to the rebellious states, and the federal government assumed the obligation of preventing the southern states from rendering the proclamation null and void. Three new amendments of the Constitution were adopted—the Thirteenth, Fourteenth, and Fifteenth. The Thirteenth Amendment prohibits slavery or involuntary servitude except as punishment for a crime of which the party

has been duly convicted. The Fifteenth Amendment asserts that no citizen's right to vote shall be denied on account of race, color, or previous condition of servitude. These two amendments were obviously intended to protect the recently freed slaves.

The Fourteenth Amendment is considerably more complex in its provisions than the Thirteenth or Fifteenth. In the area of civil rights, however, it is the first section of this amendment that is important. It defines citizenship in national terms and forbids any state to abridge or restrict the privileges or immunities of United States citizenship. The amendment continues: "nor shall any State deprive any person of life, liberty, or property, without due process of law; nor deny to any person within its jurisdiction the equal protection of the laws." This amendment was undoubtedly designed to guarantee to the recently freed slaves equal legal status with the whites in the southern states. Court decisions based on this amendment would give a different and broader meaning to the "due process of law" clause, as we shall see, by applying it to corporations as well as to persons, and by using it to channel the Bill of Rights into the area of state legislation. Thus the federal government would assume the role of protector of civil rights. In other words, the rights defined in the Constitution to *limit* federal power would be upheld *by* federal power against state or local violations of them. This statement will become clearer as we proceed.

After World War I. War is always a great enemy of civil rights and liberties. President Lincoln had used the executive power far beyond its constitutional limits in order to prevent obstruction or sabotage of the Union's war against the southern states. Similarly, the federal government during our participation in World War I refused to allow civil rights to hamper the war effort, and many things

The defense of our civil liberties, especially to criticize our government according to the dictates of our conscience, is dramatically shown here, "To silence criticism is to silence freedom." (William Sharp in the New York Times*)*

were done that would have been illegal in peacetime. After the war, fear of Communist revolutionaries inspired some doubtfully legal actions by the United States Attorney General's office and a number of state laws that went against both letter and spirit of constitutionally defined civil rights. In these circumstances a number of legal cases arose which produced some very important decisions of the Supreme Court.

Notable Court decisions. The Court evolved the "clear and present danger" norm for deciding whether legislation restricting freedom of speech, press, and assembly was constitutional. Such restriction, the Court held, violated the First Amendment unless the danger to be averted would clearly and directly result from the act for which the defendant was prosecuted. In 1919 Justice Holmes (in *Schenck* v. *United States*) stated the doctrine in these words: "The question in every case is whether the words used are used in such circumstances and are of such a nature as to create a clear and present danger that will bring about the substantive evils that Congress has a right to prevent. It is a question of proximity and degree."

In 1927 (in *Whitney* v. *California*) Justice Brandeis elaborated the doctrine.

There must be a reasonable ground to believe that the danger apprehended is imminent. There must be reasonable ground to believe that the evil to be prevented is a serious one. . . .

The wide difference between advocacy and incitement, between preparation and attempt, between assembling and conspiracy, must be borne in mind. In order to support a finding of a clear and present danger it must be shown either that immediate serious violence was to be expected or was advocated, or that the past conduct furnished reason to believe that such advocacy was then contemplated.

These and a series of similar decisions protected a person's right to criticize his government and to advocate changes in it as long as he did not incite his listeners to immediate violence. Some such line had to be drawn. Otherwise the government could justify its suppression of free speech, of freedom of the press and assembly, on the grounds that it was exercising its right to provide for the public safety. In this way it could suppress all criticisms.

In a series of decisions beginning with the *Gitlow* v. *New York* case of 1925 the Supreme Court interpreted the Fourteenth Amendment as applying certain "substantive" rights of the Constitution to the states.[1] (To understand that this is a revolutionary interpretation, we must

---

[1] Substantive rights are those which inhere in a person and must be respected by the government. They are principally freedom of religion, speech, press, and assembly. Procedural rights entitle a person to benefits arising from things being done in a specified way. These rights relate chiefly to the obtaining of evidence and its use in court, to trial by jury, and to the method of assessing punishment for crimes proved against a person.

An elderly gentleman reads his carefully prepared speech at a New England town meeting. Actual participation in the affairs of his goverment is his best safeguard against encroachment of his civil rights. (Standard Oil Co., N.J.)

remember that the federal Constitution was originally thought to limit only the federal government.) In the Gitlow case Justice Sanford stated: "For the present purposes, we may and do assume that freedom of speech and of the press—which are protected by the First Amendment from abridgement by Congress—are among the fundamental personal rights and liberties protected by the due process clause of the Fourteenth Amendment from impairment by the states."

After 1925, Supreme Court decisions in cases of personal freedoms against the states followed this principle. Such phrases as these constantly recur: "It is no longer open to doubt that the liberty of the press and of speech is within the liberty safeguarded from invasion by state action." "The First Amendment, which the Fourteenth makes applicable to the states . . ." "Moreover, since the First Amendment has been read into the Fourteenth, our problem is . . ."

At the present time, however, there is no complete agreement on how much of the federal Constitution is made applicable to the states by the Fourteenth Amendment. The general line of division taken by the Supreme Court seems to be that substantive rights are protected from

invasion by the states but that procedural rights are not. The reason, as given by Justice Cardozo, is that "few would be so narrow or provincial as to maintain that a fair and enlightened system of justice would be impossible without them (procedural rights)." Justice Cardozo was speaking of indictment by grand jury, trial by jury, protection from compulsory self-incrimination, and other such procedural rights guaranteed against federal encroachment in the Bill of Rights.

Two more decisions may be mentioned to show the trend of Supreme Court opinion. Both were handed down in 1937. In the case of *Herndon* v. *Lowry*, Herndon was freed from a twenty-year sentence imposed on him by a lower court for "incitement to insurrection." Herndon, who was a Communist, had conducted meetings and possessed literature intended to promote the Communist cause in America. The Supreme Court held that no "clear and present danger" of insurrection resulted from his action, and therefore his freedom of speech had been impaired by the lower court's decision.

In the case of *De Jonge* v. *Oregon,* the Supreme Court reversed the state supreme court of Oregon for upholding De Jonge's conviction for participating in a public meeting held under the auspices of the Communist party. Quoting a previous decision, Chief Justice Hughes asserted: "The very idea of a government, republican in its form, implies a right on the part of its citizens to meet peaceably for consultation in respect to public affairs and to petition for a redress of grievances." Since the meeting was peaceable and there was no incitement to immediate violence, the Supreme Court declared that De Jonge's right to attend an assembly for discussing public matters had been violated by Oregon authorities.

On the whole, it may be said that the Supreme Court in the 1920s and 1930s showed a most tender and solicitous regard for the maintenance of civil rights, and this has continued to be the temper of the Court.

Federal protection of civil rights. The advance of communism, nazism, and fascism in Europe in the decade before the outbreak of World War II made Americans more and more aware of the importance of their own civil rights. Over wide areas of the world the individual person seemed to be losing all power to vindicate his rights against growing tyranny. Moreover, the New Deal administration of President Roosevelt was engaged in promoting the greatest reform program through the instrumentality of federal power in all our history. There was a great fear that the machine of government was getting away from control by the people and that in time this might make the citizen helpless before the power of the state. Moreover, the federal government made a vigorous protection of civil rights, and the enlargement of powers to that very end, a part of its reform program.

Thus it was that in 1939 the Civil Rights Section of the Department of Justice was established by order of the President.[2] The order creating this section asserted that it was "to make a study of the provisions of the Constitution of the United States and Acts of Congress relating to civil rights with reference to present conditions, to make appropriate recommendations in respect thereto, and to direct, supervise, and conduct prosecutions of violations of the provisions of the Constitution or Acts of Congress guaranteeing civil rights."

The creation of the Civil Rights Section revealed further how the role of the federal government had changed as regards civil rights. In the twentieth century it clearly had assumed the role of protector of civil rights against local officials and state governments. Attorney General Frank Murphy stated this point strongly when the Civil Rights Section was added to his department: "In a democracy," he said, "an important function of the law enforcement branch of Government is the aggressive protection of the fundamental rights inherent in a free people. . . . It is the purpose of the Department of Justice to pursue a program of vigilant action in the prosecution of infringements of these rights."

The Civil Rights Section has been most active in protecting the civil and political rights of persons in the southern states. A number of convictions have been obtained for the crime of peonage and involuntary servitude. In 1941 the Civil Rights Section obtained the conviction of a worker at the polls in New Orleans for falsifying the returns at a primary election. The grounds for this conviction were that the right to vote included the right to have one's vote counted honestly.

World War II gave an immense new stimulus to the activity of the federal government in behalf of civil rights. Even before the United States entered that conflict as an active belligerent, President Roosevelt, in January 1941, stated to the Congress:

In the future days, which we seek to make secure, we look forward to a world founded upon four essential freedoms. The first is freedom of speech and expression—everywhere in the world. The second is freedom of every person to worship God in his own way—everywhere in the world. The third is freedom from want—which, translated into world terms, means economic understandings which will secure to every nation a healthy peacetime life for its inhabitants—everywhere in the world. The fourth is freedom from fear—which, translated into world terms, means a world-wide reduction of armaments to such a point and in such a thorough fashion that no nation will be in a position to commit an act of physical aggression against any neighbor—anywhere in the world.

---

[2] The *U. S. Government Organization Manual* lists and explains all government divisions. The student should use this handy volume to find in which department each division is located and what its functions are.

The ideal of the "four freedoms" to a great extent inspired the American war effort and the creation of the United Nations. It also generated efforts to reform certain conditions in the United States which many believed were not fully in harmony with the spirit of the four freedoms. Further stimulus to these efforts was supplied by the menace of Soviet power and international communism after the war had ended. Many prominent Americans contended that this menace could be met successfully only by a vigorous defense of civil rights both at home and abroad.

In 1946 President Truman appointed a Committee on Civil Rights to investigate and make recommendations for new national policies. Headed by Charles E. Wilson, president of the General Electric Company, this committee included Bishop Francis J. Haas of the Catholic Church, the Right Reverend Henry Knox Sherrill, presiding Episcopal bishop, two university presidents, and a number of other prominent American citizens. The committee made a thorough study of the status of civil rights in the United States and recommended certain additional ways and means of safeguarding those rights. The committee came to two important conclusions: (1) positive action by the federal government is needed to protect persons in their civil rights; (2) most violations of rights arise from discrimination against certain racial, religious, and nationality groups.

With respect to the first conclusion, the committee insisted that government action alone could not guarantee that civil rights would never be violated. The American people must understand the importance for human development of respecting the rights of their fellow Americans. But, the Committee insisted, additional legislation against discrimination and additional work by the Civil Rights Section of the Department of Justice would contribute toward a more gen-

Bishop Francis J. Haas was awarded a plaque by the Michigan CIO Council for his distinguished service to the cause of civil rights. The former chairman of President Roosevelt's Committee on Fair Employment Practices (1943) and President Truman's Committee on Civil Rights (1946), Bishop Haas is a well-known leader in civil-rights movements. (Religious News Service)

eral respect for human rights by the American people. Spontaneous action by the people, the committee held, should supplement increased activity by the government.

President Truman's Committee on Civil Rights listed and studied a number of rights not explicitly stated in the Constitution. These included the right to vote, the right to employment, and the right to education. The extension of the American citizen's rights to these additional areas is one of the general developments in civil rights in the middle of the twentieth century.

Desegregation in the schools. Since World War II federal activity has done much in certain parts of the country to safeguard the exercise by Negro and Indian citizens of their right to vote. Racial discrimination has been virtually ended in the armed forces. In 1954 the Supreme Court outlawed (by declaring unconstitutional) the practice of racial segregation in the public schools throughout the country. Previously the Court's position had been that school authorities in control of tax-

Southern reaction to the Supreme Court's decision on non-segregation in public schools is shown in this cartoon. The decision presented many practical problems, both legal and social, for the southern states. (Cal. Alley in the Memphis Commercial Appeal—*Associated Press Newsphoto)*

supported schools had only the obligation to maintain "equal facilities" for the white and Negro races. Now, however, the nation's highest tribunal declared that the doctrine of "equal but separate" facilities was a fiction impossible to achieve in reality. Therefore, segregation of pupils according to race was condemned. The Court did not order immediate desegregation, but has allowed school authorities time to work out an orderly change.

Conclusion and summary. In the 165 years since the Bill of Rights was adopted we have developed a way of life and a code of practices in which freedom and civil rights play an essential part. A free society cannot remain free, however, unless the persons composing it are willing and anxious to safeguard their freedom. No one's freedom is secure unless everyone's is protected. Charles Evans Hughes was president of the American Bar Associa-

tion in 1925. In his presidential address he said:

The most ominous sign of our times, as it seems to me, is the growth of an intolerant spirit. It is the more dangerous when armed, as it usually is, with sincere conviction. . . . It can be exorcised only by invoking the Genius which watched over our infancy and had guided our development—the American spirit of civil and religious liberty. Our institutions were not devised to bring about uniformity of opinion; if they had been we might as well abandon hope. . . . The interests of liberty are peculiarly those of individuals and hence of minorities, and freedom is in danger of being slain at her own altars if the passion for uniformity and control of opinion gathers head.

Since Hughes spoke these words, there have been two striking tendencies at work in the whole sphere of civil rights. The first has been a tendency to enlarge the scope of civil rights to include as "rights" some things that formerly were considered as privileges or the rewards of hard labor. Thus the "right to vote" is read into citizenship as a right instead of a privilege. The "right to employment" and the "right to education" are fre-

Poll taxes range from one to five dollars in the various states and, in several, result in disenfranchising those without means. Since the poll tax is cumulative it is possible to run up a bill in delinquent taxes, impeding further an individual's opportunity to vote. (Pierotti)

quently spoken of as civil rights. In a certain sense these are moral or human rights for those who take the trouble to earn them, but whether they can be guaranteed by government in a free society is an open question. Guaranteeing such "rights" could lead to a regimented society under an oppressive government.

The second tendency has been for the federal government to assume the role of supreme protector of civil rights. Certain of these rights were originally defined in the Constitution as a check upon the federal government; but now that government undertakes to promote and defend these rights, as well as others, against state and local civil authorities. President Truman affirmed his conviction of the rightness of this in 1947: "We must make the Federal Government a friendly, vigilant defender of the rights and equalities of all Americans. . . . The extension of civil rights today means not protection of the people against the Government, but protection of the people by the Government." This was the theme of the Committee on Civil Rights appointed by President Truman in 1946: stronger action was needed, both in the administration and in legislation, to make the federal government a powerful protector of the people's rights.

There is a danger in this development: the danger that we may rely too much on our federal government to be our "big brother" instead of standing on our own two feet. We must remember that civil rights are *ours* and that governmental agencies are only the means we have devised for protecting them. No government agency bestows our rights upon us. It can only protect rights already established.

Moreover, there is always the very real danger that a benevolently inclined national government can overprotect its citizens. By overprotecting them it renders them helpless and almost completely dependent on the government. The happy solution is to restrict the government to those functions that neither the individual himself nor local governments can perform.

It is most important for each one of us that our American society remain a society of free men—since only then can we live as human beings should live. It is also important for the success of American foreign policy that civil rights and human freedoms be respected in this country, which has taken the lead among the free countries of the world in the struggle against Soviet domination. In our generation our American civil-rights record has assumed international implications, whereas in former times it was a matter only of national concern.

REVIEW

8. Civil Rights and the Power of the Federal Government

A. Indicate the correct and wrong notions of freedom. Why must the government be limited in order to insure the individual's freedom?

B. The basic rights and liberties of the American people are to be found principally in the Bill of Rights. Where else are these found? Why was it felt necessary to enumerate these rights?

C. List the rights which are found in the Bill of Rights. What is the importance of the Ninth Amendment?

9. The Federal Government as Guardian of Civil Rights

A. When did the protection of civil rights begin to be a concern of the federal government? Briefly summarize the amendments that indicated this concern.

B. Show how during periods of war an individual's rights are often infringed upon.

C. What does "clear and present danger" mean in regard to civil rights?

D. What is meant by "substantive rights"? How did the *Gitlow* vs. *New York* case of 1925 affect these rights? Show by Supreme Court cases how the Fourteenth Amendment has been applied to the states concerning these rights.

E. The creation of the Civil Rights Section of the Department of Justice shows the role of the federal government concerning civil rights. Where has the federal government been most actively concerned? What did the Civil Rights Committee of 1946 recommend concerning civil rights?

THE CHAPTER IN REVIEW

A. Why was the new American nation of 1787 concerned with the question of rights? What did they do about it?

B. Show how the Supreme Court's concern for the protection of individual rights has developed over the last thirty-five years.

C. Compare the federal government's attitude in the eighteenth century with that of the present toward civil rights. What brought about this change?

D. The Fourteenth Amendment has been used for many purposes. Show how both the federal government and the Supreme Court have expanded its original purpose.

SELECTED READINGS

The historical development of the Constitution in its political and social setting is contained in Marshall Smelser and Harry W. Kirwin, *Conceived in Liberty*. More specific treatment of constitutional development can be found in Carl B. Swisher, *American Constitutional Development* (Boston: Houghton Mifflin Co., 1943), and in the two-volume work of Charles Warren, *The Supreme Court in United States History* (Boston: Little, Brown & Co., 1937). In addition, the following works should prove helpful for a fuller understanding of the Constitution and the Bill of Rights. Edward S. Corwin, *The Constitution and What It Means Today* (Princeton, N.J.: Princeton University Press, 1954), is an excellent analysis of the Constitution by America's outstanding constitutional scholar. Somewhat more popular is Howard L. McBain, *The Living Constitution*

(New York: The Macmillan Co., 1942), and William Kottmeyer, *Our Constitution and What It Means* (St. Louis: Webster Publishing Company, 1949).

Charles Warren, *The Making of the Constitution* (Boston: Little, Brown & Co., 1937), helps one understand the setting and the reasons for the Constitutional Convention. John C. Miller, *Crisis in Freedom: The Alien and Sedition Acts* (Boston: Little, Brown & Co., 1951) is a good study of civil rights in their first crisis in American history. The problem of civil rights during the Civil War is handled by James G. Randall, *Constitutional Problems under Lincoln* (New York: D. Appleton Co., 1926). The problem of preserving civil rights in the period immediately after World War I can be understood from reading J. M. Mecklin, *The Ku Klux Klan* (New York: Harcourt, Brace & Co., 1924).

The report of the President's Committee on Civil Rights, *To Secure These Rights,* (Washington: Government Printing Office, 1947) is essential for any study of the subject since World War II.

The rights discussed in this and the next chapter are constitutional rights. It is interesting to compare them with a list of human rights arrived at philosophically. For this purpose the student should use Rev. John A. Driscoll, O.P., *Rights and Duties—Their Foundation* (New York: The Paulist Press, 1950).

PROJECTS

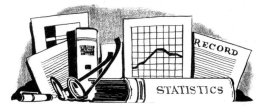

1. It would be of interest to take a copy of today's newspaper and select five news stories that illustrate the need for the Bill of Rights. How do these examples conform with or violate the Bill of Rights?

2. We have been talking a great deal about rights in this chapter. All rights carry with them obligations. Make a list of rights in addition to those found in this chapter and list the duty or obligation that goes with each of them.

3. We in America are proud of our rights. List five civil rights that are not fully enjoyed by all Americans. Discuss ways in which these rights should be extended to all.

Chapter 5. Substantive and Procedural Rights

The civil rights possessed by American citizens, as we have seen, have a philosophical and a religious foundation. Historically, these rights were given concrete expression, first in England and then in America, as the traditional rights of Englishmen and Americans. They were stated in our federal and state constitutions and in the laws based on these constitutions. They are securities against arbitrary government to which every citizen is entitled because they are guaranteed constitutionally. Roughly speaking, civil rights are personal liberties or freedoms guaranteed by the law of the land.

Liberty and civil authority. It is well to keep this definition of civil rights in mind, because in our day many people set up a false and an un-American conflict between liberty and authority. They believe that the two are essentially incompatible. They think that the individual's liberty can be safeguarded only by weakening political authority. In reality there is no real conflict between the maintenance of civil rights and necessary political authority. Civil rights are practically meaningless except in a society in which political authority is respected and is strong. Civil rights can as easily be violated under a weak government as under a strong one. It is not a question of *how strong* political authority is but rather of *what it does*.

Liberty is not unlimited. In the practical order each person's freedom must be limited in the interest of others and ultimately in his own interest. Not to limit individual liberty sufficiently is to invite tyranny. Edmund Burke stated the problem facing every government in these wise words:

> Liberty, too, must be limited in order to be possessed. The degree of restraint it is impossible in any case to settle precisely. But it ought to be the constant aim of every wise public council to find out by cautious experiments, and cool rational endeavors, with how little, not how much, of this restraint the community can subsist.

Burke wrote these words in 1777, when public leaders possessed a considerable degree of rational self-restraint. It was an age, moreover, in which the impulses of the lower classes, socially and economic-

ally, were curbed by moral and cultural controls which are less operative today. Nevertheless, Burke's advice is still pertinent. Political wisdom and respect for human dignity dictate that civil rights should be given as generous and extensive realization as possible.

Violation of civil rights. Any government action that infringes the dignity of man or woman is both wrong and dangerous. It is wrong because it violates one's right to be dealt with as a person. It is dangerous because each violation of human rights increases disrespect and contempt for persons and makes good order more difficult to achieve.

The citizen's civil rights are not generally endangered by evil-minded individuals or groups whose real purpose is to destroy liberty. They are more frequently violated by well-meaning people who are ignorant of the citizen's rights and anxious to maintain peace and order in the community. The most frequent violations of civic rights are committed by local police officials, acting perhaps with virtuous intentions but without prudent judgment. The most serious violations are committed by the majority group against racial minorities, such as Negroes or Orientals. Such violations would not be so frequent if both victims and viola-

tors appreciated the important position civil rights hold in our American way of life and if they knew specifically what these rights are. It is therefore very important for American citizens to know their civil rights.

Civil rights can be classified as substantive or procedural. The most important of our substantive rights are to be found in the First Amendment. (They are stated in similar words in almost all state constitutions.)

Congress shall make no law respecting an establishment of religion, or prohibiting the free exercise thereof; or abridging the freedom of speech or of the press; or the right of the people peaceably to assemble, and to petition the government for a redress of grievances.

The right to freedom of religion has been discussed. Let us see what the remaining substantive rights have come to mean, what limits have been placed upon them, and what problems they give rise to in our time.

Right to property. The right to acquire lawfully and to own property is assumed throughout the Constitution of the United States and has been specifically written into many of our state constitutions. According to Christian moral philosophy, the right to own property derives from the natural law whose author is

God. Wherever and whenever this right has been denied, all other rights and liberties have either suffered or been wholly extinguished. This right belongs to corporations and to the Church, as well as to individual persons.

It is obvious that if the right to property is to be enjoyed, it must have the protection of civil authority, government; otherwise, no one's property would be safe. The founders of our Republic all regarded the protection of private property as an important duty of government. This is not to say, however, that anyone may do what he pleases with his property. The use of property is regulated by law in the general interest of the local and national community. The property owner must obey building and sanitation codes, must not use his property for illegal purposes, and must bear the burden which the civil authority lays upon property.

Civil authority may exercise its rights over private property in two principal ways: (1) by taxation, and (2) by eminent domain. The government's taxing power is limited by the "due process" clause and by a number of specific constitutional restrictions. The right of eminent domain is necessary to any state's sovereignty. This is the right to appropriate private property for a public purpose. Because such a right could easily be abused, the Fifth Amendment requires that "just compensation" must be made for property so appropriated. A just price is usually reached by the courts or by administrative officials. All that is required constitutionally is that the owner of the property be given the opportunity to present evidence concerning the value he has put on his property.

In the last quarter century government in the United States (federal, state, and local) has laid a much greater tax burden upon property than ever before in our history. This has been due to war, danger of war, and to the great expansion of government to meet the needs of a vast industrial community. Similarly, and for the same reason, there has been a greatly increased resort to the right of eminent domain for road construction, government building, and defense installations. There are no limits to the amount of taxation or the use of eminent domain save in the prudent judgment of legislators and voters.

Speech and press. At the time the Constitution was drawn up Americans understood that there were two principal reasons for guaranteeing freedom of speech and press. The more basic we have already indicated: that a person has a right to communicate with others because he is social by nature. The other reason was practical: that such freedom makes for better government and encourages better the development of morality and wisdom than does a society with governmental suppression of all dissent. This practical reason is closely connected with the right to criticize the government, which is essential to healthy political life. Walter Lippmann sums up the practical grounds for freedom of speech in this way:

> If we truly wish to understand why freedom is necessary in a civilized society, we must begin by realizing that, because freedom of discussion improves our own opinions, the liberties of other men are our own vital necessity.
>
> This is the creative principle of freedom of speech, not that it is a system for the tolerating of error, but that it is a system for finding the truth. It may not produce the truth, or the whole truth all the time, or often, or in some cases ever. But if the truth can be found, there is no other system which will normally and habitually find so much truth. Until we have thoroughly understood this principle, we shall not know why we must value our liberty, or how we can protect and develop it.

The Supreme Court has never attempted to define, for once and all, the meaning of terms used in the First Amendment. It has never tried to say what "abridging" or what "freedom" means in the abstract. Nor has it ever tried to give a precise definition of "speech" or of "press." It is content to solve each individual case as it arises. In doing so, however, it has built up a body of doctrine analyzing the terms of the First Amendment. Freedom of speech and press, for example, was held in 1940 to include the right to picket during a strike and to publicize in orderly fashion the workers' side of the dispute. It can be seen that the various decisions on this subject have·developed certain general principles.

The rights of speech and press cannot be abridged or limited unless they clearly violate a recognized limit of decency, public safety, or the rights of others. Thus freedom of speech does not include the right to make political speeches in the middle of the boulevard during rush hour. The violation of public order or the attack on another's rights must be clear and certain. Thus a man cannot be prosecuted for arguing politics with a fellow passenger on the bus unless he resorts to violence, and then not for the argument but for the violence.

Reasonable limits, therefore, must be put on freedom of speech and press. Chief Justice Vinson expressed this principle in 1950 when he wrote: "Freedom of speech . . . does not comprehend the right to speak on any subject at any time." This is a principle that has consistently been accepted by the Court. Freedom of speech and press does not include libel or slander, the use of obscene or blasphemous language, the right to deceive or defraud. It does not protect one in the use of language that will incite groups to immediate violence.

The great difficulty is to draw the line between what speech or writings are protected by the First Amendment and what are not. In 1944 the Court held that a citizen who circulated an article attacking President Roosevelt's integrity and his conduct of the war had not exceeded his constitutional rights. Similar conduct

The activities of political parties have always elicited lively comment in the American press. This drawing by Homer Davenport shows Mark Hanna, the political boss friendly to "big business," replacing George Washington, whose statue stood in Wall Street.

twenty-five years earlier had been held as not protected by the First Amendment. In a series of cases in the 1940s the Court held that defendants were not guilty of contempt of court when they made critical remarks about the judge. Cartoonists and editorial writers charged with contempt for their belittling criticism of judges have sometimes been found guilty and sometimes not.

No precise line can be drawn between what is permitted and what is not. The general principles remain that freedom of speech and press are limited by public safety and the rights of others, but these limitations must be unmistakably present. Freedom of speech and press as basic rights remain, but changing conditions cause the use of these rights to expand or shrink at various times in our history.

Assembly and petition. The right to assemble peaceably and to petition the government for redress of grievances does not seem to be as much exercised today as it was in the past. Modern means of com-

Albert Kahn, co-publisher of Harvey Matusow's book False Witness *addresses a left-wing gathering in New York's Union Square. Placards express the Communist line. Guaranteed equal protection under the law, the Communists continue to exercise their* individual *rights. (International News Photos)*

munication—radio and television and telegraph—have lessened the number of assemblies and formal petitions to the government. Originally the right of assembly was subordinate to the right of petitioning the government, as if the amendment read: "the right of the people peaceably to assemble in order to petition the government." Historically, however, the two rights developed independently of each other.

A denial of the right to hold meetings would seriously hinder the free working of a free society. The holding of meetings plays a large part in the social and educational aspects of American life. Meetings are important means of developing public opinion on political questions, so much so that in 1937 the Supreme Court declared that the right of peaceable assembly is "cognate to those of free speech and free press and is equally fundamental."

Like freedom of speech and press, freedom of assembly is subject to certain reasonable limitations. Obviously we do not have the right to gather for illegal or immoral purposes. Drawing the line between legitimate and illegitimate assembling is often very difficult because of the nature of crowds. A crowd is something more than the sum of the individuals composing it. It is moved easily by appeals to passion; it can be stampeded by fear; it can be driven to commit crime by a single speech. It is necessary, therefore, to preserve the right of assembly and to erect careful safeguards around it.

In the interest of public safety, permission from the proper local authority must ordinarily be obtained for a large public meeting. Assemblies cannot ordinarily be held in such places, at such times, or in such manner as would interfere with the normal movement of the people in a city. Most communities require that certain fire and police regulations be complied with before issuing a permit to hold such a meeting. As we have already indicated, the doctrine of a clear and present danger has been the principle for deciding whether the purpose of an assembly is legal or not. The Supreme Court held in the Cruikshank and De Jonge cases that the right of assembly protects a group meeting to teach Communist doctrine or proposals for changing the structure of our government. The only restriction is that its purpose cannot be to incite people to immediate violence, nor can it follow a line of procedure which has in the past usually led to violent action.

The right to petition the government for redress of grievances has seldom been invoked in American history, although it seemed a right essential to representative government when it was adopted in 1791. The right to petition Congress for legislation does not mean that every mode of doing it is lawful. In 1894 Coxey's Army marched to Washington to present petitions to the government, and in 1932 the "Bonus Marchers" came for the same purpose. Leaders of Coxey's Army were arrested for walking on the grass, and the Bonus Marchers were dispersed by the Army when they refused to vacate condemned buildings in which they were living. In neither case was the right to petition Congress denied. Historically, most petitions of this kind for legislation have been referred to appropriate committees and allowed to die in committee.

Exercise of the right to petition the government has taken two principal forms in our time. The first of these is letter writing or telegraphing to congressmen, whereby citizens express their views on pending measures and ask their representatives to respect their opinions. In 1941 the Supreme Court held that a telegram of protest criticizing a state court was an exercise of the right of petition. The second method is lobbying, whereby groups interested in legislation maintain a paid representative in Washington to present their views to congressmen. Lobbying is a legitimate means of influ-

encing the Congress, and many groups interested in better government maintain active lobbies at the capital. Today the courts consider lobbying the most important expression of the right to petition. In 1952, lower federal courts held two laws restricting it to be unconstitutional on the grounds that they interfered with the "right to petition."

Unfortunately, lobbying has frequently been abused by groups or persons interested in purely selfish designs. Attempts at bribery and other wrongful means of influence have caused lobbyists to come under severe criticism. In 1946 Congress passed the Regulation of Lobbying Act in an attempt to control this method of petitioning the government. This law requires a paid lobbyist to register with the clerk of the House and the secretary of the Senate, giving his name and the name of his employer, as well as a sworn statement as to his salary and expenses. This law recognizes lobbying as a legitimate method of influencing Congress, but it seeks to keep it under control by the use of publicity. It is difficult to say to what extent such regulation achieves its objective.

Immunity from involuntary servitude. A third substantive civic right guaranteed by the federal Constitution is immunity from involuntary servitude. The Thirteenth Amendment prohibits slavery or involuntary servitude "except as a punishment for crime whereof the party shall have been duly convicted." Involuntary service in the armed forces, of course, is not included in this immunity. The courts have held that a man's civil rights under

No man is another man's property today. Yet 100 years ago such advertisements as this, which appeared in a Wilmington, Del., newspaper in 1854, were common. (DuPont)

this clause are not violated when he is held to the completion of a period of service for which he has contracted. But it is illegal to force a man to work out a debt under the penalty of going to jail until the debt is paid. This practice is specifically forbidden by the federal anti-peonage act. The principle outlawing involuntary servitude is clear. But it remains for the court each time to decide when sufficient force is used to render the work performed involuntary.

The right to citizenship and its privileges. Until 1868 there was considerable ambiguity about citizenship. The federal Constitution used the term "citizen" seven times, speaking sometimes of citizens of the state and at other times of citizens of the United States. The Fourteenth Amendment, however, defines citizenship in these terms: "All persons born or naturalized in the United States, and subject to the jurisdiction thereof, are citizens of the United States and the state wherein they reside." For practical purposes the two citizenships (state and national) have been merged, and we can consider them as one. There is some question as to whether citizenship is a right in the same way freedom of speech and freedom of press are rights. Since it is guaranteed to all persons born in this country or natu-ralized according to the laws in force, and since it does carry with it privileges denied to aliens, it can safely be considered as a substantive right. The federal government has the power to fix requirements for naturalization, and apparently any requirements set forth will be constitutional.

The Truman Committee on Civil Rights considered citizenship one of the American's most important rights in the twentieth century because of the privileges it entails. Only citizens may vote or hold political office. In some states noncitizens may not own real estate. In others, such professions as law, medicine, and teaching are limited to citizens. In various other ways, socially and economically, citizens enjoy advantages that aliens do not possess.

The right to vote is regulated by the several states. The Fifteenth and Nineteenth Amendments, however, forbid states to abridge or deny the right to vote because of race, color, previous condition of servitude, or sex. In other respects the states are free to fix whatever qualifications they consider reasonable. One can argue whether voting is a "right" or a "privilege," but there is no argument about its importance in our age. The vote is the ultimate means whereby the citizen

The direct vote by secret ballot is probably the best means to determine the public's reaction to a proposal. However, our elected representatives do much of America's voting—since it would be highly impractical to submit all measures directly to the people. (Standard Oil Co., N.J.)

makes his opinion felt in the government. Unless citizens have security in this right they cannot hold their representatives accountable. It therefore follows that no one who has met the requirements for the vote in any state can rightfully be refused the privilege of voting. The Civil Rights Section of the Department of Justice has adopted this principle in prosecuting election fraud cases.

The right to bear arms. This right was inserted in the Constitution to forestall the rise of a large national standing army. "The right of a people to keep and bear arms" referred to the state militia, which the authors of the amendment did not desire to be disarmed by federal action. Under the "police power" residing in the state, the ownership and use of arms by private citizens may be carefully controlled. Most states require the registration of all firearms. They forbid the carrying of concealed weapons, and they regulate the sale and use of dangerous weapons that might be used by criminals or might endanger the lives of innocent citizens.

The Truman Committee on Civil Rights interpreted the right to bear arms as a right to serve in the country's armed forces—an interpretation which is, to say the least, novel. This is a right which the committee said was not accorded equally to the various racial elements in the country. Theoretically, the committee reported, the armed forces made no distinction among the various racial groups. But in practice there were discriminations, especially against the Negroes in the Marine Corps and the Navy. When the committee reported in 1947, there were two Negro officers in the Navy and 10,000 enlisted Negro men. For every seven enlisted white men, there was one white officer. Of the 7,798 officers in the Marine Corps, none was a Negro. If, as the committee maintained, the right to bear arms includes the right to serve in the armed forces regardless of color, race,

or creed, then the armed forces were violating this right guaranteed by the Second Amendment. However, in the last decade the armed forces have made great progress toward assuring equal treatment of citizens of different races.

The right to travel. Throughout American history there has never been any question about the right of American citizens to travel freely throughout the country. No state can bar citizens of another state from travel within its boundaries. Certain well-defined limitations on the right to travel within the country have always been accepted as constitutional. Under the police power, for example, states have the right to bar diseased people from entering their borders. Again, people are not allowed free access to military establishments or to sites where secret weapons are being made. Otherwise citizens have the right to travel freely from state to state.

Prior to World War I, few Americans going abroad provided themselves with passports from the United States Government. Such documents were not needed to leave the country and return or to move freely about the countries of western Europe. Only if Americans were going to the Russian Empire or to central-eastern Europe did they as a rule obtain a passport, which is nothing but a document attesting one's citizenship and requesting foreign governments to allow the holder of the passport to pass freely and safely on his way. In czarist Russia and a few other despotic countries a passport (then and now) was conceived as also a grant of permission to the citizen or subject to leave and return to the country. But this was not the case in the United States and other countries enjoying civil and political liberty. The general disuse into which passports had fallen before 1914 was due to the general sense of domestic political security then prevailing in the Western world. A century earlier, in the period of the French

Revolution and the Napoleonic wars, the passport was widely used and strictly regulated.

War and the fear of war, revolution and the fear of revolution restored the passport system after 1914. Hence the executive branch of our government claimed the right to limit travel abroad by American citizens in the interest of American foreign policy. Within recent years this right has been challenged in a number of cases, and the courts have steered a middle course between upholding the citizen's inherent right to travel abroad and sustaining the State Department's right to refuse a passport (without which no American can travel abroad). In short, the courts have decided that the "right" to travel abroad is more than a "privilege," as the State Department has maintained. It is a right not to be denied without due process of law.

The courts have held that the State Department cannot arbitrarily refuse to grant a passport. They leave the State Department free to decide the political issues involved in foreign travel, but they require it to set forth sufficient reason for denying a passport to an individual, and they forbid it to act arbitrarily in any single case. The ruling of the courts is summed up in the statement that a passport can be denied only on "reasonable grounds," which still leaves considerable room for interpretation in each case.

Other substantive rights. There are general statements in both the Ninth and Tenth Amendments of the federal Constitution that indicate that the people retain certain rights not specifically given to the government or even mentioned in the Bill of Rights. Many people consider the right to education and to employment as among these other rights "retained by the people." Such was the view of the Truman Committee on Civil Rights, which pointed out that certain racial groups were discriminated against in the enjoyment of these "rights." In view of the federal government's acceptance of the role of guardian of civil rights, it is easy enough to see how such rights might be constitutionally protected.

The right to education means, of course, not the right to be educated, but the right to an opportunity for education. Since the public schools are supported by taxes and every citizen in some degree shares the tax burden, it surely follows that his children have a right to attend the schools. The right to employment does not mean that one has a right to a job for which he is not qualified, but rather a right to the opportunity to earn a living. This right arises from the natural law; to the state it is an elementary proposition in morality, since to deny a man that right would be unjust.

11. THE PROCEDURAL RIGHTS OF AMERICANS

Procedural rights relate to things being done in a specified way. We have already seen in the last chapter that both the federal government and the states are forbidden to pass bills of attainder or *ex post facto* laws. A typical bill of attainder was a rider attached by Congress to an appropriation bill forbidding the payment of salaries to three men in the State Department charged by the House Un-American Activities Committee with sympathizing with Communist Russia. In 1946 the Supreme Court declared the rider unconstitutional on the grounds that it punished the individuals by *ex post facto* legislation instead of by due process of law. Bills passed into law with *ex post facto* effects have usually been the result of clumsy phraseology which was corrected when its implications were discovered.

Another procedural right described in the last chapter is the *habeas corpus*. This right is invoked daily by persons arrested on suspicion and held for trial. Right to

"Depriving us in many cases of the benefits of trial by jury" was one of the objections to British rule stated in the Declaration of Independence. Some have objected, however, to the jury system on the grounds that comment by the judge on the evidence is prohibited. (DuPont)

the writ of *habeas corpus* protects the citizen from possible persecution by police officials who, for one reason or another, might desire to keep the individual in jail before he is found guilty of a crime by due process of law. Thus the citizen's right to a writ of *habeas corpus* is a deterrent against the violation of his liberties by public officials.

Jury trial. Our most important procedural rights are those which protect the innocent from a miscarriage of justice caused by fear, hatred, or prejudice, or simply by hasty, ill-considered action. These rights are often a refuge for known criminals, and Americans are sometimes tempted to consider the restrictions on the working of justice as much too severe. But the American tradition has always been that the accused is considered to be innocent until he is proved guilty; that he shall have a fair trial; and that the burden of proof rests on his accusers. Constitutional restrictions and traditional practices are all designed to guarantee the working out of these principles.

The rights whereby we are guaranteed a fair trial are stated in the Fifth and Sixth Amendments, and they are repeated in similar language in all state constitutions.

Article V. No person shall be held to answer for a capital or otherwise infamous crime, unless on a presentment or indictment of a grand jury, except in cases arising in the land or naval forces, or in the militia, when in actual service at the time of war or public danger; nor shall any person be subject for the same offense to be twice put in jeopardy of life or limb; nor shall be compelled in any criminal case to be a witness against himself, nor be deprived of life, liberty, or property, without due process of law; nor shall private property be taken for public use without just compensation.

Article VI. In all criminal prosecutions the accused shall enjoy the right to a speedy and public trial, by an impartial jury of the State and district wherein the crime shall have been committed, which district shall have been previously ascertained by law, and to be informed of the nature and cause of the accusation; to be confronted with the witnesses against him; to have compulsory process for obtaining witnesses in his favor, and to have the assistance of counsel for his defense.

The Supreme Court has defined an "infamous crime" as one punishable by imprisonment, by loss of civil or political privileges, or by hard labor. Misdemeanors, punishable by small fines, cases in equity, and cases in contempt of court are not covered by the right of trial by jury. Moreover, since trial by jury is a right intended to protect the accused, the Supreme Court has stated that the accused may waive it in favor of trial by the judge alone.

Indictment by a grand jury was adopted by Americans as a prized English common-law procedure. The grand jury, presided over by a judge, is a body of twelve to twenty-three men (or women) to whom the public prosecutor makes accusations against persons charged with having committed a crime. If the evidence seems sufficient to warrant trial, the grand jury returns a "true bill," and the accused is indicted for trial. Otherwise, the person is released. The purpose of this procedure is to save persons the expense and humiliation of being held for trial unless an informed group of their fellow citizens think such trial is warranted. This procedure has proved rather slow and cumbersome, and some states have abolished it in favor of the simple method of the prosecutor's filing an affidavit against the accused. The Supreme Court has held that such a procedure is not a denial of due process of law. Although states may dispense with the grand jury system of indictment, it must continue to be used in federal courts.

Indictment by grand jury and trial by the petit, or trial, jury do not apply to crimes committed in the armed forces or on military posts. These crimes are tried according to the procedures of military law as duly written out in the code of military justice.

The protection against double jeopardy is to keep a man from being tried again and again by a hostile government until he is found guilty. This protection does not prevent a second government from trying a person for the same offense. Kidnaping, for example, in some cases is an offense against federal as well as state law. A person may be tried for having broken federal law by kidnaping even after the state in which the crime occurred has tried the accused and found him not guilty.

The accused cannot be made to testify against himself, nor can he be made to produce private papers and documents that will help to convict him. Nor may a man's wife be compelled to testify against him. The traditional American belief has been that the state must prove the accused guilty if he pleads innocent. In some states the self-incrimination clause of the Fifth Amendment does not prohibit the use of evidence obtained by "wire-tapping," whereby the accused person's words are used as evidence to help convict him, but such evidence may not be produced in federal courts.

Most of the clauses in the Sixth Amendment are self-explanatory. Trial must be speedy and public. It should be held in the district in which the crime was committed. But the accused has a right to request a change of venue (removal of the trial to another place) if he can show that prejudice on the part of the judge or the population of the locality would infringe his right to an impartial trial.

The defense has the right to subpeona witnesses. Such witnesses are served a summons to appear in court, and their expenses are paid by the state. The defense has the right, as does the state, to cross-examine witnesses in order to credit or discredit their testimony in the interest of obtaining a fair decision from the evidence presented at the trial.

Closely connected with the rights involved in a fair trial are further rights guaranteed in the Fourth and Eighth Amendments. The Fourth Amendment states that "the right of the people to be secure in their persons, houses, papers, and effects, against unreasonable searches and seizures, shall not be violated." This suggests that there can be reasonable searches and seizures. The amendment describes them as based on warrants issued "upon probable cause, supported by oath or affirmation, and particularly describing the place to be searched, and the person or things to be seized." Under certain conditions, the Supreme Court has held, warrants need not be obtained. Search of an automobile or other vehicle can be made without a warrant, since otherwise the automobile could be driven away while the police were obtaining a warrant. Evidence obtained in violation of the Fourth Amendment is not admissible in court.

The Eighth Amendment states: "Excessive bail shall not be required, nor excessive fines imposed, nor cruel and unusual punishments inflicted." The principle behind these prohibitions is that punishment must not be arbitrary, that it must be administered equally to all, and that it must be proportionate to the crime. Precisely what is excessive bail or cruel and unusual punishment is not stated in abstract terms. In each case the court decides whether *this* bail is excessive for *this* case, basing its decision on what is customary for such cases and in what ways this particular case differs from the customary. So it is with punishments and with fines. The amendment limits the courts to reasonable punishments meted out equally to all guilty of the same crime.

The procedures connected with the right to fair trial sometimes seem unnecessarily cumbersome. They frequently tie the state's hands in prosecuting known criminals. They serve as a means of delaying or preventing justice to persons who have broken the law. These are unfortunate abuses of a system devised to protect the innocent from a miscarriage of justice. The problem is to tighten up court procedure in the interest of speedy conviction of criminals without removing the protections devised for the innocent.

Due process of law . Holding together all the rights we have been discussing above is the "due process of law" clause. The Fifth Amendment forbids the federal government to deprive a person "of life, liberty, or property, without due process of law," and the Fourteenth Amendment puts an identical limitation on the states. The Supreme Court has refused to define "due process of law." Instead it has preferred, in its own words, that "the full

meaning of the term should be gradually ascertained by the process of inclusion and exclusion in the course of decisions in cases as they arise."

The term was formerly used only in relation to procedural rights. In these cases the Court decided each time whether the defendant had been given a fair trial; that is, a regular proceeding before a proper court, with a fair hearing for both parties. Sometimes this might require a jury trial, sometimes it might require a change of venue, and sometimes it might require additional witnesses. But the principle of due process, as applied to procedural matters, was consistently held by the Supreme Court to mean a fair trial according to regular procedure.

In the last seventy-five years the "due process" clause has been applied also to substantive rights. Most cases falling in this category involve a second undefined term: the "police power" of the state. The police power is commonly held to include the regulative authority of the states and their subdivisions to safeguard and promote the public health, safety, morals, order, and general welfare of the people within the state. Under the police power various states passed minimum-wage laws, maximum-hour laws, and regulations governing working conditions. Appeals to the Supreme Court claiming that such laws deprived owners of property without due process of law were sometimes upheld and sometimes denied. The general tendency of the Court in the last twenty-five years is to restrict the meaning of "due process" and widen the extent of the state's police power.

Legislative investigations. A new problem that seems to relate to procedural civil rights has developed in the last twenty-odd years. It is the problem of protecting the citizen's procedural rights from abuses that can arise in congressional investigations. Such investigations are an integral part of good government. Neither the national nor the state legislature can function well and wisely without gathering information. Hence they must have the power to subpoena witnesses; not merely for the purpose of obtaining the necessary knowledge for making or amending or repealing a law, but for uncovering abuses that may arise in the executive administration.

Since legislative investigating committees are not courts, they cannot be bound by the strict procedures of a court. They do not seek to convict anybody, but often they run up against stubborn and unresponsive witnesses who for one reason or another are unwilling to answer questions put to them. Sometimes a witness is called for no other reason than to reveal something in his past that he would rather conceal; occasionally a witness does not tell the truth. It is right and necessary that the legislature possess the authority to cite unco-operative or dishonest witnesses for contempt or perjury and have them brought to trial in a court. But it is equally necessary that witnesses be not abused by investigating committees or subjected to undeserved blackening of their reputations. Some set of procedural safeguards, therefore, is required, and our congressional committees not only recognize this need but are striving to meet it.

Conclusion. As we conclude our discussion of this important subject we must bear in mind that our civil rights are the concrete realization of natural rights with which we are endowed by our Creator. They will therefore change continually, not in their essential nature, but in the way they are realized at each period in history. What might be necessary to fair trial at one time, for example, might be actually harmful at another time.

We should also remember that respect for civil rights is ultimately dependent on their being respected and cherished by the people of each locality. The people must cherish the rights of *all* Americans, because when one man's rights are violated, all men's rights are in jeopardy.

In a speech made at a meeting of the Four Freedoms Foundation in 1953, President Truman expressed the American tradition of civil rights in words that deserve quoting here:

The good life is not possible without freedom. But only the people, by their will and by their dedication to freedom, can make the good life come to pass. We cannot leave it to the courts alone, because many of the invasions of these freedoms are so devious and so subtle that they cannot be brought before the courts.

The responsibility for these freedoms falls on free men. And free men can preserve them only if they are militant about freedom. We ought to get angry when these rights are violated, and make ourselves heard until the wrong has been righted. . . . There are times when the defense of freedom calls for vigorous action. This action may lead to trouble, and frequently does. Effective effort to preserve freedom may involve discomfort and risk. It takes faith, unselfishness and courage to stand up to a bully; or to stand up for a whole community when it has been frightened into subjection. But it has to be done, if we are to remain free.

REVIEW

10. The Substantive Rights of Americans

A. What, in general, is meant by civil rights? What is the relationship between liberty and civil authority? What is the major reason for violations of civil rights?

B. The right to acquire private property has been limited. Why may civil government limit this right? What protection is afforded to the citizen against the government in this matter?

C. Why were Americans guaranteed freedom of speech and press? Indicate how the Court has dealt with some cases that involved these rights.

D. Explain the early historical importance of the right of assembly and petition. Why must there be limits to these rights? Show how petition today differs from what it was in colonial days.

E. When was citizenship defined? Is it a right? Indicate some rights it carries with it. Explain how the right to travel is regarded in a democratic country. How has it been challenged recently?

11. The Procedural Rights of Americans

A. What is meant by procedural rights? Describe *ex post facto* law, bill of attainder, and writ of *habeas corpus*.

B. Point out the procedural rights under the Fifth Amendment and what they mean. What was the historical background for the trial by jury and for the grand jury?

C. The Sixth, Seventh, and Eighth Amendments guarantee protection for the accused. Explain how the individual is protected by these amendments.

D. These protective measures are sometimes cumbersome. Why are they needed? What does the Supreme Court say regarding "due process"?

E. Why is there a need for legislative investigations? What safeguards must be employed in these investigations?

THE CHAPTER IN REVIEW

A. The Supreme Court has been careful in its decisions concerning the rights guaranteed in the First Amendment. Take one Supreme Court decision involving each of these rights and show how the Court has met present-day conditions in its interpretations.

B. Describe some "new rights" that have developed throughout our history and explain how they are regarded today.

C. Show how the Bill of Rights gives adequate protection to a man in his home. How is the individual protected when he is accused of a crime?

SELECTED READINGS

The readings suggested for Chapters 3 and 4 are also helpful for this chapter.

The classic study of free speech is Zechariah Chafee, *Free Speech in the United States* (Cambridge, Mass.: Harvard University Press, 1946). Vigorous and somewhat shrill defenses of civil rights are made by Alan Barth, *The Loyalty of Free Men* (New York: The Viking Press, Inc., 1951), and by Elmer Davis, *But We Were Born Free* (Indianapolis: The Bobbs-Merrill Company, 1954).

The difficult problem of protecting civil rights from abuse by legislative investigation committees is dealt with in the following articles: Robert F. Drenan, S.J., "Rights of Citizens before Congressional Committees," *Catholic Mind* (June 1954); Jerome G. Kerwin, "Fifth Amendment," *The Grail* (September 1954); and Robert McWilliams, "The Privilege against Self-Incrimination" *Catholic Mind* (October 1954).

PROJECTS

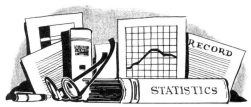

1. The federal government can exercise its right over private property by eminent domain. Find out the various steps that must be taken before the property can be taken over. Note well the safeguards that are provided for the individual owner. Make a report of your findings to the class.

2. Freedom of speech carries with it certain limitations. Make a partial list of some of these limitations and point out the reason why they are not included under the notion of freedom of speech. Inquire of the local authorities the steps necessary for making a speech in a public place. Report your findings to the class.

3. Americans have a right to trial by jury and a duty to serve on juries when called. Report to the class on the various kinds of juries and how they are selected. You might include a summary of the historical development of trial by jury.

Chapter 6. Subversive Activities and the Problem of Loyalty

12. LOYALTY AND DISLOYALTY

A just government has the right to the loyalty of the citizens. They, in turn, have the right to liberty under law and to the protection of their personal and property rights. The mutual rights and obligations of citizens and government can be clearly seen if they are discussed in terms of loyalty and subversive activity.

Nature of loyalty. Everyone knows that loyalty means being faithful to one's country and to the principles for which it stands. But there is a great difference of opinion on what this involves. Loyalty is at bottom a spiritual quality. It is an expression of love for one's country and people. Only its outward manifestations can be seen. Loyalty cannot be imposed. The man who dutifully salutes the flag is most likely a loyal American. But it is possible that he undermines the very principles which the flag represents. Again a thoughtless citizen who forgets to salute the flag when it passes in a parade may willingly give his life for his country—the supreme act of loyalty.

To understand the meaning of loyalty we must see what it does *not* involve, because there are some Americans who at times shout disloyalty—even treason—against those who disagree with them on economic or political questions. Congressmen who spoke in favor of a public housing bill, for example, were accused by a real estate lobby of being "fellow travelers" of the Communist party. Such a temper of mind is not in keeping with the American tradition that allows for a great variety of opinion on public questions while demanding agreement only on basic political principles.

What, then, does loyalty *not* mean? It is not blind submission to everything proposed by the party in power at any given time. The loyal American does not hesitate to point out what he considers the mistakes of the legislature and the administration, although he obeys whatever just laws are enacted. Loyalty is not the passive acceptance of any single idea, any given economic system, or any passing political fad. Nor is it hatred or contempt for other peoples or countries.

What does loyalty involve in a positive way? It involves faithfulness to one's country in two respects. The first is faithfulness to one's country against its enemies or its potential enemies. The second is faithfulness to the basic principles on which our government was established and on which it continues to operate. Throughout most of our history we have followed a rule of sound common sense in drawing a line between loyal opposition to the administration in office and disloyal opposition to the national interest.

In our own time, however, it has become exceedingly difficult to draw the line correctly. Today we face a serious threat to national security because of a fanatical group that rejects American interests in favor of those of another power —the Communists who are loyal to the Soviet Union and the cause of world revolution. The existence of this threat gives rise to another danger, the possibility that unscrupulous individuals may use the fear of communism as a justification for public policies that violate traditional American rights. Reckless charges of disloyalty and subversion are much more likely to hurt innocent persons than to expose the guilty. Americans must be on guard, in their fight against subversive elements in the country, not to lose the rights and liberties they seek to defend.

Liberty and security. We can readily see that civil liberty and national security seem to encroach upon each other. Each must be preserved. Neither can be destroyed in favor of the other. To blot out civil liberty in the interest of national security is the easy totalitarian solution. That is what Hitler did in Germany. That is what the Soviet Union has done. On the other hand, to endanger national security in the interest of unrestricted liberty is to invite destruction.

In time of war, restrictions on civil liberty in the interest of national security must naturally be severe. The state can rightfully make demands on its citizens that would be unjust under peaceful conditions. Since World War II came to an end without the making of a secure peace, we have lived in a sort of no man's land between war and peace. Under these conditions, which are a new experience in our history, the problem of loyalty and civil liberty becomes more difficult to solve than ever before. The tension between loyalty and liberty increases. Politicians' tempers flare up easily in this age of cold war or strained peace, and accusations of disloyalty are sometimes thrown about carelessly. Loyal opposi-

"I wants to make their flesh creep!" by *Rollin Kirby. Cartoons of the 1920s and 1930s, when this country was a fertile ground for Communist activity, viewed as alarmists and "Red baiters," those who called attention to the dangers of communism.*

tion is sometimes confused with subversive agitation.

Loyalty is a willingness to place the common interest above one's private interest. It is love of one's country without blindness to its shortcomings. It is the readiness to make whatever personal sacrifices seem necessary for the defense of the country or the preservation of its institutions. It is faithful allegiance to our traditions of freedom. It is readiness to obey and support the government when it actually safeguards those traditions.

Disloyalty. On the other hand, disloyalty is allegiance to the enemies of our country, supporting them, giving them aid and comfort. Disloyalty can also mean adhering to principles which are subversive of our institutions. In our own day disloyalty can perhaps be summed up under two headings: treason and subversive activity. Treason is defined in the Constitution as levying war against the United States, adhering to its enemies, or giving them aid and comfort. Subversive activity was defined by the House Un-American Activities Committee in 1943

as that which "derives from conduct intentionally destructive of or inimical to the government of the United States—that which seeks to undermine its institutions, or to distort its functions, or to impede its projects, or to lessen its efforts, the ultimate end being to overturn it all. Such activity may be open and direct, as by effort to overthrow, or subtle and indirect, as by sabotage."

Loyalty, as we have used the term, is true patriotism. The virtue of patriotism should not be confused with un-Christian nationalism. The latter has been condemned by right-minded men as the perversion of a virtue. It has been compared to patriotism as hate is compared to love. In 1938, for example, Pope Pius XI condemned excessive nationalism as a "matter by now of true apostasy." He used this term because excessive nationalism puts the national state in the place of God and renders it idolatrous worship.

The problem in our history. Throughout most of our history as an independent republic we have been able to take loyalty for granted. Most Americans came to this country voluntarily, or their ancestors did, to enjoy the freedoms it accorded them. There was little or no reason for them to want to overthrow the existing form of government or subvert American institutions. Of course there have always been some Americans who suspected those who held independent political opinions as being "foreign-inspired" or "dangerous-minded." But the issue of loyalty as opposed to civil liberty became a serious problem only a few times in American history before our own age.

1. *The Sedition Act of 1798* was the first such occasion. At this time the Federalists, who tended to be friendly to England and unfriendly to revolutionary France, were in power. They took advantage of our undeclared war with France to pass a series of acts which were aimed at guarding the country from French revolutionary principles. A Naturalization

Act of 1798 extended the period of residence for citizenship from five to fourteen years. It kept Irish immigrants, who almost unanimously joined the Jeffersonian Republican party, from becoming active citizens for another nine years. An Alien Act gave the President power to expel foreigners by executive decree. President Adams did not use the power conferred on him, although there were a number of radical Frenchmen who could have been expelled.

A Sedition Act was needed, for there was no federal law prohibiting conspiracy against the government or libels against high officials. One clause of this act, however, declared any defamatory speech or writing against the President or Congress, or any attempt to bring them "into contempt or disrepute," to be a misdemeanor punishable by fine or imprisonment. With the passage of these acts many American patriots temporarily lost their good sense of balance. Mobs broke into the headquarters of Jeffersonian Republican clubs. Lawyers who defended those charged with sedition were sometimes denounced by judges for "propagating dangerous principles."

Such ill-considered action provoked protest in different quarters of the country. Jefferson and Madison instigated the famous Kentucky and Virginia Resolutions for the nullification of these laws, which they held were contrary to the Constitution. In the election of 1800 the Federalists were decisively defeated by Jefferson's Republican party—partly, historians tell us, because of the unpopularity of the Alien and Sedition Acts. After the election of 1800 the loyalty obsession disappeared as quickly as it had arisen. Jefferson refused to prosecute anyone arrested for violating the Sedition Act. This act expired early in 1801, and Congress repaid most of the fines levied under it.

2. *Loyalty during the Civil War.* Neither the North nor the South found it necessary to pass a sedition law during the Civil War. But both governments acted in harsh fashion, summarily violating civil liberties in the belief that otherwise they could not carry on the war successfully. There was provocation for their actions, because sizable groups of citizens in both sections were opposed to the war and did whatever they could to prevent its prosecution.

President Lincoln acted without authorization from Congress and without constitutional authority. He proclaimed that anyone resisting the draft, discouraging enlistment, or "guilty of any disloyal practice affording aid and comfort to rebels" would be subject to martial law and trial and would be denied the writ of *habeas corpus.* Under this proclamation over thirteen thousand persons were arrested and subjected to military confinement and trial. Some were highplaced persons. The mayor of Baltimore, for example, was arrested on the suspicion of sympathizing with Southerners and he was confined in prison for a year. A Maryland judge who charged a grand jury to inquire into illegal acts of government officials was seized in his court by soldiers, beaten and dragged from his bench, and put into prison for six months. In 1867 the Supreme Court declared that such actions were unconstitutional, since no civilian could be subject to military trial when the civil courts were open, and only Congress could suspend the writ of *habeas corpus*—in time of war or rebellion.

In the conditions of the Civil War, it therefore appears that civil rights were denied in the name of loyalty. There was a dangerous tendency, moreover, among some radical Republicans to identify membership in their party with loyalty to the United States and to equate membership in the Democratic party with disloyalty. For a generation this identification was part of Republican political speeches, but gradually relations between the North and the South grew less strained and a more tolerant spirit again prevailed in party contests.

3. *Loyalty in World War I* and the years immediately following it became a real obsession for the first time in our history. The Espionage Act of 1917 and the Sedition Act of 1918 were extremely severe measures that curbed civil liberty during the war. The Espionage Act fixed a fine of $10,000 and twenty years' imprisonment on anyone convicted of interfering with the draft or encouraging disloyalty. The Sedition Act assessed the same penalties against anyone who discouraged recruiting, incited insubordination, obstructed the sale of war bonds, brought the Constitution or our form of government into contempt; or against anyone who would "willfully utter, print, write or publish any disloyal, profane, scurrilous, or abusive language about the form of government of the United States, or the Constitution . . . or the flag . . . or the uniform of the Army or Navy."

President Wilson had predicted that with the prosecution of the war "the spirit of ruthless brutality will enter into the very fibre of our national life, infecting Congress, the courts, the policeman on the beat, the man in the streets." In this spirit the Espionage and Sedition Acts were enforced. More than fifteen hundred persons were arrested for disloyalty, frequently on absurd charges for petty offenses. Unofficial "witch-hunting" went even further, as personal grudges and neighborhood feuds led people to report their enemies for disloyalty. German-Americans were the particular target of this misguided patriotism. The celebrated violinist, Fritz Kreisler, was not allowed to appear in the concert hall of a Jersey town.

Distinguished judges and lawyers protested the arbitrary violation of civil rights by the Attorney General's office during the war and immediately after its conclusion. In their published protest these jurists charged: "Wholesale arrests both of aliens and citizens have been made without warrant or any process of law; men and women have been jailed and held incommunicado without access of friends or counsel; homes have been entered without search-warrant and property seized and removed; other property has been wantonly destroyed; workingmen and workingwomen suspect of radical views have been shamefully abused and maltreated."

For a time almost any kind of criticism of the federal government was considered somewhat perilous. The Communist revolution in Russia and its threat to the rest of the world justified this rigid conformism in many people's minds. The sporadic activity of radicals in America —syndicalists,[1] anarchists, Communists, and such—further strengthened it. A return to "normalcy," however, and a period of great prosperity put Americans at ease again. The threat of subversive doctrines seemed slight and very remote.

4. *Loyalty questions and World War II.* This war was more than two years old before the United States became actively involved in it. During that period several stern measures were taken against suspected persons and organizations. The German-American Bund, a society of Nazi sympathizers headed by Fritz Kuhn, was broken up and its leader was imprisoned for violating the Smith Act of 1940. This act made it unlawful for anyone to advocate the overthrow of the government by force or the assassination of any officer of the government. It also proscribed any publication or society that advocated such actions.

Early in 1942 the panic of fear inspired by the war with Japan resulted in the creation of military areas from which any

---

[1] Syndicalists were radical trade-unionists who advocated violent direct action and the general strike as the means for seizing control of production and of the government. Their ultimate aim was to establish a socialist state. Their name derives from their alliance with unions or "syndicates" in France, where the movement began and grew strongest.

The Amache Relocation Center was one of ten established by the War Relocation Authority in 1942. The inhabitants of these centers, Americans of Japanese descent, had been excluded from the West Coast, yet were not allowed to relocate voluntarily. (National Archives)

undesirable persons might be excluded. The entire Pacific coastal area was declared to be such a military region. Living within it were some 112,000 persons of Japanese ancestry, of whom about 70,-000 were American citizens. On March 21, Congress enacted a law to punish or imprison any person who entered or remained in such a military area without authorization. Then all persons of Japanese ancestry were removed to inland "relocation centers," which were in fact concentration camps supervised by the War Relocation Authority, an agency created by presidential order. There these unfortunate people were retained for the duration of the war, although not one of them was charged with espionage, sabotage, or any form of subversive activity. Many of the young Japanese-American men were taken into the Army and performed heroic deeds. The 442nd Infantry Regiment, for example, was composed entirely of them and was one of the most heavily decorated units in the history of the American Army. The question of the legality of the government's action came before the Supreme Court in 1944, but a majority of the justices were unwilling to interfere with it. It was plain, however, that most of them had grave misgivings.

It could be defended as constitutional only by arguing that presidential wartime powers extended to the actual disregarding of the Constitution. The dreadful measure has been characterized by Edward S. Corwin, a leading constitutional authority, as "the most drastic invasion of the rights and liberties of citizens of the United States by their own government that has thus far occurred in the history of our nation." Other reputable authorities have stated that the Supreme Court's refusal to intervene in the question "virtually established the principle that any portion of the Bill of Rights, no matter how fundamental, can be set aside in wartime merely upon the plea of military necessity." Thus a most dangerous precedent for setting aside the Constitution during a war has been established.

In other respects the federal authorities displayed a remarkable concern for protecting civil rights and liberties during the war. One reason for this was the sincere desire of such men as Attorney General Francis Biddle to uphold the Bill of Rights in letter and spirit. Another reason was our military alliance with the Communist Soviet Union. American Communists, although enemies of our institutions, strongly supported the war effort because of the Soviet alliance. They appeared *temporarily* as loyal patriots, and instead of curbing their liberties the federal government allowed them to enter freely the armed services and various offices of administration.

President Truman affixed the Presidential Distinguished Unit Citation to the colors of the famous 442nd Regimental Combat Team of Americans of Japanese ancestry who distinguished themselves in combat in France and Italy. (International News Photo)

13. THE PROBLEM TODAY

The termination of World War II and of the Soviet war alliance was followed by a greater concern for security regulations. The development of the atomic bomb, together with research on even more powerful atomic weapons, seemed to require strict security regulations. The problem was further complicated by the "cold war" which developed between this country and the Soviet Union. The problem of loyalty became more complicated and more intense than at any previous time in our history.

It was obvious to any objective observer that Communists and Soviet sympathizers had worked their way into at least some government positions and that they controlled some labor unions. The exposure of a Soviet spy ring in Canada showed how successfully Soviet agents could infiltrate into high government circles. The revelations of the Alger Hiss case showed how they had found sympathizers and instruments in Washington. How to weed subversive agents out of public life without endangering the liberty of the thousands of loyal Americans became an urgent problem of the time.

As far back as 1938 a congressional Un-American Activities Committee had been created with the purpose of holding investigations to find out what legislation was needed to root out such activities. The committee held many hearings, but no substantial legislation resulted from its activity. However, its hearings did make the nation aware in some degree of the danger facing it from Communist infiltration into sensitive governmental positions. Early in 1947 the Truman administration launched its own program for protecting us against security risks.

The Truman loyalty program was set forth in a presidential executive order in March 1947, with the stated purpose of giving "maximum protection . . . to the United States against infiltration of disloyal persons into the ranks of its employees," and at the same time affording "protection from unfounded accusations of disloyalty . . . to the loyal employees of the Government."

The program called for a check on every employee of the federal government. Six criteria were listed as giving reasonable grounds for suspecting a person's loyalty. Briefly, these were (1) sabotage and espionage; (2) treason or sedition, or the advocacy thereof; (3) advocacy of revolution or violence to alter the constitutional form of our government; (4) unauthorized disclosure of confidential documents under circumstances suggesting disloyalty; (5) serving the interests of another government in preference to the interests of the United States; (6) "membership in, affiliation with, or sympathetic association with any foreign or domestic organization, association . . . designated by the Attorney General as totalitarian, fascist, communist or subversive."

The first five criteria were obviously just grounds for dismissal from federal service. The last criterion, however, caused considerable confusion and trouble. It was possible that a person could innocently have joined an organization that the Attorney General would list as subversive. This criterion involved a doctrine—so its critics claimed—of "guilt by association," by which grave injustice might be done to individuals. But, as we shall see later in this chapter, a man's associates cannot be ignored in an attempt to understand his character and behavior.

The Department of Justice furnishes the legal means of enforcing federal laws. The Attorney General heads the department; each of his assistants has charge of a division, such as the Immigration and Naturalization Service, the Federal Bureau of Investigation, and the Bureau of Prisons. (National Archives)

Investigating boards were warned to use this criterion with caution. The Attorney General drew up a list of organizations that he had reason to consider subversive. On their membership lists many perfectly loyal persons' names could be found.

Isaac Don Levine testifies before a night session of the House Un-American Activities Committee that in 1939 Whittaker Chambers offered him, as editor of an Anti-Communist magazine, evidence of Communist infiltration into the State Department. (International News Photo)

The Truman loyalty program established a procedure of investigation and was a definite recognition of a problem the administration had previously been reluctant to recognize. That reluctance was due to the fact that the discovery of Communists, subversives, and "security risks" in the government services was politically embarrassing to the administration. Hence it was not good "politics" for a Democratic administration. Nevertheless, national security dictated the necessity of removing unreliable government employees, and President Truman preferred to have them exposed by executive action rather than through congressional investigations.

The first step of his program required more than two million employees to be fingerprinted and to answer short questionnaires, which were then checked by the Federal Bureau of Investigation. If no derogatory information was found, no further investigation was made. If such information was found, the FBI then undertook a full investigation. In the first year of the program's operation more than a million names were cleared, and 777 were held for further investigation. The system continued, slightly modified by the Eisenhower administration. It works in this way:

If there is an adverse finding as a result of the full FBI investigation, the report is sent to the appropriate agency's loyalty board. If this board, after fuller hearings, arrives at an adverse decision, it sends a letter of charges to the employee. The employee has the right to answer these charges within ten days, and if the finding is adverse after his hearing he may appeal for a further hearing. Such a procedure is designed to protect the employee from unjust or summary dismissal. The need for security, however, denies the employee the usual American procedural rights. The accused employee cannot face his accuser.

John Edgar Hoover has directed the Federal Bureau of Investigation since 1924. This division of the Department of Justice examines alleged violations of federal laws. Although there are about 120 statutes which it enforces, it is widely known for its defense of internal security against treason and sabotage.

Much difficulty stems from the fact that a "security risk" is not the same thing as a disloyal citizen. The loyalty boards must try to discover whether an employee is likely to become a tool for espionage or sabotage in the future. Such intangible things as his moral attitudes, his living habits, whether he drinks heavily or not—all these things may be taken into consideration.

Generally speaking, the amount of injustice done has been small indeed when compared to the dangers that must be averted. How successful it has been in weeding out disloyal employees and security risks is a question that cannot easily be answered. The record shows that after completing its preliminary check on almost two and one half million employees the FBI found that less than twelve thousand merited full investigation. It is not possible to state how many security risks have been discovered. The number may not have been large. But a large number is not required to justify a stringent security procedure against the menace of international communism.

The Internal Security Act of 1950 (the McCarran Act) was passed by Congress over President Truman's veto because most congressmen feared that the President's loyalty program was not strict enough to safeguard our national security. The Internal Security Act of 1950 sums up much of the previous legislation against espionage and other forms of subversive activity. It has four main points: (1) registration of Communist organizations; (2) strengthening of the espionage laws; (3) stricter regulation of immigration and naturalization; (4) arrangements for detention of potential spies and saboteurs in time of national emergency.

1. Communist organizations are divided into "Communist-action" and "Communist-front" groups. The former is defined by the law as an organization "substantially directed, dominated, or controlled by the foreign government or foreign organization controlling the world Communist movement . . . and operated primarily to advance the objectives of such world Communist movement." Communist-front organizations are those controlled by a Communist-action or-

Senator Patrick McCarran (Nevada Democrat, 1876–1954), author of the Internal Security (McCarran) Act of 1950, was chairman of the Senate Judiciary Committee and Joint Committee on Foreign Economic Cooperation. He was also chairman of a sub-committee to investigate the hearings on the United States policy in the Far East, in which it was charged that Communist agents had ready access to top United States defense secrets. (Library of Congress)

ganization and operated primarily in support of communism. Front organizations must register with the Attorney General, listing their officers and financial supporters. Action organizations must do these things and also furnish a full list of their members.

2. Espionage laws are tightened according to suggestions made by federal intelligence agencies to protect scientific laboratories and safeguard the communication of defense information.

3. The Attorney General is given greater freedom in deporting undesirable aliens. Registered aliens are required to report changes of address. Aliens who advocate communism or belong to Communist-action groups cannot become citizens. No one may enter the country if he is a member of any totalitarian party or any group required to register under the Internal Security Act.

4. This portion of the act operates only in time of invasion or the declaration of war by Congress, or in case of an insurrection within the country in aid of a foreign enemy. It provides for the detention of persons found by a Detention Review Board to be likely spies or saboteurs.

President Truman vetoed this measure, charging that it would not weaken the Communists, against whom it was primarily directed, and that it constituted the greatest danger to freedom of speech, press, and assembly since the Alien and Sedition Acts of 1798. The President claimed that the bill "would actually weaken our existing internal security measures and would seriously hamper the Federal Bureau of Investigation and our other security agencies." Meanwhile, he advised Congress, "we would betray our finest traditions if we attempted, as this bill would attempt, to curb the simple expression of opinion."

Despite President Truman's objections, the bill was passed and became law in September 1950.

Existing security legislation. Let us summarize federal laws now on the statute books dealing with loyalty and national security.

Treason and sedition laws make it a crime to levy war against the United States, or adhere to and give aid or comfort to an enemy; to incite, assist, or engage in rebellion or sedition; to conspire to overthrow the government by force; or to urge insubordination or disloyalty in the armed forces.

Espionage and sabotage laws make it a crime to receive or attempt to obtain classified information with the intent to use it to the injury of the United States; to destroy or attempt to injure any defense installations or public facility useful for defense with the intention of injuring national defense preparations; to make defective munitions or equipment for defense with the intent to obstruct defense or war effort.

Security regulations limit access to defense installations and establish safeguards against accidents or sabotage; require the registration of all aliens; exclude aliens who belong to the Communist party or any of its affiliates; provide for boards to check on the loyalty of all government employees and all those working for private industries doing defense work; arrange for emergency detention of potenial spies or saboteurs in time of war or insurrection.

14. REQUIREMENTS OF A GOOD SECURITY PROGRAM

We must ask ourselves whether existing legislation goes far enough in safeguarding national security. In doing this we must remember the principle that most Americans willingly accept: security must be provided only to the extent that seems necessary, because to go further is to limit human freedoms unnecessarily. At one extreme we would have a nation

This is a typical example of the Communist view on how freedom of the press operates. The Daily Worker *cartoon shows the American press distorting for the purpose of propaganda.*

unprotected against subversive agents working for a foreign power. At the other we would have a state that denied all freedoms to its citizens.

A sound security program can more easily and safely be achieved if certain important guiding ideas are kept in mind.

1. We must remember that disloyalty and security risk are not the same thing. All disloyal persons, of course, are security risks; but all security risks are not disloyal. A drunkard, for example, is a poor security risk—but he is not necessarily disloyal. The tendency in the public mind has been to confuse security risk with disloyalty. If the distinction between the two is kept well in mind, the government can screen employees—as any corporation or other employer does—in order to secure and keep the most efficient and faithful employees obtainable. The procedure for screening such employees, moreover, is not exactly the same as the procedure for criminal trials, in which the defendant's life or freedom is at stake. Hearings should be so conducted that

dismissal from federal service as a security risk does not necessarily render a person incapable of getting another position. Hearings should therefore be private unless the person under investigation demands a public review.

2. A distinction should be made between posts that are "sensitive" and those that are not. The great majority of government positions involve routine work of a very ordinary sort. The employee in such positions has no opportunity of obtaining secret information. Screening for such positions need not be nearly so careful and thorough as for those positions of a sensitive nature, where the employee has access to confidential information.

3. A discriminating use of the doctrine of "guilt by association" seems required by the nature of the problem. The company a man keeps is always one factor used in judging his worth. His associates are not the determining factor in deciding his character, his abilities, and his inclinations, but they are good indications of these things. That is why we ask what clubs and social groups, what honor societies and professional organizations a man belongs to when he is looking for a job. It seems only reasonable to use the same criteria in assessing him as a security risk or in inquiring into his loyalty.

4. A good security program is possible only if it is administered by fair-minded men who are wholeheartedly devoted to both our national interests and our traditional freedoms. These men must be above partisan interests. They must be directed by that sound common sense which has traditionally been the day-to-day guide of our political conduct. Loyalty boards must always follow rule-of-thumb procedures. Such procedures work excellently in good men's hands. But they are subject to wide abuse in the hands of partisan or bigoted men.

5. Congressional committees have a legitimate function to investigate conditions throughout the country—in the government, in labor unions, defense plants, and other "sensitive" places like radio and newspaper work—that might reveal the need for legislation dealing with subversive activity. Such committees have been in operation since the first days of the Republic. As far back as 1792 the House set up a committee to investigate the failure of the St. Clair expedition against the Indians. Congressional investigating committees are a legitimate and a necessary means of exposing subversive activity. If their investigations are conducted properly, with due protection afforded innocent people, no complaint can be made about their work. We should also note as political scientists have frequently done, that the quality of a congressional investigating committee depends very much on the character of the men who compose it, especially on the character and personality of the chairman. No code of laws can be devised to guarantee the proper behavior of an investigating committee, as is the case with court trials. Any such set of regulations would hamper the committee's investigatory powers and render it ineffective.

Conclusion. What is the best way to deal with individuals or groups who seek to undermine American political institutions or overthrow the government by force? The attempt to make them register with the Attorney General has not proved workable. Its only achievement is to give the government grounds for prosecution against those groups who fail to register as required by law. The attempt to outlaw such a group as the Communist Party can do little more than to outlaw the name. For a new group will be organized with the same objectives, whether they are formally stated as such or not.

Many persons who have worked on this problem for a long time, such as J. Edgar Hoover, say that the law should work for the disclosure of subversive persons and groups rather than for their suppression. Such action would be an act of faith in the loyalty of most Americans, because it assumes that disclosure of subversive persons would render them ineffectual in their activity. Such faith does not seem misplaced. In the last analysis, subversive activity by a small minority eager to overthrow the government can be rendered almost completely ineffective when we have effective means for detecting such activity, adequate laws on the statute books for dealing with it, and a vigilant citizenry throughout the country.

In times past, as we have seen, the Supreme Court evolved a norm for distinguishing truly dangerous speech and action from that which was relatively harmless. This was the doctrine of the "clear and present danger." It was occasioned by cases that were concerned with individual radicals or anarchists. Since the "cold war" began we have been concerned with agents directed from abroad. Justice Jackson made this point clear in the appeal of eleven Communist leaders who had been convicted in 1949 for violating the Smith Act and who defended themselves on the grounds that their speech and activity did not constitute a clear and present danger to the country. "If applied as it is proposed here," Justice Jackson wrote, "it means that the Communist plotting is protected during its period of incubation; its preliminary stages of organization and preparation are immune from the law; the Government can move only after imminent action is manifest, when it would, of course, be too late."

The line between lawful liberties and subversive activity may not be an easy line to draw. We are all anxious to preserve our free way of life, and we realize that the preservation of freedom involves a certain element of risk as regards national security. The "cold war" and the terrible weapons invented since the last war make it necessary for us to be more vigilant than we have been in the past. Conspiracy is not a civil right but a crime.

REVIEW

12. Loyalty and Disloyalty

A. Define loyalty. What, in practice, does it mean and what does it not mean?

B. What is disloyalty? What is treason? What is subversive activity?

C. In our history we have had occasions when loyalty and civil liberty have been apparently in conflict. Briefly explain the Alien and Sedition Acts of 1798 and the reaction to them.

D. Abraham Lincoln was the first President to invade the area of civil liberties without congressional approval. What did he do and what was the Supreme Court's reaction?

E. How was the loyalty question dealt with during World War I? What was the basis for the protests of the jurists? During World War II there was an even further restriction of liberties. How did many innocent people suffer from this policy during World War II? How did the Supreme Court display weakness concerning this policy?

13. The Problem Today

A. Why has there been a strong need for security regulations since 1946? How has Congress tried to meet this problem? Describe the presidential security program of 1947. What criticism might be levelled against it?

B. Describe the procedure for discovering security risks. What difficulties have been found in discovering security risks? In what direction must the citizen be educated to appreciate the findings of loyalty boards?

C. Describe the Internal Security Act of 1950. Why did President Truman oppose it? Summarize existing security legislation.

14. The Requirements of a Good Security Program

A. What are the requirements of a good security program?

B. Why has the Supreme Court abandoned

the "clear and present danger" of Justice Holmes?

A. How did the government restrict civil liberties in 1798 and in 1861–1865? How did these restrictions endanger American freedoms?

B. Compare the restrictions on civil liberties during World War I with similar restrictions in World War II. How did the federal government go much further in 1942?

C. The danger of communism has been a *positive* threat in the United States since the 1930s. Describe the congressional and presidential measures taken to meet this threat. In security programs what safeguards should be maintained?

SELECTED READINGS

Loyalty in a Democratic State is one of the Problems in American Civilization Series published by D. C. Heath & Company. Edited by John C. Wahlke (Boston: D. C. Heath & Company, 1952), this work includes contributions by many authors—most of them critical—about the government's recent loyalty programs. It tries to achieve objectivity by including defenses of the program and additional suggestions on how best to weed subversives out of the country. It includes also an extensive bibliography.

For a better understanding of the historical development of American loyalty, consult Merle Curti, *The Roots of American Loyalty* (New York: Oxford University Press, Inc., 1946), and Percy Holmes Boynton, *Changing Ideals of American Patriotism* (Chicago: University of Chicago Press, 1936). An objective account is Roger S. Abbott, "The Federal Loyalty Program: Background and Problems" *American Political Science Review* (June 1948). A study that is critical of both the loyalty program and its "liberal" critics is Morris L. Ernst, "Some Affirmative Suggestions for a Loyalty Program" *American Scholar* (Autumn 1950).

Typical of the criticisms of government loyalty programs by "liberals" who minimize the danger of subversion are Alan Barth, *The Loy-*

alty of Free Men (New York: The Viking Press, Inc., 1951), and Elmer Davis, *But We Were Born Free* (Indianapolis: The Bobbs-Merrill Company, 1954). A study that is more sympathetic to the loyalty problem is Nathaniel Weyl, *The Battle against Disloyalty* (New York: Thomas Y. Crowell Co., 1951). The *Yale Law Journal* carried a series of articles for and against the federal loyalty program. "Loyalty among Government Employees," by Thomas I. Emerson and David M. Helfeld (December 1948), is hostile to the program; a rejoinder to this article appeared in February 1949 by J. Edgar Hoover, "A Comment on the Article 'Loyalty among Government Employees.'" A further article is by William J. Donovan and Mary Gardiner Jones, "Program for a Democratic Counter-Attack to Communist Penetration of Government Service" (July 1949).

Patriotism is discussed by Robert C. Hartnett, S.J., "Ten Touchstones of Patriotism," *America* (July 3, 1954); Sister Augusta, O.M., "Foundation Stones of Catholic Patriotism," *Catholic School Journal* (February 1955); and the pamphlet *Loyalty in a Democracy* (Washington: Public Affairs Committee, 1952).

PROJECTS

1. The Civil War was a time when loyalty was severely tested. A committee of the class can investigate and see whether the Civil War involved the question of treason.

2. In 1938 a congressional Un-American Activities Committee made an investigation into Communist activities. Prepare a report for the class on the accomplishments of this committee and any action taken on their recommendations.

3. The importance of the work of the FBI is well known. A member of the class could write to the Bureau directly to obtain literature that describes its function and the career opportunities the Bureau offers. This material, plus photographs and articles from recent magazines, could be used for a bulletin-board project that would interest the entire class.

Chapter 7. The Communist Conspiracy in America

15. AMERICAN PARTIES
AND COMMUNIST "PARTY" CONTRASTED

The two-party system. In the operations of American political life there have traditionally been two major parties contending for the popular vote. Each advocates a set of measures and policies that it hopes will meet with approval from a majority of the voters. Minor parties also play an important role in political life. They seldom hope to get control of the government, but they introduce certain issues which both major parties consider it prudent to ignore. Thus a minor party introduced the issue of women's suffrage at one time in American history, the issue of prohibition of alcoholic beverages at another, and other such measures which were adopted by a major party if or when they became evidently popular.

We must remember that all political parties accept certain assumptions about American life and that without these assumptions our party system could not work. It is necessary to remember these basic assumptions, because in the heat of political campaigns party leaders create the impression that they disagree on

everything. All American parties operate on the assumption that there is no single correct answer to questions of policy. They believe some solutions are better than others. They therefore maintain that every party has the right to propose its solution to each political issue of the day and that ultimately the people will endorse the solution they think best. Such an assumption demands freedom of political discussion carried on rationally. When one party is in power it must allow other parties freedom to criticize its measures. This is the role of the defeated party in American political life—the role of loyal opposition to the government, pointing out its mistakes, urging other measures, keeping the party in power "on its toes" politically.

This is the way our political life has tended to operate in the past. The two-party system involves other assumptions. It must assume that both parties—and minor parties as well—are interested in the national welfare, that most leaders in all parties are honest men and that their differences of opinion are honest differences. This means we must respect another's right to differ from us even

while we are firmly convinced that we are right and he is wrong. It means, moreover, that we must not put the label of treason on mere political mistakes. We must charge them up to human fallibility rather than insidious design—unless there is convincing evidence to the contrary. Otherwise a defeat at the polls would be a death warrant for the losing party leaders, and our system of free elections would become meaningless.

American political life can be carried on only because still other assumptions are generally accepted. One of these is that the Constitution provides for a good civil society. Therefore, every party agrees to respect the Constitution and operate within its framework. If any party wishes to change the Constitution, there is general agreement that it should be done according to the provisions of the Constitution itself. All parties repudiate violence

Effecting Change in Government Contrasted

This poster provides noteworthy evidence of American political freedom. The election platform, personal history of the candidates, and electoral vote tabulations are clearly stated for all to see. (Library of Congress)

and revolution as a means for changing administrations or policies. American parties have also traditionally assumed that government should serve the welfare of the nation as a whole, that every citizen is a precious human being with inalienable rights that must be respected and protected.

Political contests would soon degenerate into wild anarchy or tyrannical despotism if the participants did not all accept the basic rules of fair play. If one party resolves to liquidate its opponents when it comes to power, or even besmirch their good names in order to kill them politically, then political life becomes a deadly struggle for power. The common welfare and national interests are submerged for partisan gain, and power becomes an end in itself.

There is yet another characteristic of our party life that may be mentioned in this connection. There is nothing secret about party activity. Although the ballot is secret and no man can find out how another votes unless that other man announces it, there is no secrecy of party membership. In most states a voter must publicly enroll as a member of a party in order to take part in its primaries. Many voters, to be sure, rarely take advantage of that privilege, and many belong to no party but think of themselves as independents, voting now this way and now that way, or declining to vote when they dislike all the candidates. Our parties do not rely solely on their own members to win an election, but appeal to all the people. They are loose, rather vaguely defined and open agglomerations of people who are not controlled by party leaders. They are not disciplined organizations.

Nature of the Communist party. It is in this light that we must examine the problem of the Communist party as it has operated in this country since the end of World War II. Justice Robert H. Jackson expressed the matter well when he described the Communist party as a "conspiratorial and revolutionary" party whose aim "is to seize powers of government by and for a minority rather than to acquire power through the vote of a free electorate."

The Prohibition party was formed in the United States in 1869 as a third party to reform legislation that governed the sale of alcoholic beverages. Although never in power, the party was a strong factor in the adoption of the Eighteenth Amendment, since repealed. (D. F. Stewart in The Defender)

Supporters of the women's suffrage movement parade in downtown New York. Their objectives were realized in 1920 when the Nineteenth Amendment granted American women the right to vote. Our constitutional liberties permit dissent and agitation that lead to reform rather than revolution. (National Archives)

The Communist party was established in the United States in 1919. It was not a native party, and it was not organized by Americans to solve American problems —as was the case with the Populist party, the Free-Soilers, and other legitimate third parties. By 1919, we should remember, the Communists had come to power in Russia and had established the Comintern (Communist International), which directed the activity of Communist parties in other countries. The Comintern's headquarters were in Moscow. Its annual congresses met there, it was financed by the Soviet Government, and its activity was controlled in every respect by Russian Communists. Thus from its beginning the Communist party in this country was controlled by an agency that had the double aim of promoting revolution everywhere and serving the interests of the Soviet Government in world affairs.

For this reason the McCarran Act (Internal Security Act of 1950) identified membership in the Communist party with treason and subversion. Communists, the act states in its preamble, "repudiate their allegiance to the United States and transfer their allegiance to the

The conception below of the organization of the Communist party has been drawn from the interpretation of evidence secured over recent years. The term Secretariat in the U.S.S.R. is used for the Politburo, and in the United States it stands for the National Committee, which operates along parallel lines.

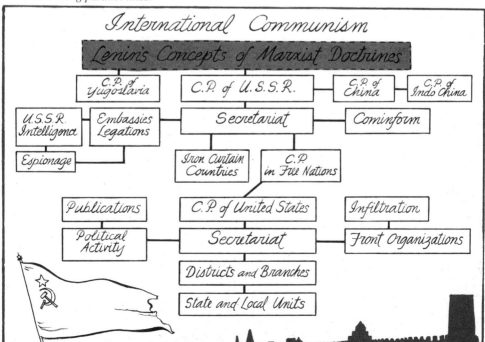

Moscow workers march in Red Square during a May Day ceremony. The Second Soviet International in 1889 established May Day as a holiday for labor, celebrated with demonstrations and parades. There is no competition here among parties—all the placards praise Communist party leaders! (Sovfoto) The Democratic National Convention of 1952 (below) furnishes a clear picture of the adequate representation of informed citizens who legally and positively choose their own candidates for political office. (Oscar and Associates)

foreign country in which is vested the direction and control of the world Communist movement." Ever since 1919, Communists have been ordered to combine deceit and intrigue with the open espousal of good causes in order to create mistrust and confusion in this country. Revolution is the goal of the party. Its aim is to destroy constitutional government in order to usher in a Soviet dictatorship.

Since the end of World War II and the creation of the Cominform (Communist Information Bureau) in 1947 the United States has been the principal objective of Communist revolutionary activity. Our country has become Target Number One. Communist activity has been pursued on a larger scale and more successfully in European and Asian countries than in the United States, but the Communist party in this country has taken on a special importance in Soviet strategy. Because it is under direction from Moscow and because it claims the freedoms accorded to other parties in our free society it becomes an especially difficult problem to handle. It is a unique problem, politically speaking, for it is the first and only political party in our history to be controlled by a foreign power. It works for the overthrow of the American political system, for the victory of the world revolutionary movement, and for increasing the power of the Soviet Union at the expense of this country.

The Communist party in the United States has never had a large membership. In the presidential election of 1924 it polled 33,361 votes, in 1936 it obtained 80,159 votes, and in 1940 it had 46,361 votes. By this last date the party was not allowed on the ballot in many states. The party attained the height of its numerical strength about 1940, when it boasted of 100,000 dues-paying members. J. Edgar Hoover, director of the FBI, testified that in 1950 the Communist party had 54,174 members.

These small figures are misleading, however, because they do not indicate the real strength of the party. Moreover, since the party was outlawed in 1954, there is no way of knowing how many persons belong to the "underground organization" at the present time. Communist leaders boast that for every member of the party there are nine who will follow the party line. Moreover, some avowed Communists find it advisable not to be members. Ben Gold, president of the International Fur and Leather Workers Union, for example, announced that he had resigned from the party to comply with the requirements of the Taft-Hartley Act that no officer of a union be a Communist. But, he announced, he still accepted the principles of the party and would act in accordance with them. In other words, he was a Communist in everything but name. There is no way of knowing how many more there are like Ben Gold in America.

Membership in the Communist party. There are no "sleepers" in the membership of the Communist party. Everyone is an active member under strict orders to follow the party line and to obey orders unquestioningly. Failure to do so means expulsion from the party. The *Manifesto and Program* of the Communist party demand that members make this sworn promise: "The undersigned, after having read the constitution and program of the Communist Party, declares his adherence to the principles and tactics of the party and the Communist International, agrees to submit to the discipline of the party and pledges himself to engage actively in its work." The concluding sentence of the pledge required of all Communists since 1935 reads: "I pledge myself to remain at all times a vigilant and firm defender of the Leninist line of the party, the only line that insures the triumph of Soviet power in the United States." The party imposes an iron discipline on its members. A member retains his good standing only by strict obedience, active co-operation with party leaders, and full compliance with orders. It is not possible for a person to be a member of the party and not work for the overthrow of the American government and our traditional way of life.

Front organizations. Membership in the party is restricted to the comparatively few who are willing to work for the Communist cause with missionary zeal. Those who are sympathetic to certain Communist objectives but are not able or willing to work fanatically for their attainment are welcomed into "front" organizations. The support of others who think the Communists are right in most things but do not like the discipline that comes with membership in the party is also obtained through these organizations, which have been part of Communist strategy since the organization of the Comintern in 1919. They are used to gain support for limited objectives from "big names" in the country, to raise funds for the Communist party, and to win possible converts who could not be approached directly.

Former Attorney General Francis Biddle gave this description of front organizations: "Testimony on front organizations showed that they were represented to the public for some legitimate reform objective, but actually used by the Communist Party to carry on its activities pending the time when the Communists believe they can seize power through revolution." Front organizations were likened to stars revolving around the sun by Otto Kuusinen, secretary of the Comintern, in his instructions to party members. "We must create a whole solar system of organizations and smaller committees around the Communist Party," he said, "smaller organizations working actually under the influence of our party."

Front organizations are not all of the same pattern. Some are purely temporary organizations for a specific purpose, perhaps to raise funds for some ostensibly good cause. Others are high-sounding committees formed to collect signatures or financial support for some permanent cause or other. Some are youth organizations that serve as recruiting grounds for the Communist party. Some are nothing more than lists of prominent names on a letterhead on which the "secretary" issues statements supporting one aspect or another of the Communist line. Typical of front organizations operated by the Communist party in this manner is the network of committees and organizations through which twenty-odd years ago over one million dollars was collected for the defense of the Scottsboro boys—seven Negroes in Alabama accused of rape. About $60,000 of the sum was actually used in defense of the case, and the rest of the money found its way into the treasury of the Communist party.

Determining a front organization. J. Edgar Hoover suggests a number of tests to be applied to any organization, and if the answer to several of them is affirmative, the organization is most likely a front for the Communist party. Among his tests, the following are the most important:

Does the group espouse the cause of Soviet Russia rather than the United States?

Does the organization feature as speakers at its meetings known Communists, sympathizers, or fellow travelers?

Does the organization shift when the party line shifts?

Does its literature follow the Communist line or is it printed by the Communist press?

Does the organization receive consistent favorable mention in Communist publications?

Does the organization denounce American and British foreign policy while always lauding Soviet policy?

Belonging to a front organization or

contributing to its support gives aid as well as comfort to the Communist party. It is a reflection on the good sense of the individual who is being exploited. It undermines the moral fabric of American society. It keeps alive the Communist cause at a time when the party must stay underground. For these reasons Americans should exercise care in joining organizations about which they know little.

16. THEORY AND PRACTICE OF COMMUNISM

The importance of doctrine. Theory plays a most important role in communism. The American Communist party's activity is conspiratorial. It does not flow logically from Marxist or Leninist theory, but it results naturally from the Marxist strategy of revolution. American Communists accept without question the original Marxist theory as modified by Lenin and Stalin. They find some way to fit their practices into the theory. We must therefore briefly outline the principal points of Communist theory so that we can understand what Communists believe and why they hold the faith they do.

Communist leaders insist on the importance of doctrine because they believe, as Lenin stated, "without a revolutionary theory there can be no revolutionary movement." Incorrect theory, they are convinced, will prevent a suc-

The face of Cardinal Mindszenty reflects the strain which his imprisonment and trial put upon him. (Religious News Service Photo)

cessful revolution. Moreover, they fear independent thought of any kind as the first step in weakening their tight control of the revolutionary movement throughout the world. No Communist, then, enjoys freedom of thought on any social, political, cultural, or other point that the party has laid down for all members to accept on faith.

The basic doctrines of communism, formulated by Karl Marx and Friedrich Engels about a century ago, are summed up in two phrases: dialectical materialism, and the surplus theory of value.

Dialectical materialism. This involves two points. The first, *dialectics,* holds that everything is in a state of constant change: social and political organizations, human life, truth itself, all reality is made up of contradictory principles. Marxists claim that they alone know the pattern whereby these contradictions work themselves out. In the field of philosophy, they hold, each truth contains its own negation or contradiction. Each society has within itself a contradictory element which expresses itself in revolution. The capitalist society in which we live, Communists hold, creates a proletarian class (the working class) that is necessarily a negation of capitalism, a class that must revolt against the existing order of things. For practical purposes, then, the term "dialectic" means "revolutionary."

Materialism, as stated by Marx and his followers, holds that ultimately everything depends on production relations. Communist materialism does not deny the reality of hopes and aspirations, ideals and self-sacrifice. It admits the reality of these non-material things but insists that they are ultimately determined by the system of class relations in the economic production of any given society. The capitalistic method of production, according to Communist theory, sets the workers off against the owners of the means of production. The two classes are locked in deadly struggle. The capitalist class tries to keep the working class from owning any of the means or tools of production. The Communist theory holds that the capitalist class controls the state. It controls the police force and the army. It controls the press and the movies, religion and education, all the means for making people think the way they do. In this way, Communist theory maintains, religion, education, all social and cultural institutions are instruments used in the class struggle whereby capitalists try to keep the workers in chains.

Communists hold that the proletariat can obtain justice only by seizing all productive property from the capitalists and putting it under common ownership. Then there would be no class struggle because there would be no exploiters and exploited. Everyone would be a worker and all would be owners. In short, there would be no classes. This conclusion seems to follow because of the Communist assumptions that classes are created by the means of production and must struggle with each other to the death.

The surplus theory of value. This theory can be described briefly in this fashion: the sole source of value in economic goods is the amount of labor put into them—the labor theory of value which Marx obtained from English economists. Thus in a competitive market the value of an automobile will be the cost of labor for everything that goes into making the automobile, from the miner who digs iron out of the earth to the painter who puts the final coat of enamel on the body. Now, Marx said, let us look at any one worker—our painter with his spray gun. Let us assume that he is paid $2.50 an hour and that he works 40 hours a week. His wages are $100 a week. If we analyze the value he has added to cars, Marx goes on, we will find that he has increased their total value $100 in the first 24 hours of labor. In the remaining 16 hours he adds another $67 to the value of the cars. Thus the owners get a surplus value of $67 from the worker's efforts, something they have not earned, something they have therefore "stolen" from the worker.

The surplus theory of value appealed to workers because it seemed true on first sight, but most of all because it seemed to pin-point the injustice of the capitalistic system and to prove how the workers were exploited. It seemed to be a scientific explanation of how the workers were cheated, and thus it had tremendous appeal to the working class. The protest ap-

Worktime Required to Buy Items in U.S.S.R. and U.S.

Moscow		New York
248 mins.	BUTTER 1 LB	26 mins.
84 mins.	SUGAR 1 LB	3¼ mins.
42 days	OVERCOAT	3 days
12 days	SHOES	1 day
24 mins.	SOAP	3 mins.
32 days	RADIO	13 hrs.

Karl Marx (right), author of the Communist Manifesto *(1848), advocated a form of socialism that relied on evolutionary development and on democratic means of attaining the liberation of all men from economic servitude. Vladimir N. Lenin (left), interpreted Marx's socialistic doctrines as advocating violence, revolution, and dictatorship as necessary steps to the future free and equalitarian society. Under his direction the Bolsheviks seized power after the outbreak of the Russian Revolution against the Czar in 1917. Joseph Stalin (below) wrested control of the Communist party after the death of Lenin. His "advance toward socialism" policy consisted of a series of Five Year Plans. He was responsible for the great purges of 1937 and 1938, to which many high officials, trusted leaders, and experienced officers of the armed forces fell victim. Stalin's position became that of a dictator. Since his death (March 5, 1953) purges and bloodshed have continued. (Library of Congress, National Archives, International News Photo)*

peal, originally based on Marx's theory of surplus value, proved so effective that Communists stressed it in all their propaganda and widened it out to include more and more "injustices."

Marxism thus became a doctrine that, to the "initiated," was apparently irrefutable. Those who criticized it, Marxists believed, were still chained to an old-fashioned kind of thinking that Marx had proved wrong. Only Marxists understood the dialectic, and only those who understood the dialectic could understand modern society. Marxism took on the aspect of a religion. It had its "infallible" body of doctrine to be found in the "inspired" writings of Karl Marx and explained in the commentaries of Engels, Lenin, and Stalin. It had its chosen people, the proletariat, and it promised a heaven on earth in the classless society of the future. Marxists took to their religion with true missionary zeal and set about the work of converting the rest of the world to their new-found faith.

Marxist view of capitalism. Marx applied his basic doctrines to an analysis of modern economic society—capitalism—in or-

der to show that revolution was both inescapable and good. His analysis turned out to be a rather grotesque caricature of capitalism, and later events have proven it wrong, but it was eagerly accepted by many as being scientifically accurate. Marx thought the capitalists would oppress the workers more and more, paying ever lower wages in order to make ever larger profits. In the course of competition, he believed, small producers would disappear until finally only a few immensely rich capitalists would be left, and all others would be propertyless workers exploited by them. "The centralization of the means of production and the socialization of labor," he wrote, "reach a point where they prove incompatible with their capitalist husk. This bursts asunder. The knell of capitalist private property sounds. The expropriators are expropriated. . . . With the inexorability of a law of nature, capitalist production begets its own negation."

Karl Marx (1818–1883) and his followers held that the revolution was bound to come but could be made to come more rapidly if the party carried out an effective strategy of revolution. He was not only a social theorist but a practical revolutionist. In 1864 he founded the First International Workingmen's Association, which aimed at organizing the proletariat of various countries. But it remained for Nicolai Lenin (1870–1924) and Joseph Stalin (1879–1953) to fashion the modern strategy of Communist revolution, which is a great deal more complex than the Marxian theory of society. That theory goes easily enough into the heads of simple, credulous, and unenlightened minds, and it is very doubtful that the leaders of international communism regard it as anything but an instrument for controlling the minds of their dupes. Communist strategy, on the other hand, calls for a close and careful study of all nations, the building and directing of subversive organizations throughout the world, and the exploitation of all opportunities to promote Communist power. The masters of international communism rule an empire in Europe and Asia, direct vast business organizations, possess the world's largest secret police and army, and even have atomic and hydrogen bombs. Every Communist party in the world is an agency of this power and does its bidding; hence every Communist party is directed by a practical and astute intelligence, not by "crackpot" theorists.

17. COMMUNISM AS CONSPIRACY

Some of Marx's first disciples believed that capitalism must develop its contradictions fully before revolution could take place. Like a pear on the tree, it must ripen naturally before it can fall to the ground. One of them, Karl Kautsky, explained their position this way: "The socialist party is a revolutionary party but not a revolution-making party. We also know that it is just as little in our power to create this revolution as it is in the power of our opponents to prevent it." Such Communists tried to co-operate with other reformist parties in each state to better the lot of the workingman and to win more converts to their doctrine.

A second generation of Communists, led by Lenin in Russia, came to emphasize the revolutionary aspect of Marxism. By stressing certain parts of Marxian doctrine they showed that the first thing to be done was to seize power in the state. Then the other classes could be liquidated, society could be pushed through a period of state capitalism, and finally the classless society of the future would be achieved. In 1917 two revolutions occurred in Russia, the second one bringing to power Lenin and his Bolshevik wing of the Russian Social Democratic party. For about three years the Bolsheviks had to fight a civil war against their opponents in order to stay in power. Meanwhile they tried to apply Marxian economic theories and achieve a state of "pure" communism at once—a state in which workers managed the factories and private ownership of productive goods was abolished. They ruthlessly defeated their opponents in the civil war and entrenched themselves in power. But their attempt at "pure" communism was a failure. Meanwhile their expectations that the rest of the European world would follow their example and have Communist revolutions were not realized.

The result was that communism, directed by Lenin from Moscow, adopted new tactics in the struggle against the capitalist world. After 1921 its aim was to strengthen the Soviet state and make it a stronghold of communism. Meanwhile, through Communist parties in other countries of the world, the fabric of capitalist society was to be weakened until revolution could come about. As leader of the one successful Communist revolution of the time, Lenin became the official interpreter of Marxian communism. In this role he developed several points which the Comintern passed on to all Communist parties as official teaching.

1. The working classes are not able or intelligent enough to revolt by themselves. They must be led by a class of professional revolutionists whose sole work in life is promoting the revolution and, when it occurs, taking over the government. This class of professionals must be hard and ruthless, disciplined and obedient, willing to sacrifice life itself for the cause they lead. In effect, they who are members of the Communist party constitute a new *élite,* the vanguard of the proletariat. Like soldiers, they must accept the party's authority unquestioningly and submit to its discipline.

2. It was a mistake, Lenin insisted, to wait for capitalism to disintegrate from its own contradictions, as Kautsky had insisted Marxists must do. The Communist party must stir up discontent, subvert society by infiltrating into the government, the army, the unions, all "sensitive" positions in the nation, such as communications work or newspaper and magazine writing. Their one objective, Lenin repeated many times, is to seize power. Every activity, the use of every front group, is to be directed toward that aim.

3. The Russian Communist party is pre-eminent among Communist parties of the world. The revolutionary movement is tied up intimately with the Soviet Union. For strategic reasons, therefore, Communists in all countries must subordinate their interests to those of the Soviet Union and the Russian Commu-

nist party. They must work for the strength and power of the U.S.S.R. against their own countries. They promote communism, they are told, by promoting what Americans would call "Soviet imperialism."

The Communists have continued to use the words of Karl Marx. But after Lenin's success in Russia, Communist theory has been little more than a façade behind which the party leaders operate. The Communist party in America today is essentially a party of conspiracy that follows without deviation the orders laid down for it by the leaders in Moscow. In this way, they are told, they promote the welfare of the proletariat everywhere and therefore ultimately in their own country.

The Communist party in this country poses a difficult problem because it does not abide by our accepted rules of morality, as do other parties and organizations in this country. It rejects American values and the standards that have made our political life possible. On the basis of Marx's dialectic, Lenin and his followers have created a morality of trickery and deceit. They advocate as good any action that furthers the cause of communism. In keeping with this theory, the Kremlin has perfected techniques of deception, propaganda, subversion, and espionage. It has trained members of the party from various countries, including the United States, in the use of these techniques.

America deals with communism. Americans would do well to maintain cool and steady minds on the subject of communism. It is a mistake to minimize the danger it presents to the country, and it is a mistake to exaggerate the danger. Either mistake plays directly into the hands of the enemy. The important thing is to know the real nature and methods of this evil and not to make wild assertions that can confuse the issue so badly that many of us may not recognize the real danger of communism when it confronts us.

In 1954 Congress passed a bill outlaw-

"The New Recruit" is the title of this cartoon, which shows the Communist method of succession to the office of Premier. Former Party Secretary Malenkov has been ousted from the position of Premier after a party purge. The powerful Party Secretary Khrushchev is installing Bulganin, the newly "elected" Premier. Another former leader, Beria, has been liquidated. (S. J. Ray in the Kansas City Star)

ing the Communist party. The law did not make it a crime for an individual to belong to the party, but it did deprive the party of legal and political status. It can no longer appear on the ballot, own property, or have a bank account. Those supporting the bill argued that the party is a tool of a foreign power, as we have seen it to be, and that it seeks to overthrow the government by force. Therefore, they maintain, it is not a political party in the true sense of the word but rather a subversive-action group that enjoyed the protection of the law until the bill outlawing the party was passed. Opponents of the bill, including Herbert Brownell, the Attorney General in the Eisenhower administration, insisted that outlawing the Communist party would not decrease its danger to American institutions. It would only drive the party underground, perhaps to emerge with a changed name and a "dummy" set of objectives that would appear perfectly legal. The Communist party can make no valid claim to existence in American political life, but the question remains as to whether outlawing it will effectively remove it from the political scene.

Another solution used rather widely throughout the country is to require oaths from all persons holding "sensitive" posts in government service, in defense industry, and in education, declaring that they are not members of the Communist party. The defect of such a measure is the assumption that Communists will tell the truth under oath and that all non-Communists will be willing to take the oath. However, Communists would not hesitate to take such an oath or make such an affidavit. The advantage of this requirement is that the Communist who takes the oath can be convicted of perjury if it can later be proved that he was a Communist at that time. Such a solution, of itself, does little to solve the problem of rendering the Communist party ineffective in America. Ways and means of screening Communists out of sensitive positions in American life must be employed, but it is doubtful that the taking of an oath accomplishes much in this respect.

Another "solution" has been tried—with very bad results. This is the use of violent, often illegal measures against people suspected of being Communists or having Communist sympathies. The city of Birmingham, Alabama, for example, required Communists to leave the city in 48 hours and imposed a penalty of $100 fine and 180 days in jail for each day a Communist remained unlawfully in town. When a Communist appeared to speak on a bill for registering Communists in McKeesport, Pennsylvania, he was escorted to the city limits and told never to return. Again, natives of Peekskill, New York, thought they were acting patriotically when they used violence to break up a concert by Paul Robeson, who had been critical of the United States and had frequently praised the Soviet Union.

Such measures do little harm to the Communists, and recourse to mob violence solves no problems at all; instead it weakens respect for the Constitution and legal procedures. It shows lack of confidence in American institutions. It reveals lack of respect for human persons. Indeed, one can well maintain that one of the dangers of communism in America is the desire it creates among its opponents to use violent, illegal means to stamp it out.

The best way to deal with Communists, in the opinion of such men as J. Edgar Hoover, is to identify and expose them and thus render them ineffective. This plan is based on the assumption that almost all Americans are loyal and that they have no sympathy with a conspiratorial party in this country. Since Communists are dangerous as subversive agents of a foreign power, they should be dealt with by the laws now on the statute books against subversion and espionage. In certain respects these laws might be tightened up and made more severe. But we have adequate agencies, such as the FBI and legislative investigating committees, and adequate laws, such as the Smith Act and the Internal Security Act of 1950, to deal with subversive elements in the country. These agencies and these laws can be used to deal with Communists as tools of a foreign power inimical to the welfare of the United States. Meanwhile the long-range fight against communism should include removing the causes of discontent in the country and increasing the loyalty of all Americans by maintaining a government and a society inspiring such loyalty.

REVIEW

15. American Parties and Communist "Party" Contrasted
A. What has been the traditional behavior of political parties in America?

B. In American politics, parties have accepted certain assumptions about "American life." Discuss these assumptions and show their importance to our political life.

C. American parties are not disciplined organizations. Explain the truth of this statement.

D. Describe the beginnings of the Communist party in America. What are its aims? Why is it un-American? Why are membership figures for this particular party misleading?

16. Theory and Practice of Communism
A. Define dialectical materialism.

B. What is the principle of the surplus theory of value?

C. How did Marxism take on the aspect of a "religion" for its followers?

D. Trace the development of the doctrine of Marx to modern times.

17. Communism as Conspiracy
A. What is involved in the present-day "line" of communism? Show how the Soviets adopted this in their relationship to countries throughout the world.

B. What points did Lenin emphasize concerning communism?

C. Point out the present danger of the Communist party to America. Why is it difficult to combat?

D. America has dealt with communism by law, by oaths, and even violent means. Why have these met with limited success? What recommendation has J. Edgar Hoover made in regard to communism?

THE CHAPTER IN REVIEW
A. How has America maintained a two-party system throughout its history?

B. Point out the evils of the Communist party and the dangers it presents to America.

C. Discuss the main theories of Marx and Engels on communism and explain how they have been modernized.

D. Communism is a conspiracy. How effective has America been in meeting this threat?

SELECTED READINGS

Communist theory is a complex subject, and there are no simple treatments of it that are not misleading. The best studies in English of this difficult subject are Charles J. McFadden, *The Philosophy of Communism* (New York: Benziger Brothers, Inc., 1939); Waldemar Gurian, *Bolshevism: Theory and Practice* (New York: The Macmillan Co., 1932); R. N. Carew-Hunt, *The Theory and Practice of Communism* (New York: The Macmillan Co., 1951); and Frank J. Sheed, *Communism and Man* (New York: Sheed & Ward, 1939). In 1937, Pope Pius XI published his classic encyclical on communism, *Divini Redemptoris,* which is published by the Paulist Press as a pamphlet entitled *On Atheistic Communism.*

Gary MacEoin has analyzed the violent opposition of Communists to religion in *The Communist War on Religion* (New York: The Devin-Adair Co., 1951), and the same subject is treated briefly by Geza B. Grosschmid, "Communism and Religion," in *Social Order* (September 1953).

Men who have left the Communist Party and tell about their former activities have written a number of exciting and informative books. Among the more important of these books are: Whittaker Chambers, *Witness* (New York: Random House, 1952); Douglas Hyde, *I Believed* (New York: G. P. Putnam's Sons, 1950); Victor Kravchenko, *I Chose Freedom* (New York: Charles Scribner's Sons, 1946); and Louis Budenz, *This Is My Story* (New York: Whittlesey House, 1947).

Communism as an American problem is the subject of a collection of essays edited by Edward E. Palmer, *The Communist Problem in America* (New York: Thomas Y. Crowell Co., 1951). The Reference Shelf has a collection of articles and speeches for and against the subject, *Should the Communist Party Be Outlawed?,* compiled by Julia E. Johnsen (New York: H. W. Wilson Co., 1949). The report of the House Committee on Un-American Activities is entitled *The Communist Party of the United States as Agent of a Foreign Power* (Washington: House Document No. 209, 80th Congress, 1st Session, 1947). Two excellent articles from *Look* and *Life,* by Dorothy Thompson and John McPartland, respectively, have been published as a pamphlet by the Queen's Work Press, *"Life" and "Look" Show Us Communism.* Louis Budenz has a comprehensive discussion of the problem in *The Techniques of Communism* (Chicago: Henry Regnery Co., 1954).

A number of other pamphlets on communism that may prove helpful to the interested student include the following: Rev. James J. Rohan, S.J., *Atheistic Communism* vs. *United Nations* (New York: The Paulist Press, 1950); Rev. William A. Nolan, S.J., *Why People Go Communist* (St. Louis: The Queen's Work Press, 1950); Alfred G. Meyer, *What You Should Know about Communism* (New York: Science Research Associates, 1953); Arthur M. Schlesinger, *What about Communism?* (Washington: Public Affairs Committee, 1950); Gregor Aronson, *Soviet Russia and the Jews* (New York: American Jewish League Against Communism, 1949); Douglas A. Hyde, *The Answer to Communism* (St. Paul, Minn.: Catechetical Guild, 1952).

PROJECTS

1. In the Constitution there are no specific provisions in respect to political parties. Yet we know that the Constitution does not forbid them. Report to the class on those sections of the Constitution which today make the party system necessary for electing our officials and guaranteeing democracy in our country.

2. In recent years many men and women who formerly held high positions in the Communist party have defected. From their published testimony and writings explain how the party operates in the United States.

3. An artist in the class might make a map of the world in 1940 and then another of the world today. The countries that are under Communist control should be indicated, and the gains made by the Communists in a very short period of time should be noted.

PROFILES

CHARLES EVANS HUGHES

BORN: Glens Falls, N.Y., April 11, 1862
EDUCATED: Brown University, 1881; private law studies and Columbia University Law School, 1884
DIED: Osterville, Mass., August 27, 1948

Hughes was a Colgate College student at the age of fourteen. He transferred to Brown University and continued a brilliant scholastic career in law after a year of teaching. He wrote an almost perfect paper in the extremely difficult New York State bar examination, then divided his time between practicing law and teaching on the law faculties of Columbia and Cornell universities, and New York Law School. Hughes entered public life as chief legal adviser to the New York State committees investigating public utilities and insurance operations. In 1906 he served as counsel to the U. S. Government's investigation of the coal trust.

That same year Hughes won the governorship of New York as a Republican despite a general Democratic landslide. He began an energetic reform of state commissions to protect the public against legal dodges developed by crafty malefactors. His active political career seemed to terminate in 1910, when President Taft nominated him to a seat on the Supreme Court. In 1916, however, he gave up his associate justiceship to run for President. Returns from the West Coast were delayed, and Hughes retired on election night apparently the President-elect, only to discover next day that he had lost California, and the presidency, to Woodrow Wilson.

In 1918, Wilson called his former rival to investigate military aircraft production, and Harding, the next Republican President, appointed him Secretary of State. From 1921 to 1925 Hughes distinguished himself by his disarmament policies. His international reputation was further enhanced by service as judge in the International Court of Arbitration, The Hague, from 1926–1930. Finally President Hoover named Hughes as Chief Justice in 1930, a position he held until retirement in 1941.

Hughes emphasized the importance of preserving constitutional rights. His most important opinions as Chief Justice applied constitutional principles to modern conditions. He upheld the New Deal National Labor Relations Act, but declared the NRA unconstitutional because Congress had delegated lawmaking powers to the President in this law. Hughes' personal integrity and reputation helped defeat President Roosevelt's efforts to "pack" the court in 1937.

For a fuller description of Hughes' career and the America of his period, Merlo J. Pusey's 2-volume biography, *Charles Evans Hughes,* is excellent (New York: The Macmillan Company, 1951). The most readily available of Hughes' own writings on topics of direct interest to social studies students are his *The Supreme Court of the United States* (New York: Columbia University Press, 1928) and *Our Relations to the Nations of the Western Hemisphere* (Princeton: Princeton University Press, 1928).

ABRAHAM LINCOLN

BORN: Hardin, Kentucky, February 12, 1809
EDUCATED: Self-educated beyond primary school; law clerkship
DIED: Washington, D.C., April 15, 1865

Lincoln's early poverty and his struggle for learning as he moved from Kentucky to Indiana to Illinois are widely known. This background, plus a varied experience as a store clerk, surveyor, and country lawyer, taught Lincoln much about Americans. He developed "the common touch" that enabled him to sway Illinois juries, half-hostile Cabinet or military officers, and the crowds at Cooper Union or Gettysburg with equal facility. His close and careful study of the Bible gave his own expressions a biblical tone.

A downstate Illinois country lawyer, Lincoln entered the Whig party, served six years in the state legislature and two in Congress without attracting any great notice. His opposition to the opening of Kansas Territory to slavery led him into the Republican party and to his debates with Douglas during the 1858 senatorial campaign, which he lost. The debates, however, won him a national reputation and the Republican presidential nomination in 1860.

Lincoln faced urgent problems from the day of his inauguration. The secession of Southern states, the questionable loyalty of the border states, and the general hesitation of many to fight to preserve the Union, all required Lincoln to act swiftly. His actions in calling for volunteers on his own authority, in suspending *habeas corpus* and suppressing newspapers favorable to the Confederacy, and in the liberal use of military courts, were all undertaken under powers he claimed as a wartime President. During the war his chief contributions to the Union were his magnificent statements of war aims in the Gettysburg and second inaugural addresses, and his careful search for a winning combination of commanders and civilian war administrators.

Lincoln's outstanding characteristic displayed during the war was his devotion to the Union; he would in no way compromise the unity and power of the U. S. Government. He resisted the urgings of many to violate the Constitution by an outright abolition of slavery, and only as a military measure did he emancipate the slaves owned by active Confederates. He urged passage of the Thirteenth Amendment, after efforts to secure compensated emancipation were not completely successful. Finally, his generous and charitable view of the defeated Confederates looked to binding up the nation's wounds. Death at the hands of a fanatic in Ford's Theatre five days after the surrender of Lee brought instead the confusion and bitter revenge that marked the so-called period of reconstruction.

The most recent full study of President Lincoln, and one of the best, is James Garfield Randall's *Lincoln, The President,* 3 vols. (New York: Dodd, Mead & Co., 1945–1952). A new and interesting book giving a detailed description of one set of events connected with him is James A. Bishop's *The Day Lincoln Was Shot* (New York: Harper & Brothers, 1955). The works of Lincoln are available in dozens of editions, the most recent revision of a complete nature being the 8-volume set edited by Roy P. Basler, *The Collected Works of Abraham Lincoln* (New Brunswick: Rutgers University Press, 1953).

J. EDGAR HOOVER

BORN: Washington, D.C., January 1, 1895

EDUCATED: George Washington University Law School: LL.B., 1916; LL.M., 1917

J. Edgar Hoover has spent a lifetime in federal service, which ranged from a part-time position in the Library of Congress to his present position as Director of the FBI. He joined the Justice Department upon graduation from law school and spent two years as special assistant to the Attorney General.

In 1924, after three years as Assistant Director, he became Director of the Federal Bureau of Investigation and began a program to improve the scientific development of information. The Bureau is charged with investigating violations of federal laws, and it has been particularly prominent in recent years in the detection and development of evidence against Communists and other conspirators against the liberties of Americans. The security aspect of the Bureau's work now extends to checking loyalty qualifications of many federal employees or applicants, and even to developing information needed to clear servicemen who are to have access to security information.

This rather highly publicized aspect of the Bureau's work has tended to overshadow other important tasks that the Bureau performs. Very little attention was attracted in the 1930s, for example, when the Bureau opened the National Police Academy in 1935. Under Hoover's energetic direction, agents of the Bureau receive special training in the techniques that law, accountancy, chemistry, and other sciences make available for detecting and identifying criminals ranging from fraudulent contractors to Communist subversives.

The National Police Academy was established to bring the special techniques developed by the FBI to the attention of police officers in the various local forces of the country. Thus federal knowledge and experience were made available under Hoover's direction for the improvement of police services throughout the nation. Although in a position to make himself a political reputation if he chose to place personal power above service to the country, Hoover has kept himself out of all political campaigns and has served with equal distinction under Democratic Presidents Roosevelt and Truman, and under Republicans Coolidge, Hoover, and Eisenhower. Public acknowledgment of his service has taken the form of honorary degrees from many universities, among them Georgetown, Notre Dame, Holy Cross, and Seton Hall.

The only generally available book describing Hoover's work in any detail is *The Story of the F.B.I.*, edited by the editors of *Look*, but including a preface by Hoover himself (New York: E. P. Dutton & Co., Inc. 1947). Hoover and his Bureau, however, are one of the most widely written about agencies in the periodical press, and specific references to the most recent articles should be sought in the *Reader's Guide to Periodical Literature*, under headings: Crime, Investigations, Hoover.

DEBATE

The question: **SHOULD THE COMMUNIST PARTY BE OUTLAWED?**

Affirmative presentation

I. Yes, to safeguard American security and American political life.
  1. The aim of the Communist party is the overthrow of the Constitution, the American way of life, and the "capitalistic system."
    a. Quotations from official party sources prove this point.
    b. The action of the party in the Soviet Union, Poland, and Czechoslovakia is further proof.
  2. The Communist party would destroy American institutions.
    a. Religion and religious bodies.
    b. Private property.
  3. It advocates, and uses, all means to achieve its end.
    a. Violence.
    b. Deceit, persuasion, and confusion.

II. Yes, the Communist party should not enjoy the protection of the law.
  1. That Communists are subversives—actual or potential criminals—has been proved.
    a. By the oaths they must take.
    b. By their conduct and record of spy rings, sabotage, and the like.
    c. By their theory.

  2. To protect them as a party is to sanction subversive activity.
    a. Puts their candidates on the ballot.
    b. Guarantees them a hearing, radio time, and newspaper space.
    c. Would help them confuse our real political issues; this is the usual Communist technique, which we would be endorsing.

III. Yes, outlawing the Communist party will entail no evils.
  1. It sets no precedent, since no other party or organization is controlled by a foreign state.
  2. It does not mean changing the Constitution by improper means.
  3. The Communist party would be outlawed for advocating criminal means and because it is incompatible with our way of life.

Negative presentation

I. No, there is no *need* to outlaw the Communist party.
  1. We have sufficient laws to punish criminal and subversive activity.
  2. Competent authorities, such as J. Edgar Hoover and Attorney General Brownell, agree that all we need do is enforce these laws, in order to have a loyal citizenry.

II. No, outlawing the Community party is dangerous.
  1. In principle, it justifies outlawing other parties and organizations.
    a. It might conceivably lead to prohibition of all third parties.
    b. Example of Hitler's outlawing of Communist party followed by outlawing of other parties, such as the Catholic Center party in Germany.
  2. This would drive subversives underground, and our aim should be to expose them, according to Hoover and Brownell.

III. No, this is not the American way to deal with the problem.
  1. We should respect the freedom of a minority group to present its case to the electorate.
  2. We must rely on the ultimate good sense of the American electorate.

Affirmative rebuttal

I. Let us not confuse the Communist party with Communist subversives.

1. We know there are good laws against subversion and crime.
2. We are concerned with outlawing the Communist party—is this a good or a bad thing?

II. What does the Communist party gain if it is not outlawed?
1. It gains official protection by law and a chance to create confusion.
2. This is recognition in the form of:
    a. A place on the ballot.
    b. Radio time to preach to Americans.
    c. Newspaper space or free advertising.
3. Protected organization to further Communist activity and plotting is a way of sanctioning subversion, treason, and revolution.

III. Why, in the negative's argument, are we to endanger our way of life?
1. We are concerned with protecting freedoms, and not "dangerous precedents."
2. Do we guarantee criminals the right to carry guns, or lunatics the right to drive cars?
3. The "clear and present danger" principle is no longer valid.

Affirmative conclusion: There is nothing to be lost in our American way of life by outlawing the party, and there is something to be gained.

Negative rebuttal

I. There is no need to outlaw the Communist party, because the doctrine of a "clear and present danger" protects us from any violence or revolution.

II. The second point in the affirmative argument confuses the issue because:
1. We assume that the Communist party will do nothing illegal. There are laws to punish Communists if they do.
2. Not all Communists advocate violent revolution; some propose peaceful change through constitutional measures.

III. The claim that this will not set a precedent is facile and not assuring.
1. The first step always makes the second easier, even if not logical.
2. Examples of history all prove this.

Negative conclusion: There is no need to outlaw the Communist party, because we have sufficient legislation to deal with the Communist danger. Outlawing the party will gain nothing;

it will only drive Communists underground; and for the little gain proposed by the affirmative, they ask us to take this un-American step and endanger our way of life. Remember what the fear of communism produced in Germany.

CLASSROOM DISCUSSION: The issues seem to narrow down to two: (1) What is to be gained by outlawing the Communist party? (2) What is to be lost? Do the gains outweigh the losses?

SELECTED READINGS

Should the Communist Party Be Outlawed?, compiled by Julia E. Johnsen (New York: H. W. Wilson Co., 1949), and *University Debater's Annual 1950–1951*, edited by Ruth Ulman (New York: H. W. Wilson Co., 1951), contain a great deal of information that the student could use, both for and against; their only shortcoming is that they are not strictly up to date. Pro and con discussions are outlined by Martin Dies and Norman Thomas, "Should the Communist Party Be Outlawed in the United States?", *Congressional Digest* (May 1954), and in "Outlaw the Reds?", *Senior Scholastic* (September 15, 1954). Another discussion of the question from both points of view is the article by T. Granik, "American Forum: Should the Communist Party Be Outlawed?", *American Mercury* (August 1954).

General background books that are against communism and the party are: Richard Crossman (ed.), *The God That Failed* (New York: Harper and Bros., 1949); Nathaniel Weyl, *Battle against Disloyalty* (New York: Thomas Y. Crowell, 1951).

Readings recommended for the affirmative side are: Frank B. Ober, "Can the Communist Party Be Constitutionally Outlawed?", *American Bar Association Journal* (August 1948); Harold E. Stassen, "Should the Communist Party in the United States Be Outlawed?", *Vital Speeches of the Day* (June 1, 1948) (debate with Dewey); "Communist Party Isn't a party, It's a Conspiracy," *Saturday Evening Post* (September 18, 1954); J. B. Matthews, "The What and How of Communist Fronts," *American Mercury* (August 1955).

Readings recommended for the negative side are: Henry Steele Commager, "Who Is Loyal to America?", *Harper's Magazine* (September 1947); Thomas E. Dewey, "Should the Communist Party Be Outlawed?", *Vital Speeches of the Day* (June 1, 1948); J. Edgar Hoover, "B-r-e-a-k-i-n-g the Communist Spell," *American Mercury* (March 1954).

UNIT THREE
American Educational Issues and Problems

Chapter 8. The American System of Education

18. RISE OF THE PUBLIC AND PAROCHIAL SCHOOLS

Americans have developed a system of education which confuses foreigners when they seek to find the "system" or rationale behind it. American education grew out of American society in answer to the needs and the demands of different groups of people throughout the country; it is not the working out of any single philosophy of education. To understand the American system of education and the problems that have developed within it, we must sketch out the way it came into being.

Establishment of the public school. The pattern on which the American system of schools was to be built emerged in colonial times. Originally the predominant form of education throughout the colonies was moral and vocational. It was administered according to colonial apprenticeship laws. In the southern colonies children of wealthier parents were privately tutored until they were ready for university work. Many of them completed their education in Europe, but some received their higher education in one or another of the early American colleges. In the middle colonies the apprenticeship system prevailed, but there were private schools attached to some of the churches in these colonies. The only school maintained at public expense in the middle colonies was the pauper school for the education of children whose parents were too poor to hire tutors.

Progress was made toward a system of public education in the New England colonies sooner than anywhere else. A Massachusetts law of 1642 required the selectmen to ascertain whether parents and masters were training their children properly and to inquire into the children's ability to read well enough to understand religion and the laws of the colony. If the children's education was neglected, the selectmen were empowered to put them out as apprentices. A law of 1647 required towns of a certain size to appoint a teacher to conduct school, and larger towns were to set up institutions of advanced learning. The towns were left free to defray the school's expenses by local taxes or by pro-rating the cost among the parents.

The first development in public schools is significant for a number of reasons. In the first place, it recognized that parents had the primary obligation of providing education for their children, and public authority sought to enforce this obligation on the parents. In the second place, therefore, it recognized the state's legitimate interest in education. In the third place, it did not try to replace but only to supplement the private school. Since most localities arranged to pro-rate the expenses of the public school among the parents, many parents preferred to send their children to privately owned schools. Throughout colonial history it was the private school rather than the public school which flourished. Nevertheless, the pattern of public schools to supplement the existing private schools was established. They were locally controlled and locally supported. Religion and morality were considered a most important part of their curriculum.

When the Constitution was adopted in 1789 the various states still took a negligible role in education. Moreover, it is obvious that the Founding Fathers never seriously considered education as one of the federal government's functions. The Northwest Ordinance had made a friendly national gesture toward education, but it was no more than a declaration of the importance of education and an encouragement for local authorities in the new western lands to open schools as soon as possible. Not only was the federal Constitution silent about education, but of the fourteen state constitutions adopted before 1800 only five mentioned education at all. The tradition then followed was that education was taken care of mostly by private academies and church-affiliated schools.

All schools at this time, public and private alike, included religious and moral education as a matter of course. Many states had religious tests for teachers, and some states delegated the administration of their schools to church authorities. There was no exclusion of religion from education in the first decades of our national history. It was in the second quarter of the nineteenth century that the public school system developed as we know it today, with its exclusion of religion from the curriculum. In these years there was growing demand for wider educational opportunities for all children. This inevitably meant schools without tuition and therefore supported out of public funds raised by taxation.

The demand for universal education grew in volume in the early part of the nineteenth century because of the developments of the time: the industrial revolution and the romantic belief in the common man. The industrial revolution required large numbers of workers who could read and write, and it gathered people together into larger towns and cities where schools were more feasible than in the country. The romantic belief in the common man involved faith in his native intelligence and moral goodness, together with an optimistic assumption that he was capable of indefinite progress if only education were placed at his disposal.

For twenty or thirty years the states tried to meet this growing demand for free education, by halfway measures. In some cases the states subsidized already established private schools so that they could take more non-paying students. In other cases the state went part way toward tax-supported schools by giving the schools money derived from the sale of public lands and from various excise taxes. In still other cases the state passed enabling legislation whereby local groups could voluntarily tax themselves for support of local schools.

City people, by and large, tended to favor public schools, whereas the rural people tended to oppose them. The working classes looked to the free public school as the doorway to higher economic and social positions; the landowning farmer saw little immediate gain from education for his son and daughter, and he feared the additional tax that would be put upon his property.

Those who opposed tax-supported

Horace Mann, whose leadership during the so-called "common school revival" as Secretary of the State Board of Education of Massachusetts advanced the cause of the public school, was largely responsible for the non-sectarian or secular status of the schools. (Library of Congress)

public schools used arguments that seem curious rather than forceful today. But they were sincerely offered, and at the time they seemed to carry considerable conviction. Many argued that a tax for the education of one's neighbors was an unwarranted interference with property rights. Others believed that a system of public schools constituted an unjustified interference by the government between parent and child. Others maintained that formal education was a luxury for those who could afford it; to provide it for poor children was to educate them beyond their social position and thus to make them discontented with their lot in life. Still others looked upon public education as the first and biggest step toward socialism, because it meant turning children over to the state for a large part of their formative years.

Against these objections to free public

The 12-grade system of today evolved slowly from classrooms such as this one of 1850, in which children of all ages "took turns" at learning. The school hours were long, from 7 to 5. The schoolmaster was frequently the minister of the local church. (Library of Congress)

education its proponents advanced forceful arguments. Daniel Webster, for example, argued that the public education of poor children at the expense of taxpayers was the best way to protect property. "We regard it," he said, "as a wise and liberal system of police, by which property, and life, and the peace of society are secured." Horace Mann, secretary of the Massachusetts State Board of Education, argued that public education would have a healthy effect in American society. "It gives each man," he wrote, "the independence and the means by which he can resist the selfishness of other men. It does better than to disarm the poor of their hostility toward the rich: it prevents being poor." Mann and his associates also argued that there is a principle of natural law "which proves the absolute right to an education of every human being that comes into the world; and what, of course, proves the correlative duty of every government to see that the means of that education are provided for all."

Faith in the common man and strong belief in the practical usefulness of education ultimately prevailed, and by the time of the Civil War the battle for free public education had been won in all the states. Meanwhile the troublesome problem of what to do about religious instruction in the public schools had been settled in about the only way possible in a country where many religious sects lived side by side. The teaching of religion was excluded from the public schools, not by the enemies of religion, strangely enough, but by its friends.

The exclusion of religion from the curriculum came about in two ways. New York exemplifies one way, Massachusetts the other. In New York the crisis was financial. The state had been subsidizing various church schools by pro-rating among them the sum of public money set aside for education. As the number of churches seeking a share of these limited

This one-room schoolhouse in New England, typical of many still in use throughout the United States, is not very different from those schoolhouses of a century ago. Least affected by changes in educational philosophy are the rural schools that maintain the traditional curricula. (Standard Oil Co., N.J.)

funds increased, the size of each share decreased. It was feared that the amount given to each church would become so small that it would be dissipated to a point of ineffectiveness. In 1842, therefore, the state decided to discontinue subsidies to private church schools and to launch its own public school system. In this public system, the state decided, no religion could be given preference over another—and the only way to achieve this was to eliminate all religious teaching from the public schools. In answer to this solution, as we shall see, Catholics enlarged their own parochial school system in New York, whereas Protestants used their Sunday schools for religious instruction and collectively supported the new public system.

The same result came about in Massachusetts in a different way. In 1827 the state legislature passed a law providing that school authorities "shall never direct any schoolbooks to be purchased or used, in any of the schools under their superintendence, which are calculated to favor any particular sect or tenet." The law was passed to keep out of schools the endless wrangling between liberal and orthodox Calvinists. Because the various church groups could not agree on religious doctrine, it seemed necessary to exclude all religious teaching from the schools.

Other states followed Massachusetts and New York in excluding religion from the public schools. It was done almost regretfully, as a measure made necessary because of the many different religions in each locality. A certain amount of religious teaching and a goodly amount of moral instruction remained in the public schools for a considerable time. Religion continued to be recognized. But only such "undenominational" religious instruction as Bible reading continued to be widespread in the public schools after the middle of the nineteenth century.

The establishment of a public school system in America did not mean the end of private schools. These increased in size and number during the decades when the public schools were being established. There were several reasons why the private school continued to prosper. In the first place, many wealthier Americans felt that sending their children to the public school with immigrant children would hurt their language, their morals, and their health. They therefore sent their children to private schools, where they could associate with children of a similar social and economic position. Others were attracted to the private school because of the superior education it provided. Both the quality of instruction and the courses offered in the private school were usually superior to those provided in the average public school.

Meanwhile the church-affiliated or the parochial school system developed in America. The most important of the parochial school systems, of course, is that maintained by the Catholic Church, and it will suffice in this brief résumé to see how it developed in the nineteenth century. An attempt was made originally to establish Catholic schools within the pub-

Bishop John Carroll in 1792 was one of the earliest of the Catholic hierarchy who pointed out the necessity of "a pious and Catholic education for the young." He hoped that graduates of the newly founded Georgetown University would become teachers in Catholic schools in their local parishes. (Library of Congress)

lic school system. In both New York and Minnesota, where the plan was tried, the state rented the parochial school building, furnished the textbooks and other school supplies, and paid the salaries of teachers. Religion was taught before the opening of the regular classes. The school conformed to all the regulations and met all the requirements set down for public schools in the state. This plan worked satisfactorily in various cities in the state of New York for about twenty years, and for a shorter time in two Minnesota towns. A majority of Catholics agreed that the plan was not permanently feasible, so it was brought to an end in both states. This plan has continued to be followed in certain isolated areas in the West, but always as a temporary policy until the local district can afford its own public school and until the local diocese can build and maintain its own schools. It works well in areas where the population is almost entirely Catholic, but elsewhere it has never seemed to be more than a temporary solution to a pressing economic problem.

Meanwhile, as the number of Catholics increased—especially in the cities—

the bishops found it generally possible to follow the direction of the Third Plenary Council of Baltimore (1884) that a parochial school be erected near each parish church. In rural areas, of course, it was frequently impossible to follow this directive. By the middle of the twentieth century, therefore, only slightly more than half the Catholic children of the country attended parochial schools. For financial reasons, or because there was no parochial school in the neighborhood, or for various other reasons, the remaining half of the country's Catholic children attended public schools.

19. THE FEDERAL GOVERNMENT AND EDUCATION

Until about the time of the Civil War the federal government showed no inclination to concern itself with education directly. Congress did nothing, for example, about Washington's proposal for a national university. Apparently the federal government held aloof from education because it believed that the Constitution forbade direct federal action in education. That the national government was benevolently inclined toward education is shown by its requirement that each new territory set aside a certain amount of public lands as an endowment for education. Moreover, when the Surplus Revenue Act of 1837 returned federal funds to the states, it was recommended that the money returned be set aside for education.

During the Civil War the government took its first step toward direct support of education. The first Morrill Act (1862) made available to each state a land subsidy of thirty thousand acres for each senator and representative the state had in Congress. In return the state was required to establish at least one college which, "without excluding other scientific and classical studies," would "teach such branches of learning as are related to agriculture and the mechanic arts." Ultimately sixty-nine land-grant colleges profited from the Morrill Act, which proved a prime stimulus toward an expanded system of state colleges and universities. Once such a college or university was established, it could count on appropriations from the state legislature to maintain it.

It should be noted that the Morrill Act

The State University of Iowa (left) is an example of the interest in higher education that prevailed after 1850. With the establishment of public elementary and secondary schools, it seemed incongruous to advocates of state universities that the public school system not include higher education. Old North (right), the oldest building in existence on the Georgetown University campus, was erected in 1795 as the initial building of the oldest Catholic college in the United States.

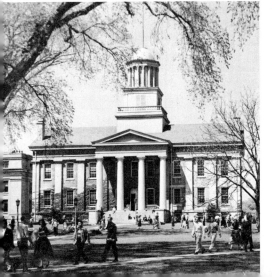

was a grant from the federal government to the states in order to stimulate a specific kind of education: practical training in "agriculture and the mechanic arts." It should be noted also that the administration of the colleges was left to the state-created agencies. The federal government, in effect, provided the endowment and allowed the states to use the interest from the sale of these public lands pretty much as they wished. Congress shied away from other attempts at this time to enter the field of education. Provision was made in 1867 for a national secretary of education, but in a few years the secretaryship was demoted to a subordinate bureau in the Department of the Interior.

Meanwhile, through the latter half of the nineteenth century, both public and private schools continued to increase in number and size. A larger proportion of the country's children attended school through the primary and secondary grades, partly because an education seemed more necessary for earning a living and partly because a larger proportion of the children lived within walking distance of a school. Most states adopted some sort of compulsory-attendance law for children under fourteen or sixteen.

The federal government restricted itself to helping education in two principal ways. It continued subsidies for limited purposes, such as the provision for agricultural experiment stations made in 1887 and for an agricultural extension service in 1914. Secondly, it maintained the federal Office of Education as a bureau in the Department of the Interior. The Office of Education was to collect statistics and other information relative to education in the country and to send such information to school authorities in the various states. The federal government's next large commitment to education was the Smith-Hughes Act of 1917, which provided that the federal government would match the states, dollar for

Henry Barnard, the first chairman of the State Board of Education of Connecticut, through his Common School Journal, *his lectures, and voluminous correspondence awakened the people to the needs of the public school. He later became the first United States Commissioner of Education. (Library of Congress)*

dollar, for money appropriated for education in agriculture and the trades in the secondary schools.

By 1917, some educators had urged Congress to create a federal department of education with a seat in the Cabinet. The general feeling in the country, however, was that federal control over education must be limited to setting minimum requirements for the use of federal subsidies by the states. Meanwhile other less obvious forces were at work nationalizing education without subjecting it to national control. The National Education Association and national societies in the various fields of learning, such as economics or history, tended to give the schools a national rather than a local approach to education. Prominent graduate schools drew students from the entire nation, and in this way they tended to nationalize education. Educational journals were published on a national scale, with the result that educational opinion and techniques were exchanged across the country. By the turn of the century, then, education remained under local control, but local differences tended to disappear under the nationalizing influences at work in all of American society.

At the beginning of this century more

than fifteen million children under seventeen were attending public schools, and about half of the remaining six million children in this age bracket were attending private or parochial schools. Universal education through primary and secondary schools was within sight. The chief exceptions were to be found in rural areas, especially in the southern states, and among city children at the top of the age bracket (sixteen and seventeen), who had left school to go to work.

Federal action in the last twenty-five years. The great depression of 1929 forced the federal government into the field of education in a roundabout fashion. Many schools closed during the worst years of the depression. Several million young people who normally would have been in school or employment were completely idle. In this crisis the federal government had the choice of taking up the employment slack by extending education in the public schools or aiding the youth directly. The latter course was taken, and the federal government set up two agencies with educational functions, the Civilian Conservation Corps (CCC) and the National Youth Administration (NYA).

Organized as an emergency measure in 1933, the CCC provided work, housing, and a degree of education for unemployed young men between eighteen and twenty-five. Scattered in twenty-six hundred camps throughout the country, these young men were paid small wages, which they had to share with their families. Directed by Army officers, they cleared swamps and forests, improved roads, and planted trees; and in their spare time they were given formal instruction in "practical" subjects. More than a million and a half young Americans were thus employed by the federal government and given a practical kind of education.

The National Youth Administration attempted to keep young people in school by giving them part-time employment on projects connected with education through the Public Works Administration, which spent $481,500,000 constructing and improving some thirteen thousand educational buildings. Many educators were alarmed when these emergency measures threatened to become a normal part of the educational pattern in America. Congress therefore took advantage of the opportunity offered by World War II to terminate the CCC. Various proposals for more direct federal subsidies to education were defeated during the war. One plan for such federal aid was defeated because it included parochial and private as well as public schools. Another proposal was defeated in 1943 because it provided equal subsidies to both Negro and white schools in the South. Neither bill was defeated on the principle that the federal government should leave the burden of education with the states.

The federal government after World War II subsidized education with a provision in the G.I. Bill of Rights to pay the tuition and help defray the living costs of veterans in accordance with the length of time each spent in the service. Tuition was paid directly to any bona fide school accepting the veteran as a student; living expenses were given to the veteran as long as he retained the status of a good student in such an institution. The subsidies thus furnished to education enabled many colleges and universities to expand in the years after World War II. Institutions of higher education continue to receive grants from the federal government for research projects carried out for the armed forces, the Atomic Energy Commission, the Public Health Service, and other similar agencies.

Education was given something like official status as a national concern in the new Department of Health, Education and Welfare created in 1953. The Office of Education was moved to this department, but nothing else was done in the next two years to give the federal government a more active role in education except to propose a vast scheme of grants-in-aid for a nationwide school-building program. The Eisenhower administration proposed a vast scheme of federal aid for education. President Eisenhower requested local groups to study their needs and to report at a White House Conference in December 1955. The conference gave strong support to the principle of federal aid, both for constructing and maintaining public schools.

Educators view this trend with mixed feelings. Some educators advocate a complete centralization of education with a system of national public schools covering the country. But most educators want to keep the federal government's role in education to the necessary minimum.

A case can be made to show that local and state governments are not able to furnish adequate education to students everywhere in America. Mississippi, for example, spent only $96 in 1952 for the education of each child in that state, whereas California spent $261 per child. Mississippi is a poor state with a propor-

tionately large part of its population of school age. In that year the income of the people of that state was $3,322 per child (the income of all the people in the state divided by the school enrollment), while in California it was $12,687. Californians, therefore, spend a smaller proportion of their income on education, but they spend much more for each child in the schools. Inequality of educational opportunity also exists within each state, and even within some communities.

In 1948 President Truman appointed a Commission on Higher Education to inquire into the national problems in this field. The commission concluded its study with the statement that "the time has come for America to develop a sound pattern of continuing federal support for higher education." It recommended that federal funds be allocated among the states in proportion to each state's need, that the states continue to administer and control their educational programs, and that the federal government restrict itself to establishing certain minimum requirements for participation in the program.

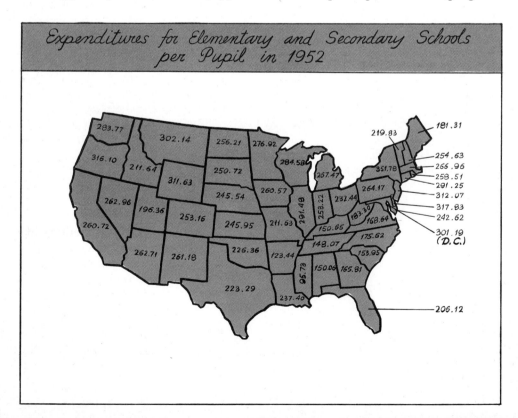

Expenditures for Elementary and Secondary Schools per Pupil in 1952

The commission also recommended that only public schools should receive federal aid, except for scholarships and research projects, in which both public and private schools should participate.

The commission's report evoked widespread criticism among educators. It was criticized for its tendency to think in something like totalitarian terms when it drew its picture of American education in the future. It was criticized for eliminating private schools from federal aid. And it was criticized for confusing training—which can be given on the job better than in school—with education in the true sense of the word. Very little criticism, however, was leveled at the general recommendation of increased federal aid.

The problem, from the school's point of view, is to receive federal aid without surrendering independence. This danger is inherent in any system of federal aid, but the tradition of local control of education seems so firmly established that the national government might find it very difficult to supplant it.

Specific ways and means of providing federal aid are many. The pattern in the past has been for the federal government to match state or local contributions. Such a dollar-matching system, however, would give the greatest amount of help to the states least needing it. Another proposal is that the federal government arrange an extensive scholarship program that would make it possible for any good student to continue his education in the institution of his choice. These and other proposals all demand of the federal government a cultural wisdom and an appreciation of education that is not commonly found among politicians. At any rate, the American tradition has been to request as little federal aid as necessary and to retain local control of the school. Traditionally, both state and national governments have restricted themselves to offering financial assistance and setting up standards for the schools.

20. MASS EDUCATION AND THE PROBLEM OF TEACHERS

A second general trend in education in the last fifty years is the increase in both the number of young people in school and in the proportions of those eligible for school. This has created serious problems of expansion in educational facilities, which unfortunately some people consider to be the only educational problem of any importance today. It is similar to the problem of any expanding business which has to adjust its facilities as smoothly as possible to increased production. There are bound to be temporary maladjustments, and a certain number of mistakes will inevitably be made. But foresight in planning and a good sense of values will enable any school system to expand with relative ease.

The basic problem involved in expanding the school system in America is the problem of preserving the quality of education while handling an increased number of students. Several thousand new school buildings will have to be erected in the next two decades. Several hundred thousand additional teachers must be trained—and this, in turn, involves expanding the facilities of higher education in every state. Let us illustrate this problem of sound expansion with a single concrete example. The best estimates are that the faculty teaching the humanities and social sciences in institutions of higher learning must be increased from the present 130,000 to 253,900 in 1970. This means training 123,000 new qualified teachers in addition to the normal number of replacements in the next fifteen years.

Expansion will not, by itself, solve the basic problems in our educational system. More education is not the answer to the problem of poor education. But because we are committed to universal education through secondary school, and because we have an increasing number of

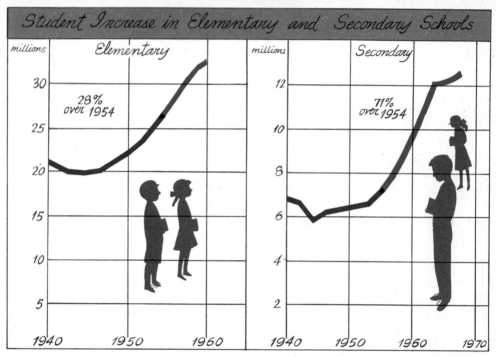

(From Teachers for Tomorrow, *the Ford Foundation Bulletin No. 2)*

children born each year, we must expand our educational facilities to accommodate additional numbers. The basic problems in American education, however, are not problems of size or numbers. Many educationists have slipped into the fallacy of arguing that all we need do is increase the number of our schools and classrooms, multiply the number of teachers and double the educational budget, and then we shall save both education and America. This is a fallacy that distracts

(From Teachers for Tomorrow, *The Ford Foundation Bulletin No. 2)*

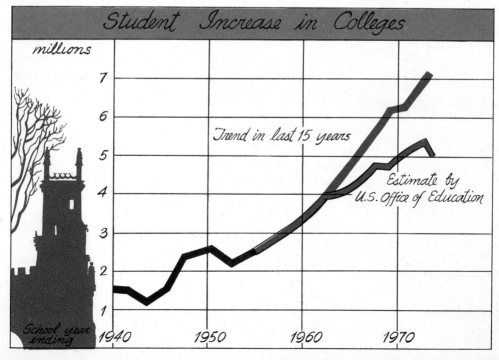

BETTER SCHOOLS
BUILD BETTER COMMUNITIES

For FREE booklet, "How Can Citizens Help Their Schools?" write Better Schools, 2 West 45th St., New York 36, N.Y.

The campaign for better schools to accommodate the largest enrollments in the history of United States education is actively supported by citizens who are conscious of the need to develop our future leadership today. Better schools, of course, mean far more than improved equipment and facilities. (Advertising Council)

us from the basic problems in American education.

The economic status of the teacher. Closely connected with the "boom" in education is the problem of paying adequate salaries to attract competent teachers in both public and private schools. From the young woman teaching kindergarten to the specialist teaching graduate students in the university, the teacher earns considerably less than persons of equal education and experience in industry or any

of the other professions. Reasons for this poor payment of teachers are fairly obvious. Few people enter the teaching profession for financial reasons. The other satisfactions they obtain from their professional work compensate to some extent for their small salaries. Most teachers in the lower grades are women, and an increasingly large number of women have entered the teaching ranks in higher education in recent years. They are able and willing to work for less than the male head of a family.

Most important among the reasons for low pay for teachers is the attitude Americans have adopted toward the teaching profession. They put great faith in education, but they tend to look on the teacher with a certain disdain. "He who can, does —he who can't, teaches," is a slogan among businessmen and schoolboys. It is unfortunately true that low pay scales have driven many capable people out of the teaching profession. Their positions are too often filled by people not competent to earn a living in some other profession. The result is that there are many thousands of capable persons in the teaching profession who work for lower

(From Teachers for Tomorrow, *The Ford Foundation Bulletin No. 2)*

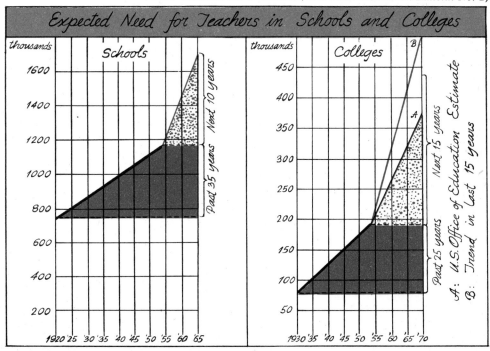

salaries than they deserve, but there are thousands more who are incompetent.

Many teachers who are reluctant to leave the field of education obtain part-time jobs to support their families. Their teaching naturally suffers. Even worse, thousands of promising young men and women who are attracted to teaching leave the profession annually for positions in industry or in government service. Unless upward revisions are made in the salary scale for teachers, both public and private schools will find it impossible to meet the requirements that additional classes will put on them in two decades.

The problem of paying adequate salaries throughout all levels of education ought to be an easy problem to solve. But it will not be solved by school administrators alone. Like so many other problems in education, this is a social problem that will be resolved one way or another according to the reaction of public opinion. State legislators who appropriate $20,000 for a football coach's salary and $7,000 for a professor of history's salary reflect the opinion of their constituents. A good beginning toward solving this problem was made in December 1955, when the Ford Foundation turned $260,-000,000 over to colleges and universities with the stipulation that the interest be used to increase the salaries of teachers of the liberal arts and sciences—the most underpaid group among college teachers.

Generally speaking, teachers should be paid a sufficient salary to free them from constant financial difficulty, to enable them to live according to their social position and be able to rear a family without taking on part-time jobs.

If the general salary level remains lower than this, the teaching staff at any school is reduced to a core of teachers willing to endure serious privations to stay in their profession. Added to this core and constituting the majority of the staff at any given time are the young men and women who teach only a few years

before leaving for other professions and the incompetents who are not able to earn more money elsewhere. Education is seriously crippled when it must operate under these conditions.

REVIEW

18. Rise of the Public and Parochial Schools

A. Briefly present a picture of education in the colonies. What two principles were early recognized in colonial education?

B. In the early days of our country what principle was common to public and private education? What two factors were leading up to universal education? Describe the early efforts of the states to accomplish this.

C. Give some reasons for the opposition to tax-supported public schools in the early 1800s. How was the problem of religious education solved? Explain how this was brought about in New York State.

D. How did tax-supported public schools affect private and parochial school systems? How did New York State effect a temporary solution to this problem?

19. The Federal Government and Education

A. Trace briefly the federal government's interest in education up to the Civil War period.

B. Before 1917 the federal government aided education in two principal ways. State what these were.

C. In what three ways did the federal government take action in the field of education between 1917 and 1941? In your answer explain the effect of these steps.

D. Since World War II we have had two innovations in the federal government, the G.I. Bill of Rights and a new Cabinet post—Department of Health, Education and Welfare. Point out the part each played in the expansion of education.

E. What has been the reaction of educators to this increased activity of the federal government in the field of education?

F. List the proposals of President Truman's Commission on Higher Education. Relate the criticism offered by educators concerning these proposals.

20. Mass Education and the Problem of Teachers
A. What are the basic problems confronting America in expanding the school system?

B. What is the significance of the economic problem of teachers? How can this be changed? What must be done to attract qualified personnel into teaching?

THE CHAPTER IN REVIEW
A. Trace the development of education in the colonies and in the early days of our Republic. Illustrate the universal acceptance of the importance of religion in education of this period.

B. Trace the development of "tax-supported public schools" and point out the effect of this change on religious education.

C. Describe the participation of the federal government in education during the periods 1789–1860, 1860–1917, 1917 to the present. What were some of the good and bad effects of this increased activity of the federal government?

SELECTED READINGS

William T. Kane and John J. O'Brien, *History of Education* (Chicago: Loyola University Press, 1954), provides good background for an understanding of current problems in American education. A popular and easy-to-read survey of these problems is to be found in Don Sharkey, *These Young Lives: A Review of Catholic Education in the United States* (New York: William H. Sadlier, Inc., 1950).

An excellent popular statement of the Catholic view of education and an excellent study of American educational problems are made by Rev. James Keller, *All God's children* (Garden City, N.Y.: Hanover House, 1953). Father Keller's book is done in his usual lively, challenging way. It proves useful for this and the following two chapters. Another useful book for all three chapters is William F. Cunning-

ham, *Pivotal Problems of Education* (New York: The Macmillan Co., 1940). More exhaustive treatment of all these problems is given in J. D. Redden and F. A. Ryan, *A Catholic Philosophy of Education* (Milwaukee: The Bruce Publishing Co., 1942).

The America Press has published three pamphlets on the role of the state in education: Robert C. Hartnett, S.J., *Federal Aid to Education;* Robert C. Hartnett, S.J., and Anthony Bouscaren, *The State and Education;* and Robert C. Hartnett, S.J. (editor), *The Right to Educate.*

PROJECTS

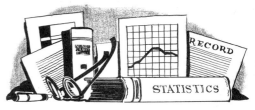

1. It would be of interest to the class to learn the requirements for entrance into college in the colonial days. Select three of the colleges that were founded before the Revolution and report to the class on entrance requirements of each. A contrast could be made with present-day entrance requirements and curriculums to see whether today's students would meet the earlier standards.

2. Religious intolerance is not a new problem for American society. Report to the class on the anti-Catholic feeling in the United States during the nineteenth century. Examine the incident of the burning of the Ursuline Convent at Charlestown, Mass., and the attendant circumstances. Tell how this incident could have been prevented.

3. Make a chart to show how important a part the Church plays in the field of education. The chart should show the total number in the various levels of educational institutions and the number of Catholics who are in Catholic schools on each of the levels. *The Statistical Abstract of the United States* and *The Catholic Directory* publish the necessary statistics.

4. There is a great need for teachers today, and we might well consider this worthy profession as our vocation in life. One way of becoming aware of this would be to make a poster to indicate the requirements for teachers on the various levels and the inducements of the teaching profession.

Chapter 9. Educational Problems of a Secular and Pluralist Society

21. RELIGION AND THE PUBLIC SCHOOLS

Educators maintain that salutary reform in the schools is impossible unless it is the result of public demand—except, of course, in such matters as teaching methods or the better budgeting of time and money. Robert M. Hutchins, former president of the University of Chicago and a severe critic of American education, concludes that "a strange-circularity thus afflicts us (which even Plato speaks of in *The Republic*). The state of the nation depends on the state of education; but the state of education depends on the state of the nation." [1]

This is so, educators maintain, because the school cannot escape the weaknesses of the society in which it operates. A society that insists on racial segregation, for example, will see to it that racial segregation is practiced in the school. A society that is materialistic will insist that its public school adopt a materialistic approach to education. The truth in this

[1] Robert M. Hutchins, *The Higher Learning in America* (new Haven: Yale University Press, 1945), p. 32.

contention should not blind us to the fact that school authorities are immediately responsible for the education they give in the schools and also that they play a large part in forming public opinion about the kind of education the community desires. Private schools can take a strong stand against ill-formed public opinion about education, for they can hope to draw a large student body from parents who agree with their stand. But public schools are very responsive to public opinion, and wise educators have the responsibility of cultivating a sound public opinion on educational matters.

We have seen that our society is committed to offering equal educational opportunities to all. In this country we have committed ourselves also, in so far as possible, to provide the maximum education that each student is capable and desirous of receiving. There is a widespread opinion that education should be available without charge from kindergarten through graduate work in college for all who can qualify to receive it at each level. This is the opinion of the commission ap-

pointed by President Truman in 1948 to investigate the problems of higher education. At any rate, public schools cannot very well refuse to shelter American youth through a large part of their waking hours. The problem of the school administrators and teachers is to see that the time is well spent. This may be considered a disheartening view to take of public education in our society, but it is difficult to see how any other view squares with reality.

Our pluralist society. Our society is "pluralist": it is made up of people of many different religious convictions. The public school system must be so organized that it treats all religious faiths with respect. It must show preference to none, and it must be careful not to ridicule or undermine the religious convictions that each student receives at home. These are convictions he brings to the classroom, and he has the right to be educated without indoctrination in favor of or against any beliefs not in accord with the religion of his home.

A pluralist society is also made up of people of different cultural heritages. Like the various religions, so the various cultures must be respected in our schools. Care must be taken that the way of life the child has acquired at home is not de-stroyed by the school as it attempts to make all children good Americans. At the same time, however, there is an element of unity in our society. This unity is civic and political. It involves loyalty to the same government, the cherishing of certain institutions, attitudes, and convictions pertaining to civil life. The motto on our coins, *E Pluribus Unum* (One from Many), is a good description of American society: political unity and cultural plurality, one nation from many peoples without obliteration of cultural differences.

It is not easy to fit a school system into this social pattern. There would be fewer problems if we had but a single religion and a single cultural pattern. Similarly, there would be fewer school problems if we had a totalitarian state. The school would then have to conform only to the government's orders and adopt the monolithic social and religious pattern of the state. But our society is more complex, and the school's social function therefore becomes more complex and delicate.

The tasks of the public school. The essential tasks of a public school in our society can be reduced to these two: (1) to guide the intellectual growth of children on the elementary and secondary levels; (2) to safeguard American unity and develop good

Detroit high school students attend a Brotherhood Institute arranged by the National Conference of Christians and Jews. A pluralist society can meet on common ground, taking stands on moral problems as citizens interested in social and political affairs while respecting individual and group beliefs.

"To safeguard American unity and develop good citizenship" are the first tasks of the public school. First-graders in a Texas school recite the Pledge to the Flag before beginning their day's lessons. (Standard Oil Co., N.J.)

citizenship. The first of these functions the public school must perform—like any private or parochial school—because it is an educational institution. The second function it must perform because it is a *public* school, a state institution with certain public functions that private schools are not bound to perform in exactly the same way.

The public school cannot have a religion or a philosophy of its own. It cannot rightfully make a religion of patriotism, as schools in totalitarian countries have done. Nor can it adopt a philosophy of secularism or any other philosophy, since this would violate the right of the student to have the religion of his home respected.

The task of the public school, then, is to adapt itself to the religions and the cultural patterns of the community in which it functions. A public school in a community of Catholics, Jews, and Lutherans, for example, should arrange its extracurricular activities and temper its classroom instruction in such a fashion as to show respect for all three groups. This means, for example, excusing the students of each religion from school attendance on their respective religious holidays. It would mean that the teachers maintain a neutral ground on disputed questions among the groups, a neutral ground that results not from indifference to religion but from a proper respect for the consciences of all persons.

This is a delicate task and it can never be perfectly performed. Nevertheless, it is the only position that the public schools can properly assume. Some educators prefer to take the easy way out by substituting their own worldly religion of secularism. It is most important for Americans to realize that secularism is a form of religion, for it offers its own explanation of ultimate values. One person has as much *legal* right to be a secularist in America as another has to be a Catholic or a Jew, and he has the right to have his conscience respected in the public school. But secularists have no right to make their philosophy the official creed of the public school—any more than Catholics or Jews have a right to make their respective religions the public school's official creed.

Religion in the curriculum. Public schools have generally found that the easiest way of handling this difficult problem is to ignore religion completely. But this is unsatisfactory in at least two major respects. In the first place, religion plays an important part in education. Knowledge of God is the most important knowledge. To ignore religious doctrine is to offer an incomplete, lopsided education. Moreover, education without religion restricts spiritual and moral development to the plane of natural morality—to speak the truth, to keep the golden rule, to treat others with respect, and so forth. These are good principles, but they do not suffice.

In the second place, the public school that ignores religion does not prepare its students for life in an American society that is still religiously oriented in many respects. The Eighty-second Congress, for example, inserted the phrase "under God" into the pledge of allegiance to the American flag. Prayers at public functions, the mottoes on our coins, Thanksgiving Day, and many American customs and institutions assume that we are a religious people. The public school that excludes religion fails, at least to some extent, to educate its students and to prepare them for living in a society that recognizes and does honor to God.

We should note that this problem is peculiar to the public school. The parochial school professes the Catholic religion to be true, and parents understand the school's profession of religion when they send their children to it. Private non-denominational schools are in a somewhat different position. Usually a private school does not profess any particular religion. The private school is therefore free to adopt whatever courses and program seem best for the religion of its students. Parents who do not approve of the school's choice can send their children elsewhere.

The public school is in a different position. Attendance is compulsory for all children who do not attend school elsewhere. Almost half the Catholic children in America attend public schools. A much higher percentage of Jewish children are in the public schools, and the children of the Protestant sects form the highest percentage. Thus a dilemma results: the public school cannot profess a religion of its own, and it should respect the religion of each of its students. At the same time, do not parents of these Catholic, Jewish, and Protestant children in the public schools have the right to demand something more than a purely secular education for their children?

Many Americans and a large number of educators are satisfied with a secular education that eliminates all religion

The Confraternity of Christian Doctrine, under the auspices of the NCWC, enlists lay teachers as well as religious in their program. The Confraternity is one of the best available ways to continue the religious training of students enrolled in public schools.

ous faiths was important for an understanding of our cultural heritage. This does not solve the problem (just as learning about baseball is not learning how to play baseball). Many teachers who would handle such a course about religion are themselves the product of religionless education; they would have to obtain a sympathetic understanding of the role of religion in history, which they do not now have.

A more radical proposal is to teach the "common core" or "least common denominator" of all religions. This proposal is radical because it advocates really *teaching* religion instead of teaching *about* it. However, an attempt to teach any common core of religion to children of all faiths is bound to lead to trouble as questions are asked and various interpretations offered of the most elementary religious doctrines. Few teachers would be able to explain Luther's position in religious history, for example, without giving offense either to Catholics or to Lutherans. Moreover, the common denominator of all religions is hardly the important and vital substance of any religion. The supreme truth of the Catholic religion is the Incarnation—our Lord, Whom the Jews do not acknowledge.

A fourth proposal is that religion be taught to public school children through a released-time arrangement. When the McCollum decision was handed down in 1948, released-time programs were operative in some twenty-two hundred communities in forty-six states, and more than two million students received religious instruction in this way. The plans varied from community to community. Essentially, however, they provided for time *within* the regular school day for students to receive instruction from church officials of the various faiths in the community. Attendance was voluntary, usually on written request from the parents, and the church officials were not paid by the school. The McCollum decision held

from the public school. Many others, however, realize its inadequacy, and they offer various proposals to get a measure of religion into public education. One suggestion is that the present religious practices followed in many schools—reading from the Old Testament (without comment), recitation of the Lord's Prayer, singing of hymns—be extended to all schools and be further emphasized. This is no solution of the problem.

A second proposal, which merits serious consideration, is that religion be included in the curriculum as a subject to be studied for its "cultural" value. The 1947 report of the Committee on Religion and Education of the American Council of Education made this suggestion in the belief that "exposure . . . to the ideas, beliefs and practices" of the vari-

such instruction *on the school premises* unconstitutional, but the later New York decision held it constitutional if offered elsewhere.

The released-time program is perhaps the most satisfactory single solution to the problem of putting religion into the public school child's education. But it has its drawbacks and is far from adequate. It creates inconveniences, and it reaches only a small percentage of the children attending public schools. It is given once a week in most places, and thus it fails to meet the ideal of making religious education the supreme principle in the entire curriculum.

The problem of putting religion into the public school curriculum in a pluralist society is basically insoluble. The community can only seek the most effective means of filling up the vacuum created by a religionless education.

22. THE PRIVATE AND PAROCHIAL SCHOOLS IN THE AMERICAN SYSTEM

The existence of private and parochial schools side by side with public schools is an integral part of the American system of education. It is incorrect to speak of either public or private schools as being more "American" or more important. In numbers of students, of course, the public school is more important than the private school on the elementary level, but considerably less important on the higher level. About one elementary student in each nine attends a private or parochial school, but more than half the students in colleges and universities are in private schools.

The importance of the private school in America does not depend on the number of students who attend it. This is not to minimize the quantitative effect of private and parochial schools, for there were an estimated 4,240,000 students in Catholic schools in this country in 1955.

Reading from the Bible is still continued in many public schools. Many educators deplored the omission of religious training in the schools and welcomed released-time programs as a safeguard to the community's moral health. (Mineola, N.Y., School System)

A total of 3,348,300 of them were in elementary school, 639,600 in secondary schools, 219,706 in institutions of higher learning, and 32,394 in major and minor seminaries. The American interested in public affairs should be interested in the welfare of these private and parochial schools because the future of America depends to some extent on the kind of work they do with the students now committed to their care.

We should remember that the private school has played an outstanding role in the history of American education. It has produced a disproportionately large number of leaders in American political, professional, and business life. It has maintained a standard of learning that public schools find impossible of attainment.

Sacred Heart Church at the University of Notre Dame is a prominent landmark on the campus. Each of Notre Dame's residence halls has a private chapel where the students may make daily visits to the Blessed Sacrament.

this point concretely in the following words:

State colleges and universities have frequently been jeopardized by the arbitrary acts of those who hold political power. When that time comes the private institutions must be counteracting agencies to keep the light of freedom burning. When Governor Talmadge terrorized the University of Georgia it was the institutions like Emory University, Agnes Scott College and Mercer University that maintained in the state the basic decencies of independence. The steadying influence of Tulane University in the days of Huey Long in Louisiana cannot be over-estimated. When the Board of Regents in Texas recently threatened the integrity of the state institutions, it was Rice Institute and the Southern Methodist University that held the banner of free scholarship.

In like manner, one could add that the freedom of midwestern state universities depends, to a large extent, on the existence in their midst of such private universities as Notre Dame, Northwestern, St. Louis, and Chicago.

The saving to the taxpayer . Americans take for granted that several million students should attend privately supported schools each year. They forget the almost incalculable sums of money this saves the taxpayer annually. Father Henry V. Walsh, pastor of the Sacred Heart parish in Philadelphia, calculated that in 1953 his parish school saved the taxpayers of Philadelphia $286,015 and that the Catholic schools of the city save Philadelphia over $33,590,000 in a single year. If the Catholic schools of any major city in America ceased to function and their students jammed into public schools, the public school system in that city would be hopelessly overcrowded. Taxpayers would be assessed hundreds of millions of dollars to expand the public schools to accommodate the additional students, and they would have to pay millions of additional dollars annually to maintain the expanded system.

We see, therefore, that the average American citizen who sends his children to the public school should have an inter-

It is the principle of the private school, then, rather than the numbers enrolled that constitutes its primary importance. The private school can maintain high standards because it need not defer to public opinion. It can more readily pursue special interests than can the public school. More important, its existence makes impossible a monopoly of education controlled by the state. One might say that the private school acts something like salt and yeast in the bread of the American educational system. It gives it a distinctive flavor and a quality it would not otherwise have. And it plays a part in safeguarding the freedoms we cherish in this country. Without educational freedom our other freedoms would be in serious jeopardy. Raymond Fosdick, author, diplomat, and former president of the Rockefeller Foundation, put

est in the maintenance of a good system of parochial and private schools. Parents of children who attend parochial or private schools have a more direct and immediate interest in them. These parents support public schools by paying taxes. They have a right to send their children to them. Why do they assume the double burden of supporting two educational systems? The reasons are varied. Some parents want their children educated with others of the same social and cultural background, and this can be done only in private schools catering to people of a particular class. Others want their children given a more thorough education in smaller classes, in schools maintaining higher standards than they believe the public schools can offer.[2] Most of them, however, believe that only in the parochial school can their children be properly educated, for they understand that religion is an important part of education and that their children's spiritual development should not be neglected.

Opposition to parochial schools. Some Americans oppose private and parochial schools as being wasteful and "un-American." Let us see briefly what they mean by these charges. They contend that the parochial school system in any large city duplicates the public school system and adds to the total cost of elementary and secondary education in the city. The total number of schools would be cut down, they argue, if they were all in one system.

There are two fallacies in this "waste" argument. The first fallacy is this: Even if the total cost were reduced, the taxpayer would still have to pay considerably more for an expanded public school system. The saving would go exclusively to those who support parochial and private

The Harper Memorial Library of the University of Chicago is the focal point of this famous school's educational life. The university has a unique program of studies for exceptional students, who may enter immediately after elementary training and progress as rapidly as their talents and mental capacities will allow.

schools *voluntarily* by sacrifices they think well worth the cost. To deny such parents the right to spend money on their children's education instead of on more clothes or entertainment is hardly eliminating "waste."

The second fallacy lies in forgetting that the cost of education is measured primarily in the number of *classrooms* maintained and teachers employed than in the buildings used. Eliminating parochial schools would not reduce the number of classrooms unless the already filled classrooms were overcrowded even more; and thus the maintenance of educational standards would become even more difficult.

The charge that private and parochial schools are "un-American" is the conclu-

---

[2] It must not be assumed that all private and parochial schools are better than all public schools. Far from it. Some public schools maintain exceptionally high standards. These outstanding schools are in communities that value good education, and they usually draw good students from a society more or less homogeneous socially and economically.

sion of a number of assumptions that are simply untrue. One assumption is that private and parochial schools are divisive of American unity. Those who subscribe to this assumption believe that Catholics somehow do not think and act politically in the same way that children from the public schools do. Political records—voting, running for office, joining neighborhood improvement associations and the like, and records in the armed forces in time of war—show that the graduate of the private or parochial schools is, on the average, like the public school graduate in all these respects.

The second assumption behind the charge of "un-Americanism" against private and parochial schools is that all American children must receive exactly the same education in order to produce a classless, uniform society. If anything is un-American, it is that unattractive ideal. The danger to our society is not the danger of disunity but of enforced conformity. Enforcing the same education on all children might produce uniformity—but it would be the faceless uniformity proper to a totalitarian state rather than to our free society. One who advocates such conformity through education takes an incorrect view of man, of the role of education in his formation, and of the relation of the human person to the state.

People who desire public schools to monopolize education in order to make all Americans conform to the same pattern forget that education belongs primarily to the parents. By reason of their relationship to their children parents have the obligation to rear their children physically, mentally, and spiritually. Proper education is part of this obligation. Parents do not surrender it when they send their children to school, a point clearly recognized by the Supreme Court in the Oregon school case of 1925. In this case the Court declared an Oregon law unconstitutional because it was designed to make it impossible for parents to send their children to private or parochial schools. In rendering this opinion the Supreme Court stated:

The fundamental theory of liberty upon which all governments in this Union repose excludes any general power of the State to standardize its children by forcing them to accept instruction from public-school teachers only. The child is not the mere creature of the State; those who nurture him and direct his destiny have the right, coupled with the high duty, to recognize and prepare him for additional duties.

The duty of the state. The state, of course, has a legitimate interest in education, as it has in all matters that involve the common welfare of its citizens. Just as the state has the right to safeguard public health, so it has the right and duty to take necessary measures to safeguard and promote the intellectual development of its

A group-study class in American history at Fort Myer, Va., is made up of drafted and career personnel who continue their education in their leisure time. The armed forces place considerable emphasis on education as the business of defense becomes more technical and requires greater training. (U. S. Army Photograph)

An absent member (right) of a class of crippled children (left) participates with them every day by means of the school-to-home intercommunicating system. The physically handicapped are not denied an education in this state, in which a relatively high amount of money is spent for education each year. (Los Angeles City Schools)

citizens. The state has a legitimate interest, moreover, in seeing that the school system produces good citizens. The state has also a legitimate interest in seeing that the taxes collected for education are well spent, that the taxpayer is given a fair return for each dollar taken from him for the support of the public schools.

The state has the duty of making available the specialized types of education that parents are unable to give their children. It would seem to have the duty, too, of supplying the general kind of education given in the primary and secondary grades, because at least this much education is generally required of everyone who must earn his living in modern society. Most children cannot receive such an education from their parents, nor can they afford to go to private schools. There is no agency left except the state to make such education available to most children.

It would seem that the state has a right to make education compulsory up to a certain point, for only in this way can it protect some children from parental irresponsibility. In short, the child has a right to a certain amount of help in the business of being educated, and the state has the obligation of protecting this right by making education both available and compulsory. It does not follow, however, that the state may establish an educational monopoly by prohibiting church or private groups from conducting their own schools. If the state does this it abandons its proper protective and supplementary role and forcibly substitutes itself for the parents. The state is not properly a teacher.

A state monopoly of education, moreover, is dangerous to the freedoms that are part of our American tradition. For a monopoly of educational institutions would produce a people whose minds were formed and whose thinking could be guided by the government. A century ago, in 1859, John Stuart Mill wrote: "A general state education is a mere contrivance for molding people to be exactly like one another. . . . In proportion as it is efficient and successful, it establishes a despotism over the mind, leading by natural tendency to one over the body."

Problems of private and parochial schools. The

very existence of private and parochial schools has become financially precarious in recent years. Tax legislation, coupled with rising costs of maintenance, has threatened many privately supported schools with insolvency. Tax laws passed since 1933 have made it extremely difficult for persons to accumulate large fortunes. Consequently, schools cannot look to the rich for large contributions as they formerly did but must rely more and more exclusively on tuition and occasional fund-raising drives to support the school. Private schools find that increasing tuition cuts down the enrollment and makes the cost of education for each student higher. Any attempt by the private school to operate with income from tuition alone means that the school will eventually price itself out of business.

Parochial schools are somewhat better situated. Here it is not the parents of the school children alone who bear the expense of the school, but all members of the church community (the parish or whatever the unit may be) bear a share of the expense. Of course many parochial schools meet a large part of their expenses out of tuition charges, which puts a severe burden on parents of large families. However the costs may be divided, parochial school systems find it increasingly difficult to maintain buildings and equipment in good repair. The salary problem used to be less serious in the past, but parochial systems throughout the country now find that they must hire an increasingly larger number of lay teachers to supplement the religious teachers.

Faced with this problem of getting additional financial support, many exponents of the private and parochial school system have turned to the state for help. Some crumbs of tax-raised funds are given to parochial and private schools at the present time, more in some states than in others. Most important is the exemption from taxation, which amounts

in effect to an annual subsidy of millions of dollars to private and parochial schools. Transportation to parochial schools at public expense is provided in many states. A federal school lunch program operates in parochial as well as public schools. Research contracts, exchange fellowships, and other such federally supported projects use private colleges and universities as well as public institutions. The G.I. Bill of Rights provided for the veteran's continued education in the school of his choice, private or public. None of these measures of help destroyed the independence of the private school.

It therefore does not seem either wrong or inadvisable for private and parochial schools to look to the state for additional help. These schools, as much as the public schools, are committed to the task of educating young people so that they can mature into good Americans, live useful lives, and thus make this country an even better land in the future.

A reasonable amount of additional state aid, moreover, would seem the most expedient way to handle the problem created by the increased number of students. A dollar goes farther in the parochial system than it does in the public school system, because the members of religious orders work for practically no salary. A few thousand dollars spent in keeping a parish school in operation would save the taxpayers the several million dollars required to build a new public school—which must then be maintained out of taxes raised for that purpose every year.

Stout defenders of the parochial school system shy away from state aid on the grounds that such help means state control. The state has the right to see that its money is properly used, of course, but it is debatable whether this would mean additional state control of parochial schools. The state already fixes minimum standards, requires certain courses, demands certain qualifications for teachers, and in many other ways "interferes" with the freedom of the parochial or private school. Past experience with state aid, especially from the federal government, suggests that there is little reason to fear that help from the government would spell the end of the prized independence of the parochial and the private school.

23. ACADEMIC FREEDOM
AND RACIAL SEGREGATION IN THE SCHOOLS

Ever since the time of Socrates teachers have jealously prized their academic freedom—the right to search for the truth and to teach it. In these last twenty years the problem of freedom in research and teaching has become serious. Public schools are financially dependent on legislators who have shown an increased tendency to interfere in education. Private schools are more or less dependent on wealthy benefactors who sometimes wish to control the teaching their gifts make possible. The infiltration into the academic field by Communists who mix propaganda with teaching has further complicated the problem of academic freedom.

Any fruitful discussion of academic freedom must begin by admitting that the teacher has no rights *against* the truth. Academic freedom flows from the teacher's devotion to the truth—to discover it and to transmit it to his students. In the first place, the teacher has not only the right but the duty to discover the truth according to the established methods within his field. Historians, for example, work with records and documents. By following certain established rules of evidence, the historian tells the story of the past from these records and documents. Academic freedom involves the right to investigate and to experiment freely in one's field of competence.

Freedom to teach the truth is not un-limited. The teacher (at least in primary and secondary schools) is said to be *in loco parentis*, one who takes a parent's place, and he must therefore use prudence with regard to both the manner and the extent of his teaching. No student should be taught what he is not yet ready to understand. There is a time for all things. The mind must grow in wisdom and understanding before it is ready to receive certain kinds of knowledge.

Academic freedom is the right to communicate to the student what the student ought to know. It is a corollary to the fact that education is helping a student to grow in knowledge and to develop intellectual and scholarly habits of thinking. The use of propaganda, therefore, is not included in academic freedom. A teacher who subordinates his teaching to his own "pet" ideas and preferences has perverted the function of teaching and abuses his right to academic freedom. In most fields of knowledge, especially in the social sciences, there are many propositions that cannot be labeled simply "true" or "false." Points of view must be transmitted as points of view, not as objective truth, and other points of view should be respected.

Some teachers have abused their position and have used the classroom as a place for indoctrinating young people with propaganda for some cause or another. Such teachers have invoked the right of academic freedom to justify such "teaching." This gives rise to the question of what limits the state or the church or any other outside agency can rightly put on the teacher's transmission of knowledge to the student. No teacher has the right to teach what is false. The teacher is a human person, of course, and is subject to error. But no outside agency —state, church, or private benefactor of a school—can rightfully order a teacher to teach error. Second, matters of opinion that are *probably true* must be taught as such. They cannot rightfully be disguised as *absolute truth,* and no agency can rightfully force the teacher to violate his professional function in this respect.

There remains the matter of *not* teaching some things that are true and of teaching others. Here both state and church have a proper regulative function. The state has such a function because teaching is a social matter and it is related to the common welfare, which the state is entrusted to promote. The church has such a function because it has been divinely appointed as guardian of religious and moral truth. Benefactors of a school, finally, have a right to require that certain subjects be included in the curriculum if their gifts were accepted for that purpose. Nevertheless, prudent educational policy requires that outside regulations of teaching be kept to the necessary minimum.

An illustration of the abuse of academic freedom is the case of Communists who appealed to the right of free teaching when they were fired from their jobs. According to the principles we have discussed above, anyone who joins the Communist organization surrenders his right to teach because he is no longer committed to teaching the truth. He takes an oath to teach the "party line," not to question it, not to criticize it, but to pass it along to his students. In other words, he has surrendered his freedom of inquiry and his dedication to the truth.

Racial segregation in the schools. The problem of racial segregation in public schools was brought to a head by the momentous decision of the Supreme Court on May 17, 1954, that such practices were unconstitutional because they denied the right of all children to equal educational facilities. There is nothing wrong with segregation in principle, but it has generally worked out in such fashion as to discriminate against certain racial groups, notably the Negro and the Mexican. Let us therefore see how segregation came about in public schools and why the Supreme Court declared it unconstitutional.

There are three principal ways in which forced segregation originates. The first is by state law. In 1954 seventeen states and the District of Columbia required that Negro children be educated in separate schools. Four other states had laws permitting segregation if the local community desired it. The second method is social. There are many areas in the country where different races are forced by custom and tradition to attend their own schools. This kind of segregation is enforced not by law but by popular feeling. It exists only where there is strong feeling about "not crossing the color line." The third method of segregation in the schools is residential. It is more accidental than intentional, and it usually lasts for only a generation or two. Residential segregation results from different racial

Although some states immediately complied with the Supreme Court decision regarding desegregation, opposition to the decision ran high in others. Parents withdrew children from the schools and formed picket lines, and some students went on "strike." (Wide World)

or cultural groups living exclusively in one part of a city and therefore attending the same school. This type of segregation is fairly common in the North and the Midwest.

Social and educational segregation is most widespread in the South, where a double school system was established to conform with the "separate but equal" doctrine enunciated by the Supreme Court in 1896. This doctrine asserted that Negroes could constitutionally be excluded from schools for white pupils as long as they were offered equal educational facilities in their own schools. The southern states established a double system of schools, one for white children and another for Negroes, which they maintained under the "separate but equal" doctrine.

A double system of schools is said to decrease the quality of education for both whites and Negroes because it uses public school money in wasteful duplication of facilities and in various unnecessary expenses. It took $1,225 of the taxpayers' money each year in Missouri, for example, to drive a single Negro student 50 miles back and forth daily because he was not allowed to attend the nearby white students' school. Even if forced segregation is not discriminative, it appears to be costly.

Segregation has almost always worked out in discriminative fashion. The President's Commission on Higher Education reported in 1948 that:

The schools maintained for the Negro are commonly inferior to those for the whites. The Negro schools are financed at a pitifully low level, they are often housed in buildings wholly inadequate for the purpose, and many of the teachers are sorely in need of more education themselves. Library facilities are generally poor or lacking altogether, and professional supervision is more a name than a reality.

One concrete example will illustrate the truth of this statement. In 1946 the value of school property in the District of Co-

lumbia for each white child was $250, and the annual expenses for each white child were $104. The value of school property in the Negroes' schools was $48 per child, and the expenses were $57. The attempts of some southern states to provide "separate but equal" education in such professions as law and medicine were not successful.

In a series of decisions after 1945 the Supreme Court repudiated the "separate but equal" doctrine by insisting that separate or segregated education could not be equal. In 1950 the University of Texas was ordered to admit a Negro to its law school on the grounds that graduate professional schools cannot be duplicated. In the same year the Supreme Court declared (in *McLaurin* v. *Oklahoma*) that a university cannot segregate a Negro within the university after having admitted him as a student.

On May 17, 1954, the Supreme Court climaxed a series of non-segregation rulings by declaring that "in the field of public education the doctrine of separate but equal has no place. Separate educational facilities are inherently unequal. Therefore, we hold that the plaintiffs (Negro parents) and others similarly situated for whom the action has been brought are, by reason of the segregation complained of, deprived of the equal protection of the laws guaranteed by the Fourteenth Amendment."

The Supreme Court did not set a time or require any particular method for ending segregation in the seventeen states where it was required by law. Reaction in the states concerned was not uniform. The District of Columbia announced at once that it would integrate its educational system in the fall of 1954. Six states prepared to accept the Supreme Court's ruling and integrate their schools within a year. These states were West Virginia, Kentucky, Delaware, Maryland, Oklahoma, and Arkansas—all states with a comparatively small Negro population.

Missouri, Tennessee, Texas, and North Carolina indicated they would follow the Court's ruling, but they would integrate their schools gradually in a step-by-step process. In some localities there was strong feeling against desegregation, but in many others the first steps toward implementing the Supreme Court's decision were taken without difficulty. Usually, it should be noted, little change took place in primary and secondary schools because residential requirements naturally resulted in a measure of social segregation.

Virginia and the six states of the "Black Belt"—South Carolina, Georgia, Alabama, Florida, Mississippi, and Louisiana—denounced the Court's decision as based on social theory rather than constitutional law. They therefore set about finding ways and means of maintaining segregated schools. Some proposals were extreme, such as passing and enforcing clearly unconstitutional segregation laws until they were acted on by the Supreme Court, at which time a new set of similar but not identical laws would be put on the statute books. Other less rebellious methods prevailed in some states. Mississippi planned to abolish the public schools altogether and reconstitute them as private schools, thus creating a system of schools exempt from the Supreme Court's decision. Louisiana proposed to invoke the police power of the state to require segregation "to promote and protect public health, morals, better education and the peace and good order in the State, and not because of race."

Such resistance to the Court's decision creates many problems in education—as does the decision itself. Prejudice and discrimination are social factors not changed overnight by judicial decisions. The solution to discriminative segregation is the ending of prejudice and the sincere desire to practice Christian justice and observe constitutional rights in the treatment of all racial and cultural groups in the country. In some ways, perhaps, the Court's desegregation decision has hampered the slow evolution toward greater justice in the treatment of Negroes in this country. In the long run, if we can judge by the way Catholic schools have approached the problem, the segregation problem will be solved by the American people.

REVIEW

21. Religion and the Public Schools

A. Our society is "pluralist." How is this true of the educational systems of America? What is the element of unity in our society?

B. Point out the twofold task of the public school. How does the mission of the public school differ from that of the private or parochial school?

C. Some have found that the easiest way to handle the problem of religion in the public school is to ignore it. Give two reasons why this is unsatisfactory.

D. List four proposals made to prevent the elimination of all religion from public education.

22. The Private and Parochial Schools in the American System

A. Describe briefly the role that the private school has played in American education.

B. The savings to the taxpayer by private and parochial schools are not always known. How is this saving realized? Why do people endure "double taxation"?

C. Show that the view that private and parochial schools are "un-American" is entirely unfounded. Point out the dangers behind this view and the theory that all education must be the same.

D. The state has some obligations in the field of education. State what these are and the limitations involved in them.

E. List some of the problems that face private and parochial schools. How are some of these being solved?

23. Academic Freedom and Racial Segregation in the Schools

A. Define academic freedom in its full meaning.

B. Point out some abuses of academic freedom. How have Communists tried to invoke this in order to retain their jobs in education? Why is this attempt on their part an abuse of the term academic freedom?

C. Describe how forced segregation originates. How has the Supreme Court decided these laws in cases since 1945? How have the southern states reacted to these decisions?

THE CHAPTER IN REVIEW

A. The teaching of religion in the public schools presents many problems. Indicate some of these problems and the attempts made to solve them.

B. Point out the contributions of the private and parochial schools to America. Indicate the opposition to the private and parochial schools and state why the opposition is basically "un-American."

C. What federal aid do private and parochial schools receive at the present time?

D. Academic freedom and racial segregation are present-day problems. Describe each of these problems at the present time. What solutions have been offered for these problems?

SELECTED READINGS

The following are useful for dealing directly with the problem of education in a pluralist society. *Education for Democracy: The Debate over the Report of the President's Commission on Higher Education* (Boston: D. C. Heath & Company, 1952). This is a book of readings edited by Gail Kennedy. It includes key parts of the Commission's report and various reactions to the report. The professional educator's point of view on these matters can be found in two works: *The Function of the Public School in Dealing with Religion* (Washington: American Council on Education, 1953), and *Moral and*

Spiritual Values in the Public Schools (Washington: National Educational Association, 1951).

James B. Conant, *Education and Liberty* (Cambridge, Mass.: Harvard University Press, 1952), argues that American institutions are not safe unless public schools are given a monopoly on the education of young people. He is answered in an article by James M. O'Neill, "Education and Liberty," *Social Order* (September 1953). Also useful is O'Neill's *Religion and Education under the Constitution*, mentioned in the reading list for Chapter 3.

A good article on the subject of religion in education is that by Frederick J. Zwierlein, "Religion in Schools," *Social Justice Review* (January 1954). *America* handled the problem thoughtfully in a series of three editorials in the issues of July 17, 24, and 31, 1954.

PROJECTS

1. Educational facilities have grown rapidly over the past twenty years. Draw up two charts for your own town or city—on one include all the educational facilities available in 1940 and, on the other, the facilities at the present time. Include on these the schools, summer schools, kindergartens, adult courses, etc., and the number of students. Observations can then be made by the class concerning the future needs of the community.

2. The *World Almanac,* the *Statistical Abstract of the United States,* and other sources in your library contain statistics on education throughout the world. The entire class would profit from a committee report on the nature and scope of education in foreign countries. The role of the United States in the Point Four program and the role of UNESCO should be included in this report.

3. The class will be interested in learning the story of those public schools that were run by Catholic religious. A research report, made from secondary sources, on these schools might include information on how they came to be, some of the results of this system, and the occasions for discontinuing them.

Chapter 10. The Basic Problem in American Education

24. OLD AND NEW EDUCATIONAL AIMS

Americans traditionally have had great faith in education. From earliest times our forefathers connected it in some way with the better life for each individual and the betterment of society as a whole. George Washington believed that the national government should establish a university, and Thomas Jefferson insisted that free government was impossible if the people remained generally ignorant. "The general mind," he wrote, "must be strengthened by education" if free, republican government was to succeed.

Our forefathers had a clear understanding of education and its relationship to good government. They understood education to mean a "diffusion of knowledge" and a "refinement of the mind"; in short, an intellectual and moral development that comes from hard study of mathematics, literature, logic, and science. This education was to be universal, in the sense that it was to be available to all who were able and willing to receive it.

Education was not to be restricted to an aristocracy of birth or of money. If there was to be an American aristocracy it must be an aristocracy of talents, because our forefathers had no idea of lowering educational standards to accommodate inferior minds. They believed—perhaps too optimistically—that all normal people were capable of receiving a good education. To put the matter another way, our forefathers thought universal education differed in terms of the persons to be educated, not in terms of the subjects to be mastered or the method of teaching to be employed. They meant to raise the "common man" up through education, not to pull education down to fit the inferior mind.

American faith in education has persisted until our own time. We have generously and faithfully supported our public schools. The average child today is in school twice as long as he was a century ago. Today we spend nine times as much on the education of a single child each year as we spent in 1870. We spend about one hundred times as much on education

as we did a century ago, and we have more than four times as many children in school. Americans have invested more money in education than any other people in the world because they believe that in some way education will make better citizens of a better country.

Our government can prosper only if people are generally well educated. American society requires that every adult be able to read, write, and think. If the schools fail to produce graduates able to do these things, the assumptions on which our government is based become invalid, and popular representative government is in serious danger of being undermined. A prominent university professor declared in 1953:[1]

A republican system of government requires citizens who are highly literate, accurately informed, and rigorously trained in the processes of rational and critical thought. If the schools fail to raise up a nation of men and women equipped with these qualities of mind, then self-government is in danger of collapse through the sheer inability of its electorate to grapple intelligently with the complex problems in science, economics, politics, and international relations that constantly come up for public decision.

[1] Arthur E. Bestor, *Educational Wastelands* (Urbana, Ill.: The University of Illinois Press, 1953), p. 12.

A cursory glance at contemporary society suggests that something is seriously wrong with American education. Almost every American child finishes eighth grade, and most of them complete another four years of school. But fewer graduates read serious books and magazines than at any previous time in American history. The most popular form of reading in the Army is the comic book. A large proportion of applicants for business and secretarial jobs can neither read competently nor spell commonly used words. We have longer school years, better equipment in the schools, and supposedly more advanced methods of instruction. But many graduates of the modern school approach illiteracy. Is there a connection between this fact and the fact that fewer students take fundamental courses in grammar, Latin, mathematics, and foreign languages than in former years? What is the reason that many freshmen entering a good university recently could not do a problem in long division or exercises in English grammar?

Many scholars and many parents in this country answer these questions by asserting that new trends in education are destructive of the very purpose for which schools exist. They maintain that a

Two of the many books that have awakened Americans to a new appraisal of their school systems in recent years are (left) by Arthur Bestor, professor and eminent historian, and (right) Rudolph Flesch, Austrian immigrant and critic of modern trends. Criticism stems from disillusionment with the new methods of teaching and the neglect of worth-while subjects in the curriculum.

group of educators who do not really believe in human intelligence have obtained control of many schools and have used their position to undermine sound educational programs. These assertions have been made by men who believe that most Americans can be trained to use their minds independently, to read and to write, and thus to become responsible American citizens. One of them, Arthur E. Bestor, an eminent historian at the University of Illinois, has written:[2]

The issue is drawn between those who believe that good teaching should be directed to sound intellectual ends, and those who are content to dethrone intellectual values and cultivate the techniques of teaching for their own sake, in an intellectual and cultural vacuum . . .

Across the educational world today stretches an iron curtain which the professional educationists are busily fashioning. Behind it, in slave-labor camps, are the classroom teachers, whose only hope of rescue is from without. On the hither side lies the free world of science and learning, menaced but not yet conquered. A division into two educational worlds is the great danger that faces us today. American intellec-

tual life is threatened because the first twelve years of formal schooling in the United States are falling more and more completely under the policy-making control of a new breed of educator who has no real place in—who does not respect and who is not respected by—the world of scientists, scholars, and professional men.

Professor Bestor has stated the case in strong language, but what he says has been said by many other university professors, by many businessmen, by many thoughtful parents, and by many school-teachers throughout the country. A paradoxical situation seems therefore to have arisen in America: The American people have great faith in the power of education to improve the country, and they have invested billions of dollars in it. Yet education has been devalued and degraded by professional educators so that it fails to accomplish the objectives which Americans have a right to expect of it. Let us inquire how this paradoxical situation has come about, and let us analyze the nature of our basic educational problem so that we can take measures to solve it.

---

[2] *Ibid.,* pp. 11, 121.

To put the matter briefly: the "old" system of education was in need of reform and improvement. Advances in psychology showed that old methods failed to achieve fully the aims of education. A group of educators therefore worked out an entirely new method of teaching called the "progressive" method. At the same time they developed a new philosophy of education, and they created a profession called pedagogy. The pedagogues, or specialists in educational methods, soon came to exercise a very large influence over the public schools (and a considerable measure of influence in many private schools) through their schools of education and through state requirements that teachers take courses specified by the pedagogues.

Starting out with the legitimate aims of improving teaching methods, they ended up changing the curriculum, throwing out standard courses in mathematics or languages which did not fit into their system, and pretty much dictating not only *how* the student was to be taught but also *what* he was to be taught. Educators who value liberal education therefore complained that the progressive school threw the baby out with the bath. In the process of reforming educational methods, the educators threatened to get rid of education itself. Let us see in more detail what is meant by these serious charges.

Our forefathers did not think that education consisted of pouring information into empty heads until they were filled to capacity. They understood that education aimed at the intellectual and moral development of the student. It is to enable the student to grow in wisdom as he matures physically. Our forefathers further believed that the study of certain subjects achieved these ends and at the same time gave the student basic information in the most important fields of knowledge: mathematics, natural and social sciences; grammar, rhetoric, and literature; logic, philosophy, and religion. Education in these subjects should enable the student to put other subjects into proper focus, to see the breadth and depth of social problems, to bring the wisdom of the past to bear on the problems of the present.

Such education as this was not aimed at making men good butchers or good bankers or good candlestick makers. Its aim was to make good men who could think soundly. Our forefathers understood that we needed a nation of butchers and bankers and candlestick makers who could think independently and effectively

In the classical tradition of education, Robert Frost, one of America's foremost poets, conducts an English seminar at Dartmouth College. (Standard Oil Co., N.J.)

about public matters, and they realized that mathematics and Latin and logic were proper subjects to educate such free men. They expected butchers to learn to be good butchers and shoemakers to be good shoemakers—but not in school. School was the place where all students learned to use their minds; its primary purpose was intellectual, not vocational.

A young person was adjusted to life by his home, his church, and many other agencies. The school's specific purpose was to develop his mind so that he would become an independent, intelligent, and responsible person. The older education, then, possessed a higher utility than training stenographers to take shorthand or cosmetologists to apply make-up. Cardinal Newman has explained its usefulness in this stately sentence:

> If then the intellect is so excellent a portion of us, and its cultivation so excellent, it is not only beautiful, perfect, admirable, and noble in itself, but in a true and high sense it must be useful to the possessor and to all around him; not useful in any low, mechanical, mercantile sense, but as diffusing good, or as a blessing, or a gift, or power, or a treasure, first to the owner, then through him to the world.

This is the sense in which our forefathers expected general education to serve our country. Its aim was to develop all Americans intellectually.

Origin of "progressive" education. Education in fundamental subjects was sometimes badly handled in the past. Frequently teachers stressed rote learning at the expense of comprehension and analytical thinking. Some teachers made memory work the sum and substance of education. In short, there was room for considerable improvement in teaching methods in order to allow for differences among students and to guide their individual intellectual growth. Normal schools were established to fill this need. Future teachers, who presumably knew the subjects they were to teach, received training in better methods of instruction.

The normal school was a legitimate vocational school—like a barber school or a dental school—where practitioners in teaching taught others how to teach. But within a short time normal schools became schools of education in the universities, and education took its place as a legitimate subject with a supposedly educational content instead of being regarded as a "how-to" course to develop a particular skill. Professors of education have combined with public school superintendents and officials in state departments of public instruction to form what Professor Bestor calls "the interlocking directorate of professional educationists."[3]

This group has presumed to redefine the aims of education. They have departed radically from the purposes and the curriculum followed for the education of free men for centuries, and they have substituted courses designed to "adjust" students to their environment. They are entrenched in power in most states through legislative requirements that exclude from teaching positions anyone who has not accumulated a number of "education" courses under their control. Any educator who hopes to advance in the educational system must do graduate work in "education." Ironically, those best qualified under these requirements often are those with the least real education, for they acquire many courses in "how to teach" and few in the subjects they are supposed to teach.

The interlocking directorate of which we speak has usurped control of education, which properly belongs to parents. It determines not only *how* courses are to be taught but also *what* each child is to learn. One progressive educator recently stated: "As a rule, parents wish only the best of school conditions for their children; determination of what is best, however, is not a matter for parents to decide, but is the responsibility of the regularly

[3] *Ibid*, p. 102.

constituted school authorities."[4] Sensible parents realize that they should respect the opinion of educators on school matters, but they cannot surrender their God-given responsibility for the education of their children by turning them over blindly to public school authorities who claim that they alone are qualified to decide what a student should learn.

The interlocking directorate of educationists has driven many excellent students out of teaching and into other fields. If it tightens its system of control and undergoes no improving reform it will discourage more and more prospective good teachers from entering the profession. Comparative figures show that by 1950 students majoring in education in college (and therefore destined to be teachers) were distinctly inferior to those in other fields. To cite only one example, when almost 100,000 freshmen took the draft-deferment tests, 53 per cent secured a passing grade. Whereas 68 per cent of those in engineering and 57 per cent of those in social sciences passed, only 27 per cent of those majoring in education passed—by far the lowest category of all.

Responsibility for this state of affairs rests squarely upon the professors of education who have damaged the American educational system by giving it new aims and a novel curriculum. But the American public cannot escape some share of responsibility. Robert M. Hutchins, a caustic critic of progressive education, insists that public schools are sensitive to public demand and that when people expect state universities or city high schools to train drum majorettes or good mambo dancers such courses are added to the curriculum. They can be added, let us remember, because the proper object of education has been denied and a new aim substituted. If the school conducts a life-adjustment program instead of training

Teacher education courses in special methods are often devoted to activities that are extremely elementary and present little challenge or satisfaction to the serious college student. Preparing to teach biology, the students spend their time in graphic arts courses.

students to think, the mambo may have as good a claim as algebra to a place in the curriculum.

25. NATURE AND PHILOSOPHY OF "PROGRESSIVE" EDUCATION

This system of education is described by its adherents as "student-centered" instead of "subject-centered." Whether this new focus of attention is sound or not depends on what these phrases connote. If they mean that the teacher should focus his attention on developing the student's intellect, there is no ground for objecting to them. If they mean that subject matter is unimportant and that the teacher is to concentrate on keeping the student happy and occupied with trivial things, then they subvert the purpose of education as it has been understood in our civilization for many centuries.

Also, this system of education stresses learning by experience rather than from books. Progressive educators insist that the student does not really understand

[4] Quoted by Albert Lynd, *Quackery in the Public Schools* (Boston: Little, Brown and Company, 1953), p. 47.

anything that he has not experienced. Therefore, they organize field trips to study social matters. Learning in the classroom is through projects and discussion rather than from reading books, going to the library, consulting the opinion of experts, and gathering the wisdom of the ages to focus it on the problem under study. When these "progressive" methods are used to arouse student interest and are harnessed to legitimate educational subjects they can improve instruction considerably. But when experience is substituted for book learning, as it is in many places, recreation replaces education. One does not understand the industrial system from an hour's tour through a steel mill. Nor does a student understand the nature of democracy from counting "ayes" and "nos" in the classroom. Within limits, then, the new techniques can improve educational methods—as long as they remain techniques designed to achieve the proper aim of education and do not replace it.

But progressive education goes much farther. It sets forth revolutionary new aims for education. Let us see what these aims are as stated by the most prominent advocate of "progressivism," Professor William Heard Kilpatrick of Teachers College at Columbia University, and his disciple-biographer:[5]

... if we wanted rich, meaningful learning we must start with the students' present knowledge, wishes and interests, whatever they may be and wherever they may lead.
Kilpatrick from now on sought "a living good," good in terms of whether it made life better or richer or happier. . . .
But books as the beginning and the end of education are a sterile and meaningless kind of education that shrivels up life, and denies all that is good and creative in an ongoing, pulsating, creative life.
To Kilpatrick, education meant better adjustment, richer, happier, increasingly creative

---

[5] Samuel Tenenbaum, *William Heard Kilpatrick: Trail Blazer in Education*, quoted by Albert Lynd, *op. cit.*, pp. 231–232.

living. For this kind of education it was necessary that the child immerse himself in the actual process of living. "We have in mind," he said, ". . . growth in the richness of life and growth over experience. . . . From this point of view education is good when life is continuously made richer and richer and richer."

Let us try to interpret these words to make sense in the light of other pronouncements on the aims of progressive education. Advocates tell us that they satisfy the student's "real needs" and that they guide his "life adjustment" to the society in which he lives. A moment's reflection suggests that this is a bold presumption on the part of professional educators, for parents can well inquire by what norm the superintendent decides that students need a "democratic" solution to their lunch-money problem but they do not need the Fourth Gospel or Shakespeare's *Hamlet*. The new aim of education—to satisfy "real needs" and to manage "life adjustment" for the student —is a radical departure from the purpose of the school. It is obnoxious to our way of life, for Americans have traditionally assumed that the home, the church, and local institutions all have a part in helping the student satisfy his real needs and adjust himself to his environment. For the school to seize this role for itself is to give it an exclusive control over the student which is both un-Christian and un-American.

This system is also a failure as an educational device. The school does not and cannot directly solve "real-life" problems. Its proper function is to train people to think so that when they are confronted by real problems they will be able to solve them. The school is the proper place to learn principles, to develop habits of right thinking, to obtain a broad view of things so that the student can proceed to acquire his vocational training without sacrificing the independence of thought which is proper to free men. The men who drafted the Constitution received a

A high school agriculture class is shown visiting a nearby farm to get experience in culling poultry. Across the country, courses of study in the schools will vary according to the needs of the individual and the community. (Standard Oil Co., N.J.)

liberal education in the wisdom of their forebears. They did not take field trips to colonial legislatures or work "democratically" on classroom projects to make constitutions for student councils.

Progressive education is based on a pragmatist philosophy called *instrumentalism*, which was best expounded by John Dewey. It will be sufficient for our purposes to state those theories on which instrumentalist education is based. Dewey held that there are no eternal truths, that knowledge is changing and subjective. He regarded the human being as an animal constantly developing and always adapting itself to its environment. Albert Lynd points out that Dewey denied the existence of God and of the human soul as understood by Christians:[6]

Many of Dewey's education disciples may be coy or confused, but the master himself is clear enough in his writing about the implications of his philosophy. It excludes God, the soul, and

----
[6] *Op. cit.*, p. 206.

all the props of traditional religion. It excludes the possibility of immutable truth, of fixed natural law, of permanent moral principles.

If there are no absolute values or eternal truths, what claim can philosophy or literary classics have over "how-to-drive-cars" courses? As a matter of fact, the latter seems more directly connected with the student's biological adaptation to his environment. If the student is a mere animal organism adjusting to its environment rather than a person composed of body and soul, it is logical for schools to aid his "life adjustment" and cater to his "real needs" rather than educate him in an outmoded wisdom of the past.

An outstanding educator and a critic of progressive education, Reverend Francis C. Wade, S.J., has summed up Dewey's educational thought:[7]

1. Thinking begins *only* where facts or things appear as a challenge to or a difficulty felt by the individual.
2. Definite concepts are not intellectually gripped and retained unless something practical is done with the object.
3. Theoretical knowledge, which is remote from direct use, is an outgrowth of practical knowledge immediately directing activity.
4. The mind is a growing thing, not a receptive faculty like a plastic disc which will receive and give back whatever you put into it.
5. Teaching that begins with a set content, chosen and arranged according to the demands of adult thought, is only indoctrination, not real instruction.
6. Teaching must begin with a problem that presents a challenge to the individual, as touching his felt needs or interests.
7. The result of proper teaching is not a set of dead contents that encourage dogmatism and unjustified conservatism, but a method of knowing, similar to the method of the physical sciences, that emphasizes critical judgment and faith in progress.

Instrumentalist education has created many serious problems in the American

----
[7] See Reverend Francis Wade, S.J., "Child-Centered School—Doctrine or Heresy," *Bulletin of National Catholic Educational Association* (Washington, D.C.: August 1955), pp. 201–202.

John Dewey (1859–1952), American philosopher and educator, is credited with originating the "progressive" system of education. His principal theories as outlined in this chapter have been attacked for their pragmatism and for bringing into the schools matter that is not proper to them. Stressing what is immediately practical, he advocated vocational training and had little regard for content courses in the school curriculum.

schools. Let us analyze some of the most serious of these problems. The greatest arises from the development of a pronounced *anti-intellectualism* in the schools.

26. ANTI-INTELLECTUALISM IN THE SCHOOLS

Progressive education makes no distinction between courses that should develop the intellectual virtues and those that satisfy passing popular whims. In a formal address to the National Association of Secondary-School Principals, a principal from Illinois proclaimed:[8]

Through the years we've built a sort of halo around reading, writing, and arithmetic. We've said they were for everybody. . . .

---

[8] A. H. Lauchner, "How Can the Junior High Curriculum Be Improved?", *Bulletin of the National Association of the Secondary-School Principals* (March 1951).

When we come to the realization that not every child has to read, figure, write and spell . . . then we shall be on the road to improving the junior high curriculum.

Between this day and that a lot of selling must take place. But it's coming. We shall some day accept the thought that it is just as illogical to assume that every boy must be able to read as it is that each one must be able to perform on a violin, that it is no more reasonable to require that each girl shall spell well than it is that each one shall bake a good cherry pie.

In the same vein, another progressive educator says that arithmetic is "just a distasteful medicine he [the student] is forced to take because of the discredited notion that it is 'good for him.'" For that reason, he insists, in modern schools "square root is out the window." [9]

Such thinking is consistent with the view (strange for educators to take!) that students have no minds and that the job of the school is to adjust these biological organisms to their environment and thus to make them happy. The president of the New York State College for Teachers put the idea frankly when he said: "Education is not even primarily intellectual, certainly not chiefly intellectual. It is the process by which the emotions are socialized." [10]

The new "education" does not stop at mere indifference to things intellectual. It has consistently revealed hostility to them. Whereas teachers were formerly supposed to know the subjects they taught, nowadays there is a definite trend in progressive schools to pick teachers who have not been good students, on the grounds that they will fit into the system better. This is an amazing development which requires ignorance rather than knowledge from the teacher!

Educational trivia. Quite logically, the new education has scuttled the subjects long

---

[9] Wilbur A. Yauch, "How Good Are Your Schools?", *American Magazine* (September 1951).
[10] Quoted by Robert M. Hutchins, *Education for Freedom* (Baton Rouge, La.: Louisiana State University Press, 1943), p. 20.

considered the core of any sound educational program and substituted for them whatever the educators or the students might want to do. Professor Kilpatrick is quoted by his biographer as saying, "It is first, last, and all the time not subject matter which must immediately concern us, but life and personality and their best growth." The biographer continues:[11]

> For that reason he wanted no curriculum set in advance, nor did he want teachers to "sell" or foist subject matter on the child. Once you have a curriculum set in advance, the child is forgotten, and those who do not meet standards or who deviate from set patterns are corralled back to the set enclosures. Under this arrangement there is the ever-present and inherent danger that the child will be coerced, and coercion "seldom builds desirable habits."

Kilpatrick was consistent in saying that he did "not see how we can teach traditional mathematics in conformity with a modern philosophy of education." For any mathematics beyond making change for a dollar has nothing directly to do with "life adjustment." It is an old-fashioned subject which develops habits of hard thinking and teaches students how to deal with abstract quantities. In similar fashion, progressive educators rule out physics and foreign languages.

What takes the place of the standard subjects that are "thrown out the window"? Typical of the new curriculum is the fairly widely adopted program on "Home and Family Life," which has units on how families play games together, how to conduct outings, how to care for family pets, and how to organize the family democratically. A study on

curriculum made by progressive educators in Illinois listed fifty-five possible "real-life problems" for study in high school. These included such subjects as improving one's personal appearance, selecting the family dentist, collecting art objects, and doing parlor stunts. All these things may play a significant part in growing up, but the intelligent student might well ask what connection they have with real education. Is it in the home or in the school that a young person should learn parlor stunts and how to choose the family dentist? Such a program is an arrogant intrusion by educators into affairs that do not properly concern them.

The extent to which these ideas have entered into educational circles can be appreciated by anyone who reads the report of the President's Commission on Higher Education (1948). This report states that it assumes eleven objectives for higher education. Besides certain traditional aims, such as acquiring the ability to think critically and constructively, it lists others such as these: to attain a satisfactory emotional and social adjustment; to maintain and improve one's own health and to co-operate actively and intelligently in solving community health problems; to acquire the knowledge and attitudes basic to a satisfying family life.

As a result of these educational aims, the school is overburdened with trivia from primary grades to the university. This development has come about because of the philosophy underlying progressive education and because of a wide-

[11] Samuel Tenenbaum, *op. cit.*, p. 179.

The objects of the criticism of many educators are courses such as this, in cooking. A young person can learn such things in her home and devote her school time to more valuable studies.

spread belief that schools are to train students in order to increase their earning power. Vocationalism has loaded educational institutions with thousands of subjects which should be self-taught or learned on the job. This is partly the fault of the public, who demand that the schools have a "practical" curriculum and that they prepare students to take well-paying jobs upon graduation. But it is largely the fault of educators who are supinely responsive to public demand. When journalism becomes a popular thing, schools of journalism pop up everywhere like mushrooms. So it is with almost every trade—which should be learned by the applicant after he has finished his formal schooling.

The most obvious result of the trend toward progressive education, then, is that it replaces the wisdom of the human race with "life-adjustment" projects in the lower grades and vocational training programs on the higher levels of education. This trend has not worked out as completely as its advocates would like because it has been resisted by the hundreds of thousands of sensible teachers throughout the land—and whole school systems in many areas—who faithfully

teach their students how to distinguish truth from error, fact from fancy, right from wrong. These are teachers who believe that democracy in education means that no one should be debarred from receiving as sound an education as he is capable of acquiring, not that it means lowering the standards so that less and less is taught to more and more students.

As we have seen, the education of the nation's youth by no means belongs exclusively to the educators. Society in general has a stake in the educational programs throughout the nation. Most recently have the nation's scientists and industrialists expressed their dissatisfaction with the educational schemes that deny sound scientific training. The scarcity of qualified science teachers and the small number of science majors graduated from our colleges each year are cause for anxiety among those who realize that the scientific progress of the United States might very shortly fall behind that of other nations. The second half of the twentieth century promises to be the period of the greatest acceleration in scientific development. It is no wonder, then, that representatives of the major chemical and engineering companies in the United

(From Teachers for Tomorrow, *the Ford Foundation Bulletin No. 2)*

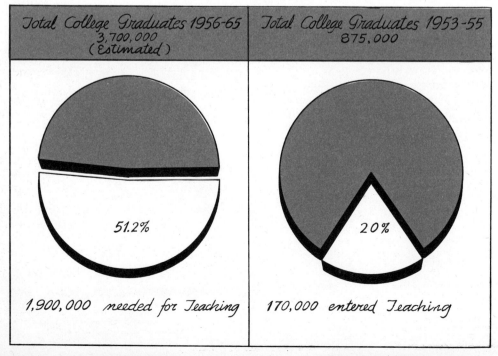

Total College Graduates 1956-65 3,700,000 (Estimated)	Total College Graduates 1953-55 875,000
51.2%	20%
1,900,000 needed for Teaching	170,000 entered Teaching

States are visiting campuses in an effort to recruit engineers for their firms and to encourage the study of science in general.

Grants-in-aid that provide for joint sponsorship of research projects, endowments for laboratories, and scholarships to deserving students are evidence of the concern of our country's industries in the science programs of our universities. Such efforts, however, can be rewarding to only a minimum degree if the elementary and secondary schools encourage the effortless surrender of their students to the less difficult courses of study. Mathematics, physics, and chemistry must be taught as such, for no "appreciation" courses or "life-adjustment" courses can prepare students for further study in these subjects. In their retreat from "indoctrination" courses progressive educators have retreated from areas of learning that are sorely needed to augment the ranks of our country's scientists. Indoctrination courses are the "bugaboo" of progressive educators, although it is only in recent years that "to indoctrinate" meant anything but to teach subject matter. Today, for the progressive educator "to demand that a student learn a set content as true as in mathematics, physics, and chemistry is the educational sin that cannot be forgiven." [12]

Joel H. Hildebrand, president of the American Chemical Society, in a criticism of progressive education stated, "A civilization that intelligence has built requires intelligence to manage." [13] The aims of education cannot be so compromised that the nation's youth are prepared for second-best positions in a society that will soon need their leadership. The complexity of the atom age has already raised the necessary minimum of scientific intelligence for all people. This fact, in turn, is awakening leaders in gov-ernment, industry, and business to the fact that intelligence itself must again be the hallmark of our schools. The traditional belief that knowledge, skill, and intelligence are proper to academic pursuits is thus being restored, at least in the minds of the most objective observers of our educational programs. It is therefore deplorable in the extreme that in many of our schools the "content" courses, which include the sciences, are being de-emphasized in the times of their greatest need.

When the deciding factors in a student's course of study are his likes and dislikes, as certainly is true in many instances, it is no wonder that the student's talents are rarely discovered, his potential hardly tapped, his development incomplete. It is a grave underestimation of the business of public life to believe that courses in home decor and gardening offer proper preparation.

Conclusion. The problems we have discussed in these last chapters seem to reduce themselves, in the last analysis, to the single one of having the school perform well the task for which it is fitted and to shun the tasks that properly belong to the family, the church, industry, and other agencies. American parents have grown to expect the school to do almost everything—to teach their children manners and social graces; in kindergarten, how to brush their teeth properly and how to tie their shoelaces; in high school, how to drive a car and how to put on cosmetics. The new educators believe that these are properly the aim of education and they willingly embrace them. Inevitably they discard the subjects proper to education because they tend to interfere with the new aims of education.

American parents have the right and the power to effect reforms within the public school systems. Indignant parents can force school authorities to abolish trivia, as they have done in a few places in the country, and to re-establish a

[12] See Reverend Francis Wade, S.J., *op. cit.,* p. 204.
[13] Joel H. Hildebrand, "Intelligence Is Important," *Chemical and Engineering News,* October 17, 1955, p. 4415.

sound curriculum. If parents once again assume fully their duty of rearing their children, and if religion again takes its proper place in the home and in society, then the school will surely be forced to assume again its proper place in the educational picture. The school's proper function is difficult enough to accomplish well, since it must aid parents in guiding the student's intellectual development. It must help the student develop his intellectual skills, guide him toward a love of truth, and thus enable him to grow in wisdom. If it does this well, the school can let other agencies assume the other burdens it has improperly assumed in the last half century.

REVIEW

24. Old and New Educational Aims

A. To what educational principle did Americans commit themselves during the first half of the nineteenth century? How has this been achieved in the twentieth century?

B. Are we really a *literate* nation? Illustrate your answer. What has caused the conditions that exist?

C. "Progressive" methods have been charged with bringing about the present condition of education in the United States. Point out how this is true. What was our forefathers aim in education? How was this to be brought about?

D. How did progressive education originate? How did it succeed? What is meant by Professor Bestor's term, "interlocking public school directorate"?

25. Nature and Philosophy of "Progressive" Education

A. What are some of the principles of progressive education? What are some of its "new" aims in the field of education? Show how these ignore the real purpose of education.

B. What is the false philosophy upon which progressive education is based? Give some of its principles.

26. Anti-intellectualism in the Schools

A. How do "content" subjects fit into this "new curriculum"? Show how the school loses its purpose with "trivia."

B. What has been the reaction of the country's industrialists and scientists to progressive education? Why is their concern of great importance today?

THE CHAPTER IN REVIEW

A. Universal education has become very important to the future of America. What is the paradox that exists in respect to the American people's attitude toward education? What did our forefathers believe would be the result of education?

B. Progressive education as expounded by John Dewey is essentially "learning by doing." What is meant by this phrase? What are the weaknesses of this system?

C. How does progressive education develop an anti-intellectual attitude? What are the dangers involved? What is meant by educational trivia?

SELECTED READINGS

The theory of progressive education is best stated by John Dewey, *Democracy and Education* (New York: The Macmillan Co., 1916), and by William H. Kilpatrick, *Source Book in the Philosophy of Education* (New York: The Macmillan Co., 1934). A Catholic critique of progressivism is to be found in Joseph McGlade, C.S.C., *Progressive Education and the Catholic Church* (Westminster, Md.: The Newman Press, 1953), and in Geoffrey O'Connell, *Naturalism in American Education* (New York: Benziger Brothers, Inc., 1938).

In addition to Redden and Ryan's *A Catholic Philosophy of Education,* one should consult the shorter work of William J. McGucken, S.J., *The Catholic Way in Education* (Milwaukee: The Bruce Publishing Co., 1934), and the same author's pamphlet, *The Philosophy of Catholic Education* (New York: America Press, 1936). There are many pamphlet editions of Pope

Pius XI's encyclical on education, "The Christian Education of Youth." The best defense of liberal, Christian education remains the series of lectures delivered by Cardinal Newman and published as *The Idea of a University.* The best of many editions of this work is the one edited by Charles Harrold (New York: Longmans, Green & Co., Inc., 1947).

Criticism of the progressive system of education is soundly made by Arthur E. Bestor, *Educational Wastelands* (Urbana, Ill.: University of Illinois Press, 1953). A more readable criticism is that of Albert Lynd, *Quackery in the Public Schools* (Boston: Little, Brown & Co., 1953). Although popularly written, this book is based on sound common sense. Robert M. Hutchins has written three small books, all of which contain essentially the same arguments against progressive education. These are *The Higher Learning in America* (New Haven: Yale University Press, 1945); *Education for Freedom* (Baton Rouge, La.: Louisiana State University Press, 1943); and *The Conflict in Education in a Democratic Society* (New York: Harper & Brothers, 1953). Another good criticism of modern education is that of Bernard Iddings Bell, *Crisis in Education: A Challenge to American Complacency* (New York: Whittlesey House, 1949).

PROJECTS

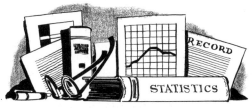

1. There is constant discussion of the value of a classical education. Two students with opposite views can write a brief report upholding their opinions. The class will profit from a discussion of the question after the reports have been read in class.

2. It would be most valuable to read the encyclical of Pope Pius XI on education. An artist in the class could prepare a poster that lists the aims, purposes, and end of education as seen by the Holy Father. Include the obligations of the parents, the Church, and the state.

3. The present conditions of overcrowded classrooms and the shortage of teachers have opened new vistas for television in the field of education. Prepare a plan for a lesson in this course, which you have adapted for a television program. You need not write a script for the lesson but include the various means that you would use to illustrate and teach. Invite the class to discuss the merits of your plan.

BISHOPS' STATEMENT OF 1955

"To preserve freedom America must teach freedom," was the keynote of the statement of the American bishops at their annual meeting in 1955. In this we have a clear declaration on the rights of the private and church-related schools in the United States. From 1792 to 1919 there were thirteen pastorals of the American hierarchy. Since the 1920s the bishops have issued an annual statement on some current issue that they believed was in need of clarification. Recognizing the dangers that secularization was bringing to the school systems, the bishops at the First Plenary Council in 1852 and at the Third in 1884 recommended, and then enacted as law, the parochial school as the necessary safeguard of the faith of the children. In 1955 it was again necessary for the bishops to state their position, which the following excerpts clearly illustrate:

"It [the Catholic school] is no foreign importation, no alien growth, but a sturdy native plant, a conspicuous example of a common religious impulse working under the favorable condition of our Republic.

"Let this be fully understood: Private and church-related schools in America exist not by sufferance but by right. The right is implicit in the whole concept of American freedom and immunity from totalitarian oppression and in the constitutional framework of our Federal government and of the several states. Under attack it has been rendered explicit by the decision of the Supreme Court of the United States in the celebrated Oregon School Case.

"Indeed, it is worth remarking that while the state may usefully engage in the business of education, as demonstrated in our national experience, it has no authority either to monopolize the field or arrogate to itself exclusive privileges and powers. The state, by definition, is not itself primarily an education agency.

"What, then, is the place of the private and church-related schools in America? Their place is one dictated by nothing more than justice and equity, and accorded the recognition of their worth. They have, we repeat, full right to be considered and dealt with as components of the American educational system. They protest against the kind of thinking that would reduce them to a secondary level, and against unfair and discriminatory treatment which would, in effect, write them off as less wholly dedicated to the public welfare than the state-supported schools. The students of these schools have the right to benefit from those measures, grants, or aids, which are manifestly designed for the health, safety and welfare of American youth, irrespective of the school attended."

PROFILES

ARCHBISHOP JOHN HUGHES

BORN: Annaloghan, County Tyrone, Ireland, June 24, 1797
EDUCATED: Mount St. Mary's College (Seminary), Emmitsburg, Md.
ORDAINED: 1826; consecrated bishop, 1838; archbishop, 1850
DIED: New York City, January 3, 1864

The Hughes family managed to provide elementary training for the future archbishop before emigrating to America, where he later joined them as a laborer at the seminary for a year before entering as a student. A talented debater and thinker, Fr. Hughes served a number of Philadelphia parishes before being named Coadjutor Bishop of New York. He succeeded the French-born Bishop Dubois in 1842.

Bishop Hughes founded a number of child-caring institutions and dozens of churches; this phase of his work was crowned by the construction of the beautiful St. Patrick's Cathedral on Fifth Avenue in New York City.

The growth of the Catholic population of New York with the migration of thousands of Irish and German Catholics in the late forties was shown in 1850, when New York was established as an archdiocese, with Archbishop Hughes as its first head. He established the diocesan seminary, St. John's College, at Fordham, where it eventually became Fordham University, one of America's largest Catholic institutions of learning.

Education was a much debated topic during Archbishop Hughes' lifetime. The public School Society of New York was active in developing a system of schools under private auspices for public use, and the Archbishop objected strongly to Protestant tendencies in these schools, such as Bible study from the King James Version. Finally the Public School Society turned over its schools to the government, and the strictly Church-supported Catholic school system was pressed forward by the Archbishop.

Hughes had to defend himself and his flock against very bitter attacks by misled and sometimes vicious proponents of nativism. His national reputation, however, was attested by the invitation to address Congress in 1847, tendered by such diverse political leaders as John Quincy Adams, Stephen A. Douglas, and John C. Calhoun. His unswerving devotion to the United States led President Lincoln's government to send him to Europe to represent the Union cause in Catholic countries. He returned to exert his influence in calming the draft riots in New York in 1863.

There are no recent biographical studies available. Background material may be found in Ray Allen Billington's *The Protestant Crusade, 1800–1860* (New York: Rinehart & Company, Inc. 1952), which traces the anti-Catholic movement Hughes had to face, and *The Catholic Church in the United States,* by Theodore Roemer, O F.M. Cap., Ph.D. (St. Louis: B. Herder Book Co., 1954). A well-written scholarly study by Henry J. Brume, "The Archdiocese of New York a Century Ago," is available in research libraries, good public libraries, and in the libraries of institutional members of the United States Catholic Historical Society: *Historical Records and Studies,* Vol. 39–40, pp. 129–190 (New York: U.S.C.H.S., 1952).

BORN: Cork, Ireland, September 23, 1786
EDUCATED: Law studies and seminary at Carlow College, Ireland
ORDAINED: 1808; consecrated, 1820
DIED: Charleston, S.C., April 11, 1842

John England distinguished himself in Ireland as a brilliant lecturer and scholar; he taught at St. Mary's Seminary and was president of the theology faculty there. He founded and edited a newspaper, the *Chronicle,* which was a powerful ally of O'Connell's Catholic emancipation movement. His work in Ireland included also the establishment of free schools for impoverished students and protectories for Catholic girls.

In the midst of his career as an Irish priest, writer, and educator, he was named Bishop of the understaffed see of Charleston, South Carolina. Immediately, he determined to become an American citizen, and when he was consecrated in Cork he refused the oath of allegiance expected of Irish bishops prior to embarking for what was in effect a mission field in the United States.

At Charleston, Bishop England's talents as a speaker, writer, and editor were pressed into service in an almost one-man administration of the diocese that covered a very large area. Although the diocese had only two priests in 1820, Bishop England established Catholicism as a vital force in his diocese. He founded and taught at the diocesan seminary, organized new parishes for immigrants and newly won converts, and started the first American Catholic newspaper, the *United States Catholic Miscellany.* This paper, started in 1822, continued publication until the beginning of the war in 1861.

Bishop England won a reputation among non-Catholics by his careful and scholarly exposition of Catholic doctrine and practices, which turned away much of the ill-advised actions of nativists. South Carolina's dormant Philosophical Literary Association revived under the influence of the dynamic scholar from Ireland. His adopted country demonstrated its respect for him when, in 1826, he was invited by an almost entirely Protestant membership, to speak before the United States Congress.

The bishop returned to Europe on visits and persuaded Irish Ursulines to establish and staff schools in his diocese, but he turned down opportunities to return to Europe permanently on Church service. His habit of ministering personally to victims of yellow fever and dysentery epidemics in Charleston finally cost him his life in 1842.

A recent, well-balanced study of Bishop England is Dorothy F. Grant's *John England, American Christopher* (Milwaukee: Bruce Publishing Company, 1949). A more liberal sprinkling of quotations from the bishop is included in Peter Keenan Guilday's 2 volume *The Life and Times of John England* (New York: The America Press, 1927). Some Catholic reference libraries may contain copies of the Missal he prepared for American Catholics with explanation of the liturgy.

DEBATE

The question: **SHOULD THE FEDERAL GOVERNMENT GIVE FINANCIAL AID TO ALL EDUCATIONAL INSTITUTIONS?**

Everyone agrees that the federal government should promote the common welfare by taking whatever just measures are proper, but this question resolves itself into two topics about which there is serious disagreement. The two questions on which the debate hinges are: (1) Is federal aid desirable for *any* educational institution, public or private? (2) Should such aid, if desirable, be given to private and parochial as well as public schools, or should the former be excluded?

Affirmative presentation

I. The affirmative should answer the first question by showing its necessity and propriety.
  1. There is a need for federal aid to all kinds of schools.
    a. Some localities cannot furnish funds for good schooling.
    b. Good schooling is needed in America to produce good citizens and productive workers and to allow each person to develop his faculties fully.
  2. Federal aid for education is similar to

federal assistance for roads, housing projects, and similar programs.
  a. It is the American way of helping.
  b. It leaves the control of schools in local hands.
  3. Federal aid is an efficient way to accomplish the government's role in education, helping, encouraging and fostering it.
II. The affirmative answers the second question by showing the equality and fairness of such a measure.
  1. Private schools are as deserving of aid as are public schools.
    a. They perform the same public function.
    b. They save taxpayers billions of dollars a year.
    c. Without federal support many of them will collapse.
  2. Not to give aid to private schools is to discriminate and to injure our American pluralist system.
  3. To give aid to public schools alone is to promote a state monopoly of education by aiding already aided public schools.

Negative presentation

I. The negative should answer the first question by showing that federal aid is unwise and detrimental to the interests of education.
  1. Federal aid to local schools, public or private, is a dangerous step toward ending our system of locally controlled education.
    a. Control always follows support.
    b. Federal government must control spending of its funds.
  2. This is a step toward totalitarian control.
    a. The federal government is in a position to control the formation of the minds of all Americans.
    b. The temptation to insist on indoctrination is overwhelming.
II. The negative should oppose including private schools on these grounds:
  1. It is contrary to the idea of separation of church and state. Taxpayers' money would be used for the support of a religion.
  2. Private schools should oppose receiving money from the federal government.
    a. It will lead to federal control of private schools.

  b. Private schools will become pawns in the political game.
  c. This will lead to "uniform" education and cultural monism.

Classroom discussion: The class should determine the following: (1) whether this is a misunderstanding of the church-state issue; (2) whether there is any real danger of federal control of education; (3) whether the issue of needing federal aid is a real one or not: Do 'poor' states have money for other things? Do we go to the federal government for everything we need?

SELECTED READINGS

Background information on this subject can be found in the following: C. D. Hutchins and others, "Educational Expenditures of the Federal Government," *School Life* (October 1954); W. W. Brickman, "Federal Aid to Education in 1954," *School and Society* (March 6, 1954); C . A. Quattlebaum, "Federal Aid to School Construction," *Journal of the National Education Association* (November 1954).

The issues are discussed pro and con in the following articles: J. Burkhart, "Dangers of Federal Aid to Education, " *School and Society* (September 17, 1955); "Taxes for Tuition?", *Senior Scholastic* (April 30, 1952); "Federal Aid for Schools," *Senior Scholastic* (February 23, 1955); "Federal Subsidies for Higher Education?," *Congressional Digest* (August 1955); J. L. Morrill, "Dilemmas for Decision," *Vital Speeches of the Day* (November 15, 1954); E. Fuller and B. Johnson, "Federal Aid to Education?", *Rotarian* (June and August 1955).

The question whether federal aid should be restricted to public schools alone is treated in the following articles: James B. Conant, "Unity and Diversity in Secondary Education, "*Vital Speeches of the Day* (May 15, 1952); James M. O'Neill, "Religious Education and American Democracy," *Vital Speeches of the Day* (April 15, 1952); W. E. McManus, "Agnes Meyer on Parochial Schools," *Catholic World* (February 1954); John B. Sheerin, "Eisenhower and Parochial Schools," *Catholic World* (April 1955);"Federal Roles in School Aid," *America* (February 26, 1955); "State Barriers to Aid to Private Schools," *America* (March 19, 1955); D. M. Knight, "State Regulation of Independent Schools," *America* (June 4, 1955); V. A. McCrossen, "Public Aid to Parochial Education," *Catholic Educator* (September 1953); R. L. Stokes, "Senator Taft on Catholic Schools," *Catholic World* (July 1952).

UNIT FOUR
Social Problems
in an Expanding Society

Chapter 11. Population and Immigration

27. THE NATURE OF SOCIETY AND THE GROWTH OF POPULATION

As we approach the subject of social problems we should keep a correct view of society in mind. Society, we must remember, is not made by man. It is natural. Man needs society, first of all, in order to satisfy his material and spiritual wants. But social life is founded on something more than individual needs. Man is social because he is rational and because he can love. He can communicate his ideas and do good (or evil) to others. In society, man's rationality and personality are more effectively realized, and thus man develops more perfectly as a person.

Although society is natural, specific social institutions are devised by man at a given time and place in history. These institutions are good if they achieve their purpose of elevating human nature; they are bad if they harm human nature— morally, intellectually, or physically. The family, for example, is a natural institution. But each individual family is created by a man and woman who enter into the married state to help each other, to perfect each other as human persons, and

to rear the children with which their marriage may be blessed. As we shall see in a later chapter, one of the basic American social problems is that of restoring the family to its rightful place in society.

Our approach, therefore, is to examine some of the social problems created by defects in our institutions and to see in what way they can be improved so that everyone may have the opportunity to live in freedom, justice, and security.

Natural social groups. The 165,000,000 people in this country are not merely that many individuals. They are social persons related to each other in myriad and complex ways. Let us draw up a list of the principal ways in which people group together into social organizations.

1. The *family* is the basic, natural social unit. Everyone is a member of a family actually in existence or broken up through death, divorce, or some other means.

2. People group together *geographically* into neighborhoods or local communities. This grouping is a natural one in so far as people residing in the same locality have a general interest in community welfare and have certain problems in

common, such as those arising from a need for police and fire protection and recreational and educational arrangements.

3. *Political* groups range from the village and the city through the county and state to the nation as a whole. Each unit exists because there are certain problems that the people within it have in common to the exclusion of others. People in the city of Cincinnati, for example, have certain local problems common to the residents of that city but in which residents of Cleveland or Columbus have no immediate interest.

4. *Occupational or vocational* groups are natural because people in the same trade or occupation have many interests in common. Lawyers in New York City have common interests and problems with lawyers in Albany, and it is therefore natural for them to form associations of some sort on the basis of these common interests. So it is with coal miners, doctors, teachers, longshoremen, and people in the various other occupations.

5. *Socially,* people join together to promote interests that the members of each group have in common. These interests may be simply ones of taste or of mutual convenience, or they may be a more serious attempt to promote some aspect of the common good. Thus we have hundreds of societies like the Elks, the Knights of Columbus, or the Rotary Club.

6. *Religiously,* of course, people join together with those of like faith for the communal worship of God.

7. People of the same *ethnic* group sometimes band together because of similar viewpoints, similar cultural backgrounds, and similar problems.

Some of these groups are permanent and others are temporary. Some permanent groups, like the city or the village, are composed of a changing membership based upon residence, whereas others are of a somewhat more permanent membership, as the family or the ethnic group. The 165,000,000 who make up this nation are not a static population in any sense. Geographically, Americans are a fluid people. Some families move from one place to another. Between 1950 and 1954, for example, Nevada showed a 33 per cent increase in population, whereas West Virginia lost 2.9 per cent of its population. Not very many people moved out of California, but more than a million moved into that state.

This constant movement of the people of America modifies the nature of each social problem. The general trend of Ne-

This poster has been used in an organized campaign to promote tolerance and understanding among all Americans. (Institute for American Democracy)

gro migration into the northern states, for example, tends to make the problem of white and Negro relations a national rather than a regional problem. The influx of large numbers of Puerto Ricans into New York City and other urban centers, again, creates serious local problems. Population problems change in any city when a racial group, such as the Poles in Detroit or Milwaukee, loses its distinctive features and melts into the rest of the population.

Population changes. In the last few decades improvements in medicine have increased life expectancy to more than seventy years. There is now a much more sizable proportion of our population above sixty than ever before in history. A new field of specialization in medicine, geriatrics, or the care of the aged, has consequently come into being, and institutions are developing to care for this new segment of the population. Population changes are sometimes sudden and severe in the occupational order. In the last decade there has been a tremendous influx of men into electronic work, and there has been a rapid drop in the number of coal miners. Such changes involve a number of social problems. People even "melt out" of ethnic groups, usually in the course of several generations, and in so doing they solve some problems and create others.

We can see, then, that American society is a complex set of relationships that are constantly in a state of flux as people move about, take up new occupations, join new groups, and otherwise establish new relations with other sets of people. These changes of population structure create problems that must be solved as well as possible.

The problem of expanding population. Ever since the time of the Greeks there has been a haunting fear that the time will come when there will be too many people in the world, or in some given part of it, to share the food supply. Put in simplest terms, the fear comes to this: A farmer and his wife own a ten-acre farm on which they can raise food enough to support ten people. Suppose they have four children, who grow up and marry and all of them live on the ten acres. When the four married couples have children, there will be too many mouths to feed with the food that is produced on the farm. Now extend this picture to an entire country, or to the entire world, and you can imagine a grim situation for the human race.

Until the late eighteenth century this fear remained in the back of men's minds because the population did not increase very much. Infant mortality was high; epidemics and famines were frequent; war and disease and the resulting shortness of life carried off a high proportion of people before they reached the age of thirty-five. Beginning about 1750, better agriculture, improved sanitation, and other changes associated with the industrial revolution caused a sudden increase of population. This brought to the front of men's minds again the old fear of too many people in the world.

Thomas Malthus (1766–1834) formulated a famous "law of population." Malthus stated that food supply tends to increase at an arithmetical ratio (1, 2, 3, 4, 5, 6, 7), whereas population tends to increase at a geometric ratio (1, 2, 4, 8, 16, 32, 64). According to these ratios, Malthus explained, one could expect the population to double in about twenty-five years and to increase to sixty-four times its original size in 150 years. Meanwhile the food supply would increase to only seven times its original amount.

Such actual increase of the population had not taken place because of war, disease, and famine, he admitted, but if these checks did not operate to limit the population, then starvation inevitably would face mankind. Men should therefore adjust themselves to this law of population, Malthus argued, by the use of "moral restraint": refusal to marry, late marriage, or the practice of restraint in marriage.

Subsequent history proved Malthus a poor prophet. For one thing, industrial and agricultural developments after 1800 created an abundance of food and other goods that Malthus never dreamed of. Machinery, fertilizer, railroads, electricity, and man's other inventions solved—at least for the time—the problem of producing enough goods to enable all people to live decently. Especially in this country there was no shortage of food, and there were always the still uncultivated fields to the west where more food could be raised if needed. In the next place, many factors other than food supply entered into population trends in the nineteenth century: the quickened tempo of life; urbanization; social and economic competition that discouraged early marriage—these and many other factors brought about a declining birth rate in the nineteenth century and an even sharper decline in the first four decades of this century.

Birth and death rates. Let us look at the population statistics to see what was happening in this country. But first let us distinguish between *birth rate* and *number of births.* The birth rate is the number of children born per thousand people. At certain times, as we can see in the chart on page 174, the birth rate can decline while the actual number of births increases.

Until about 1850 the birth rate in this country was over 50 per 1,000 population. The rate declined, first gradually, then more rapidly until it reached the fig-

Thomas R. Malthus (1766–1834) viewed human suffering, such as war, famine, and pestilence, as population checks. He predicted that the population would eventually outrun the world food supply. Despite his pessimism and incorrect predictions, his study contributed to the development of sociology, or the science of group living. (Library of Congress)

ure of 30 per 1,000 in 1900. In 1920 it was 23.7, by 1930 it had declined to 18.9 births per 1,000, and in 1940 it was 17.9; although during all this period the *number* of births each year steadily increased. This was because of immigration and a rapid decline in the death rate, which caused the total population to increase. In 1920 the death rate had reached the new low of 13 per 1,000 population, in 1930 it had fallen to 11.3, and in 1940 it was only 10.8. Thus more people were living longer. The total number of births increased each decade, but because the population was larger the rate was lower.

Population prophets. Demographers (students of populations) twenty-odd years ago predicted a declining population for this country. Some experts believed the decline in actual numbers would not set in until after the food supply had become insufficient. In 1923, for example, the expert Edward M. East insisted that our country's agricultural resources could not support a population of more than 166,000,000—a number we have almost reached. But the experts did not see any possibility of such an increase in population. On the basis of population trends,

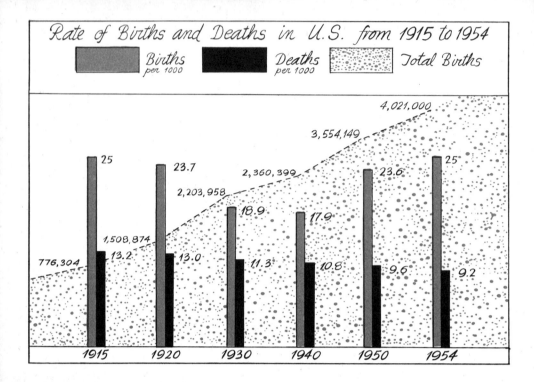

Rate of Births and Deaths in U.S. from 1915 to 1954

Births per 1000   Deaths per 1000   Total Births

4,021,000
3,554,149
2,360,399
2,203,958
1,508,874
776,304

25   23.7   18.9   17.9   23.6   25
13.2   13.0   11.3   10.8   9.6   9.2

1915   1920   1930   1940   1950   1954

their estimates of this country's maximum population varied from 136,000,000 to 148,000,000, this maximum to be reached, according to various estimates, between 1955 and 1970. Then a decline would begin. (We give here the lowest and highest estimates and the earliest and latest date set for the maximum population.) Demographers expected a gloomy future for America because of the declining birth rate.

The census figures of 1950 proved the pessimistic demographers to have been no better prophets than Malthus. The birth rate increased from 17.9 in 1940 to 23.6 in 1950, and it reached 25.2 in 1954. The number of births increased to 4,000,000, a figure at which it seems to have become more or less stabilized. As late as 1947, population experts insisted the maximum population of this country would be 164,500,000, to be reached in 1990. This figure was reached early in 1955.

These figures have been given to show that forecasting is a dangerous business

and that prophecies based upon expected population trends are not well grounded. The most recent census figures do show that since 1940 we have been in the midst of a population revolution. The birth rate has increased, while the death rate continues to fall. This means that we have a larger proportion of older people and a larger proportion of infants in the population. As a result, medical practice, educational institutions, employment opportunities, and recreational facilities must be adopted to care for these enlarged segments of the population. The 1950 census revealed also a continued drift of people away from the farm. The only states to show a net loss for the ten-year period ending 1950 were predominantly agricultural states: Arkansas, Mississippi, North Dakota, and Oklahoma. There was a general drift of the population westward, especially to the Southwest, with California, Texas, and Arizona all making gains far above the average. Another noticeable population shift was to the suburbs. Large cities showed less gains than expected, but the suburban areas showed the greatest gains of all.

It is easy to see that a rapidly expanding population creates many interrelated social problems. The rapid growth of suburbs, for example, has changed the make-up of the metropolitan community. The suppliers of goods and services have had to adjust their business to reach over wider areas. We should keep in mind the impact of an expanding population on the social and economic problems we discuss in the following chapters.

The error of the Neo-Malthusians. As a result of the most recent trends in population statistics some experts (called Neo-Malthusians) are now forecasting that within a comparatively short time the world, and this country too, will be overpopulated. That is, they say, there will be too many people for the food supply. Most Neo-Malthusians therefore advocate limiting the population by preventive means, including artificial means of birth control. Otherwise they see a world teeming with people who cannot obtain enough food.

Overpopulation is largely a phantom problem. At some remote time it might become a real problem, but at the present time—especially in America—there is no ground for fear of imminent overpopulation. The problem is rather to devise social and economic methods for distributing the means of life equitably among the people. Neo-Malthusians make their fearful predictions and advocate limiting the population because they refuse to consider a number of factors that should be kept in mind:

1. Artificial means of birth control are always wrong. Such prevention of birth is unnatural, since it defeats the primary purpose of marriage and it weakens the unity of the family. Not only is it a wrong solution to the problem—if there is a problem—but it is a defeatist approach to the whole problem of population. What Neo-Malthusians do not realize is that every one of the persons whom they compute in statistical terms is made to the image and likeness of God. The birth of each person, therefore, is in itself an abidingly good event. Limiting the population because of vague and phantom fears disobey's God's command: "Increase and multiply, and fill the earth."[1]

2. New sources of food are constantly being discovered, but population-maintenance estimates are made on existing scales of food production. The soy bean, alone, for example, proved sufficient to upset Malthus' worst predictions. Unknown in this country thirty years ago, it is now our fourth largest crop and is used for all sorts of food preparations. Experiment is now being conducted with various sea-grown plants which will make available enough food to support millions of people. The chemical industry has made it possible to grow food without using soil at all. What the future will bring no one knows. At least we do know that population forecasts must be for the immediate future and are subject to a large degree of error.

3. There are areas in the world where backward agriculture and an undeveloped economy make overpopulation a real problem, one to be dealt with seriously and systematically. But the economy of the United States—even if it were to develop no further in the years to come—is capable of supporting with a reasonable degree of comfort as large a population as is foreseeable at the present time.

28. PROBLEMS AND POLICIES OF IMMIGRATION

At first glance immigration seems to be a simple matter: how many and what kinds of people shall we admit to this country each year? But it became increasingly clear at the end of the war in 1945 that our immigration policy was in need

[1] *Genesis* 1:28.

of serious revision and that the problems involved were among the most complicated facing us as a nation. In 1952 the McCarran-Walter Act was passed, and it remains the basic immigration law of the land today.

Problems of American immigration must be considered in their world setting. They are primarily national problems, of course, but they are also part of the world migration problems. We must think not only in terms of how many immigrants we need and can absorb in this country but also in terms of high- and low-pressure areas of the world's population, in terms of people who, for one reason or another, must migrate somewhere. In considering American immigration problems we must also keep in mind American foreign policy and our need for friends abroad.

General principles. There are a few general principles to remember when we talk about our immigration problems. First, the government's right to control immigration is inherent in the government's obligation to protect and promote the common good. In the second place, the government may not in good morals exercise this right in arbitrary fashion. No people can intelligently maintain their own interests and security if they disregard the general interests of the whole of mankind. Where there is room for needy and decent people, they ought to be admitted if they are willing to respect and cherish the institutions of the country that opens its doors to them. Although there are economic and political aspects to these problems, as we shall see, nevertheless immigrants cannot be considered mere commodities to be imported to fill some need or excluded because they are not required by the American economy.

Historical development of our immigration policy. When this country won its independence from England it had no immigration policy. Nor did there seem any need for formulating one. Until about 1876 the individual states were free to set up whatever local regulations they desired to restrict or encourage immigration across their borders. The national government saw no need for federal action.

Free immigration before the Civil War created racial and social problems that played an important part in American history. The great bulk of immigration in this period came from Ireland and Germany. A fairly large number came from Britain, and smaller numbers came from the Scandinavian countries, from Italy, and from Austria-Hungary. Nativism was a reaction of older Americans chiefly against the Irish immigrants, who were Catholics, and to a less extent against German immigrants, who were suspected of radicalism and of drinking too much lager beer on Sundays. Nativism was more than mere fulmination against "foreigners." It gave birth in the 1840s to local political parties that demanded a restriction of immigration, twenty-one years' residence for naturalization, and the limitation of office-holding to native Americans. This was hardly surprising in view of the fact that annual immigration jumped from 84,066 in 1840 to 369,980 in 1850. The chief causes of this were famine in Ireland and political persecution in Germany. The annual figure increased until it reached 427,833 in 1854.

Nativist feeling reached its climax in the 1850s in the organization of the Know-Nothing party. This party was successful in some state and local elections and attempted to run a presidential candidate in 1856. The Know-Nothing party's platform included a demand that paupers and criminals be denied admittance to the country, that public lands be sold only to citizens, that state laws permitting unnaturalized foreigners to vote be repealed, that twenty-one years' residence be required for naturalization, and that officeholding be restricted to Americans by "birth, education and training." None of these proposals was enacted into law.

Nativism seemed to disappear when the issues of the Civil War occupied men's minds, so that this first wave of anti-foreign feeling passed without leaving a deep permanent mark on America. Nevertheless, the annual number of immigrants increased steadily. In the two decades after the outbreak of the Civil War the annual figure varied from a low of 91,918 in 1861 to a high of 459,803 in 1873. In these twenty years slightly more than five million people emigrated to the United States, drawn by the economic opportunities of our expanding industrialism.

Before 1876 there was only one federal law relating to immigration: the act of 1819, which provided for assembling immigration statistics and established some regulations to protect steerage passengers crossing the Atlantic. Lack of federal legislation, however, encouraged immigration. Anyone who wanted to come to America and who managed to cross the Atlantic was allowed to enter. Railroad companies and other organizations wanting a large labor supply were free to recruit workers abroad and bring them into America. The immigrant then worked out his passage in the period of labor he had contracted to perform.

A Supreme Court decision of 1876 practically forced the federal government to pass measures regulating immigration. The Court declared unconstitutional state laws that taxed immigrants and the ships on which they came into the country. Such laws were construed by the Court as attempts to regulate foreign commerce, a function reserved by the Constitution to the federal government. In 1882 Congress passed the first general immigration law. Two policies were established by this law. The first was to collect a head tax from each immigrant. The second was to exclude undesirables from entry into the country. Undesirable were described as lunatics, idiots, criminals, and persons likely to become public charges.

Joseph Bulova, a Czech immigrant, developed highly efficient systems of manufacturing precision instruments on a large scale. (Bulova Watch Co.)

Subsequent legislation before World War I tended to follow these two policies, by increasing the head tax and enlarging the undesirable categories. The head tax increased from an original fifty cents to eight dollars. The law of 1891 excluded those who could not meet certain health standards, and it excluded polygamists as undesirable. Agitation by natives on the Pacific coast to exclude all Orientals as undesirables was only partly successful. After a new treaty between China and this country in 1880 it was possible to pass the Chinese Exclusion Act of 1882, whereby only teachers, students, travelers, and merchants of Chinese origin were allowed to enter the country.

Similar legislation could not constitutionally be passed against the Japanese because Japan refused to surrender its treaty rights by which Japanese were to receive equal treatment with the nationals of other countries. A literacy test had

William Knudsen came from Denmark to work in an American factory. Eventually he became president of one of the world's largest corporations. During World War II he directed production for the War Department. (General Motors Corp.)

been proposed in Congress as a means to exclude another class of "undesirables" —those who were not already educated. Although the bill passed through Congress several times it was killed by presidential veto, until in 1917 a nervous Congress mustered the necessary two-thirds majority to pass the literacy requirement over President Wilson's veto.

The annual waves of immigrants grew larger in the four decades before World War I. Five million arrived in the 1880s, and almost nine million came in the first decade of the twentieth century. In earlier years most of the immigrants came from western and northern Europe. After 1890 most of them came from the countries of southern and eastern Europe— Bulgars, Poles, Russians, Italians, whose names and languages made them much stranger and more foreign-sounding to the average American than were the Irish or the Germans. One result of this new and enlarged mass of immigrants was a

fresh wave of nativism, the American Protective Association of the 1890s and the revived Ku Klux Klan of the post-World War I era. Some people believed the new immigrants would "destroy our government . . . and divide our property." Others feared that the country simply could not absorb a million newcomers a year, and the clannish way in which the immigrants lived in large cities seemed to make the fear reasonable. Religious and racial bigotry also played a part in fomenting the new demands for further restrictive legislation.

World War I and immigration. This feeling was intensified by the nervous strain of participating in the World War, and it created the state of mind that made possible Congress's passing the Immigration Act of 1917 over presidential veto. Besides providing a literacy test for all over sixteen years of age, this act doubled the head tax of immigrants and excluded all natives from southeastern Asia by setting up an "Asiatic Barred Zone." No doubt a major cause of this act was the arrival here in 1914 of 1,218,480 persons, the largest number for any year in our history. Many were in flight from military service in Europe.

Immigration was limited by shipping facilities during the years immediately after the war, but by 1920 conditions in Europe made it apparent that a new wave of immigration would soon develop on a scale never seen before. Steamship agents were quoted in 1920 as saying that they could book passage for ten million immigrants if the space were available. The head tax and the policy of excluding undesirables were not sufficient to curtail immigration to the number that some believed the nation could absorb annually. Powerful groups, such as the American Legion, the American Federation of Labor, and the National Grange, demanded effective legislation to restrict or even stop immigration.

A number of restrictionist bills appeared in Congress, which passed as the Emergency Quota Act in May 1921. This act marked a turning point in American immigration policy. Formerly we had adopted the policy of freely admitting anyone who did not fall into one of the "undesirable" categories. The new policy restricted immigrants to a quota assigned to each country, the quota to be based on the number of persons of that nationality in our country at a given time in the past. The Emergency Quota Act of 1921 allowed the annual entry from each country of 3 per cent of the number of its nationals resident in the United States at the time the 1910 census was compiled. If all quotas were filled, a maximum of 357,000 immigrants would enter annually. Nevertheless, our official immigration statistics show that 403,001 persons entered in 1920 and 706,896 in 1924.

Since 1921 our policy has been to control immigration in two ways: (1) to restrict the total annual number through the quota arrangement; (2) to select the immigrants through various criteria of admissibility. Legislation since 1921 has consisted of a number of revisions of the quota system and several amendments to the exclusion provisions of the Immigration Act of 1917. A new quota Act of 1924 reduced the quotas from 3 per cent to 2 per cent of the base population elements in the country (thus reducing the total by one third) and assigned quotas on the basis of the 1890 census instead of the 1910 figure. This change gave larger quotas to the countries of northern and western Europe than to the countries from which most of the recent immigrants had come. That is, it provided for a preponderance of English, Irish, Scandinavians, and Germans. The northern and western countries of Europe had an annual quota of 125,853, whereas southern and eastern European countries were allotted 24,648. These quotas went into force in 1929.

Effect of economic depression. As a result of the revised quotas and of the great economic depression in our country, there was a sharp decrease in immigration from 1930 to 1935. The annual number dropped from 241,700 in 1930 to 34,956 five years later, and the allowed quotas were not filled. The northern and western European countries filled an average of 18 per cent of their quotas, and the other countries filled an average of 41 per cent. Doubtless the dismal outlook for economic advantage in the United States provides the explanation of these facts. The figures mounted rather sharply from 1936 to 1939, owing in part to the Nazi political persecutions in Germany and the danger of war in Europe. During this decade, of course, many thousands of immigrants came in from the countries of the Western Hemisphere that were not under quota limitation.

29. THE IMMIGRATION PROBLEM SINCE WORLD WAR II

Immigration tended to decline, naturally, during the war years of 1939–1945, but after 1945 the situation in Europe was such as to fill many quotas. The desolations of war and the hundreds of thousands of "displaced" persons from central-eastern Europe who because of political reasons would not or could not return to their own countries created one of the greatest of social problems. Where were they to go? Allowed to go where they wished, most of them would have elected to come to the United States, which appeared prosperous and unscarred by the war. But it was impossible for them to be admitted in great hordes, and the likelihood of their including some political subversives dictated a close screening process in filling up legal quotas. At length, in June 1948, Congress passed by voice vote and the President signed the Displaced Persons Act, which admitted 205,000 European displaced persons to the United States without regard to quotas.

McCarran-Walter Act. After long legislative hearings and study, Congress in 1952 passed the McCarran-Walter Act to bring our immigration law up to date. It stirred up a great deal of controversy. President Truman vetoed it, but his veto was overridden by Congress. Under the law, certain modifications have been made in quota admissions, although the basic national quota of the 1924 act remains unchanged. A small quota was extended to each of the Asiatic countries for the first time. Preference was given, up to half the quota for each country, for relatives of immigrants already dwelling in this country. This is a humane provision which aims at reuniting families. Preference is also given to those whom the Attorney General designates as urgently needed by the United States because of special skills or training that can be an asset to this country. The law drastically tightened up the screening process to guard against politically dangerous immigrants.

Criticism of the act. There has been widespread criticism of the McCarran-Walter Act on several different grounds. Some critics charge that it sets a limit far below the number of people we can absorb annally and need to maintain industrial leadership. Others have bitterly assailed the quota distributions, charging unfair discrimination against the peoples of southern and eastern Europe to the advantage of northern and western Europe, and even alleging a preference for Protestants over Catholics. It is true that the countries of Europe that have fallen under Communist domination in general are given quotas that are low in comparison with the number of American citizens whose stock originated in those countries. However, special legislation has allowed a large number to come in who were displaced persons, and by and large the annual quotas are about the same as the average annual numbers who came to

ANNUAL QUOTAS ALLOTTED AND QUOTA IMMIGRANTS ADMITTED BY QUOTA AREA—1954

QUOTA AREA	QUOTA	ADMITTED
Belgium	1,297	1,445
Denmark	1,175	1,128
France	3,069	3,044
Germany	25,814	28,361
Great Britain and Northern Ireland	65,361	21,092
Iceland	100	109
Ireland	17,756	5,169
Luxembourg	100	79
Netherlands	3,136	3,208
Norway	2,364	2,195
Sweden	3,295	1,803
Switzerland	1,698	1,634
TOTAL NORTHERN AND WESTERN EUROPE	125,165	69,267
Austria	1,405	1,056
Bulgaria	100	52
Czechoslovakia	2,859	2,005
Estonia	115	156
Finland	566	555
Greece	308	571
Hungary	865	801
Italy	5,645	6,042
Latvia	235	203
Lithuania	384	311
Poland	6,488	4,851
Portugal	438	496
Rumania	289	308
Spain	250	329
Turkey	225	190
U.S.S.R. (Russia)	2,697	1,887
Yugoslavia	933	778
Other southern and eastern Europe	700	332
TOTAL SOUTHERN AND EASTERN EUROPE	24,502	20,923
EUROPE—TOTAL	149,667	90,190
ASIA—TOTAL	2,990	3,286
AFRICA—TOTAL	1,400	350
OCEANIA—TOTAL	600	272
ALL QUOTA AREAS— TOTAL	154,657	94,098

this country during the 1930s. If the Greek and Italian quotas are smaller than is desired by the Greeks and Italians now in the United States, it should be remembered that the United States since 1945 has spent billions of dollars on the economic rehabilitation of Greece and Italy, and the relief of the peoples of these countries has been accounted for in other ways. Even so, Italy has the fifth largest quota; it is exceeded only by the British, German, Irish, and Polish quotas. The allotted number for Poland undoubtedly appeared so small as to be totally out of proportion, but this injustice promises to be corrected in some degree by the operation of the 1953 Refugee Immigration Act, which provides for the admission of 214,000 refugees in the succeeding three years. Many of these will be Poles unable or unwilling to return to their country, which is ruled by Communists. The carrying into effect of the 1953 act appears to have been slow, owing to the careful screening process. Two years after its enactment there was widespread criticism of this slowness.

Two general stands on the immigration question. People tend generally to take one stand or another in regard to immigration. One stand is restrictionist: that it is necessary to limit the number of immigrants severely or perhaps even to stop immigration altogether. The other stand is to increase immigration to as large a number as can possibly be absorbed by our economy and our American society. No one holds for letting in everyone, but the estimates of those opposed to tight restrictions is that we can absorb two to three times as many as the McCarran-Walter Act admits.

Arguments against increased immigration. Restrictionist arguments should be considered carefully. The government's primary responsibility is to provide for the common good of its citizens, and an immigration policy that ultimately hurts the common good is not defensible. In the

Alexander Graham Bell was a Scottish-born educator who invented a system of visible speech for deaf persons, as well as a modern necessity, the telephone. (Harris & Ewing)

past, labor leaders took a strong stand against free immigration. Their argument, briefly, was that unrestricted immigration furnished too large a supply of workers and thus lowered wages.

The effect of immigration on labor conditions is difficult to estimate. Many other factors enter into determining the workers' standard of living. We must remember that the government now sets minimum wages by law, regulates working conditions, and sets maximum hours that a laborer may work. Moreover, unions now bargain collectively for many employees. Thus there are few occupations held by the laboring class for which an individual worker bargains with an individual employer. But the labor argument against immigration assumes that neither the government nor the unions play any significant role in setting wages or working conditions. Close study of the problem does seem to show that there is this much to the labor argument against immigration: when unemployment is general, then a flood of immigrants does add to the number of unemployed. However, the very condition of unemploy-

Andrew Carnegie, Scottish-born bobbin boy in a cotton mill, rose to the head of Carnegie Steel Company. His "Gospel of Wealth" had as its keynote the idea that wealth was a "trust" to be administered for the public good. (U. S. Steel Corp.)

ment tends to discourage foreigners from coming to this country.

This leads us to another charge made against a generous immigration policy, the charge that immigrants in large numbers end up on relief rolls and thus become a burden to the taxpayer. Census statistics show that the percentage of unnaturalized Americans (immigrants who have not yet become citizens) receiving relief is only slightly higher than the percentage of native Americans in any given year. Moreover, twenty-three states require either citizenship or a long period of residence for old-age assistance, a fact that throws many immigrants on other forms of public relief. Finally, we should remember that under the law no immigrant is admitted if he cannot show that he is not liable to become a public charge, and if he does so within five years, he is automatically deportable.

In recent years labor leaders have taken a less severe stand in regard to immigration. Both the CIO and AFL leaders came to believe that the quota system set up in 1921 and subsequently modified gave labor more than enough protection. When hearings were conducted in 1946 by the House Committee on Immigration and Naturalization on a bill to cut quotas in half, CIO leader Leo Goodman testified:

Naturally, a labor organization representing 6,000,000 American workers would not be inclined to support measures which would threaten the job security of its own members. However, the CIO realizes, from past experience, that immigration is automatically checked in periods of unemployment while it rises in periods of prosperity; that in the past, immigrants have contributed in innumerable ways to the wealth and well-being of this country; that a large proportion of immigrants are not potential job seekers but women and children; that new blood in industry, agriculture, business, and professions enriches our national life; that the best and most enlightened thought on this subject opposes arbitrary, prejudiced, and superficial legislation to curtail immigration into the United States.

The AFL took a stand in favor of maintaining immigration quotas as set up in 1924. "The American Federation of Labor," its representative testified, "feels that we should maintain our present immigration quotas as an indication to the world that we intend to remain an active participant in world affairs, believing that to do otherwise, and especially to reduce our immigration quotas, would indicate that we are not willing to accept the responsibility of leadership." In the hearings of 1947 and 1948 both labor organizations favored the admission of large numbers of displaced persons outside the regular quotas.

Another argument advanced against a generous immigration policy can be stated in this way: Immigrants come to this country to get better jobs and enjoy the freedom we have preserved at great expense, but they refuse to shed their old attachments and really become Americans. Thus they set up "little Italies," "little Polands," "little Rumanias" in this country, expecting the protection of American law but refusing to be like other Americans. This is essentially the same argument used by nativists against the Irish immigrant in 1840 and against the German immigrant in 1917. Objective study of immigration suggests two lines of argument against this charge. There is no doubt that many immigrants do generally settle in more or less closed communities, "little Italies" and "little Polands," where they continue to speak Italian or Polish and practice their Old World customs. But this is a transitional stage in the process of naturalization.

Immigrants are Americans by choice, and they are generally anxious to become thoroughly American. But they cannot easily discard a way of life and a set of values with which they were raised. The children of immigrants are confronted with difficult social problems, as we shall see, but their grandchildren turn out to be as thoroughly American as the descendants of colonial stock. Schools, movies, and all the other things that form men's minds play a role in Americanizing the immigrant. The argument that immigrants do not really become Americans, therefore, applies only to those recent immigrants who are in the process of adapting themselves to their new home.

The strongest argument for a cautious and strictly limited immigration policy is from the standpoint of the danger of admitting too many persons who have had no previous experience of ordered liberty and government of the people, by the people, and for the people. Our political, legal, and civil institutions are complex. They are a growth of more than three hundred years, and back of that lie four or five centuries of English experience and development of institutions for safeguarding freedom. It is not easy for a person who has never known any kind of government but arbitrary tyranny to master the ways of civil life in the United States. It is not easy to shed overnight a natural preference for dictatorial government or a natural submission to it. Immigration policy should be kept always subordinate to the high interest of preserving the civil and political institutions of our country.

Arguments in favor of enlarging the immigration quotas. Most arguments for a more liberal immigration policy are reducible to three: (1) that we need more immigrants; (2) that immigrants have made sizable contributions to our culture and we can expect them to do so in the future; (3) that we have a moral duty to accept a fair share of those who must leave their present homelands.

The first of these arguments stresses our need for skilled technicians as well as a large number of laborers in order to maintain technological progress and to maintain a high living standard. This argument can be used to justify suspending or temporarily modifying our immigration quotas, but it does not seem to justify any basic change in policy. The argument of need, in other words, means that we should encourage immigration as long as we need certain kinds of skills that some immigrants possess—but no longer.

The second argument appeals to history. It points out that the economic contribution of the immigrant has been especially important. Imported Irish labor helped build the great railroad system that crossed America in the nineteenth century. Slav labor played a large part in doing the hard work in the steel mills. Germans and Scandinavians turned much of the Midwest into a rich farming area. Italians and Portuguese furnished a large part of the labor for the New England textile mills. In general, much of the hard work involved in building a rich America was performed by immigrants.

They have done more than this. They have been among the greatest of our inventors and our skilled technicians. Many leaders in industry, in the arts and sciences, were born abroad and emigrated to America. The list of such immigrants is long. In any list of industrialists, such names as these would be included: Andrew Carnegie (Scot) in the steel industry, John Jacob Astor (German) in the fur industry, Joseph Bulova (Czech) in watches, Charles Fleischmann (Hungarian) in yeast, William K. Knudsen (Dane) in the automobile industry. Any list of inventors would include Enrico Fermi (atomic power), John Ericsson (ironclad ship and screw propeller), David Lindquist (electric elevator), David Thomas (blast furnace), John Garand (Garand rifle), and Alexander Graham Bell (the telephone). These lists could be multiplied to show that immigrants made many individual contributions to American wealth and culture. Without them this would have been a poorer nation, materially and culturally—for much of our culture has been transplanted from Europe, and each generation of immigrants renews and enriches the contribution.

It therefore seems that immigration has been helpful to America in the past and that it would be unwise to restrict it unduly until it is shown that we are unable to absorb sizable numbers of additional immigrants each year.

The third argument—that we have a moral obligation to accept our share of displaced persons—is intimately interwoven into foreign relations, which we shall study later. Here it is enough to say that the obligation is binding in so far as immigration is not of such quality or quantity as to injure the welfare of American citizens. It is a matter of giving shelter and means of life to those who are in need and willing to work.

30. THE PROCESS OF IMMIGRATION AND NATURALIZATION

When a person desires to migrate to America to live he must apply to the

Future Americans are shown attending a citizenship class. Courses in American history and government, reading and writing, and English prepare them for their citizenship examination. (Board of Education, City of N. Y.)

American consul in the city nearest to his residence for a permanent visa. The American consul conducts a preliminary investigation as to the applicant's qualifications for American citizenship. If he is found to be unobjectionable he is placed on the waiting list, and when a place within the quota is found for him he is allowed to come to this country. Here he is examined by immigration officials and, if cleared, he is allowed to enter the country.

After entering the country the immigrant may file a declaration of intention to become an American citizen. He must wait five years, and then he may appear in court to obtain his citizenship papers. Meanwhile the Immigration Service again investigates the immigrant to determine whether he is likely to be a good American citizen. The Immigration Service then prepares a recommendation to a court of law. To obtain citizenship papers the immigrant must be able to read and speak English reasonably well and have a basic knowledge of American history

Youngsters in Old World Ukrainian costumes are shown absorbed in New World comic books while attending the Women's International Exposition in New York. (Wide World Photo)

and government. He must renounce all allegiance to the country of his birth, swear that he will be loyal to this country and be willing to bear arms in its defense. No one may become a citizen if he voluntarily belonged to a totalitarian party in the previous ten years or if he believes in the overthrow of the government by violence. The person who possesses the necessary qualifications and passes the tests administered by the court is then given his citizenship papers.

The problems of the immigrant. Socially, the immigrant finds Americanization more difficult. Immigrants are American by choice, but they frequently find it difficult to renounce the old way of doing things in favor of the American way. For immigrants from non-English-speaking countries, language is often a great difficulty. Thus the process of assimilation is slowed down. It is easier for the immigrant to accept the big changes in his life than the little day-to-day alterations.

A study of how a group of displaced persons settled down in St. Louis is revealing.[2] The study revealed that within five years the group had made a successful economic adjustment. They had good jobs, and many (28 per cent) of them had bought their own homes. Eight of the

[2] Rev. John C. Reed, S.J., "DP's Find Homes," *Social Order,* October 1954.

twenty-five who had married since coming to this country had married Americans. Most of them had purchased something or other on the installment plan. Of the 221 interviewed, 219 said they intended to become citizens; the other two left the question unanswered. On the whole, then, this group adjusted quickly to American living. But difficulties were encountered. Language came first among these difficulties, then came difficulty with some of our laws and customs—such things as the way people greet on meeting, the way American children act toward their elders, and the red tape encountered in getting a loan. One immigrant who married an American girl found his most difficult adjustment was getting used to washing the dishes, but this could hardly have been his duty!

The immigrant, then, is forced to change his pattern of living when he comes to America, and the best intentions in the world cannot eliminate the difficulties involved in this adjustment. The children of immigrants also face social difficulties. They attend school with children of American stock. The standards of behavior, the norms of judgment, everything is determined by the Amer-

Jacob August Riis, Danish-born immigrant, implemented social welfare by his use of newspaper campaigns to effect the clearance of New York slums. (Library of Congress)

ican children and their parents. The immigrant's child usually feels embarrassed because his parents speak English badly or because they seem to act awkwardly with other people. He tends to repudiate the culture his "foreign" parents represent. He wants to be as "American" as the child of native parents.

Frequently the immigrant's child finds himself in social difficulties. His parents may keep much of the culture of the country from which they came, and they can live contentedly in this country even if they are not accepted socially by native Americans. The child, even though abandoning his parents' culture, frequently finds that Americans still look down on him socially. He is not fully accepted in the country in which he was born. As a result, the child of immigrants is sometimes hostile to American society.

The solving of personal difficulties by each immigrant is a story of long-range success interrupted by occasional failure. Immigration as a national problem, of course, is the sum total of these daily problems of adjustment faced each day by each immigrant. From the national point of view the problems can be looked at geographically, politically, and economically.

Geographically, immigrants tend to settle in certain parts of the country. Certain cities and states are therefore faced with the immediate, practical problem of absorbing immigrants, whereas other localities are affected only remotely by the problem. Six states have consistently had the largest alien population: New York (24 per cent), California (14 per cent), Texas (7 per cent), Michigan (6 per cent), New Jersey (5 per cent), and Massachusetts (5 per cent). Three out of every five immigrants settled in a large city, and most of the remainder settled in urban areas larger than 25,000. The problem of absorbing the immigrant, therefore, is largely an urban problem, and it is most general in states along the coast and in Michigan.

Politically, the problem is to adjust the immigrant to American civil life and to make him a participating citizen. Naturalized citizens (like many native Americans) tend to support the party and the candidate who promise to do the most for them. Because they are not accustomed to the way our parties operate, they have frequently been the prey of unscrupulous politicians. Most states have enacted legislation to curb these abuses, but the immigrant citizen remains a voter who is less likely than the native American to understand the spirit of American party politics. His is more likely, therefore, to be the raw voting material on which the political machine feeds.

Economically, the immigrant's position in American life is varied. Today, as in the past, some of our most skilled technicians and some of our best scholars have come from abroad. Many able professors in our American universities were born abroad. But the great mass of immigrants occupy the same position economically that their predecessors have throughout American history. They live in the cities and they furnish the manual labor required in factories and mills in urban areas. This is a generalization, of course, for there are thousands of skilled tradesmen among the recent immigrants. There are some farmers and there are some businessmen.

Preference has been given to the farm laborer and to certain skills needed in America today. But studies of recent immigrants show that the farmers and members of the professional and managerial class tend to migrate to the cities, where they take laboring jobs. In the study of immigrants to St. Louis, for example, of the sixty-two farmers who came to this country, only eight were still farmers after five years. Although only eight entered the country as unskilled workers, after five years there were sixty-five in this class. Of the nineteen who entered as professional or managerial persons, only nine were still in this class after five years.

Expelling the undesirable alien. The federal government reserves the right, as it must, to expel any immigrant who proves that he will not make a good citizen. This right is stated in the Internal Security Act of 1950 and in the McCarran-Walter Act of 1952. By these laws the Attorney General is empowered to deport any alien engaged in or intending to engage in activities "prejudicial to the public interest." No definitions are given to limit the Attorney General's power. No proof of guilt is required. No provision for a hearing is made. In effect, the alien has no civil rights and may be deported without ever being informed of the charges made against him. Such a procedure is hardly consistent with our free institutions. Because the government is not required to prove guilt against the immigrant it wishes to deport, its power can be and has been exercised in painful and unjust ways.

More than three hundred immigrants have been deported or subjected to denaturalization hearings in the first year and a half of the Eisenhower administration. Because the Supreme Court has ruled that sovereignty gives the government the legal right to fix qualifications for citizenship, the immigrant does not enjoy any civil rights the government does not choose to give him. The President's Commission on Immigration reported in 1953 that the McCarran-Walter Act "fails to conform to the generally accepted standards for fair hearings." In almost identical words Archbishop Cushing testified before the commission that this law "fails to provide for an independent, fair hearing for people who are threatened with denaturalization and deportation." Archbishop Cushing advised that the law "should be amended to purge it of several un-Christian and un-American provisions."

Conclusion. Most of the critics of the present immigration law agree on the following points: (1) That we can absorb a larger number of immigrants than are now permitted to enter the country annually. It would therefore be in our interest—both to promote our prestige abroad and build our strength at home—to admit more immigrants than we now do. (2) That we should abolish or revise drastically our quota system. That any revised quota system should allocate visas without regard to national origin, race, creed, or color. That any other system is unworthy of America and is ultimately prejudicial to our interests and our ideals. (3) That we should improve our deportation proceedings in order to provide a system of fair hearings in which the accused would have the opportunity of defending himself against specific charges made against him. (4) That steps should be taken to make easier the process of naturalization from beginning to end. Such steps should involve preparing the immigrant for the America he is to enter before he leaves home, explaining

American customs more thoroughly to him during the course of his first years in this country and setting up additional agencies to help him in his difficulties. Such action could best be performed by non-governmental agencies such as church-affiliated organizations, civic clubs, or perhaps the American Legion —patriotic organizations that wish to help Americans-by-choice become good American citizens.

In his veto of the McCarran-Walter Act, President Truman observed: "I am sure that with a little more discussion in this country, the public conscience and the good sense of the American people will assert themselves, and we shall be in a position to enact an immigration and naturalization policy that will be fair to all." Such a policy cannot result from a reckless throwing open of our doors. It must result from calm deliberation, which gives rise to legislation made in a spirit of justice and generosity, and for the primary purpose of promoting the welfare and preserving the institutions of our Republic.

REVIEW

27. The Nature of Society and the Growth of Population
A. Why is man social? What are the principal ways in which man has grouped together into social organizations?

B. How are Americans geographically a fluid people? How do new industries affect population?

C. What was Malthus' theory? How has history treated this? How accurate were the prophecies of the demographers?

D. Why must the theories of the Neo-Malthusians be rejected? Explain three factors that must be kept in mind in this regard.

28. Problems and Policies of Immigration
A. State several general principles in regard to immigration problems.

B. What was the policy of the United States before 1876? What problems were brought about by this policy?

C. What changed our immigration policy in 1876? Summarize important immigration legislation before 1921.

D. After 1921 the United States instituted the quota system for immigration. Describe this system. Why was it said to be discriminatory?

29. The Immigration Problem Since World War II
A. What was the purpose of the Displaced Persons Act?

B. The McCarran-Walter Act of 1952 codified our immigration laws. Cite some of the main provisions of the act. Why has it been criticized? What later act has been passed?

C. Summarize the two main, current views on immigration. What is labor's present position? Why? What is the argument concerning slow assimilation?

D. List the arguments and reasons of those who desire more immigration.

30. The Process of Immigration and Naturalization
A. Describe the steps required for naturalization.

B. Briefly describe some of the problems of the immigrant. Where do most immigrants settle?

C. Show how the undesirable alien is expelled. Why is the present method objectionable?

D. On what points do present critics of our policy agree?

THE CHAPTER IN REVIEW
A. What are the errors of the Malthusian theory? Note particularly the moral aspect of this theory.

B. In the nineteenth century there were many problems concerning immigrants. Discuss the social, economic, political, and religious aspects of these problems.

C. The following periods were important in regard to legislation for immigration: the 1880s, the 1920s, and 1952. Summarize the immigration laws of these periods and show how legislation has become more restrictive in regard to immigration.

D. An immigrant is faced with many problems. List some of these problems and the solutions offered for them.

SELECTED READINGS

Bishop Haas, *Man and Society,* and Eva J. Ross, *Basic Sociology,* suggested in the reading list for Chapter 1, develop points covered in this chapter. Also useful is Rev. Raymond W. Murray, C.S.C., *Introductory Sociology* (New York: F. S. Crofts & Company, 1946).

The Neo-Malthusian view of population problems is frequently written about in Catholic journals. Among the more recent studies are the following: an editorial, "Pope Pius XII on Population," *America* (October 9, 1954); an editorial, "Catholics and Population Problems," *Commonweal* (July 9, 1954); James Vizzard, S.J., "Our Growing Population," *Social Order* (September 1951), an excellent study of population experts and the 1950 census; J. B. Kelley, "Too Many People?", *Catholic World* (June 1954); L. T. King, "Over-population, Fact or Fallacy?", *Catholic World* (December 1948); and C. J. Enzler, "Overpopulation Bogey," *Sign* (November 1948).

The standard survey of immigration in this country is G. M. Stephenson, *A History of American Immigration,* 1820–1924 (Boston: Ginn & Company, 1926). The same material is covered in more popular fashion and with strong sympathy for the immigrant by Carl Wittke, *We Who Built America* (New York: Prentice-Hall, Inc., 1939). The process of assimilation is handled well by Thomas J. Woofter, *Races and Ethnic Groups in American Life* (New York: McGraw-Hill Book Co, 1933), and in somewhat more informal fashion by Bertram Schrieke, *Alien Americans* (New York: The Viking Press, Inc., 1936), and William C. Smith, *Americans in the Making* (New York: D. Appleton-Century Company, Inc., 1939). The contributions of immigrants to American life have been related enthusiastically by Louis Adamic in *A Nation of Nations* (New York: Harper & Brothers, 1947), and by A. H. Eaton, *Immigrant Gifts to American Life* (New York: Russell Sage Foundation, 1932). The problem of alien rights and deportation is thoroughly analyzed by Milton R. Konvitz, *Civil Rights in Immigration* (Ithaca, N.Y.: Cornell University Press, 1953).

Both sides of the current controversy over the McCarran-Walter Act are presented in *Immigration: An American Dilemma,* edited by Benjamin Munn Ziegler as one of the Problems in American Civilization Series (Boston: D. C. Heath & Company, 1953). Most of the arguments for and against our current immigration policy found in Clarence A. Peters (editor), *The Immigration Problem* (New York: H. W. Wilson Co., 1948), are still current. The discussion on the American Forum of the Air program by Senator Paul Douglas and Congressman F. E. Walter is available in pamphlet form, *Is the McCarran-Walter Immigration Law Fair?* (Washington: Ransdell, Inc., 1953). The position taken by the National Catholic Welfare Conference and most bishops is given by Msgr. John O'Grady, "Christian Immigration Policy," *Catholic Mind* (August 1952), and the same author's "Number 1 Problem: Immigration," *America* (January 10, 1953).

PROJECTS

1. An interesting study can be made of the population growth in your own town. Draw up a chart showing the population changes in your town, state, and in the nation. Is your community matching the growth of the nation? Use the years 1930, 1940, 1950, and, if possible, the present year for your chart, and report your findings to the class. What reasons can be offered for the rate of growth of your town?

2. It would be well to note the vast scientific changes that have helped to increase the world's food supply in the last thirty years. A class committee can select several items common to the dinner table and determine how advances in science have affected the production, supply, and cost of these items.

3. To grasp the true problem of immigration, we should observe it at its peak and note the variations of other years. Examine the immigration statistics for each ten-year period beginning with 1800 and account for the periods of major increase and decline by supplying reasons that would encourage or discourage immigration into the United States.

"GIVE ME YOUI
YOUR HUDDLED MASSE
THE WRETCHED REFUSE O:
SEND THESE, THE HOMELES
I LIFT MY LAMP BESII

Chapter 12. Relations of Racial, Cultural, and Religious Groups

31. OUR CULTURAL PLURALISM

Because the United States originated historically in the British colonies of North America and, in expanding, carried wide the English language and legal and civic institutions of British origin, the dominant culture of our country is that of the English-speaking peoples. It became distinctively American yet never was torn completely loose from its origins. In becoming American, it absorbed many elements from peoples of non-British origin, so that even the "American language" came to differ from English.

When our nation was formed, the great majority of the citizens were white or Caucasion in race (English, Irish, Scottish, Dutch, Swedish, German), Protestant in religion, and English-speaking. The next largest racial element was the Negroes, whose ancestral home was in Africa and who were almost all slaves. After the Negroes came the Indians, numerically. There were very few Jews. Although Catholics had played the leading role in the early explorations of the Mis-

sissippi Valley and the Southwest, those regions had not yet been incorporated in the union of states. Only Maryland and Pennsylvania had then a sizable number of Catholics, but these were in a minority of the whole population of those states. Most Americans seem to have assumed that our country was a predominantly white, Protestant Christian, and English-speaking country, although even then it was "pluralistic" in its racial, cultural, and linguistic character.

Today, although "American" English is still the dominant language and our civic and political institutions have undergone no fundamental change, the country has become much more pluralistic in racial, cultural, and religious composition. A great number of our people are now of Polish, German, French-Canadian, Russian, Lithuanian, Italian, and Spanish-Mexican cultural origins. The Negroes are free and have civic equality with the whites. There are five million Jews. Although probably a majority of Americans belong to or have a background in the Protestant religious de-

IRED, YOUR POOR,
EARNING TO BREATHE FREE,
OUR TEEMING SHORE.
HE TEMPEST-TOST TO ME,
HE GOLDEN DOOR!"

nominations, the Catholic Church has become far and above the largest religious body in the country. Almost one fifth of the American people today belong to the Catholic Church. These developments, coming along with the industrialization of the country and the increase of the population, give rise to many problems in racial, cultural, and religious relations.

The distinctively American (and Christian) solution to problems that arise between racial, religious, and cultural groups in our pluralist society assumes as an ideal that all groups should be treated freely and equally, that none should be made to conform to a single pattern or be so thoroughly mixed as to lose their identity. To deny Indians, for example, the right to maintain their distinctive culture and to force them to be like other "Americans" is worse than a failure to solve the Indian problem. It is a positive injustice, a cultural totalitarianism, to force them to "mix" into American society. To mix cultural, racial, or religious groups forcibly is not in the American tradition, nor is it a Christian solution to the problems. Segregation practices in this country have been wrong only because they have been discriminative and harsh.

Many problems in intergroup relations are largely the result of bad manners, ig-norance, and ill temper. The problems are sometimes legal or constitutional, but generally the root of the trouble is to be found in lack of charity and mutual understanding among the various groups. They spring from a lack of tolerance of cultures other than our own and a lack of understanding of the very nature of our American pluralist society. Unless Americans respect the various cultures and religions and races in their midst, problems that arise from such group relations will become more difficult.

In his first encyclical Pope Pius XII spoke of

a marvelous vision which makes us see the human race in the unity of one common origin in God, "one God and Father of all, who is above all and in us all"; in the unity of human nature, which in every man is equally composed of material body and spiritual, immortal soul; in the unity of the immediate end and the mission in the world; in the unity of dwelling place, the earth, of whose resources all men by natural right avail themselves to sustain life and develop life; in the unity of the supernatural end, God Himself, to whom all should tend; in the unity of means to secure that end.

From its beginning our country accepted something like this "marvelous vision" of which the Pope speaks, although many Americans have often failed to live up to the ideal it held forth. We have seen that the Declaration of Independence was based on principles of equality and of natural rights and that American ideals included the principles of justice and freedom for all. The Constitution and the Bill of Rights contain guarantees for these ideals.

Unfair prejudice. Sociologists who have studied group prejudice tell us that it is a very complicated matter. It almost always involves mistaken judgments by people of one group about those of another. Such judgments are based not on factual knowledge but on hearsay, hasty generalizations, incorrect conclusions, and, most of all, lack of understanding of the problem. Typical of mistaken judgment is the statement that by heredity Negroes are mentally inferior to whites, and therefore it is a mistake to try to provide higher education for them. Another typical mistaken and prejudiced assertion is that Catholics cannot be loyal Americans because they recognize the religious authority of the Pope.

Plain ignorance still accounts for considerable unfair prejudice. Probably there are still some Americans who believe that Jews have concocted a scheme to overthrow governments throughout the world, and some still believe that Catholics are somehow bound to a "medieval institution" and will overthrow the Constitution and establish the Inquisition if they become numerous enough to impose their will on the nation. There has been a general decrease of such prejudice based on plain ignorance about various racial and religious groups in the country. Nevertheless, genuine understanding of various groups' positions is still far from achieved by most Americans. Only the best-educated Protestants, for example, understand the Catholic doctrine of papal infallibility or the American Catholics' stand on the church-state problem. If there were genuine understanding of these things, prejudiced attacks on the Catholic Church would make little or no appeal.

A second element in prejudice is termed "deviant will attitudes" by the sociologist. This means that prejudiced people are willfully unjust in their approach to other groups. It is a matter of bad will. It results largely from the desire of many people to find a group on whom they can place the blame for their own shortcomings. Prejudice against the Negro, for example, is found to be most intense among those whites who fear that the Negro will compete with them economically if discriminations are removed. A recent study of prejudice found that tension between racial and cultural groups was uniformly more severe when economic insecurity was involved.

Prejudice operates in a most complicated way to create conditions on which it justifies itself in its own eyes. A racial or cultural group suffering from discrimination tends to develop what might be called "ghetto traits," which set them off from the rest of American society. For example, when Jews are excluded from the country clubs and other social organizations in a community, they are forced to form their own clubs and organizations. When they do this they are accused of clannishness, and the original prejudice seems to be justified. The Negro who has received a good education and is qualified in every way for a good position in industry finds in some regions of society that when his color is discovered on the application blank he must take an "adaptability" test which he invariably "fails." Eventually he ends up running an elevator or handling freight. White people who are prejudiced against Negroes then tell each other that an education is wasted on a Negro because even college graduates end up running elevators. Meanwhile the Negro graduate becomes surly and resentful of the society that discriminates against him because of his color. If such surliness is manifested in the Negro's behavior with white people, the prejudiced white people then decide that all an education does for Negroes is to make them resentful and surly. It is better, they conclude, that Negroes stay in their "natural" place. Thus prejudice increases by feeding on its results, and it seems to justify itself as it grows.

Development of anti-social attitudes. Cultural and racial groups which suffer from prejudice and discriminative treatment sometimes tend to develop anti-social qualities. This is often the unfortunate result of the poverty to which prejudice condemns many in these groups. But the group does not thereby entirely escape blame for its anti-social attitudes. Leaders of these groups can improve group relations by working among their own people to remove the anti-social traits which seem to justify prejudice.

Statistics reveal that cultural and racial groups suffering from discrimination commit more than their share of crimes, such as robbery, assault, and murder. There is more juvenile delinquency among such groups, and their children receive less education. Moreover, they tend to develop bad manners—which a highly integrated society such as ours can ill afford to tolerate.

A little reflection on this sad situation reveals that its cause is not racial. The grinding poverty and the terrible living conditions to which Negroes are condemned in the rural South and in most northern cities naturally lead to malnutrition, lack of education, lack of moral instruction. Abject poverty leads to social

Booker T. Washington (Library of Congress)

and financial irresponsibility. The sub-human living conditions of Puerto Ricans in New York are conducive to sub-human, anti-social actions. Any group living under similar circumstances and suffering from similar discrimination would behave badly.

The harm to society. The mistreatment of racial and cultural groups has a bad effect on all society, on those who belong to the so-called white majority as well as on those suffering from discrimination. Society as a whole suffers when the talents and the abilities of people in "minority" groups are not fully developed. The nation loses the contributions that might have been made by members of racial and cultural groups suffering from discrimination. Who knows how many potential Booker T. Washingtons shined shoes or picked cotton for life because of discrimination against the Negro?

As we suggested in the chapter on civil rights, discrimination against "minorities" has hurt American reputation abroad. The lynching of a Negro in Louisiana or the bombing of a Negro's house in Chicago is given more attention in Paris or Moscow than in Louisiana or Chicago.

Finally, and perhaps most important, prejudice and discrimination against any group has a moral effect on the rest of the population. It corrodes their conscience and develops a moral callousness. It debases our manners, our good taste, and our sense of honor.

General Benjamin O. Davis, highly decorated Air Force officer, is shown receiving his brigadier general's star, the first Negro so honored. His father was the first Negro officer in the United States Army. (Air Force Photo)

Race relations between white people and Negroes have frequently been called America's number-one social problem. Study of this problem soon reveals that it breaks down into several distinct problems. There are approximately fifteen million Negroes in the United States today, about half of whom live in rural areas in the South. They are mostly tenant farmers or sharecroppers whose income is miserably low. Connected with the racial problem in the South and forming part of it, then, are such problems as tenant farming, sharecropping, and the poverty associated with this way of life.

In the last four decades Negroes have been moving northward and westward in large numbers. The Negro population of the South increased only a fraction of 1 per cent in the decade between 1940 and 1950, but the national total of Negroes showed a growth of 15.8 per cent. Negroes leaving the South tend to settle in larger northern cities such as Chicago, Detroit, and St. Louis. The problems connected with race relations between whites and Negroes in the cities center around poor housing, segregation in the schools, entertainment, and various forms of social discrimination. It will suffice for our purpose in discussing the Negro problem in America to keep two principal problems in mind: (1) that of Negro-white relations in the South, which is largely rural; (2) that of relations between the two groups in large cities throughout the rest of the country, which are largely but not exclusively northern.

The development of the Negro problem is familiar to all of us who have read American history. Whereas other immigrants came here freely, the Negro was captured in Africa, shipped to this country, and sold on the slave block upon his entry into the land of the free. From the beginning, America was for the Negro, the land of the slave owner, and the overseer. By 1860 there were about four million Negroes in this country, and only a tiny fraction of them were free. The great majority lived severely restricted lives. They were exploited for the forced labor on which plantation owners believed their cotton economy depended.

Official national policy toward the Negro changed drastically and suddenly with the Emancipation Proclamation of 1863 and with the North's victory in the Civil War. The Fourteenth and Fifteenth Amendments were, in effect, terms of the peace imposed on the South by the North. They were constitutional guarantees that the Negro should enjoy the same rights and freedoms as the white man. No preparatory steps had been taken to make the Negro's transition from slavery to freedom a smooth one socially, politically, and economically. Since neither white nor Negro was prepared to live according to the Thirteenth and Fourteenth Amendments, and since they were passed against popular feeling in

Champions in the sports world are helping to dissolve racial and religious prejudice in this country. This victorious basketball team of Duquesne University, a Catholic men's college, is an excellent example.

the South, the national policy they embraced was not realized in fact. When "white supremacy" was re-established in 1877, Southerners knit together a social, legal, economic, and educational system devised to "keep the Negro in his place." These codes were rigidly enforced. No white man who desired social standing in the community dared violate the "black code" of the community.

Details of the code differed from state to state, but essentially it was the same everywhere. Negroes were deprived of the vote by various subterfuges, such as poll taxes, "educational" requirements, and "grandfather clauses" (that no one might vote unless his grandfather voted, which eliminated all Negroes). Thus they were excluded from political life. They were discriminated against economically. Negroes were restricted to menial jobs and to farming. They were forced to use separate—and terribly inferior—restaurants, buses, trains, theaters, and all other social facilities. They were kept in their own churches and not allowed to attend school with white children. The code worked successfully; it kept the Negro in an inferior position from which he could not rise of his own efforts. The Constitution said he was legally the equal of the white man. But American society said he was not. All political experience shows that no constitutional provision can be enforced unless it is accepted by society.

In the North the Negro suffered from discrimination and forced segregation that were legally less severe than in the South but in fact were sometimes more severe and harsh. No one in the North felt the same social responsibility for the Negro that better people felt in the South. The Negro was allowed to fend for himself, with the result that he was exploited by the northern landlord and factory owner. He was forcibly segregated in slums, kept out of respectable hotels, schools, restaurants, churches, and hospitals. Meanwhile he was to be reminded that he had been set free from his master.

The progress of the Negro. The history of the American Negro since 1877 is the story of his gradual attainment of the constitutional privileges to which he is legally entitled. For a considerable time progress was slow, for prejudice dies hard. The Negro could do little to help himself. Without help from white groups he could change the system only by armed revolt—which takes money, organization, and leadership. A few white groups took up the Negro's cause. A long series of decisions by the Supreme Court declared unconstitutional one form of discrimination after another. Two wars and booming industry enabled the Negro to find better jobs and to live in places where the "black code" was not rigidly enforced.

In the years since 1940 the Negro has made progress that would have been unbelievable at any previous time in our history. Each gain has been small, but all the gains add up to a significant progress. Negroes were admitted to boxing and to big-league baseball, for example, and one by one good hotels and restaurants began to accept their patronage. Restrictions against Negro doctors practicing in general hospitals were quietly dropped in large cities such as Indianapolis and St. Louis. A number of Negroes were elected to state legislatures; others were appointed to political positions. More recently the segregation of Negroes was ended in the Army and the Air Force.

Not less important in the long run, perhaps, are the Supreme Court decisions which reversed the long accepted theory that "separate but equal" facilities were sufficient to implement the Fourteenth and Fifteenth Amendments. The reasoning behind these decisions, as we have seen, is not that segregation itself is wrong but that forced segregation is bound to be discriminative. At the present time, segregation in interstate transportation is virtually forbidden by Court decisions. Segregation in publicly maintained higher education was prohibited by a series of decisions. Finally, as we saw in the chapters on education, in May of 1954 the Supreme Court declared that forced segregation in public education on any level was unconstitutional. Discrimination against the Negro worker has been lessened by the federal government's withholding contracts from companies that practice such discrimination.

These have been great gains in solving the Negro problem. They have been made in remarkably short time and with a minimum of friction. The natural impatience of some Negroes in improving their housing conditions, in getting better jobs, and in securing real equality of education has resulted in local situations that sometimes slow up the solving of this problem.

Present position of Negroes. Let us try to describe the Negro's position in America in 1955. Southern states have on their statute books a code of laws that are under constant review in the Supreme Court, and several of them are declared unconstitutional each year. In general, they forbid intermarriage between Negroes and whites; they provide for separate education of the races, separate waiting rooms, restaurants, hotels, and other public facilities in which contact might be made between the races. Social contacts are forbidden by city ordinances and county custom, and the laws are enforced on the grounds of preventing "disorderly conduct" or "vagrancy."

This is the general picture, but a closer inspection reveals a few more examples to illustrate the present conditions. Court decisions have outlawed segregation in Pullmans, dining cars, and interstate coach travel. Most trains carry a coach to which the Negroes are directed, but a persistent Negro can sit where he pleases with little likelihood of being ejected. On buses segregation is universal, even though it is illegal in interstate travel. Libraries, however, are generally unsegregated. Most professions have separate

societies for Negroes, but a few of the national societies admit both Negroes and white members. We can conclude, then, that segregation is general in the South but it is not complete.

Segregation is not easily ended, nor is it always undesirable. In some activities it is perfectly proper for Negroes to group together to the exclusion of whites, and vice versa. What is unjust is the discriminative and harsh segregation that has been forced on the Negro in the South and—in different ways—in the North. For segregation is not confined to the South. In northern cities Negroes are generally confined to one or more sections of the city. In recent decades they have managed to move out of these sections in some cities, but not in others. Custom and education tend to confine the Negro to certain jobs. Negroes are never hired as clerks in stores that cater to white customers, for example, but they run elevators and serve as deliverymen in the same stores. With rare exceptions, Negro doctors and lawyers are compelled by social pressure to restrict their practices to Negro clientele.

This subtle discrimination is practiced throughout the country. It is frequently more a matter of custom than of true prejudice. Many otherwise fair-minded people have so long been accustomed to think of the Negro as moving only in certain spheres of life that they regard menial work as his rightful place and are shocked when he tries to move "out of his place." Many people with no real prejudice are not shocked at the racial discrimination in the crime reporting of many American newspapers, which identify criminals by the word "Negro" if he is a member of the Negro race, but do not identify others as "white."

Effects of discrimination. Americans are so accustomed to this kind of discrimination that many do not recognize it. But the combination of subtle prejudice and discriminative segregation has its effect on the Negro. Only one possessing heroic virtue can save himself from bitterness and cynicism about the land of the free in which he lives. Unfortunately it is the best-educated and most intelligent Negroes who suffer the most, because they would be able to rise socially and economically if it were not for racial discrimination. One reaction of the Negro has been to slide across the color line whenever the opportunity presents itself. Accurate statistics are not available on how many light-skinned Negroes slide into the white population annually, but the number is considerable.

Frequently these persons create for themselves a set of difficult social problems, especially when they are rejected by their own people as deserters and not accepted by the white population with which they hope to be identified. Occasional intermarriage between Negroes and white persons also creates a serious social problem that must be faced with heroic courage to prevent such marriages from being a failure. These are the individual problems—each one a serious problem in itself—that millions of Americans face daily because of the social barriers that white people have erected against Negroes in American society.

One of the most serious but perhaps least noticed results of discriminative segregation is the effect it has on family life. In rural areas the high cost of marriage licenses and the Negro's aversion to the white man's court make common-law marriage a normal thing. Working conditions—cotton picking and crop gathering—require the labor of both men and women. As a result the grandmother tends to become the dominant, stabilizing influence in the rural Negro home. The father's position suffers from his inability to support the family by his own labor. In cities the oldest boy tends to assume headship of the family because he "knows his way about." He becomes the tutor and guide of the younger children

as the father is pushed into the background. In similar fashion, the girl tends to emancipate herself at an early age from her mother's control as she learns white people's ways. Thus parental control and guidance for the children are weakened dangerously at an early age.

The Indian problem. The American Indians are a cultural group which presents problems considerably different from the typical cultural-relations problem in this country. This follows from the fact that their history differs from that of the immigrant cultural groups. The Indians were the original inhabitants of this country, and from the very beginning a bitter warfare developed between the white settlers and the Indian inhabitants. Indians found that their way of life, based on a hunting, pastoral, and nomadic economy, was broken up by the white man's farm and personal, permanent ownership of the land. The Indians resisted the white man's advance westward, and they therefore came to be regarded as the enemies of civilization. Whereas the Spanish Goverment grappled with the problem of converting and "hispanizing" the Indian, the English generally adopted the simpler solution of exterminating him or driving him into the wilderness.

About the middle of the nineteenth century our national policy in regard to the Indian changed from one of simple extermination ("the only good Indian is a dead Indian") to one of isolation and concentration. The Indians were allotted certain lands (reservations) where they were to live apart from the white settlers, who were free to take the remaining lands. This policy was harshly enforced. When farmers, ranchers, or miners discovered that land reserved for the Indians was valuable, the Indians were dispossessed and moved to some poorer territory. That is why President Hayes indicted American treatment of the Indian in these words: "When the Indians had settled upon land assigned to them by

Primitive living conditions are vividly shown in this winter scene on a Navajo Indian Reservation. The plight of the Indian is not generally this severe, but the Indian problem will require the attention of our government for many years. (Dept. of the Interior)

compact and began to support themselves by their own labor, they were rudely jostled off and thrust into the wilderness again. Many, if not most, of our Indian Wars have had their origin in broken promises and acts of injustice on our part."

Our Indian policy was revised basically by the Dawes Act of 1887. This act permitted the division of the tribal reservation into family farms, each Indian to own his own farm as private property. His children were to be educated in government schools. Citizenship was to be awarded to those Indians who applied and who had sufficiently "Americanized" themselves. This law was apparently based on a naïve view of the "acculturation" process, and it assumed that a modicum of education and good will could transform an Indian into an "American."

This attempt to force the Indian into our common cultural and social pattern was not successful. Indian children were forced to give up family customs and tribal languages. They were educated as though they were "little New Yorkers" or "little Philadelphians." The result was a tragic failure—for the Indian child educated this way was a lost person, neither an integral Indian nor an integral "American." Economically the Indians fared worse. The Indians lost more than 100,000,000 acres of their privately owned land to speculators and buyers. Most of their remaining land was close to worthless, although some tribes held onto valuable oil, timber, and mineral lands.

In the 1920s our government adopted a new policy for gradually Americanizing the Indians. This task was entrusted to the Office of Indian Affairs in the Department of the Interior. Indians who are judged competent are given full property rights, but the government continues to act as legal guardian for the others. In 1924 full citizenship was conferred on all Indians, and serious attempts were made to improve their condition, to revive their crafts, and to find markets for their products. Recent education has not tried to impose the white man's civilization on the Indian but to teach him how to take care of himself. Most Indians still live on reservations, but there has been an accelerated tendency for the younger members of the tribe to move off the reservation and to melt into American society.

Present position of the Indians. Today there are about 350,000 Indians owning about 56,000,000 acres of land. They are found chiefly in the Southwest and in the Dakotas. Arizona had 65,761 Indians in 1950, Oklahoma 53,769, New Mexico 41,901, and South Dakota 23,344. Indians are scattered in small numbers in every state in the Union.

A move to terminate federal protection of the Indian's separate culture came to a head in 1952. More than a hundred bills nominally designed to "free" the Indian were introduced in the Eighty-third Congress. Proponents of termination legislation argue that by ending federal services and breaking up reservations they will "emancipate" the Indian and force him to become a "first-class" citizen. Opponents of these bills insist that termination of federal protection must come about slowly and that it should not be accomplished until the Indians are integrated into American society. Moreover, they maintain, it should not be accomplished by force. Indians should be left free to maintain their own culture, to hold land in common on reservations, and to follow their chosen way of life freely. President Eisenhower pledged "to consult with the Indian people of this country and to give them every opportunity for a full expression of their desires, suggestions, hopes and aspirations."

Comparative studies of the social, religious, and educational life of Indians on reservations and of those who have moved into American society suggest that life on the reservation is richer for the Indian than life in the city. He participates more fully in educational, religious, and community affairs on the reservation. White people who are genuinely interested in the Indian's welfare therefore claim that an abrupt termination of the reservation system would work hardship on Indians to whom the federal government has pledged its protection.

33. OTHER PROBLEMS, INCLUDING THOSE OF RELIGIOUS BODIES

Other cultural or ethnic groups in America constitute serious local problems for a time in one area or another, as the Puerto Ricans do in New York City or the Mexican-Americans do in New Mexico and Arizona, or the Japanese in the Pacific coast states. Each of these problems has its own peculiar nature, but they all follow this same general problem: the group is alien to the society in which it is situated; it speaks for a time a different tongue; it comes from a different culture, where it has learned a different set of values and different ways of do-

ing things. Its members must earn their living in this new American society. Usually recruited for menial work of one kind or another, they are poorly paid, badly housed, and denied many of the advantages that social life affords to the other Americans in the locality.

Ways of combating prejudice. One of the outstanding American authorities on this subject, Father John LaFarge, states that three elements are required "for reaching harmony among the various conflicting groups in this country." These elements are (1) accurate information and intelligent publicity to mitigate prejudice; (2) honest co-operation among the various groups; and (3) the grace of God. Father LaFarge considers this last element most important, although it is usually overlooked by the professional expert in social relations.

Studies in the psychology of intergroup relations made under the auspices of the American Jewish Committee found that the lack of religion played an important part in the building up of prejudice. These studies found that the secularization of American life created an atmosphere in which prejudice could flourish. They also found from the committee investigations that Christianity, wherever

St. Michael's High School for Navajo Indians in Arizona graduated its first students in 1950. One of the four graduates is shown here with Most Reverend Bernard Espelage of Gallup, N. Mex. (Marquette League for Indian Missions)

Reverend John LaFarge, S.J. At right, Father LaFarge addresses the Catholic Interracial Council. Their program is designed to release accurate information and intelligent publicity to mitigate prejudice. (Kay Bell; Layne's Studio)

it is thoroughly understood and put into practice, is an effective antidote to prejudice. The first step in combating this evil, then, is to look beyond outward appearances—language, color of skin, and such—and see every person as our fellow human being created by God.

This first element, which should give us a new attitude toward intergroup relations, is therefore basic to any lasting social reform. But of itself it is not enough. More than good will is needed. Intelligent legislation can accomplish a good deal toward ending discrimination.

The Catholic Church has been active in ending compulsory discriminative racial segregation in the South and in the border states. Catholic, Protestant, and Jewish committees of various kinds have studied the cause of prejudice and have suggested various ways of combating it. Among these ways is the preparation of material in printed form, the selection of speakers for organized groups like labor unions, women's clubs, and business organizations. Religious groups have also taken the lead in developing human-relations "workshops." These "workshops" gather together, study together, and work together so that they can understand each other better. They are supposed to bring this improved understanding back to their respective communities. Legislation and the work of private organizations have done much toward solving the problem of racial and cultural relations.

All such efforts can avail little, however, unless they are aided by an improvement in the manners of the general run of people and an elevation of the spirit of justice. This means a larger and finer courtesy and a widespread gentlemanly conduct, in contrast with which all racial prejudice and unjust discrimination appear base and contemptible.

The National Federation of Catholic College Students has sponsored a pledge that sums up practical lines of action which high school seniors would do well to adopt and practice.

As a student, I recognize my responsibilities and obligations in regard to interracial justice and charity; therefore I pledge myself:

To have an intellectual approach to interracial relationships;

To study seriously in order to find their real foundation;

To recognize my obligation to reshape my life in conformity with these facts;

To protest with courage and discretion any statement or action which expresses or implies discrimination or derogation toward any minority group;

To affirm my intention to foster the cause of interracial justice and charity, in accordance with my capacities, throughout the balance of my life.

Relations among religious groups. Although the Catholic Church in 1955 numbered about thirty-two million persons in the United States, the various Protestant denominations taken together total more than fifty million, and probably a majority of the seventy million who have no church or synagogue affiliation are of a Protestant ancestral background. The rural regions of the country generally and the southern states are predominantly Protestant in temper and disposition.

There has always been a strong tendency among Protestant sects to divide into new denominations, so that there are several hundred Protestant churches. Within each sect there has been a tendency for one group (fundamentalists) to hold fast to particular doctrines as the essential part of religion, whereas another group (modernists) have tended to minimize doctrinal differences and to stress moral conduct and the social importance of religion. To counteract the tendency toward division and form a united front in the face of a secularist and considerably dechristianized society, some Protestant leaders inaugurated an "ecumenical movement," which is an attempt to unite various Protestant sects in a sort of federation. The movement has taken many forms, but the general plan has been to promote co-operation in matters wherein they can all stand together as Protestants. This movement encounters difficulties in that it can appeal only to those religious bodies that tend to consider religion more as an attitude toward social and political life than as a creed, a code, and a cult.

The Catholic Church, which is even more sensitive to the moral problems arising from the advance of naturalism, pragmatism, and secularism in American life, stands as a rock of unity in our country and the main blockade against these malignant forces. More and more, Catholic leaders have shown a disposition to co-operate with Protestant and Jewish leaders in civic questions wherein all share a common moral principle. They have frequently found themselves taking a common stand on certain measures af-fecting the rights of the working class, immigration, and similar matters that have direct moral implication. They do this, however, not as official representatives of the Church but as fellow countrymen and citizens who are alive to moral issues in American society. The activity is civic and social, not ecclesiastical.

Relations among the various religious bodies in this country are not always harmonious. Although the old suspicion and prejudice against Catholics that was once widespread in America is now confined mainly to poorly educated people, nevertheless a latent prejudice in some Protestant leaders occasionally breaks out on some specific problem. The outstanding example of such prejudice in recent years is the PAOU (Protestants and Others United), which was organized ostensibly to protect separation of church and state. Capitalizing on suspicion and ignorance of its followers, the PAOU has opposed many measures endorsed by community leaders as promoting the common welfare because these measures also helped the Catholic Church. Tensions among the religious bodies in America result mostly from ignorance. They will probably always exist to some degree, but a campaign of information—assuming good will and loyalty to the ideal of American pluralism by men of all faiths —will do much to eliminate the prejudice from which these tensions arise.

Although Catholics must defend the just interests of the Church whenever these are attacked, it ill becomes members of the universal Church—the grand bearer and custodian of the whole body of Christian truth—ever to display resentment toward their Protestant fellow countrymen. They ought to be large-minded enough to understand the pathetic excuse that ignorance gives to bigotry. No doubt some Catholics, too, are bigots, but they ought not to be, for they are taught to practice perfect charity and to respect tenderly the human conscience.

Nothing is more odious than quarreling between religious groups who in their hearts know that it is contrary to the spirit of Christianity.

The fact is, there really are no very serious problems in our country arising out of pluralism in religion, and as long as we are all loyal to our civil and political institutions, none can arise.

34. E PLURIBUS UNUM

American society is basically healthy. We study its weaknesses because only in this way can we see how to improve it. But we must not let our concentration on weaknesses blind us to the fact that we are fortunate to live in a free society —and to be free to examine it critically and suggest ways of improving it.

The American form of the English language is a rich language because it has absorbed words and phrases from many tongues, from Latin, Greek, French, German, Spanish, Indian, and many others. In a similar way, American society is rich and vital because it has absorbed many

The feast day of St. Patrick on March 17 is the occasion of an impressive parade along New York's Fifth Avenue, in which Americans of Irish descent honor the patron saint of Ireland. (American Irish Historical Society)

peoples without destroying their various cultures. America has valued differences among people and understood that respect for these differences is requisite for the free development of each American. As these different cultures are taken into American society they lose some measure of their distinctness, but they preserve a good portion of their individuality. Archbishop Cushing of Boston explained it this way:

It would be unfortunate continually to isolate one racial strain from all the others and persistently to dwell upon its characteristics, whether good or bad. At the same time, it would be unfortunate to accept the "melting pot" theory of American life and to suppose that the individual characteristics of the races which comprise America have been lost by their indiscriminate fusion into a completely neutral and homogeneous American character. America is not a "melting pot"; the races which have come here have gladly blended in the harmonious whole that is America their several characteristics but they have not on that account entirely lost them. It is the glory and the strength of America that she enjoys the united loyalty of the members of many racial families. It is no less her glory and her strength that she permits racial and cultural differences to survive in those who are legitimately attached to these traditions. As distinguished from all Fascist national unities and all Communist classless societies, America has never pretended nor attempted to be a monolithic society. . . . In this house of America, as in that of heaven, there are many mansions!

Our country thus stands fast against the ideal of cultural uniformity in what is sometimes called "monolithic society." This means a society in which all are educated in the same school system, trained to think alike, hold the same standards of value, and are conditioned to react in the same way to any given stimulus. An attempt to reduce all persons to the level of a monolithic pattern was made by Hitler and the Nazis in Germany in the 1930s, and something close to it is still being tried in the Soviet Union. Some American educators who are fanatically attached to an idea of democracy that is far from consistent with American traditional democracy urge measures that would tend toward a single cultural pattern of life in our country. They imagine that all our social and political problems would be easy to solve if all Americans were educated in the public secular schools and there taught to think exactly alike.

Americans have traditionally prized their freedoms and respected their differences too strongly to surrender them to a state-controlled monopoly of education. There is always the temptation to surrender freedom as too burdensome a thing to maintain in complex modern society, but most Americans are individualistic enough to resist any overt attempt to steal their freedom from them.

"Creeping conformity." The greater danger, perhaps, is what we might call "creeping conformity," that increasing fear of being different from the rest of men. This is the tyranny of public opinion, the fear people have of not being just like others or of not thinking and acting with the crowd. The popular press, radio, and television have changed the scope of conformity in the last fifty years. Movies, radio, and television programs, and national magazines in this country have done a great deal to make all people speak alike, want the same things, do the same things in the same way, and even think alike. Children all over America imitate the mannerisms of the same movie hero. Men and women all over America are told it is smart to have certain brands of shoes or hats. Conformity on a national scale tends to destroy the social and cultural differences that identified various communities in this country. As these differences gradually melt away we lose the richness of culture that comes with variety.

There is no sinister plot to rob us of our cultural heritage. But we are confronted with a real problem: how to keep our American way of life the rich and di-

Colorful traditions such as the Greek Orthodox practice of diving for a cross on the Feast of the Epiphany, enrich American cultural life. (Religious News Service Photo)

versified thing it is and not slide into a monolithic culture in which all people conform to the same pattern. Let us put the problem another way: We are the richest country in the world because we have developed mass production and mass distribution of consumer goods. Automobiles, furniture, cigarettes, shoes, and almost everything we use are all available in great abundance because they are "factory-made." Mass production of goods is possible only if millions of Americans are taught to want exactly the same thing. It is almost impossible for us to have the wealth of goods we enjoy unless most of us wear uniform clothes, use uniform furniture, live in uniform houses with standardized gadgets throughout. The problem, then, seems to be a choice between conformity with a high standard of material comforts and independence of taste with a lower standard.

Perhaps the choice is not that simple. Perhaps when Americans reflect on the problem of cultural monism they will discriminate between the goods that should be factory-made and those that should not. Why, for example, should not all cars be alike if the alternative is an automobile costing more than most people could afford? On the other hand,

The Threat of Cultural Monism

should the American public be satisfied with standardized romances showing in thousands of movies throughout the country at the same time? Perhaps this is buying entertainment at too high a price —for we surrender individual judgment of good plays to see what producers believe will have mass appeal.

Cultural conformity comes about slowly—something like creeping paralysis—and its results are socially unhealthy. Gradually a passive kind of person emerges, one composed of a spectator body and a spectator mind. This is the man who cannot entertain himself with good reading or healthy exercise. He has learned to watch passively while the professional actors work out the great scenes from literature for him. Thus he surrenders his intellectual initiative and his physical vigor. Moreover, he tends to lose his independence of will.

A danger lurks behind this trend toward cultural monism. It is a remote danger, but it is one that we should see distinctly so that if it ever becomes proximate we can be on guard against it. The danger is this: People who have surrendered individual tastes and independent thinking are the material from which totalitarian dictatorships are made. Social conformity can lead to political conformity. Moreover, the means of communication are now so completely centralized that the same image and the same voice can appear in every home in this country at the same second. The physical means to create a monolithic society are therefore present. If Americans are willing to surrender their social and cultural initiative and their political independence, all that is necessary for dictatorship is a government willing to assume the task. Our traditions are all against it, but if these traditions grow weaker and conformity increases at the expense of social and cultural independence—then the danger will be less remote.

A depersonalized society. A problem closely related to the one of cultural monism, which we have been discussing, is the tendency in modern society to establish relationships between people as though they were things instead of persons. This is frequently called, for the sake of convenience, "a depersonalized society." Americans traditionally have had great respect for the human person, and the ultimate basis of this respect is the belief that man is created to the image and likeness of God. There has been a tendency at work in American society—slowly but steadily—to forget the worth and dignity of the person and to treat him more and more like a thing. This tendency is due partly to industrial developments, partly to the growth of large cities, and partly to a loss by many Americans of the concept of the person.

A little reflection will enable us to realize how far this tendency toward a depersonalized society has already gone when we contrast relationships between persons today with those of a century ago. Society has become so complex that business enterprises, hospitals, social-service groups, and other organizations tend to pigeonhole customers and employees into

Civic pride and community co-operation are illustrated as students clean a littered area for a playground. (Department of Sanitation, City of New York)

classified groups and then to deal with individual persons as members of a certain group or class. Employers are aware of this fact, and many of them have taken steps to counteract it. But the problem remains. The complexity of modern society, especially in the large city, makes it almost impossible to deal with every customer and every employee as though each were a unique person. Nothing but a strong consciousness of the sacred worth of the human person can successfully counteract this tendency.

It is important for us to realize that a pluralist society like ours depends upon our appreciating the unique worth of each person and his ability to contribute something to society. Without such realization we are likely to do a measure of injustice to the persons with whom we come in daily contact in the city: the bus driver, the clerk in the store, the maid who cleans our house once a week, the mechanic who repairs our car. If we forget the unique importance of each person, our pluralist society will lose much

of its richness, and people will be reckoned in purely statistical terms—now as voters, now as consumers of pork sausage or candy mints, now as wearers of shoes or occupiers of hospital beds. Such statistical calculation is necessary in the modern world, of course, but if we forget the unique importance of each person he is likely never to be treated as more than a number.

Conclusion. What can we do specifically to work out a solution to this problem? Let us remember first of all that the problem will never be finally solved. There will always be tension between the need for unity and the desire for diversity. We shall do our daily task well if we continue to be loyal Americans who respect the cultural differences we see about us. If each of us prizes his independence of judgment and acts from sincerity, then we shall be better citizens, conscious that anonymity among Americans is neither traditional nor desirable.

In the second place, we should jealously safeguard our political institutions.

Americans generally understand that division of power in the government protects them from tyranny by any one branch of government. Sometimes we forget that the primary division of authority—that between church and state—protects our freedom even more basically than does the division of power within the government. As long as the government does not control our consciences and as long as it does not decide what is morally right and wrong, there will be effective limits on its power and its functions. Another division of power and functions basic to the American life is the division between federal and local government. We should jealously preserve for local government whatever functions it can successfully perform.

Finally, as individual Americans we should develop ourselves individually and socially. Our society is healthy when we engage actively in social, cultural, political, and religious life. Such activities are the means for developing initiative and self-reliance in the citizenry of this country. They enable us to achieve our purpose in society: to develop ourselves on the natural and supernatural planes to the full perfection desired for us by our Creator.

REVIEW

31. Our Cultural Pluralism
A. What is meant by a "pluralist" society? How is American society pluralist today in contrast to the society of the colonial period?

B. What is the distinctively Christian and American solution to the problems that arise in a pluralist society? What did Pius XII say concerning this in his first encyclical?

C. What are the factors that account for prejudice? List some of the results of prejudice on the subjects themselves.

D. How does poverty produce "anti-social" conditions? How does prejudice harm all society?

32. Negroes, Whites, and Indians
A. What was meant by the "black code"? How did the Negro fare in the North immediately after 1863?

B. What were the major causes for the improved status of the Negro?

C. Supreme Court decisions have helped the Negro by forbidding discriminatory practices. Explain the fallacy present in the "separate but equal" concept. How has this been changed?

D. List some of the restrictive laws that are still present in the South. What are some of the restrictions prevailing in the North? What are some of the effects of these discriminations against the Negro?

E. What was our government's policy in the nineteenth century toward the American Indian? How was this changed by the Dawes Act of 1887? Why was this act unsuccessful?

33. Other Problems, Including Those of Religious Bodies
A. What other groups constitute present problems? According to Fr. John LaFarge, what three elements are required for overcoming prejudice?

B. How have religious groups aided the fight against prejudice? What remains to be done today?

C. Summarize the pledge of the NFCCS toward combating prejudice.

D. Cite the major religious divisions in the United States. Show how they co-operate on problems in America. List some of the present difficulties in relations among various religious groups.

34. E Pluribus Unum
A. List some ways in which American society has been enriched by its cultural pluralism. How did Archbishop Cushing point out that cultural conformity is not desirable? What would cultural uniformity result in?

B. What is "creeping conformity"? What has tended to bring this about? What are the unhealthy results of this conformity?

C. What is a depersonalized society? How is this exemplified today?

D. How will a recognition of the unique worth of the individual counteract the idea of a depersonalized society?

THE CHAPTER IN REVIEW

A. What is the Christian attitude toward prejudice? Explain how the Negro suffers socially, politically, and economically from discrimination.

B. In our history the treatment of the American Indian during the nineteenth century has been summarized as a "century of dishonor." Point out the truth of this statement and explain what steps have been taken to change this situation.

C. Cultural, economic, and political monism present a number of dangers to American society. How can they be avoided?

SELECTED READINGS

A vast literature has been produced on racial groups in America and the associated topics of prejudice and racial antagonisms. A classic book on this general subject is Rev. John LaFarge, S.J., *No Postponement: U. S. Moral Leadership and the Problem of Racial Minorities* (New York: Longmans, Green & Co., Inc., 1950). Also helpful for giving a general view of the problem are R. M. MacIver (editor), *Group Relations and Group Antagonisms* (New York: Harper & Brothers, 1944); Stewart G. Cole and Mildred Wise Cole, *Minorities and the American Promise* (New York: Harper & Brothers, 1954).

Catholic morality on race relations is given by Father LaFarge, and it is stated in the following pamphlets and articles: Rev. Daniel M. Cantwell, *Catholics Speak on Race Relations* (Chicago: Fides Publishers Assn., 1952); Rev. Yves M. J. Congar, O.P., *The Catholic Church and the Race Question* (New York: UNESCO and Columbia University Press, 1953); Rev. Paul J. Hayes and Rev. Edward J. Hayes, *The Catholic Church and Race Relations* (New York: America Press, 1955).

Reaction to the Supreme Court's decision against segregation in the schools is recorded in C. Dowdey, "A Southerner Looks at the Supreme Court's Decision on Segregation," *Saturday Review of Literature* (October 9, 1954); M. M. Clarke, "Our Constitution Is Colorblind," *Catholic World* (January 1955); and E.

V. Hollis, "The Supreme Court Decision on Segregation," *Vital Speeches* (November 1954).

There is very little written directly about cultural monism, but it is treated in some fashion by many writers who are concerned with the cultural drift in America today. One of the best of these works is Bernard Iddings Bell, *Crowd Culture: An Examination of the American Way of Life* (New York: Harper & Brothers, 1952). The relationship of religion to culture is analyzed by Christopher Dawson, *Religion and Culture* (New York: Sheed & Ward, 1949).

The effect of industrialization on culture is well handled by Walter Marx, *Mechanization and Culture* (St. Louis: B. Herder Book Co., 1941). Lewis Mumford's *In the Name of Sanity* (New York: Harcourt, Brace & Co., 1954) is a thoughtful work which reverses the author's formal approval of technology as found in his *Technics and Civilization* (New York: Harcourt, Brace & Co., 1934). The "new Mumford" is analyzed by Frederick D. Wilhelmsen, "In the Name of Sanity," *Social Order* (January 1955). Wilhelmsen also wrote an article, "Technics and Totalitarianism," for *Commonweal* (April 23, 1954), which provoked considerable correspondence in the following issues of that journal. A provocative approach to this problem is taken by Herbert Marshall McLuhan, *The Mechanical Bride: Folklore of Industrial Man* (New York: Vanguard Press, 1951).

PROJECTS

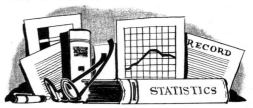

1. The work of the Catholic Interracial Council to combat racial prejudice has been outstanding. A report on the activities of this group, which has councils in many of the larger cities throughout the United States and in many of the colleges throughout the eastern states, would explain what can be done in regard to this important problem.

2. The daily newspapers very often carry stories that show evidence of unfair prejudice. Select some examples of this and explain how such prejudices can be overcome. In some instances the prejudice may exist in the very manner in which the story was written.

Chapter 13. Crime and Punishment

35. INCREASE AND CAUSES OF CRIME

There has been an alarming increase in crime in America in the last half century. This increase, especially among young people, is explained by some sociologists as the result of unstable social conditions. Increasing crime in the 1920s was blamed on social dislocations caused by World War I: families temporarily or permanently broken up, young men's careers interrupted by service in the armed forces, personal stability destroyed by the war's tensions, and other such disrupting factors. The unemployment and the poverty of the depression were blamed for much of the crime in the 1930s. World War II was cited, as was the preceding war and for the same reasons, as a cause for increasing crime since the 1940s. Finally, these sociologists hold, upset world conditions and lack of secure peace are conducive to crime today.

This explanation contains a large measure of truth, for crime waves have always followed war. But it is not an adequate explanation of the increasing amount and rate of crime in this country. The greatest deterrent to crime—the

moral sense rooted in religion—has grown steadily weaker through the twentieth century. Most Americans avoid criminal acts because they are wrong. But an increasing number of Americans seem to have little or no moral sense at all. For them the only deterrent to crime is the punishment meted out for it. This means that the educative agencies in the community—the home, the church, and the school—have failed to keep alive and strong the religious and moral sense. We know that, when religion breaks down, disruptive factors like war and depression have more harmful results on society.

The volume of crime in America. The Federal Bureau of Investigation reported at the end of 1953 that more than two million major crimes had been committed in this country. This was a new high, an increase of 4.5 per cent over the previous year and an increase of almost 40 per cent over the average year before World War II. In addition to major crimes, such as murder or robbery, there were countless minor crimes or misdemeanors. More than four million people were arrested in American cities, and more than three million were committed to jails and prisons.

The FBI report for 1954 showed that crime was still increasing. The population increased 2 per cent over 1953, but the crime rate increased 8.5 per cent. On an average day in 1954, 35 persons were feloniously killed, and there were 252 felonious assaults; 197 robberies and 1,454 burglaries were committed and 608 cars were stolen. Two facts are especially worth noting. First, the increase of crime was greatest in rural areas, 11.9 per cent against 7.2 per cent in urban areas. This is probably due to greater preventive measures taken against crime in the city, but it shows that the social and moral breakdown leading to crime has worked its way into rural areas. Second, a greater proportion of crimes are committed each year by juveniles. Almost half the burglaries in 1953 were committed by people under eighteen, and one-third of them were committed by those under sixteen. Over half the car thieves were juveniles.

The cost of crime in this country is enormous. First of all, there is the cost in wrecked lives and in moral degradation which accompany crime. The loss in terms of money is also enormous. J. Edgar Hoover, director of the FBI, estimates that the annual cost of crime in this country has risen to over fifteen billion dollars, more than three times the money spent on education. This estimate includes the direct loss, of course, as well as the expense of detection and punishment.

Serious crimes are called felonies, and they are punishable in most states by imprisonment for one or more years. Typical felonies are murder, robbery, assault,

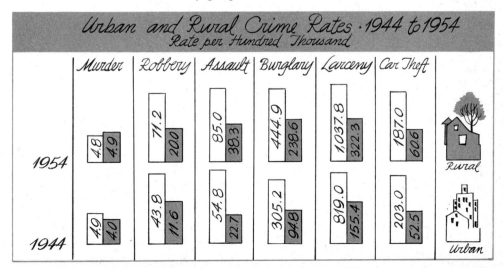

Urban and Rural Crime Rates · 1944 to 1954
Rate per Hundred Thousand

	Murder	Robbery	Assault	Burglary	Larceny	Car Theft	
1954	4.8 / 4.9	71.2 / 200	85.0 / 38.3	444.9 / 238.6	1037.8 / 322.3	187.0 / 606	Rural
1944	4.9 / 4.0	43.8 / 11.6	54.8 / 22.7	305.2 / 94.8	819.0 / 155.4	203.0 / 52.5	Urban

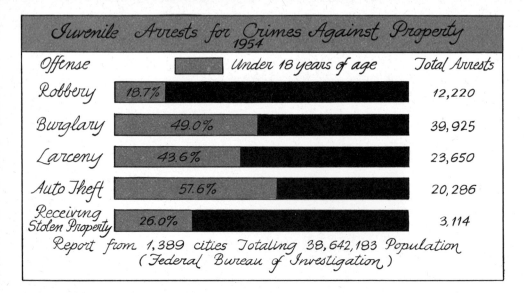

Juvenile Arrests for Crimes Against Property
1954

Offense	Under 18 years of age	Total Arrests
Robbery	18.7%	12,220
Burglary	49.0%	39,925
Larceny	43.6%	23,650
Auto Theft	57.6%	20,286
Receiving Stolen Property	26.0%	3,114

Report from 1,389 cities Totaling 38,642,183 Population
(Federal Bureau of Investigation)

or arson. Minor infractions of the law are called misdemeanors, and they are usually punishable by fines or short terms in prison. Typical misdemeanors are speeding, parking violations, and disorderly conduct. Crimes can also be classified according to their perpetrators. Organized crime, as the name indicates, is a business in which a syndicate or gang of criminals is engaged for profit. Organized crime deals in forbidden goods or actions, such as dope, vice, liquor (in areas where there is prohibition), and even in the business of murder. Individual crimes are either premeditated or spontaneous crimes of passion. These distinctions are helpful in deciding what degree of punishment should be meted out to the convicted criminal.

In his address on crime and punishment in 1954, Pope Pius XII said:

The criminal act is always an opposition of one person against another, both when the immediate object of the crime is a thing, as in theft, and when it is a person, as in murder; further, the Ego of the person who becomes a criminal is directed against higher Authority, and therefore in the end always against the authority of God. . . .

Causes of crime. There is no single general cause of crime. Poverty is a factor in some kinds of crimes. But juvenile delinquents sometimes come from wealthy homes, and millionaires occasionally commit murder. Psychological disturbance is a factor. Many criminals are maladjusted persons with a grudge against society. A high proportion of criminals in prison are psychopaths, sex deviates, and other abnormal persons. But many criminals are apparently perfectly normal persons who rationally elected to commit a criminal act. Environmental factors other than poverty are cited as causes of crime: slum conditions, lax community attitudes toward certain kinds of crimes, bad example of "respectable" citizens who violate the law successfully or admit no moral code in business practices. These environmental factors play a part in the prevalence of crime, but they fail to account for the incidence of crime in the way that an adequate cause accounts for a result.

A study of criminals sentenced to penal institutions indicates that we can isolate three principal causes of crime. (These are not the only causes, let us remember, but three concrete causes about which each community can take remedial action.)

Poor education. There are two aspects to this cause. One is the lack of sufficient education; the other is the lack of the right kind of education. A study at the

Charlestown prison in Massachusetts for a ten-year period (1938–1947) showed that of the 2,865 inmates whose cases were studied approximately 2,000 had a formal education ending between fourth and eighth grade. Only 74, or 2.5 per cent had been to college, and of these only 29 had graduated. This latter group consisted mostly of doctors and lawyers who had abused their profession and were imprisoned for the first time. Most of the poorly educated criminals had been convicted of crimes such as robbery, larceny, and rape.

Education does not necessarily make a person good. But the evidence shows that it tends to make him law-abiding. The criminal population generally has a substandard education. Students of this subject point out, however, that an unbalanced education—one that teaches skills without teaching religion or developing the student's moral sense—can make a clumsy criminal a skilled criminal. This is the danger of an education that leaves out moral principle.

Broken homes or immoral family life. More important than lack of good education as a cause of crime is the failure of the family to perform its task of rearing and educating its children properly. Parents may fail here in many ways, but there are three that seem most frequent: neglect, lack of parental discipline, and bad example. Rearing children properly in the modern world is a difficult task that requires patience and a considerable part of the parents' time. Children are neglected in homes broken by death or by divorce when the remaining parent must earn a living. Homes in which immorality or drunkenness is regular, in which parents are constantly quarreling, are schools of vice for the growing child. Children in such homes spend a great deal of time on the streets, where the occasion of crime more frequently arises.

Other parents harm their children by grossly spoiling them. Children who do not learn to respect authority, who do not learn that they cannot always have their way, grow into adults who cannot obey the law. Lack of parental discipline in the home breeds selfishness in the children, and selfishness is an essential ingredient of crime. The failure of the home is so widely recognized as a cause of crime that many judges have suggested legislation enabling them to punish parents for their children's delinquent acts.

Creating interests in educational hobbies is a vital part of a well-regulated recreation program for juveniles. The Stamp Club attracts pre-adolescents and occupies their time in a wholesome way. (Standard Oil Co., N.J.)

211

Lack of religion. Less generally recognized by modern criminologists and social workers as a cause of crime is the lack of religion. Failure to recognize this fact is hard to explain except by saying that many criminologists and sociologists do not believe in religion, although many more understand the close connection between practicing one's religion and being a law-abiding citizen. One criminologist, after studying the record of Charlestown Prison for ten years, concluded: "Indifference to religion (whatever that religion may be) or lack of any religious practice at all is an almost universal characteristic of those who daily move into the prisons of the land." Estimates for the nation as a whole reveal that more than 80 per cent of the prison population did not practice any religion before coming to prison.

In addition to these three basic causes of crime, of course, there are many stimuli that suggest wrongful acts to the potential criminal. Comic books, movies, radio and television programs that glorify crime or even deal with criminal life as exciting adventure are inducements to crime for the morally unstable person. The connection between violence and crime in entertainment and the rising volume of crime in the country is now established. Efforts are being made to reduce these incitements to criminal and violent acts, but the success of any drive to improve comic books or movies depends on continued effort through the years and on general public support.

36. CRIME PREVENTION

Because of human imperfection there will always be some amount of crime. Crimes of passion will never be completely eliminated as long as people can become passionately angry. The prevalence of organized crime and of those individual crimes that are not purely spon-

A problem of American cities is to provide their young citizens with recreation under safe and properly supervised conditions. A well-organized recreation program is one of the most effective deterrents to juvenile delinquency. (Standard Oil Co., N.J.)

taneous depends pretty much upon public opinion and morality. A lenient or tolerant attitude toward certain kinds of lawbreaking makes it almost impossible for the police to enforce strict observance of the law.

Public disapproval of crime, then, is the most important ultimate means of crime prevention in a community. Widespread sympathy for criminals as unfortunate victims of their environment creates an atmosphere that breeds more violations of the law. A stern but understanding public opinion is the first element in crime prevention.

A second is good laws. Laws must be reasonable, both in what they allow and forbid and in what penalties they prescribe for violation of the law. A law that is unreasonable cannot be well enforced. The failure of prohibition in this country is an excellent example of what happens to unreasonable laws. Many localities have a few archaic laws that have become unreasonable and therefore are not observed—such, perhaps, as a five-mile speed limit in parks or the prohibition of outdoor play on Sunday.

The third element in crime prevention

is rigid but reasonable enforcement of the law. Certainty and strictness of punishments are deterrents to those who are not prevented from violating the law by any moral or religious considerations. Punishment need not be automatic. Each violation is a special case, of course, and it involves a unique human being. Each case should be treated individually, then, with full consideration of the circumstances in which it occurred. Considerate enforcement is not lax enforcement.

Other crime-prevention measures seek to eliminate the factors that contribute to the prevalence of crime. Social factors, we have seen, are such things as slums and poverty. Each of these is a problem or a series of problems in itself. Any measures that eliminate slum areas or relieve drastic poverty ought to do something toward reducing the amount of crime in the country. The early detection, at school or in the home, of neurotic tendencies in a youngster may result in effective treatment that will make the child a healthy, normal person.

More specific preventive measures can be taken with the three specific causes of crime we have already examined: the lack of education, the absence of healthy home life, and the lack of religion. Strict enforcement of minimum education laws in the various states would help decrease the amount of crime to some extent. Balanced education that included moral and spiritual development of young people would do even more good. Whatever helps to develop healthy home life will help prevent crime. In similar fashion, whatever develops active religious life in society will decrease the extent of crime.

Rehabilitating criminals. The rehabilitation of convicted criminals is a difficult and frequently disheartening task. In days past, criminals were treated as hopelessly lost, as men who had forfeited all social rights and were to be kept in prison as long as possible to protect society from their misdeeds. In the last thirty years progress has been made in looking upon most criminals as reformable, and steps have been taken to prepare them for normal life when they re-enter society. Rehabilitation work involves a pre-sentence investigation, attention to the criminal while he is in prison, and supervision for at least a time after he leaves prison. The pre-sentence investigation enables the judge to decide what kind of imprisonment will most benefit a particular individual: whether he should be put with hardened criminals or segregated from them, whether he can be put on probation, whether he needs psychiatric treatment, other medical treatment, or special handling of any kind. Rehabilitation in prison involves the work of psychiatrists, chaplains, educators, and others who can help the individual find out what is wrong with himself and develop both skills and attitudes that will enable him to live a normal, productive life when he is let out of prison. Supervision after release from prison is designed to help the ex-convict in the difficult job of readjusting to a normal life in which he is responsible again for his acts.

In his address on crime and punishment Pope Pius XII advocated the use of trained experts in rehabilitating prisoners, but he warned that no rehabilitation is possible without a change of heart; that is, without a religious change.

Boy-meets-girl problems are ironed out at teen-age dating forums. This is an important phase of the CYO social activities program. (CYO photo by Bill Linge)

We hope [the Holy Father stated] that all the solid results produced by investigation and experience in the field of psychology, psychiatry, pedagogy and sociology, will be used to the advantage of the imprisoned. This naturally presupposes a thorough professional training in those called to such work.

No one who is in any way familiar with the actual application of punishment will nurse utopian dreams of great success. The good will of the prisoner must match any outside influence, but that cannot be gotten by force. May divine grace arouse and direct that good will!

A high percentage of prisoners (about 50 per cent in the best institutions with selected prisoners; higher than 80 per cent in ordinary prisons) commit crimes after parole and are convicted again. But rehabilitation work justifies itself if it salvages only one in a hundred of the human wrecks who go to prison.

Punishment. In breaking the law, a criminal upsets right order, and justice requires that he suffer for the wrong he has committed. Such punishment must be administered, of course, by the proper authorities in any society. Society has the right of self-protection, and in pursuance of this right it has empowered its properly constituted authorities to punish wrongdoers by imprisoning them or by whatever effective means seem advisable. Punishment is also the legitimate means of deterring other potential criminals. Finally, punishment is a legitimate means of reforming those criminals who can be reformed. Modern communities expect punishment to do three principal things: (1) to protect the innocent; (2) to deter potential criminals; (3) to rehabilitate as many convicted criminals as possible.

Various forms of punishment. Prior to the establishment of criminal penitentiaries the most common forms of punishment were flogging, mutilation and other forms of corporal punishment, exile, and fines. Flogging seems to have had the double purpose of punishing a person for his crime and deterring him and others from similar crimes in the future. Mutilation had the same double purpose, frequently

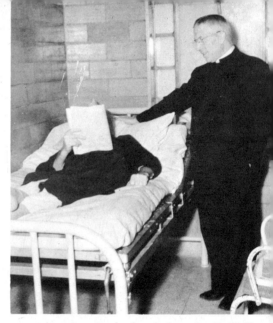

A patient in the hospital at the United States Penitentiary, Terre Haute, Ind., is visited by his chaplain. Attention to the prisoner's spiritual needs aids in his reform and rehabilitation.

with the added feature of rendering the culprit incapable of performing the same crime again. Thus spies had their eyes gouged out, thieves had their hands cut off, the tongues of blasphemers were pulled out.

The extreme form of corporal punishment, of course, is capital punishment or death. Various methods of execution have been used throughout the world, such as poisoning, infliction of snakebites, breaking on the wheel, or throwing the victim to wild animals. In modern times capital punishment is inflicted by hanging, shooting, beheading, electrocuting, or suffocating in the gas chamber. Some criminologists regard capital punishment as an anachronism (a survival of the past) which serves no good purpose and occasionally claims an innocent victim. Others defend it for its deterrent effects.

Exile served the double purpose of punishing the guilty individual and protecting society. Exile was used as punishment chiefly for political offenses. Sometimes it meant exile from one's home town or province or from the capital of the country. Sometimes it meant exclusion from one's native country, and sometimes it meant transportation to a penal colony—a form of punishment called "the dry guillotine" in France. Fines have been the most frequent of all penalties. They have historically been the commonest way of punishing for minor offenses, and they have frequently accompanied other punishment for major offenses. Their convenience is that they involve no expense for the state, as does imprisonment, and they are a source of income.

Imprisonment. Prisons came into general use toward the end of the eighteenth century. Until that time jails were places of detention for persons awaiting trial and sentence. Prisons were first operated as punitive institutions. Accommodations and food were designedly bad. The prisoners were persons who were sent to prison to pay a debt to society by confinement and by suffering. It is important to remember this idea because it persists among a large number of Americans today. It is true—but it is not all the truth. A second concept of prisons developed in the latter part of the nineteenth century: that the prison should be a place of reform.

These two concepts struggle for control of prisons today. It is difficult to reconcile the two ideas in practice, though not impossible. We can easily see that the program of a prison, its discipline, organization, and treatment of inmates, will depend on whether it is to punish them or reform them. The best criminologists have adopted a middle position of trying to work out a program that does both. They try, by separating the hardened criminal from the first offenders and others who seem redeemable, to reform the latter and protect them from the bad influence of the former. Sanford Bates, one of the country's outstanding criminologists, tells us that "a desire to coddle the criminal is as bad as a vengeful attitude towards every person who has received a sentence." And another leading criminologist, Austin H. MacCormick, says: "It is difficult to say which is worse in prisons in the long run, extreme laxity or excessive severity."

Prisons are expensive institutions. No one knows how much jails and lockups cost the taxpayers of the various cities and counties throughout the country; however, we have statistics on federal and state prisons. There were 172,729 inmates in these prisons at the end of 1953, about the same number as in each of the previous twenty years. A conservative estimate is that the cost of operation of these prisons is $125,000,000 a year. This does not include the cost of construction or of building additions to the original buildings. The cost of keeping a man in prison varies from the low of $172 in Arkansas to the high of $1,890 in a model California institution. The national average cost per inmate is estimated at anything from $650 to $1,500 a year, depending on whether one includes the bare cost of operating the prisons or all the associated expenses of probation, the use of other state services, and so forth.

A survey of the federal and state prisons indicates that only a few of them are thoroughly bad and only a few can be considered really good. Most of them are mediocre, not as bad as some reformers picture them, but not organized or staffed to achieve the purposes for which they exist. Many of them are ancient structures, poorly ventilated, and so built that no sound segregation policy can be followed in them.

37. NEED FOR PRISON REFORM

Modern criminologists describe a good prison as one that has maximum security arrangements for the small number of criminals who require them and sufficient freedom within confinement for those who can benefit from a measure of responsibility? Men should be lodged one to a cell in blocks or divisions peopled by prisoners of a similar nature. In a good prison the inmates are given daily an hour to three hours of recreation or exercise outdoors. They have occasional access to a library and to the commissary. They are kept occupied a good part of the time with classes, some form of labor, and social activity conducive to their rehabilitation. They may receive visitors occasionally (once or twice a month), and they may communicate periodically by letter with the outside world. (Such letters are censored by the prison authorities.) They receive regular visits from a chaplain, a physician, a psychiatrist, a social worker, and other staff members who may aid in their rehabilitation. Unless prisons are so maintained, they become much costlier to society because they otherwise would be breeders of crime. They are a distinct social liability if they turn out more hardened criminals than they receive.

That something is seriously wrong with most of our prisons was indicated by the epidemic of riots that occurred in the eighteen months from April 1952 to September 1953, and broke out again in the summer of 1954 and 1955. The epidemic of riots hit every kind of prison in the country. There was a riot in Massachusetts' 148-year-old Charlestown Prison and in California's prison at Soledad opened in 1951, at one of the largest (the 6,500-man prison at Jackson, Michigan) and one of the smallest (the 500-man prison in Utah), at one of the worst (the Louisiana Penitentiary) and one of the best (the federal reformatory for young men at Chillicothe, Ohio). Some of the riots were easily quelled, and some of them were ended only after several days of siege, the loss of several lives and millions of dollars' worth of property.

The riots followed a similar pattern. Unrest was stirred up for a considerable time by a few ringleaders, usually younger prisoners, and the riot was set off by a seemingly trivial incident, most often food badly prepared. The ringleaders were supported by part of the prison population, who seized some of the guards as hostages and held out in the desperate hope of having their demands met by the administration. Most of the prisoners refused to co-operate, and the riot was usually confined to one or two cell blocks. Eventually the riot was quelled without concessions being made by prison authorities.

The American Prison Association's Committee on Riots studied the problem and reported on the epidemic of riots in 1953. The committee placed the blame for the riots on the following causes:

1. Inadequate financial support from the legislature, and indifference to good prison management on the part of officials and the general public.
2. Substandard personnel caused by lack of funds.
3. Enforced idleness from lack of a good work and education program.
4. Lack of professional leadership and professional programs, such as good pre-parole investigators and competent psychiatrists.
5. Excessive numbers in each prison and serious overcrowding.
6. Political domination of management, with officials chosen because of political connections instead of professional training.
7. Unwise sentencing and parole practices.

These causes boil down to a lack of sufficient funds to maintain a good institution with a sound program and adequate personnel and a failure on the part of the politicians and the public to understand what a prison needs to accomplish its purpose.

Punishment and rehabilitation program. It is safe to say that, with a few exceptions, prisons do not accomplish much rehabilitation of criminals. Instead of being assets, the prisons are, by and large, liabilities for which the taxpayers spend a great deal of money. They are part of a larger program of punishment and rehabilitation that begins before the criminal is sentenced and does not end until long after he has been released from prison. Let us look at the principal phases of this program:

Investigation should take place before the criminal has been sentenced to punishment for the crime he has committed. Such an investigation will show the judge what factors induced the individual to commit crime, what his educational and vocational background has been, and what kind of punishment is most likely to rehabilitate him. Such investigation is also sound economically, because on the basis of the information given to the judge he can put some of the guilty individuals on probation instead of sentencing them to prison. This not only saves the taxpayer's money but also saves redeemable persons from the contamination of prison and the confirmed life of crime that so often begins there.

Loss of political and civil rights accompanies conviction of a felony and imprisonment, but the loss of these rights and their recovery differ from state to state. Seventeen states still employ the penalty of *civil death* for convicts sentenced to prison for life. One who is dead *civilly* cannot sue, own property, or buy or sell anything. Most states suspend civil and political rights during time of imprisonment. They are recovered as a rule at the time of parole, although in some cases pardon by the governor of the state is required to restore rights lost by conviction of a crime. Other rights also are generally lost at the time of conviction. In thirty-six states conviction of a felony is grounds for divorce. It is usually grounds for exclusion of the convict from his profession or his trade—frequently for life.

Induction and classification of the new convict is perhaps the most important single step taken within the prison. A good induction and classification service includes physical, psychological, and mental examinations, as well as interviews with a chaplain and others on the professional staff. This staff decides what sort of program will best achieve the purposes of imprisonment for the individual under consideration. A good classification service protects first offenders from the bad influence of hardened criminals. It segregates various kinds of psychopaths, and it puts those who are not likely to create trouble or try to escape into work that does not require as close confinement as other groups of prisoners.

Competent personnel is necessary for a well-run prison. The pay of prison guards in most institutions is low. Such saving is costly in the long run. The starting salary in the Missouri State Penitentiary in 1954, for example, was $154 a month as compared with the starting salary of $280 at the Stateville Penitentiary in neighboring Illinois. A riot in the Missouri penitentiary cost more than three million dollars in destroyed property alone, enough money to pay guards good wages for many years. In addition to competent, well-trained guards, a prison needs a pro-

The dormitory quarters of the Federal Correctional Institution in Tallahassee, Fla., provide freedom within confinement for selected prisoners. Such living conditions ease the transition the individual must make upon his return to society. (Bureau of Prisons)

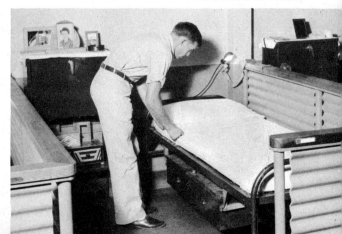

fessional, educated staff of social workers, chaplains, physicians, and psychiatrists.

A labor and education program is essential for any well-run prison. Long hours of enforced idleness are unnatural, because man was created to be active, to use both his mind and his body to work and to create. Enforced idleness, which is common in many American prisons, breeds perversion and sullenness and is the principal cause of prison trouble. Labor programs serve the double purpose of keeping prisoners busy and helping support the prison and also the convict's dependents. A good labor program gives the working convict small wages, which play a part in rebuilding his self-respect and his responsibility. Opposition to labor programs by labor unions and manufacturers resulted in legislation in many states that prohibited various forms of prison industry. This legislation, most of which was passed during the depression of the 1930s, prevents the administration in many prisons today from maintaining a reasonable work program.

Investigating committees have universally recommended, after the study of each prison riot, that a work program be devised in each prison and that legislation be passed requiring various state institutions to purchase such articles as soap and furniture that can be manufactured in prison. Such an arrangement is a saving to state agencies and it is a means of partial support for the prison. Most important, however, it keeps the prisoners out of trouble that is bred by enforced idleness.

, Education is woefully inadequate in most prisons. A good educational program must aim at making up the deficiency in formal schooling that we have seen is general among prisoners. It should also develop a skill or a trade for each prisoner so that upon release he can be gainfully employed. Most important, an educational program should be designed to develop the prisoner morally and spiritually so that true reform is possible.

Probation and parole are seriously neglected features of the prison program. The mere serving of a certain number of years in prison does not automatically prepare a man to return to society and stay out of trouble in the future. Careful preparation of the prisoner is necessary. Obtaining employment for him and providing him with certain helps during his first year or so of freedom remove one of the major causes of crime. A good rehabilitation program within the prison has small chance of achieving permanent results unless the prisoner is released at the right time and under proper supervision.

Substitutes for imprisonment. Two alternatives to confinement in prison have been tried with varying success. The first of these is probation (usually of first offenders), whereby the convicted person is given a suspended sentence and put on his good behavior. He must report periodically to a probation officer and account for his actions. Probation has not yet been given a good trial in this country. It cannot operate successfully without a fairly large staff of competently trained individuals who have a sincere interest in the persons under their charge.

A good probation system operates at much lower cost per person than does a prison. The total custodial staff in federal and state prisons for 167,000 inmates is 15,000. To this must be added the 400 wardens and deputy wardens and about 7,500 other employees. This is a ratio of one employee to every seven inmates. For the 675,000 persons on probation throughout the country there are about 3,000 probation officers, or one for about every 225 persons cared for. Contrasted with the $1,500 spent to keep each person in prison, the cost per person of probation varies from $20 in some states to $150 in others. A good probation system would cost considerably more, because it would involve a larger staff of better-trained officers who would therefore have to be better paid. Criminologists estimate that a good probation system would cost from $150 to $200 a year for each person handled, a sum that still contrasts favorably with the amount needed to maintain a person properly in prison. The best possible probation system, however, would not be a complete substitute for prison confinement, which is absolutely necessary for hardened criminals and those guilty of the gravest crimes. The defense of the law-abiding public is even more important than the rehabilitation of criminals.

The second alternative to the typical prison is the "open prison" or camp to which carefully selected prisoners are admitted. The open prison is very much like the Civilian Conservation camps of the 1930s. It has a minimum of security provisions, no walls, and no locked doors. Reliance is placed instead on the honor and the co-operation of the prisoners. Open prisons have been tried in various places in this country and with varying degrees of success. The open prison is less expensive to operate and it has generally enjoyed a better record than the confining prison; but statistics on escapes and rehabilitation records are a poor basis for comparison because the open prison has accepted only the better type of prisoner.

Jails and lockups. More than three million persons are committed to jails and lockups every year. The jail population is about sixty thousand on any given day in America. Considerable attention has been given to prison reform but very little to reform of the jails and lockups. The jail population consists of a motley crowd of vagrants, drug addicts, drunkards, prostitutes, sex deviates, and accused persons awaiting trial. The lockup, usually called "police station" in the cities, has a similar crowd. Jails are also used as the place of imprisonment for short sentences.

Jails and lockups are generally worse than prisons for their indiscriminate and unsystematic treatment of the inmates. Their only saving feature is that the individual inmate does not remain in them as long as in prison. In most jails no classification or segregation system is used, except the segregation of males and females. Mingling of all types of criminals in this fashion breeds additional crime. Jails are frequently antiquated buildings that have become firetraps. They are unsanitary, the food is bad, and often the staff personnel are merely qualified for their roles as peace enforcement officers.

The community has the duty of protecting the jailed individual's natural rights and treating him as a human being.

"Open prisons" such as the Federal Correctional Institution in Seagoville, Tex., admit only carefully selected prisoners. These prisons concentrate on reforming and rehabilitating prisoners. (Bureau of Prisons)

This is particularly true of the many jailed individuals who have committed no serious crime. Many are held because they cannot or will not pay the fine charged against them for a misdemeanor. Committees investigating conditions in various jails in the country have made recommendations that can be summed up under these headings:

1. There should be classification in each jail to separate males and females, juveniles and adults, harmless and dangerous, well and diseased.

2. Each prisoner should have a separate cell maintained in sanitary fashion.

3. Jails should be secure places of confinement in modern fireproof buildings.

4. Staff personnel should be adequately trained, and they should be employed under Civil Service regulations instead of political preference.

5. Unregulated punishment—the "third degree"—should be prohibited by law.

6. Provision should be made for periodic inspection of jails by interested citizen groups and by various officials.

There is a great public indifference toward jails and prisons since the public rarely hears of them until a riot or some other scandal within a prison comes to light. Then public indignation is aroused, reforms are discussed and occasionally adopted, and then the public becomes indifferent again. Such indifference does not recognize that prisons and jails are expensive institutions, in terms of human life and taxpayers' money. We should expect to receive in return both adequate protection and a measure of correction. Secure confinement is comparatively easy to achieve, but rehabilitation is difficult and uncertain. If, however, only a small percentage of the persons committed to prison are reformed, rehabilitation programs are justified.

Reform institutions. The juvenile (a child under eighteen in most states) is treated as a child by the law; that is, as a person who is not as responsible for his action as an adult. For that reason special courts,

probation officers, and institutions for confinement have been established in this country for juvenile criminals. Because the law does not hold the child responsible in the same way that it does the adult, his offense is referred to as a delinquent act instead of a crime. Any child who has reached the age of reason, however, is morally responsible for his acts.

Reform schools or training schools aim more at rehabilitating the juvenile criminal than at confining him. The theory that most criminologists work upon is that no one under eighteen can be considered a hardened criminal beyond hope of reform. Good reform schools are staffed by competent educators, vocational instructors, psychiatrists, and others who play special parts in preparing the juvenile offender for a useful social life when he is released. The proportion of inmates who are permanently reformed differs from institution to institution, but it is considerably higher in the juvenile schools of correction than in the adult prisons. Like crime, however, rehabilitation is a personal thing with juveniles as with adults. Reform is accomplished by the individual delinquent's willfully changing his attitude and his way of life.

REVIEW

35. Increase and Causes of Crime

A. Give some reasons for the increase of crime in the twentieth century. What is the strongest reason? Why?

B. How are crimes classified? Explain the statement of Pope Pius XII in regard to crime.

C. Explain briefly three of the principal causes of crime.

36. Crime Prevention

A. List some of the more effective ways of preventing crime.

B. Explain how attacks on the causes of crime will aid the prevention of crime.

C. Describe the change in attitude of the public toward the criminal in the past thirty years.

D. Contrast the new and old concepts of prisons.

37. Need for Prison Reform

A. Describe the conditions that exist in a good prison.

B. List the findings of the American Prison Association in regard to conditions in prisons.

C. Describe the recommended program of punishment and rehabilitation.

D. Describe two substitutes for imprisonment and point out the merits of each.

E. What specific reforms should be made in regard to the jails and lockups of our communities?

F. What special problem does the juvenile criminal present? What is being done for him? Why is this a serious problem at the present time?

THE CHAPTER IN REVIEW

A. A decline in public morality is most often the cause of a widespread increase of crime. Discuss the causes of crime that stem from such decline in public morality.

B. What is the purpose of punishment? Why does society have the right to punish?

C. Today juvenile crime is a serious problem. Discuss the means to overcome it and the safeguards necessary to prevent delinquent youngsters from becoming hardened in crime.

SELECTED READINGS

General treatments of the problem of the criminal are to be found in Mabel A. Elliott, *Crime in Modern Society* (New York: Harper & Brothers, 1952), and Sir Norwood East, *Society and Criminal* (Springfield, Ill.: Charles C Thomas, Publisher, 1951). The penologist,

John A. Gavin, treats religious laxity, broken homes, and poor education as basic factors in crime in an article entitled "Three Factors in Crime," *Social Order* (January 1952). The May 1954 issue of *The Annals of the American Academy of Political and Social Science* is devoted to the problem of the criminal.

Probation and parole programs instead of imprisonment are studied by Paul W. Keve, *Prison, Probation or Parole* (Minneapolis: University of Minnesota Press, 1954). Keve's studies are restricted to the area around Washington, D.C., where he handles parole programs, but his remarks can be seen to apply to the national problem of imprisonment and parole.

Juvenile delinquency is the subject of many studies. The following are among the more sensible treatments: Clement S. Mihanovich, *Principles of Juvenile Delinquency* (Milwaukee: The Bruce Publishing Co., 1950); Rev. Kenneth Morgan, *Juvenile Delinquency Again!* (New York: The Paulist Press, 1951); Ruth Strang, *Facts about Juvenile Delinquency* (Chicago: Science Research Associates, 1952).

PROJECTS

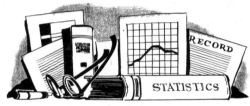

1. Local governments have set up commissions to study crime, and youth boards have been set up in many areas to stem juvenile delinquency. A committee of your class can offer valuable suggestions toward reducing crime, after studying the programs for crime prevention that are present in your own community.

2. The history of most notorious crimes includes many of the factors that have been discussed in this chapter. Select one of these crimes (or even a recent crime that is currently publicized in the newspapers) and see what started the criminal on the road to crime. Caution should be employed, however, in order not to pre-judge any given case.

3. A class discussion on the extent that newspapers, comic books, movies, and television may, in some instances, contribute to crime will be rewarding if suggestions for the curbing and control of these influences are made.

Chapter 14. Health and Welfare

38. CARE OF DEPENDENT PEOPLE

In every community there are some people who are in need of help from others. These are the dependent classes —the sick, the aged, the disabled, and the orphaned children who must rely on other members of the community for support. Dependents may be classified as those who are temporarily disabled and those who are chronically unfit (or too young) to be active, self-sufficient members of the community. The temporarily disabled suffer from diseases or other disabilities of which they can be cured and restored to active life, such as measles, tuberculosis, or broken limbs. The chronically disabled require treatment for disabilities that cannot be cured, such as heart trouble and some forms of mental illness. The problem with the chronically disabled is to render their lives as nearly normal as possible and to find a place for them in society, if possible, so that they are not completely inactive.

Ideally, dependent people should be taken care of by their families. But this ideal is often impossible to realize because of the expense involved or because of the nature of the care required. The local community is obliged, in justice and charity, to help families care for their disabled. When the local community is unable to provide adequate care for its dependent members, state agencies and the federal government are obliged to help.

Three lines of endeavor present themselves in dealing with the problems of dependent classes in a community. (1) *Preventive action* strives to reduce the number of persons falling into the dependent class to the minimum. This includes such action as safety campaigns to reduce the number of accidents, inoculation for immunity against certain diseases, and periodic health examinations. (2) *Treatment* cures as many victims who fall into the dependent class as possible. This includes such things as hospitalization, effective use of the best medicine and the best trained personnel, and health-insurance plans to enable an individual to afford adequate care. (3) *Rehabilitation* tries to prepare the victim for returning to as active a life as possible. This includes such things as providing artificial limbs, teaching certain skills to the blind, or training a person with heart disease for a less

strenuous but productive occupation.

The social cost of physical disability. Accidents and sickness cost our nation billions of dollars a year. It is estimated that the average worker loses about ten days on the job a year because of illness. This involves a considerable loss in the production of goods and services which constitute our national income, in addition to the large expense for hospitals, medicine, and medical services. The best estimates are that the total annual cost of sickness is about ten billion dollars. About two million serious accidental injuries occur annually. About twenty thousand of these injuries are fatal or cause permanent disability. A large percentage (we have no way of estimating accurately how large) of disabling sicknesses and accidents is avoidable.

The number of physicians in this country has increased constantly, but many more are still needed. There were 145,000 physicians in 1920, 175,000 in 1940, and 218,500 in 1953. Meanwhile, however, the population was increasing at about the same rate, so that there was one physician to every 735 people in 1920 and one to every 730 in 1953. There are about 91,000 dentists, or one to every 1,725 people, approximately the same ratio for the past thirty years. Medical and welfare authorities agree that this is not enough physicians or dentists to care for the health of the nation. Moreover, they are not well distributed. In some rural areas there are no hospitals, doctors, or dentists within a radius of many miles, whereas there are hundreds of doctors and many hospitals in each of the larger cities.

The President's Commission on the Health Needs of the Nation reported in

Year	Total Disability Work-Injuries	Total Loss (Estimated) of Man-days	Future Loss (Estimated) of Man-days because of these accidents
1954	1,860,000	38,000,000	190,000,000
1953	2,034,000	41,000,000	206,000,000
1952	2,040,000	41,000,000	206,000,000
1951	2,100,000	42,000,000	219,000,000
1950	1,952,000	40,000,000	212,000,000
1949	1,870,000	39,000,000	204,000,000
1948	2,019,900	41,000,000	219,000,000
1947	2,059,000	447,000,000	233,700,000

Cost of Accidents to American Industry

Dr. Jonas E. Salk developed the polio vaccine that may banish the threat of paralytic polio. Throughout America, school children participated in the federally sponsored inoculation programs. (Natl. Foundation for Infantile Paralysis)

1952 that there was no prospect of a sizable increase in the number of physicians or dentists in the near future. There are only seventy-nine medical schools and forty-three dental schools in the country. They are filled to capacity, and they cannot easily accommodate more students because of the nature of medical and dental education. Expensive equipment and hospital facilities are required. Expert teaching staffs are needed. Moreover, medical and dental schools must depend on grants-in-aid and private philanthropy to continue operation, because tuition never pays more than a small part of the expenses. Increasing the capacity of our medical schools appears impossible without some kind of public aid. Finally, nine to fifteen years of training after high school are required before a young man can start practicing medicine. The problem of increasing the number of physicians·and dentists in proportion to a rapidly expanding population is therefore a serious one.

The number of hospitals in the country has not increased greatly in the last thirty years, but the accommodations within

the hospitals have vastly increased. In 1920 there were slightly more than 800,000 beds for hospital patients, and now there are almost twice that number, more than 1,500,000. Moreover, the functions of the hospital have multiplied in the last thirty years with the addition of clinics and other outpatient departments. The President's Commission on the Health Needs of the Nation described the modern hospital as "the basic institution providing technical facilities for the promotion of health, the diagnosis and treatment of disease, and the rehabilitation of the disabled. More and more, it is becoming responsible for a continuing flow of health services to the community, supplying preventive services in health centers at one end of the line and rehabilitative and home care services at the other end."

The record of American medicine. The accomplishments of American physicians and their associates—research men, nurses, social workers, public health specialists, and the like—have been truly wonderful. Research has discovered a number of "wonder drugs"; better medical education has given us more expertly trained practicing physicians; public health work has eliminated many causes of disease, such as contaminated food;

Orphaned children receive loving care in foundling homes sponsored by religious communities. These privately supported institutions augment government agencies in caring for dependent persons. (Catholic Charities)

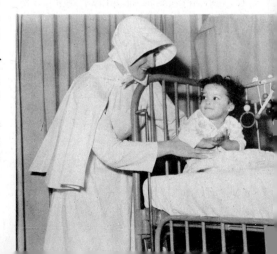

The Veterans Administration of the federal government operates 173 hospitals, which have an average daily patient load of 110,893, according to VA reports for November 1955. The hospitals are excellently staffed and equipped, and they provide services to veterans at minimum costs. (Veterans Administration)

and campaigns by private agencies, like the Heart Fund, have done much to diagnose diseases in their early stages and to cure them. As a result we have reduced infectious diseases almost to the vanishing point. The tuberculosis death rate, for example, dropped from 194 for each 100,000 people in 1900 to 27 in 1950. The death rate from pneumonia for the same period dropped from 202 to 34, and the diphtheria rate dropped from 40 to less than one. Between 1900 and 1950 the death rate for all infectious diseases dropped from 676 to 79 for each 100,000 persons.

Death rates in maternity cases dropped in about the same proportion, largely because of better prenatal care given to the mother and hospitalization during the time of delivery. In 1915 there were 61 maternity deaths for each 10,000 live births, and in 1949 the number had dropped to nine. The infant death rate also fell considerably, but the death rate of infants less than a year old is still high, partly because many communities do not have the expensive equipment necessary to save lives of babies born prematurely. Death rates have fallen sharply in the children and young people's age groups,

because these were the classes that were hardest hit by infectious diseases.

The result of these advances in medicine is that the average American's life expectancy is increased to a new high— for women, 72.6 years; for men, 66.6 years. There is some misunderstanding about the lengthened life expectancy. People 65 years of age cannot expect to live a great deal longer than people who were lucky enough to attain the same age a century ago. But a much larger proportion of the people reach the age of 65. The victory of medicine over infectious disease and other medical accomplishments are changing the age composition of the population. People over 65 will no longer be rare exceptions. They will make up a sizable part of the population.

Credit for these accomplishments must be shared by men and women in many different fields of work. The practicing physician, dentist, nurse, and social worker have saved countless lives and have instructed their patients in preventive medicine. Americans can take pride in the selfless devotion that most physicians have given to their work. Many industries and labor unions have adopted health programs that helped to raise the

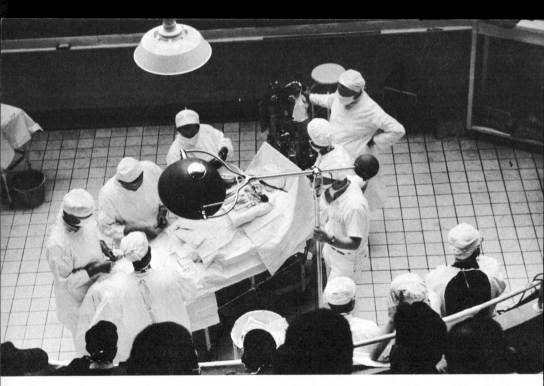

This photo of a modern operating room in a medical-college hospital helps to explain the high cost of surgery. In attendance are doctors, nurses, and technicians, whose service fees added to the laboratory and hospital rates make the expense prohibitive for many. (Abbott Laboratories)

health standards of the working class in this country. Various local, state, and federal agencies have played a valiant part in the battle against disease. Public health programs include sanitation measures, periodic physical examination of school children, immunity shots against certain infectious diseases, and enforced quarantine of those who have contracted such diseases.

Two other groups have done less spectacular but very effective work in this battle against disease. They are the private organization and the medical researcher. An education campaign has been undertaken by private organizations to teach people the causes and the early symptoms of such diseases as cancer, diabetes, heart trouble, and tuberculosis. Early diagnosis of such diseases makes possible a cure or at least an arrest of the disease. Finally, the scientist working in the laboratory has played an important —perhaps the most important—role in defeating disease. It is in the laboratory

that the causes of disease have been found, and it is there that the new medicines and the new treatments have been perfected. It has been by teamwork and co-operation, then, that these different people in health work have increased our life expectancy and enabled us to avoid many diseases that formerly filled people with dread.

The successes we have just recounted, however, have created new sets of problems. We have already indicated one of them: the problems connected with the aged and those afflicted with chronic illnesses. A person can live many years with heart trouble nowadays, but he cannot live as if his heart were perfectly sound. An increasingly large number in each community suffer from one or another of the chronic diseases, and they present a set of social problems to the community.

Although great progress has been made in medicine in the last half century, much yet remains to be done. The cause and cure of some diseases, such as muscular dystrophy, are still completely unknown. Heart disease and cancer are the leading causes of death at the present time. Research and studies are being conducted to discover the causes of these diseases and meanwhile to retard their fatal effects by early diagnosis and treatment. The number of young men rejected for military service in World War II for physical disability shows that the health problem is still serious. More than 15 per cent of the men called up for the armed services since the war have been rejected for physical reasons even though the requirements have been lowered.

The financial problem of obtaining adequate medical services. Medical services are necessarily expensive. Let us take the case of a high school student who is rushed to the hospital with acute appendicitis. His appendix is removed within an hour. He remains in the hospital for a week and returns home, cured. He incurs the obvious expense of board and room for the week, but in addition there are many other costs involved. The anesthetic, drugs, and medicine administered to him are expensive. A number of tests must be taken before and after the operation. Each of these tests involves a corps of laboratory workers whose salaries must be paid. The physician and the nurses involved in the case must charge fees that, spread out over a number of years, pay for their expensive training. The hospital must charge rates that will help pay for its costly equipment and many special services.

This is a simple and a relatively inexpensive case. Catastrophic illness, such as tuberculosis, heart disease, or mental illness, that strikes the head of a family incapacitates him from earning a living for a long time and costs him thousands of dollars for adequate care. These are unavoidable expenses. Hospitals and doctors must have good equipment, costing thousands of dollars, which they must pay for from patients' fees. Wealthy people can afford occasional catastrophic illnesses, and poor people can obtain care in clinics and through various public health programs. The American in the middle-income bracket, however, is not eligible for clinic treatment and he often is not able to afford adequate medical treatment when afflicted with an illness like cancer.

Various insurance programs and prepayment plans have been worked out to spread the financial burden of illness and enable the patient to obtain good medical care without going into serious debt. The best-known prepayment plan is the Blue Cross, whereby employees of a participating company make monthly payments to the Blue Cross, for which they are entitled to hospital care under certain conditions. The employee pays so much a month to the Blue Cross. In return, he and the members of his family receive normal hospital care, including most of the services like laboratory tests and use of the operating room. The President's Commission on the Health Needs of the Nation recommended the extension of prepaid health plans to as many people in the country as possible. It recommended also that these plans provide outpatient care for their participants. The Blue Cross and most other plans require a participant to be in the hospital at least overnight. As a result, many hospital beds are occupied by people who could be treated within an hour or two and sent home. Similar plans, such as the Blue Shield, take care of surgeons' and doctors' fees up to a certain amount for hospitalized cases.

The prepayment method takes care of ordinary medical expenses, such as operations, childbirth, and hospitalization for treatment of accidents. But it is not devised to deal with catastrophic illness. This sort of illness is more like a fire or an airplane accident. It hits relatively few people, but it is destructive financially when it strikes. Months of hospitalization

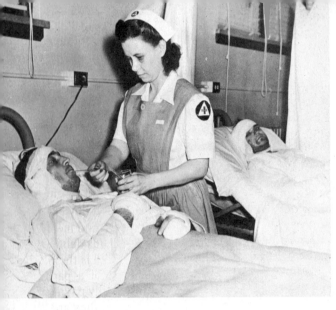

Disasters such as the one that occurred in an Ohio gas plant and hospitalized these victims are covered by factory insurance policies. A gas explosion in the home, which could inflict just as serious injuries, would be classified as a catastrophic accident and would cause great hardships in suffering, expense, and loss of income. Group insurance plans are designed to cover these emergencies. (American Red Cross)

are frequently required when a person is seriously injured or suffers a nervous breakdown. Loss of earnings and medical expenses run into thousands of dollars in such a case. An insurance policy, similar to fire or accident insurance, is one way to deal with catastrophic illness. Most insurance companies have such policies at the present time. For a certain annual premium the insured has all his medical expenses paid above a certain amount (about $300) if these expenses result from one of the catastrophic illnesses covered by the policy.

Prepayment plans and insurance methods of paying medical expenses operate on actuarial principles—the calculation of premiums on a statistical analysis of the risk taken by the company with each policy. Statistics indicate, for example, that out of each thousand people in a given area a certain number will be hospitalized for a certain number of days and require a certain total of services. This cost is spread among the thousand participants and the premium set at a figure that will cover the estimated cost. These plans distribute the burden among those who can afford to participate. People with little income, however, can rarely afford the $100 to $500 in premiums that

adequate protection will cost them. Some other method needs to be worked out for people in the lower-income groups to obtain adequate health services. Perhaps no scheme can be worked out that would not involve more disadvantages politically and socially than the good it might accomplish. A vast amount of free medical service is given by doctors or paid for by charitable institutions. But the problem of adequate care for the health of all citizens remains.

39. THE STATE, THE DOCTORS, AND MEDICAL INSURANCE

"Socialized medicine." There has been much debate in this country on whether we should adopt a national plan of compulsory health insurance. In the heat of argument the real medical needs of the nation are frequently overlooked. Health insurance can be of many kinds, as we have already seen, and the nub of the argument about "socialized medicine" is whether the insurance should be compulsory and whether it should be administered by the federal government.

Americans do not seem to want anything as extreme as a federal system of compulsory health insurance. We seem committed to our system of private medicine and voluntary insurance, which has worked well in the past. A partial answer to our need is found in group practice, a system whereby a number of specialists combine their skills and their expensive equipment to offer expert medical care to their patients at considerably lower cost than if each practiced individually. In days gone by American physicians resisted group practice more or less instinctively, but medical practice in the armed forces served to change many a young doctor's mind. More than half the doctors who served in the armed forces stated that they intended to enter group practice when they left the services. In 1952 the President's Commission on the Health Needs of the Nation found more than six hundred groups practicing throughout the country, and a large number of additional groups have begun practicing each year since then.

The advantages of group practice are obvious. In each group are such specialists as an internal medicine physician, a surgeon, a nose and throat man, perhaps a dentist, a pediatrician, and an obstetrician. By pooling offices and expensive equipment these men reduce their overhead and thereby the fees they must charge to make a reasonably good living. Moreover, by pooling skills they can offer the patient adequate expert treatment for ordinary ailments. Such a method, therefore, combines the advantages of expert treatment and low cost. This method of group treatment has been adopted by many companies and labor unions as the best way to serve the health needs of a large number of employees. When the companies or the unions are too small to support a group, they frequently use its services at special rates, and the group of doctors supplements this income by general practice.

Various group-practice plans, combined with voluntary health plans worked out by large companies and unions, cover about 15 per cent of the American working force today. The Cooperative Health Federation of America, which sponsors such plans, has grown steadily since its inception in 1946. It publishes and distributes literature concerning health problems and sends out to its members a monthly information bulletin on the progress of health plans throughout the country.

Most of these health plans are financed by contributions made by management according to labor contracts negotiated with the union. This is one of the "fringe benefits" that unions have obtained from management. One of the model health plans is the Labor Health Institute of St. Louis, which serves the AFL teamsters' union and the CIO local of warehouse workers. Management contributes 3.5 per cent or 5 per cent of the employees' wages. For the smaller amount, medical, dental, and hospital services are provided for the employees, and for the larger amount the same services are provided for the employees and their families. More than two hundred shops in St. Louis have subscribed to the full family plan. Among other services, all members are entitled to an annual medical examination which includes all the X-ray and laboratory tests used in a thorough medical checkup.

Most employers and personnel managers of the shops using the plan are satisfied that it serves a good purpose and that it benefits both management and labor. A survey showed, for example, that absenteeism among employees covered by the plan was less than half the absenteeism among those not covered. Moreover, adequate medical protection removes a major cause of worry among employees and thereby increases their efficiency on the job. Institutions similar to the Labor Health Institute of St. Louis have been set up by the Hotel Trades Council in New York and the Central

Labor Union of Philadelphia. Some industries have set up their own independent health and welfare funds for employees and their dependents.

The fact remains, however, that a large number of workers are not covered by any health plan and cannot afford good medical service. Various public health services have tried in different ways to help these people. The interest of the national government in the health of the nation was increased when more than 40 per cent of the men called up for service in World War II were rejected for medical reasons on first examination. In 1953, Congress created the Department of Health, Education and Welfare. The law creating the department set up an office of special assistant to the department secretary on all matters relating to public health and medicine. The special assistant has complete responsibility for reviewing all health and medical programs of the department and recommending any needed changes. He also reviews all legislative

Sterility testing of serum samples submitted by pharmaceutical manufacturers is one of the services of the Biologics Standards Division of the federal government. (Dept. of Health, Education and Welfare)

proposals relating to health and medicine and is responsible for formulating department policy on these matters.

Preventive and rehabilitative medicine. We have accomplished a great deal in the diagnosis and treatment of diseases. We have made considerably less progress in the two fields of preventing illness and rehabilitating the partially disabled person. Only a small percentage (about 6 per cent) of our health bill is spent on research and preventive medicine. Most communities, however, have recently increased their expenditures in this direction. Local public health service in most communities now includes milk, food, and water inspection services to protect residents against contamination of these sources. It also provides for periodic examination of school children, for quarantine of homes with infectious diseases, for inspection of public dining places, and for various educational means whereby the public is acquainted with the cause and treatment of different diseases.

The federal government enters the field of preventive medicine by inspecting tourists and immigrants entering the country, requiring them to have immunization shots and to be free of infectious disease. The federal government also inspects animals and plants that might bring infectious diseases into the country, and it regulates the distribution and sale of drugs and foodstuffs that might be harmful to the user's health. Moreover, it inspects such food as meat to ensure the consumer of an uncontaminated food supply.

Less has been done in the field of rehabilitation. Dr. Howard A. Rusk, chairman of the Department of Rehabilitation and Physical Medicine at New York University, claims:

Today our problems of chronic disease and physical disability have reached such proportions that they cannot be solved by any single individual or group of individuals. They are community problems involving medical, social and economic factors, and they can be solved

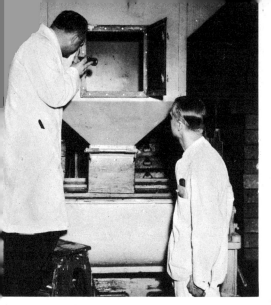

The Food and Drug Administration of the federal government establishes sanitary codes for food-processing plants and conducts regular inspections of factories. Here an inspector examines equipment in a large bakery. (Dept. of Health, Education and Welfare)

only by community action to which each individual and group within the community contributes his own particular skills and experience.

The problems of rehabilitation differ with each disability. But a few general principles can be suggested that apply to all types of cases. (1) Skilled workers are needed who can teach the individual to adjust mentally and physically to his new condition—how, for example, to use artificial limbs, or how to read Braille and prepare for work that one can do when blind. (2) The community must provide jobs for the disabled so that they can earn at least part of their livelihood, regain their self-confidence, and make their contribution to the community's welfare. (3) Careful thought must be given to each case so that the individual can be prepared for the kind of work he is able to do well. (4) A series of tests should be used to discover each individual's skills and aptitudes so that his talents do not remain buried.

At the present time we do not have nearly enough doctors trained in preventive medicine or social workers trained in rehabilitation. Nor is there sufficient public interest in the problem to create and equip rehabilitation centers in every large community. Especially in the field of mental illness, which we shall discuss later in this chapter, is there need for personnel and funds to enable these patients to regain a useful role in society.

One approach to the problem has been disability insurance, whereby payments

Although there is no known cure for polio, there are various types of treatment that help patients to take up again the life they knew. At the Warm Springs Foundation in Georgia this young man is learning how to operate an electric typewriter with the assistance of an occupational therapist. (Natl. Foundation for Infantile Paralysis)

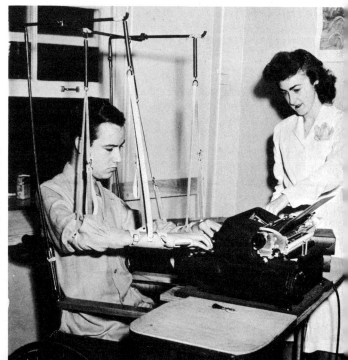

are made to the disabled to make up for his loss in earning power while he is recovering. Compulsory insurance against injuries on the job, the best remedy against disability-caused loss of income, has been in effect in some states for half a century. Today almost every state has some form of workmen's compensation. Most states set a maximum number of weeks beyond which compensation is not paid.

More recently, disability insurance has been extended in four states (Rhode Island, New York, New Jersey, and California) to cover injuries incurred off the job. Eleven states have bills in committee to provide for compulsory disability insurance similar to that of the four states mentioned above. Although they differ in details, these bills provide a minimum of $10 a week and a maximum of $25 or $30 for a limited time, usually half a year. This type of disability insurance does not aim at giving adequate coverage for total disability but rather at providing temporary benefits to cover a relatively brief layoff from work. For that reason some persons, such as Senator Paul Douglas of Illinois, propose federal legislation.

Mr. Douglas sponsored a bill to "make rehabilitation services available to individuals, so that they can, whenever possible, get back on their feet." The Doug- las bill provides that if the worker cannot earn a living again he will receive regular monthly payments until he reaches the age of sixty-five, when he will become eligible for social security. Whether the Douglas proposal is practicable is a matter for argument. But it does seem that some combination of disability insurance and rehabilitation is needed to protect persons disabled by accident or illness and to salvage their abilities—both for their personal sake and for the social good.

40. ACCIDENTS, INSANITY, ALCOHOLISM, CARE OF THE AGED

Accidents. The fourth leading cause of deaths in this country is accidents. They are the leading cause of death among children and young people. Altogether, between 90,000 and 100,000 people die annually from various kinds of accidents: traffic accidents, drownings, burns, falls, explosions, and other such happenings. Two facts make the accident picture even worse when it is examined closely: (1) Most accidents need not happen; they are the result of carelessness. (2) Accidents strike young people more frequently than older people, largely because the young are more careless. Consequently, society is hurt more severely by accidents

The "bird cage" around this press is used as a safeguard to prevent the operator from getting his hands injured. Industrial accidents have been decreasing steadily since 1952, when only 22.3 per cent of the country's total accidents were occupational. (General Motors)

than by any other leading cause of death.

In addition to fatal accidents, of course, there are more than a million accidents each year which cause temporary or permanent disability to the victim. The cost of accidents each year is incalculable, but conservative estimates are that it amounts to at least seven or eight billion dollars. We must reconcile ourselves to the fact that we shall always have a large number of accidents. We live in a world of machines and we are human beings with fallible judgment and weak bodies. The best safety observance will reduce fatal accidents to a minimum—a figure much lower than the present total of 90,000 to 100,000 a year—but some drivers will occasionally miscalculate speed or "black out" momentarily, something will go wrong with the brakes of an automobile, or someone will slip at the top of the stairs.

The National Safety Council insists that "the techniques of accident prevention are known and proved. All that remains is their vigorous application." Community action in the form of safety programs, such as the Safe Driving Day

The mining industry, which for many years was plagued with accidents resulting from the collapse of timbering used to support tunnels, now uses expansion bolts to hold ceilings in place. The development of new safety devices and the emphasis on accident prevention have helped America's industries to reduce the number of man-hours lost because of accidents.

Stillwater, Okla., is justly proud of its excellent safety record. All bicycles in Stillwater are licensed and registered, thereby aiding the police in impressing on the children their responsibility as operators of licensed vehicles who must obey all traffic signals. (Standard Oil Co., N.J.)

inaugurated in 1954, do something to remind us of the unnecessary death toll taken by accidents every day. But final responsibility for reducing accidents to the minimum possible in our industrial society rests with each individual. It is a sign of maturity when we calculate the risk involved in "taking a chance" and when we avoid "chances," realizing that one mistake may snuff out our own or someone else's life.

Mental illness. Along with accidents, mental illness has become much more prevalent in the last half century. This is due partly to our recognizing and treating mental illnesses that were ignored or hidden in the past. Nevertheless, there seem to be more mental disorders in proportion to the population than there were at the beginning of the century. One cause of this increase is undoubtedly the fast, nervous pace that is forced upon us by modern civilization. Mental illness accounted for more draft rejections and more medical discharges than any other physical ailment in World War II. It is estimated that one out of every twenty people will be treated in an institution for mental illness sometime during his life. In 1931 there were 352,000 patients in mental hospitals, or 284 for every 100,000 people. In 1951 the number had increased to 584,500 patients, or 387 for every 100,000. Feeble-minded patients had increased in similar proportion, from 77,500 in 1931 to 137,000 in 1951.

A distinction should be made between mental illness and mental deficiency or feeble-mindedness. Mental deficiency involves such lack of judgment and intelligence that the individual can never fully care for himself. He must receive institutional or home care throughout his life. There are three generally accepted grades of feeble-mindedness. The idiot has practically no intelligence. The imbecile has the intelligence of a seven-year-old child or less. The moron has an intelligence between that of an eight-year-old child and one of thirteen. All three classes of feeble-minded are custodial problems to society because they are not responsible for their actions. Morons can live something like normal lives if they are carefully supervised, but idiots and imbeciles require confinement and close supervision when they are away from home. There is no known effective treatment for any of these mental deficients.

Mental illness, on the other hand, is an acquired disease which can frequently be cured. The two principal types of mental illnesses are neurosis and psychosis. The former can be treated successfully by a competent doctor or psychiatrist if the patient co-operates. Neurosis is the failure to adjust properly to life's problems, and it results in unreasonable fears, anger, or worries. Neurotics do not function efficiently in society. They can be cured, or at least helped, by removing the causes of their unreasonable fears or anxieties. Such treatment is usually long and expensive.

Psychosis is a serious mental illness which is either organic or functional— that is, caused by physical disease or injury (organic), or by tensions and anxieties which cause complete mental breakdown (functional). Some progress has been made in the last twenty years in the treatment and cure of psychoses. Surgery, various kinds of shock treatment, and psychotherapy have all been used with some measure of success. More research is needed in this field, however, and we must expect mental illness to be a serious social problem for at least a few more generations. The community's problem is to provide adequate institutional care for mental defectives and those mentally ill, for two purposes: (1) to protect the community and the mentally ill person from his irresponsible acts; (2) to treat those who can be cured in order to restore them to normal life.

Alcoholism. Another class of dependents who are a burden and a problem for the community are the alcoholics. "Alcoholism" is considered a disease by most physicians; but it is also a moral problem because it involves the loss of the distinctively human attributes of freedom and rationality. How responsible the alcoholic is for his compulsive drinking is a matter for speculation, but personally he bears a large degree of responsiblity for contracting the disease of alcoholism.

Alcoholism is a serious national problem in terms of lives wrecked and time lost from productive work. Excessive drinking is said to cause industry a loss of about one billion dollars a year. Many homes are broken up each year because of drinking, and it is a leading cause of accidents.

Most people who drink, drink moderately. They do not drink enough at any one time to become drunk; that is, to lose control over their minds, their bodies, and their wills. Neither do they drink so frequently that they cannot do without liquor. They are "social drinkers" who drink moderately at parties and other social events. It is estimated that there are about four million "problem drinkers" in the country and about one million alcoholics. "Problem drinkers" are those who drink too much on occasion or who drink too frequently and to excess. Drink is a source of trouble to "problem drinkers." It interferes with their family life and their social relationships. It causes them to lose time at work, perhaps to be involved in traffic accidents, and in general to be less reliable persons. "Problem drinkers" can cure themselves by the exercise of will power and extreme caution as to the time of drinking and the number of drinks they take.

The alcoholic is faced with a much more serious problem. The only solution is for him to give up drinking altogether, because for the true alcoholic drinking is compulsive; that is, he has no control over his appetite after he has taken the first drink. The alcoholic keeps on drinking until he loses control over himself morally and physically. Various methods have been employed to help the alcoholic give up drinking permanently. Drugs that create an aversion to alcohol have been used with some success. Psychiatric treatment has been successful in some cases. Alcoholics Anonymous has had more success than any other group in curing excessive drinkers because it approaches excessive drinking primarily as a moral problem with psychological and physical overtones. Through prayer and a frank admission of one's weakness and dependence on God and through mutual help Alcoholics Anonymous has cured 100,000 drinkers. Each member pledges to refrain from drinking for the day—and he renews the pledge each day of his life.

Addiction to narcotics. Even more serious than alcoholism is addiction to drugs. There are not as many drug addicts as there are alcoholics, but the number seems to be increasing more rapidly, especially among the young people. It is more serious than alcoholism because it leads to the complete moral, physical, and social disintegration of its victims— and it is more difficult to cure. The drug addict finds it easy to start. Soon his system demands more—stronger drugs and at more frequent intervals. Within a short time he cannot get along without drugs. He will steal or even commit murder to get a few days' supply. Since drugs are illegal, the drug addict soon finds himself in the clutches of the organized crime syndicate that can supply him.

Drug addicts can be cured with institutional care, but only about 40 per cent stay cured permanently. Strong will power is required after release if the individual is not to become an addict again. Preventive action, therefore, is the only sure way of handling this serious social problem. Co-operation among local, state, and national agencies in the enforcement of existing laws is necessary to crack down on the organized criminals who exploit the drug addict's weakness. Compulsory institutional treatment seems advisable for the victims, so that they can be restored to normal life.

The care of the aged. Until recently, most old folks lived with their children's families, and the rest were taken care of at little cost in an "old folks' home." The success of the medical profession in saving us from the fatal effects of infectious disease and other illnesses has created a new problem for us—the problem of a large proportion of the population being over 65. In 1900 only 4.1 per cent of the population was over 65; in 1950 the percentage had increased to 7.6. There were more than twelve million persons over 65

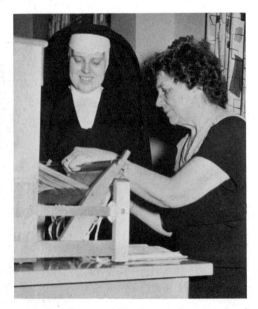

cative facilities to the aged to enable them to live active, happy lives after retirement.

Gerontology is in its infancy. Until many intensive studies now under way are completed we shall not have the factual data on which action can be based. Meanwhile we know that the problem of adjusting social institutions to a changing population is a continual problem for society.

In St. Patrick's Home for the Aged, women are taught various skills, such as weaving, which enable them to lead useful and productive lives that are also personally satisfying. (Catholic Charities)

in 1950, and it is estimated that this number will increase to more than twenty-one million in 1975.

A new science has developed within the last decade to deal with the problem of the aged. It is called gerontology, and it studies the problems of the aged in the fields of medicine, economics, sociology, and psychology. Generally stated, the problem is to enable people over 65 to continue to lead useful, productive lives that will also be personally satisfying. Work in these various areas began only a few years ago. There are now a number of doctors who specialize in geriatrics—the study and treatment of the "degenerative" diseases common to the aged. Some economists are now studying the problem of providing retired needy persons with an adequate income, and modifying job requirements in order to postpone the age of retirement. Some communities have begun to study ways and means of offering recreational and edu-

REVIEW

38. Care of Dependent People

A. Define dependents. What is the obligation of the community toward the care of dependents? What three means can be taken to deal with the problem of dependent classes in the community?

B. What are the basic reasons for the shortage of physicians in the United States today?

C. List some of the accomplishments of American medicine.

D. Name some of the means by which the high costs of medicine, doctors, and hospitals are met by individuals.

39. The State, the Doctors, and Medical Insurance

A. What is meant by socialized medicine? What kind of health program do Americans seem to prefer? What is group practice? List some of the advantages of it.

B. Describe how labor has made use of the various health plans. What are some of the benefits of such plans?

C. What caused the increase of the government's interest in the health of the nation? What has Congress done about it?

D. What has been done in the field of preventive medicine? Describe the role of the federal government in this field. What are the accomplishments of the states in the field of rehabilitation? What has Senator Douglas proposed?

40. Accidents, Insanity, Alcoholism, Care of the Aged

A. What are the distressing facts shown in the accident record in this country? What, ultimately, must be done to prevent accidents?

B. What are the causes for the increased number of mental illnesses? What is meant by feeble-mindedness? How is mental illness classified? How is each type treated?

C. Alcoholism is both a disease and a moral problem. Why is it a serious national problem? What is a "social drinker"; a problem drinker; an alcoholic? What methods have been employed to cure the alcoholic?

D. Why is drug addiction such a serious problem today? What solutions are there for this problem?

E. Why has gerontology become an important science today? Describe the work started in behalf of the aged.

THE CHAPTER IN REVIEW

A. How can accidents be prevented? Describe the various ways whereby one may meet the extraordinary expenses of illness or accidents.

B. How have medical authorities, industry, labor, and government tried to meet the problems of accident prevention?

C. Summarize three additional problems in the field of health today and describe what is being done toward their solutions.

they should, but he does not advocate "socialized medicine" as the solution. This book is reviewed in an article by Edward Duff, "Medicine, a Public Utility?", *Social Order* (March 1954). An objective study of this subject is offered by George W. Bachman and Lewis Meriam, *The Issue of Compulsory Health Insurance* (Washington: The Brookings Institution, 1948). Other methods of paying for medical care are discussed in: "A Voluntary Approach to the National Health Problem" (Washington: National Catholic Welfare Conference, 1949), and A. H. Scheller, S.J., "How Co-op Health Plans Work," *Social Order* (October 1953).

Many pamphlets have been written on problems of mental health, alcoholism, and narcotics. The following are recommended: Rev. John C. Ford, S.J., *Alcoholism, Education for Sobriety* (New York: America Press, 1950); Frank A. Riley, *Alcoholics Anonymous* (St. Louis: The Queen's Work Press, 1947); Raymond G. McCarthy, *Facts about Alcohol* (Chicago: Science Research Associates, 1951); Alton L. Blakeslee, *Alcoholism—A Sickness That Can Be Beaten* (New York: Public Affairs Committee, 1952); George Thorman, *Toward Mental Health* (New York: Public Affairs Committee, 1950); Victor H. Vogel and Virginia E. Vogel, *Facts about Narcotics* (Chicago: Science Research Associates, 1951).

SELECTED READINGS

Building America's Health, a report to the President by the President's Commission on the Health Needs of the Nation (Washington: Government Printing Office, 1952), is a basic document on the subject of health and government policy.

The question of adequate medical care and the government's role in providing it for the people are examined by James Howard Means, *Doctors, People, and Government* (Boston: Little, Brown & Co., 1953). Dr. Means believes Americans do not get as good medical care as

PROJECTS

1. Prepare a report on the five major causes of death from disease in the United States. Outline the ways in which these diseases can be prevented and the number of deaths from them lessened. Your report should include a summary of the services, organizations, and educational programs that have been enlisted in the fight against these diseases.

2. The Blue Cross plan for providing for medical care is one of the well-known plans to ease the cost of illness. A committee from the class could make a worth-while report on the benefits of such a plan. The additional services of Blue Shield and other plans should be incorporated in this report and the findings made known to the class by use of the bulletin board.

3. The unions in many instances have their own health plans. Another committee in the class could write to one or more of the larger unions and obtain a copy and explanation of their health programs. An interesting comparison with the second project can then be made.

PROFILES

BOOKER T. WASHINGTON

BORN: Hale's Ford, Franklin County, Va., April 5, 1856
EDUCATED: Hampton Institute, 1875; advanced studies at Wayland Institute, Washington
DIED: November 14, 1915

A slave boy who was seven years old before he actually slept in a bed, Booker T. Washington is an outstanding example of what patience, study, and talent can accomplish. Years of hard labor in extreme poverty made possible his education at Hampton Institute, where he was janitor as well as student. Washington entered on a teaching career upon graduation, bringing to his classes the same determination to impart learning that he had demonstrated in acquiring it.

After several years teaching elsewhere, he returned to his alma mater as a teacher. There he received his first administrative assignment, being charged with the task of integrating Indian students admitted to Hampton on an experimental basis. Two years later, in 1881, Washington was appointed head, and only teacher, of a new school at Tuskegee. The school existed by act of the Alabama government, on paper only: Tuskegee had no building, no land, no assets except its founder.

Given such a forbidding prospect, Washington's great talents as a school organizer and administrator were challenged. With his stu-

dents and his gradually growing staff he actually built the buildings for his school. He added courses, enlarged the faculty, and he earned a national reputation. A prudent person, Washington set as his ambition the creation of a trade and technical school to provide Negroes with the skills that would open the way for economic security and self-sufficiency. To insure the success of his project, he also addressed himself to the development of an institute to train other Negro teachers who could teach and inspire future generations of young Negroes.

Washington's excellent administration developed Tuskegee from a struggling school into a prominent technical institute, attracting widespread attention. His talents as a speaker were displayed before more and more audiences that sought after him to hear his ideas on vocational education and on ways to help Negro Americans develop their abilities. He lent his organizational skills to such groups as the National Negro Business League, which encouraged small independent Negro businesses. A highly successful organizer, a powerful speaker and popular writer, Washington is best remembered as an original and dominant contributor to Negro education.

The Negro educator's own story of his life, *Up from Slavery* (New York: Doubleday, Page & Co., 1901), is a splendid introduction not only to his career and the problems of Negro education but to the personality and philosophy of the man himself. Basil Mathews' *Booker T. Washington: Educator and Interracial Interpreter* (Cambridge, Mass.: Harvard University Press, 1948) stresses his major contributions to society, while his speeches have been collected in E. Washington's *Selected Speeches of Booker T. Washington* (New York: Doubleday & Company, Inc., 1932).

REVEREND JOHN LAFARGE, S.J.

BORN: Newport, R.I., February 13, 1880
EDUCATED: Harvard, 1901; University of Innsbruck, 1905
ORDAINED: 1905

John LaFarge, son of one of the really outstanding artists in United States history, left the country after graduation from Harvard to study for the priesthood at the University of

Innsbruck, Austria. While at Innsbruck he determined to enter the Society of Jesus, and, after ordination on July 26, 1905, he returned to the United States to enter the Jesuit novitiate, Poughkeepsie, N.Y.

After completing his training in the Society of Jesus, Fr. LaFarge entered on years of mission service in poverty-stricken rural areas of Maryland. This life, in contrast with his family's literary and artistic circle of friends, which included such figures as Theodore Roosevelt, challenged him to harder work to develop the latent talents and encourage the spiritual, educational, and social welfare of his charges.

His priestly services were devoted to Negro parishes in Maryland and to mixed populations both there and in New York. These experiences led him to use his eloquent pen and attractive personality to draw the attention of other Americans to the social and economic problems raised by racial questions in the United States. The plight of the Negro struck him forcefully, and the fact that large numbers of Americans were unconcerned led Fr. LaFarge into organizing Catholic Interracial Councils. These councils concerned themselves with the study of race relations and methods of solving the social tensions in that field.

Fr. LaFarge led such organizations as the Catholic Laymen's Union in the study of papal encyclicals on social questions, and his clear and vigorous writings on these topics frequently appeared in pamphlet form as well as in articles. Skillful writing and well-organized articles on questions of social morality marked his contributions as editor and writer for the Jesuit weekly, *America*, with which he was associated for a quarter century. Other work in the literary field included leadership in the magazine *Interracial Justice*, and several books that present clearly and forcefully the truth that charity and justice to fellow men are not only good Americanism but essential Catholic dogma.

The best way to study the contributions of Fr. LaFarge is to read his own writings. His autobiography, *The Manner Is Ordinary* (New York: Harcourt, Brace & Co., 1954), is a superior piece of writing and a fine introduction to his life and work. Two of his books present the substance of his thinking on proper relations between members of the different races: *Interracial Justice* (New York: The American Press, 1937) and *No Postponement: U.S. Moral Leadership and the Problem of Racial Minorities* (New York: Longmans, Green & Co., 1950).

BISHOP JAMES HEALY

BORN: Georgia, April 6, 1830
EDUCATED: Holy Cross College, 1849
ORDAINED: 1854, Paris; consecrated, 1875
DIED: Portland, Maine, August 5, 1900

Son of an Irish settler and a Georgia slave girl, James Healy had a surprisingly close family life as one of ten children. His education was remarkably good and included studies in a Quaker school in New York before he and his brothers entered the new college of the Holy Cross in Worcester, Mass., in 1844. In this year he and his brothers had been baptised. The young graduate, who ranked first in the college's first graduating class, pursued his vocation in Sulpician schools in Montreal and Paris.

A year after his return to serve in the Archdiocese of Boston he was appointed chancellor, and pastor of St. James' Church, the largest parish in the city. Because abolitionist agitation was strong in the city, Fr. Healy found himself in a difficult position: he would not support violent measures, yet he suffered difficulties in dealing with certain Bostonians because of his color and ancestry. His bishop and his two brothers, one a Jesuit at Holy Cross, the other a parish priest of the diocese, provided mutual support in these trying times.

Fr. Healy was consecrated second Bishop of Portland, Me., in February 1875, beginning a quarter century of service to the people of that see. A bishop, two priests, and two nuns in a family of ten children—this was a proud record for any family of any age in America. His parentage again was used by cruel or unthinking people as a means of diminishing, if they could, his influence for good, not only for Catholics, but for all the people of the area. Bishop Healy's example of steadfast disregard of such mean tactics and his zeal in ministering to his people tore down their poorly constructed walls of prejudice and established a more just and equitable basis for race relations in his area. The special object of his interest was the welfare of children in his diocese: he was a strong supporter of the parochial schools, the founder and patron of orphanages and other child-caring institutions, and the solicitous guide and friend of the sisters who staffed them. By the time of his death he had earned the respect and love of the people of Portland as an outstanding American bishop.

The best reference generally available about the life and times of Bishop Healy is Albert S.

Foley's *Bishop Healy: Beloved Outcaste* (New York: Farrar, Straus & Cuhady, 1954). This book not only traces Bishop Healy's career but gives an excellent picture of nineteenth-century American city life.

DEBATE

The question: **SHOULD THE IMMIGRATION POLICY OF THE UNITED STATES AS EXPRESSED IN THE MCCARRAN-WALTER ACT OF 1952 BE CHANGED?**

Both sides can agree (1) that the federal government has, as its primary obligation, the protection of its citizens, and therefore it has a right to make whatever laws are necessary to afford this protection without working positive injustice on anyone; and (2) that the federal government has a less immediate but a real obligation to do for human persons outside its boundaries whatever justice imposes and charity suggests, as long as it does not thereby fail in its primary responsibility. The conclusion, from which the real debate should issue, is that the question is whether the McCarran-Walter Law is the best means of achieving these two objectives.

Affirmative presentation

I. The law is detrimental to the nation's best interests.
  1. Denies us our greatest wealth, people
  2. Contribution of immigrants
  3. A poor, sparsely settled nation, if it were not for immigrants
II. The law is contrary to the interests of world peace.
  1. Need of thousands for a "home"
  2. The obligation to let in more immigrants, since it can be shown that this policy will not hurt us
III. The quota system is a fairly recent innovation.
  1. Quota system is discriminatory.
  2. Quota system is an artificial way to arrive at the total number of immigrants

Negative presentation

I. The law protects American citizens.
  1. From too great an influx of immigrants
  2. From undesirable immigrants
II. The law is an effective regulation on immigration.
  1. Relatively severe regulations on entry and deportation
  2. Systematic control by quota
III. The quota system is reasonable and just.
  1. Humane and just as conditions permit
  2. Complementary to our foreign aid program

CLASSROOM DISCUSSION: Admitting that some ceiling must be put on the number of immigrants, the class should determine: (1) Does the McCarran-Walter Law set too low a figure? (2) Are the right classes excluded; right ones admitted? (3) Are the provisions and the method of enforcing them more severe than conditions demand? (4) Is the national quota system the best principle for setting the total number to be admitted?

SELECTED READINGS

Background material may be found in *The Immigration Problem,* edited by Clarence A. Peters (New York: H .W. Wilson Co., 1948).

Readings recommended for the affirmative argument are: "Immigration and Christian Morals," *America* (June 4, 1955); Msgr. John O'Grady, "Number 1 Problem: Immigration," *America* (August 29, 1953); "Action Wanted on Immigration Law," *America* (May 23, 1953); "Dimensions of Mercy; Refugee Legislation" (February 19, 1954); "These Inaccessible Shores; Refugee Relief Act and McCarran-Walter Act" (September 24, 1955); Msgr. John O'Grady, "Christian Immigration Policy," *Catholic Mind* (August 1952); O. Handlin, "We Need More Immigrants," *Atlantic Monthly* (July 1953); R. Elliott, "Revise McCarran Act," *Christian Century* (March 25, 1953); W. A. W. Krebs, Jr., and C. P. Ebb, "New Immigration Law," *Science* (March 20, 1953); Clement S. Mihanovich, "Proposed New Immigration Law," *Social Order* (November 1953) .

Arguments supporting the negative side may be found in J. B. Matthews, "Immigration, 1956 Issue," *American Mercury* (October 1955); W. Peterson, 'Scientific Basis of Our Immigration Policy," *Commentary* (July 1955); F. E. Walter, "The Truth about the Immigration Act," *Reader's Digest* (May 1953).

UNIT FIVE
Family and Community

Chapter 15. The Family in American Society

41. NECESSITIES AND DIFFICULTIES

The family is the basic social institution in all human society. Each of us is born into a family which is the world to us during our infancy. The infant is cared for by parents who guide his early development. The child who learns to play with neighbor children goes out from the home as a member of a family. He "comes from a family" when he goes to school. When he enters the larger society of his community it is as a member of a family rather than as an isolated individual. He carries his family name and with it whatever reputation the family has earned.

The attitudes he holds and the abilities he has developed are largely the product of his family training. Most young adults establish their own families by marriage, and they find that their new family dominates their interests and controls their activities as thoroughly as did their parents' family when they were children. Married men and women make their most important decisions as fathers and mothers, as husbands and wives, not as isolated individuals.

We can therefore see that the family plays a dominant role throughout our lives. Society can be healthy and vigorous only when the family is healthy; that is, when it performs its functions properly and when it is generally accorded its proper place in the organization of society. A country's need for healthy family life is explained by the sociologist, Reverend John L. Thomas, S.J.:

In the first place, since the human infant is born utterly dependent upon others, society must provide a suitable milieu where it can be nourished, protected, and trained over a considerable span of years. This is the function of the family. In order to do this the family must have stability, a certain degree of economic security, and the cooperation of other institutions such as the Church and the school. The nation is vitally interested in this function of the family, since the quality of its future citizens will depend on how well the family performs its task of preparing the child to take its place in society. The Church is greatly concerned also, since training in and practice of the faith during the most formative years of the individual's life takes place in the family circle. The primary right and obligation of educating children rest with the parents. It is the function of the Church and state to assist the parents in this function. The term "assist"

should be underlined. The Church and state cannot replace the parents. In the exceptional cases where the parents cannot or will not fulfill their task, these secondary institutions may have to interfere, but this interference must always be recognized as regrettable.

The importance of the family for sound society has been generally recognized throughout American history. The increased number of divorces and otherwise broken homes in the last twenty years has attracted the attention of political and social leaders. In 1950, President Truman wrote to the National Conference on Family Problems:

Intelligent and practical concern for a sound and successful family life invites the interest of all who look to the good of society. And it is always a matter of profound importance. However, there seems special need for such concern for the family today. The times are disturbed. There is all about us an unrest that lays everything open to question. This extends even to the most consecrated traditions and fundamental beliefs, including those pertaining to the family.

This conviction was expressed in different words by Dr. Carl Binger, professor of clinical psychiatry at Cornell University, when he addressed the Child Study Association. "Nothing in contemporary life," he said, "not even the atom bomb should demand more of our best

thought and energy than the preservation of the family. I want to make it clear that children need loving, manly fathers and strong, womanly mothers actively in their lives from the moment they are born; and that nurses, schools, play groups, and all the other educational paraphernalia of our day may supplement but never replace this primary need." The Catholic bishops issued a formal statement on the family in 1949 in which they said: "No nation can be greater than its families. The state measures its true strength by the stability of family life among its citizenry."

Thinking persons realize that the traditional form of the family, as it has existed in America and the rest of the Christian world, is undergoing a profound and disturbing experience in our time. This is why the major religious bodies have set up special organizations for dealing with marriage and family problems. Judges and jurists have given serious thought to revising marriage and divorce laws. Various marriage-counseling services, such as the American Institute of Family Relations, have been established in thirty-five cities.

The nature and the functions of the family. The family is a natural society established by God as a means for man's growth and perfection. A particular family is brought into existence by marriage, which is the permanent union of a man and a woman with a view to common living and the procreation of children. When a man and a woman voluntarily consent to form a life partnership, their consent establishes marriage and thus founds the family. It is important for us to remember that the union is, under the law of God, indissoluble except by death. Moreover, it must be entered into freely by a man and a woman who are eligible to marry; that is, who suffer from no legal, moral, or physical impediments to marriage.

The purpose of marriage is twofold: (1) the procreation of children; (2) the mutual perfection and help of the two partners. The first purpose includes not only the birth of children but also their training and education, the development of all a child's faculties until he has reached maturity. The second purpose involves mutual help and satisfaction— all covered by the general term "love"— that a man and wife should give to each other. They have the obligation of helping each develop physically and emotionally and spiritually as human persons made to the image and likeness of God. These purposes can be attained only if the family is a permanent society. Neither purpose can be completely achieved in anything less than a lifetime of living together.

In order to achieve its purpose the family must have certain things. First of all, it must enjoy economic security. The goods of this earth do not of themselves bring true happiness. But it is obvious that a family cannot perform its functions of rearing children properly unless it has a certain amount of material goods at its disposal. The father must earn a living wage, and he must be able to set aside enough to meet such emergencies as normally arrive in any family's life—such as the birth of children and expenses from illness and accidents.

Second, a family must live in a healthy environment. This means it should live in decent quarters—a home or apartment— in a neighborhood that is physically and morally clean. A family not so situated has little chance to rear its children properly or to pursue the social life that all normal people should enjoy.

Third, a family needs educative help in rearing its children. The father and mother are not equipped in our modern world to educate the child in a systematic and adequate way. This help must be furnished by state or private institutions on such terms that the parents can afford to use them. Outside agencies must, moreover, furnish such education as will help develop the child spiritually as well as intellectually.

Fourth, the family cannot easily achieve its purposes without the aid of religion. It is difficult to overcome the crises in family living unless all members of the family love and understand each other in a religious way. Unless, in short, their life together is supernaturalized by grace, the members of a family will find it impossible to attain fully the purposes of family life.

Finally, the family needs the support and protection of the government and of other social institutions. The children's lives must be protected by vigilant enforcement of traffic laws; the family's property must be protected by the police; the respect for family life must be pro-

Reciting the Family Rosary should be a practice in every Catholic home. Family unity is nurtured by this form of social prayer. (Religious News Service)

tected by the schools and newspapers. The family is not self-sufficient. It needs the help and the protection of such other social agencies as the state and the school and the church.

The family in modern American society. Modern developments all seem to have conspired against the family. They have made it more difficult for the family to maintain its integrity and to achieve its natural purposes. For the sake of convenience we can discuss these developments that are hostile to the family under the headings of (1) industrialism, (2) urban life, (3) feminism, (4) individualism, romanticism, and secularism. These developments are mutually interacting, of course, but we shall discuss them separately for the sake of understanding more clearly how they have affected family life.

Industrialism. Only a few generations ago the family was an economic unit, with each member having a duty to perform. This economic unity was one of the factors holding the family together. The introduction of the factory system destroyed this. Whereas families used to raise their food and preserve it themselves and add to their income by spinning wool or weaving cloth together, the factory system took people out of the home to earn their livelihood. Many factory tasks could be performed by children and women as well as by men. Wages were pitifully low in the early years of the industrial revolution. It was necessary for women and children to supplement the father's income in order to support the family.

The worst abuses of child labor and the employment of women have been corrected, but the factory system still works against healthy family life. The father is usually away from home all day, thus throwing the entire burden of caring for the children on the mother. Women are encouraged to take positions in the modern industrial system—sometimes they must in order to supplement the hus-

Nursery schools for children of working mothers offer a next-best substitute for maternal care. Families with inadequate incomes have attempted to solve their difficulties with the wife's supplementary salary. (Standard Oil Co., N.J.)

band's inadequate wages. This discourages the presence of children in the household, and if there are children they are frequently turned over to day nurseries or other inadequate substitutes for a mother's care. Moreover, factories are built and workers are offered jobs with little or no consideration for family welfare. Labor and industry still bargain for wages and working conditions as though the workers were isolated individuals instead of family men.

Urban life. American cities apparently grew up without any thought given to the workingman's family. Although serious attempts are currently being made to correct these evils, as we shall see in the next chapter, the fact remains that most urban families do not have adequate living quarters or sufficient recreational area for healthy family existence. Cities offer easy substitutes for parental guidance and control of children—movies, neighborhood clubs, local gangs, and the like—which set norms of conduct and codes of behavior for the growing children. In the midst of the many outside distractions offered by the average city environment, parents find it increasingly difficult to perform the functions imposed on them by family life.

Feminism. Women were formerly in a

position subordinate to men legally and politically—a position in which they did not as a rule suffer when the Christian idea of the family and of woman's special dignity was strong. But when those ideas grew weak, women were frequently exploited and taken advantage of. As a result, a movement set in to give them legal rights equal to those of men. The feminist movement may have accomplished some good, but at the same time it had some evil effects. Its worst effects were to weaken the family and to make women second-rate men rather than first-rate women. The feminist movement tended to throw women into economic life to compete with men. It tended to take women out of the home to find their place in the business world.

This feminist movement seemed to argue that equality between the sexes meant identity of function. It forgot that the sexes have specific characteristics that are not identical but mutually complementary, that man and woman are made to help each other rather than to compete in the same functions. The full development of persons of each sex requires that society respect these special physical and spiritual qualities. That is why the modern attempts of women to imitate men have prompted two modern social scientists to call them "the lost sex." Women's proper place in society is well summed up by Pope Pius XII:

In both states alike [marriage and celibacy] woman's sphere is clearly outlined by qualities, temperament and gifts peculiar to her sex.

She collaborates with man but in a manner proper to her according to her natural bent. Now the sphere of woman, her manner of life, her native bent, is motherhood. Every woman is made to be a mother: a mother in the physical meaning of the word or in the more spiritual and exalted but no less real sense.

For this purpose the Creator organized the whole characteristic makeup of woman, her organic construction, but even more her spirit and above all her delicate sensitiveness. Thus it is that a woman who is a real woman can see all the problems of human life only in the perspective of the family. That is why her delicate sense of her dignity puts her on guard any time that a social or political order threatens to prejudice her mission as a mother or the good of the family.

Unfortunately the tendency of feminism in the last half century has been to deny woman these special qualities the Pope described without obtaining anything of real value to replace them. This denial has weakened the structure of the family in modern times.

Individualism, romanticism, and secularism. In days gone by marriages were more or less arranged for young people by their parents with a view to economic security and social suitability. Such an arrangement was far from perfect, though in many instances it may have worked out fairly well. In several ways American developments changed this pattern of courtship, so that young people took it upon themselves to "fall in love" and become engaged to be married. Such marriages are often ideal, but sometimes the "love" both felt turns out to have been temporary infatuation. When this is the

Women leaders in the nineteenth century gained a number of legal rights for their sex. This emancipation movement, however, tended to deny women their proper role in the family. (National Archives)

The first Women's Rights meeting, which laid the foundation for Woman Suffrage, was held under the courageous leadership of Elizabeth Cady Stanton in Seneca Falls, N.Y., July 19, 1839

case, the modern marriage fails if it has no other support than romantic love. Such functions as farming, fishing, cloth-making, education, and religious worship —which helped hold families close together in the past—have been taken over by other agencies. The tendency to look on marriage in romantic terms exclusively therefore leads to frequent disillusion-ment and to the breakup of many young families.

The idea of the family as a divinely created society has gradually given way (among people who have abandoned Christianity) to looking at it more or less as a "necessary evil" or a "social conven-ience." This new concept of the family has come about wherever people tend to judge things in purely secular, materialis-tic terms. When all consideration of God as the "third partner in marriage" is elim-inated, a new set of secular standards is set up for judging a family's worth and function.

42. THE DIVORCE EVIL

The outstanding Catholic authority on the family today, Father Thomas, con-cludes that, while all these trends we have discussed are important in weakening the family, "there is widespread family disor-ganization today primarily because man's ideas about the family have changed." Father Thomas's studies show that the most important change was from looking on marriage as a sacramental union to considering it a civil contract entered into by two persons—pretty much like buy-ing a house or an automobile. "Once di-vine sanctions were removed from the family," he concludes, "it was a short step to by-pass all social control and to consider marriage as a private affair con-cerning only the individuals involved. Thus the institution of the family was es-tablished on the unstable basis of per-sonal satisfaction."

A considerable body of legislation was passed in this country on the basis of this changed concept of the family. Many states passed laws that allowed divorce not only for specified causes but also "for any other reason which the court shall deem necessary." Many states grant di-vorce on the grounds of "incompatibil-ity"—which seems to mean that when two persons would like to quit the life they promised to follow till one of them died there is no reason for their not do-ing so. The prevalent idea here seems to be that marriage and divorce are purely civil acts which two persons should be free to enter into with a minimum of state interference.

Divorce. Americans have the reputation of being the most married and the most divorced people in the world. The median age for men at the time of marriage in this country is 22.7 and for women 20.3. This means that a fairly large percentage of the men and women marrying are less than 21 and 20, respectively. The divorce rate has risen steadily throughout the century. In 1890 there were 33,461 di-vorces recorded in this country, or one divorce for each 2,000 population. In 1920 the figure had risen to 170,505, or slightly more than three for each 2,000 persons in the country. The percentage was slightly higher in 1940, with a total number of 264,000 in that year, or four for each 2,000 population. In the next decade there were almost 4,500,000 di-vorces affecting almost 9,000,000 persons and their children.

Although there has been a decline from the peak of 1946, when a record number of 610,000 divorces were granted —because of hasty war marriages and general upset conditions—nevertheless, between 300,000 and 400,000 persons are divorced each year. This means that about 10 out of every 1,000 married cou-ples are divorced annually. If the current divorce rate continues, approximately one marriage in three will end in divorce.

We must remember that recorded divorces do not tell the whole story of the breakdown of marriages in this country. It is estimated that there are about 50,000 desertions each year, usually by the husband, and while the deserter sometimes returns, nevertheless many of these desertions are "poor men's divorces."

The social significance of this large number of divorces cannot be grasped unless we remember the children involved. Although a large number of divorces occur early in married life between childless couples, about 40 per cent of the divorced persons do have children. In 1948, for example, 313,000 children were involved in the 410,000 divorces granted, and about two-thirds of these children were less than ten years old. The effect of this breakup of families on the children can easily be imagined. Statistics reveal a close connection between juvenile delinquency and broken homes, to say nothing of the immeasurable emotional disturbance suffered by children who must renounce one or another parent and be denied normal family life.

The confusion in family life caused by frequent divorce and remarriage is vast. There is legal confusion, first of all, caused by the fact that divorces in some states are not recognized in others. The easy residence requirements of such a state as Nevada are not recognized as valid in some of the other states. In this way a divorced person who remarries does not know whether or not he is a bigamist. Moreover, it is not known who his *legal* wife is and this raises questions regarding inheritance rights. The confusion is even worse for the children involved. They come to have two "fathers"—one adopted and one natural—and each makes a claim for their loyalty and affection. Or they may have two "mothers" competing for their filial love. At any rate, normal family life is impossible when divorce has broken up what Christ commanded that no man put asunder.

Causes of divorce. Why do people obtain divorces? Sociologists have studied this problem carefully in the hope that by discovering the causes of divorce they could correct what everyone admits is a serious defect in American society. The first striking fact they discovered is that 40

Marriages and Divorces 1940 to 1953					
Year	Marriages	Divorces		Marriages	Divorces
			Rate per 1,000 Population		
1942	1,772,132	321,000		13.2	2.4
1943	1,577,050	359,000		11.7	2.6
1944	1,452,394	400,000		10.9	2.9
1945	1,612,992	485,000		12.2	3.5
1946	2,291,045	610,000		16.4	4.3
1947	1,991,878	483,000		13.9	3.4
1948	1,811,155	408,000		12.4	2.8
1949	1,579,798	397,000		10.6	2.7
1950	1,667,231	385,144		11.1	2.6
1951	1,594,694	381,000		10.4	2.5
1952	1,539,318	392,000		9.9	2.5
1953	1,546,000	390,000		9.8	2.5

per cent of the divorces granted are given to couples married less than five years, and 25 per cent to couples married from five to nine years. The causes of marriage failure in the early years of married life differed from the causes breaking up families after ten or more years together. "Maladjustment," including "in-law trouble," is the most frequent cause of divorce in the earlier years, whereas excessive drinking and marital infidelity are the most frequent causes after ten years. It is to be expected that a couple who have overcome the problems of adjustment to married life will not separate for trivial reasons after ten years.

A study by Father Thomas of some 7,000 failures in Catholic marriages furnishes helpful information on the cause of separation or divorce among people who consider marriage a sacramental union for life. According to the study by Father Thomas, 14 per cent of the failures in marriage occur in the first year, and about 43 per cent occur within five years. "In-law" trouble is the leading factor causing failure in the first year of married life, but after the first five years it is a negligible factor. Irresponsibility and problems connected with sex relations are major factors only in the earlier years of married life. The two major causes of marriage failure, drink and infidelity, become more significant after the first five years of marriage, although the other causes of divorce—such as temperament, irresponsibility, and "in-law" trouble—never completely disappear.

This study suggests that marriage is a dynamic union requiring constant adjustment to changing situations. The popular idea that a bride and groom must adjust to a new kind of life after marriage is true, but the implication that once the initial adjustment is made everything will be smooth is not true. The coming of children, changes in social or economic standing, poor health of one partner, these and many other things require fresh adjustment on the part of the married couple. A good start in marriage is a big step toward establishing a successful family, but it is no guarantee that all problems of a family life will automatically solve themselves through the years.

As long as marriage is considered a purely civil contract entered into by two individuals, each pursuing his own self-interest, divorces will continue to weaken family stability in this country and thereby weaken the fabric of society. Something can be done on the purely natural level, however, by schools and public agencies to show the social evils of divorce and to show statistically that people who fail the first time in marriage seldom succeed the second or third time.

The frequency of divorce can be cut down somewhat by wise counseling before marriage. Divorce is most frequent among those who marry in haste. Solid premarital education in the seriousness and the responsibilities of married life should have at least some good effect among thoughtful young men and women. Some wise person should tell every engaged couple the great secret that romantic love is but the prelude to the greater and more abiding love they will have for one another many years

Cana and Pre-Cana Conferences are designed to educate young Catholic couples to the spiritual and temporal responsibilities of married life. A model conference is shown in session at an annual Eastern Cana Institute at Seton Hall University, New Jersey. (Religious News Service Photo)

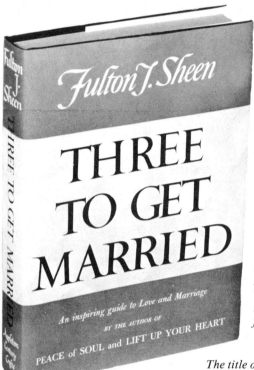

Millions of viewers of all faiths listen to Bishop Fulton Sheen's weekly telecast, "Life Is Worth Living." In his talks Bishop Sheen examines the nature of man from many aspects. (Raymond Hellriegel)

The title of Bishop Sheen's guide to love and marriage refers to the special place that God has in the union of man and wife. (Appleton-Century-Crofts)

later, if they live according to the laws of God. Marriage counselors believe that marriages would be more stable if they were considered soberly by young people instead of looked at as though they were romantic adventures. Love conquers all easily in a movie or a novel, where the author can arrange things as he wishes. But in real life a great deal more than romantic love is required of the partners of a successful marriage.

Finally, the evil of frequent divorce can be mitigated by more severe state laws on marriage and divorce. The trend in recent years is toward requiring a waiting period between application for a marriage license and the marriage ceremony. Such a waiting period will prevent the worst kind of hasty marriage. Divorce laws that respect marriage and require real cause to be shown for legal separation will help make married people settle difficulties that now drive every third married couple to divorce and break up

normal family life for about one million children every three years.

43. THE PROBLEM OF LOW FAMILY INCOME

The family cannot perform its functions unless it has an adequate supply of material goods: living quarters, food, clothing, money for medical and dental care, education, and a generous amount of recreation. There are many families in America whose income would be sufficient if it were properly spent. This involves more than simply keeping a budget. It involves a correct standard of values so that money is spent to achieve the purposes of family life rather than to frustrate them.

Right spending. Specifically, this means that money must be used first of all for children—their procreation and their rearing, which means food, clothing, education, and the other necessary expenses. Family income must be used also for the personal development and perfection of husband and wife in a physical, psychological, social, cultural, and religious way. The standard of living in a Christian family should take into consideration not only material comforts but also spiritual and cultural values. The spending of family income should also be guided by the classification of economic goods into absolute necessities, relative necessities, and superfluities. Absolute necessities are those which nature imposes on us, and they must be taken care of first. Absolute necessities, according to Christian social teaching, mean a sufficient amount of food, clothing, shelter, health, education, recreation, provisions for accidents, disease, unemployment, old-age security, inheritance, and the support of religion.

Relative necessities are those goods a family needs to maintain its rightful social standing in a community. This would include such things as house furnishings, an automobile, and whatever other goods are commonly owned by families in similar social circumstances. Superfluities, obviously, are things over and above what is needed for adequate comfortable living. Parents have the obligation of providing for absolute necessities first, then relative necessities, and finally, if any money is left, they can rightfully indulge in superfluities.

Even low-income families frequently violate these norms of right spending. A family that cannot "afford" another child but can afford a new automobile or a second television set is not spending its income with prudence. A family that cannot "afford" milk or proper medical care for the children cannot afford to go to the movies every week. Records of relief agencies and charitable organizations show that many families applying for the bare necessities of life are spending part of their income on superfluities. The proper use of family income is the first step toward mitigating the problem of low family income.

Inadequate incomes. The 1950 Census Bureau figures show that over half the families in the United States received less cash income than is required to maintain the City Worker's Family Budget, which is what workers consider necessary for a family of four. Fifty per cent of the families in this country—19,596,000—received less than $3,100 cash income, and the minimum cost of the family worker's budget for that year was $3,295. This means that half the families in this country did not receive a minimum family income.

The median income (that earned by the family at the middle of the income scale) had increased to $3,890 in 1952. But, owing to rising prices, real income (income in money adjusted to the change in prices) rose very little. Of the families earning less than $2,000 in 1949, about one-third were farm families whose income was increased a great deal by non-cash items such as food and shelter. Almost one-fourth of the families in the low-income group were headed by persons over 65 years of age, and a fairly large number of the low-income group were broken families headed by women as the result of divorce, widowhood, or desertion. After these subtractions are made, however, the fact remains that inadequate income is a pressing problem for many American families. It is estimated that, in 1950, 4,300,000 families were struggling to raise three or more children on less than $3,000 income a year.

One bad effect of this condition is that other members of the family find regular employment to supplement the father's wages. The increase in family income that has occurred since 1939 is due largely to the employment of wives. In 1949 more than half of all non-white families had more than one wage earner—usually husband and wife, sometimes one or more of the children. About two-fifths of the white families in the city had two or more earners. The largest percentage of employed wives is found in families making over $6,000 a year. Normal family life suffers, of course, when the mother is forced to take a job outside the home in order to supplement her husband's income.

Inadequate family income is especially serious because larger families average lower incomes than smaller families. The accompanying table and chart show that the median income for the one-child family was $4,109 in 1952 and only $3,045 for the family with six or more children. Even where incomes are the same, parents must pay severe economic penalties for having several children. Let us see what happens to the income of several different persons earning $75 a week or $3,900 a year. A single man pays federal income taxes of $605 and therefore has $3,295 left. A married man with no children pays $467 in taxes and therefore has $3,433 left for himself and his wife, or $1,717 apiece. A worker with five children pays no income tax, but his salary provides only $557 for each member of the family. If he has another child the income per person will drop to $488. A glance at the accompanying table shows that the median income for families of six or more children is only $3,045—or something less than $375 per person for the year.

These figures indicate a close relationship between inadequate family income and the number of children in a family. For this reason many persons favor a family allowance plan such as Canada has, whereby the government would pay a monthly allowance to families for each child over a certain number. Such an allowance is not charity. In the words of Father Edgar Schmiedeler, O.S.B., director of the Family Life Bureau of the National Catholic Welfare Conference, it is "a recognition of a nation's greatest responsibility, its responsibility to its children. In other words, the grants that are given should be a practical recognition of the fact . . . that a country's children are its greatest asset."

Family allowances. Many countries have provided some kind of family allowance for children. Canada gives from five to eight dollars a month for each child under sixteen. Similar allowances are given for children by New Zealand and Sweden, while four countries (Australia, France, Ireland, and the United Kingdom) give allowances to all families with two or more children. Altogether, there are twenty-six countries with allowance programs established by national governments, and nineteen have some kind of voluntary system administered by private agencies.

Those who favor a system of family allowances argue that this is a most effec-

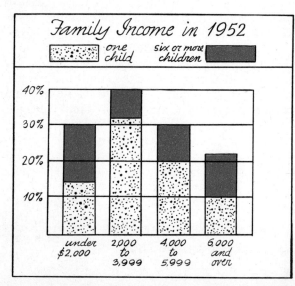

Family Income in 1952

one child / six or more children

	under $2,000	2,000 to 3,999	4,000 to 5,999	6,000 and over

Family Size and Income 1952

Children under 18	Median Income
1	$4,109
2	4,268
3	3,817
4	3,765
5	3,206
6 or more	3,045

The influx of women in industry during World War II has continued into the post-war era. According to Department of Labor statistics, more than half of them use every dollar of their wages for daily living. (Westinghouse Photo)

tive way to enable low-income families to perform their proper function and maintain the common good of society. There are, however, strong counterarguments. To pay such allowances the state must raise additional money by taxation, and taxes are already a heavy burden, even on low-income families. Ought such allowances to be paid for all children to all families? If so, some families will get allowances who do not need them. If only the needy families were to receive this aid, there would have to be some kind of means test; that is, some way of finding out who are the needy. This would mean additional government officials prying into the affairs of the family to ascertain whether the need was real and if so to make sure that the parents actually used the allowances for their children instead of squandering them for their own pleasure. To some extent a system of family allowances is actually in existence through the operation of the graduated income tax and the exemptions provided for each dependent child. An enlargement of such exemptions would probably be the most prudent way for the government to aid the low-income families.

Other family problems of national importance. Every family faces problems—sometimes of critical importance—of adjustment to new conditions. The successful solving of these problems depends on whether the parents and children have developed a sound sense of values and appreciate the importance of the family as a social unit in each person's development. A satisfactory solution of problems facing the family and threatening its existence as a sound social unit cannot be achieved until men and women recapture the Christian idea of the family.

The employment of women. In the modern industrial system women can perform many tasks as efficiently as men. Female employment outside the home has therefore increased rapidly in the twentieth century. In 1900 there were 5,-000,000 women so employed, and they constituted 18 per cent of the work force in business. In 1930 the number had risen to 10,400,000, and in 1954 it was almost 20,000,000, or 31 per cent of all workers. From a purely individualistic point of view there would seem no reason for not encouraging women to seek employment outside the home, because in this way the labor supply is increased and the production of additional wealth is made possible. Moreover, the employment of women would seem to offer them an eco-

There are few fields of work not open to women today. The country's need for engineers has attracted many women into career positions in this profession. (Westinghouse Photo)

institutions, such as Rockhurst College in Kansas City, Missouri, pay an additional amount to employees with a certain number of children, but such institutions are exceptional. Employees are normally looked upon as individual workers who are paid for the labor they perform regardless of their family status. Moreover, working conditions and hours of employment are settled with no other thought than industrial efficiency. Neither employers nor unions think of workers as being primarily the heads of families. Until they think also in family terms, the problems of family life will not be solved on a national scale, and workers with families will continue to find society working against them.

nomic security they would not otherwise enjoy. But when female employment outside the home—except in unusual circumstances—becomes general, the family is weakened. Such employment interferes with ideal relations between husband and wife, and it makes the proper rearing of children almost impossible. It encourages childless or one-child families, and it necessarily turns over many family functions to other agencies, such as the school or the private nursery.

The determination of wages. Normally wages are determined in this country by the market and by bargaining between employer and employee, either individually or collectively. Some businesses and

REVIEW

41. Necessities and Difficulties
A. Show why the family is the basic social institution in all human society. Why must family life be healthy? Why are serious-minded people worried about family life today?

B. What is the nature of the family? What is the purpose of marriage? List those essentials that a family must have in order to achieve its purpose.

C. It is said that modern American society seems to have conspired against the family. Briefly explain each of the reasons given for this statement.

42. The Divorce Evil
A. What has been the most important change in regard to the concept of the family in present-day marriage?

B. List some of the social implications of divorce. List some of the causes of divorce.

C. What can be done to prevent bad marriages?

43. The Problem of Low Family Income

A. What considerations should be taken into account in regard to the spending of the family income?

B. How do some countries provide for families with children? What are some of the drawbacks to these plans?

C. How does the employment of women affect family life?

THE CHAPTER IN REVIEW

A. Family life has been seriously threatened in modern America. Explain the factors that have brought this about and indicate some of the possible solutions to this problem.

B. How have present-day conditions tended to increase divorce? Why is divorce a social evil; a moral evil?

C. Favorable economic conditions contribute toward a successful family life. State two ways by which family incomes can be supplemented without endangering family unity.

subject: John J. Kane, *Marriage and the Family, A Catholic Approach* (New York: The Dryden Press, Inc., 1952); Rev. Edgar Schmiedeler, O.S.B., "The Family, A School of the Virtues" (Washington: National Catholic Welfare Conference, 1949); Emerson Hynes, *Seven Keys to a Christian Home* (Des Moines, Ia.: National Catholic Rural Life Conference, 1947); Ed Harrington, *Cana Catechism* (St. Louis: The Queen's Work Press, 1950); and Mr. and Mrs. John J. Farrell, *This Is Cana* (St. Meinrad, Ind.: Grail Publications, 1952).

The problem of family allowances, with a strong endorsement of the plan, is presented by Francis J. Corley, S.J., "Family Allowances: U.S. Plan," *Social Order* (April 1953), and by the same author, "Why Federal Family Allowances," *Social Order* (June 1954). The Institute of the Social Order has published a study "American Low-Income Families," *Social Order* (February 1952). Another good article on this subject is R. and H. Cissell, "Case for Family Allowances," *America* (October 16, 1954).

SELECTED READINGS

The sociology books suggested in previous reading lists (Bishop Haas, *Man and Society;* Eva J. Ross, *Basic Sociology;* and Rev. Raymond W. Murray, C.S.C., *Introductory Sociology*) all have good chapters on the family as the basic social unit in society. Various family problems are treated from the Catholic point of view in the magazine *Family Digest.* Rev. John L. Thomas, S.J., is a sociologist who has specialized in the problems of the modern Catholic family in America. He has published a series of articles under the general title, "The Catholic Family in a Complex Society," beginning in the December 1954 issue of *Social Order.* Another good article is by a layman who has specialized in family-life problems, A. H. Clemens, "Values in Family Living," *Social Order* (March 1953).

There are many books and pamphlets on the Christian family. The following are typical of some of the good literature on this important

PROJECTS

1. Every member of the class should be familiar with the encyclical of Pope Pius XI on marriage. You will learn the true nature and purpose of marriage as well as the obligations of married life if you summarize the main points of this important document.

2. A class committee could make a worthwhile report on the laws of their state concerning child labor. The committee should find out the basis for these laws by examining the conditions that existed in the state fifty years ago.

3. The incomes of persons engaged in certain professions and occupations are higher than the incomes of others. The *Statistical Abstract of the United States* lists the average incomes from many different kinds of work. Study these and report to the class on any inequities that you believe exist. Take into consideration the amount of formal training, years of experience, and particular skills or talents necessary for the various fields.

Chapter 16. The Urban Community

44. TOWN AND COUNTRY

A person's life is ordinarily spent in a community—in the city or in the rural community where he lives, works, goes to church, and spends his leisure time. Within the community he obtains most of the goods he needs, material things like food and clothing, as well as immaterial goods like education and entertainment. It is therefore a matter of immediate importance to each person that his community be sound, that it operate with a true sense of values; in short, that it be conducive to his living the good life.

A community may be considered as a group of families living within a certain geographic area and united by a number of common interests. Sociologists distinguish two kinds of communities, urban and rural, in which almost all Americans live. The urban community is the city, of course, with its peculiar problems. The rural community is a group of farms centering around a village in which the church, the school, and the store are found. A closer look at American society suggests that many of us live in communities that are midway between urban and rural, cities of five to twenty-five thousand persons who enjoy some of the advantages and some of the disadvantages of both rural and urban living.

Nevertheless, it is accurate enough to divide American society into urban and rural communities. The kind of life led in each community, together with the problems each must continually face, tends to develop what may be called the "urban mentality" and the "rural mentality." The people of each community are familiar with different things, think in somewhat different terms, have different sets of values, and in many ways behave differently. The 1950 census showed that 64 per cent of the population were urban dwellers, and 34 per cent lived on farms and in rural communities of less than 2,500 people. About 30 per cent of the population lived in large cities of 100,000 or more, and about 34 per cent in cities of from 100,000 down to villages of 2,500. About half the rural population lived on farms and about half in small villages of less than 2,500. (A small percentage of non-farm people live in open country.)

Urban v. rural. There has always been a certain amount of tension between the

urban and the rural population throughout the country and in each of the states. Each group has its own particular interests. Historically, the urban population has been "underrepresented" in Congress and in most state legislatures. This is because our system of representation contains a principle of territorial as well as popular representation. There is a wise necessity in this. If only people and not great public interests were represented, the city populations of the country would soon destroy, without realizing what they were doing, the agricultural interest upon which the cities depend for their life. Nevertheless, the cities are not without some just complaint against "underrepresentation." Many find themselves unable to solve their problems without sympathetic assistance from the state governments, which have granted the cities their charters. It is important, then, that rural people try to understand urban problems, for the key to their solution often lies in the action taken by Congress and by state legislatures, with representatives from rural areas often holding the decisive votes.

One other general idea should be kept in mind. Differences between urban and rural communities have grown less marked in the last half century. The automobile and the delivery truck have brought farmers into the city. The radio and television bring the farmer and the city dweller the same news and the same entertainment. Rural and urban schools use the same textbooks and have the same curricula. Rapid transportation and modern science, then, have tended to merge together urban and rural communities in at least some respects. Greater identity of interest and greater mutual understanding seem possible than at any time in the past. The same developments that make for cultural monism can have the good effect of bringing about a meeting of the urban and rural minds so that farmers and city dwellers can become mutually aware of each other's problems and help in solving them.

The haphazard growth of American cities. Medieval cities, centered around the church, the guildhall, and the market place, were usually hemmed in by a fortified wall and well situated on the local terrain. Most cities of medieval origin were in little need of renewal for centuries because the citizens' daily lives changed very little, the population was relatively static, and therefore the city still served the same needs as when it was built. American cities, on the other hand, grew rapidly in a changing industrial world

This aerial view of the financial district of New York City (above) is an example of how a city with a minimum of space must grow. Office space in buildings at the center of the district command high rent and are rarely unoccupied. The photo below of the East Side of New York shows two of the zones of a metropolitan area. In the background are the office buildings, hotels, and transport terminals that make up the central area. In the foreground is the residential area. (Standard Oil Co., N.J.)

and have been in a perpetual state of obsolescence, renovation, and expansion. The New York City plan of 1811, for example, assumed that internal traffic would move east and west and that river traffic was of primary importance. This assumption soon proved wrong, as north and south traffic became more important and sea traffic far outdistanced river traffic. Oklahoma City, again, began as a boom town made up of temporary structures which soon proved inadequate.

When the United States won its independence, no city had a population of 50,000. At the time of the Civil War only Greater New York could claim a metropolitan population of 1,000,000. Philadelphia had passed the 500,000 mark, and only six other cities had as many as 100,000 inhabitants. Within the next forty years the New York area had tripled its population, Chicago and Philadelphia had more than 1,000,000 each, and three other cities had passed the 500,000 mark. Fifty years later, in 1950, there were five cities with a population over 1,000,000, thirteen more with more than 500,000, and eighty-eight with more than 100,000 apiece. The number of urban dwellers increased by 22,000,000 in the decade between 1940 and 1950.

This extraordinary growth of American cities was neither foreseen nor planned. It resulted, naturally, in dislocations and inconveniences of different kinds in each city. Among the differences, however, we can discern a pattern of development more or less common to all American cities. At first the area of the city extended no more than two miles from the center. This limit was fixed by the mode of transportation—pedestrian, horseback, or horse-drawn vehicle. There was no need for streets to be wide or regular. Increased population made it necessary to pack more people into each square block, since it was impracticable for people to live at a great distance from the center of the city.

Between about 1880 and 1910 the cable car and streetcar increased the feasible area of the city to a line extending five miles from the center. Meanwhile larger numbers of immigrants poured into the city, and the overflow population from rural areas settled down to jobs in the city's growing industrial establishments. At the same time the elevator and steel construction made skyscrapers possible. Whereas the population tended to spread out from the center of the city to live in outlying districts, the business activity was concentrated in a smaller area. Thus the intermediate sections of the city fell into decay. The lower-income families continued to live here in crowded, unsanitary, and often unsafe dwellings.

A third stage in the growth of cities, from about 1910 to the present day, was made possible by the automobile and the truck. The urban area now extends fifteen or twenty miles in any direction from the center of the city. Thus cities have tended to develop in contradictory fashion: the heart of the city maintains a constantly larger working population who live farther away from their place of employment. Meanwhile the expanding intermediate zones continue to become blighted areas or slums occupied by low-income or racially segregated groups.

Effects of haphazard growth in the cities. The bad results of the rapid, haphazard growth of American cities are apparent. The city dweller finds that living in cramped quarters in unsanitary, neglected buildings creates serious moral and physical problems that make normal family life almost impossible. Those who are financially able flee from the city to homes in the suburbs, usually outside the city's legal boundaries, creating a serious loss in taxes to the city and making it more difficult for the city administration to perform its necessary functions. A large and relatively wealthy class of people has collected in the suburbs around each city. These people use the city's streets and cultural facilities. They work in the city and enjoy its safety and sanitary services. But they pay little or nothing in taxes to support these services. Thus the city finds itself in the difficult position of having to perform additional functions with a declining revenue.

More easily observable results of the haphazard growth of American cities can be summed up in this way: (1) inadequate streets for handling mass automotive traffic, streets that are too narrow and laid out with no relation to the needs and functions of the city today; (2) congestion of buildings, with resulting congestion of traffic, noise, smoke and gasoline fumes, crowded transit lines, and difficult sanitation problems; (3) lack of zoning regulations, with the result that residence, factory, and commercial facilities are all intermingled; (4) lack of playgrounds and parks, inasmuch as the area around the central part of the city seemed too valuable to set aside for recreation when the city was growing; (5) blighted and slum areas for rental to the low-income group who are not in a position to demand that they be made decently habitable; (6) the growth of the metropolitan area, in which the original urban population spills over into suburbs not incorporated into the city and uses city facilities but pays nothing for their maintenance.

45. CITY PLANNING

The political unit of the city is seldom conterminous with the social unit of the urban or metropolitan area. The artificial city limit separating the city proper from an incorporated suburb does not destroy the community of interests between neighbors who live on either side of the city's boundary. They attend the same theaters, go to the same churches, shop in the same stores, and have a common interest in a healthful neighborhood.

They pay taxes to different local authorities, it is true, and they usually enjoy protection from different police and fire departments. But otherwise they belong to the same community.

Let us therefore center our attention on the urban or metropolitan area rather than the city proper. Each metropolitan area is made up of a cluster of independent suburbs, semi-rural districts, and smaller cities which encircle the major city of a region. Thus St. Louis is surrounded by cities and unincorporated villages extending to the south, west, and north in Missouri and spreading out through southern Illinois on the other side of the Mississippi River. The New York metropolitan area extends into Westchester County, New Jersey, and out into Long Island. During the decade 1920–1930 metropolitan communities increased in number and size to such an extent that it was felt that they would soon include a majority of this country's population. Since 1938, however, the trend has changed. The percentage of the country's population living in metropolitan areas with more than a million people has declined slightly. Cities from 10,000 to 100,000 in size showed the greatest population gain since 1930. The 1950 census listed 85,000,000 people living in 171 metropolitan areas in this country.

The villages and cities constituting a metropolitan area are reluctant to merge their facilities and to attack their common problems together. There are some notable exceptions of combination in specialized functions. The union of forty-one communities in the Los Angeles area sewage system is an outstanding example. So is the New York Port Authority, and the Missouri-Illinois Bi-State Development Agency organized in 1949 to make plans for streets, highways, sewage and drainage, and to initiate action in respect to railroad-terminal facilities, airports, and bridges and tunnels for the St. Louis metropolitan community. The three

The Kolping House in Los Angeles provides interim housing facilities for boys who migrate to the city. Much more, this Catholic society offers them a true home environment, caring also for their spiritual needs. (A. L. Ellerkamp)

counties in which the Denver metropolitan community is located maintain a common health department, and smoke abatement is handled on a county-wide basis in the Los Angeles area.

But co-operation has been only in specialized areas. The obvious solution of annexing the outlying villages and cities to the central city has not proved practicable for a number of reasons. State legislation which prohibits such action except by majority vote of both communities, intervening state boundaries, and the tax differential between outlying districts and the central city are some of the more common obstacles to political consolidation. The only exceptions are in Texas, where growing cities have had the foresight to annex surrounding land before it is incorporated into a civic entity; and in Virginia, where annexation takes place upon a favorable finding by a special court set up to review the problem.

Make-up of a metropolitan area. A metropolitan area is normally divided into five rather well-defined zones: (1) *the central area,* in which are located the main business district, hotels, and the terminals of both intracity and intercity transport; (2) *the transitional area,* characterized by tenement districts and slums, rooming houses for transients, and quarters for the lowest income group in the city (this is the most dismal area in the city, the locale of most vice and crime and juvenile delinquency); (3) *the area of workingmen's homes,* some of them owned by the occupant but many of them rented (this is the blighted area in most cities, in need of repair and renewal); (4) *the residential area* of private homes and better apartment houses, which gradually melts into the (5) *suburban or commuters' zone,* which may extend some twenty or thirty miles away from the heart of the city.

It is well for us to recall at this point that a metropolitan area is a dynamic community. The boundaries between the zones we have indicated in the previous paragraph do not remain fixed for any length of time. Slum areas, for example, are often in what were the finest residential parts of the city in its earlier days. The city will go on changing to meet new conditions, like those created by increased automobile traffic or the recently developed trucking industry, or it will decline.

The general tendency of business in most American cities since World War II has been toward decentralization. The large department stores have established branches in outlying areas in order to cope with the loss of trade from a wider dispersion of people into the suburbs. Industrial establishments have likewise found it advisable to move out of the congested heart of the city into suburban areas along convenient transportation lines. Cities have therefore tended in the last ten years to break up into a cluster of communities within the large metropolitan community—and have created a new set of problems in doing so.

Since metropolitan areas are constantly

changing communities, the general problem facing the inhabitants of any such area is that of intelligent adaptation to changing needs. Such adaptation involves foresight and planning on the part of the community so that no section of the city becomes a slum area or falls into comparative disuse. Without such intelligent planning American cities face the continual problem of clearing out slum areas and renewing blighted sections, only to see the same problems develop anew in a few years.

Urban planning. Most American cities, like Topsy, just grew up. Factories and railway terminals were erected in the most convenient location. Oil wells were sunk in the heart of some midwestern cities. In general, little thought was given to the city's future or to the ugliness which was the price of quick profit. By the turn of the century Americans realized that their cities were both ugly and inefficient. The Chicago World's Fair of 1893 and the resurrection of the L'Enfant plan for Washington in 1900 made Americans realize that cities which are built by men can be planned by men. Several large cities had planning commissions by 1910. The first approach to planning was to create a beautiful city. Results of such planning are the Chicago lake-front area, civic centers in cities like San Francisco and St. Louis, and beautiful residential areas like Roland Park in Baltimore and River Oaks in Houston. Zoning laws were adopted by almost all cities in an effort to make new develop-

ments pleasing to the eye. These laws controlled the height and size of buildings within various zones, the kind of material to be used in their construction, and the distance they must be from each other and from the street. Planned traffic control began about 1920 with the introduction of automatic electric signals, one-way streets, boulevard priority, and other such measures to dissolve the congestion of trucks and automobiles choking every urban area.

Such planning proved inadequate. At best it eliminated an evil that had grown up in the city. But it failed to get at the causes of slums or of traffic congestion. It failed to consider all the problems of urban community living and provide a solution that would enable people to live together in a city with a minimum of inconvenience and a maximum of advantage. What was obviously needed was a planning agency for each urban area to work out general aims and objectives (the "master plan") to which all changes in the city should conform. By 1950, 18 cities over 500,000 had such agencies actively functioning, and 650 cities of 10,000 or more had planning commissions supported by the city budget.

Planning commissions are usually composed of interested citizens from various professions and businesses, such as an engineer, a lawyer, a banker, a retail merchant, an industrialist, a real estate man, a priest or minister, and a housewife. In this way different points of view and different special interests are repre-

Planning of this federal housing project included play areas and parks. Strict zoning regulations ensure a healthy environment for the residents. (Gottscho-Schleisner)

sented. The commission assembles factual information about the urban community, considers its needs and its functions, and from this data it prepares the master plan. The trend within the last ten years has been to organize metropolitan planning commissions, for it was found that city planning commissions were helpless when the surrounding communities did not co-ordinate their changes with the central city's plans. The control of traffic in the city of San Francisco, for example, is impossible unless the nine counties in the San Francisco Bay area co-operate to regulate and direct traffic flowing in and out of the city proper.

A step toward co-ordinated planning was taken by the establishment of the San Francisco Bay Area Council. In 1948 the Detroit Metropolitan Area Regional Planning Commission was established to develop highway, utility, and land-use plans for the entire region. A Los Angeles Regional Planning Commission has full jurisdiction over planning, zoning, and subdivision of unincorporated areas in Los Angeles County. A model interstate planning commission was created in 1949 in the Missouri-Illinois Bi-State Development Agency. Metropolitan planning commissions must be authorized by state legislation in most states, and failure of the state legislature to take action on this problem has hindered many metropolitan areas from taking this step.

Objectives of good planning. What do planning commissions hope to have the urban community provide for its inhabitants? The magazine *Platform* lists these objectives:[1]

A good community life. In the modern American city this seems to require neighborhoods of from 3,000 to 10,000 people, insulated from through traffic, grouped around a shopping center, churches, schools, and perhaps theaters. The purpose of this arrangement is to

[1] Adapted from *Platform*, April 1947, pp. 2–4.

make the neighborhood a vital thing so that people can know their neighbors, become friendly with them, and live a richer social life.

A pleasant environment. Provision should be made in each neighborhood for parks and playgrounds, for wide streets and walks with trees and grass parkways. Strict zoning regulations are necessary to achieve this objective.

Convenient location of schools. These must be within walking distance for all children and so located in reference to through traffic that children can reach them without hazard. The use of underpasses and overpasses must be planned before a school is located.

Cultural and civic centers. Some of these can be distributed in the neighborhoods, such as theaters or bowling alleys. Others, such as municipal auditoriums and music halls, must be located conveniently near the center of the city, served by public transportation, and near adequate parking accommodations.

Traffic engineering. Every modern city is faced with the problem of regulating traffic in order to provide both speed of travel and safety for its inhabitants.

Renewal of depressed areas. An adequate master plan must provide for clearance and rebuilding of slum areas in order to achieve the other objectives of the plan. Consideration must also be given to the constant renewal or rehabilitation of areas that begin to decay in order to prevent the formation of slums in the future.

46. MAKING THE GOOD LIFE POSSIBLE IN THE CITY

Slum clearance. Slum clearance is not an isolated problem. It is intimately connected with problems of sanitation, adequate housing, juvenile delinquency, and general civic welfare. Everyone agrees on the need for slum clearance in most big cities, but two difficult problems present themselves at once. First, what to do with the people living in the slum area? They must be housed at approximately the same rent while the clearance and rebuilding go on. Second, how to pay for the project? No city is able to clear slum areas and rebuild them with funds out of its ordinary revenues. Special bond issues can furnish the funds, but in most states they must be approved by the citizens of the area—and eventually paid for in taxes. People are reluctant to assume new tax burdens even for projects they admit are worth while.

We do not realize, unless we look closely at the problem, that slums are costly to maintain. A survey of two areas of the same size in San Francisco, one slum and the other a good residential section, showed that the slum area paid the city only $368,000 in taxes, whereas its bill for fire, police, and welfare services was $712,000. The planning association therefore concluded: "It takes money to eliminate the Geary-Fillmores [slum area surveyed] of this and other cities. But it also takes money to keep them. Whether or not we San Franciscans will devote our time and dollars to supporting misery or to supporting human happiness is entirely up to us."

Knowledge of this fact minimizes the objection that slum clearance costs a large sum of money which the city does not possess. But it does not eliminate the problem. The money must still be raised. The trend in the last decade has been for federal, state, and municipal governments to co-operate in eliminating slums and rebuilding the cleared areas. The federal government has devised a program of financing part of the cost for clearance programs that receive approval from the proper federal agency. Private institutions with large accumulations of capital, chiefly insurance companies, have been encouraged to invest in the cleared area. The Stuyvesant Town and Riverton developments of the Metropolitan Life In-

surance Company in New York are typical of the projects developed by private capital when it is attracted (by special tax provisions) to invest in civic renewal enterprises.

Legislation for slum clearance. State legislation to encourage the renewal of deteriorated areas began in 1940 with the Illinois Neighborhood Redevelopment Corporation law and New York's Urban Redevelopment Corporations law. Both laws enabled owners of property in a decadent area to pool their interests for the purpose of general redevelopment and to form a corporation with the right of eminent domain to acquire the rest of the property in the area. By 1950 some kind of urban redevelopment legislation had been adopted in twenty-seven states and the District of Columbia.

Bills for federal aid for urban redevelopment were introduced in Congress in 1943, but the first measure to pass into law was the part of the Housing Act of 1949 that provided federal grants and loans to assist cities in clearing blighted areas and preparing them for rebuilding. This measure provided half a billion dollars for capital grants to absorb two-thirds of the loss suffered by the city in preparing a blighted area for rebuilding. It also furnished one billion dollars for loans for the development. These grants and loans were restricted to areas that were designed by the urban planning authorities principally for housing developments. The Housing Act of 1954 continued these provisions.

Since 1949, urban rehabilitation projects have generally been devised to take advantage of federal aid. In doing so, urban authorities have been forced to concentrate on slum clearance and rehabilitation in conjunction with building low-rent public housing projects. The Housing and Home Finance Agency directs the federal redevelopment program and sets down the standards to which participating urban communities must comply.

Government co-operation with private institutions has resulted in a vast program of slum clearance. Housing projects, such as Stuyvesant Town and Peter Cooper in New York which accommodate 8,755 middle-income families, have replaced slum areas. (Standard Oil Co., N.J.)

The agency requires that the community must have prepared "a general or master city plan for the development of the locality as a whole" and that, in examining the plan, the agency will consider the plan's treatment of "existing and proposed land use, population, and the economic base of the community, highways, streets, public utilities, community facilities and services, zoning, and of community programs for slum clearance and urban redevelopment and capital expenditures."

Other parts of the law require a general approach to the whole problem of civic renewal. The federal administrators, in studying applications for grants and loans, will consider action taken by local communities for the improvement of building codes, the elimination of restrictive practices in the building industry, and the prevention of "the spread or re-currence of slums and blighted areas through the adoption, improvement, and modernization of local codes and regulations relating to land use and adequate standards of health, sanitation, and safety for dwelling accommodations."

The success of any urban redevelopment plan depends on the foresight of the planning commission and the enthusiasm with which the people of the community adopt the plan. Notable slum-clearing and slum-prevention work has been done in Milwaukee and in Baltimore. Other cities, like Chicago, New York, and St. Louis, show what can be accomplished on a smaller scale.

The functions of the urban community. Let us summarize briefly some of the functions of the urban community in enabling its inhabitants to live a reasonably good and productive life:

Safety. Each city must devote a considerable part of its resources to preventing crime and protecting people from the ravages of fire, flood, or other disasters. Each city tries to maintain adequate fire-fighting equipment and a modern police department armed with the latest technical resources for apprehending criminals.

A more serious problem—because it is more difficult to solve—is the traffic problem, which daily endangers the lives of urban inhabitants. The report of the Twentieth Century Fund stated in 1953: "The task ahead is staggering because the traffic problem has developed much more rapidly than the techniques for its solution, because the cost of the solution is tremendous, and because, even while improvements are in process, the problem continues to grow beyond calculations. No city has yet mastered this crucial problem." Highways that skirt the city proper, tunnels and bridges, with which New York has accomplished wonderful results, help solve the traffic problem. Express highways to carry high-speed traffic through areas without congesting local streets are another partial solution tried

The Port Authority Bus Terminal in the heart of New York City serves 130,000 bus travelers each weekday. Rooftop parking and a complex ramp system for buses relieves the heavy traffic in this part of the city. (The Port of New York Authority)

by Los Angeles and Seattle. The combination of private automobile and public transportation has been tried successfully by St. Louis. Municipal parking lots are used by almost half the large cities in the country to keep private automobiles off the streets of the central area throughout the day. These and other measures tend to relieve the traffic problem, but they have not by any means solved it.

Sanitation. Sewage and waste disposal must be handled efficiently if the urban community is to live healthfully and pleasantly. This problem, like many other urban problems, seems to have grown faster than the technical means of coping with it. Constant research and experiment with new sewage-disposal plants have resulted in marked improvements since World War II. The same kind of progress has been made with garbage-disposal plants.

Smoke abatement is another problem of sanitation which all large cities face. Pittsburgh and St. Louis, at one time considered the smokiest cities in the nation, solved this problem by rigid inspection laws requiring certain kinds of relatively smokeless fuels and certain kinds of burners to eliminate smoke from bad combustion. A full solution of the smoke problem cannot be achieved by a city acting alone, since it requires co-operation by all subdivisions within the metropolitan area. St. Louis, for example, still suffers from smoke palls when the wind is from the east, because the cities in southern Illinois still use unwashed soft coal.

In addition to the smoke problem is another closely related to it but as yet hardly recognized; the pollution of the air by the gasoline exhausts in motor traffic. What the effect of these poisonous fumes may be on public health has not yet been determined, but the subject is being studied by students of lung cancer, a disease that has been growing at alarming rates and particularly in the cities.

Noise is another nuisance about which

This modern sewage-disposal plant is one of a series that provides sewage and waste disposal for the city of Cincinnati. Regular re-appraisal of the community's sanitation facilities is necessary for the health and well-being of the inhabitants of the city.

there has been much discussion in urban communities, but as yet there has been little effective action.

Welfare agencies. Each community tries to do whatever it can to care for the sick, the unemployed, the underprivileged, and those who cannot care for themselves. The local community has the responsibility, in so far as it is able, to care for such people. More specifically, urban communities have the serious and burdensome task of maintaining hospital facilities, institutions for the aged, the insane, and others whose immediate families are unable to care for them. In recent years many cities have worked out excellent health and welfare programs with hospitals and medical schools, as well as with social-work schools and private relief agencies located within the urban area.

Education. Traditionally, as we have seen in Unit Three, education is a local responsibility. Each urban community, therefore, has the responsibility of helping the parents educate their children and prepare them for their role as adult citizens. Communities should not only provide adequate school buildings but also pay high enough wages to attract good teachers and thus ensure good educational systems. The trend in higher education in the last twenty years has been away from secluded college towns and toward urban universities. An increasingly large number of urban universities are financed and controlled by the city, such as Wayne University in Detroit, Oklahoma City University, and the Municipal University of Wichita, Kansas.

Since 1946, adult education has become an increasingly serious problem for urban communities. Adults have additional leisure time, and it is a community responsibility to help them use their time advantageously. Nothing would seem to be more in keeping with the purpose of community living than help for persons who are anxious to continue their education and to develop their intellectual and manual skills.

Cultural and recreational activities. The urban community has the responsibility of providing adequate parks, civic centers, and other healthy means of recreation and entertainment. The obligation follows from (1) the fact that failure to provide such facilities makes it likely that

The picture at right, taken exactly five years later than that at left (at the same time of day), vividly depicts the great improvement the Bureau of Smoke Prevention of the city of Pittsburgh has effected. (Newman-Schmidt Studio)

many persons will spend their time in harmful recreation, like gambling or excessive drinking, and (2) even if they do not fall into bad habits, the failure to find healthy recreation is a hindrance to their full personal development. Urban communities with sufficient funds and a large enough population should also be aware of cultural opportunities that can be made available to their inhabitants, such as traveling opera companies, symphonies, and ballet companies.

47. THE PROBLEM OF ADEQUATE HOUSING

We have seen that the general problem facing urban communities is that of planned rehabilitation. The most pressing aspect of this problem is adequate housing. For a number of reasons—chiefly the advancing cost of building and the inability of low-income families to purchase homes—household construction has for many years lagged behind the increasing number of families. Between 1920 and 1950 the number of families in the country increased from 24,500,000 to 38,788,000. In that same time only about 9,000,000 homes were built—less than the number of additional families. When

we remember that several million houses had to be replaced to keep the number constant, we realize that the people of this country were not as well housed in 1950 as in 1920.

The biggest boom in house construction in our history began in 1950, but the housing problem remained acute. The President's Council of Economic Advisers reported in 1950 that "the objective over the next few years should be to build, on the average, about 1½ million new residential units annually." However, many low-income families are still inadequately housed. Many families are doubled up, sometimes even six and seven persons sleeping in one room in congested urban areas. Normal family life and proper personal development are impossible under such conditions.

In 1954, President Eisenhower reported to Congress that the need for public-financed housing projects was still urgent. The President told Congress that his comittee of twenty-three housing experts informed him that 19,000,000 of the 37,-000,000 homes and apartments in the country were more than thirty years old and that we needed 1,400,000 new units annually for the next eight years to deal adequately with the housing shortage.

The President's aim was to see that "opportunities are provided every American family to acquire a good home," because "good housing in good neighborhoods is necessary for good citizenship and good health among our people." President Eisenhower therefore outlined a program that would (1) deal effectively with slum areas, (2) encourage more home construction by private builders and purchases by individual families in the low and middle-income brackets, and (3) provide additional low-rent public housing for the poorer people in each urban community.

The need for additional and improved housing is generally admitted. There is disagreement, however, on whether the federal government should supply this need. Arthur W. Binns, president of the National Home Property Owners' Foundation, opposed government action on housing.

Actually the issue is not between public and private housing [he stated], it is drawn and very sharply drawn, between public enterprise and private enterprise. . . . If the government now takes over the housing of the nation under a bill which provides at the beginning twice as much public housing as we had prior to Pearl Harbor, we have started down a path which can only lead to the nationalization of all property.

Senator Taft, on the other hand, favored public housing financed by the federal government to the extent of 135,000 units annually for six years. In 1952 he explained his stand to the National Housing Conference.

It is no reflection on private industry to say that it never has, and probably never will, meet the serious low-income problem in the housing field. The general theory that the government has a duty to assist the lowest income groups has been accepted in every state in the Union and it does not involve any departure in principle from that which we have pursued during the 150 years of life of the Republic.

Federal aid to housing. The accepted American solution seems to be in favor of federal aid for low-income families. The decision to use federal aid was made during the Great Depression. In 1932 a Federal Home Loan Bank was established to extend credit to savings and loan institutions for mortgage loans. In the following year the Home Owners' Loan Act was passed to grant long-term credit to home owners who needed assistance against foreclosure of their mortgages. The National Housing Act of 1934 created the Federal Housing Authority (FHA) to insure lenders against loss on loans for house repairs and residential home mortgages. The FHA, then, facilitates the repair and improvement of residential units throughout the country.

The Wagner-Steagall Act of 1937 created the United States Housing Authority to provide financial assistance to local governments in the elimination of unsafe and unsanitary housing and in providing good low-income housing. A number of emergency housing acts were passed during and after World War II, but the first comprehensive housing bill in a decade was passed in 1949. The Housing Act of 1949, as we have seen, provided one billion dollars in loans to be made by the federal government over a period of five years for slum clearance and redevelopment and another half billion in grants to cover two-thirds of the local governments' losses from slum clearance. These loans and grants were closely tied in with low-income public housing projects. The Housing Act of 1949 further provided that the Public Housing Administration may authorize local housing agencies to start building 135,000 low-rent units each year over a period of six years, the federal contribution not to exceed $308,000,000. Finally, provision was made for research to lower the construction costs of housing.

By this housing act the federal government does not go directly into the business of public housing and slum clearance. It declares itself ready to help local governments meet their housing problems if they in turn meet certain federally set requirements. High building costs, rising prices, and priorities for defense work during the Korean War, all combined to prevent the law from working out as completely as Congress intended. In the first year, for example, only about 10,000 dwelling units were started instead of the 135,000 permitted by law.

A new comprehensive housing act was passed in 1954. Again the provision for slum clearance was tied in with low-income housing. Federal aid was provided for 35,000 new dwelling units. Terms for obtaining FHA loans were broadened to enable more middle-income families to purchase homes.

Federal aid does not solve the housing problem. It eases it somewhat, but construction and repair of homes must still be paid for—and construction costs are unreasonably high. These higher costs are due partly to higher wages and higher costs of material, but they are also due in part to certain abuses on the part of builders and unions: collusive bidding by electrical, plumbing, and other contractors; feather-bedding by unions (requiring a certain number of unnecessary workers on the job); insistence on six-hour workdays with overtime pay for additional work; exorbitant profits for the builder. Elimination of these and other abuses will enable Americans to build and repair more homes. But the problem of adequate housing will remain.

To a considerable extent the building of low-priced housing by private enterprise was slowed up by the maintenance of rent controls for a long period after World War II. During the war, prohibitive restrictions were placed on the building of anything not directly connected with the war effort. This created a serious housing shortage. Throughout the war, the number of inhabitable units actually decreased because no new units were built to replace those that fell into disuse. Meanwhile the number of families looking for housing increased considerably. To prevent the exploitation of renters, the government froze rents at existing levels during the war. The law provided that a renter could obtain triple damages from any landlord who put his property on the "black market" and charged higher than the legal rent for any dwelling unit covered by rent-control regulations.

When the war ended in 1945 the housing shortage became temporarily worse than it was during the war. Millions of returning veterans looked for places to live, and millions of other families who had been doubling up in single-dwelling units wanted to separate. The result was an increased demand for housing that the building trade was unable to accommodate. Wage disputes, shortage of materials, and the attempt by some builders to take advantage of market conditions, all combined to raise the price of new units. Meanwhile rent controls were maintained by popular pressure from the big cities. Those who lived in low-rental units therefore enjoyed preferential treatment for several years, because rents in controlled areas did not keep up with the general rise in prices.

Rent controls seemed temporarily

Army quonset huts and barracks were used for temporary housing for veterans' families after World War II. These emergency accommodations, used during the worst housing shortage in history, were gradually emptied as the building industry enjoyed its greatest "boom" period. (New York City Housing Authority)

necessary to protect the renter who was not able to build his own home from paying the rent that an unscrupulous landlord could demand if there were no controls. But the system of controls put honest landlords at a disadvantage, because they were not free to adjust rents to changing price levels. And the controls slowed up the building of low-price units because renters had no desire to buy them when they enjoyed preferential treatment under the rent-control system.

Various attempts were made to adjust rent controls to rising prices in order to alleviate the obvious injustice to many landlords. One provision was to allow a 15 per cent increase in rent by voluntary agreement between tenant and landlord. Another was to allow the landlord to increase his rent if he could prove that he was not earning a fair return on his investment. Some landlords, especially small ones who owned a single home or two purchased when prices were high, suffered from the continuance of rent controls. Others used such devices as forcing tenants to paint and repair the units at their own expense. Because all units were occupied at all times, many landlords were better off than they had been in the years of free rental before the war.

The problem was obviously a difficult one to solve. It was necessary to remove rent controls in order to encourage building, and still they could not be removed precipitately in any area where there was an acute housing shortage in low-price units, for then many who could have least afforded an increase would have had to pay for one or be evicted. Landlords argued that if controls were removed houses would be built quickly and rents would not increase. In the three years after 1948, however, rents increased by 19.8 per cent in the areas where they were decontrolled and only 3.5 per cent in areas kept under control. The biggest advance, when a local area was freed from rent control, was in the lowest brackets.

Congress was faced with the dilemma of satisfying landlords and renters every time the rent-control law was due to expire. The eventual solution was to keep controls only in those areas that requested them. By the summer of 1955 a combination of public and private housing had done much to alleviate the housing problem. In many large cities throughout the country there were more units available than needed, and the problem of rent controls was no longer urgent. The continuance of controls for an unnecessary length of time, however, prolonged the eventual solving of the housing-shortage problem.

Conclusion. The basic problem of the urban community will never be finally and definitively solved. This basic problem breaks down into myriad smaller, more specific problems caused by the concentration of a million or more persons into a single metropolitan area. Decentralization encourages sociable, neighborly living in a cluster of communities that pool their resources for certain civic functions but remain autonomous in other ways.

Growth in each metropolitan area, it seems, should be guided by a master plan that takes into consideration the community's needs and functions. To cite a single concrete example, it seems reasonable to require each new office building or store erected in the city to include provision for adequate parking for the workers and customers who will use the building.

A pressing problem confronting each city is to find new sources of revenue. Each city has been forced to assume additional functions that involve huge expenditures—police departments, hospitals, schools, libraries, garbage disposal, sanitation, and the like. These functions must be financed from taxes paid by the inhabitants of the city. Suburbanites, we have seen, use the central city's facilities but escape paying most of the taxes assessed against those who live within the city. The result is that taxes become disproportionately high within the city proper, and more people move to the suburbs to escape paying them.

This problem will remain as long as the outlying districts in the metropolitan area resist incorporation into the central city. There seems no immediate likelihood of such incorporation taking place on a general scale. A partial solution of this problem was achieved by St. Louis when it received permission from the Missouri legislature to assess an earnings tax on all persons employed in the city. By means of this tax (one-half of one per cent of the income of each individual earning his income or wages in the city) St. Louis secures some revenue from those living outside the city boundaries but using the city's facilities during the day.

A general awareness on the part of the inhabitants of an urban community of their immediate problems of daily living is the first step toward solving such problems as admit of solution. National and international problems seem more important to us—and frequently they are—but their importance should not blind us to the fact that urban and rural communities also have their problems. And a community can usually do something toward solving them if it is willing to spend the necessary time and money.

REVIEW

44. Town and Country
A. What is meant by the "urban mentality" and the "rural mentality"?

B. What is the value of having a geographic as well as popular basis for representation in Congress?

C. Why have most American cities grown in a haphazard fashion? What are a few of the economic factors that have aided the growth of our cities? List some of the effects of this rapid growth?

45. City Planning
A. What is meant by a metropolitan area? Why is there often a lack of co-operation within these areas? List the five well-defined zones of a metropolitan area?

B. What is meant by decentralization?

C. Why is there an urgent need today for planning commissions in our cities? What members of a community generally serve on such a commission? What good objectives of planning were listed in the magazine *Platform?*

46. Making the Good Life Possible in the City
A. Why is slum clearance an important problem today? In your answer indicate the social and economic aspects of this problem.

B. Briefly show how state and federal legislation has recognized the problem of slum clearance. What is the function of the federal Housing and Home Finance Agency?

C. What are some of the problems faced by the urban community in enabling its citizens to live a good and productive life? Explain each briefly.

47. The Problem of Adequate Housing
A. Why is adequate housing such a problem today?

B. Outline the beginnings of federal aid to housing. What did the Housing Act of 1949 provide? The Act of 1954? List some of the housing problems that still exist.

C. Why were rent controls necessary after World War II? List some problems that rent controls created for the landlord.

THE CHAPTER IN REVIEW
A. What has been the cause of tension between urban and rural communities? Why has this tension decreased in more recent years?

B. What are the major problems that face city planning commissions today? What solutions have been offered for each of the problems listed?

C. State how slum clearance and adequate housing are problems that are closely related. Review the steps taken by the federal government to solve these problems. What recommendations can be made for safeguarding the future growth of American cities in order to avoid problems of housing, congestion, and inconvenience?

SELECTED READINGS

The greater number of social and economic problems Americans encounter are connected with the urban community. The monthly, *American City,* is a journal devoted to the problems of American cities. Most sociology textbooks devote a section to urban problems. A college text of considerable value for this subject is *Dynamic Urban Sociology,* edited by William E. Cole (Harrisburg, Pa.: The Stackpole Co., 1955).

Increased population and rapid technological progress made our cities suddenly seem outmoded after World War II, and many books on urban redevelopment appeared. Among the better books on this subject are: Guy Greer, *Your City Tomorrow* (New York: The Macmillan Co., 1947); Gerald Breese and Dorothy E. Whitman (editors), *An Approach to Urban Planning* (Princeton, N.J.: Princeton University Press, 1953); Svend Riemer, *The Modern City* (New York: Prentice-Hall, Inc., 1953); and Coleman Woodbury (editor), *The Future of Cities and Urban Redevelopment* (Chicago: University of Chicago Press, 1953). The Chamber of Commerce published a pamphlet, *City Planning and Urban Development* (Washington: Chamber of Commerce of the United States, 1952). The most authoritative book on the subject, however, is Miles L. Colean, *Renewing Our Cities* (New York: The Twentieth Century Fund, 1953). The religious and human element necessary for sound urban development is discussed by J. Dennis Clark, "Human Community Planning," *Social Order* (September 1952).

The housing problem is well analyzed by A. Schalk, "America's Housing Headache," *Catholic Mind* (August 1952), and by an editorial in *America,* "House against Federal Housing" (April 10, 1954). The need for federal action to provide housing for poor people is explained by T. J. O'Dwyer, "Case for Low-Income Housing," *Catholic Mind* (February 1953), and by Rev. John R. Mulroy, "Shall the Poor Have Homes?", *Catholic Charities Review* (March 1954).

Editorials in Catholic journals on the problem of slums include: "Expensive Slums," *Social Justice Review* (March 1954); "Slums and Social Justice," *Ave Maria* (December 19, 1953); and "The Making of a Slum," *The Sign* (August 1954).

PROJECTS

1. Review the history of your own or a nearby town or city and see what factors contributed to its growth. Was it because of a nearness to railroads, rivers, marketing centers, or harbors? Suggest several reasons for the location of industry, markets, or other economic pursuits in this area. A report to the class on this phase of local history will provide a good background for understanding local problems that are mentioned daily in newspapers and on the radio or television.

2. Set up your own planning commission and see what can be proposed in regard to traffic controls, new public buildings, and recreational facilities for your town. The commission should take into consideration the rate of population growth in the town (information from the population report made in Chapter 11 will be helpful here) and the existing facilities of the town.

3. Criticism has been directed against the different housing programs that are supported by federal, state, or city governments because of the maximum incomes established for the families so housed. These maximums need to be reviewed frequently to avoid discriminating against families on certain income levels. A member of the class could submit a report on the housing restrictions for a nearby housing project. A class discussion would bring out some interesting aspects of the problem as needs, incomes, family sizes and apartment accommodations are examined.

Chapter 17. The Rural Community

48. DIMINISHED AGRICULTURAL POPULATION

The industrial revolution, which began shortly after we won our independence from England, changed us gradually from a predominantly agricultural to a predominantly industrial nation. The 1950 census found that only 16.6 per cent of the population lived on farms and about another 20 per cent lived in rural communities—towns and villages with less than 2,500 inhabitants.

This is a decline that has reached serious proportions in recent years and threatens to unbalance our social economy. In 1920 about 32,000,000 people (30.1 per cent of the population) lived on farms. In 1940 the farm population had fallen to 30,500,000, or 23.2 per cent of the national total. In 1950 there were only 25,000,000 living on farms, and the number has decreased considerably since the last census was taken. Meanwhile the total population of the nation had increased. Between 1940 and 1950 the rural population—those on farms and in communities of less than 2,500—dropped from 57,500,000 to 54,500,000, whereas the urban population increased about

22,000,000 in the same decade. The rural population in 1955 was about 34 per cent of the national total, and about 15 per cent lived on farms.

Decline in proportionate numbers has not made the farm population and the rural community less important segments of our nation. Agriculture is one of man's basic occupations. It supplies us with our food, and it furnishes much of the raw material from which we are clothed, sheltered, and kept warm. Whether we live in the city or on the farm, then, we have a direct interest in the welfare of the farmer and the other people who live in the rural community and depend immediately on the farmer for a livelihood. The welfare of the nation is intimately tied up with the welfare of the rural population.

There is still another reason why we must solve the problems of rural life satisfactorily in this country. An estimated 70 per cent of the world's population is engaged in agriculture. If the United States is to maintain the great role in world affairs which events have thrust upon us, we must be able to offer guidance and example in solving the problems of rural life. We must do more than

teach technical efficiency to nations that wish to learn from us. We must also show them how to integrate the rural community into the increasingly industrialized society that is being so rapidly created in Asia, Africa, and other parts of the world. This can be more effectively achieved if we make our own rural communities places where people can develop their human faculties to the fullest and live the good life.

Therefore, it is important for all of us to understand the problems of the rural community and to support whatever measures help solve them. Monsignor Luigi Ligutti, executive director of the National Catholic Rural Life Conference, stated at the conference's 1954 convention that "my greatest hope is that the city people and the rural people will be-

come more conscious of the importance of agricultural people, agricultural production, and living conditions on the land." *The Manifesto on Rural Life*, published by the National Catholic Rural Life Conference, concludes with this appeal for thoughtful action by all Americans toward solving rural-life problems:

The rural problem is complex and varies in type and in intensity with geographical areas. Wrong attitudes toward agriculture and wrong appraisals of what constitute fundamental values, deeply rooted in the thinking of both rural and urban groups, are barriers that must be surmounted. . . . The rural problem is so important that it should engage the greatest minds of the nation.

Complexity of the "rural problem." The "rural problem," as seen by the National Catholic Rural Life Conference and other

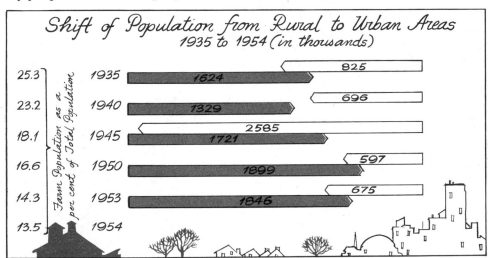

Shift of Population from Rural to Urban Areas
1935 to 1954 (in thousands)

Farm Population as a per cent of Total Population

		Rural	Urban
25.3	1935	1624	825
23.2	1940	1329	696
18.1	1945	1721	2585
16.6	1950	1899	597
14.3	1953	1846	675
13.5	1954		

Monsignor Luigi Ligutti, executive director of the NCRLC, has championed the cause of the farmer and has helped many Americans to a better understanding of agricultural life.

groups who understand the needs and rights of human nature, is not the simple problem of getting more from the soil and raising the farmer's income. It is a complicated problem, as complicated in many ways as the problem of successful living in the city. We shall consider its social aspects in this chapter and look at its economic aspects in a later chapter. Let us remember, however, that dividing the rural problem this way is somewhat arbitrary. We do it so that we can understand the problem better by looking at it from two different viewpoints—social and economic. In this chapter, then, we shall discuss problems connected chiefly with how the farmer and other rural people live. Later we shall discuss problems connected with how the farmer earns a living.

There is an intimate connection between the way a farmer lives and the way he earns his living. The average urban dweller has separated his work from the rest of his life. He works six or eight hours a day as a mechanic or a clerk or a bricklayer. The rest of the time he lives pretty much like the urban dweller next to him, who might be a teacher or a bus driver. In the rural community, however, family life and social life are intimately connected with the business of farming.

It is difficult to generalize about farmers and rural communities throughout the country. The potato grower in Maine faces different problems and lives a different kind of life than does the citrus-fruit grower in southern California. The wheat farmer in Kansas has little in common, it seems at first glance, with the cotton sharecropper in Alabama.[1] Running through all these differences, nevertheless, are certain common elements and certain common problems.

The farmer and those rural dwellers whose welfare is intimately connected with him depend on elements over which they have no control. They are at the mercy of the weather. Too much rain breeds crop-destroying insects. Insufficient rain brings a drought that will burn up the fields. Floods and soil erosion are constant threats. If the farmer is fortunate and has a bumper crop, it is likely that everyone else will be equally fortunate and the market will be glutted with the goods he has raised. Unless the government acts to safeguard a steady and worth-while price for his crops, he may be ruined by events over which he has no control. Consequently, he must adjust his

---

[1] For a full discussion of this subject, which we cannot do here, see Charles P. Loomis and J. Allan Beegle, *Rural Social Systems* (New York: Prentice-Hall, Inc., 1950), or Carl C. Taylor and associates, *Rural Life in the United States* (New York: Alfred A. Knopf, Inc., 1950). These are excellent treatments of rural life and its problems.

The general store in this Vermont rural community serves as a clearinghouse for ideas during the winter months. The discussion of topics which range from sports to politics in this "hot-stove league" supplies recreation that cannot be found in the big city. (Standard Oil Co., N.J.)

The good life is not difficult to achieve on the farm as families are more closely knitted together. Their work and recreation are family co-operative projects and their tastes tend to be more simple. (SCS Photo)

life to an uncertain future. Long-range planning by the farmer is not impossible, but his life involves a larger element of uncertainty than does the urban worker's life.

Farming is a hard life. The hours of work are long, especially at certain seasons of the year, and the work to be performed is hard manual labor. Machinery has helped man with his manual labor on the farm, of course, but it has not reduced the farmer's task to one of pushing buttons and simply repairing his machines. Some farmers can ordinarily expect a large income, but most of them earn considerably less cash income than do most urban workers. Farming is a hazardous undertaking. Yet the fact is that it attracts many intelligent people who work long hours at hard labor for no very large income. Many of these people could earn considerably more money in the city. We might ask, then, why they are attracted to the land.

Farming is a way of life. Thoughtful farmers would agree with Monsignor Ligutti's statement at the 1954 National Catholic Rural Life Conference:

In all the work of the farmer he must consider himself as a partner with God. He must regard his profession as noble. As Cicero said, "Of all the occupations by which a living is made, none is better than agriculture, none more delightful, none more becoming to the dignity of a free man." Farming is more than money making. It contributes to the development of the farmer's personality and in a special way to the formation and the Christian training of his family.

Farming requires no degrading work. Nor is it monotonous labor which depersonalizes the worker, as is the case with so many of the urban workers' tasks. The farmer co-operates with the Creator in bringing forth the fruit of the earth, and from his work he can derive a very great satisfaction.

Farming tends to knit families closer together. The family is the economic unit on the farm, because farming is essentially a co-operative enterprise in which father and mother and children take part. Not only the actual manual labor but also the planning of each project is naturally a family affair on the farm. There is a common interest in the enterprise and a community of knowledge about farm problems—things that members of the urban worker's family rarely enjoy. Many rural families are far from exemplifying these truths. But their failure is not the fault of their occupation and way of life, as is frequently the case with urban families.

The revolution in the rural community. Both farming and life in the rural community have undergone revolutionary changes in the last century. Originally the farmer tried to support himself and his family by raising his own food and by keeping chickens and a few cows. He grew a surplus of one crop or another to market for cash, with which he bought the necessaries and comforts of life he could not

Today labor-saving devices afford the farmer more leisure time than ever before. Machinery also saves the farmer the expense of hiring extra hands, thereby increasing his income, which can now be spent for his children's education, necessities, and some luxuries. (U.S.D.A. Photograph)

produce himself. These were comparatively few, because the farmer was also a carpenter, a mechanic, and several other kinds of craftsmen. The revolution in farming turned the farmer away from self-sufficient farming into one-crop farming for cash profits. Cash-crop farming for profits, combined with the introduction of labor-saving machinery, changed the size of farms in America. Farms grew larger in size and fewer in number, a trend that has continued to the present time. In 1920 there were 6,518,000 farms in this country, and by 1950 the number had fallen to 5,596,000. During that same time more than 200,000,000 additional acres had been put under cultivation. Obviously this meant the acreage per farm had increased. More important, large farms had increased more than had medium-sized units. In 1920 there were 67,405 farms each of more than 1,000 acres. In 1950 there were 121,362 of these giants.

Labor-saving machinery continued to be introduced on the farm through the twentieth century, thus making a larger farm product possible each year with a smaller working force. In 1941 there were 1,675,000 tractors on American farms; in 1953 there were 4,400,000. In 1941, 225,000 combines and 120,000 corn pickers were in use; in 1953 the numbers had increased to 940,000 and 635,000, respectively. In 1953 more than three times as many farms (700,000) used milking machines as had in 1941. Since World War II, then, a second industrial revolu-

tion has taken place on American farms.

Another part of the agricultural revolution was to make farm labor more efficient. A century ago one farm worker could produce enough to provide for four people. In 1920 he could provide for ten, and in 1948 he could provide for fourteen people. The introduction of machinery thus added momentum to the migration from the rural community to the city, inasmuch as fewer hands could manage a large farm efficiently; and therefore in the rural community doctors, lawyers, merchants, and others served a smaller farm population. Many villages disappeared or dwindled to a store or two.

The industrialization of the nation changed the rural community in still other ways. The automobile and the bus changed the center of rural life from the village to the larger town. Distance grew shorter in terms of time. Therefore, the community could spread out geographically. A study of this problem showed that in 1905 it took a total of 1,000 minutes to reach the school, church, lodge, bank, drug- and grocery stores. In 1930 it took only 276 minutes to reach the same places. The average distance to these places had increased by about half, but the time spent reaching them had been cut to almost one-fourth.

A more recent industrial development is further changing the character of the rural community. In recent years many large industries have begun a process of decentralization whereby factories are built in open country or in small towns.

Without electrification on the farm, the many chores are doubled. However, despite the hard work, farm life has many advantages, not the least of which is knowing that one is working for himself. (Standard Oil Co., N.J.)

This brings urban workers and professional people into the rural community. The most notable example of part-time farming and decentralized industry, of course, has occurred in the TVA region. A harmonious integration of these urban people into the rural community can be profitable to the rural populations.

The results of all these revolutionary changes have been both good and bad for the rural dweller. Radio, television, city-trained teachers in the rural schools, ease of communication between rural and urban areas, all combine to "urbanize" the rural dweller. The farmer does not have to contend with city traffic every day or worry about smoke palls, but in many respects he thinks like a city dweller and has adopted an urban set of values. He listens to programs and advertisements aimed to satisfy urban tastes and desires. A greater proportion of his time is spent in the urban community than formerly, because he must now go to the city to secure the goods and services he formerly obtained in the local village. If the current population trends continue, we can expect the rural community of the future to consist of a small city at the center, surrounded by farms and small shopping areas extending many miles from the central city. The biggest

population gains between 1940 and 1950 were in cities between 10,000 and 100,000 population, and this same trend has continued since the 1950 census.

The agricultural revolution we have been discussing, then, has changed both the enterprise of farming and the character of the rural community. The farmer has become a cash-crop industrialist; the rural community has thinned out and dispersed itself over a wider area. In the process of this revolution many rural communities lost a considerable part of their social and personal values. Carl C. Taylor summed up the losses in these words:[2]

The things we have lost in rural life during the process of these transitions, or at least the things we want re-gained or built into rural life, are apparently: (1) not only the economic but social and psychological security which we had in the period when self-sufficient agriculture prevailed; (2) the richness of rural life which many less commercial agricultures have because of their art, music, drama, folk recreation, and community participation; (3) those qualities of personality and the social values which we think grow only out of family and neighborhood life.

We might put the problem this way: As a result of the revolution in agricul-

[2] Carl C. Taylor, "The Restoration of Rural Culture," in *Catholic Rural Life Objectives*, (Des Moines, Third Series, 1937), pp. 89–90.

Migration from the farms is usually an economic matter, but many young folks are lured to the city because of better cultural opportunities. The bookmobile is one of the many innovations of recent years that have been designed to increase cultural activity in the rural areas. (Standard Oil Co., N.J.)

ture, an attempt has been made to apply urban standards to the rural community. The result of such an attempt could never be successful. At most, it would turn rural dwellers into second-rate urbanites. The problem is rather to make a first-rate rural community; that is, to realize as fully as possible the rural community's potentialities.

49. THE GOOD RURAL COMMUNITY

There are many excellent rural communities throughout the country where a great part of the population lives a full, satisfying human existence. But in some rural areas the sense of community is weak, largely because the farmer looks at his occupation as a job instead of a way of life. He looks to the city for his recreation, his culture, and many of the services that should ordinarily be obtained in his local community.

A good rural community cannot exist without a right attitude toward rural life. Some city people think of rural life as a series of barn dances and chicken dinners, of fresh air and sunshine and the simple life of a century ago. They ignore the hard work and scientific planning that are necessary for success on a modern farm. A wise approach to the problems of rural life realizes that life on the farm is hard—that is, does not pay large profits in cash—but that its rewards are large in social and personal life.

There is no reason today why every farmer must *live* on his farm. With the motorcar at his disposal, he can live together with other farmers in a nearby village. This is the pattern followed in many other parts of the world. American farmers have never taken strongly to this form of rural life, although many have now come to do so. There are, of course, certain disadvantages in living off the farm: loss of time spent going to and from work, and transportation costs.

The corresponding social and cultural advantages, however, might outweigh the disadvantages. Neighbors would be nearer. Schools would be better. Shopping would be easier, and professional services would be more readily available. Living conditions would be better and cheaper because utilities, such as gas, light, water, and sewage disposal, would be available at less cost. Finally, as *The Manifesto on Rural Life* explains, "religious activity would be intensified . . . organization would be stronger and more active; the spirit of solidarity and cooperation would grow among the villagers and townspeople."

Whether the farmer lives in the village or on his farm, however, the composition of a good rural community is pretty much the same. Besides farmers, it includes merchants, a banker, perhaps an editor, teachers, a priest and ministers, and some lawyers and physicians. At the 1954 convention of the Catholic Rural Life Conference, Monsignor Ligutti stated: "The rural areas need more professional people —doctors, lawyers, bankers, writers, clergy. Your minister, your priest, your banker, your lawyer and your doctor are the backbone of the rural community, the natural leaders."

Part-time farming. A rural community need not be dependent exclusively on farming. Various experiments have been worked out successfully to combine part-time farming with part-time industrial employment. Three different plans for part-time farming have proved successful: (1) living on small acreages in or reasonably near a town, working regularly at an industrial job and farming the small acreage as a hobby or extra source of income; (2) living on a relatively small farm or in town and dividing time between farming and employment in some industry that does not require full-time work; (3) living on the farm and developing some sort of home industry as an additional occupation.

This photo of the Granger Homestead Settlement shows the tracts of land these miner-farmers work to stretch their incomes by raising their own food supply. (NCRLC)

The small dairy farm in the picturesque New Hampshire country is an example of what the U.S.D.A. calls a good farm. There is less migration from owner-operated farms such as this. (U.S.D.A. Photograph)

All of these possibilities offer obvious financial advantages. They save the farmer from "putting all his eggs in one basket," and thus cushion the effects of crop failure or other farm disaster. Moreover, they enable the small farmer to increase his meager cash income so that he can improve his farm and enjoy some of the reasonable comforts of life. Careful planning by persons with both industrial and agricultural experience is required to establish a community that is semi-agricultural and semi-industrial.

One notable example is the Granger Homestead Settlement in Granger, Iowa, developed under the leadership of Monsignor Ligutti. Granger was originally a coal-mining area where the workers suffered from low wages and seasonal unemployment. The average annual wage of families selected for the Granger settlement in 1936 was $908. The families suffered from inadequate housing, low living standards, and a drab social life. Fifty families were carefully selected for experiment. Most of them were miners' families, and all had had farming experience. Aided by government funds, they purchased modern homes with large enough tracts of land to raise much of their own food supply. Since the period of inactivity in the mines was from April to September, the workers were able to devote sufficient time to their small farms. The aggregate wage income of the members of the Granger community decreased in three years about 10 per cent, but this decrease was more than taken care of by the products from their small farms. More important than the economic gains, however, were the social and moral achievements of this community that enabled a depressed group to live a better life than was possible when they were dependent exclusively on their jobs in the mines.

In a rural community persons of divergent religions and racial backgrounds must learn to co-operate as Americans and neighbors with a large number of common interests. Rural resettlement programs—like the Granger Homestead group—can select their members. In such cases, experience shows that it is wise to have people of the same religion and the same general background. When this is done, the parish can perform its proper function of serving as the center of social and cultural as well as religious life.

Prosperity of the farmer. The prosperity of the rural community—merchants, bankers, professional people, and tradesmen who serve the farmer—depends on the farmer's having sufficient cash income to purchase goods and services. The farmer's cash income need not be as large as an urban worker's with the same-size family, because it is supplemented by the food he grows for his own use and by the services he performs for himself.

During World War II and in the years afterward, the farmer was prosperous. The demand for his products was large at home and abroad. Since the all-time high of 1947, however, the farmer's income has declined somewhat while his costs for wages and machinery have increased. Farmers' net income in 1953 decreased by one billion from the previous year and dropped $4,300,000,000 from 1947.

Improvement of the small farmer's lot is not easy. More efficient farming can help some of them. Others can be aided by easy credit arrangements to enable them to buy a farm large enough to support a family decently. Education in farming technique and expert help in planning crops and marketing them can also increase the farmer's income. This is a problem for the best farm leaders to work on systematically through the years in the hope of enabling the small farmer to earn a living family wage in his combined cash and self-subsistence crops.

Importance of the rural school. Cultural development in rural communities depends much on the rural school. Rural leaders used to point out that the rural school is not adapted to the needs, the outlook, or the way of life proper to the rural community. The same textbooks, written by city people as a rule and assuming an urban outlook on the students' part, are used in the city and in the rural community. Frequently the teachers are people reared in the city and educated in an urban university. This criticism, however, is less valid today than it was ten years ago.

Rural leaders want their schools to develop in the student a love of farm life and an appreciation of the values of living in a rural community. They desire training in home arts and crafts, in scientific farming, and in other matters related to wholesome and successful farm life. They desire the rural school to be a center of social activities for young people that will "counteract the lure of the city." Experience has shown that a good rural school can do much to improve the rural community when the necessary factors—such as good land well located in reference to markets—are present.

The rural school is helped in attaining these objectives by federal legislation and federal funds. Hundreds of vocational agricultural departments have been established in schools throughout the country, pursuant to the Smith-Hughes Act. Through its county agents the Department of Agriculture's Extension Service carries on what has been called the great-est adult-education project in history. It supplies interested persons with printed information on hundreds of topics related to farming and rural life. Educational work is also done by agencies within the Farm Bureau, the Grange, and the Farmers Union.

Co-operatives in the rural community. The immediate aim of farmers' co-operatives is economic: to help them market their crops advantageously or to buy at lower costs. But co-operatives are social by nature. They involve a common approach to solve a common problem, and thus they bring people together for discussion and action. Their successful operation illustrates the value of social action to the farmers. Moreover, a co-operative frequently branches out into such activities as education or recreation.

Farmers' co-operatives take many different forms. Producers' co-operatives are organized by farmers to market their crops. By collective action farmers can bargain more effectively, advertise if necessary, and generally market their goods more advantageously. In consumers' co-operatives the farmers organize to buy collectively and thus at less cost than if each one purchased his gasoline, machinery, or other goods separately. Credit co-operatives operate in similar fashion to make money available to the farmer at lower rates of interest and easier arrangements for repayment of the principal.

The first permanently successful co-operative was that of the Rochdale Weavers, a group of poorly paid factory workers in the English town of Rochdale, who joined together in 1844 to stretch their low wages by collective buying of food and other necessities. The principles on which the Rochdale experiment operated have been followed by almost every successful co-operative in this country. (1) Each member, no matter how much stock he owns, has one vote. (2) Goods are sold at current prices or slightly less. (3) The surplus, or profit after adminis-

The town auction attracts people from the surrounding countryside to purchase needed articles or simply to socialize. Auctions are often run for the benefit of churches and fraternal organizations and the articles are donated by the townspeople. (Standard Oil Co., N.J.)

trative expenses are paid, is divided annually, with each person receiving a share proportionate to his purchases throughout the year. This rebate is the saving effected by patronizing the co-operative. (4) A fixed and limited return is made on capital investment—the shares of stock purchased by the members with which the co-operative buys its goods, pays its employees, and takes care of other operational expenses.

At the beginning of 1955 there were about 7,500 consumers' co-operatives serving rural communities, and they did a total business of $2,800,000,000 in sales. One billion of this was in feed. There were about 7,000 marketing co-operatives that did an annual business of $9,250,000,000 in such products as cotton, grains, livestock, nuts, poultry, fruit, and tobacco.

The economic advantages of the co-operative to the farmer are obvious. And they are his primary consideration when he joins either a producers' or a consumers' co-operative. But co-operatives can be used for more than economic benefits. Under intelligent, dynamic leadership they can be used to reorganize a rural community's social life and play an important part in taking a common approach to the solution of local problems. By discussion of local health and sanitation problems, by co-operative study of market trends, by a general program of adult education, co-operatives can be used to raise the intellectual and cultural tone of the community. The co-operative approach to local problems enables the people in a rural community to solve at least some of their own problems instead of turning to state or federal agencies to do it for them. In this way co-operatives can be used to develop an active, informed group of people without which no community can flourish.

50. TENANT FARMING, THE LURE OF THE CITY, THE MIGRANT WORKER

Tenant farming has long been a serious agricultural problem. Farmers who went into bankruptcy frequently remained on their farms as tenants of absentee owners —insurance companies or more prosperous farmers. Farm tenancy threatened to become a general thing during and after the depression of the 1930s. Prosperity caused by World War II mitigated the tenancy problem because the farming population profited from the mistake made after World War I. During that first world war the farmer invested his profits in more land in order to extend his holdings and thus increase his profits. The agricultural depression of 1921 found him with heavy mortgages on newly acquired land.

During World War II, on the other hand, the farmer invested his profits more wisely. He paid off his mortgage to obtain full ownership and he bought modern equipment. Many tenants managed to buy the farms which they worked. In 1935, 2,350,000 farms were mortgaged, only 1,714,000 in 1945, and the number had dropped to 1,480,000 by 1950. A similar trend is observed in farm tenancy. In 1930, 2,664,000 farms were operated

The plight of the migrant worker is dramatically depicted in this photograph, which shows the itinerants having a roadside meal in New Mexico. (Ewing Galloway)

by tenants, in 1945 the number was 1,858,000, and by 1950 it had fallen to 1,444,000.

Tenancy is harmful to the tenant, the soil, and even the urban communities that are ultimately dependent on farm production for their food and other items of comfortable living. A report of the Department of Agriculture, *Disadvantaged Classes in American Agriculture*, has this to say about the social effects of tenant farming:

At its worst, tenancy forces family living standards below levels of decency; develops rural slums; and breeds poverty, illiteracy, and disease. In such circumstances, tenant families live in houses of poor construction, almost universally in need of repair, often without doors and windows, with leaky roofs, and sometimes even without floors. Seldom are these houses equipped with running water, electricity, bathrooms, or indoor toilets. The surroundings are usually unsightly and devoid of beauty. The poorer tenant family's food is simple, lacks in variety, and often lacks some of the essentials of good nutrition. Their clothing, in a great many cases, is inadequate for the mere protection of the body, much less to provide any sense of satisfaction. The incessant movement from farm to farm and from community to community of families living under such conditions constitutes a disintegrating influence upon all social institutions and all forms and types of social participation. Systematic church attendance is impossible, neighborhood relations are constantly disrupted, and the children of tenant parents find their school attendance periodically interrupted.

Tenant conditions are not always as bad as those described by the Department of Agriculture's report. But even under the best conditions tenancy is not an ideal way to operate the farm. The tenant cannot have the same interest in safeguarding the future of the farm as can the owner. His interest is solely in a profitable crop, even at the risk of impoverishing the soil.

Migration to the city. The rural community is continually weakened by the migration to the city of men and money. The farmer who obtains credit outside the rural community sends interest payments to the city. The farmer who purchases services and goods in the city sends his money out of the rural community. If he sends his children away to school, he must support them in the city where they live. When such spending becomes general among the population of a rural community, the business and professional people in the community find that they cannot earn a decent livelihood. Their only recourse is to leave the community and make a living elsewhere. Thus the rural community becomes less self-sufficient and a less fit place for living.

More important, as agricultural people continually insist, is the migration of the best young people to the city. It has been normal all through history for the rural communities to populate cities by migration. But the rural community suffers if *most* of its young people leave it for good. In 1954, Secretary of Agriculture Ezra T. Benson reported the following facts about the migration of young people to the city. The rate of migration is higher for women and girls than for men. It is higher from low-income farm areas and from areas where the proportion of children to adults is large. It is higher from tenant-operated farms than from farms operated by the owner. These facts indicate that migration to the city is largely an economic matter, that young people go to the city because they cannot obtain an adequate livelihood on the farm.

There does not seem to be any direct solution to the problem of losing the young people by migration from the farm. They will stay on the farms and in rural communities when they can make a good living there and when rural life is culturally and socially more attractive.

The migrant worker. The very nature of large-scale, single-crop farming has created a class of part-time workers who migrate from one area to another as the crops ripen. These people, who have no permanent home, are called migrant workers. They belong to the agricultural population but not to the rural community.

Farming is seasonal work, especially on the large one-crop farms. Preparing the soil and planting a crop requires many man-hours of labor. But with the help of modern machinery and with good planning the farmer can spread this work out over several weeks. In this way he does not have to hire many extra workers. Gathering the crop presents greater difficulties. It ripens at the same time on all farms in a given area, and the best time for picking the crops may be as short as one week for soft fruits to as long as seven or eight weeks for cotton. If his crop is not gathered within the given time the farmer faces failure for the year. Ingenious man has not yet built machinery that can replace human hands in picking peaches out of the trees or grapes off the vine efficiently and with little damage to the crop. Because such machinery has been built for harvesting, shucking, sorting, and packing grain crops, the migrant worker does not constitute a problem on the large grain farm.

Farmers who cannot employ efficient machinery to harvest their crops resort to human labor in large quantity for a short time, a matter of days or at the most a few weeks on each farm. These workers are recruited and brought into the area, where they live in temporary quarters until the crop is picked. Then they move on to another area where another crop is ripening. The migrant worker is paid comparatively low wages. There are no minimum-wage laws for farm labor, and the migrant worker is unorganized and hence in no position to bargain successfully with the farmer. None of the other benefits that are enjoyed by most workers throughout the country are available to the migrant worker. He is not covered by social security. Therefore, he receives no unemployment insurance, no protection of any kind for himself or his family in time of emergency.

Out of a total of four and one-half million farm laborers in the country, somewhat more than one million are migrant workers. This group is constantly enlarged by Mexican workers—"wetbacks"[3] —who come across the border at certain seasons at the rate of about 10,000 a week. Employment is not steady for the migrant worker, of course, and living conditions are bad. Novels and occasional newspaper and magazine articles do something to arouse the public conscience to an awareness of the hard life led by migrant workers, but for some reason the American people have not been aroused sufficiently to force state and national governments to improve the migrant worker's lot.

The condition of the migrant worker resembles somewhat that of the factory employee in the early years of industrialization. Migrant workers suffer from economic and social evils because of the nature of their work, because they are not organized for collective action on their own behalf, and because they have been consistently excluded from sharing in the benefits of social legislation. If crops are late or if weather is bad, the migrant worker must remain idle without pay. In Michigan, 90,000 migrant workers were kept idle in the summer of 1954 because the sugar-beet and fruit crops were late. The editor of the *Michigan Catholic* reported, after a visit to one of the migrant workers' camps: "In three hours I saw more misery than I have seen in all my thirty years in Michigan."

The misery he saw can be observed wherever migrant workers live: malnutrition, overcrowding, unsanitary living conditions, poverty, all resulting in widespread disease and a high death rate, especially among children. Eighteen infants

---

[3] "Wetbacks" are Mexican workers who enter this country illegally, usually by wading or swimming across the Rio Grande at night. Hence the name.

died from malnutrition in twenty days in two California counties during the 1949 cotton-picking season. A physician reported to a presidential commission that his survey in Texas showed that 96 per cent of the children in the camp at Mathis had not drunk any milk in six months and that 80 per cent of the adults had not tasted meat in the same time. A county health department director in Florida reported that in one nursery maintained for migrant workers' babies —so that mothers and children also could work—he found forty-eight babies in a small room on two beds. Two of them died later. In most camps there is no sewage system. People are crowded together in temporary, inadequate quarters. Sometimes fifteen or twenty men, women, and children of various families live in a single room.

One of the worst evils attendant upon migrant labor is the community's inability to provide education for the migrant worker's children. To provide adequate schooling seems almost impossible, because the migrant camp moves to a new locality every few weeks. The result is that the children do not usually attend school. Instead they work in the fields with the parents, often performing long hours of work.

Aiding the migrant worker. Such conditions, of course, are inhuman. They continue to exist (1) because of general public apathy, (2) because the one million migrant workers are unorganized and without corporate representation, and (3) because there is a vested interest of large-scale farm operators (about 2 per cent of the nation's farmers) whose profits depend on exploiting the migrant farm laborer. From time to time religious and humanitarian groups stir up interest in the migratory workers' plight, but the large-scale farmers have successfully blocked legislative action by national or state governments to improve the migrant worker's condition. Meanwhile religious

and humanitarian groups have distributed food and clothing and tried to care for the sick in some of the camps. But these relief measures do not solve the problems.

A federal Interagency Committee on Migrant Labor studied the problem extensively in 1946 and 1947 and made the following recommendation:

It is recommended that local, state and national citizen action be encouraged and stimulated by the dissemination of information in a form which can be used by civic, labor, church and educational agencies toward the end of mobilizing the intelligence and conscience of as wide a group and as many groups as possible for the progressive attack on the problems of migrant workers. This effort should not only result in needed legislation but also make it possible for migrant workers and their families to have an appropriate place in the life of the communities in which they are employed.

A bill to improve the migrant workers' condition was introduced into the House of Representatives shortly after this report was published in March 1947, but the opposition killed the bill in committee. No further legislative action has been taken, and the condition of the migrant workers has continued to be deplorable. In June 1950, President Truman appointed a Commission on Migratory Labor to inquire into social, economic, health, and educational conditions among the migrant workers. The commission conducted hearings on these conditions for ten months in Washington and in nine states where the greater part of migratory farm work was concentrated. Its report gave a comprehensive picture of the problem of migrant farm labor and made a series of recommendations for drastic reforms.

Meanwhile it became evident to the reformers that strong interests were opposed to any real reform. Agricultural committees of various state chambers of commerce sent out calls for Mexican workers and stated, in effect, that they

The tragedy so often associated with the lives of migrant workers is easily understood from a study of these pictures. The parents are forced to neglect their children. There can be little "home life" in shacks such as these. (National Archives)

would abide by immigration laws only if the federal government allowed them to recruit as many Mexican workers as they thought necessary each season. Food processors and owners of the big "factory farms" insisted that any reform of the migrant workers' condition would ruin them economically. The farm interests are so strongly represented in the Congress that they can block any legislation that does not have overwhelming public support behind it.

Recommendations so far offered for solving the migrant farm worker problem can be summarized in this fashion:

1. Enforce strict federal control of immigration of alien workers into this country and the interstate transportation of native workers. Much of the evil is associated with methods of recruitment, experts say, and strict regulation of recruitment practices would attack the evil at its source.

2. Extend the benefits of Social Security legislation to migrant farm workers.

3. Provide, by appropriate state and federal legislation, for stringent licensing and inspection of labor-recruiting agencies, of labor camps, and farm working conditions.

4. Enact and enforce in each state mini-mum-wage requirements for farm labor, as well as laws on child labor and school attendance.

5. Extend to farm workers the protection of the Labor-Management Relations Act, which would facilitate their self-protection through collective bargaining. Many students of the problem see this as the indispensable long-term solution.

6. Promote in the farm areas small workshops and decentralized industries to employ the migrant worker during the period when there is no work available on the farm.

No single recommendation, if applied, would end the social evil of migrant workers' subhuman existence. A long-range combination of most of these recommendations seems necessary. The problem is full of difficulty. The cotton farmer and the fruitgrower need a large force of pickers for only a short time each year. They cannot be expected to pay an annual living wage to as many men as they must have on hand at picking time. On the other hand, if their continued operation depends on the ruination of lives, those who support the system are forced to ignore the human values which lie at the heart of American society.

REVIEW

48. Diminished Agricultural Population

A. What is the danger in the decline of the country's rural population?

B. State some of the problems over which the farmer has no control.

C. Why is farming a way of life? How does it help family life?

D. What revolution in farm life took place during the last century? What changes in farming methods were a result of this revolution? How have they affected the farmer's social life?

49. The Good Rural Community

A. What are some of the advantages to be enjoyed by a farmer who lives in a community away from his farm?

B. What are some of the plans that have been worked out for part-time farming? Name a few advantages of this program. Describe briefly what has been accomplished in this regard at Granger, Iowa.

C. What do rural leaders expect of the rural schools? How are these schools attaining their objectives?

D. What are the principal values of farmers' co-operatives?

50. Tenant Farming, the Lure of the City, the Migrant Worker

A. What is tenant farming? Why is it lessening today? What are some of its social evils?

B. Why have farmers migrated to the cities? What must be done to make farm life attractive?

C. What is a migrant worker? Where are they generally found? Why are they generally at a disadvantage?

THE CHAPTER IN REVIEW

A. Describe the agricultural revolution of the past hundred years and show some of the social and economic effects of it on farm life.

B. Describe the various kinds of farmers co-operatives and how they are managed.

C. What are the recommendations of the Federal Interagency Commission on Migrant Labor? How have these recommendations been blocked? Summarize some of the suggestions to aid these workers.

SELECTED READINGS

The two generally accepted basic works on rural life are Carl C. Taylor and Associates, *Rural Life in the United States* (New York: Alfred A. Knopf, Inc., 1949), and Charles P. Loomis and J. Allan Beegle, *Rural Social Systems* (New York: Prentice-Hall, Inc., 1950). An excellent historical study of the relationship of the farmer to the federal government is given by Murray R. Benedict, *Farm Policies of the United States, 1790–1950* (New York: The Twentieth Century Fund, 1953).

Church authorities on rural life have issued a statement of their policies and have discussed Catholic social thought on this subject in their *Manifesto on Rural Life* (Milwaukee: The Bruce Publishing Co., 1939). Also basic for Catholic thinking on the subject is Msgr. Luigi G. Ligutti and Rev. John C. Rawe, *Rural Roads to Security* (Milwaukee: The Bruce Publishing Co., 1940). The conclusions reached by an International Catholic Congress on the Problems of Rural Life are published as a pamphlet, *Christianity and the Land* (Des Moines: National Catholic Rural Life Conference, 1952). The NCRLC has also published a pamphlet, *The Pope Speaks on Rural Life* (1947), and two pamphlets which bring their *Manifesto* up to date: *The Land: God's Gift to Man* and *For This We Stand.*

The Farm Foundation has published a number of pamphlets that are instructive on rural-life problems. Among them are: *Human Relations in Agriculture and Farm Life* (Chicago: Farm Foundation, 1950); *Reaching the Grass Roots* (1952); and *Increasing Understanding of Public Problems and Policies* (1952).

The "invasion" of the rural community by industry is the subject of an article by Neil Hurley, "New Profile of Industrial America," *America* (February 5, 1955).

Co-operatives have been the subject of much writing. Rev. Leo R. Ward, C.S.C., has edited an excellent study of co-operatives, *United for Freedom* (Milwaukee: The Bruce Publishing

Co., 1945). Also informative are: *Catholic Churchmen and Co-operatives* (Des Moines: National Catholic Rural Life Conference, 1944); Jerry Voorhis, *The Co-operatives Look Ahead* (New York: Public Affairs Pamphlets, 1952); and four pamphlets published by the Government Printing Office: *Why Co-ops?* (1948); *Organizing a Farmers' Co-operative* (1945); *The Story of Farmers' Co-operatives* (1951); *Agricultural Co-operation in the United States* (1947).

A basic document for the study of the problem of migrant workers is the Report of the President's Commission on Migratory Labor, *Migratory Labor in American Agriculture* (Washington: Government Printing Office, 1951). Two pamphlets that contain valuable information on the subject are Varjen Fuller, *No Work Today!—The Plight of America's Migrants* (New York: Public Affairs Pamphlets, 1953), and Lowry Nelson, *Migratory Workers* (Washington: National Planning Association, 1953). A discussion of the difficulty of obtaining legislation to improve the migrant workers' condition is an article by Raymond Bernard, S.J., "Run-Around for Migrants," *Social Order* (October 1951).

PROJECTS

1. American agriculture provides the world's greatest variety of food products and raw materials. To understand the breadth of our agriculture, an artist in the class could draw an outline map of the United States and indicate the areas of the country that produce the various agricultural products consumed at home and abroad.

2. A committee of the class could write to the Catholic Rural Life Conference for information regarding its beginnings, purposes, and accomplishments. A report could then be made to the class or a display of the Conference's publications could be made on the bulletin board.

3. The *Statistical Abstract of the United States* contains figures that show the decline in the farm population since 1920. An interesting report can be made to the class about the present number of farms being operated in the United States, their ownership, and their output according to size. Class discussion that would follow this report might include a comparison between farm ownership and large industrial corporations.

PROFILES

ROBERT F. WAGNER

BORN: Nastatten, Germany, June 8, 1877
EDUCATION: City College of New York, 1898; New York Law School, 1900
DIED: New York City, May 4, 1953

Wagner's family moved to the United States when he was only eight years old, and his education was therefore almost entirely in American schools. He had to work part time while in school because of straitened family finances. While still a college student he became very interested in the law as a profession, and in politics as a practical means of influencing lawmaking. Consequently he participated in Democratic party activities and began a career in elective office as a member of the New York State Assembly in 1905.

He became Democratic floor leader of the Assembly and later acting lieutenant governor. An associate and friend of Alfred E. Smith, Wagner centered his attention on reforming the legal status of laboring people in New York. His chief contribution in this direction was the framing of a workman's compensation law, which was adopted largely with Smith's aid and has served as a model for other states in protecting laborers from the economic catastrophe that accompanies severe injury. His ambition as a lawyer seemed satisfied in 1919, when he was chosen Justice of the New York Supreme Court. He was elevated in 1924 to the Appellate Division, which is a higher court in New York State.

In 1926, Wagner was elected to the Senate where he served continually until 1949, through four successive elections. His senatorial service made him an internationally known legislator. His name is most intimately associated with the Wagner-Connery Labor Relations Act, although his legislative service was directly responsible also for introducing measures to collect and publish unemployment statistics. He was a leader in establishing the United States Employment Service and the Social Security Administration. Always interested in such projects as eliminating slums, Wagner approached this problem in constructive collaboration with such Republicans as Senator Robert Taft. Forced to restrict his activities more and more in later years, he retired from the Senate and finally redeemed a long standing pledge to himself, by taking instructions and entering the Catholic Church shortly before his death.

Biographical sketches of Senator Wagner are included in *Current Biography* (New York: H. W. Wilson Co.) for the years 1941 and 1953. For informative articles on Senator Wagner the student should consult the *Reader's Guide to Periodical Literature.*

PIERRE CHARLES L'ENFANT

BORN: France, August 2, 1754
EDUCATION: French military schools and institutes
DIED: Prince George's County, Maryland, June 14, 1825

Lieutenant L'Enfant, a highly skilled military engineer, arrived in America in 1777. His professional training made him almost unique in the American forces, commanded chiefly by ex-militia officers; most of the other European volunteers were rather glamorous troop leaders than technicians. L'Enfant improved Fort Mifflin on the Delaware River, which established his reputation when it withstood one of the most concentrated British sieges of the war: it was strong enough to resist heavy cannonading, and its own fire ports commanded all approaches. Impressed, Washington made L'Enfant chief of his engineers. Congress by special resolution raised him to the rank of major.

After the war Major L'Enfant elected to remain in America and employed his constructive abilities in civilian architecture. He designed the adaptation of New York's old City Hall for use by the First Congress, as well as that of Federal House in Philadelphia. When the new national capital city was under discussion Major L'Enfant seemed the logical choice

to entrust with the task of planning it, and his appointment was endorsed by both Washington and Jefferson.

L'Enfant's street plan differed considerably from the checkerboard type that had marked earlier American town and city planning. He broke up the grid with a series of diagonal avenues, which would intersect at park-like areas and key public buildings; these avenues, in his plan, would be named after the states of the Union. The basic L'Enfant plan has, in fact, been followed: it was flexible enough to provide for gradual growth outward from the Capitol, and the broad avenues and many parks that he called for are characteristics of the city today.

However, L'Enfant quarreled with his superiors over releasing his plans to the public before all the details were settled: he charged that land speculators would profit unduly from such information. Discharged, and generally unappreciated, L'Enfant refused his fee for the plans, retired to private life, and even spurned Madison's later offer of the chair of engineering at West Point. After his death his great vision was recognized, and, in a final tribute, the plans for Washington, D.C., were engraved on their designer's gravestone.

L'Enfant's life and work have not been made the subject of any recent full-length book; however, the high point of his career is described by Elizabeth S. Kite in *L'Enfant and Washington, 1791–1792* (Baltimore: The Johns Hopkins Press, 1929). A study is available in a scholarly publication by H. Paul Caemmerer, "The Life of Pierre Charles L'Enfant," in *Columbia Historical Society Records,* Vol. 50 (1948–1950), (Washington: The Society, 1951), pp. 323–340.

THE NATIONAL CATHOLIC WELFARE CONFERENCE

The headquarters for the National Catholic Welfare Conference are located at 1312 Massachusetts Avenue N.W., Washington 5, D.C. It was established in September 1919 and began as a continuation and broadening of the work of the National Catholic War Council formed to co-ordinate the work of Catholic groups during World War I.

A voluntary association of the bishops of the United States, the NCWC, according to its founders, has grouped together the various agencies "by which the cause of religion is furthered. Each of these, continuing its own special work in its chosen field, will now derive additional support through general co-operation."

An Administrative Board of ten archbishops and bishops is chosen each year, and together with the American cardinals they head the various departments.

The *Executive Department* co-ordinates the activities of all the NCWC departments and directs the following activities: the Confraternity of Christian Doctrine, the Bureau of Information, the Publication Office, the Bureau of International Affairs, the Inter-American Bureau, the Office of UN Affairs.

The *Department of Education* collects data concerning Catholic education, furnishes information to school officials and the general public, advises Catholic educational institutions, and generally represents the interests of Catholic schools in educational circles and before national and international groups.

The *Press Department* aids the Catholic press through releases, articles, pictorial service, editorial information service, a weekly news letter, special texts of Catholic documents, and biographies. This service is made available also to the secular press in this country and throughout the world.

The *Social Action Department* makes known the social teachings of the Church and under the guidance of the bishops interprets the application of these teachings to the social problems of the day. The Department works in the following fields: industrial relations, international peace, family life, race relations, social welfare, and rural life.

The *Legal Department* serves as a clearinghouse for information that is needed by Church officials on governmental and judicial matters. It keeps up with current legislation and decisions of the courts that might touch Church interests. It handles religious and social matters that need to be discussed with government officials or before congressional committees, and it interprets legislation for the bishops and other Catholic authorities.

The *Immigration Department* aids the immigrants by giving them advice and assistance in their many problems. The department brings the immigrant in contact with local Catholic organizations and maintains contact with the various agencies of this government and of foreign nations that are concerned with these matters.

The *Youth Department* helps to promote youth work on a diocesan and college basis. Its work embraces the various diocesan youth councils and, on the college level, the National Federation of Catholic College Students and the Newman Club Federation. These function under the National Council of Catholic Youth, a federation of approved Catholic youth groups supervised by the department, which tries to strengthen present organizations without absorbing them.

The *Department of Lay Organizations* consists of the National Council of Catholic Men and the National Council of Catholic Women, whose chief functions are co-ordinating, promoting, and assisting the activities of the Catholic lay organizations of the country and providing them with the guidance of the hierarchy. It seeks to affiliate and unite all fraternal, social, and religious societies of Catholic men and women.

The *War Relief Services* was established in 1943 to administer a program of relief and assistance to refugees, prisoners of war, displaced persons, victims of war, and merchant seamen in the United States and in more than sixty foreign countries. The National Catholic Resettlement Council was established to find homes for the many thousands of displaced persons emigrating to the United States. The Annual Bishops' War Relief Fund has distributed over $200,000,000 throughout the world to all in need.

The *National Catholic Community Service,* a member of the USO, was established to co-ordinate the work of serving our armed forces and ministering to their material and spiritual needs. It has been maintained in the post-war period to meet the needs of our peacetime forces.

The *Mission Secretariat,* the newest department of the NCWC, is designed to aid all U.S. religious societies that send missionaries to foreign lands. It provides a means of contact among all these groups and helps them in their relationships with agencies of the United States Government and of foreign governments that touch on mission work.

In addition to these departments there are a

number of special committees under the auspices of the NCWC that deal with the propagation of the faith, protection of morals, and special problems of a sociological nature.

For an excellent summary of the NCWC, the *National Catholic Almanac* (Paterson, N.J.: St. Anthony's Guild) is recommended.

DEBATE

The question: **SHOULD THE FEDERAL GOVERNMENT ADOPT A NATIONAL FAMILY ALLOWANCE PLAN?**

Affirmative presentation

I. Yes, we need some kind of support for low-income families.
 1. Statistics prove that a number of families do not have an adequate income.
  a. Lowest-income families tend to have more children.
 2. Inadequate income hurts and even destroys family life.
  a. Material means (food, clothing, shelter) necessary for preserving family life cannot be had.
  b. Children cannot be raised properly without good education and environment.
  c. Parents are discouraged from having children.
  d. Mothers are forced to work outside the home.
II. Yes, a federal family allowance program is the best form of assistance.
 1. It has worked well in other countries.
  a. It has not resulted in abuses.
  b. There is very little criticism of it in these countries.
 2. It is endorsed by religious and social authorities.
 3. It is the most direct, effective way of giving assistance where it is most needed.
  a. A small monthly payment is suggested for each of the first three children.

 b. Payment is automatic—no "poverty" qualification.
 4. It would help to promote the common welfare.
  a. Children would obtain the necessaries of life.
  b. Families would hold together.
  c. Healthier communities and a healthier nation would be the result.
III. Yes, because a simple plan like this entails no serious problems or difficulties.
 1. The outlay is a "drop in the bucket" compared to other outlays.
  a. The "drop" is in the right place, where it will do the most good.
 2. There would be no strings attached to it; no need to fear "government control."
 3. A federal family allowance program would work like any other federal subsidy, such as veteran benefits.
  a. How could the same amount of money be better spent?

Negative presentation

I. No, although the negative admits the need of some families for some kind of assistance, this need is not as great as affirmative makes it.
 1. Low-income families can stretch dollars by right spending.
  a. Big cars, liquor, and television sets are not necessary to family life.
 2. Low-income family statistics are deceiving.
  a. They include only *cash* income; wages of young, newly married couples; semi-retired persons who don't have to work hard.
 3. Why give "child checks" to people (the greater number) who have adequate income?
  a. The dilemma: Either give most of the money to those who don't need it. Or set up "means tests," which even the affirmative does not want.
II. No, federal family allowances are bound to have bad psychological and social effects.
 1. There is the parallel of relatives or friends who help support children and tend to take over management as well.
 2. Public assistance tends to destroy family independence.
  a. It hurts the legitimate pride of father as provider for the family.

b. Children are made partial wards of the federal government.
3. It would encourage laziness on the part of those content with subsistence.

III. No, the negative has its own proposal: a radical readjustment of the income tax allowance.
1. The negative proposes giving larger exemptions for each dependent child.
2. This supports a family, in part, by allowing it to keep its earnings.
3. This is, in every way, a healthier, more American solution to the problem.

Affirmative rebuttal

I. Let us localize the issue before us:
1. Both sides admit that low-income families need assistance of some kind.
2. The negative offers its alternative of increased allowance on income tax for dependents.
II. Let us compare these proposals and decide which is better.
1. People most in need of support do not pay any income taxes and will not be helped at all by the negative plan.
2. Negative plan is to help the rich and ignore the poor.
3. Let us see how two families would make out under each plan. Both have six children; income for one family is $4,000; for the other it is $10,000.

Affirmative conclusion: Family allowances are not a dole but a matter of distributive justice. Plan gets help where it is needed and without social opprobrium. Society is the ultimate beneficiary.

Negative rebuttal

I. Let us get down to the basic issue:
1. Should a family support itself?
2. Should a family depend on the federal government?
II. The affirmative takes the second alternative.
1. What are its implications? Selling the family's soul for a mess of pottage.
III. The negative takes the first alternative.
1. We admit some material hardships, but the prize of family integrity and freedom is worth the price of occasional temporary hardship.

Negative conclusion: A program of this kind is another step toward the cradle-to-the-grave subsistence plan of an encroaching government—frequently called "creeping socialism."

CLASSROOM DISCUSSION: The class should determine the following: (1) Can we agree that there is enough suffering from low income to make some form of public assistance desirable? Review the arguments of the debate. Re-examine the statistics on family income. (2) If there is need for public assistance, which way is better?

SELECTED READINGS

Very little has been written in opposition to this plan. This, however, should not be misconstrued as suggesting unanimous endorsement of such a plan. On the contrary, those who oppose it do not consider the plan likely to win enough support to cause them to write against it. The following readings, therefore, are favorable to the plan, but many arguments against federal allowances are contained in them.

The following articles written by Francis J. Corley, S.J., appeared in *Social Order:* "Family Allowances: U.S. Plan" (April 1953); "Why Federal Family Allowances?" (June 1954); "Family Allowances: Dole or Wage?" (February 1954); "Taxes and Family Allowances" (March 1954). Articles appearing in *America* are: Robert E. and Frances I. Delany, "Family Allowances" (July 20, 1946); Mary T. Waggaman, "Whys and Wherefores of Family Allowances" (March 20, 1948); Robert and Helen Cissell, "The Case for Family Allowances" (October 16, 1954). *Commonweal* carried the following articles pertinent to this topic: Harold Maslow, "Family Security in America" (June 16, 1939); John C. Cort, "Wages and Big-Family Men" (March 20, 1951).

In addition to the above, Senator Richard L. Neuberger, who has sponsored such a program in Congress, wrote an interesting article on the success of the program in Canada, "Canada's Social Security System for Children," *Reporter* (April 27, 1954). Edgar Schmiedeler, O.S.B., an authority on social problems, is the author of "Family Allowances for the U.S.A.?", *Homiletic and Pastoral Review* (September 1945). An article by Senator Paul H. Douglas, who has sponsored social welfare bills, is an early comment on such federal allowances, but it is nevertheless related to the present conception of the plan, "The Family Allowances System as a Protector of Children," *Annals of the American Academy of Political and Social Science* (September 1925). Two articles by F. Emerson Andrews should also be mentioned here, "What Price Children," *Atlantic Monthly* (November 1943), and "How About Family Allowances?" *Parents' Magazine* (June 1944).

UNIT SIX
National Economic Problems

Chapter 18. Principles and Problems of Management

Our economic problems are even more complex, in some ways, than the social problems we have been analyzing. They can be simplified and studied like arithmetic problems, but then they are no longer the real problems of economic life in America. In this unit we shall investigate four sets of problems: (1) those dealing with business, or the problems of management in the American economy; (2) problems facing labor; (3) the farmer's basic problems; (4) the problems of preserving our natural resources. As was the case with social problems, so economic problems do not admit of any easy solution. But they must be studied and they must be solved as thoroughly and as equitably as possible.

Economics can be defined as a social science that deals with the production, exchange, distribution, and consumption of wealth. Economic activity is concerned with making things useful—either by producing them or by making them available to the consumer. Both farming

and making ladies' hats are economic activities because they produce goods or wealth used by the consumer. Railroads and candy stores engage in economic activity because they make goods available to the consumer.

Economic activity is governed to some extent by certain so-called "laws." These laws are not to be confused with the "laws" of natural science. They are rather tendencies than laws. One such economic law, for example, is that when the supply of a certain commodity increases, the price decreases. This tends to work out if no other factors intervene—such as a change in the demand for the commodity or an agreement among the producers of the commodity to keep up the price. It is necessary for us to understand these basic economic "laws" or principles if we are to make wise decisions in trying to solve some of our economic problems.

Basic economic principles. Let us imagine that you are in a position to start a small business of your own. After surveying the market you decide to make chairs. Your first decision involves two basic economic

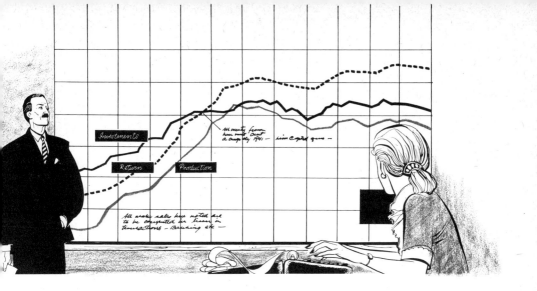

judgments: (1) chairs are useful goods; (2) there is a *market* for them. Your economic activity of manufacturing chairs consists of getting *raw material* from the forests, *transforming* it into useful chairs by *labor,* and *selling* your product to retail merchants or directly to the consumer. You can set up your chair factory only if you have enough money or can borrow enough to buy the necessary machinery and pay your employees until you start selling the chairs. This money is called *capital.* The machinery you have purchased is also called *capital.*

We see, then, that four elements enter into the production of chairs: (1) materials, (2) labor, (3) capital, (4) yourself, or the enterpriser—the organizing factor that brings the other elements together to achieve a certain economic end, here the production of chairs. Let us see a little more about each of these elements.

1. *Materials* ultimately come from the land and the sea and the air. To have economic value they must be relatively scarce, either in amount or in location. Air is free because it is relatively unlimited in amount. Salt, on the other hand, has economic value because in its usable form it is relatively scarce. The material you use in your chair factory will cost more than the trees in the forest. It costs more because of the labor involved in cutting the trees into boards, drying them out, and transporting them to your factory. Accumulated labor costs in these operations are the principal factor in determining the price you must pay for your material.

2. *Labor,* we have seen, adds to the value of the tree by transforming it into usable lumber in your factory. The labor element within your factory transforms the lumber into a more valuable and a more useful product—the chair. Other kinds of labor are equally "productive" in the economic sense: the lawyer who defends a client in court, the barber who cuts your hair, the teacher, the physician, and the maid, all perform services that are economically valuable.

Labor's right to wages is based on two principles. The first is the *performance principle.* An upholsterer in your chair factory, let us assume, upholsters one chair an hour. You compute that by his labor, not including the cost of material, he increases the value of each chair $5.00, or $40 a day the value of your product.

You could not afford to pay him a sum equal to the whole value that his labor added to your chair; nor would that be just, because you have invested your capital (and risked it) in providing the

In 1904 there were 1,752,187 children between the ages of 10 and 15 at work in the United States, or 18 per cent of all children of those ages. A great number of these worked as bobbin girls and coal breakers. Today the employment of children is strictly controlled by federal and state law, much of which was brought about by the activity of the unions. (Lewis W. Hine Photo, National Child Labor Commission; Press Association, Inc.)

room or factory, probably also the tools, which provide your employee with his opportunity to earn a living. It is likely that you have also paid to insure him against accidents. Hence you are rightly entitled to retain enough from the value he has added to the chair to give you a profit or interest on the investment of your capital. However, since you monopolize his full working time—eight hours a day—you have a moral duty to pay him what is called a living wage. He and his family have the right to live, and to live decently; so that if he devotes *all his productive time* to your business, he has a right—equal to yours—to a livelihood from your business.

Precisely how much a living wage may be will vary with time and circumstances; it can be defined only in particular cases. In our times it has probably been defined in the contract negotiated between you and the trade union of which your employee probably is a member. If you cannot pay him this living wage without losing money, you have no right to monopolize his working day. There is something wrong with your business; you have not invested your capital wisely. This doctrine of a living wage applies of course only to full-time employees, not to babysitters nor to the boy whom you hire once a week to mow the lawn.

3. *Capital* is of two kinds: *money capital* and *capital goods*. Money capital consists of savings that are invested in a productive enterprise. Both money capital and capital goods are productive. Without such capital goods as plows and seed, the farmer could grow very little indeed. Capital or investment, therefore, claims a share of your factory's income on the grounds of productivity. Another ground for its claim to income is that the investor denies himself the satisfaction of spending his money on consumer goods in order to invest it. He is therefore entitled to payment for having sacrificed a pleasure. Practically speaking, unless capital earns money, a highly developed free economy becomes impossible.

4. *Management* is the fourth productive element in an economic enterprise. You bring together the material, the labor, and the capital into your chair factory. If you organize these elements well enough to compete with your rivals, if you get a right mixture of the three elements, then your factory will show a profit. Profit is the reward of the enterprise—yourself in the chair factory—after you have paid yourself a salary and have taken care of all other production costs: material, wages for labor, interest for capital, depreciation, and taxes.

The *price* of each chair you produce in

your factory depends on several items. Demand, or how much people are willing to pay, is one important factor. Another is the *cost of production*. Unless you can sell chairs at a price high enough to cover your total cost of production, you cannot stay in business for any length of time. As the manager of an enterprise, then, you are interested in keeping the cost of production as low as possible. If you are able to withstand your competitors, you will make good profits, the difference between cost of production and income from sales. If you are not able to compete successfully you will go bankrupt.

Division of labor. So far we have considered economic principles dealing with production in a single enterprise. Now let us widen our view to take other producers into consideration. Your chair factory makes only chairs. Other factories specialize in making glassware or silverware or rugs or some other single product. Moreover, within each factory there is division of labor into specialized tasks. You find that you can produce more chairs each day if one man does all the sawing, another the sanding, another the painting, and so on. If each man took a piece of lumber and stayed with it until the chair was finished, you would produce very few chairs and you would have to charge a high price for them.

Division of labor is the first step in developing our complex economy. It increases the productive efficiency of labor and makes possible a wealthy economy. Division of labor in this country has taken four interrelated forms: (1) *specialization by products* (one factory makes only tin cans or shoes or ladies' hats); (2) *division of labor in making any one product* (one man sands your chairs, another paints them, and so on): (3) *division of labor in the total productive process* (your factory is only one step in getting the maple tree into the buyer's kitchen. A lumber company cuts the tree; a railroad transports it to your city; a retailer buys

it from your factory; perhaps a delivery agency takes it from the store to the ultimate user's house); (4) *division of labor within the fields of enterprise* (management in large companies has sales departments, personnel departments, research departments, accounting and office administration departments).

This high degree of specialization makes an economy highly productive, but it creates innumerable problems. The more we specialize, the more we depend upon each other. If the painter in your chair factory refuses to paint any more chairs, everyone else must stop working until he is willing to paint more chairs. If banks refuse to lend you money to buy more lumber when you need it, you will have to shut down your factory. Many men will be out of work. It is therefore necessary for us to keep our economy as stable as possible. This, we shall see, is one of our primary economic problems.

Competitive economy. Another thing we notice when we withdraw from your chair factory and take a wider view of our economy is that it is a *competitive economy*. You decided to make chairs because you thought you could make them profitably. Now you find that several other firms make chairs very much like your own. You find that you must sell your chairs at about the same price as theirs, and therefore you must operate your factory efficiently. Soon you find that competition is not limited to the firms making chairs from wood and cloth. If all of you agree to hold your prices up, you soon find that people are buying steel and plastic chairs. Or perhaps they are using their old chairs and buying other things instead.

Competition is therefore an important means of keeping business efficient and keeping prices down. It is called a "control" within the economy. But competition cannot operate with absolute freedom. Unless it operates in a moral and social framework, it leads to economic

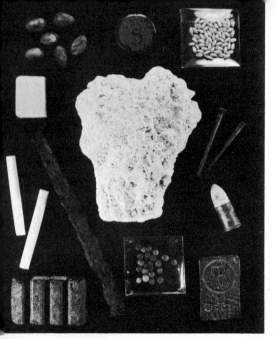

Cocoa beans, candy, grain, cheese, salt, nails, cigarettes, and other items are still used in some parts of the world as a medium of exchange. (The Chase National Bank Museum of Moneys of the World)

anarchy. If some competitors believe that "anything goes" in cutting costs of production—using inferior material, paying starvation wages, and the like—then the morally good competitor is put at a disadvantage.

Money economy. Finally, ours is a *money economy*. Economists explain the role of money by taking the simple example of a village merchant who exchanges his wares with neighboring farmers, so many bushels of wheat or so many dozens of eggs for a pair of shoes. Because such a system is clumsy, a common medium of exchange—*money*—is introduced. Money serves three functions in our economy. (1) It is a medium of exchange. Instead of getting wheat or eggs for shoes, the merchant gets money, which, in turn, he uses to purchase goods he needs. (2) It is a standard of value. The market value of various goods is measured in terms of a single item, money, instead of various other commodities. Shoes, for example, are said to cost ten dollars instead of three and one-third bushels of wheat or twenty-four pounds of beef. (3) It is a convenient way of storing up value. The farmer who raises a good wheat crop can sell it at once and bank his money.

52. THE AMERICAN ECONOMIC SYSTEM

The basic economic principles we have discussed in the previous section did not develop in the abstract. They developed in an American social and political setting which gave us a distinctively American economy. The social conditions in which our economy developed can be summarized under the following:

Our society is free. A person is free to live where he wants, to follow the trade or profession he prefers, to work or not to work. There are limits on this freedom set by law and custom, but it is nevertheless true to say that we enjoy freedom of labor, freedom of contract, free enterprise, consumers' freedom of purchase, and a system of prices more or less freely set by supply and demand.

Most property is privately owned and, within certain limits set by law and custom, a person is legally free to use his property as he wishes. The state owns considerable property, of course, and in some cases even competes with private enterprise. But we look upon this as a deviation from our normal way of life which must be justified by unusual circumstances.

Our economy can be controlled or modified by legislation. Child-labor laws, for example, prohibit the employment of children under a certain age in most states. Other laws fix minimum wages or set the hours an employee may work in a given industry. These laws are passed in the general interest or to protect a certain class who might otherwise be exploited. Such legislation is now considered part of the American way as long as it is not unjustly discriminatory.

Custom is an important factor in our economy. Custom has come to encourage the employment of women in professional and executive positions and to discourage the employment of young people, even where such employment is allowed by law. Custom, again, is an important factor in determining what food we shall eat and what kind of clothes we shall wear. Custom changes, we know, and what is not acceptable at one time may come into demand at another. It is now customary for women to smoke cigarettes if they care to, and cigarette companies must think of women as potential customers. This changes their "sales approach," their packaging, advertising, and even to some extent the kind of tobacco used in the cigarette.

We see, then, that economic laws work out in a social and political setting. Economics recognizes only money profit as a motivating force in our economy. But workers will frequently take less well-paying jobs in a better climate or quit one job because they do not like the foremen or their fellow workers. Similarly, some people buy goods at a slightly higher price in the neighborhood drugstore because they like the proprietor or because they believe independent drugstores should be supported instead of chain drugstores.

The national income. Measured in terms of production, our economy is the most successful the world has ever known. Our national income has increased from $81,600,000,000 in 1940 to almost $240,000,000,000 in 1950, and over $305,000,000,000 in 1953. This figure is somewhat deceptive, as the accompanying chart shows, because goods and services cost more in 1950 than they did in 1940. Measured in terms of real value instead of money value, nevertheless, our gross national product has more than doubled since 1929.

The total national product—or the national income, which is essentially the same thing—is not the only criterion for judging an economy's soundness. Distribution of that income is an important factor. Justice requires an equitable distribution of the national income, and prosperity is impossible without it because markets will contract when large numbers cannot purchase the goods that are produced, resulting eventually in employment cut-backs. In the last twenty years the low-income groups have gained much more proportionately than those in the high- and middle-income groups. The income of the top 1 per cent in the country has actually declined, and that of the remaining 99 per cent has more than doubled. These figures indi-

Money of the American colonies that are collectors' items today include such fascinating coins as the pine-tree shilling (1652) and the Fugio cent with the typical Yankee maxim, "Mind your business" (1787). The famous Spanish "pieces of eight" (1766), used along the Gulf Coast, were halved and quartered to make change, and became known as four bits and two bits. (The Chase National Bank Museum of Moneys of the World)

cate not only a constant increase in national income throughout the past twenty years, but also a more nearly even distribution among the economic classes.

The ideal economic system. Before we examine some of the more important economic problems of this age let us summarize the requirements of an *ideal economic system*. (1) It should produce *sufficient goods and services* to meet the reasonable needs of everyone in the community. (2) It should produce *needed goods and services* first, and supplement them with such conveniences and luxuries as it can manage to produce without skimping on any necessities of life. (This obviously requires a sound community set of values, which economic considerations by themselves do not adequately provide—they must come from other sources, such as religion and social tradition.) (3) Goods and services should be so distributed throughout the economy that extreme poverty is eliminated. (4) Production, exchange, and distribution of goods and services must be so accomplished that justice is done to all members of society.[1] (5) Balance must be maintained between the production of goods and their consumption so that a stable economy can be achieved. These are ideals which can never be completely realized, but they should be kept in mind as we discuss our economic problems and think of ways to solve them.

Different forms of enterprise. Legally, there are three kinds of businesses: the proprietorship, the partnership, and the corporation. The proprietor is the sole owner of a business firm. As owner he bears full legal responsibility for his busi-

[1] There are different kinds of justice. In general, justice is the virtue of rendering to every man what is due to him. *Commutative justice* is that which prevails between two equal, completely separate persons. The purchaser of a horse, for example, is required under commutative justice to pay a price equal to the value of the horse. *Legal justice* requires a citizen, who is part of civil society, to fulfill the right which belongs to the whole civil society. The obligation to pay taxes falls within the purview of legal justice. *Distributive justice* gives the citizen a right to his share of the common goods which belong to the community. The right to a living wage or the right to property is ordinarily a matter of distributive justice. *Social justice* requires each member of a group to help other members of society secure their rights. Social justice requires us, for example, to help those who need it to receive their due rights as citizens and as human beings in this country.

National Income and Cost of Living · 1945–1954

National Income (in millions)		Consumers' Price Index (1935–39 equalling 100.)	
1945	181,248	1945	128.6
46	179,577	46	139.5
47	197,168	47	159.6
48	221,641	48	171.9
49	216,193	49	170.2
50	239,956	50	171.9
51	277,041	51	185.6
52	289,537	52	189.8
53	303,648	53	191.3
54	299,673	54	191.9
Dept. of Commerce		Bureau of Labor Statistics	

Money Income Received by Families and Single Persons

Families and Single Persons Ranked by Income	Average Money Income in Dollars of 1948 Purchasing Power		Per cent Increase in Average Income 1935-36 to 1948
	1935-36	1948	
Lowest Fifth	534	893	67
Second	1,159	2,232	93
Third	1,810	3,410	88
Fourth	2,734	4,711	72
Highest	7,083	9,911	40

ness, and he has a right to all its profits. Proprietorship is ordinarily limited to small businesses that can be owned and directed by one person, such as drugstores, filling stations, or small industries employing relatively few persons. The advantages of a proprietorship are obvious for small businesses that require personal attention by the owner to customer relations and to quality of work, as would be the case with a photographer or a jeweler.

The partnership is another form of enterprise suited to relatively small business. A partnership is formed when two or more persons pool their resources—money, skills, good will, and such—under terms of a binding agreement to carry on a business. The terms state how much each is to contribute in the way of money, labor, or other resources, and what share of the profits each is to receive. The advantage of a partnership over a simple proprietorship is that it pools together a larger amount of capital and a wider range of skills so that the business can operate on a larger scale with larger potential profits. Partnerships are common among lawyers, architects, and financiers, because in these instances various specialties can be combined for more effective business.

The disadvantage of partnership lies in the nature of each partner's legal responsibility. Any one partner can be held responsible for the entire debt of the firm.

The corporation is the third common form of enterprise. A corporation is a legal person chartered under law—by articles of incorporation—to carry on a business as though it were a real person. Thus a corporation can sue or be sued at law. A corporation is formed by a group of people who issue stock which they buy themselves or sell to others. Each person is liable only to the amount of stock he has purchased, and the company is liable only to the extent of its capitalization. This is called "limited liability." The organizers of the corporation must give cer-

Corporation

Formed by a group; controlled by its stockholders.

Partnership

Formed by two or more.

Private Enterprise

Individually owned.

tain information about their proposed company to the authorities of the state in which they wish to incorporate. When the corporation is once established it continues to live as a legal person until it is dissolved.

Large businesses are almost always organized as corporations for two obvious reasons: (1) no one person has available the millions of dollars required as capital for a large enterprise; (2) it is easier to accumulate a large sum when the risks are limited. Each stockholder in a corporation invests as much as he thinks he can reasonably risk. His losses are limited to the amount of his investment, we have seen, and his profits are ordinarily limited to some proportion of his investment, depending on the nature of the corporation—whether it is engaged in risky business like prospecting for oil, or in a relatively safe and stable enterprise like a chain grocery store.

Large-scale and small-scale businesses. There is a general tendency for small enterprises to assume the form of proprietorship or partnership and for a large enterprise to be a corporation. Sometimes, however, the small concern finds it advantageous for various reasons to incorporate. It is nevertheless generally true that the size of an enterprise will determine its form of organization. And the size of any enterprise will be determined

to some extent by the nature of the business. Automobiles, for example, cannot be manufactured on a small scale. Millions of dollars must be invested in machinery, and a profit can be made on such a sum only by producing thousands of automobiles annually. A repair shop, on the other hand, requires very little investment and few employees.

Other businesses, like grocery stores, can be organized as large-scale or small-scale enterprises. There are advantages and disadvantages to each form of organization. The large firm enjoys these advantages: It can purchase its materials in quantity and therefore more economically; it can invest in machinery and therefore produce most goods more cheaply than the small firm can; it can invest in advertising and in research for better products and more efficient methods of production.

The disadvantages of large-scale production are sometimes economic, but more frequently they are social and political. A large firm tends to become impersonal in dealing with its customers, its workers, and even its minor executives. Each employee tends to become a cog in the giant industry, with profit the determining factor in each policy decision. When a company becomes gigantic in size it tends to dominate its field and sometimes exercises undue influence over even the government. Sometimes however, a company finds that it has become too large to operate efficiently. It is something like a basketball player who has grown so tall and heavy that he has lost his agility and his speed. The company that is too large tends to develop inertia. It cannot readily change production to meet changed market conditions; its commitment, in terms of investment, is too heavy to make alterations easily.

Small-scale business is advantageous whenever personal attention is required, where investments need not be large, and where the market fluctuates rapidly. Florists, jewelers, delicatessens, and most of the services are ordinarily organized as small-scale businesses. In certain enterprises, notably grocery stores and drugstores, the advantages of large-scale and small-scale organization offset each other. A large grocery-store chain can purchase its goods more economically or even manufacture some of them, but it must operate impersonally, refuse to extend credit to its customers, and allow for inefficient operation by some managers. The independently owned store can afford to operate on a neighborly basis, extend credit to most customers, and cater to individual tastes. For these advantages the customer will usually have to pay more than he would at the chain store.

Looked at from the combined social and economic point of view, a mixture of large-scale and small-scale businesses is a good thing. The large-scale enterprise keeps prices low for the consumer who must stretch his dollar as far as possible. The independently owned enterprise is part of the local community and most of its profits are spent there. A goodly number of independently owned enterprises keeps a community healthy. Small businesses can overcome some of their disadvantages by co-operative buying and advertising, by promoting research through trade associations, and by identifying themselves with community interests.

53. BIG BUSINESS AND MONOPOLY

There has been a definite trend toward the large corporation in American business in the last half century. Corporate enterprises do almost all the manufacturing and they create over three-fourths of our national product. In 1950 some 140 corporations produced nearly half the national product. In 1952 there were twenty-four corporations with assets over one billion dollars each, among them Bell Telephone with assets of ten billion, Standard Oil of New Jersey with five billion, and General Motors with four. Large business corporations dominate our economy except in the fields of agriculture, construction, and professions, such as law or medicine. We can see, therefore, that we must solve economic problems in terms of large organized groups rather than individuals. The problems of the businessman and the laboring man must be solved as corporation and union problems.

We shall discuss these problems from the union's point of view in the next chapter. Here let us see them from the company's viewpoint. Corporate assets are owned by stockholders. Anyone who buys a share of stock in, let us suppose, Bell Telephone Company has purchased title of ownership to a certain amount of that company. Thus the owner of one share of stock in a company that has issued one million shares owns one millionth of the company and has a right to one-millionth of the profits. Statistics revealed that in 1952 there were six and a half million stockholders in the country. Further study shows that this apparently wide distribution of ownership is more concentrated than appears at first glance. Stock is owned by only 7 per cent of the families in the country, and 1 per cent own about 80 per cent of the stock.

Control of large-scale business. Control of most large companies rests in the hands of a few large stockholders and of management. Each share of stock represents one vote. Shareholders vote at business meetings either by being physically present or by entrusting their vote to a proxy.[2] Among the two hundred largest non-financial corporations surveyed in 1940, for example, 1 per cent of the stockholders owned more than 60 per cent of the stock. We see, then, that a few individuals usually have the power to control each corporation and therefore the other stockholders' investments. With control of the stock goes the power to choose the board of directors, who, in turn, select the management and determine the policies of the company.

Recent studies show that control of most large corporations passes into the hands of managers who may or may not own shares of stock. By controlling proxy votes and by keeping sizable blocs of stock from accumulating in one person's hands, management can maintain a kind of dictatorship within the corporation. Generally management runs the business honestly and efficiently, but the owners have nothing to say about the company's policies, and the likelihood is that all they know about their company is what they read in the newspapers. The divorce of control from ownership of large corporations presents moral and social as well as economic problems. Legally, of course, the stockholders can take over control of a company from management, and occasionally they do. But it is exceedingly difficult to organize a group of stockholders scattered throughout the country, and it is difficult for anyone but management to secure a large number of proxy votes.

The device more frequently used by many companies with scattered owner-

ship is to avoid stockholders' meetings by not soliciting proxy votes at all. Since no quorum is present, no stockholders' meeting is held and management is not required to make accounting to the owners of the company. Most stockholders, we can assume, are content with their annual dividends. They have neither the desire nor the ability to tell management how to run the company. Sometimes stockholders do not even know what their company produces. But ownership of stock carries with it responsibility and the right to a voice in the management of the stockholder's property. Corporations seem to require strict regulation by the Securities Exchange Commission so that the stockholder can be informed of company matters and can vote on them at the annual stockholders' meeting if he wishes to exercise his proprietary rights.

Monopoly in the American economy. Strictly speaking, a monopoly exists when one company or a combination of companies working together have exclusive control of the supply of some commodity or service. The Temporary National Economic Committee of 1943–1944 defined monopoly in more elastic terms: "Appreciable monopoly power is said to exist whenever a single seller or a number of sellers acting in unison control enough of the supply of a broadly defined commodity to enable them to augment their profit by limiting output and raising prices."

Monopoly has taken various forms in our history. The simplest form is for one company to "corner" the supply of a service or a commodity. Examples are public utilities in most cities, where there is a single telephone system, one gas company, one electric-power company, or one company with a monopoly of water supply. A second form of monopoly is the trust. It consists of a group of companies controlled by a single board of trustees who own or control the voting stock of each company. The board select the management of each company and

<hr>

[2] A proxy to vote shares of stock is an authority given by a shareholder, who has a right to vote, to another to exercise this right at his own discretion. Management in some companies encloses a form with the notice of shareholders' meetings which, when signed and returned in the self-addressed, stamped envelope, gives management the authority to act as the signator's proxy.

co-ordinate their policies in order to secure the greatest profit for the trust.

When trusts were declared illegal, a new device, the holding company, was used to achieve the same monopolistic arrangement. The holding company is a separate corporation formed to buy and hold a controlling bloc of stock in a number of formerly competing firms. The holding company conducts the business of the several companies in the interest of the holding company rather than of any single company it controls. Another form of monopoly is the merger. A merger is the combining or merging of two or more firms into one. It becomes a monopoly when all the firms in an industry, or a preponderant part of them, are swallowed up by a single corporation. All these forms of monopoly eliminate competition and limit production to the amount that will give the largest profits.

Natural monopolies. In some areas monopoly is a necessary thing. Five competing telephone companies in Chicago, for example, would serve no good purpose at all. They would create endless confusion, and they would be much costlier than the monopoly that exists there now. Anyone engaged in business would have to have five phones in order to be available to everyone. Generally speaking, public utilities are "natural monopolies."

Experience has developed two methods of handling natural monopolies. One method is to grant the monopoly to a privately owned company on certain conditions and to regulate the company by a government commission. The monopoly is granted in a charter which specifies the amount and quality of goods or services the company must furnish, the taxes it must pay, and other obligations it assumes. The commission fixes the rates or price the company may charge for its services, the rate being such as to cover the cost of production and furnish a fair profit to the stockholders.

The second method of handling natural monopolies is for the government to own and operate them. The post office is an example of such a government-owned monopoly. During the 1920s and 1930s there was a general trend toward public ownership of gas and electric companies. Cities, states, and even the federal government entered the public utility business when it was felt that private companies had abused their privileges of monopoly. There has been much argument about the relative merits and the relative efficiency of public and private ownership of natural monopolies. A survey of various publicly and privately owned companies suggests that the efficiency of each company is determined less by the abstract principle of public or private ownership than by the competency and honesty of management in each case.

"Competitive monopolies." Monopoly in other fields—those that should be competitive—ordinarily entails limited supply of the commodity at unnecessarily high prices. The company is interested in the highest profits possible, which can ordinarily be attained by limiting the quantity of goods that reach the market. The history of the aluminum industry illustrates this point. Between 1925 and 1940, when aluminum was a monopolistic industry, production costs were about eleven cents a pound and the product sold for nineteen to thirty-eight cents a pound. The government entered the field during the war, and when the war was over it sold out to a number of competing firms. For several years aluminum sold at fourteen cents a pound and was put to many new uses.

Americans have maintained a traditional hostility to monopoly. Because it smothers competition and tends to fix prices as it wishes, the monopolistic company has been the object of legislative attack several times in our history. Both political parties pay lip service to small business and to competition, and both favor rigid enforcement of the Sherman and Clayton anti-monopoly laws. Experience has shown, however, that it is almost impossible to enforce competition by law. Holding companies, interlocking directorates, price agreements, and various such understandings by all companies in a certain industry cannot effectively be prevented by law.

A close study of our economy reveals that there are few effective monopolies. Most business enterprises neither are perfect monopolies nor are they perfectly competitive. They operate under conditions of imperfect competition. When there are few firms in the field, prices are settled easily. A leading firm sets the price and the others fall in line. On the other hand, apparent monopolies must meet competition from other areas. Railroads, for example, must compete with trucking concerns, bus companies, and airlines for their freight and passenger traffic. Oil must compete against gas and coal, steel against copper and aluminum. In none of these cases, you will note, is competition perfect, because the competing products are not exactly the same. But if one of them becomes too expensive it will lose much of its business to the others. Thus we see that in very few fields is there opportunity for a monopoly to make exorbitant profits for any length of time. Strict regulation of rates by government commissions seems the best way to prevent abuses in the few truly monopolistic industries.

54. CONTROL OF THE BUSINESS CYCLE

In normal times business goes through a succession of ups and downs, a period of prosperity followed by a period of depression. The cycle of prosperity-depression-prosperity has been interrupted by the armed truce under which we have lived since the end of World War II. This armed truce has kept a large number of potential workers in the military forces,

and it has maintained an artificially large proportion of capital and manpower in defense industry. If "normal," peaceful times return within our lifetime we can expect to be confronted with the problem of preventing depression and maintaining our economy at adequate production.

Prosperity is a period, of course, when nearly all workers are employed gainfully and most firms earn good profits. Depression, on the other hand, is a period of considerable unemployment, losses instead of profits for business, and a comparatively small volume of business throughout the country. Why we go through the cycle repeatedly has long been a mystery to business analysts, but intensive study of the subject after the Great Depression of the 1930s suggests at least some causes of depression and some preventive measures for avoiding a serious depression.

Financial, economic, and psychological factors all interact to cause periods of prosperity or depression. In time of recovery from depression there is considerable investment in heavy-goods industries. Families replace worn-out automobiles and refrigerators; industry replaces worn-out machines and even builds entirely new plants. This spending has a snowball effect in that it means more jobs and more wages. More wages mean more money spent on food, clothes, entertainment, and other consumer goods. To meet the new demand, many industries expand and new ones are started. This creates a demand for additional heavy goods and therefore additional jobs. Eventually the market tends to reach a saturation point and it becomes difficult to sell any more automobiles or refrigerators. Many industries will have overexpanded and overproduced in anticipation of a long-maintained large demand. In order to get something from the goods they have produced, many businessmen will cut prices. Others will cut production, and still others will go out of business. Cutting production cuts consumer income, and consequently markets shrink even more. Further market shrinkage forces additional cuts in production—and so on, until the country is back in a depression.

Maintaining prosperity. There is general agreement on what must be accomplished to avoid depression. Prosperity will continue as long as manpower and capital are profitably employed, and this is possible only under two conditions: (1) that workers are justly paid; (2) that savings can be invested profitably. If workers are not justly paid, their purchasing power will shrink, the market will contract, and production will be cut back. If savings cannot be invested profitably, the capital necessary for industrial operations will not be available. To put the problem another way, wages and profits must remain high enough to keep the economy operating at a capacity adequate to sustain the whole society in its material needs.

Difference of opinion is sharp on ways and means to maintain adequate production. Some authorities believe that free enterprise is the best means of achieving stable prosperity; others believe that government planning and direction are necessary. Business groups, such as the United States Chamber of Commerce, the American Bankers' Association, and the National Association of Manufacturers believe that attempts by the government to take positive action to prevent depression are more likely to do harm than good. The Chamber of Commerce puts it this way:

The primary function of government is to preserve opportunity for individual enterprise, to protect against crime and predatory incursion, and to preserve a sound money system. Where necessary, government sets up regulation to prevent actions inimical to the public interest; but at times such regulation dries up private initiative and investment, which may do more harm than good, in that case.

Labor unions and many professional economists believe that the government must take a positive role to prevent depressions because free enterprise, they claim, inevitably goes through the cycle of prosperity-depression-prosperity unless outside intervention takes place. In its 1949 convention the CIO resolved:

The government, acting as agent for the people, must accept responsibility for stabilizing production and employment, and must plan for steady growth in production, year after year, so as to assure full employment to the growing labor force and to achieve ever higher standards of living.

The problem of maintaining prosperity is not, of course, merely a national problem, for the United States is not a self-contained unit. Many important and even indispensable raw materials for our industries must be imported; and many of our industries are geared to such gigantic production that even the great American market is not big enough to use all that they produce. The same is true of American agricultural production. The United States must trade with other nations, and this necessity has become greater since we have become the world's foremost manufacturing country. Hence a tariff policy and an expanding foreign trade are necessary for the maintenance of economic prosperity.

The role of the government in maintaining prosperity. In any event, the government must take a stand on the business cycle. Either it must believe that by allowing the greatest leeway possible to free enterprise it will assure continued prosperity, or it must assume that by positive action the government can control the business cycle. Whether we like it or not, the government cannot remain entirely aloof from American economic life. It takes a stand on economics with every tax measure, for it must tax some kinds of income and some kinds of business. Tax measures will encourage spending or saving, consumption of goods or capital investment. Taxes will encourage some industries and discourage others even though this may not be their purpose. Taxes, combined with social security and various other welfare disbursements, shift income from one economic group to another. The inflationary or deflationary effect of any proposed tax measure must be considered by the government.

Again, the government is a gigantic consumer. It spends billions of dollars annually on defense and on domestic programs. This biggest single consumer in the American economy can decide whether to retrench or to spend liberally each time the budget is prepared. The amount of government expenditure in any one year will have considerable influence on prices—and therefore on the business cycle. The government is also a big lender. A recent survey indicated that the federal government has outstanding loans and guarantees totaling almost $60,000,000,000. Tightening or loosening credit terms will have a marked effect on the business cycle. Finally, the government is in business on a tremendous scale. It owns power projects like the Tennessee Valley Authority, the Grand Coulee, and the Bonneville developments. It owns 2,078 hospitals containing three-fourths of the hospital beds in the country. It employs 6,000,000 civilians, one out of every nine in the total work force, and its annual civilian payroll is $11,000,000,000. Its assets total $126,000,-000,000, as compared with General Motors' $4,000,000,000.

It is easy for us to see, then, that the federal government's policies have an important effect on the business cycle. As a producer, a financier, an employer, a consumer, it plays a leading role in our economy. It therefore seems that the government should take thought of the effect each of its moves will have on the American economy. This will not always be the deciding factor, of course, but it should always be kept in mind and given the weight it deserves in each case. A decision to increase the armed forces, for example, should be made primarily on the basis of foreign policy needs. A decision to increase the pay schedule for all civilian employees, on the other hand, should be based in large measure on its effect on our economy.

The Council of Economic Advisers. For these reasons, in 1946 Congress authorized the President to appoint three men to serve as his Council of Economic Advisers. The council is required by law to report semiannually to the President on the economic condition of the country. The report is based on the council's study and interpretation of economic developments. In the light of this study the council must appraise programs and activities of the government that have any effect on employment and the business cycle. Finally, the council is to formulate and recommend national economic policy to promote employment, production, and purchasing power in a free economy. The nature of these recommendations is inevitably colored by the council's economic philosophy. Thus President Truman's council gave one kind of advice, and President Eisenhower's another.

The council's function is purely advisory. The President may incorporate its recommendations in his annual message to Congress, and he may propose legislation to put these recommendations into law. But he is also free to ignore them. The purpose Congress had in mind in creating the Council of Economic Advisers was primarily to take preventive action against unemployment (the CEA was created by Section 4 of the Employment Act of 1946), and secondarily to smooth out the business cycle by co-ordinating government measures that have a noticeable effect on the country's economy. The council is committed by law to a philosophy of free enterprise and the promotion of the common welfare.

55. MANAGEMENT RESPONSIBILITIES

Management has obligations to three groups: (1) the stockholders or owners of the enterprise; (2) the employees; (3) the consumers. Management is hired by the owners to produce goods or services at a reasonable profit; in accepting his position the manager implicitly contracts to make a profit for the owners. His obligation to his employees is stated specifically in the labor contract. From the social and moral point of view, management is obliged to treat employees as human beings deserving of respect and to make wages and working conditions fit for human beings. Management is also obliged to treat the potential consumer justly. Dishonest advertising or fraudulent claims ought not be made for the product. Moreover, management has an obligation to produce its goods or services at a just price. It is easy to see that these obligations may sometimes work against each other. Fair profits, just wages, and just prices at times may not all be possible of attainment. Unless all three can be achieved, management has failed and the enterprise will not survive.

Co-operation of management and labor. In the last twenty years an increasing number of managers have come to realize that the enterprise is more than an economic unit. It is also a social unit in which labor and management participate under whatever terms the labor contract includes. In 1931, Pope Pius XI insisted that a work contract providing only for wages and hours and certain working conditions was not sufficient. "In the present state of human society," he wrote, "we deem it advisable that the work contract should, when possible, be modified somewhat by a contract of partnership. . . . In this way wage-earners are made sharers in some sort in the ownership or the management, or the profits." In 1949, Pope Pius XII put the same idea in these words: "In the economic domain, management and labor are linked by a community of action and interest. . . . They are co-operators in a common task. They eat, so to speak, at the same table."

Plans of effective co-operation between labor and management have been tried with remarkable success in some instances. In two articles in *Fortune*, Russell Davenport told of his findings on the subject.[3] The essential point, he found, is that the worker needs a sense of belonging to the enterprise. This sense of belonging comes only from real participation. "Only the personal participation of the employee in both the profits and that part of management which has to do with production can evoke from him the kind of dynamic cooperation that the enterprise system now needs." Mr. Davenport found that "real participation consists in finding means by which to reward labor for any increase in productivity, and then building around this formula a working relationship between management and labor that enables them to become a team." Once the team is present, "labor's prime interest, just like that of management, becomes productivity."

Such co-operation between management and labor is not easy to obtain. It requires the right disposition from both managers and labor leaders, considerable skill in human relations on the part of management, and a certain amount of social vision from both managers and the workers in the enterprise. But its successful accomplishment is essential to a healthy development of the individual enterprise in the American economy.

Business leaders also stress the fact that management must train and develop a more effective personnel on the lower executive levels. Through the last two decades management has had to concentrate on dealing with unions so much that it has tended to neglect the lesser executives—down to the level of foreman and supervisor—who are not included in negotiations with the union. The result is

[3] "The Greatest Opportunity on Earth," *Fortune* (October 1949), and "Enterprise for Everyman," *Fortune* (January 1950). The latter article was published in abridged form in the *Reader's Digest* (April 1950).

These workers are participating in an in-service course that will teach them what is required in the organization and management of any business. It's Your Decision, *a motion picture that is followed by a lecture, shows employees the different points of view of the firm, stockholder, and employee. (Westinghouse)*

that the natural leaders of the work force in the enterprise have not been trained to play their part effectively. Better personnel relations with these employees and better training programs must be devised by management as a step toward teamwork in the enterprise.

Management and profits. The very nature of large-scale enterprise creates a series of problems for management which seem to defy any lasting solution within our capitalistic system. Management has the obligation to see that both men and machinery are kept occupied if a factory is to operate at high efficiency. Wages must be paid to a man, whether he works productively or stands by idle, and interest must be paid on an expensive piece of machinery, whether it is idle or employed. Management has the obligation of maintaining peak production, since otherwise an enterprise geared to peak production will operate at a loss.

Production at full capacity raises few problems as long as the market can readily absorb all the goods produced. The problem, then, is simply one of efficient, economical production. But the very success of producers of certain goods creates serious economic and moral problems, because, as we have indicated, production cannot readily and easily be cut back when demand falls off. In the years after the war, the market absorbed all the auto-

mobiles and refrigerators and other heavy goods that industry could produce. But within a given time in each industry this demand was met and the market came to be "glutted." In this situation management was faced with a series of problems. It could not cut back production easily because of wage contracts and because of the heavy investment most industries had made in full-scale production.

Large machines that at one time required individual operators are now controlled by automation equipment that calls for the service of one man. The operator sits before a light panel that tells him instantly if one or more of the number of machines that the equipment controls is not functioning properly. (Black Star)

Creating the "demand." The only alternative was to "expand" the market to keep it up with continued full-scale production. Various devices of questionable morality present themselves to management as methods of keeping up demand. High-pressure salesmanship is used to convince people that they really want a new car or a new television set or a new refrigerator, even though the present one serves them well. The American desire "to keep up with the Joneses" is exploited by salesmen in the heavy-goods industries in order to get people to buy new models before the old ones are worn out. Closely affiliated with high-pressure salesmanship is immoral advertising to create an artificial "need" for goods that people would otherwise not buy. Some businessmen defend such advertising as creating "a higher standard of living," but there is no doubt that much of it creates an artificial demand for goods without which people would be perfectly happy.

Associated with these two practices is installment buying. This is a device to induce people to purchase goods they cannot afford and to mortgage their salaries to pay for these goods. Installment buying is especially vicious because in effect it raises the purchase price by as much as 50 per cent. A fourth device to keep up an artificially high demand is the practice of manufacturing so-called durable goods cheaply so that they will wear out or become obsolete within a short time. A variation of this is to change styles in automobiles, clothes, and other such products so that an item which could serve for several years becomes "obsolete" within a season or two.

Business executives often denounce these practices of creating "demands," but they are reluctant to cut back the employment of labor and machines. Such non-profit associations, however, as the Better Business Bureau and the Advertising Council work to correct these abuses. The former reviews the sales methods of

Some ways by which a Demand is created

business firms and investigates consumers' claims of misrepresentation and other unethical business practices. The Advertising Council contributes great sums of money and time in order to lay before the American public facts about the national life. Its efforts are directed toward offering courses of action for the people of America in five vital areas: national defense, national economy, human resources, natural resources, and overseas relations.

One last device used by big industry is to lobby for tariffs that maintain high prices in home markets and make possible the disposal of goods abroad at a loss.

So far we have discussed only the most important problems confronting management. There are many others—problems that must be solved daily as part of management's task. Such problems as packaging and distributing the enterprise's product, customer relations, meeting competition from similar products must continually be solved if management is to be successful. Long-range plans to cope with problems of supply of raw material, the labor force, power and transportation, and even decentralization for insurance against atomic attack must be regularly reviewed.

Conclusion. We have seen in this chapter that our economy is neither perfectly free nor completely regimented. It is held in delicate balance by a set of economic "laws" or trends that cannot be successfully flouted. But these economic laws do not work out with mechanical exactitude or with the inexorability of physical laws. Our economy operates in a social and political environment which is distinctly American. It is subject to moral, social, and legal controls which result in an economy of "imperfect competition." Our discussion of the various economic problems facing us should lead us to conclude that an economy can be healthy and productive in the long run only if it operates with a sound set of ethical values and realizes that material resources are intended by the Creator to serve man rather than to be his master. Our basic economic problem is to develop and maintain an efficient, productive economy that accepts these social and ethical controls as conditions of operation.

REVIEW

51. Definition of Terms and Principles
A. Define economics.

B. List the four major economic judgments that you make when you start a business.

C. When do materials have value? How does labor add to the value of a product? Why has labor a right to a living wage?

D. Why is capital necessary for production? How does the management of a business affect the profit on products?

E. Name and briefly describe the four types of division of labor. How is competition a "control" within our economy? Point out three functions of money in our economy.

52. The American Economic System
A. Briefly describe some of the social aspects of our economy.

B. Describe how our national income has changed. What groups have been most affected by this change?

C. What are the requirements of an ideal economic system?

D. Define proprietorship, partnership, and corporation. Point out several advantages and disadvantages of each.

53. Big Business and Monopoly
A. Indicate how large corporations dominate our economy today. How are these controlled today? How does management maintain control of a corporation?

B. What is a monopoly; a trust; a holding company; a merger?

C. Why is a monopoly necessary in some cases? How does the government control monopolies?

54. Control of the Business Cycle
A. What is the business cycle?

B. What are some of the ways to avoid a depression?

C. How does the government help to maintain prosperity? How much of a part does the government play in business?

D. What are the purposes and functions of the President's Council of Economic Advisers?

55. Management Responsibilities
A. Point out and briefly describe the obligations of management to the stockholders, to employees, and to the consumers.

B. What have recent Popes declared concerning management and labor?

C. What problem faces management in our recent technological development? How does management create a market or demand?

THE CHAPTER IN REVIEW
A. Describe how labor, capital, and management all contribute to the value of an article.

B. Describe the workings of a corporation, a trust, and a monopoly.

C. When did the government first participate

in the regulation of business? Why are government controls necessary in business today?

D. Our society is a great deal more than a set of economic relations and processes. Explain the truth of this statement in light of the principles outlined in this chapter.

SELECTED READINGS

An encyclopedic work that proves most valuable as a reference tool for the subject matter of this chapter is J. Frederick Dewhurst and Associates, *America's Needs and Resources* (New York: The Twentieth Century Fund, 1955). A general understanding of economics in this country can be obtained from Horace Taylor and Harold Barger, *The American Economy in Operation* (New York: Harcourt, Brace & Co., 1949), or Rev. John F. Cronin, S.S., *Economic Analysis and Problems* (New York: American Book Company, 1945). These two books are college texts, but they should not prove too difficult for high school seniors. Shorter explanations are to be found in three pamphlets: Seymour L. Wolfbein and Harold Goldstein, *Our World of Work* (Chicago: Science Research Associates, 1951); *Capitalism: Way of Freedom* (New York: Comet Press Books, 1952); and *Understanding the Economic System and Its Functions* (Washington: Chamber of Commerce of the United States, 1953).

Catholic social principles do not automatically solve American economic problems. They are right principles which can be applied to economic conditions in this country to work out solutions. These principles can be found in the following: Mary Lois Ebert, C.H.M., and Gerald J. Schnepp, S.M., *Industrialism and the Popes* (New York: P. J. Kenedy & Sons, 1953), a collection of papal statements relative to industrialism and the industry council plan; Pope Leo XIII, *The Condition of Labor,* and Pope Pius XI, *On Reconstructing the Social Order,* both published by the National Catholic Welfare Conference in 1942; Pope Pius XII, *Six Social Documents of His Holiness, Pope Pius XII* (Huntington, Ind.: Sunday Visitor Press, 1953); *The Church and Social Order*

(Washington: National Catholic Welfare Conference, 1941); *Bishops' Program of Social Reconstruction* (Washington: National Catholic Welfare Conference, 1939).

A defense of big business is made by James Truslow Adams, *Big Business in a Democracy* (New York: Charles Scribner's Sons, 1945), and a more critical study of the subject is David E. Lilienthal, *Big Business: A New Era* (New York: Harper & Brothers, 1953). A valuable work is A. D. H. Kaplan, *Small Business: Its Place and Problems* (New York: McGraw-Hill Book Co., 1948). A critical treatment of big business in the period 1861–1901 is Matthew Josephson, *The Robber Barons* (New York: Harcourt, Brace & Co., 1934).

A simplified explanation of the business cycle is found in "A B C's of the Business Cycle," *United States News and World Report* (April 29, 1949), and "Turns in the Business Cycle," *United States News and World Report* (February 27, 1948). Management's and labor's points of view on the subject are given in *Sustaining Prosperity* (Washington: Chamber of Commerce of the United States, 1953), and *Maintaining Prosperity* (Washington: Congress of Industrial Organizations, 1953).

Automation in factories is the subject of John Diebold, *Automation: The Advent of the Automatic Factory* (New York: D. Van Nostrand Co., Inc., 1953).

PROJECTS

1. A living wage is necessary for a full-time employee. A class committee could examine the wage scales for two major industries. A report to the class should include minimum and maximum wages that have been paid by the industry, as compared to the price index for the year of each and the annual median wage for similar work.

2. Write to the New York Stock Exchange for information regarding its operation. Report to the class on how to read stock quotations, the way in which stock prices fluctuate, how transactions are made, and the role of the stockbroker.

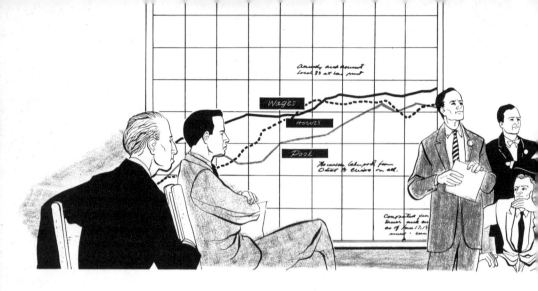

Chapter 19. The Problems of the Worker

56. RISE OF LABOR UNIONS

We have seen that man has a right to work, because this is the way most people earn a livelihood. We have also seen that the worker has a right to a living wage, just as the businessman has the right to a reasonable profit as the means whereby he earns his living. As a human being the worker has an additional right —the right to working conditions and treatment worthy of a human being. He has the right, therefore, to the respect which is his due. It follows that the workingman has the right to use whatever legitimate means he can to achieve and protect these rights. The means most commonly employed in the last century has been unionization for the purpose of collective bargaining.

The workingman's need to organize in order to bargain successfully with management is generally recognized. In the first test case of the National Labor Relations Act in 1937, the Supreme Court put the matter simply and clearly:

Long ago we stated the reason for labor organization. We said that they [unions] were organized out of the necessities of the situation; that a single employee was helpless in dealing with an employer; that he was dependent ordinarily on his daily wage for the maintenance of himself and family; that if the employer refused to pay him the wages that he thought fair, he was nevertheless unable to leave the employ and resist arbitrary and unfair treatment; that union was essential to give laborers opportunity to deal on an equality with their employer.

Unions are especially necessary when a recession or a depression occurs, because in such times there are more workers than jobs, and management could drive wages down to a bare subsistence level if it bargained with each worker individually. A large company does not need any *one* worker as much as the worker needs his job. That is the basic reason why there is no equality of bargaining power unless workers act collectively.

Moral philosophers are not in complete agreement as to whether a worker has the duty to join a union. The weight of opinion seems to be that he does have such a duty as long as the union is organized to achieve good objectives and does not use wrong means to attain its purposes. If he has such a duty, it does not rest on economic grounds alone. It arises

from man's nature and from the nature of society. Each of us has an obligation to promote the common good, and the ordinary way of doing this is through co-operative activity in organizations and other social institutions. Moreover, such institutions are means whereby the individual can more fully develop his social faculties. Finally, because others make sacrifices through the union to obtain good wages, hours, and working conditions, a man is obliged to do his share in gaining these. Such considerations suggest that workingmen, like business- and professional men, have the duty to work together through established institutions in order to achieve their legitimate objectives peacefully. It does not mean that they must join this or that particular union. Other considerations, as we shall see later in this chapter, might outweigh this duty and make it imperative for the workingman to refrain from joining some particular union.

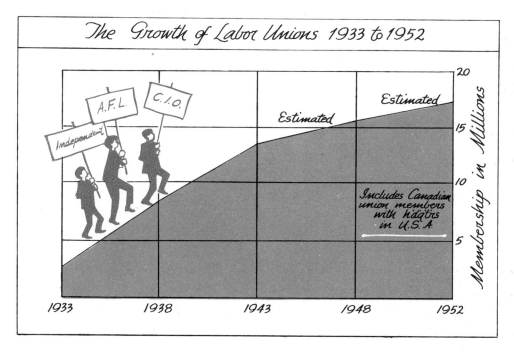

The rise of unions in America. The powerful unions in this country today are distinctly American. The American Federation of Labor and Congress of Industrial Organizations (AFL-CIO), and independent unions like the United Mine Workers of America, differ in certain important respects, but they all aim at bettering the workingman's condition within the framework of the American economy. This point should be kept in mind because there is considerable misunderstanding about the nature and conduct of unions in this country. In most European countries unions became entangled with Socialist and Communist agitation and were the tools of various radical parties. European refugees to this country tried to carry on the class struggle here, but they were never fully accepted by the workingmen of this country. Their agitation and their writings, however, made many professional and business people believe that the union movement in this country was Socialist or anarchistic.

Let us therefore see briefly how and why unions came into being in this country. Then we shall be in a better position to understand both their good and their bad points. Originally we were an agricultural country. A farm laborer could bargain effectively with his employer because his labor was needed by the farmer about as much as he needed the job. In the cities and villages the workers were in a good bargaining position because there was always a shortage of workers. Moreover, the dissatisfied worker could always move on to another job or stake out a homestead on the frontier. In such a setting there was little need of widespread unionization for collective bargaining. Moreover, in an agricultural setting the workers are too widely dispersed to make unionization feasible.

A glance at the accompanying table

GAINFUL WORKERS OR EXPERIENCED CIVILIAN LABOR FORCE

YEAR	POPULATION	TOTAL	FARM OCCUPATIONS		NONFARM OCCUPATIONS	
			Number	*Percent*	*Number*	*Percent*
PERSONS 10 YEARS OLD AND OVER						
1820...............	6,487,815	2,881,000	2,068,958	71.8	812,042	28.2
1830...............	8,639,412	3,931,537	2,772,453	70.5	1,159,084	29.5
1840...............	11,629,006	5,420,000	3,719,951	68.6	1,700,049	31.4
1850...............	16,452,835	7,697,196	4,901,882	63.7	2,795,314	36.3
1860...............	22,429,625	10,532,750	6,207,634	58.9	4,325,116	41.1
1870...............	29,123,683	12,924,951	6,849,772	53.0	6,075,179	47.0
1880...............	36,761,607	17,392,099	8,584,810	49.4	8,807,289	50.6
1890...............	47,413,559	23,318,183	9,938,373	42.6	13,379,810	57.4
1900...............	57,949,824	29,073,233	10,911,998	37.5	18,161,235	62.5
1910...............	71,580,270	37,370,794	11,591,767	31.0	25,779,027	69.0
1920...............	82,739,315	42,433,535	11,448,770	27.0	30,984,765	73.0
1930...............	98,723,047	48,829,920	10,471,998	21.4	38,357,922	78.6
PERSONS 14 YEARS OLD AND OVER						
1930...............	89,100,555	48,594,592	10,161,212	20.9	38,433,380	79.1
1940...............	101,102,924	51,742,023	8,833,324	17.1	42,908,699	82.9
1950...............	112,354,034	59,015,464	6,837,652	11.6	52,177,812	88.4

shows that the non-agricultural work force became larger than the agricultural work force between 1870 and 1880. The first permanently successful federation of unions (the AFL) was organized in 1881. Unionization was held back through most of the nineteenth century by the mobility of social and economic classes in this country. Every worker could aspire to become an owner in time, or at the very worst to have his children move into the "capitalistic" class. Gradually, however, millions of workers came to realize that most of them would remain workers for life. By the time of the Great Depression most workers had come to accept their status, and they naturally turned to ways and means of improving it. Unions seemed an obvious means to accomplish that purpose.

Industrialization and unionism. Another factor conducive to the growth of unions in this country was the concentration of business in larger and larger units. No matter how considerate and humane its policy may be in dealing with employees, a corporation employing many thousands of workers cannot deal with them in the same personal way that an employer can when he owns a small plant and employs five men. The concentration of thousands of employees into a single working center gives them a sense of having much in common. It is easy to develop in them the realization that in combination they have great strength, whereas singly they are of little consequence.

We can see, then, that the development of unions was almost inevitable when this country became highly industrialized. Until fairly recently in the twentieth century, nevertheless, many professional and business people considered the union movement "un-American." It did not seem to fit in with traditional American ideas of self-help, of unlimited opportunities for advancement for the ambitious individual, and of the liberty for both workingmen and businessmen to follow their own self-interest. Unions therefore developed in a hostile atmosphere. Injunctions, court decisions, and legislation all tended to prevent the peaceful growth of unions and to push union leaders into violent action. Developing in this hostile atmosphere, incidentally, gave unions a tradition of violence that poisoned some of them after public opinion and government policy had turned in their favor.

The first powerful labor organization in this country was the Knights of Labor. Organized in 1869, it included 700,000 members within a short time. The Knights enlisted all kinds of wage earners, skilled and unskilled, in a loose organization that was poorly led. Failure in a series of major strikes hurt the Knights, and the withdrawal of craftsmen's locals spelled their ruin. Meanwhile the American Federation of Labor had been organized along different lines, and from the beginning it adopted a different social and political policy.

The great labor organizations. The AFL claims 1881 as the year of its beginning. At that time representatives of about forty-five thousand craftworkers met at Pittsburgh to organize a new federation of trade unions. Five years later they took the name of the American Federation of Labor. By 1900, AFL membership had passed the half-million mark, and by 1910 it had risen to a million and a half. During World War I its membership

The large company's loss of personal contact with the employee and the great concentration of labor in one plant are conducive to union growth. The advantage of collective bargaining is only one of the merits of the unions. (Ford Motor Co.)

swelled to more than four million, but the prosperity of the 1920s combined with intensive anti-union drives to cut AFL membership to less than three million by 1930.

The AFL avoided affiliating with any political party or committing the organization to any class-conscious economic or social theory. It accepted the American economic system and tried to win for the workingman his due share of the income. It limited itself to working for specific objects: better wages, shorter hours, better working conditions. It backed candidates who "voted the right way" on various measures it favored or opposed, and it withdrew its support from candidates who voted against its measures. The AFL was not concerned with the workingman-in-general. Its membership was made up of skilled craftsmen, the "aristocracy of labor," and it did nothing directly to promote the interests of the unskilled laborer.

Because the unskilled worker was especially in need of help in wage-and-hour bargaining, many labor leaders felt that the AFL needed serious structural reorganization so that it could make room for these semi-skilled workers in its ranks. Unskilled workers, of course, outnumbered craftsmen. Their addition to the organized workers' force would enable

Terrence Powderly, Grand Master Workman of the Knights of Labor, was so conscientious a union organizer that he lost his job as a machinist and was blacklisted by his employer. At great personal expense he built the organization's membership from 28,000 to 700,000 in six years. (Library of Congress)

Samuel Gompers, the first President of the AFL, organized a War Committee on Labor that helped to unify the war industries of the country. He strongly opposed political activity of a partisan nature by his union. (AFL)

union leaders to achieve legislative objectives more easily. The depression, with millions of workers idle, convinced more and more labor leaders that workers should be organized according to the plant or factory in which they worked instead of the trade they pursued.

Passage in 1935 of the National Labor Relations Act, better known as the Wagner Act, cleared the way for a new type of union. This act, as we shall see later, gave governmental protection to unionizing activity within each plant. As a result, the Congress of Industrial Organizations (CIO) was organized. The CIO set about organizing workers in the steel and auto and rubber industries and in many smaller industries in which the workers were still not organized. Most members of the CIO were new union men, never before organized. The AFL continued to enlist everyone who could fit within its craft framework. The drive toward unionization caused bitter and frequently violent clashes between the two big federations, but it more than doubled the number of men in union ranks. In 1935 there were about three million members in the AFL, and in 1940 there were almost eight million in the combined ranks of the AFL and CIO. Unaffiliated unions had also increased their membership from some 600,000 to slightly more than a million. World War II swelled union membership to about fourteen million.

Union membership today. Figures on union membership can be misleading in several ways. In the first place, unionized workers represent only a fraction of the workers in America. The labor force at any given time includes all those fourteen years and older who are able to work for wages or profit or in family enterprises like farming. In 1955 the labor force consisted of 67,700,000 persons out of a total population of 165,000,000. Changes in the nature of the labor force have changed the problem of unionization. Farm laborers, for example, have declined greatly in number, whereas people in clerical and sales work have increased in number. The net result of these changes is that many workers are still not members of unions. Unions must organize "white-collar workers" if they are to include all wage earners in their ranks.

Another change that will alter the composition of union ranks in the near future is the upward trend in numbers of skilled, semi-skilled, and educated workers. Unions must adapt themselves to a better educated and more highly trained membership than in the days when the CIO was organizing the steelworkers. Educated members are more articulate and more likely to be critical of abuses within the unions. They are also more likely to be critical of management and more insistent on successful action by union leaders.

Somewhere between 16,500,000 and 17,000,000 workers out of a total work force of perhaps 67,700,000 are in unions. (The number is uncertain because locals understate membership in reporting to the AFL-CIO, inasmuch as dues are charged against the affiliated local on the basis of its stated membership.) Between 1,800,000 and 2,000,000 workers are in independent unions. The most important of the unaffiliated unions are the United Mine Workers, with about 600,000 members, and the railroad brotherhoods, with about 430,000. One of the problems still facing unions, then, is that of enlisting as many as possible of the still ununionized workers in the country. Labor leaders consider this a pressing problem, and they have organization drives under way in some parts of the country and among certain kinds of workers at all times.

We have already seen that the AFL and the CIO were originally independent unions and organized along different structural lines. The AFL had been traditionally organized on a craft or trade basis. Bricklayers working for twenty or thirty different construction companies were organized into a local. The locals belonged to a national union or brotherhood of bricklayers. The AFL was made up of a federation of these national craft unions. In similar fashion patternmakers in a steel casting plant were organized with patternmakers in other neighboring plants into a single local. The CIO local, on the other hand, consisted of all employees in a given plant. The men were organized on the basis of the place where they worked or who their employer was. All auto workers in the Ford plant in Detroit, for example, are members of Local 600 of the United Auto Workers. This union, then, was affiliated with the CIO.

These lines of difference tended to become blurred in the last twenty years, so much so that by 1955 union leaders found

William Green succeeded Gompers as president of the AFL in 1924 and continued the labor policy of the former president. He believed in the craft unions and strongly opposed all efforts to organize the AFL on an industry basis. (Ransdell Photo)

it possible to talk of merging and setting up a single central office. The AFL had found it necessary to break down the rigid craft line in local membership ranks, and the CIO had found it occasionally advisable to incorporate unions on a craft instead of an industrial basis. In December 1955, the AFL and CIO merged, becoming the AFL-CIO, the largest union in the history of labor. The merger was hailed by the majority of members and termed by George Meany, the union's new president, as "the most important trade-union development in our time." The International Brotherhood of Teamsters (1,229,000 members), the largest union in the AFL, insisted that it be accepted as part of the new union's industrial department, which is made up primarily of former CIO unions. The other departments are those former AFL crafts groups: building trades, metal trades, and the like. The merger of the two unions (a total of 15,000,000 members) was made smoothly after months of planning, but differences in the structures of the two groups still showed through.

The AFL-CIO, like its components formerly, is made up of unions and not of individual persons. The teamster who carries a union card does not himself belong to the AFL-CIO. He belongs to a teamsters' local, and the Teamsters International[1] is affiliated with the AFL-CIO. These affiliates—some of them with a membership of more than a million—

Labor leaders of rival unions were photographed March 21, 1951, at a Washington defense-program conference of 700 AFL and CIO state and local leaders. Left to right are: William Green, Philip Murray, George Meany, and Walter Reuther. In December 1955 the AFL and CIO merged to form the largest union in the history of labor, with former AFL president George Meany as head of the 15,000,000-man AFL-CIO. (Nate Fine)

have their own dues, manage their own affairs, discipline their own members, make their own contracts with management, and call their own strikes. They can withdraw from the Federation whenever they wish. The United Mine Workers had been in and out of both the AFL and the CIO, and at present they are an independent union. The right of the International to withdraw makes it difficult for the Federation's central office to enforce too tight a discipline on the individual unions—a point generally overlooked when former CIO and AFL leaders found themselves criticized for not expelling Communists from some of the member unions' ranks.

57. UNION AIMS, METHODS, AND RESTRAINTS

Aims of labor. Unions, we have seen, accept the American political and economic system and try to operate within its framework. Their aims have traditionally been to obtain a greater share of the national income. They have consistently

John L. Lewis led in the formation of the CIO and concentrated on the mass-production industries such as automobiles, steel, and textiles in his organization drive. He was elected first president of the CIO. (International News Photo)

---

[1] "International" is a misleading term. The Teamsters International is a nationwide federation of teamsters' local unions. It should be properly called "The National Federation of Teamster Unions."

worked for higher wages, shorter hours of work, and better working conditions. Recently they have added "fringe benefits" as another objective. Typical "fringe benefits" are vacations with pay, health plans paid for by management, sick leave, and plans for the higher education of the workers' children. The apparently simple aims of higher wages and shorter hours grow complex in some industries. Higher wages might involve the demand of a guaranteed annual wage in an industry in which seasonal employment makes a high hourly wage more or less meaningless. This is the avowed goal, for example, of the United Automobile Workers at the present time. Demands for shorter hours might involve conflict over "split shifts" for the bus drivers, as when a bus company asks the driver to work four hours early in the morning and four more in the early evening. If we keep these possible complications in mind, however, we can safely say that unions continue to seek good wages, good hours, and good working conditions for their members.

Newspaper interest in sensational news has combined with the traditional hostility to unions on the part of some people to give us a distorted picture of union activity. As a general rule union leaders achieve their objectives by peaceful and even friendly negotiations. Frequently contracts are renewed automatically. Sometimes they are drawn up for long periods, as was the case of the five-year agreement entered into between General Motors and the United Automobile Workers in 1950.

Friendly negotiation is the usual means whereby unions and management settle their differences. Experience has shown both labor and management that they cannot be completely selfish and disregard the other's interest. Management has learned that workers must be given fair pay and decent working conditions if they are to remain productive workers.

And workers have learned that management must operate at a profit or the plant will have to close down. Both parties try to drive as hard a bargain as they can within what they consider the bounds of reasonableness and justice. Both are represented by experts who present their arguments as convincingly as possible in order to come to an agreement that union leaders can defend to the workers and management can defend to the shareholders.

Labor's bargaining methods. The central aim of unions throughout their history has been to bargain collectively with the employer. Unless the union representative speaks for every worker in the plant or every worker within the given craft in a certain area (locals still maintain the former CIO or AFL character) he weakens his bargaining power. His ultimate threat during negotiations is to take the men off the job, and this is not an effective threat if the employer can replace them by non-union men or if they are so small a part of the labor force in the plant that production can go on in their absence. It is for this reason that unions have tried to achieve "union security," of which there are three kinds: (1) the *closed shop,* in which only union members are hired; (2) the *union shop,* in which all workers must join the union; (3) *maintenance of membership,* in which all union members must retain membership during the life of the contract. Union security is also promoted by the *preferential-hiring* agreement, whereby the employer agrees to hire union members first whenever they are available. These measures restrict the freedom of management and workers alike, but are weapons without which unions in some instances could not bargain effectively.

Unions are created, we have seen, to bargain collectively. Ordinarily this bargaining takes place in closed session between union and management representatives. Occasionally, when the two parties cannot agree on contract terms, they agree to accept a mediator. The mediator is a disinterested third party who meets with both sides separately, listens to their arguments, and weighs them carefully. He then makes recommendations which labor and management are free to accept or reject. The government has established a Federal Mediation and Conciliation Board that disputing parties may utilize if they wish. The success of mediation depends on the ability of the mediator, his powers of persuasion, and his fair-mindedness.

Arbitration is used to settle another kind of labor dispute. The arbitrator sits like a judge in the case: he listens to the arguments of both parties and then hands down a verdict which both labor and management have agreed beforehand to accept. Arbitration is not used in contract negotiations. It is used to settle disputed points of interpretation as to the enforcement of a contract already signed. Both mediation and arbitration are successful ways of settling labor disputes without resorting to the workers' ultimate weapon—the strike.

The strike. Strikes are costly to management, to labor, and to the general public. They occur when labor and management come to a deadlock in contract negotiations or when labor believes management is violating a provision of the contract in force. Strikes sometimes seem to occur over trivial things, but as a rule an important matter is at stake when union leaders resort to a strike. A long strike becomes an endurance contest between management and the union. In the past, strikes frequently wrecked unions by depleting their reserves and by driving desperate men out of union ranks so they could find work before their families starved. Strikes have also wrecked businesses, especially the smaller concerns that do not possess large reserves of capital and credit.

Frequently strikes occur when the matter of wages is not at stake. The workers concerned might lose several days' or even several months' wages over such a matter as a ten-minute coffee break in the afternoon. The failure of a strike to increase the worker's wages enough to pay for his lost wages does not

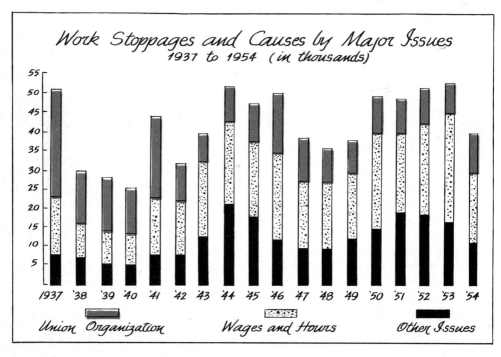

Work Stoppages and Causes by Major Issues
1937 to 1954 (in thousands)

Union Organization   Wages and Hours   Other Issues

The primary purpose of a "sit-down" strike was to discourage management from employing non-union workers to replace striking union members. The possible violation of property rights is a serious consideration in determining the justification of this type of strike. (Library of Congress)

mean, however, that strikes have not "paid" the workingman. Through the last half century he has made remarkable gains in wages and in better working conditions. Other factors enter into the workingman's increased prosperity, of course, but collective bargaining with the strike as a final weapon has played a significant part in bettering the workingman's condition. To ask him to surrender the right to strike is to ask him to give up his most effective bargaining weapon. To ask him to use this weapon reasonably is another matter.

We have said that long strikes become endurance contests between management and labor. Both sides lose, although one or the other may gain in the long run. The general public never gains. Our economy is so complex that a strike in one industry soon ties up many other segments of economic life. A strike in a carburetor plant, for example, will soon paralyze a large part of the automotive industry. A strike cannot be justified, then, unless it is over a serious matter— a matter of principle connected with collective bargaining, or a serious adjustment in wages or working conditions. Nor can a strike be justified unless union representatives have tried conscientiously to achieve their objective by peaceful negotiations.

We should remember, however, that it is often difficult to tell who is ultimately responsible for a strike. Very often responsibility is divided between the union and management. Unless one knows the details of the case one should suspend judgment on which side is responsible for the strike.

In all labor-management negotiations justice requires that both sides consider the broad interests of the public. When a nationwide union negotiates with the managers of a nationwide industry, there may be a temptation for the latter to capitulate to the union leaders' demands and then simply pass on the resulting increased costs of production to the public. This is not real bargaining between labor and management, but collusion between them at the expense of the public.

Government policy on the labor question. Until the New Deal, the federal government and most states followed a policy that was unfriendly to labor unions. Court injunctions were frequently used to prevent strikes. Sometimes the armed forces were employed to keep the plant in operation and to break picket lines. It was generally felt that unions interfered with American enterprise, that they were radical importations from Europe, and that they were inimical to the progress that had made America great. It was also generally felt that strikes violated management's property rights. The Great Depression changed public opinion considerably on unions and strikes. A corresponding change took place in official government policy.

The Wagner Act. The National Industrial Recovery Act of 1933 spelled out the new policy. Workers were given the right to bargain collectively through representatives of their own choosing, and management was prohibited from interfering in any way with labor's right to organize. When the NIRA was declared unconstitutional, the workers' right to organize and to bargain collectively was incorporated into the National Labor Relations Act, or Wagner Act, of 1935. This act is frequently called "the Magna Charta of labor." The Wagner Act contained this statement of policy:

It is hereby declared to be the policy of the United States to eliminate the causes of certain substantial obstructions to the free flow of commerce and to mitigate and eliminate these obstructions when they have occurred by encouraging the practice and procedure of collective bargaining, and by protecting the exercise by workers of full freedom of association, self-organization, and designation of representatives of their own choosing, for the purpose of negotiating the terms and conditions of their employment or other mutual aid or protection.

Under the protection of the Wagner Act union membership increased from 3,500,000 to 9,000,000 within five years, and in another five years it grew to almost 15,000,000.

The Wagner Act provided for a National Labor Relations Board which was to enforce the act's provision. The NLRB consists of five members appointed for five-year terms by the President. The Board can hold elections in plants or industries in order to determine whether the workers want union organization and, if they do, which union is to represent them. It studies charges brought by labor or management to decide whether

William Green, former president of the AFL, is shown conferring with Senator Robert Wagner, author of the National Labor Relations Act. (International News Photo)

either group is guilty of unfair labor practices. Unions guilty of unfair labor practices or violation of other laws are denied protection of the law. Managements guilty of unfair labor practices, such as racial discrimination or interference in union elections, are excluded from consideration for government contracts and penalized in various other ways.

The Taft-Hartley Act. Many non-labor people—farmers, professional people, businessmen, and consumers—felt that the government had gone too far in its protection of labor. They believed that management was at a serious disadvantage in dealing with labor, that the "umpire" was on labor's side instead of being neutral. This feeling was increased by the imprudent conduct of some labor leaders and by the disclosure that communists had infiltrated a number of unions. Agitation for amending the Wagner Act continued for several years and finally resulted in the Taft-Hartley Act of 1947. This act,

A threatened tie-up of the port of Philadelphia was averted when the Reverend Dennis J. Comey, director of the Institute of Industrial Relations at St. Joseph's College, told 200 dock workers that their "wildcat" strike was wrong. Some 125 of them went back to work immediately and the others soon followed. (Religious News Service)

which was passed over President Truman's veto, is officially known as the Labor Management Relations Act.

Union leaders opposed the Taft-Hartley Act as being "anti-labor," and representatives of management praised it for striking a proper balance between the two; in other words, for being impartial. After eight years of operation the Taft-Hartley Act seems neither as disastrous for labor as union leaders said it would be nor as favorable to management representatives as they had hoped it would.

Let us see what the Taft-Hartley Act provides. First of all, it is an amendment of the Wagner Act, and it retains both the statement of policy we have seen and a guarantee that workers may bargain collectively through unions of their own choosing.

Second, it aims at protecting the worker from excessive domination by union leaders; that is, by preventing these leaders from becoming "bosses." This is accomplished by several provisions: (1) The union may not charge excessive initiation fees. (2) It must make an annual financial report to its members. (3) No one has to join a union in order to apply for a job within a unionized plant. (4) The union cannot use dues for political purposes without express authorization from the individual members. (5) It cannot collect dues by check-off, which means having them deducted from the worker's pay check without his express authorization. (6) Members may not be expelled from the union except for non-payment of fees, dues, or assessments.

Third, unions are put under new controls by a number of provisions. (1) Union officers must swear that they are not Communists. (2) Officers must report their manner of election and their salaries. (3) Unions can be sued for damages if they violate terms of the contract with management. (4) Union health and welfare funds may not be irresponsibly administered by union officials.

Fourth, the Taft-Hartley Act contains provisions to protect the public from un-

ion activity. (1) Strikes are forbidden against innocent firms that supply the firm with which the union has a dispute. (2) Strikes to remedy conditions for which management is not responsible are forbidden. (3) Restrictions are imposed on strikes that endanger national health or safety. (4) Strikes are now forbidden in jurisdictional disputes (when two unions claim the right to represent the workers in a given plant).

Most experts in labor economics say that the Taft-Hartley Act contains a number of excellent provisions. Some, however, hold that other provisions undermine its stated purpose: to encourage collective bargaining and to protect the worker from domination by union leaders. In other words, although the act is supposed to guarantee both collective bargaining and democracy within the union, certain provisions are said to be directed against effective collective bargaining. First, management is free to hire non-union employees. If the workers in a plant vote for a union shop, however, all employees must join the union within a reasonable time. Moreover, workers are required to vote on management's last offer before a strike can be called in any dispute that might affect national health or welfare. The worker also has the right to settle his own grievances with management. These restrictions on union leaders seem to assume that they do not truly represent labor. In the first four years of the Taft-Hartley Act's operation, however, workers voted 97 per cent in favor

Representative Fred Hartley (R., New Jersey), Senator Robert Taft (R., Ohio), and Senator Irving Ives (R., New York) are shown meeting to revise the original Hartley Labor Bill. Hartley and Taft later drafted the law which bears their name. (International News Photo)

"I'll Be Hanged—!" The "right to work" laws adopted by a number of states are bitterly opposed by labor unions. These laws allow management to hire non-union workers (sometimes at lower wages than the union scale) without the new workers being obliged to join a union. (Seaman in Justice)

of the union leaders' demands in 46,146 polls conducted by the National Labor Relations Board.

"Right-to-work" laws. Laws that are less friendly to unions have been passed in many states, especially in the South, where anti-union feeling is strong. At the beginning of 1955 seventeen states had adopted so-called "right-to-work" laws which prohibit union shops. These laws permit management to hire non-union workers without their then being obligated to join a union. If management is hostile to unions, it is obvious that non-union employees will be given preference over union men. The "right-to-work" laws therefore drive men out of the union. Those who condemn these laws argue that: (1) they infringe the workers' right of association, which is a legitimate means to attain good wages; (2) they practically force labor and management into conflict. The term "right to work" is misleading, inasmuch as the laws do not guarantee jobs for anyone. Their only guarantee is that a worker does not have to belong to a union to keep his job, which in some instances is equivalent to guaranteeing him lower wages.

58. CRITICISM AND PROSPECTS OF ORGANIZED LABOR

Some union leaders, as well as the rank and file of some unions, have been guilty of selfish practices that have antagonized the rest of the American people. As a rule, only a small minority have engaged in such practices, but they attract attention and enable non-union people to conclude erroneously that unions generally engage in such anti-social practices. The result is that opponents of the unions have developed a number of generalizations, each of which is only partly true:

1. That unions will not give a good day's work for the good day's pay they demand. Workers loaf on the job. They insist on "feather-bedding," or the hiring of more men than are needed to do a certain piece of work. It is true that these abuses are rather common in the building trades and with musicians; that is, among workers whose employment is seasonal and who tend to stretch each job out as long as they can. Most unions co-operate with management and try to get a good day's work out of their members.

2. That union officials are racketeers who exploit the workers for their own selfish purposes. No one will deny that some union leaders have used their position for selfish purposes, and some of them have been convicted of extortion—demanding money as a condition for supplying management with the labor needed. Only a small percentage of union officials are guilty of such practices—perhaps about the same percentage as that of businessmen guilty of corrupt practices. Union members have the opportunity to repudiate their leaders whenever an election is held under the auspices of the National Labor Relations Board. Their endorsement of their officials by about 97 per cent of the vote is an indication that very few workers think

they are being exploited by their union.

3. That unions are "soft" on Communists; that they are the agencies through which Communists operate most successfully in this country. This general statement is an oversimplification of a very complex development in union history in the last three decades. In 1920, William Z. Foster organized the Trade Union Educational League in order to revolutionize the unions. The strategy was to "bore from within" and to place Communists in key spots in existing AFL unions. But AFL leaders were generally successful in defeating these attempts.

The rapid increase of union membership in the midst of struggle between the AFL and the CIO created the kind of confusion on which communism thrives and grows. The CIO secured hundreds of thousands of recruits monthly, and they needed trained men to staff the new units. A number of the persons they hired turned out to be Communists. In time Communists came to dominate at least eleven CIO unions and to have considerable influence in the CIO central office. Beginning in 1948, however, the CIO set about cleaning house, and by 1950 all Communist-controlled unions had been expelled from the CIO. No AFL union was known to have fallen under Communist control. Communists dominated a few locals, like hotel and restaurant workers in New York, but they never controlled a national AFL union.

A more serious, because more valid, criticism of union labor in recent years has been the extraordinary political activity of the leaders. Some of them have gone far beyond the legitimate defending of the interests of the labor unions in national and local legislatures and public administrative offices. Such leaders have sought to influence their followers, and even to use union funds, to promote general political objectives having little or no direct relation to laboring interests; e.g., questions of foreign policy, recruitment of the armed forces, the national budget, and taxation laws. In all such political issues union workers have, of course, an interest, but as citizens of the United States, not as members of a particular union. Unions have a right to expect that their members as voters will support measures that serve the right interest of the union. But they have no right to attempt to sway their members in support of public policies that either do not affect union interests or go against some other interest of the workers, any more than managers of large companies have the right to control the political conscience of their employees.

The prospects for unions in America. The union member must give up a measure of his freedom to obtain the security that unions can offer him. He must abide by the vote of the majority in the union or operate in a state of economic anarchy. The place of the worker within the union has been excellently stated:[2]

Employee freedom can be protected without destroying or weakening collective bargaining. The workers should continue to be permitted to decide by democratic means whether they want collective bargaining, and the law should guarantee this right by preventing all interference by the employer and by limiting the union to normal educational channels. Once the majority has spoken, the individual worker should not be permitted to countermand the desires of the majority and to weaken the union's bargaining strength by refusing to join the union or to participate in

[2] Dr. Gladys W. Gruenberg, "Unionism at the Crossroads," *Social Order*, January 1955, p. 12.

Sidney Hillman, appointed chairman of the Political Action Committee of the CIO in 1943, believed that the unions of America should take a more active part in politics. (Library of Congress)

its activities. No society can operate under a system of anarchy. This is as true of the industrial plant community as it is of the political community.

As a minority, however, the individual union member should be guaranteed his right to speak and to appeal to some outside agency if his democratic rights are violated. But he should not retain the right to act contrary to the wishes of the majority. This conforms with normal orderly democratic processes in that all of us are obliged to obey laws even though we retain the right to vocalize our opposition to them.

There are reasons for optimism in regard to the relations between unions and management in the future. The wave of "right-to-work" laws and other anti-union legislation was a natural reaction to the period of indulgence by the government toward unions—which had followed a period of anti-union policy. We can reasonably expect a long period of normal relations between management

"Still Racing His Shadow." The problem of meeting the higher cost of living in time of prosperity causes labor to ask for new wage demands. What could be a vicious circle, in which increased wages bring on increased prices, has caused some economists to prescribe "fixed" wages and "ceiling" prices. (Shoemaker)

and unions in the future, because management in large industries and workingmen have generally accepted unions as the normal means for workingmen to achieve their just objectives. Management in most plants admits that unions serve a necessary purpose in the American economy and that, if they are led by reasonable men, they are an advantage to management as well as to labor.

Principles of industrial peace. The fact that unions and management get along peacefully in many industries caused the National Planning Association to appoint a committee to study the causes of *industrial peace* in the hope that other industries and unions could adopt them. The committee discovered that the following conditions prevailed in those establishments that enjoyed industrial peace:

1. Management fully accepted collective bargaining and the union as an institution.
2. The union fully accepted private ownership of the business and the role of management in administering it.
3. The mutual relations of the union and the employer were characterized by trust and confidence.
4. Labor-management consultation and sharing of information were highly developed.
5. Grievances were settled speedily on a flexible and informal basis.
6. The union was strong, responsible, and democratic.
7. Management recognized the difference between a trade union and a business organization.
8. Management placed great stress on personnel administration.

Better labor-management relations. It is now realized that collective bargaining through unions is not the complete answer to the labor problem. Largely through the influence of papal pronouncements on labor, social thinkers—Catholic and non-Catholic—have come to insist on the need of the workingman's being dealt with as a person instead of as a commodity. A just wage is his first need, of course, and this he can obtain through collective bargaining. If the

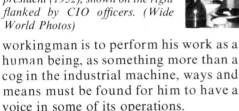

In an office in the White House, labor and management negotiate a settlement of a steelworkers' dispute. In the national interest, the President urged representatives of Jones and Laughlin, United States, and Republic steel companies to meet with Philip Murray, CIO president (1952), shown on the right flanked by CIO officers. (Wide World Photos)

workingman is to perform his work as a human being, as something more than a cog in the industrial machine, ways and means must be found for him to have a voice in some of its operations.

Various plans have been tried in some plants to achieve this result. They have met with varying degrees of success or failure, depending largely on the quality of labor leaders and the sincerity of management in the plants where they have been tried. One plan is *profit sharing,* whereby the interests of the workingmen have been merged with the interests of management and owners in running a business at a good profit. Workers are paid an annual bonus out of the profits, and it is therefore to their interest to effect economies, to eliminate waste, and in general to promote the company's profits for the year. They are thus encouraged to take a real interest in producing. Many union leaders, however, are suspicious and fearful of this practice, lest the worker transfer his interest from the union to the plant.

Another plan which has been tried with less success up until now is that of *co-management.* It calls for labor representatives sitting down with management and formulating business policies: whether to cut back production, whether to open up new markets, whether to change models, and other such matters as these. With certain outstanding exceptions, neither management nor labor has so far taken well to co-management. Management is reluctant to share its policy-making responsibilities, and it maintains that labor

representatives do not have sufficient knowledge or a sufficient sense of responsibility to help make wise decisions. On the other hand, many workers maintain that co-management makes heavy demands on them for which they are not paid: much study and reading, long hours of discussion, and in general assuming a share of management's responsibility for which management alone is rewarded. Many practical difficulties face any company that wants to achieve the ideal of co-management.

Industry councils. Principles for working out ideal relations between labor and management have been outlined in Pope Pius XI's encyclical "On Reconstructing the Social Order." In this letter the Pope described what is known in this country as the "Industry Council Plan," whereby each industry would form councils to solve common problems and promote the general welfare. Labor and management would both be represented in these councils, which would furnish a large measure of self-regulation to each industry. Government regulation would thus be kept to the minimum. The industrial community would regulate itself to avoid the evils of excessive competition and of monopoly and to give labor and management just treatment. The Pope, of course, did not lay down a blueprint on how the Industry Council Plan could work out in this or any other country. He stated only a principle. Its application here would involve many serious problems, and it can be achieved only after much serious thought and considerable experiment. It is an ideal, nevertheless, that gives both labor and management their due. Moreover, it joins them together as co-operating partners instead of antagonists, and it offers the general public a good chance to escape from paying the bill, as it has had to do so often, for the continual struggle between labor and management.

REVIEW

56. Rise of Labor Unions

A. Why is there a need for workers to organize? Why do many philosophers maintain that a worker has a duty to join a union?

B. Why, in the early days of our country, was there no real need for unions? List some of the factors that aided the rise of unions.

C. Trace the beginnings and early growth of the AFL. Give some reasons for its success. What group did it ignore?

D. What proportion of the total work force in the United States are members of unions? Describe how the CIO and the AFL organized their unions before 1955.

E. What are some of the important effects of the merger of the AFL & CIO in 1955?

57. Union Aims, Methods, and Restraints

A. What are "fringe benefits"? How do unions and managements generally settle their differences?

B. How does a union achieve "union security"? Why is mediation or arbitration necessary at times to settle labor disputes? Briefly describe each of these.

C. What is a strike? Why do unions and management try to avoid strikes? Describe the situation that must be present before a just strike may be called.

D. What was the government's general attitude toward labor before 1933? Describe the major advantages gained by labor from the Wagner Act of 1935.

E. Why was the Taft-Hartley Law passed in 1947? What are some of its provisions? What are "right-to-work" laws?

58. Criticism and Prospects of Organized Labor

A. What are some of the criticisms directed at unions which are half-truths?

B. Why is labor criticized for entering politics?

C. Why must a worker give up a measure of his freedom in order to obtain union security?

D. Why is there reason for optimism regarding future management-union relations? Describe the atmosphere in a company where there is industrial peace.

E. How has dealing with the worker as a human person affected relations with management? What is the aim and work of an industrial council?

THE CHAPTER IN REVIEW

A. What brought about the need for unions in the United States after 1850? Why was unionism slow to grow? What hostility did it encounter?

B. Trace the beginnings of the AFL and the CIO and show how they differed in purposes and aims. Account for their growth and present strength.

C. What are some of the differences between the Wagner Act of 1935 and the Taft-Hartley Act of 1947?

D. Describe some of the plans in operation today which treat the worker more as a partner in the industrial endeavor.

SELECTED READINGS

The problem of the employee's relationship to his employer has become terribly complicated in modern society, and a vast literature has grown up around the subject. Useful background studies are: Foster Rhea Dulles, *Labor in America: A History* (New York: Thomas Y. Crowell Co., 1955), for a good study of the union movement in American history; Florence Peterson, *American Labor Unions: What They Are and How They Work* (New York: Harper & Brothers, 1951), for a sympathetic explanation of unions; W. S. Woytinsky and Associates, *Employment and Wages in the*

United States (New York: The Twentieth Century Fund, 1953), for an encyclopedic reference work on labor matters.

Frequent articles on labor problems appear in *America* and *Commonweal.* Rev. Benjamin L. Masse, S.J., is labor editor for *America* and John C. Cort for *Commonweal.* These experts keep their readers up to date on current developments. Good articles on the general labor question include Father Masse's "Causes of Industrial Peace," *America* (February 13, 1954), and John C. Cort, "The End of the Testy Titans," *Commonweal* (July 23, 1954), in which the author discusses the proposed merger of the CIO and AFL. The practical problems of industrial relations are discussed by A. A. Ahner, "Human Labor Relations," *Social Order* (March 1951); and Gladys W. Gruenberg, "Unionism at the Crossroads," *Social Order* (January 1955), examines the effect of the Taft-Hartley Law on labor relations.

The technique of collective bargaining—an important element of labor relations—is demonstrated in Selwyn H. Torff, *Collective Bargaining* (New York: McGraw-Hill Book Co., 1953), and Walter Hull Carpenter, *Case Studies in Collective Bargaining* (New York: Prentice-Hall, Inc., 1953). Opposing points of view on a worker's obligation to join a union are presented by William A. Durbin, "The Right Not to Join a Union," *Social Order* (September 1952), and Rev. William J. Smith, S.J., "The Duty to Join a Union," *Social Order* (November 1952).

Catholic thinking on the union movement is to be found first of all in Pope Leo XIII's *Rerum Novarum* (1891) and Pope Pius XI's *Quadragesimo Anno* (1931), both of which have appeared in translation in many pamphlets and in collections of both Popes' writings. (See the reading list at the end of Chapter 36.) On this subject the following pamphlets are also useful: Norman J. McKenna, *The Catholic and His Union* (New York: The Paulist Press, 1948), and Rev. William J. Smith, S.J., *The Catholic Labor School* (New York: The Paulist Press, 1941). Rev. John F. Cronin, S.S., discusses the subject in two different and excellent books: *Catholic Social Action* (Milwaukee: The Bruce Publishing Co., 1948) and *Catholic Social Principles* (Milwaukee: The Bruce Publishing Co., 1950).

Specific problems in labor relations are treated in the following:

1. *Guaranteed annual wage:* Rev. Joseph M. Becker, S.J., "G.A.W. for Auto Workers," *Social Order* (June 1955), analyzes the advantages and disadvantages of the guaranteed annual wage in dispassionate fashion. A longer treatment of the same subject is made by Mary Waggamann, *The Case of the Guaranteed Annual Wage* (New York: The Paulist Press, 1954). A Chamber of Commerce pamphlet, *The Economics of the Guaranteed Wage* (1953), presents industry's point of view on this subject.

2. *Profit sharing:* Rev. Leo C. Brown, S.J., "Profit Sharing Pays," *Social Order* (February 1951), makes a study of how profit sharing worked well in a single plant. A more general treatment is James A. O'Brien, "Profit Sharing and Organized Labor," *Social Order* (March 1954), and Rev. Joseph B. Kenkel, C.Pp.S., *Sharing Profits with Employees* (New York: The Paulist Press, 1952).

3. *Co-management:* Different points of view on this subject are presented by Rev. Joseph B. Kenkel, C.Pp.S., *Sharing Management with Employees* (New York: The Paulist Press, 1953), and Henry K. Junckerstorff, "Co-Management: A Trojan Horse," *Social Order* (January 1953).

4. *Right-to-work legislation:* Catholic bishops and priests in labor work are almost universally agreed that these bills are misnamed and that they are an attack on unionism itself. Rev. Leo C. Brown, S.J., "Right-to-Work Legislation," *Social Order* (March 1955), admits abuses in union activities but demonstrates that these laws are no solution to the admitted abuses.

PROJECTS

1. Invite representatives of labor and management from a local company to present concrete evidence of good relations and how they are maintained. A class committee could obtain the same information by visiting the plant of a local company.

2. If a student of the class is a member of a union, he could report to the class on how unions work to gain benefits for their members. A similar report can be made by a student whose father or other relative is a union member or organizer.

Chapter 20. Agriculture in the American Economy

59. THE RECURRENT PROBLEM OF FARM INCOME

Agriculture is the foundation of our economic system. It furnishes the food consumed by the nation and much of the raw material on which industries depend. If the farmer does not receive the equivalent of the worker's just wage or the industrialist's fair profit, then our economic system is unbalanced and serious injustice is done to the farmer. If such unbalance continues for a long time, the nation as a whole suffers economically and socially. Moreover, if farmers do not receive a fair price for their products, their purchasing power is reduced and the market for many goods is curtailed.

The farmers' income in 1929 was $5,-700,000,000 out of a total national income of $87,400,000,000. In 1940, it was $4,900,000,000 out of $81,300,000,000, or about 6 per cent of the national income. In 1953 farm income was $12,400,000,-000 or somewhat less than 4 per cent of the total national income. It is estimated that about 43 cents of each dollar spent

for food eventually reaches the farmer. The remaining 57 cents pays transportation costs, marketing expenses, and profits for middlemen. It is obvious, therefore, that agriculture is not properly integrated into the American economy.

This has remained an unsolved problem since the development of one-crop farming for profit after the Civil War. As long as we were essentially an agricultural nation and each farmer tended to be self-sufficient, the farmer's problems were comparatively easy to solve. But when the farmer began to raise a cash crop for profit, he put himself at the disposal of economic forces over which he had little or no control. He had to make heavy investments in land and equipment. He depended on a good market each year, because if his crop did not command a good price he could not pay his debts and finance next year's crop. He depended on various middlemen to market his crop, especially the railroads and the owners of warehouses and grain elevators. He was seldom in a position to bargain with them successfully, because

if he refused to pay whatever rates they charged his crop rotted in the field.

The farmer's efforts to relieve his plight. In the last half of the nineteenth century the farmer's problems became acute and he tried various ways to solve them: the Grange, the Farmers' Alliance, legislation to control the railroads and the middleman, the formation of a third party, and finally various kinds of national legislation to improve the economic status of agriculture. Let us review the main points of this development so that we can see how the agricultural problem has changed in the last century.

Grain farmers in the Midwest were severely exploited in the years after the Civil War. The railroads charged excessively high rates for transporting the farmers' grain to market. Elevators and warehouses, often owned or controlled by the railroads, also overcharged the farmer. The farmer was desperate when he found that a successful crop hardly paid him the expenses of raising and marketing it, and he was ready for radical action. At this point (1867) Oliver Hudson Kelley, a clerk in the Department of Agriculture, organized the Patrons of Husbandry, or the Grange, as a society to spread information on scientific farming. The Grange grew rapidly when the farmers found it an agency through which they could attack the railroads. By 1875 the Grange had 850,000 members.

The Grange proposed to regulate the railroads by state law, even to fixing minimum rates. Within a few years Granger-dominated legislatures in Illinois, Wisconsin, Iowa, and Minnesota passed laws which strictly regulated railroads and storage elevators. In the historic *Munn* v. *Illinois* case (1876) Granger legislation was vindicated on the grounds that a state has the right to regulate a business "that is public in nature though privately owned and managed." State regulation later proved ineffective, but Granger action had shown how some abuses from which the farmer suffered could be corrected through state and national legislation.

The acute distress suffered in agricultural areas in the 1870s and 1880s made the farmer realize that exploitation by the railroads and warehouse owners was only part of his problem. A decline in prices ruined the farmer who had purchased his farm and equipment "on time" at high prices and then had to continue payments with money received from the sale of his annual crop at low prices. The farmer clearly belonged to

ALL FARM FOODS
IN BILLIONS OF DOLLARS

Year	Farm Value	Retail cost	Marketing bill
1945	12.6	24.4	12.5
1946	15.7	30.8	15.6
1947	18.7	36.4	17.7
1948	19.2	38.9	19.7
1949	17.1	37.8	20.7
1950	17.7	38.7	21.0
1951	20.3	43.0	22.7
1952	20.2	44.6	24.4
1953	19.3	45.2	25.9
1954	18.8	45.6	26.8
*1955	18.3	46.3	28.0

* Preliminary estimate.

While marketing charges have risen, the value of the farmer's product has dropped since 1951. Higher prices paid by the consumer for farm products since 1951 therefore do not mean that the farmer's real income has increased. Consult the table above for the differences in the retail cost of farm foods and their farm value. Since 1948 the marketing bill has been higher than the farm value. For only five years since 1918 has the farm value exceeded the marketing bill (1943–1947).

the debtor class, and he therefore wanted "cheap money." By cheap money he meant high prices, because the more you pay for a pair of shoes or a bushel of wheat, the cheaper your money is relative to commodities. The farmer therefore came out for various inflation schemes, such as greenbacks and the free coinage of silver. Of course he wanted high prices for what he had to sell, not for what he had to buy. His prime wish was to pay his debts with cheap money.

The Farmers' Alliance, which grew strong by 1890, demanded currency inflation and strict regulation of the railroads. In 1890 the Alliance ran a ticket of candidates in every state where they were strongly organized. Alliance candidates for governor were elected in three states; two senators and about forty representatives were Alliance men; and at least eight states had legislatures controlled by the Alliance party. The various local Alliance parties united in the next year to form the national Populist party, which was primarily the party of agrarian discontent. Among other "progressive" measures like the referendum and initia-

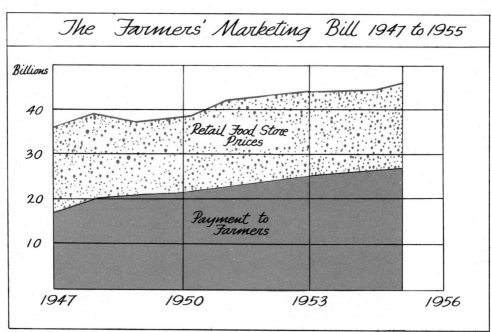

The Farmers' Marketing Bill 1947 to 1955

Billions

Retail Food Store Prices

Payment to Farmers

40

30

20

10

1947   1950   1953   1956

This newspaper cartoon (1887) reflects the skepticism of many over the regulation of railroads by the Interstate Commerce Commission. This legislation was the result of the popularization of the farmer's plight by the Grange, the Farmer's Alliance, and the Populist party. (Library of Congress)

tive, the Populist party demanded currency inflation and government ownership of the railroads.

Farmers looked to the Populist party as the agency for solving their economic difficulties. But when parts of the Populist program were adopted by the Democratic party, the threat of a third party with agricultural backing diminished. Moreover, the farmer enjoyed increasing prosperity from 1898 until the end of World War I. Meanwhile the Interstate Commerce Commission was empowered to regulate railroad rates. Agricultural

discontent therefore subsided until the depression of 1921.

This depression found the farmer heavily in debt for the land and equipment he had acquired to meet the great need for food during World War I. To pay these debts, farmers increased production and thus built up a surplus of farm goods. The price of agricultural goods fell even more. Through the 1920s the price of manufactured goods was protected by high tariffs, which were of no advantage to the farmer. He therefore had to pay high prices for clothing

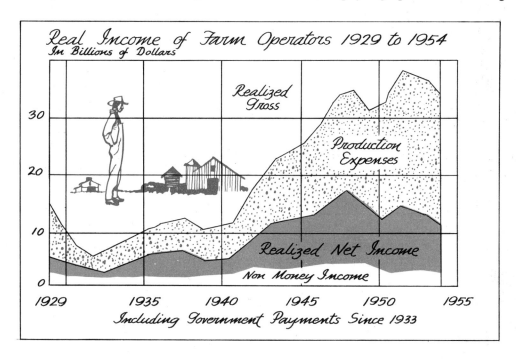

Real Income of Farm Operators 1929 to 1954
In Billions of Dollars

Realized Gross

Production Expenses

Realized Net Income

Non Money Income

30

20

10

0

1929   1935   1940   1945   1950   1955

Including Government Payments Since 1933

and manufactured goods, while his annual income grew smaller. In 1919 farm income had been sixteen billion dollars, in 1929 it had fallen to eleven billion, and in 1932 it was only five billion dollars. The farmer realized, at last, that he could not operate successfully under such conditions. The nation could not consume all the food that was produced, and the farmer had to face stiff competition in world markets.

Federal legislation to relieve the farmer. The Agricultural Marketing Act of 1929 established a Federal Farm Board to buy surpluses of each farm product. The surplus was to be stored until the demand was strong enough to keep prices up when the surplus goods were released for sale. The Federal Farm Board in 1933 had spent almost two hundred billion dollars and yet failed to solve the farmer's problem. The farmer continued to produce, overloading the Board with unsalable surpluses.

New Deal farm legislation tried to correct this fault of the Federal Farm Board by limiting the amount of goods the farmer could produce. This was the basic idea of the Agricultural Adjustment Act (AAA) of 1933. This law tried to restore the farmer's purchasing power of the prosperous 1909–1914 period by limiting his production of certain basic crops and thus forcing up prices. Farmers were to be paid a cash bounty for reducing production of six staple crops: cotton, corn, wheat, tobacco, rice, and peanuts. After four years of AAA bounties, farm income increased two billion dollars—the result of higher prices of the staple farm products.

The Supreme Court declared the AAA unconstitutional in 1935, but Congress quickly passed the Soil Conservation and Domestic Allotment Act to achieve the same objective by slightly different means. Farmers were paid for planting alfalfa and other soil-nourishing crops instead of such basic commodities as

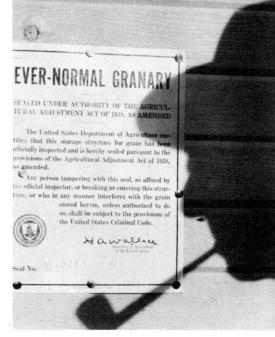

A government seal "locks" a store of surplus grain for future use. Under the second AAA the farmer was allowed to insure his entire crop with the government, who stored it for him and granted him a loan which was slightly below the crop's "parity" value. Thus the country's ever-normal food supply was maintained and the farmer was guaranteed a fair income despite price changes. (U.S.D.A.)

corn, wheat, cotton, and tobacco. The new law therefore also limited production of basic commodities in order to sustain their prices, and paid farmers a bounty for substituting crops that would not be sold on the open market. Incidentally, soil conservation was promoted to some extent by the measure.

A new Agricultural Adjustment Act was passed in 1938. Its purpose was to restore the farmer's purchasing power of 1909–1914 by controlling the production and marketing of farm goods. It continued the direct subsidies provided by the Soil Conservation and Domestic Allotment Act, provided for acreage allotments for all participants in the plans, and organized the Commodity Credit Corporation, which supported farm prices by allowing farmers to retain their produce. The law sought to stabilize farm income and at the same time to insure the nation of an adequate food supply at a fair price.

Rising prices and a world-wide demand for American farm products brought prosperity to the farmer with World War II. This prosperity continued until 1948 because of the unsettled world situation and Europe's slow recovery from the war's devastation. Since then the farming interest has been supported by artificially maintained food prices; that is, by using government money to buy farm goods to be kept off the market. The farmer is convinced that his position in the American economy is basically unsound. He prospers without government subsidy only in time of war or national emergency.

Let us see how this is so. The farmer's principal expenses are (1) purchases and repair of equipment; (2) interest on his mortgage and other debts; (3) farm wages; (4) taxes. His sole income, from which he must meet his expenses, consists of the sale of his crop. A fall in farm prices hurts the farmer because his expenses remain more or less constant. Whether wheat sells for $2.00 or $1.00 a bushel, his expenses are about the same. The farmer is therefore dependent on receiving a good price for his crop. He cannot cut expenses by curtailing production, as the manufacturer can, or convert to some other product that continues to obtain a good price on the market. A wheat farmer, for example, cannot change in the middle of the season to cotton or tobacco. The climate, his equipment, his initial outlay are all aimed at a wheat crop.

60. THE FARMER'S NEED FOR GOVERNMENT SUPPORT

The farmer therefore operates at a disadvantage in the American economy—unless he obtains *some kind of government support*. His basic economic problem seems to be that of obtaining the equivalent of the worker's guaranteed minimum wage. In practice this has meant stabilizing his return at a safe level so that he can plan expenses with the same degree of certainty with which the industrialist plans his outlay and return.

Parity prices. In recent decades the federal government has tried to solve the farmer's problem by maintaining "parity prices" for his products. "Parity prices" have been called minimum wages for the farmer. Parity is defined as the "ideal relation between what the farmer receives for his products and what he has to pay for the things he needs." In order to determine fair prices for farm products, the government looks for a period when farmers were fairly prosperous. The 1909–1914 period is taken as the base for determining parity prices, since crop prices then compared favorably with the cost of goods and services the farmer bought at the same time. This shows us the farmer's purchasing power during the base period. This ratio is then adjusted to changes that have occurred in the price of farm goods and the general price.

Let us take the price of wheat for an example. The average price of wheat in 1909–1914 was 84.4 cents a bushel. With this amount of money the farmer could buy about two and a half times as much as he can today. So the parity price of wheat would be $2.11. The government

Among the many aids to farmers is the crop-dusting service. Although this is more feasible on large farms, where dusting can be done from small aircraft, small-farm owners whose farms are contiguous often share this expense. (U.S.D.A.)

339

can secure this price in one or both of two ways: (1) It can purchase wheat on the open market until the price rises to $2.11. The wheat purchased by the government can be stored, shipped abroad, used by the armed forces, or even burned. (2) It can make loans to the farmer up to a certain percentage of parity (usually 90 per cent) if he stores his wheat. Then the farmer sells his wheat when the price goes up to parity, but if prices stay down he is allowed to default on his loan.

The difficulty with a parity-price program is that huge surpluses may accumulate. To avoid this difficulty the government has used two devices. The first is to lower the percentage of parity given to the farmer as prices of his crop decline. This encourages him to turn to other products and to curtail production of the crop that is in surplus on the market. The second device is to have the farmers participating in the program curtail production voluntarily. If they fail to vote in favor of reducing their acreage, government support of that crop is drastically reduced. In the summer of 1953 the Secretary of Agriculture called for a reduction of 16,600,000 wheat acres for the 1954 crop. Wheat farmers voted by more than 87 per cent to curtail production as Secretary Benson requested. Government support was therefore continued at 90 per cent of the parity price for wheat.

The government's agent in this price-support program is the Commodity Credit Corporation, a part of the Department of Agriculture. The CCC is capitalized at $100,000,000 and empowered to borrow up to $6,750 million to carry out its program of purchasing surplus commodities or making loans for curtailment of production. The CCC is required by law to support the prices of certain basic commodities, such as wheat and cotton, and to keep up the price of other products that the Secretary of Agriculture thinks need support. The Agriculture Act of 1954 replaced the fixed 90 per cent of

parity price support set in 1949 with a sliding support of from 75 per cent to 90 per cent.

There seems to be general agreement among Americans now that some sort of government support is necessary to assure the farmer an adequate income. Whether this support must use the parity-price formula is a matter of debate, but no better method has won general acceptance as yet. Farm experts and government men also argue whether the support should be fixed or flexible. Another part of the government's support program that is frequently criticized is the limitation of production. Many people feel there is something wrong with a system that must limit the production of basic foods when some Americans are hungry and millions of people throughout the world are starving. Others justify limitation of production in the interest of soil conservation but not as a means of maintaining high prices.

The NCRLC proposals to relieve the farmer. The National Catholic Rural Life Conference, at its 1954 convention, declared: "We regret to hear from many voices in this country a growing chorus of alarm over what is called 'surplus' production. We believe that the concern is misplaced. The real matter for alarm is that the 'surplus' is not recognized as a great blessing and a rare opportunity." The real problem, then, is not production but rather distribution. The National Catholic Rural Life Conference believes that the price-support program satisfies neither the farmer nor the consumer, and it is unjust to the consumer.

The NCRLC therefore proposes a new approach to solving the farmer's basic problem. It believes that a workable solution is a system of "carefully planned direct subsidies to farmers." Farmers would produce anything they liked and sell it in the open market for whatever price it would bring. The government would compute the parity price—as we

Agronomists and agricultural engineers at Cornell University, in co-operation with the Federal Agricultural Research Service, have developed a system of "mole drainage." This plow digs out underground tubes in a field for better drainage.

turn, they expect that the American people would be enriched by many articles and services imported into this country in payment for the farm exports. In criticism of this proposal, it may be said there would be danger of piling up still more surpluses, because world agricultural recovery since the end of World War II has drastically limited the American farmer's market. Other food-growing countries would not relish the dumping of United States products in *their* markets.

61. ADDITIONAL MEANS OF AUGMENTING FARM INCOME

Many farmers manage to operate their farms at a comfortable profit year after year. They have reduced the risks connected with agriculture to a minimum by intelligent planning and by using the various means at their disposal for operating their farms efficiently.

Scientific farming. Until about two centuries ago "scientific farming" consisted mainly of selective breeding and crop rotation. Modern developments in genetics and chemistry have enabled the farmer to enrich the soil, rotate crops, plow in order to retain moisture and prevent erosion; in short, to increase the yield per acre many times without impoverishing the soil. Research and experiment are the methods of developing better farming techniques. The individual farmer cannot afford expensive experiment or research, but the results of such work are available to him at little or no cost. Both the federal government and most states maintain experimental stations and conduct intensive research to improve farming. They supply the farmer with printed matter and, on occasion, send experts to help him with a difficult problem. They have perfected better seed, discovered effective methods of killing insects and pests, improved animals by scientific

have been discussing it—for each farm product. It would then pay the farmer in a direct subsidy, up to a certain limit, the difference between the market price he received and the parity price for that year. In that way the consumer would have to make only one additional payment for his food: the tax required for the subsidy. Now, of course, he has to pay the higher parity price for his food and still pay taxes to support the parity program. In other words, he is paying for crops that are not grown or are not consumed after having been raised.

This proposed solution of the farmer's basic problem involves an attitude toward world trade that we shall discuss later. Its proponents assume that surplus farm produce would be exported to markets where food is badly needed. In re-

The large farms, producers of three-fourths of the country's farm produce, employ machinery not found on small farms. This fleet of combines is shown in a Texas wheat field. (U.S.D.A.)

breeding, analyzed soils, and produced materials to enrich them.

Most states furnish technically trained experts to advise the farmer as to the quality of his soil and what crops he can best grow. Often it is the simple matter of plowing at the right depth for the crop to be grown on a particular farm, and according to the contour of the land.

Increased mechanization. We saw in Chapter 17 how machines had supplemented human labor on the farm in recent decades. The small farmer cannot own a combine, of course, but he can increase his efficiency by using various other mechanical devices, from the jeep to the milking machine and the electrically heated incubator. Mechanization increases the capital investment on a farm, of course, but the additional yield more than pays for the investment in machinery. Statistics show that, although it costs four dollars more an acre to grow corn now than it did thirty years ago, the increase in yield has reduced the production cost per bushel by one-third.

Suitable credit arrangements. The farmer with a poor piece of land finds himself in an apparently vicious circle: his land does not yield a crop profitable enough to enable him to buy the materials and equipment with which to improve it. And until he improves the soil, he will never enjoy a profitable year. The only way he can break out of this difficult position is to obtain credit with which to finance improvements. The credit must be on terms especially adapted to the farmer, however, because he does not earn a weekly wage with which he can pay back the loan in regular installments. Moreover, the possibility of crop failure makes the farmer a bad risk to the creditor who is

naturally inclined to demand high interest to cover the risk.

The problem of obtaining sufficient credit at low interest rates has been perennial with the American farmer. Let us look at his credit needs first—for they differ from the ordinary consumer's or industrialist's credit needs. The farmer needs three kinds of credit: (1) long-term —from ten to twenty years, (2) intermediate—from one to three years, and (3) short-term—less than a year. He needs long-term credit to buy his land, build his home, barns, and other permanent buildings. He must obtain this credit at a reasonably low rate of interest and on terms of repayment adjusted to his cash earnings, which for most farmers come when the major crop is marketed or livestock is sold. He needs intermediate credit to buy machinery, farm animals, fertilizer, and other capital improvements in the land. And he needs short-term credit for seeding and to provide him with sufficient funds to carry and market his crop.

The individual farmer is not in a position to obtain the credit he needs at the rate of interest he can afford to pay. Two methods have been followed to provide him with credit at a reasonable cost. The first method is through co-operative credit associations. These associations have worked most successfully in the comparatively prosperous farming localities where the individual farmers can pool their resources to obtain credit at low interest and on convenient terms.

Government-insured loans to the farmer. Government-insured loans are generally made in the poorer farming areas and in those rural communities in which co-operatives have not developed. A series of government measures, beginning with the Federal Reserve Act of 1913, makes credit available to the farmer at fairly low rates. This act made provision for the financing of short-term loans. The Federal Farm Loan Act of 1916 facilitated long-term credit by creating a National Farm Loan Association from which the farmer could borrow up to 50 per cent of the value of his farm and 20 per cent of the value of his permanent improvements. The debt is repaid in annual or semiannual payments, and it is carried at a low rate of interest (which varies with changing financial conditions).

The Federal Intermediate Credit Act of 1923 created twelve intermediate credit banks to assist local banks and co-operatives in granting the farmer loans of from six months to two years in duration. These basic farm-loan acts have been supplemented by loan provisions in various agricultural laws passed in the last twenty years. The farmer, whose credit needs were unscrupulously exploited in the nineteenth century, is now in a position to obtain needed credit at fair rates of interest.

Federal legislation has created a number of credit institutions to take care of the farmer's various needs. The Farm Credit Administration, a bureau in the Department of Agriculture, supervises most of these institutions. Production Credit Associations make short-term loans, especially to cover crop and livestock production and marketing. In 1953

The co-operative elevator associations assist the farmer in storing and marketing his crops. Crops are sampled and graded, as shown here, when they are delivered to the elevators. (U.S.D.A.)

they extended farmers more than $1,200,-000,000 in credit. Special banks were created by the Farm Credit Act of 1933 to lend money to farmers' co-operatives. The Farmers Home Administration was created in 1946 to "provide supervised credit for farmers who cannot get it elsewhere at adequate terms and under reasonable conditions." The credit problem seems about as well solved as it can be.

Co-operatives. We have already seen the important part co-operatives play in developing the rural community. Economically, they are important because they increase the farmer's purchasing power and they help him market his produce advantageously. Consumer co-operatives increase his purchasing power in two ways. First, they provide him with consumer goods at a low price and thereby enable him to buy more with his money. Second, they do something to keep other stores in line on prices, services, and quality of merchandise. Producer co-operatives perform the service of marketing which no single farmer has the capital and the facilities to do for himself.

Effective political organization. In the two-party system which we have in this country it is impossible for any single economic group to control a party. It is therefore necessary for each group, such as manufacturers, workingmen, and farmers, to have some agency to represent them to the parties and to the state and national legislatures. These lobby groups, as we shall see in a later chapter, present their points of view on various proposed bills to legislative committees and argue for or against legislation that will affect them.

Farmers are well represented by the National Grange, the American Farm Bureau Federation, and the Farmers' Union. The Grange, after its initial radical venture into politics, settled down to a conservative promotion of social and fraternal life among farmers. Its opinion is respected by congressional leaders and by legislatures in the agricultural states. The Bureau was not organized until 1919, but its membership has grown rapidly. In 1946 it passed the million mark, and at the present time it has more than one and a half million members.

Farmers need to be represented on more than issues that deal directly with agriculture. Tariffs, tax laws, labor laws, and all measures touching the national economy will have an important bearing on agricultural prosperity. A high tariff on manufactured goods always works to the disadvantage of the farmer because it tends to raise the price of goods he must buy without effecting a corresponding increase in agricultural prices. Farmers have an interest in seeing that tariffs do not discriminate against them. In similar fashion, failure to tax intangible wealth proportionately puts a larger burden on land and on income. The farmer is therefore interested in a tax bill that will burden him with no more than his share. Farmers also have an interest in legislation that will affect wages, for ultimately wages go into the cost of goods and are paid by the consumer.

Conclusion. By the very nature of our economy, farmers find themselves in a difficult position. They need continual government support and some measure of government control to avoid producing in a highly competitive market while buying in a restricted market. A greater measure of co-operation and more highly developed sense of common interest will enable farmers to forgo shortsighted gains for long-term security. Although farmers need cash income to live comfortably in modern America, nevertheless more attention to self-sufficiency would increase both the farmer's economic security and his social independence.

Any sound approach to the farm problem, it would seem, should seek to achieve the following objectives: (1) secure for the farmer an adequate stable income which is proportionate to the national income and adjustable to the changing price level; (2) give aid to low-income farmers and eventually enable them to achieve the equivalent of a living wage by improving or enlarging their holdings and increasing their efficiency by adopting new techniques and modern machinery; (3) pass on a fair proportion of the saving from increased efficiency to the consumer in the form of lower prices; (4) encourage the farmer to conserve and enrich the soil; (5) adjust production to changing habits in food and dress.

The most pressing of these objectives is relief to low-income farm families. More than one million families earn less than $1,000 a year in cash income. Much farming, like industry, is concentrated in the hands of a comparatively few big producers. Twenty-five per cent of the farmers in this country produce more than three-fourths of the farm product, and the remaining fourth is divided among middle-sized and small farmers. Agricultural experts advocate various measures, such as a progressive land tax, to discourage large-scale farming in favor of middle-sized farms. They also advocate educational measures and easy credit terms to enable the small farmer to enlarge his holdings and to work them more efficiently.

REVIEW

59. The Recurrent Problem of Farm Income

A. Why is the farmer's income a concern of the entire nation?

B. When did the farmer begin to have economic difficulties or problems? Why was the Grange movement started? How did it begin to achieve its purpose?

C. Why has the farmer always favored cheap money? What groups were organized to try to achieve this?

D. What new problems faced the farmer in the 1920s?

E. How did the New Deal try to solve these problems of the farmer? How did World War II affect the farmer? Why does he need government support?

60. The Farmer's Need for Government Support

A. How has the technological revolution affected the farmer and his farm?

B. What are "parity prices"? Why does the farmer want these? What problems do parity prices create?

C. How does the Commodity Credit Corporation work? What proposals have the National Catholic Rural Life Conference made to help the farmer?

61. Additional Means of Augmenting Farm Income

A. Describe present-day scientific farming. How does the government promote scientific farming?

B. Why does the farmer need credit? Describe the different types of credit for farmers. How has the government aided farm credit?

C. How are the farmers represented politically? What are some national problems in which the farmer has a vital concern?

THE CHAPTER IN REVIEW

A. Show why the farmer has the problems today that he did not have a hundred years ago.

B. Point out how the farmer has become more and more dependent upon the government since 1933.

C. List the basic objectives that must be found in a sound solution of the farm problem today.

SELECTED READINGS

The reading list for Chapter 17 applies to this chapter as well. In addition to that list,

the following works are helpful for the economic aspects of the farm problem.

A basic work is Earl O. Heady, *Economics of Agricultural Production and Resource Use* (New York: Prentice-Hall, Inc., 1952). A history of the development and the changes in agriculture is W. H. Clark, *Farms and Farmers* (Boston: L. C. Page & Co., 1945). Leland Fryer, *The American Farmer* (New York: Harper & Brothers, 1947), is a good discussion of the farmer's basic problems.

Louis Bromfield discusses the new scientific agriculture in *Out of the Earth* (New York: Harper & Brothers, 1950). A good discussion of a sound government farm policy is Benjamin L. Masse, "Farm Program for Abundance" *America* (February 5, 1955). The question of price support is debated in the special issue of *Senior Scholastic* devoted to "The American Farmer" (February 16, 1949).

Credit for farmers is explained in two pamphlets published by the Government Printing Office: *Farm Credit Instruments* (1951), and *ABC's of Credit for the Farm Family* (1950).

PROJECTS

1. Write a brief report contrasting farm life of 1850 with that of the present day. Indicate what the farmer of today must possess materially, intellectually, scientifically in order to run a successful farm.

2. Science has been able to make many uses of farm products as substitutes for other materials, and in the manufacture of plastics. A group in the class could find out some of the recent developments of scientific research with farm products and make a report on their findings to the class.

3. Imagine that you are a farmer. A bill is being proposed to end all government aid to farmers. Draft a letter to your congressman protesting this, stating your reasons.

Chapter 21. Conservation of Natural Resources

62. WASTE AND RESTORATION

A nation's wealth and power can be reduced to three elements: (1) its people, which are its greatest wealth; (2) its natural resources, the earth and its natural products, such as water, forests, minerals, and oil; (3) the wealth that people create by applying labor and human ingenuity to these natural resources—our agricultural and industrial goods. The greatness of a nation depends on the respect it has for its human and natural resources and on the intelligent use to which it puts them.

The earth was created by God for man's use and for his support. Coal and iron and oil are not buried in the earth to be kept from man. They are there for his use. But use and abuse are not the same thing. To waste our natural resources is to squander our wealth and invite national poverty in the future. Our problem, then, is to make intelligent, planned use of our natural resources so that we do not leave an impoverished country to our children. President Taft, an early leader in conservation work, defined it in these words: "Conservation is the preservation of our natural resources for economical use, so as to secure the greatest good to the largest number for the longest time."

A statement entitled "Man's Relation to the Land" was issued after two interdenominational meetings of Catholics, Protestants, and Jews in 1945. The statement reads, in part:

God created the world, of which the earth is a portion, with a purpose, and through His loving Providence He maintains the world for the good of human beings. Therefore, all human beings possess a direct natural right to have access to created natural resources. . . .

Land is a very special kind of property. Ownership of land does not give an absolute right to use or abuse, nor is it devoid of social responsibilities. It is in fact a stewardship. It implies such land tenure and use as to enable the possessor to develop his personality, maintain a decent standard of living for his family and fulfill social obligations. At the same time, the land steward has a duty to enrich the soil he tills and to hand it down to future generations as a thank offering to God, the Giver, and as a loving inheritance to his children's children. . . .

Efficiency in land use is not to be judged by material production but by a balanced consideration of the spiritual, social, and material values that redound therefrom to person, family, and society.

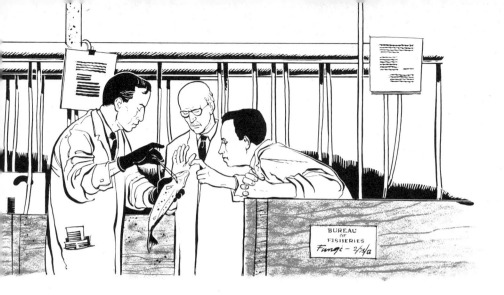

Natural resources differ with regard to their use. Some can be used without being destroyed. Soil and trees, like air and water, can be used generation after generation without loss if each generation is careful to replenish what it takes out of the soils and the forests of the land. Other resources are limited in quantity and are destroyed when used. There are only so many billion tons of coal remaining in the earth. Each ton burned means one less ton left. New coal beds may be found, but the supply is limited at some definite amount. So it is with oil and stone and the various minerals.

Sound conservation practice in regard to each item of natural wealth depends on three things: (1) whether it is replenishable; (2) if it is not, what is the estimated remaining amount and how much must be used annually in a reasonably plentiful economy; (3) whether substitutes can be developed without injuring our economy, as oil and natural gas have largely replaced coal, and as it is likely that atomic energy will be used commercially within twenty or thirty years.

From wealth to scarcity. The pages of history tell of the ruins of once great nations that declined because they abused their human and their natural resources. North Africa was once fertile land, the granary of the Roman Empire, but failure of rainfall, destruction of forests, and human neglect turned this land into a desert. Centuries of intensive farming have impoverished the soils of China and India and have intensified the problem of poverty and even of starvation in those two lands. Exploitation of the land and its resources has been one of the consistent causes of the decline and ruin of great empires.

This same pattern of exploitation was followed in this country until recently. The story is well known by everyone who has studied American history: how the early settlers found a rich land waiting to be used, how they cleared the forests for farms, how they raised crops with no thought to the future, and how when they had impoverished one plot of land they moved on to a fresh one. This exploitation for immediate profit occurred in farming, in the lumber industry, in mining, in petroleum, and in wildlife.

The result is that in a century and a half our ancestors destroyed much of our natural wealth. It is estimated that almost a fourth of our good agricultural land has been destroyed beyond restoration. Another fourth has been so badly damaged that it will take a generation of careful conservation work to restore it to its original fertility. The remaining half was saved by our realization of how rapidly we were destroying our natural heritage. A few early leaders, notably Washington and Jefferson, understood that Americans were destroying their natural resources. "Our lands were originally very good," Washington wrote to a friend, "but use and abuse have made them quite otherwise. . . . We ruin lands that are already cleared and either cut down more wood, if we have it, or emigrate into the Western Country."

The successful movement toward conservation was begun by Theodore Roosevelt early in this century when it became apparent to all that there was a limit to our natural resources. Conservationists have succeeded in getting through their message to American farmers and to most of the urban public as well. We can say, therefore, that the problem of soil conservation is more a problem of ways and means to accomplish the program than of deciding to make the effort. It is to the farmer's interest to save the soil from which he earns his livelihood, and he is therefore happy to co-operate with such government agencies as the Soil Conservation Service and the Bureau of Reclamation.

Not all people are agreed on the need for conservation practices with our other resources. Some government experts predict a critical shortage of domestically produced oil within twenty years. Many oilmen, on the other hand, insist there is no foreseeable shortage for centuries to come. In similar fashion, some lumber cutters insist there is no conservation problem in regard to our forests, whereas most government specialists demand stringent laws to regulate lumbering practices. Harnessing our water power and controlling floods raise still other problems: the national government would more naturally assume responsibility in the latter case, but opinion is divided on the water-power question. Let us briefly outline some of the main problems that challenge our conservation program in the middle of the twentieth century.

Saving the soil. Soil conservation involves the double task of reclaiming eroded or impoverished soil and preventing erosion or impoverishment of soil that is still fertile. Over half our cropland suffers from erosion, and perhaps one-fifth of it is ruined beyond repair. Each day, it is estimated, enough soil is eroded from our fields by wind and water to make a farm of eight thousand acres. Put in other terms, as a nation we suffer a loss of three to four billion dollars a year from soil erosion.

Erosion is caused by wind or water taking away the fertile topsoil and depositing it as silt in river bottoms or blowing it onto other lands. When the protective covering of trees and plants has been stripped off the land it is unable to absorb rainfall or to resist damaging winds.

Mistaken practices that leave the soil subject to erosion must be corrected. One-crop farming without adequate fertilization weakens the soil. Overgrazing of pasture land strips the land of its protective grass. Indiscriminate cutting of woodland destroys the land's best cover and cuts down nature's most effective windbreak. Indiscriminate planting of certain crops, such as corn or beans, which require open soil around the stalk, bares the soil to washouts from heavy and sudden rains.

Soil-conservation practices seek to prevent these abuses and to enrich a weakened soil. The preventive measures are the following:

1. Crop rotation to preserve the soil's plant food. (Each plant takes different elements of nourishment from the soil, and some plants put certain elements back.)

2. Strip-cropping to tie down the soil and hold water—planting alternate rows of ground-covering crops like alfalfa or clover between rows of ground-exposing crops like corn or beans.

3. Contour-plowing to prevent water wash-

ing topsoil downhill—terracing of the hillside to hold water, and plowing according to the contour of the land to guide the water to prepared outlets.

4. Planting winter crops to bind down the soil and protect it from wind erosion and from springtime washouts.

5. Planting tree windbreaks to cut the sweep of the wind.

6. Building waterways to guide off excess water and to prevent gullying.

Soil building consists of putting into the soil the food that plants take from it. Fertilizers are either natural material, such as soybeans that are plowed under to nourish the soil, or artificially prepared chemical matter. Different soils lack different elements, depending on locality and crops. Government technicians will analyze the soil of a locality to determine what it needs to produce a certain crop profitably. Fertilizer is one of the farmer's largest items of expense, but farmers realize that failure to use it will not only cut the size of their crops but impoverish their soil permanently. Another method of soil building is to improve its composition. Some soil is too sandy and some is too hard. In either case, the soil is not productive, and it is subject to erosion because it does not absorb rainfall well. Technological developments since World War II give promise that new chemicals may enable the farmer to reclaim poor soil, thus increasing its productivity and protecting it from erosion.

The role of federal agencies in soil conservation. Both the national and state governments have taken an active part in soil-conservation practices in the last twenty years. The conservation program of Theodore Roosevelt and Gifford Pinchot almost fifty years ago was directed mainly at preserving wildlife and forests. But the terrible dust storms of the depression era (1931–1937) made the farmer in Maine and the clerk in Philadelphia realize that a formerly fertile part of this country was turning into a vast desert. Public opinion

This abandoned farmstead in Baca County, Colo., stands in ruins from blasting winds which have shifted topsoil from the fields to cover the house and barns. The old turning plow in the foreground was left at the end of a row in the field. (U.S.D.A.)

urged national action to reclaim the "Dust Bowl" for productive farming.

In 1935 Congress created the Soil Conservation Service to co-ordinate soil- and water-conservation work and to advise farmers on conservation practices. At President Roosevelt's suggestion the various states enacted soil-conservation measures, and by 1947 every state had set up some kind of program to deal with the problem. The federal government has divided the country into soil-conservation districts which will soon include every farm and ranch in the country. In 1950 there were 2,285 districts including 1,253 million acres of land, and in 1953 there were 2,549 districts taking care of 1,404 million acres.

The Soil Conservation Service prepares land maps to include all data needed for farm planning and watershed protection. Its experts show farmers how to strip-plant, contour-plow, and practice other soil-conservation measures. They prepare conservation plans for groups of farmers who agree to co-operate in irrigation, drainage, and general erosion

A soil scientist makes notes on an aerial map as he takes inventory of the land to see for what purpose the soil is best suited. This soil map, when completed, is the basis for soil planning. (U.S.D.A.)

control. They also conduct experiments on about seven million acres of submarginal land the Service owns and is treating. They have experimented with seeding over burned-out forest areas and in developing other methods of soil and water conservation.

Several other federal agencies co-operate with the Soil Conservation Service in protecting the land. The Forest Service, as we shall see, plants trees for windbreaks and to maintain our watersheds. The Farm Security Administration and the Agricultural Adjustment Agency encourage soil-conservation practices by the farmers in their programs of crop control and incentive payments. The Federal Extension Service educates farmers in the latest techniques of farming, many of which are concerned with soil conservation.

The problem of soil conservation, then, is one that has been fairly well solved. It is necessary to educate each new generation in conservation practices, however, to continue to improve methods by experiment and research, and to maintain consistent support from Congress and the state legislatures.

Flood control is closely linked to soil conservation. The danger of floods is diminished when the soil is able to soak up rainfall. But we must always provide for means of controlling excess water. Water is a powerful servant, as any hydroelectric plant proves, but it is a terrible destroyer when it breaks out of control—as spring floods throughout the country show every year. Water keeps us clean and slakes our thirst. It nourishes our crops and keeps the land green. It runs our factories and keeps our lights burning. It serves as an inexpensive means of transportation. But when it gets out of control it washes away farms, tears out bridges and destroys roads, clogs up rivers and inundates cities at the cost of millions of dollars and hundreds of lives. Control of our water resources is therefore a most important means of promoting our national welfare.

Conservation of water resources involves many interrelated problems. Maintaining reserves to irrigate lands that do not receive enough rainfall is part of any water-control program. Sufficient water must be available for each urban community, for consumption, for domestic sanitation, and for industrial uses. Control of water erosion involves a system of ditches and canals to lead water harmlessly into rivers. The dredging of silted rivers is required to make them navigable. Dams are required for flood control and to furnish hydroelectric power in great quantities each year.

Some of these problems are fairly easily solved. Most cities in the country have an adequate reservoir system to maintain sufficient water in reserve for the city's use. With some cities, however, this is a continual and a pressing problem. Cities located in arid areas usually restrict the consumption of water to essential uses in the dry seasons. Purification of the water is satisfactorily done in almost all cities by the use of sedimentation tanks, by filtration, and by disinfection. In rural areas the water problem can be satisfactorily handled in most areas by careful planning. The use of septic tanks has become quite general in the last ten years to prevent pollution of the water supply. Increased consumption of water and several dry seasons have created a shortage of underground water in many localities. When artesian wells dry up, water must be supplied from another source—a problem that can usually be solved, but frequently at great expense to the individual person or the local community.

The Tennessee Valley Authority. Providing for water reserves, flood control, irrigation systems, and the control of water power are interrelated problems that seem to require a general and comprehensive solution. The notable example of such an attempted solution is the Tennessee Valley Authority (TVA) set up in 1933 to harness the waters of the Tennessee River and its tributaries, control its floods, provide for its navigation, and furnish the inhabitants in this area with electric power. The accomplishments of the TVA are impressive. It has reduced flood damage and saved inhabitants in its region millions of dollars. It produces billions of kilowatt hours of electric energy so that the use of electricity in the TVA area has increased about eighty-fold. It has also produced a million tons of fertilizer, developed improved methods of drying hay and grain, studied problems of community planning, and contracted for various other services.

There is considerable argument as to whether the accomplishments of the TVA are purchased at too high a price. The opponents of the TVA argue that any such government-owned enterprise spends the taxpayers' money to compete unfairly with private enterprise. The TVA can operate at a loss, they point out, and have its deficiencies made up by congressional appropriations. They also argue that the work done by the TVA belongs, in our American system, to private enterprise and to local government. The manufacture of electric power and of fertilizers, for example, is best done in our economy by private ownership; flood control and irrigation projects, again, should not be imposed on people by national bureaucrats but should come from locally controlled government agencies.

Supporters of the TVA claim regional control of water resources is logically a federal project because it always includes several states. Anything less than a unified system for an entire river system, they insist, is ineffective as a means of

The havoc wrought by a flood is shown in this aerial view of the city of Hannibal, Mo., as the flood waters of the Mississippi engulfed it. Disasters such as this can be prevented or at least minimized by proper forest controls and the building of dams. (U. S. Weather Bureau)

flood control and cannot guarantee adequate irrigation or sufficient hydroelectric power. Finally, backers of the TVA point to the corporation's record to show that it has consistently co-operated with local people and that community participation in its projects has always been enthusiastic. They advocate setting up similar projects in each of our great valley basins—such as a Missouri Valley Authority, a Columbia Valley Authority, and an Ohio Valley Authority.

There seems to be general agreement that the federal and state governments should build dams for flood control. Ultimately this would involve a series of dams in the upper waters of each valley system to control the seasonal release of water on each watershed. But is it wise to build a dam for flood-control purposes alone? Why not at the same time provide for power development, irrigation, and navigation? Many people believe that a government which does all these things is encroaching on the right of individuals to do such things themselves. Others claim it is the government's duty to promote the people's material welfare as the TVA has done.

Maintaining our forests. The commercial need for wood must be balanced against the conservationist need for standing trees in order to satisfy both requirements as well as possible without causing either to suffer irreparably. We have already seen how forests are necessary to prevent soil erosion and to control floods. The need for cut lumber increases annually. In 1940 we used twenty-nine billion board feet of lumber. In 1950 we used thirty-eight billion board feet, and the Forest Service estimates that we shall need at least forty-two billion a year in the future.

American pioneers and after them commercial lumbermen cut down our forests recklessly. Instead of selective cutting, they cut forests clean; the pioneer to clear a tract for his farm, the lumbermen to get the quickest profit. By 1909 less than half our original timber land was left. Forest fires and continued overcutting of the timber supply have reduced the stock each year. Fire destroyed twenty-three million acres of forest in 1940, fifteen million acres in 1945, and seven and a half million acres in 1950. Meanwhile, the Forest Service reported, we are cutting more than eighteen and a half billion board feet more than is being replaced by new growth each year. Wood supply is short the world over, so we cannot depend on foreign sources to make up for our domestic shortage of wood. We must find ways and means of replenishing our own supply and handling it with sound conservation methods in the future.

Poor cutting practices create an unnecessary tree shortage. When lumbermen

The Grand Coulee Dam is shown here with its pumping plant, discharge pipes, feeder canal, north dam, and lake forming in the Upper Grand Coulee equalizing reservoir. The aim of this series of dams is to control the upper waters of each valley system to eliminate the seasonal releases of water upon the valley below. (Bureau of Reclamation)

cut a plot clean by stripping off every tree, they make it impossible for nature to produce a second growth on the land. The Forest Service tells us that 64 per cent of the loggers employ poor cutting practices—cutting seed trees or spoiling trees by dragging chains against them.

Forest-conservation methods have been perfected in the last twenty-five years to such a degree that there is no need to deplete our forest reserves to obtain the wood we need. The Norris-Doxey Act of 1937 and Cooperative Forest Management Act of 1950 furnish expert help to small operators to put their woods on a permanent yield basis by selective cutting. These acts provide technical services and expert advice on the management of forest lands and the cutting, marketing, and processing of forest products. In this way the amount cut is kept equal to the new growth so that the forest sustains itself. Tree planting is now being done at an increased rate. About 150,000 acres are planted annually, and that amount must be increased many times if we want to reforest our denuded lands.

Adequate fire protection is another important forest-conservation measure. It is estimated that 90 per cent of the forest fires are caused by negligence. With vigilant observation by means of watchtowers and helicopters, fires can be put out before they do extensive damage. In 1952 only 58,000,000 acres of forest land out of a total of 270,000,000 acres were unprotected by adequate forest-fire service. Over 7,500,000 acres of unprotected forest lands (13 per cent) were burned out, and only 281,000 acres (about one tenth of 1 per cent!) of protected lands were lost by fire. The cost of fire protection is saved many times over by the prevention of a single forest fire.

No one objects to tree planting as a conservation method, but some commercial lumbermen refuse to adopt a program of selective cutting. They are inter-

The approved method of cutting Douglas fir trees results in open, clear-cut blocks which will be reseeded by the green timber surrounding them. This system of harvesting is recognized by both private industry and government agencies as the best means of forest conservation.

ested in immediate profits, and selective cutting is both more difficult and more expensive than cutting a plot bare. Some commercial lumbermen defend their logging practices on the grounds that the supply of trees in this country is inexhaustible. Most lumbermen, however, admit that compulsory conservation methods are needed because some companies and individuals will always slash into forests for quick profits.

Lumbermen generally prefer state rather than federal regulations on cutting practices. Advocates of federal legislation propose that when a company decides to cut a plot it be required to have an expert from the Forest Service mark the trees which sound conservation practice allows to be cut. The government's right to regulate cutting practices in privately owned forest lands is undeniable, because bad cutting causes soil erosion and floods, and it depletes our forest reserve. If voluntary action or state regulation is not clearly effective, then the federal government has the unmistakable duty of taking action to protect our remaining forest reserves.

The practice of selective cutting—felling only full-grown trees—is one of the most important methods of forest conservation. Here a forest ranger measures the girth of a ponderosa pine which has been marked for cutting. (U.S.D.A.)

64. OIL, COAL, AND OTHER MINERALS

So far we have been discussing resources that are replenishable—soil, water, and trees—but now we are concerned with a form of natural wealth that is limited in amount. A barrel of oil pumped from a well and consumed as fuel is one less barrel in our oil stock. America runs on oil. Our industrial efficiency and our military power are built on oil. We use it for fuel, lubrication, asphalt, the preparation of synthetic rubber and other products, for cleaning fluids and medicinal products. Substitutions for oil can be employed for many things, such as heating fuel, but no other material is an adequate substitute for oil as a lubricant.

Consumption and production of oil. Consumption of oil in this country has increased by leaps and bounds since World War I. In 1950 we used almost six and a half million barrels of crude oil a day, an increase of 11 per cent over the previous year. This increase continued, and a new record for the consumption of oil was set each year. Increased industrial production was one reason for our consuming more oil. Moreover, many more trucks, buses, and automobiles are on the road. More machines are used on the farms. Many industrial plants and private homes have converted from coal to oil to obtain cleaner, more even, and—in some localities—less expensive heat. These in-

creased uses of oil put our economy in a precarious position. An end of our oil supply, or a sharp reduction of the annual supply, would stall our machine economy.

Oil production, however, has kept pace with increased demand. Dire estimates have been made in the past as to the amount of our national oil reserve. If they had been right we would long since have used up our last barrel of oil. But they have been revised annually on the basis of newly discovered fields and more efficient methods of extraction and refinement. Both the amount of production and the proved reserve have increased annually. A little less than two billion barrels were produced in 1950. In 1951 the figure had risen to two and a quarter billion barrels, and in 1952 it had increased another forty-two million barrels. Meanwhile the proved oil reserve in 1952 was almost twenty-eight billion barrels, an increase of half a billion over the previous year.

The amount of oil in our national reserve is limited, although we do not know what the amount is. We know that the pessimistic estimates of the past have been belied by recent discoveries. But we also know that the oil industry has been operating on a policy that is not to the best national interest. The Temporary National Economic Committee estimated in 1939 that the supply of petroleum in this country would be exhausted in thirteen years. Such an estimate has proved wrong. TNEC hearings found the oil industry's policy to be: to keep crude oil flowing to consumers at low prices as long as possible, to encourage its wide use without imposing arbitrary restraints, and to rely upon the technological ingenuity of future generations to solve the inevitable problems of scarcity and higher prices. Such a policy is unsound—as unsound as your parents would be if they spent all their earnings on the assumption that you could raise and educate yourselves.

Sound policy lies in a proper adjustment between current demand and future needs. Estimates of future oil supply must consider the probability of additional discoveries of domestic fields, including tideland oil deposits. Also to be considered are imports from foreign sources and the possibility of producing oil synthetically. Concerning oil production, certain facts must be borne in mind. New fields produce large quantities of oil and natural gas. As they are worked for a time, they grow old or "tired" and produce a small quantity daily and, eventually, the fields run out. Improved methods increase production in two ways: by extracting a greater percentage of the deposit (e.g., using air or water pressure to pump oil out of a well when the natural gas pressure has fallen) and by eliminating waste in the conversion and refining processes (e.g., constructing leak-proof and evaporation-proof pipe lines and storage tanks.

Everyone interested in the oil problem seems agreed that production should be efficient and that waste should be eliminated. Men in the oil industry are satisfied that they have done a remarkable production job in the past, and they feel that they can do an even better job in the future. They are opposed to government regulation of the oil industry on the grounds that a young and changing industry needs the utmost freedom to develop. They are also opposed to government-sponsored imports of foreign oil and to the government's development of a synthetic-oil industry. Their opposition is justified, they say, on the grounds that they are producing all the oil we need each year and synthetic oil is too expensive for industrial or domestic use.

Those who fear that increased oil consumption will soon exhaust our proved and even our potential reserve advocate three lines of action. (1) They believe the government should conduct foreign trade arrangements to give preference to the importing of oil from the large sources in the Middle East and the Caribbean area, especially Venezuela. As we shall see in a later chapter, this is a complicated matter of foreign relations, but it certainly merits serious consideration. (2) They urge the government to sponsor research in synthetic-oil production as a source of oil especially in time of war, when we cannot rely on foreign sources of supply. Experimental plants to make oil out of coal and shale have been established in Louisiana, Mo., and Rifle, Colo., but at the present time they are expensive to operate as compared to the processes of refining natural oil. (3) They insist on a number of conservation practices in the production and consumption of oil.

Oil-conservation practices. Regarding the production of oil, good conservation practices include: (1) the limiting and spacing of wells in any given area to be drilled (to prevent the rapid depletion of an oil pool, making it uneconomical to extract the last portion of the pool, since too many wells are in operation and thus run up the expense of extraction); (2) improving prospecting methods to eliminate "wildcat" or exploratory drilling, which runs up the cost of production; (3) regulating the amount of gas that can be produced with each barrel of oil (the gas loss in California was thus cut from 40 to 60 per cent in five years); (4) improving

This oil well is situated seven miles offshore in the Gulf of Mexico, has quarters, storerooms, storage tanks, and all necessary facilities for maintenance. The oil is taken off by barges and brought to the mainland. (Standard Oil Co., N.J.)

methods to extract the entire oil pool in a field, such as using gas or water pressure; (5) promoting unit operation, whereby the various producers over a given oil pool combine their interests to develop the field co-operatively. (Thus they reduce expenses and increase oil recovery by as much as 30 per cent.)

Regarding the consumption of oil, good conservation practices include: (1) encouraging the use of substitutes for oil wherever practical, such as using coal instead of oil for heating purposes; (2) promoting agreement among the big oil companies not to "sell" oil to consumers for every purpose but to reserve it for more essential uses; (3) fixing an annual quota, which should be reasonable, for the domestic consumption of oil products; (4) eliminating waste in the transportation and consumption of oil products by developing such things as more efficient furnace burners and automobile motors.

Conservationists find the biggest problem is to convince the American public and the oil industry that the production of large quantities of oil at a low price endangers our economy and defense potential of the future. Accurate statistics are lacking on which to base any calculation of when our reserve will be exhausted. In each case the attempt to calculate future reserves is met with un-

known or intangible factors which defy precise conclusions. Nevertheless, prudence would seem to dictate as careful a daily consumption of our oil reserve as is compatible with a healthy, productive economy that meets both reasonable domestic and military demands.

Conserving our coal and mineral reserves. Like oil, coal has many uses. It is one of our chief sources of heat and power, of course, but it is also the base material from which such things as lipstick, perfume, and nylon stockings are made. There are two kinds of coal: anthracite or hard coal, and bituminous or soft coal. Anthracite coal is found only in a small area in Pennsylvania, but bituminous coal is found in many places throughout the country, especially in the Appalachians and the Rockies and in such midwestern states as Illinois and Kentucky.

In our changing economy oil and hydroelectric power are replacing coal as a source of heat and power. The annual consumption of coal has remained more or less constant throughout the last sixty years, whereas the annual consumption of oil and natural gas has multiplied many times in the same period. At the present rate of use our coal reserves will last several thousand years. Conservation practices are prudent, nevertheless, because much of our reserve is inferior coal and difficult to extract. Methods of mining and transporting coal have been devised to eliminate waste. Improved furnaces and stokers have reduced combustion loss, and more efficient smelter, engine, and boiler designs have increased the efficiency of coal as a source of heat and power.

The "coal problem" is not, strictly speaking, a problem of conservation. It is rather the problem of the coal industry's competing with more efficient sources of power, petroleum and natural gas. Continued research and continual application of new techniques can do something to increase efficiency in the production and use of coal, but present indications are that coal will play a less important part in our economy than it has in the past.

As for other mineral resources—iron, aluminum, cobalt, uranium, granite, tungsten, and the like—each involves its own set of problems. Here we have space to suggest only a few problems common to many of them. Some minerals are in large supply, such as iron and sulphur, and the chief problems in their regard are those of efficient production, elimination of waste, use of by-products, and development of a larger market. Others are in short supply. The chief problem, especially in the case of tin and nickel, is to make favorable trade arrangements with the countries controlling the principal source of the world's supply of each metal. Some metals we need in large amounts, like tin and aluminum, and others we need only in small quantity, such as manganese and zinc. Most metals are essential for our maintaining a strong economy and defense program. Molybdenum, for example, is used to temper steel. Great quantities are not required, but our economy and our defense efforts would be seriously impaired if the supply of molybdenum were suddenly cut off.

Conclusion. Certain general conclusions can be stated about our natural resources.

They are God-given wealth intended for our use, but they are not to be squandered for quick profit. Future needs should always be balanced against immediate demand. Common sense dictates continual improvement in method of production and use of each resource so that waste is reduced to a minimum and efficiency is increased. Research should be undertaken to find possible substitutes for each material that might be soon exhausted or become so scarce as to be uneconomical to mine. Natural resources of foreign countries, such as tin or oil in the Middle East, should enter into our considerations in foreign relations. The United States has been richly endowed by God with natural wealth, but no country can

One of the principal ways of conserving oil is by proper transportation. A striking contrast is presented between the picture above of flatboats on Oil Creek, Pa., laden with barrels of oil (1861) and the picture below of a modern cross-state pipe line in Montana (1955). (Drake Museum; Standard Oil Co., N.J.)

maintain the high standard of living we enjoy without a large foreign trade.

Tremendous increases in production since 1914 have caused this country to use up more of certain basic raw materials than were consumed by all mankind throughout recorded history before 1914. There is every reason for us to expect annual increases in our need for raw materials in the future. It therefore is prudent to use our natural resources carefully, to avoid waste and get-rich-quick schemes, and finally to restore what we use of such natural resources as soil, forests, and water power.

REVIEW

62. Waste and Restoration

A. Why must we conserve our natural resources? What responsibilities has an owner of land in this regard?

B. In regard to our natural resources, what three principles should we keep in mind when we use them? Cite some lands where resources have been ruined. What did our early settlers do concerning conservation?

C. Who was the leader of the conservation movement? How has the soil of our country been harmed? How can we prevent this in the future, and in fact improve our soil?

D. Briefly describe the federal government's role in conservation during the last twenty-five years.

63. Water and Forests

A. How is flood control related to soil conservation?

B. Describe the aims, functions, and accomplishments of the Tennessee Valley Authority. Give some of the criticisms leveled against it.

C. Why is there a need for preserving our forests? List several ways our forests have been heedlessly ruined. How has the government aided forest conservation? Why has fire protection proved so beneficial?

64. Oil, Coal, and Other Minerals

A. Account for the increase of oil production in this century. Why does the oil industry object to government regulation?

B. Give some ways in which production and consumption of oil can be safeguarded.

C. What is the "coal problem"? What conservation problem is common to all minerals?

D. What basic ideas must a good citizen have concerning our natural resources?

THE CHAPTER IN REVIEW

A. Why is there a need today for conservation? How was this need brought about?

B. Discuss the advantages and disadvantages of the Tennessee Valley Authority. Could the benefits be achieved in other ways?

C. Show the importance of conservation in regard to forests and minerals. What has the government done concerning these?

SELECTED READINGS

There have been thousands of books and articles written on the conservation of natural resources since Theodore Roosevelt and Gifford Pinchot focused the nation's attention on the problem early in this century. Here we shall list (1) some of the later general works on American natural resources and their conservation, and then a few special treatments on (2) soil conservation, (3) forests, (4) oil, and (5) the TVA and similar proposed projects.

1. Axel F. Gustafson and Associates, *Conservation in the United States* (Ithaca, N.Y.: Comstock Publishing Associates, 1949); Guy Harold Smith (editor), *Conservation of National Resources* (New York: John Wiley & Sons, Inc., 1950); S. V. Ciriacy-Wantrup, *Resource Conservation* (Berkeley, Calif.: University of California Press, 1952); and Henry B. Wales and H. O. Lathrop, *The Conservation of Natural Resources* (Chicago: Laurel Book Company, 1947). These books are all by strong advocates of conservation. They include a chapter or two on the way Americans squandered their natural resources and how conser-

vation began; then they devote a chapter to each of the major forms of conservation. The subject is well summed up by Bill Reiche, "Uncle Sam Weighs His Resources," *Popular Mechanics* (March 1948).

2. Hugh H. Bennett, *Elements of Soil Conservation* (New York: McGraw-Hill Book Co., 1947), by the former chief of the Soil Conservation Service; W. Van Dersal and E. H. Graham, *The Land Renewed* (New York: Oxford University Press, Inc., 1946), a pictorial exposition of soil conservation. Constructive suggestions are made by Louis Bromfield, "We Don't Have to Starve," *Atlantic Monthly* (July 1949); and Herbert L. Marx, Jr., describes the work of the Soil Conservation Service in "Saving Our Soil," *Senior Scholastic* (November 9, 1949).

3. Conservation of forests is the principal subject covered in Edward G. Cheyney and Thorvald Schantz-Hansen, *This Is Our Land* (St. Paul: The Webb Publishing Co., 1946), and Martha S. B. Bruere, *Your Forests* (Philadelphia: J. B. Lippincott Co., 1945). *Life* (November 3, 1947) has a good editorial treatment of "The Vanishing Forest" and suggests a program for conserving the remaining forest areas of the country.

4. Oil conservation today involves the problem of tidelands oil deposits and whether their ownership is vested in the national government or in the states. This problem is discussed from the historical and legal point of view by Ernest R. Bartley, *The Tidelands Oil Controversy* (Austin, Tex.: University of Texas Press, 1953), and by J. Wraight, "Geography of Tidelands Oil," *Social Order* (April 1953). The amount of Tidelands oil is described in "Race for Undersea Oil Riches," *United States News and World Report* (May 7, 1948). Various aspects of the oil problem are discussed in a series of articles in *Senior Scholastic* (January 12, 1948). North Bibee, "Why We aren't Running Short of Oil," *Reader's Digest* (January 1950), explains how improved methods have saved billions of barrels of oil.

5. The classic defense of the TVA is the book by its former head, David E. Lilienthal, *TVA: Democracy on the March* (New York: Harper & Brothers, 1944). Both sides of the question are examined by Carl J. Armbruster, S.J., "TVA: Blight or Blessing?", *Social Order* (May 1954), and in the Reference Shelf volume for debaters edited by Walter M. Daniels, *Should We Have More TVA's?* (New York: H. W. Wilson Co., 1950). The latter work discusses not only the TVA but also the pros and cons of

Columbia Valley, Missouri Valley, and St. Lawrence Seaway projects. Arguments for and against such projects are condensed in "More Authorities for Our River Valleys?", *Senior Scholastic* (May 4, 1949).

PROJECTS

1. We must be well aware of conservation in our daily lives. Each class member could list three ways in which he as a high school student can aid conservation.

2. Our nation has been blessed with many natural resources. Make a chart, indicating the extent of our resources in contrast with the world's total supply of the items. You could include such items as lumber, oil, coal, and precious minerals.

3. We must realize how much we are dependent on our resources. For example, study the part the forest plays in our daily lives. What limitations and additional expenses would be placed on our industry if our forests no longer existed?

PROFILES

ANDREW CARNEGIE

BORN: Dunfermline, Scotland, November 25, 1835
EDUCATION: Primary schooling in Scotland
DIED: Lenox, Mass. August 11, 1919

Carnegie was the son of an impoverished Scottish weaver whose hand-loom business was ruined when steam power was applied to the textile industry in the early nineteenth century.

The family emigrated to America, and a very youthful Andrew Carnegie entered American industry as a plant helper. Probably the turning point of his career came with a change of employment, when he became a telegraph messenger.

Eager to improve himself, Carnegie changed his position and became a telegraph operator. Carnegie later left the telegraph company for employment with the Pennsylvania Railroad, just as railroads were beginning to pay serious attention to communications. His on-the-job training and experience, plus his ability to organize and exploit opportunities earned him assignments as train dispatcher and later as superintendent of the Pittsburgh Division. Even at these relatively early stages of his career Carnegie made shrewd investments, putting money into industries that were beginning to show promise: sleeping-car manufacture and oil extraction, both closely related to his railroad interests.

The Civil War opened a great opportunity to show his talents for industrial organization and wise investment. After a period of service to the Union as a director of eastern military railroads, Carnegie left government and direct railroad service in 1862 to organize his first company, the Keystone Bridge Company. He had observed experiments with iron railroad bridges, and his company began to specialize in these structures, which he correctly forecast would be in great demand. Step by step, he proceeded to organize a massive steel empire, building or buying control of iron furnaces, rolling mills, and Bessemer steel plants. Eventually he sold his interests for $500,000,000 to United States Steel, organized by J. P. Morgan especially to buy him out, and retired to supervise the philanthropic disposition of his capital.

Carnegie is practically the model of a "rugged individual" corporation head: he opposed combinations of labor, would not recognize unions, and operated at all times to secure his own company's maximum profits; he drove competing firms out of business and used every device to corner the markets in his commodities. All these measures, and the general philosophy to defend this attitude of extreme individualism and the amassing and distribution of wealth, he summed up in a series of books, the most famous of which was *The Gospel of Wealth*.

A readable biography that will hold the interest of high school students is Burton J. Hendrick's *Life of Andrew Carnegie* (New York: Doubleday & Co., Inc., 1932). *Social Darwin-ism in American Thought, 1860–1915* (Philadelphia: University of Pennsylvania Press, 1944), by Richard Hofstadter, is a challenging book that discusses the notion of the survival of the fittest in economics, government, and society in general, a pattern which Carnegie fitted very well.

SAMUEL GOMPERS

BORN: London, January 27, 1850
EDUCATION: Primary schooling only
DIED: San Antonio, Texas, December 13, 1924

One of the most important labor leaders in world history, Samuel Gompers arrived in the United States at the age of thirteen to begin his career in American labor as a poorly paid helper. Eventually he developed sufficient skill to qualify as a full-fledged cigar maker. Ordinary labor experience, however, was not to be his future: he was vitally interested in his union's activities.

By 1877, Gompers was so esteemed by fellow unionists that they elected him president of the cigar makers' union, which was then very much concerned in the general problems of organization that were confronting American labor. Foremost among these problems was the question of whether labor unions should be made up of men who did similar work or simply be associations of all workingmen in a given area. The Knights of Labor, a widespread and widely publicized organization, stood for organization to include all workers, regardless of craft or trade.

Gompers, however, led his cigar makers into a new organization, the Federation of Organized Trades and Labor Unions, in 1881. He was himself one of the chief organizers of this Federation, which later changed its name to the American Federation of Labor. The chief idea behind the organizational structure of the Federation was to encourage the development of unions of men in like employment, with similar interests and objectives. The Federation itself would serve as a mutual-support unit, which would solve organizational problems that might arise, co-ordinate joint drives and programs, and assist individual unions whenever possible. After a brief period of exploring organizational techniques, the AFL dominated organized labor. Gompers served as its president every year but one from 1886 to his death in 1924.

Gompers' unique contributions to the cause of labor were along the lines of guiding policy into moderate lines, choosing objectives that were generally within labor's reach, and methodically pursuing them until they were accomplished. Among his organization's chief accomplishments was the drive to eliminate sources of labor that would depress general wage levels: he favored limitation of immigrant labor, an extended compulsory school law, and elimination of convict-labor products from the market. At all times Gompers was careful to steer the AFL clear of anti-capitalist movements and clear of commitment to any political party.

The autobiography of Samuel Gompers was edited by Mathew Woll and published in two volumes (New York: E. P. Dutton & Co., Inc., 1943). An interesting book that analyzes the contributions of Gompers to American labor is *The Labor Philosophy of Samuel Gompers,* by Louis S. Reed (New York: Columbia University Press, 1930).

PHILIP MURRAY

BORN: Blantyre, Scotland, May 25, 1886
EDUCATION: Schooling in Scotland, honorary degrees from American universities
DIED: San Francisco, Calif., Nov. 9, 1952

Attendance at a labor meeting at the age of six and employment in the mines at ten gave this leader of the CIO an early acquaintance with labor and working conditions. In 1902 his family moved to the United States and settled in Pennsylvania. While working in the mines he became involved in a labor dispute that cost him his job but rewarded him with the presidency of his local union.

He rapidly ascended the organizational ladder of the labor union and in a short time became vice-president of the International Union of United Mine workers under John L. Lewis. He served in this position for more than twenty years.

Murray received recognition from several Presidents, particularly Wilson, Harding, and Franklin D. Roosevelt, who appointed him to various labor commissions and called upon him to help with contract negotiations. He was recognized early for his ability as a peacemaker and is credited with helping to draft the Guffey-Snyder Coal Act of 1935.

One of the early organizers of the CIO, Murray in 1936 was chosen to head the Steelworkers Organizing Committee. In 1937 he succeeded in negotiating a contract with "Big Steel" companies although he had never worked in a steel mill. He had, however, acquired in a short time a vast knowledge of the industry. In 1940 he was elected president of the CIO, a position he held until his death. It was during this period that the CIO grew to great strength and the campaign against Communist infiltration of the unions was waged.

Philip Murray was the recipient of the Hoey Award of the Catholic Interracial Council in 1943. In 1952 he received the Quadragesimo Anno Award given to an individual who has made an outstanding contribution to the Christian solution of industrial problems.

Philip Murray played an important role in the rapid growth of unionism that coincided with the beginning of the New Deal. A man of principle, respected by all, including those with whom he disagreed, Murray was largely responsible for the more favorable reputations that labor leaders now enjoy. His ability to negotiate helped to settle many difficulties between labor and management and to avert needless loss in time, production, and wages during his long career.

The volumes of *Current Biography* for 1949 and 1952 contain brief, concise summaries of Philip Murray's life. The *Reader's Guide to Periodical Literature* will direct the student to many articles that have been written about Murray.

DEBATE

The question: **SHOULD THE GOVERNMENT CREATE AND SPONSOR MORE PROJECTS OF THE TVA TYPE?**

Both the affirmative and the negative should study the history and development of the TVA to see the investment involved, the farming interests and industries affected, and what changes it has effected in the Tennessee Valley.

Both should also read the criticisms of the "philosophy" of the TVA, its operation, and any bad effects it has had.

The next point is to study similar projects that have been proposed to see whether they can work out as TVA has done. (There is no point in arguing about any *one* project, such as the Columbia River Valley or the Missouri River Valley. It is the *principle* of having the federal government sponsor such projects wherever feasible that is being discussed.)

Affirmative presentation

The affirmative should develop the following three arguments:

I. There is need to develop certain regions in the United States on a valley or interstate basis.
  1. A full economy, a growing population, and a higher standard of living, all demand such development.
II. Federal authority is the only means for such valley-wide development.
  1. States have done nothing; by their very nature they won't.
  2. Only the federal government has the funds and the know-how for such development.
  3. Only federal authority can extend over interstate developments.
III. As it has worked out in the TVA, it is the American system in action.
  1. There is considerable local participation and, on some levels, direction.
  2. Farmers, businessmen, and *all* inhabitants have prospered.
  3. The people have ultimate control of the TVA.

Negative presentation

The negative should admit material advantages of TVA and offer a counterproposal.

I. The best way is for the states concerned to set up a bi-state or tri-state authority for the project.
  1. States have been doing more and more of this on smaller projects.
  2. They have a more immediate interest than the federal government.
  3. Projects would be more susceptible to local control.
II. Federally created and sponsored projects entail certain very real dangers.
  1. They are in unfair competition with private business.

2. They put government in business—never a proper role for government.
3. They are a form of "creeping socialism."

III. Since the TVA pays no federal taxes, the whole country is taxed for the sake of those who receive benefits from the TVA.

CLASSROOM DISCUSSION: Discussion should begin by eliminating all but the crucial points. Everyone will admit that such gigantic projects should not be sponsored unless needed; that the federal government should not sponsor them if other agencies can and will, and if they will do the work well. This seems to settle to a discussion on two questions: (1) Can only the federal government feasibly sponsor such projects? (2) Will the setting up of several such projects under federal sponsorship entail serious dangers to our American way of life?

SELECTED READINGS

Both sides of the issue are presented in the following discussions: Walter M. Daniels (ed.), *Should We Have More TVA's?* (New York: H. W. Wilson Co., 1950); Carol L. Thompson, "More Authorities for River Valleys?", *Senior Scholastic* (May 4, 1949); C. J. Armbruster, S.J., "TVA: Blight or Blessing?", *Social Order* (May 1954).

An objective, scholarly study of the problem was made when proposals for additional TVA projects were first seriously entertained. It is excellent background material. Wesley C. Clark, "Proposed 'Valley Authority' Legislation," *American Political Science Review* (February 1946).

The most eloquent defenses of projects like the TVA have been made by two former directors of the TVA, David Lilienthal and G. R. Clapp: David Lilienthal, *Democracy on the March* (New York: Harper & Brothers, 1944) and "An Alternative to Big Government," *Reader's Digest* (May 1947); G. R. Clapp, *TVA: An Approach to the Development of a Region* (Chicago: Chicago University Press, 1955).

Among the various criticisms of the TVA type of project, the following should be consulted: John T. Flynn, *Road Ahead: Creeping Socialism* (New York: Devin Adair, 1949); Dean Russell, *The TVA Idea* (Irvington-on-Hudson: Foundation for Economic Education, 1949); Howard Bloomfield, "The Government Didn't Have to Do It," *Reader's Digest* (April 1950); Henry Hazlitt, "Seamy Side of TVA," *Newsweek* (August 1, 1955).

POLLING
PLACE

UNIT SEVEN
Government and Politics

Chapter 22. Our Democratic Republic

65. MORAL BASIS OF OUR GOVERNMENT

In our discussion of social and economic problems we saw the government frequently play an active role in solving them. All through history governments have exercised "sovereign power," which is the ultimate human power in civil society. But it is only in the last century that governments have assumed the extensive social and economic functions they now perform. Our American governments, from the city and the county to the federal government in Washington, do many things that were undreamed of when the Constitution was written. The city of New York, for example, spends many times as much annually as the national government did in 1790.

Traditionally, Americans have not liked too much government. With the exception of a comparatively small number of people who advocate what is called a "welfare state" or some form of socialism, most Americans wish to keep government down to what they consider a necessary minimum. Some of these people argue that goverment is "a necessary evil." They believe that its only function is to protect people's lives and property, to restrain evil men from committing wrongs against their neighbors. They therefore conclude: "That government is best which governs least."

Government not a necessary evil. Others who wish to keep government to the necessary minimum do not look upon it as a necessary evil. They consider government both necessary and natural. Government is needed to establish and enforce order. It is the necessary supreme power that every society must have if men are to enjoy order, prosperity, and safety. To achieve such order today, the federal government must be strong. It must protect us from potential enemies within and outside the country; it must regulate problems of interstate and international commerce; it must solve problems related to large-scale labor disputes and similar social and economic issues. Obviously, government must have whatever power is needed to accomplish its functions.

Necessity of strong government. In recent years some Americans have erroneously imagined that weak government is good

and strong government is bad. If anything, the reverse of this proposition tends to. be true. Any government not capable of handling the difficulties put to it is not a good government. The Fathers of the Constitution were clear-minded on this point. They tried to create a government with power to accomplish its purposes. In other words, they tried to create strong government. But they tried to limit that government to its proper functions, to doing what it was created to do. This, they believed, would protect Americans from the tyranny of weak government that is either unable to enforce the laws or becomes incompetent by becoming big, corrupt, and oppressive without being powerful.

The confusion between strong government and oppressive government has been clearly stated in this way:[1]

Civil power is derived as a necessary adjunct to political authority. Whenever the exercise of political power is reasonable and just, *ipso facto* the use of coercive power proportional to the seriousness of the matter is reasonable and just. Power, then, both moral and coercive, is a property of authority itself and without it authority itself is essentially changed.

There is no reason to fear power as such if

[1] James V. Schall, S.J., "The Necessity of Government," *The Commonweal,* November 26, 1954, pp. 215–217.

this be the case, rather what must be feared is the unjust use of power, not, however, because it is power but because it is unjust. The attempt to limit the power of a government in terms of a constitution or basic law of the land must not, therefore, be understood to mean the actual lessening of a real power. Rather it means the attempt to define the limits in which the use of power is just.

The purpose of government. Governments have the same essential functions to perform in all countries: the defense of the country's legitimate interests in the international community and the maintenance of order, security, and justice at home. What these basic functions involve differs from time to time, of course, but they always involve the co-ordinating of lesser groups in order to promote the common welfare. In America today we find that this includes such things as providing adequate military defense, protecting our civil and political rights, and providing common services for the community, such as good roads and adequate supplies of water. These are some of the concrete tasks performed by our government as it seeks to achieve the purpose for which it exists.

Let us therefore inquire into the purpose of government so that we can more judiciously decide just what things the government should do and what things it should leave to citizens or other groups within the country.[2] Let us remember, first of all, that man is formed by nature to live in an organized community. The state, then, is founded on natural law because a multitude of men cannot live together in society to the mutual benefit of all unless there is an authority to direct them and to maintain order. This authority resides in the state and in the government. Political authority is therefore rooted in human nature. It is natural, and its ultimate foundation is in God.

The state exists to promote the common good. This might seem to be an obvious statement, but it involves very delicate reasoning since a mistake might end up justifying totalitarian government on the one hand or weak and incompetent government on the other. The common good cannot be separated from the welfare—spiritual, cultural, material—of each individual in the state. The state exists to provide the means whereby individual human beings can develop their faculties and live in justice and security. But the common good is something more than this, just as an orchestra is something more than the sum of players who comprise it. It is the good of all persons within the group and the good of the group as a whole. Bishop John Wright says it "is not only a collection of advantages and utilities; it is strongly moral and ethical in its content. It includes elements of rectitude and honor. Only on condition that it embraces these is the 'common good' truly good; the good of a people living in a community, the good of an organized human city, rather than the booty of a pack of thieves or common hoard of a mob of gangsters." These words restate a truth clearly recognized and affirmed by all the great political

Bishop John Wright, of Worcester, Mass., has brilliantly described the attributes and virtues of what is known as "the common good"—the goal of good government. (Charles River Press)

thinkers of the past, from Aristotle and Cicero to St. Thomas Aquinas and on to Edmund Burke and John Adams.

As far as government is concerned the common good can be looked at under two broad aspects. The first of these is *protective or negative.* The government must defend all citizens in the exercise of their rights. It must protect them from aggression by enemy states and from all forms of injustice within the state. The second aspect of the common good is *positive or promotional.* The state has the responsibility of furthering the intellectual, moral, and material welfare of its people. There is practically no dispute about the first or negative aspect of the common good, for everyone agrees that the state must protect its people from injustice. There is considerable disagreement, however, about the positive role that the state should play.

Let us see if we can arrive at a correct statement of general principle before determining what positive or promotional functions our American government should properly assume. These functions are generally referred to under the term of "the general welfare," and they have been well defined as "the sum total of all those conditions and facilities which are necessary to enable all the members of the state to provide for their basic phys-

[2] An excellent book on general political principles analyzed from a Christian point of view is Henry J. Schmandt and Paul G. Steinbicker, *Fundamentals of Government* (Milwaukee: The Bruce Publishing Co., 1954). Our discussion in this chapter leans heavily on this book.

ical and moral needs."[3] Looked at this way, they include three categories: (1) material goods that are essential to maintain a good standard of life; (2) intellectual goods, or the knowledge and culture of the mind; (3) moral goods, or those virtues that constitute the highest achievement of men on this earth. To achieve the conditions under which these goods can be realized is the positive or promotional function of government.

Enlarged function of government. In years past there was little need for the government to perform many positive or promotional functions to achieve the common good. Its role was confined largely—though not exclusively—to the negative function of protecting the safety and rights of citizens in a less complex society. The industrial revolution, however, developed an economy in which interdependence of person on person has increased, and economic insecurity is the lot of very many unless the economy as a whole continues to function satisfactorily. Under modern conditions the state has to play an active role to maintain society in justice and security.

Before World War I, a former professor of government said after his experience as governor of New Jersey:[4]

In the old-fashioned days when life was very simple we used to think that all government had to do was put on a policeman's uniform, and say, "Now don't anybody hurt anybody else." We used to say that the ideal of government was for every man to be left alone and not interfered with except when he interfered with somebody else; and that the best government was the government that did as little governing as possible. That was the idea that obtained in Jefferson's time. But we are coming now to realize that life is so complicated that we are not dealing with the old conditions, and that the law has to step in and create new conditions under which we may live, the conditions which will make it tolerable for us to live.

[3] Schmandt and Steinbicker, *op. cit.,* p. 139.
[4] Woodrow Wilson, *The New Freedom* (New York: Doubleday, Page & Company, 1913), pp. 19–20.

Woodrow Wilson defended the need for a strong government in this complex age in his book, The New Freedom. *(U.S. Treasury)*

In somewhat similar fashion Pope Pius XII stated in his first encyclical letter of 1939, *Summi Pontificatus:* "No one of good will and vision will think of refusing the State, in the exceptional conditions of the world of today, correspondingly wider and exceptional rights to meet the popular needs." But the Pope went on to warn us: "Even in such emergencies, the moral law, established by God, demands that the lawfulness of each such measure and its real necessity be scrutinized with the greatest rigor according to the standards of the common good."

American government and the natural law. Our Constitution provides for *republican government.* This means that we have *representative government,* not direct democracy. In our government there are three essential functions: legislative, executive, and judicial, and power is so divided. The executive branch is charged with the duty of enforcing and administering the law, dealing with other countries, protecting us, maintaining law and order. Its function is to govern. The legislative branch makes law; consents to executive proposals or it rejects them; it criticizes and resolves; it represents the people as a whole and their vast variety of interests. Its function is not to govern but to represent the people and to see that government does not become oppressive. The work of the judicial branch is to administer justice in particular cases and, if necessary, to guard the Constitution against violation by either the legislature or the executive.

The authors of our Constitution recognized the reality of natural law ordained by God for the moral welfare of man and society. The Founding Fathers believed that one could find the content of the natural law by right reason. They therefore believed that rational men would agree that some things are right and some things are wrong, that there are natural, inalienable rights, that there are norms for judging whether a government is good or bad. Because they believed these things they were confident that they could state general principles of good government in a basic doctrine to which American governments should always seek to conform. This basic doctrine is our Constitution. Although it is not correct to identify it *as* natural law, nevertheless many of its basic principles derive from the precepts of natural law. Our government is one that respects and protects individual human rights.

The principle of subsidiarity. Nowhere in the Constitution is a complete list given of the functions or the duties of the federal government. Certain general functions are specified and others, as we shall see later, are implied. Are there any general principles by which we can determine what the federal government should do and what it should leave for the individual person or for other private agencies to do? Is there a principle for deciding, for example, whether the federal government should provide medical services for all people? Or employment? Or schooling? This is one of the basic problems in American political life in the middle of the twentieth century, and various schools of thought have developed answers to it.

One extreme answer is *individualism.* Individualists would limit the government to the negative function of maintaining order, enforcing legal contracts, and protecting individual freedom. They believe that the common good can be more closely achieved by individuals pursuing their respective interests than by the state assuming any positive functions. Individualism was a common attitude in earlier American history, but comparatively few persons subscribe to extreme individualism in our age. An editorial in the *Freeman* states the case for individualism in these words:[5]

We are convinced that freedom is inherent in the individual, the gift of God, and that the function of government, the only function for which it has any competence, is to protect the individual in the enjoyment of that endowment. If it goes beyond that field, if it invades any area of human activity, it necessarily transgresses the freedom of some or all of the people.

[5] A clear statement of individualism can be found in the first number of *Freeman* (October 2, 1950), in an editorial, "The Faith of the *Freeman*," and in an article by George E. Sokolsky, "Freedom—A Struggle."

· Pope Pius XI on Subsidiarity ·

" . . . those in power should be sure that the more perfectly a graduated order is kept among the various associations, in observance of the principle of 'subsidiary function', the stronger social authority and effec— tiveness will be and the happier and more prosperous the condition of the state."

Such a view, we have already seen, is based on a wrong concept of man and of society. Individualism forgets that man is a social creature and that individualistic development is not sound or rounded development of the human person. Individualism is therefore wholly impractical and has never actually been practiced except in a limited way.

The other extreme answer is _collectivism._ All collectivist theories are reactions to individualism, and they go to the other extreme of turning all social functions over to the state in the belief that the state can perform them better than individuals or other agencies. There are different kinds of collectivism, of course, from moderate forms of socialism to the extreme of communism. Any government that exercised the broad powers most Socialists would give it would tend to become bureaucratic and irresponsible and perhaps even totalitarian. Individuals would tend to become wards of the state, completely dependent on governmental initiative and enterprise for their economic, social, and cultural welfare. Such a regime, then, would tend to stifle human development, which is the purpose of men's living together.

Somewhere between the extremes of individualism and collectivism each government must steer a course which is best adapted to the time and circumstances in which it operates, to the character of its people, and to the problems with which it is confronted. It can neither categorically renounce all positive functions nor automatically assume them all, for either program would defeat the purpose of good government. Experience has discovered a principle for deciding which functions government should assume and which it should leave to individuals and to lesser groups. This principle, which is an essential part of the Christian tradition, is called _the principle of subsidiarity._ It was well described by Pope Pius XI in _Quadragesimo Anno:_ "Just as it is wrong

His Holiness, Pope Pius XI, contributed greatly to the proper understanding of the function and scope of a good government in his renowned encyclical, Quadragesimo Anno. (United Press)

to take from the individual and hand over to the community what the individual can accomplish by his own initiative and enterprise, in the same way it is an injustice, a grave evil, and a disturbance of right order to transfer to a greater and higher society what can be effected by smaller and lower groups."

This principle has guided our reasoning on the social and economic problems we discussed in the first half of this volume. It is equally applicable to political problems. The federal government should not assume any function that local communities or state governments can perform adequately. But it has an obligation to perform those necessary functions which private groups and state agencies are clearly incompetent to handle. Regulation of the railroads, to take an obvious case, can be handled only by an agency of the federal government. Again, a regional water-power and irrigation project, such as the TVA or a projected Missouri River system, cannot be handled by any one state. But the federal government cannot properly assume such a function until it is demonstrated that local enterprise cannot do the job adequately and equitably.

Why should government follow the restrictions set down by the principle of subsidiarity? The answer is that otherwise the purpose of government tends to be thwarted. "The origin and primary scope of social life," Pope Pius XII explained in his Christmas message of 1942, "is the conservation, development and perfection of the human person." Men will most closely approach that development and perfection accordingly as they are free to do things themselves, either individually or in groups they have formed. They have little chance to develop if they simply take orders from a government that decides all things for them. While it is true that modern technological and economic developments have put additional functions on the state, nevertheless the principle remains sound that it should undertake only those functions that lesser groups cannot perform well.

66. OUR GOVERNMENT AS DEMOCRACY

The structure of our government is republican, but its character or nature is democratic. At the time of the adoption of the Constitution, the Republic was more aristocratic than democratic. Almost everywhere property qualifications for voting limited the electorate, and it was the habit of the people to choose distinguished, well-to-do men for government; that is, to choose the men who came naturally to the front in the society of that age. Among such men the word democracy was in bad odor; it suggested the rule of the mob—the kind of political disorders that were breaking out in France at the very moment our federal government was beginning to function. Thus the followers of Thomas Jefferson who considered themselves to be the purest republicans were stigmatized by their opponents as democrats.

As the years passed, the aristocratic Republic became democratized; that is, it became more responsive to popular sentiments and opinions and based on a larger electorate. Property qualifications for voting were swept away, and popular participation in government increased. The Republic came to be, in the immortal words of Lincoln, "of the people, by the people, for the people." The meaning of this is that the whole citizenry acts politically through its qualified voters and elected representatives and executives. In other words, all the voters chose some of the people to act with the authority of all of the people in regulating the public affairs of the entire nation, in accordance with the fundamental limiting and empowering rule of the Constitution.

Good government in our Republic now depends not only on the wisdom and justice of comparatively few people but on the active, intelligent, and virtuous participation of all citizens. Democracy can be the best kind of government or the worst, depending on the morality and political intelligence of the people.

At its best, democracy draws all citizens into the life of the state, promotes political education and civic virtue, and nourishes a noble spirit of community and liberty. At its worst, it degenerates into folly, extravagance, and lawlessness and breeds dictatorship for the salvation of a minimum degree of order in society. History is strewn with the remains of democracies that failed for want of a wise democratic citizenry.

Principles of democratic citizenry. Experience and reason have shown that certain principles must be respected by the people if democratic government is to flourish.

1. There must be reverence and respect for law and the rule of right reason in the enactment of laws. For this reverence and respect to endure, religion is necessary to remind all citizens constantly that civil authority and just law rest ultimately upon God and the natural moral law. A godless democracy will respect no law but that of its own will and passions, and therefore will go to ruin.

2. The citizenry must keep themselves

well informed on public issues and government problems, so that they may act from opinion instead of mere sentiment. All good government is controlled ultimately by public opinion, but there is a great difference between opinion and sentiment. Opinion is the result of reason working on information; sentiment may be generated by ignorant fancy and will, unguided by reason. When the Congress enacts a law after prolonged study and hearing testimony from all informed persons, we have government by public opinion. But when Congress responds to the pressure of mass fanaticism, we do not have government by public opinion. Democratic government requires the expression of all honest opinion and attentive respect for it, not only on the part of those in government but on the part of the citizenry.

Russian soldiers carry icons and other religious objects down the church steps as they desecrate the Seminova Monastery in Moscow. The party is the power in a totalitarian state as it directs the military, which overruns the land and does the party's bidding. (International News Photo)

Two Catholic churches once stood on this site in Budapest where the Hungarian Communists have erected a massive monument to Premier Stalin, the late Soviet ruler. (Religious News Service) In strong contrast (right), policemen direct the crowds to allow the Girl Scout troops to enter St. Patrick's Cathedral in New York to observe Girl Scout Sunday. (CYO Photo by Bill Linge)

3. The people as a whole must be interested in promoting the common good and in putting it above their immediate selfish interests. Here true patriotism comes to the aid of good citizenship; for true patriotism is love of one's country, willingness therefore to sacrifice for it, and never seeking a narrow selfish interest instead of the good of the local or national community. Some may believe that, if every citizen pursues his own interest and votes accordingly, the common good is automatically achieved in the electoral process. But the common good is not realized that way; it is attained only when the preponderant majority of the citizenry is actuated by the ideal of the common good. No selfish citizenry ever sustained a great and noble republic.

4. The most important principle of all is that of electing virtuous, honorable, and intelligent men to public office. There is no such thing as good government in the hands of bad men; there is no good law that cannot be perverted from its principle by dishonest or unintelligent administration. "There is no qualification for government, but virtue and wisdom," wrote Edmund Burke. This is as true in the democratic twentieth century as it was in the aristocratic political life of the eighteenth century. In its original sense the word *aristocracy* did not mean government by a hereditary nobility, but government by the wisest and best men. Such men, if they possess the talent of leadership, form a natural aristocracy in every society. Democracy cannot dispense with its natural aristocracy.

Voting. In our federal Republic each state, it will be remembered, has the authority to determine which citizens possess the right, or privilege, of voting, subject only to the constitutional restriction of not denying the franchise to anyone because of sex, religion, or race. All states have established requirements of age, citizenship, and residence for voters. Supplementary qualifications of education, ownership of property, and sex are occasionally urged by some people today. The age requirement in forty-six states is twenty-one, Georgia and Kentucky having fixed the age for voting at eighteen. Some age must be set, for children cannot understand issues at stake in an election and cast an intelligent vote for one candidate or another. When do children acquire sufficient social and political wisdom to cast an intelligent vote? A question like this can never be answered perfectly. The age set should be the one at which most young people acquire enough maturity of mind to think on political matters. The argument has been made that if a young man is eligible for military service at eighteen he should also be eligible to vote, but this is not logical.

Southern Russia's Don River still serves as an outdoor laundry for these residents of Rostov, who carry wash baskets uphill after pounding family wash on the river's shore as their ancestors did for centuries. (Wide World) The high standard of living enjoyed by Americans is evident in the photo at right of customers in a community laundermat who admire the art work of the proprietor as machines clean their wash. (United Press)

Military service does not require the same abilities as voting.

The assumption behind citizenship and residence qualifications is that aliens and transients do not possess the loyalty, the interest, and the knowledge of local political conditions necessary for a mature, responsible vote. Such qualifications used to vary greatly from state to state, but now all states require that voters be citizens, and most states fix a one-year residence requirement for eligibility to vote. A few southern states have a two-year residence requirement to eliminate Negro migrant workers. As long as states allow persons to become citizens within a reasonable time and do not set unreasonably long residence requirements, these two requirements are prudent means for screening out irresponsible voters.

The question of additional requirements for responsible voting is easy to settle theoretically but very difficult to work out practically. Is education necessary for intelligent, informed voting? At first glance it would seem that ability to read and write are absolutely necessary and that additional education should enable a person to understand political issues more thoroughly and vote more intelligently. But many well-educated people have no interest in political matters, do not inform themselves on the issues, parties, and candidates at each election, and therefore display no unusual intelligence in voting. On the other hand, some uneducated people show political interest and acumen of high quality, and they are well qualified to cast an intelligent vote. They can keep abreast of political developments by listening to speeches, by using the radio, and by "cracker-barrel" discussions.

The argument that a person should own property in order to qualify as an interested, responsible voter is seldom advanced seriously nowadays, except as a qualification for voting in certain kinds of elections, such as bond issues or en-

Radio, television, and the press carry the news of political elections to the people as fast as it happens. In our democratic Republic the people are truly represented, enjoy a free vote and a free press. (United Press)

abling acts for additional property taxes. The argument is that property owners have a larger investment in society than propertyless people, that giving the vote to the poor would enable them to rob the rich legally by adopting socialistic measures, and that withholding the vote from propertyless people would induce them to be industrious and saving in order to qualify for the vote. In somewhat similar fashion it is held by some people today that allowing non-property owners to vote additional levies on property gives them the power to despoil owners of their property.

There was a good deal more in this argument two hundred years ago than today. Historically, the franchise has expanded almost exactly at the rate that the rank and file of people have demonstrated their worthiness to exercise it. To withdraw it from people long accustomed to exercise it would be an insane reaction; indeed, it would be impossible. The democratic franchise—universal suffrage for all men and women who meet age, citizenship, and residential qualifications— is an established American institution. It is morally right and politically wise.

People who have no voice in civil society are never fairly treated. All have a right to be heard, to be consulted; otherwise they will feel no sense of loyal membership in the nation. Democracy, so understood, nourishes patriotism and civic virtue, without which the nation would sink and go to pieces.

The percentage of eligible voters who actually make use of their right is often comparatively small. A presidential election that stirs up great interest and excitement usually brings out a fairly large body of voters, although even in 1952 the high public interest in the contest between Dwight Eisenhower and Adlai Stevenson (with the Korean War as a major issue) aroused only 62 per cent of the voters to go to the polls. Much smaller percentages turn out for state and local elections, although such elections often affect the citizen's pocketbook more directly than a national election. This is not good citizenship. Many people neglect or decline to vote because they see no differences between the parties or the candidates and hence do not think it makes any difference who wins. Many others refuse to vote when their party comes under the leadership of men whom they disapprove. Still others are just not interested.

Some reformers advocate compulsory voting, with a fine to be levied against all eligible voters who do not show good reason for failing to vote. Compulsory voting is permitted by a few state constitutions, but no legislature has passed a law to require it. Some foreign countries have compulsory voting, but experience shows that it does not awaken an uninterested electorate. On election day an epidemic of "colds" and other "minor ailments" seemed to hit such a country as Austria, where there was compulsory voting. In the Soviet Union there is compulsory voting; more than 90 per cent of the people are brought to the polls to vote as the government tells them to

vote. Indeed, it is likely that any government that possessed the power to compel all voters to vote would use that power to make them vote as the government wished. Compulsory voting is hardly compatible with free institutions. If people are not interested in political affairs, their votes are not worth casting. If candidates and parties debate honestly and intelligently, injecting reality and not nonsense into political contests, there will be a larger public interest.

REVIEW

65. Moral Basis of Our Government

A. Why is civil government a necessity? What is the basic difference between a strong and an oppressive government?

B. What are some basic functions of government? What does Bishop Wright say concerning the common good? Give the positive and negative aspects of the common good.

C. What are the three categories of "general welfare" that the state should endeavor to provide for? What caused the increase of the government's activity in this field? How did Woodrow Wilson describe the increased need for the federal government's concern? Pope Pius XII?

D. What are the three branches of our government? Briefly state their functions.

E. How has the principle of subsidiarity been described by Pope Pius XI? Give a positive and negative example of this principle.

66. Our Government as Democracy

A. Briefly list four principles which must be recognized by the people if a democracy is to survive.

B. Who determines the qualifications of voters in our country? What is the voting age in the forty-eight states? Why are there resident and citizenship qualifications?

C. What percentage of voters exercised their right in the presidential election of 1952? Why do some not vote? Why would compulsory voting be undesirable?

THE CHAPTER IN REVIEW

A. What is meant by the phrases "common good" and "general welfare"? Why have they taken on added meaning in the twentieth century?

B. Describe individualism; collectivism; principle of subsidiarity in government.

C. Summarize the voting qualifications existing today. List a few of the reasons why all who are eligible to vote should exercise this privilege.

SELECTED READINGS

A basic book setting forth the general Catholic principles regarding government is Heinrich A. Rommen, *The State in Catholic Thought* (St. Louis: B. Herder Book Co., 1945). This book is difficult reading for a senior high school student, but those who are going on to college should know about it. Father Keller's *Government Is Your Business* is very easy reading. Chapter IV is particularly pertinent to this discussion. Msgr. John A. Ryan and Rev. Francis J. Boland, C.S.C., *Catholic Principles of Politics* (New York: The Macmillan Co., 1940), has long been considered the standard and most widely used work on this subject. It can be supplemented by Rev. A. J. Osgniach, O.S.B., *The Christian State* (Milwaukee: The Bruce Publishing Co., 1943). A good collection of statements by the Popes since Leo XIII on the nature of government is Rev. Francis J. Powers, C.S.V., *Papal Pronouncements on the Political Order* (Westminster, Md.: The Newman Press, 1952). The following pamphlets offer brief analyses of Catholic thought on government: Rev. Gerald C. Treacy, S.J., *Catholic Political Philosophy* (New York: The Paulist Press, 1947); Rev. James M. Gillis, C.S.P., *God in Government* (New York: The Paulist Press, 1943); Msgr. John A. Ryan, *Citizen, Church, and State* (New York: The Paulist Press, 1941).

The best recent treatment of government from a Christian-Thomist point of view is Henry J. Schmandt and Paul G. Steinbicker, *Fundamentals of Government* (Milwaukee: The Bruce Publishing Co., 1954). This book offers a systematic discussion of the theory of government and of political institutions. Discussion of the basic problem of government in this country is given in two excellent and readable books: Walter Lippmann, *The Public Philosophy,* and Ross J. S. Hoffman, *The Spirit of Politics and the Nature of Freedom,* both mentioned in the reading list for Chapter 2. A comprehensive study of American government is James M. Burns and Jack W. Pel Fason, *Government by the People* (New York: Prentice-Hall, Inc., 1952).

The need for strong but limited government is well put by James V. Schall, S.J., "The Necessity of Government," *Commonweal* (November 26, 1954). The meaning and workability of the principle of subsidiarity is explained by Henry J. Schmandt, "State Intervention—When?", *Social Order* (December 1954), and Rev. John F. Kenney, S.J., "The Principle of Subsidiarity," *American Catholic Sociological Review* (March 1955).

PROJECTS

1. The class should discuss ways by which the citizens can be alerted to use their voting privilege. A group might offer their services to the two major parties in the community for the purpose of distributing literature. One very practical way for students to demonstrate their interest in the voting privilege is to vote 100 per cent in the annual school elections.

2. Assume that you are living in 1792 and that you are over 21. Look up the qualifications for voters in this period. Compare them with the qualifications today and report the changes to the class.

3. Make a chart of our presidential elections since 1900, showing the voting percentages. On the same chart show the voting percentages for Congressional elections. Explain your chart to the class pointing out the lesson that can be drawn from a comparison of the figures.

Chapter 23. Political Parties and Pressure Groups

67. THE PRINCIPLE OF PARTY AND THE NATURE OF PARTIES IN AMERICA

The Constitution makes no provision for political parties, although they have played an essential role in American political life from the beginning of our national history. You will remember from American history that during Washington's administration people found themselves aligning into two parties: the Federalist, led by Hamilton, and Republican, led by Jefferson. These parties differed on certain questions of policy and on their evaluation of different men to promote the common welfare of the new nation.

Because Washington had seen party strife carried to the violence of war, and because the new federal Constitution required a spirit of unanimity on fundamental political principles, he saw an ominous tendency in the party contests between Federalists and Republicans. In his Farewell Address he warned that the "common and continual mischiefs of the spirit of party are sufficient to make it the interest and duty of a wise people to discourage and restrain it." It is obvious, however, from the whole extent of his re-

marks on party politics that he was thinking of what the eighteenth century called "factionalism." A faction is a body of men seeking to obtain office for their own advantage rather than for the general good of the country. Washington feared that factionalism might tear apart the country and open the door to foreign influence and corruption. But he did not deny, but rather agreed, "that parties in free countries are useful checks upon the Administration of the Government, and serve to keep alive the spirit of liberty." He knew that men tend to divide in opinion over measures and principles for the public welfare, and therefore tend by nature to form political parties wherever they are free to do so. Hence he said of the party spirit that it was "a fire not to be quenched; it demands a uniform vigilance to prevent its bursting into a flame, lest, instead of warming, it should consume."

Parties and factions. As we turn to a study of political parties, it is of the utmost importance that we understand what a true party is, as distinguished from a faction. A genuine party is a political group or organization that strives to convince the

public that its principles or proposals are for the general good of the whole nation; that *general good* must be its aim. A faction, on the other hand, is a group that is out for itself; it seeks power for selfish reasons—to get jobs, or government contracts, or some other things for the sake of the faction, not for the sake of the country. There are still other groups that might be called political sects, which center their whole energy upon some pet scheme of reform and have no interest in the broad and general welfare of the nation. Some political sects may be at war with the fundamental principles of the Constitution; such are the Communists, whose so-called party has never been a true party but a revolutionary sect. A genuine political party may have to face the necessity of making broad reforms in the state, but it always defends the general constitution of society, seeks the public welfare, and therefore always commands the support of a very large body of voters. The true principle of party can flourish only where political freedom prevails; therefore, it has flourished best in the English-speaking world, which possesses an ancient tradition of civil and political liberty.

In Washington's time two general attitudes toward the Constitution and the role of the new federal government developed, and it was natural for men of either persuasion (loose constructionists and strict constructionists[1]) to join with others of like mind to influence the government and, if possible, to control it. This meant they must elect men to office who accepted their point of view. Parties are the means whereby individual voters are organized with others of like mind to make their influence felt and to have their policies adopted by the government. Only through the instrumentality of political parties can any policy emerge from a mass of independent voters.

Parties soon became necessary for a second reason. The separation of powers provided in the Constitution was devised to prevent the accumulation of power in any one man's or any one group's hands. Some means was needed to harmonize the two principal branches of government and to direct their activity toward the same specific ends. Congress and the executive department might agree that they want to promote the common welfare, but unless they agree on what spe-

---

[1] Loose constructionists interpreted constitutional grants of power to the federal government "loosely," or generously. They tended to favor the federal government's assuming many functions. Strict constructionists, of course, took the contrary view.

Gladys Dickenson, union vice-president, is shown testifying before the House Education and Labor Committee on the subject of minimum wages. The common good is served when representatives of business, labor, agriculture, and other groups aid the country's legislators in this way. (Amalgamated Clothing Workers of America AFL-CIO)

cific measures will accomplish this objective, very little can be done. The Constitution provides no effective method of joining the executive and legislative branches for effective teamwork. The political party filled this need, and although it sometimes seems woefully inadequate in this respect it is still the best means we have to bring Congress and the President together to accomplish the purpose of government.

Our party system. Edmund Burke wrote the classic definition of a political party in 1770 when he called it "a body of men united for promoting by their joint endeavors the national interest upon some particular principle in which they are all agreed." Burke was thinking, however, of a comparatively small group of active political leaders in the eighteenth-century British Parliament, not of the great popular parties in this democratic age. Party, as Burke understood it, still exists but operates only among leaders and groups within our parties. A few years ago, for example, Governor Dewey of New York and Senator Taft of Ohio each headed what Burke would have called a party, and these "parties" contested against each other for the commanding influence in the national Republican party. Our parties today certainly reflect in a vague way differing attitudes on certain important political issues, but essentially they are organizations to combine, compromise, and unite a variety of interests and opinions for the purpose of winning elections. The party system has been defined "as an institution, supplementary to the government, aiding the electorate in the selection of official personnel and in the determination of public policies, and in the larger task of operating or criticizing the government."[2]

Some of the general characteristics of our party system are as follows:

Membership is voluntary. People join one party rather than another for a variety of reasons, such as family allegiance, one's economic position, or, in some places, local tradition. The Democratic party today tends to attract city people, the working class, and those of more "liberal" views. Since the Civil War and the reconstruction policies of the Republican party, the Democrats have enjoyed a near monopoly in the South. The Republican party is stronger among the farmers, the business classes, and those of more "conservative" view. In recent decades there has developed a "liberal" and a "conservative" wing within each party, with the result that division within the parties is sharper than between them. At any rate, a person is free to change from one party to another as long as he conforms to the law in his state. Usually this requires his

[2] C. E. Merriam and H. F. Gosnell, *The American Party System* (New York: The Macmillan Co., 1949), p. 464.

party identification to vote in party primaries. Even elected officials are free to change party membership, as Senator Wayne Morse of Oregon did in 1954, but they must accept the consequences at the polls in the next election and the "discipline" of party leaders.

A party has an official program or platform. This is a statement of what policies the party promises to adopt if its candidates are given control of the government. Parties have been notoriously deficient in putting their programs into law, and many people question whether the platform is a statement of policy or merely a device for attracting votes. Party leaders undoubtedly write their platform with an eye to winning the election, but the platform cannot easily be brushed aside if voters are truly interested in the issues, if it is clear that the party's platform has played a decisive part in winning the election for its candidates, and if the people persist in making the party leaders translate their promises into law. All parties adopt platforms as statements of policy, but whether they are to be taken seriously or not depends on a number of circumstances and on the determination of the electorate. Unfortunately, platforms are often so vague and general that they tend to become meaningless. Party leaders are anxious not to offend any interest or any group in the country, so unless there is widespread demand for a specific policy they will write a platform that "straddles" issues and can be interpreted almost any way one wishes to interpret it.

A party has an organization designed to put its candidates on the ballot and to secure their election to office. The organization begins in the precinct and the ward, and it is designed to "get out the vote" in favor of its candidates. The organization attempts to get loyal party men nominated in the primary so that a true "party man" is on the ballot at election time. Party workers include the professional politicians, part-time workers who hope to obtain a job or some other favor from the victorious candidate, and any number of other people who have some reason to work in favor of one party rather than the other. Party organization follows the pattern of elective offices. Each party has a national committee to work for its candidate's election to the presidency, a state committee, and similarly constituted committees for every congressional, legislative, and senatorial district of the state. These committees are all concerned exclusively with the election of candidates to office and the general development of popular support for the party in their respective districts.

Each party also maintains good organization within Congress and each of the state legislatures. The purpose of this organization is to try to maintain party solidarity on legislation, enforce party discipline, and pass out rewards in the way of committee assignments and the nomination of party friends to appointive positions in the government. Although the President and the governors are not members of the formal party organization, they are usually looked upon as party leaders and party spokesmen in the country at large and in each of the states.

Additional functions of the party. We have seen that a party is a group of men organized to elect its candidates to office and secure control of the government. What other functions does such an organization perform in American political life?

1. Parties help inform voters on political issues. Their information is obviously one-sided; it is designed to be persuasive rather than educational. But the intelligent voter can listen to both sides, hear arguments for and against many proposals, and from the welter of information and opinions offered to him he can emerge a better-informed citizen.

2. Parties select candidates for office, and thus they simplify the voter's prob-

lem of electing someone—for without party organization it is difficult to see how the voter would be able to vote for anyone but friends or acquaintances. In this way parties assure most successful candidates that they will receive a majority of the votes in the electorate rather than a mere plurality.[3]

3. Parties help legislatures to insure the working out of some kind of program, and they effect co-operation between executive and legislature when both are of the same party.

4. They provide constant criticism of the government and act as a kind of surety that no mistakes will pass unnoticed by the voters. Thus the defeated party keeps the victorious party on guard and prevents it from ruthlessly exploiting its victory in its own interests instead of providing for the national interest.

68. THE PARTY SYSTEM

Countries with a well-developed political life have generally had only two principal parties. Since the early days of our history we have fairly consistently maintained a two-party system. Many

[3] A majority is more than half the total vote. A plurality is more than any other candidate received. If there were three candidates, for example, and A received 40 per cent of the votes and B and C each 30 per cent, A would have a plurality of votes but not a majority.

additional parties have been formed, of course, and they can occasionally serve an important function in political life. The two-party system is defended for producing a responsible government endorsed by a majority of the people. The party with a majority in Congress and with its candidate elected President is responsible to the country for the government's conduct. In the multi-party system, on the other hand, a government must be made up of coalitions of various parties, and none of them is responsible for the government's activity.

The two-party system is criticized for offering the voter little real choice, either of candidates or of policies. Critics maintain that both parties appeal to a large majority in the country. They therefore adopt platforms so general as to be meaningless, and they advance candidates on a basis of popularity instead of real political worth. There is a measure of truth in this criticism, as a review of history would show, but it tends to ignore the fact that all political life is a series of compromises between different groups, and legislation is the result of many compromises. In the two-party system these compromises take place in party conference and convention *before* election. Let us see how this works.

A party in a large country like ours operating with the two-party system is made up of many elements: rural and ur-

State delegates march in a swirl of campaign signs following the nomination speech entering the name of Senator Robert Taft in the Republican balloting during the convention in Chicago in 1952. (United Press)

blican Ticket

SIDENTIAL ELECTORS

For President
WIGHT D. EISENHOWER

For Vice-President
RICHARD M. NIXON

Democratic Ticket

FOR PRESIDENTIAL ELECTORS

| DEM. | For President
ADLAI E. STEVENSON |
| | For Vice-President
JOHN J. SPARKMAN |

Prohibition Ticket

FOR PRESIDENTIAL ELECTORS

| PROHI. | For President
STUART HAMBLEN |
| | For Vice-President
ENOCH A. HOLTWICK |

Socialist Labor Ticket

FOR PRESIDENTIAL ELECTORS

| SOC'L
LAB. | For President
ERIC HASS |
| | For Vice-President
STEPHEN EMERY |

Progressive Ticket

FOR PRESIDENTIAL ELECTORS

| PROG. | For President
VINCENT HALLINAN |
| | For Vice-President
CHARLOTTA A. BASS |

(Indiana Board of Election)

ban, wage-earning and property-owning, business, professional, and laboring classes. Each of these elements has its own special interests, and each subscribes to larger national interests that it tends to identify with the common welfare. It is the function of the party to reconcile these interests and to work out compromises between them in such a way as to keep all groups within the party. This reconciliation of interests makes for a rather vague and general platform as a rule, but on occasion the party will take a definite stand on some issue. When the party secures a majority in the legislature it is expected to translate its platform into law, and the various elements in the party are expected to be more or less satisfied with the results.

In the multi-party state, each party can take a definite stand on the issue that gives it a reason for existence. On the basis of this stand it will secure the election of a certain number of candidates—as will be the case with other parties in the country. A government is formed from a coalition or a bloc of parties receiving the most votes, but the government cannot adopt the policies of any single party. It must compromise among them until it arrives at some program on which a majority is willing to agree.

Compromise takes place, then, *after* the election, but it is just as surely compromise as that within parties in the two-party system. Generally speaking, government under a multi-party system is less stable than under the two-party, in which the winning party clearly controls the government until the next election. Responsibility and stability, then, are two great advantages of the two-party system when it works properly.

Third parties play an important role in the two-party system. They have historically served to introduce issues upon which both major parties were afraid to take a definite stand. Third parties have introduced such issues as woman suffrage, prohibition, government control of railroad rates, and various political innovations like the initiative and the referendum.[4] By crystallizing dissenting opinion in a particular issue and submitting it to the voters, a third party forces the major parties to take a definite stand on the issues. This often means the political death of the third party—as you will remember, this was the case of the Populist

[4] Initiative and referendum are forms of "direct legislation" used in many states for constitutional amendment and statutory legislation. Initiative is the process whereby people, by means of a petition, force the legislature to act on a measure. Referendum is the procedure of submitting a proposed law to the electorate for approval or condemnation.

party when the Democrats in 1896 adopted most of the Populist issues—but it also means that the third party has performed an important service. If neither major party adopts the third party's program and it proves popular with a large percentage of the voters, then the third party may become a major party by replacing one of the others. Thus in American history the Republicans replaced the Whigs, and in English history the Labour party replaced the Liberals as one of the two major parties.

Local elections and national parties. Our two major parties—the Democratic and the Republican—are organized on a national basis and they are concerned primarily with the national government and its policies. But these parties take part in state and local elections. It is as adherent to one or the other party that most state legislators, mayors, aldermen, sheriffs, and like officers are elected. Many people believe that this is harmful to local and state government because there is usually little if any connection between local problems and national policies. Although there is a closer connection between national policy and such local problems as child labor, slum clearance, and interurban bridges than formerly, it remains a fact that local offices should be filled on the basis of local issues and the ability of the candidates to solve these problems. Often local winners "ride to victory on the coattails" of the national victor.

Various attempts have been made to separate local from national elections so that each can be decided on its own merits. One method is to hold local elections at a different time from the national election. This involves additional expense, of course, and it calls the voters out at least one additional time. Moreover, it is only partly successful. It does prevent local officials from riding in on presidential coattails because people usually vote a "straight ticket." But it does not prevent local Republicans or Democrats from using the party label, identifying themselves with national leaders, and winning office by evading local issues.

Another method is the non-partisan ballot, which bears no indication of party affiliations of the candidates running for office. The non-partisan ballot is supposed to put each candidate on his own reputation and his own merits. It has worked successfully in small communities, where candidates are likely to be known personally by the electorate. In larger communities, however, where party organization was strong, both Democratic and Republican party workers knew which candidates belonged to the organization and were to be supported. Another difficulty with the non-partisan ballot in large communities is that lack of party identification for the candidates left most voters in even greater ignorance of their policies than if they had been identified by a party label.

Neither the separate election nor the non-partisan ballot is a final solution of the confusion between local and national issues by the great mass of voters. The only adequate solution seems to lie in voters interested and intelligent enough to inform themselves of the local as well as national issues in each campaign and to determine, as well as possible, where each candidate stands on the pertinent issues. The better newspapers throughout the country and such organizations as the League of Women Voters try to get definite statements from all candidates on the pertinent issues and make such information available to the voters.

In the last analysis, it is evident that the principle of party politics can never be kept out of any election in the civil community. The familiar party labels may be dropped, but every candidate has his backers, and for that occasion these backers form his party. Rare is the candidate who runs totally unconnected from a corps of friends, associates, or backers; rarer still is the election of such a candi-

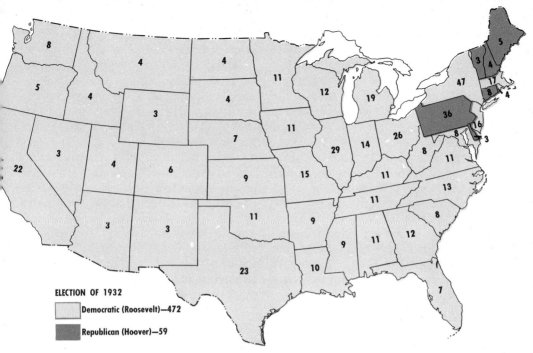

ELECTION OF 1932

Democratic (Roosevelt)—472

Republican (Hoover)—59

date. Voters, therefore, are almost never offered a simple choice of determining which candidate is best fitted for the office, because when they vote for a man they in reality vote also for the group of men with whom their candidate is associated, even though the names of such men do not appear on the ballot.

Controlling party finances. A political party in a state or national campaign assumes that it must spend millions of dollars to get its candidates elected. Large sums are spent for radio and television time, for billboards, direct-mail advertising, handouts on election day, and other such means of advertising. Moreover, na-

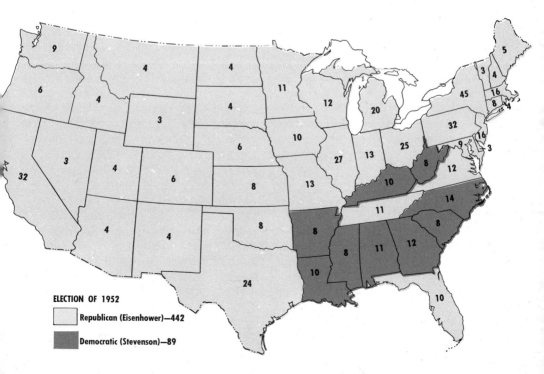

ELECTION OF 1952

Republican (Eisenhower)—442

Democratic (Stevenson)—89

tional, state, and local headquarters must be maintained during the campaign; workers must be hired and various other expenses paid in getting out the vote. Such expenses are entirely legitimate, but they are subject to abuse and they therefore constitute a problem in American political life.

The problem of party finance seems to divide itself into the amount of money spent and the source of funds collected. No official records of campaign expenditures were published until 1908. Since that time, expenses have mounted rapidly, and by 1936 they seemed to be getting out of control. A Senate investigating committee reported early in 1937 that in the previous year the Republican National Committee had spent almost nine million dollars and Republican state committees almost five million, or eighty-five cents for each vote polled by the national ticket. Democratic party expenses were $5,600,000 for the national committee and close to three million for the state committees, a total of thirty-three cents for each vote polled.

Where does this money come from? It must come from voluntary contributions, since American political parties have no dues, as do most European parties. These voluntary contributions will obviously come from persons and organizations that believe they have an interest in the outcome of the election. Small contributions are obtained from some citizens who believe that one party or the other best represents the national interest. Others have a personal interest, as wage earners, property owners, or businessmen, in seeing a party's program put into effect. They are willing to "invest" in the campaign. Large contributions come from business associations, and naturally these expect their beneficiaries will favor them if they are elected. Some "voluntary" contributions in the past were practically assessments, especially from those on public payrolls who had to pay a per-

centage (1 or 2 per cent as a rule) of their salaries if they wanted to keep their jobs.

Publicity connected with party finance revealed that the major political parties were in danger of "selling out" in order to obtain finances for a campaign. Although it is too much to say that either party would enact policies it thought detrimental to the country in order to reward a generous contributor to the campaign, such contributors could easily come to wield undue influence over party policy and personnel. A series of corrupt-practices acts were therefore passed by state legislatures and by Congress to limit the total amount that can be spent on a campaign, the amount that any one candidate can spend or have spent on his behalf, and the amount that he can obtain from any one source. The corrupt-practices acts also regulate the uses to which the money can be put and require each candidate to make a public financial accounting of his campaign expenditures.

A study of campaign expenses suggests that there is no great need to fear that money alone will win a campaign. The Republicans have consistently spent much more than the Democrats since 1925 but in that time have won only two presidential elections to five for the Democrats. Nevertheless, some kind of reasonable limit on campaign expenses enables a man to run for office without becoming financially indebted to groups that will try to influence him unduly after election. More important, however, is the control over the amount that any one person or organization can contribute to a candidate's campaign expenses. Most states have detailed restrictions on sources and amounts of contributions, prohibition of bribery and other corrupt means of soliciting votes, and a requirement of publicity in campaign expenditures. These state laws are too diverse to analyze here. In general they are similar to national legislation which, of course, is applicable only to campaigns and elec-

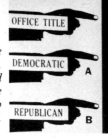

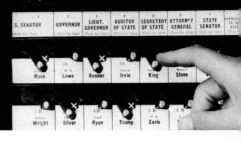

Automatic voting machines are widely used in the United States. Fewer ballots are invalidated and greater secrecy assured with the use of these machines, which speed up voting and tabulating. (William I. Siegfried)

tions involving congressmen and the President.

Federal legislation on party finances. National legislation can be summarized under three heads: (1) *Limitations on the raising of money.* No one on relief rolls, no federal employee, no corporation or union may lawfully contribute to a campaign fund. No one may contribute more than five thousand dollars to the campaign of any single candidate for federal office. (2) *Limitations on the amounts that may be spent.* Senatorial candidates may spend twenty-five thousand dollars and candidates for the House five thousand dollars in a campaign. These limitations do not apply to primary campaigns or limit friends and other supporters of the candidate. Moreover, items of "personal," expense like stationery, postage, and circulars, are exempted from this limitation. (3) *Requirement of publicity.* Every candidate is required to file an account of his contributions and his expenditures with the secretary of the Senate or the clerk of the House. A similar report of financial operations is required periodically of all party committees and other organizations receiving or spending money for political purposes.

The corrupt-practices acts were beneficial, but they did not end all abuses in party finance. In 1939 and 1940 two more laws (known as the Hatch Acts after Senator Hatch of New Mexico, who introduced them) were passed to correct the remaining abuses. The first measure sought to protect persons on the federal payroll from intimidation in elections. It also prohibited the solicitation of funds from people on relief and tried to eliminate the use of relief funds to coerce vot-

ers. The second measure extended protection against partisan coercion to all persons on state and local government payrolls whose salaries were paid in part from federal funds. It also limited each national party committee to expenditures of three million dollars in any one year.

There are still loopholes in both federal and state laws. The limit of five thousand dollars for any individual contribution is evaded by those who contribute that much to each of several state committees, which then assume expenses formerly borne by the national committee. The limit of three million dollars' expenditures for any one national committee is evaded by creating mushroom organizations, each of which stays within the legal limit. If it is wise to control party finance by legislation, as most Americans seem to think it is, effective legislation still remains to be found.

69. PRESSURE GROUPS AND THE COMMON GOOD

Closely allied to the financial problem is the problem of pressure groups attempting to control a party in order to obtain favorable legislation and favorable consideration from the executive in the national or state governments. A pressure group is any organization seeking to effect the course of government without actually nominating candidates for office. Occasionally pressure groups have decided to put candidates into the field, and then they became parties. Thus the Nonpartisan League remained a pressure group in Montana and the Dakotas, but it became the Farmer-Labor party in Minnesota.

Pressure groups serve a legitimate purpose in a democratic country, and it would be wrong to try to abolish them. Indeed, to do so would in effect be to abolish democracy, for they are means through which individuals bring their influence to bear on government. Political, social, and religious groups try to influence party platform makers to adopt reforms and promise laws that they think are for the general welfare. Thus the Social Action Department of the National Catholic Welfare Conference has urged such things as good minimum-wage laws, and the Farm Bureau has requested any number of measures favorable to farmers. Party platforms take into consideration these different requests to win the favor of as many groups as possible.

As long as no one pressure group can dominate the party's policies or personnel, there is little danger to American political life from their existence. The main pressure groups threatening to be strong enough to constitute a danger to free democratic government are the economic groups, combined business interests on the one hand and labor interests on the other, or the alliance of both against the public interest.

Business interests, represented by the United States Chamber of Commerce and the National Association of Manufacturers and various smaller associations, have been influential in the Republican party for many years. Generally speaking, Republican legislation has been favorable to business groups, which in turn generously support Republican candidates in election campaigns. Labor, as represented by the big union federations, has been influential in the Democratic party, and in the period of Democratic ascendancy laws favorable to unions were passed. Business interests and unions repeatedly insist that they are interested in the common welfare and that their measures are not selfishly devised to promote their own interests. Business believes quite sincerely that what is good for business is good for the country as a whole. Unions believe, again quite sincerely, that what helps unions and the workingman helps the entire nation. Each group has assembled evidence and arguments to defend its contention, but the fact remains that situations can develop where group interests run counter to national interests. Responsible business and union leaders tell us that when such a situation does arise they will loyally support national interest instead of their own group interest.

Political parties and the common good. The basic problem of American political life is to identify as closely as possible, the party's objective with the common good. We must admit that this has never been done perfectly in the past, nor does it seem possible in the future. Neither party in a two-party system can represent all the interests in the nation or identify perfectly its objectives with the common welfare. The aim of the party is to elect candidates to office and thus to control the government. To accomplish this objective it must try to accommodate as many interests as possible—which can never add up to the same thing as the national interest or the common good.

The clothing workers and their CIO locals supported F.D.R. for re-election in 1944. Unions more actively participated in campaigns with the establishment of the Political Action Committee of the CIO in 1943. (Amalgamated Clothing Workers of America AFL-CIO)

You will remember that Edmund Burke said that a party is "a body of men united for promoting by their joint endeavors the national interests upon some particular principle in which they are all agreed." The same sagacious political philosopher observed that "all government . . . is founded on compromise and barter." A major political party in America approaches the promotion of the common welfare to the extent that it reconciles conflicting interests and, when it is in power, promotes each within the bounds of justice. Parties are frequently condemned for being "all things to all men," for taking vague and general stands on controversial issues, and for not committing themselves as advocates for one group or class in the nation. This condemnation misses the mark, however, because it does not understand one of the principal functions of a major party in the American political system.

It is the business of political philosophers and of students to define the common good and to specify what measures are necessary to achieve it. It is the function of the political party to reconcile the interests of different groups in the country in such fashion as to approach as close as possible to the common good. The degree to which both parties do this, therefore, is the degree to which American political life will approach perfection. Politics is a practical art of working with many men of diverse interests. The good politician should, by persuasion and other means that are proper for leading human beings, convince groups of divergent interests that they must compromise with each other so that political life can be pursued by free men organized democratically. The alternative, of course, is authoritarian control of individuals and groups by the government so that social order can be maintained and the national interest promoted.

A conservative and a liberal party. An often heard criticism of our party system is

"The Man to Head the Line" is the title of this cartoon, which shows that the general welfare of the nation must come before the private interests of various segments of the population. (Carmack in the Christian Science Monitor)

that the two parties are too much alike, that they differ too little. Why, therefore, it is asked, ought not all the conservatives in both major parties unite to form a conservative party, while the so-called liberals in each party unite in the same way? Those who think this should be done believe that it would lead to clearer division on issues and introduce more reality into party debate; they also point to the fact that on most important issues in both national and local legislatures the parties show no solid front against each other and the lawmakers do not divide along strict party lines. Republican "progressives" often vote with the "liberal" northern Democrats, while conservative southern Democrats are found voting with conservative Republicans.

The answer to the question raised here is a little complicated, but very important. In the first place, it may be said that it is well for the country that the rival parties are in agreement on all fundamental questions that go toward the structure of society and the Constitution. Let them differ as much as they like on concrete measure and policies, but let them not strain the bonds that unite all Americans. As the parties are now formed, there is enough conservatism in the Democratic party to prevent its being captured by extreme radicals, and there is enough liberalism in the Republican party to keep it from being an instrument of reaction. Hence both parties are restrained from taking political directions that could lead them to extreme mutual hostility. To use again the words of Washington, they are kept in that state in which they "warm" our civil life without "consuming" it. Finally, it is worth pointing out that *conservative* and *liberal* are not very useful *political* words in America, and indeed have never been employed here as party names. We are all liberals to the extent that we love liberty, and all conservatives to the extent that we cherish our Constitution and the liberties which it secures as a great heritage to be held in trust for our posterity.

Conclusion. Ultimately, healthy political life in the American system depends on an active, intelligent electorate. Unless voters are interested in political matters and are willing to use the time and energy necessary to inform themselves of the issues at stake and the qualifications of at least the candidates of both major parties, political affairs are surrendered to those whose interest is likely to be narrowly selfish. By the very nature of things, there will always be the danger of serious abuses in the party system. Party politics is primarily a job of "selling" candidates and policies to the majority of the people at each election. Unless the people as a whole are intelligent enough to understand issues and the worth of candidates, party organizations will obviously confuse issues and select popular rather than good candidates. Since parties are successful only if they win elections, the people can force sound policies and good candidates upon them—or by their indifference or their lack of political wisdom the people can force wrong policies and poor candidates on any party that will sacrifice principle to win an election.

Although parties are subject to abuses and will never be perfect, they play an essential role in American political life. It is impossible to conceive how our government and our politics could operate if parties were abolished. They select candidates for office and inform the public of the issues at stake. They bring about cooperation between the executive and the legislature, and they provide the means for operating the government effectively and criticizing it helpfully.

REVIEW

67. The Principle of Party and the Nature of Parties in America

A. Why did Washington warn against party strife? What is the general purpose of a political party? What is a faction? A political sect?

B. What was Edmund Burke's classic definition of a political party? Has this any validity today?

C. What are some characteristics of our party system? Briefly explain each.

68. The Party System

A. What is the advantage of having only two main parties? Give one criticism of having only two main parties. List two disadvantages of the multi-party system.

B. What is the major contribution of a third party? Give some concrete examples of this from American history. What is the value in local elections of a non-partisan ballot? Give a criticism of the non-partisan ballot.

C. Cite figures from the 1936 election to show that party expenditures were extremely high. Where does this money come from? Why can contributions constitute a danger to political parties?

D. What did federal legislation in general try to accomplish in limiting party finances? What did the Hatch Acts of 1939 and 1940 try to accomplish? Point out two ways in which these laws have been evaded.

69. Pressure Groups and the Common Good

A. What is a pressure group? What good can it accomplish? What danger would a powerful pressure group present to the party?

B. Why is compromise necessary in political activity? If compromises did not take place, what would be the result?

C. Why have not American political parties borne the names Liberal and Conservative?

THE CHAPTER IN REVIEW

A. Describe the organization of a political party and point out what its functions should be.

B. Show why America has stayed with two major parties although we have had many third parties which have served useful purposes.

C. Why has there been a need to limit spending by parties? Point out steps that the government has taken in this regard.

SELECTED READINGS

The outstanding textbook (for college students) on political parties was for a long time the study of Edward McChesney Sait, *American Parties and Elections* (New York: D. Appleton-Century Company, Inc., 1942). This work has been brought up to date by H. R. Penniman, *Sait's American Parties and Elections* (New York: Appleton-Century-Crofts, Inc., 1952). Two additional standard studies are C. E. Merriam and H. F. Gosness, *The American Party System* (New York: The Macmillan Co., 1949), and Hugh A. Bone, *American Politics and the Party System* (New York: McGraw-Hill Book Co., 1949).

The role of third parties is well portrayed by William B. Hesseltine, *The Rise and Fall of Third Parties* (Washington: Public Affairs Press, 1948). James A. Farley, *Behind the Ballots* (New York: Harcourt, Brace & Co., 1938), gives an interesting personal account of party operations. Party machinery on the city level is critically examined by John T. Salter, *Boss Rule: Portraits in City Politics* (New York: Whittlesey House, 1935).

Lobby groups have been the subject of much writing. Karl Schriftgiesser, *Lobbyists: The Art and Business of Influencing Lawmakers* (Boston: Little, Brown & Co., 1951), is a good formal study of the subject; an informal, anecdotal account is Mary O. Moore, *I'll Meet You in the Lobby* (Philadelphia: J. B. Lippincott Co., 1950). A study of the government as lobbyist is made by Forest A. Harness, "Our Most Dangerous Lobby," *Reader's Digest* (December 1947). A short account of lobbyists is the pamphlet by Franklin L. Burdette, *Lobbyists in Action* (Washington: National Capital Publishers, 1950).

PROJECTS

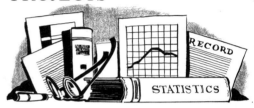

1. Make a chart showing the evolution of political parties in the United States. Indicate the principal third parties and what they stood for. This project would take some extra time to prepare, but the result would be a worthwhile reference chart for later chapters in this text.

2. A student interested in political activities of the major parties could study the election maps or returns for the elections since 1900. The former can be found in a complete American history text, and the various almanacs list the election results. Notice should be made of the inroads that one party makes from time to time into territory traditionally ascribed to its opposition. Sectional interests account for the solidarity of the vote in certain areas, and it would be interesting to the entire class to learn how such "blocs" are sometimes broken by the opposing party.

3. A student interested in modern European history could trace the changes in the government of France since World War II, indicating how the political power has changed hands so many times in this state that has a multi-party system. A class discussion should bring to light the disadvantages and advantages to the French government in its recent history brought about by this system.

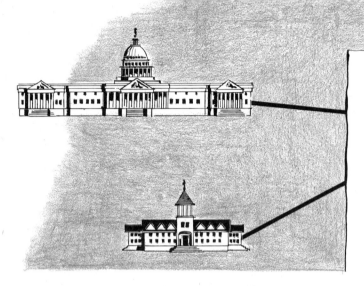

The Constitution of the United States 1787

Chapter 24. Federalism and Nationalism

70. THE FEDERAL UNION AND THE STATES

Every citizen in the United States finds himself subject at the same time to several governments—federal, state, county, municipal—all of which he must support and obey. The federal system of government is complicated, and the growth of governmental functions in the economic and social spheres in the last fifty years has made it more complicated than ever.

The nature of federal government. Political scientists classify governments as confederate, federal, and unitary. The essential differences among these three types of government are found in the location of ultimate power. The *confederate government* is one in which the individual states composing it retain their full sovereignty and independence. They delegate certain powers to the central government, which acts as their agent in certain specified matters. The central government cannot operate on the citizens directly; its relations are only with the separate states. The German Confederation (1815–1867) is an example of this type of government, as was American government under the

Articles of Confederation (1781–1789).

A *unitary government* is one in which power is concentrated in the central government, and the local units possess only the powers assigned to them by the sovereign central government. The distribution of powers can be changed by the central government in the unitary system, whereas it can be changed only by the local states in the confederate system. France and England have unitary government. In France the local units are little more than administrative agencies of the central government, whereas the British Parliament has delegated a large measure of independence to local units in Great Britain. In both cases, however, it is the central government that has effected the distribution of powers and has the authority to change the distribution.

Federal government is one in which power is distributed between the central and local units in such fashion that the distribution can be altered only by mutual consent of both central and local governments. It is a compromise between two sets of values, one central and one local, and as a compromise it sets up a form of government that is more com-

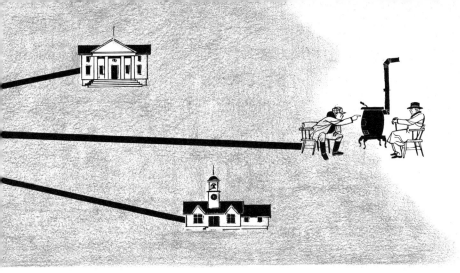

plex and harder to modify than either confederate or unitary government. In the federal system both central and local governments derive their powers from a fundamental constitution. Both operate directly on the people. Local states cannot withdraw at will from the federal union, as they can in a confederacy, nor can the central government alter the distribution of powers by itself, as it can in the unitary system.

Federal government possesses certain distinct advantages and disadvantages as compared to the other two types of government. Its chief advantage is that local units join together to create a large and powerful government without sacrificing their separate identities. Local affairs can continue to be handled locally. In the second place, such a system preserves

better the variety in laws and civil institutions which arise from varied forms of social life. In similar fashion, the federal system increases opportunities for active participation in political life. It serves, so to speak, as a "training school" in the states for people to obtain political experience before assuming positions in the central government. Finally, the federal system tends to decentralize power, and when it works properly it saves the central government from overburdening functions that are common in government today.

The disadvantages of federalism are the reverse side of its advantages. First, it entails a certain duplication of functions and services—and with this, of course, additional expense. Second, the federal system is less flexible than unitary

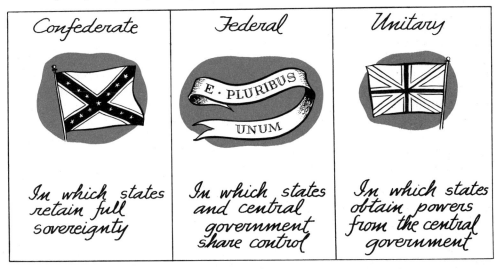

Confederate	Federal	Unitary
In which states retain full sovereignty	In which states and central government share control	In which states obtain powers from the central government

government, and in time of crisis this rigidity can become a serious handicap. Third, lack of uniformity in legislation and administration among the local units creates confusion in such matters as insurance, divorce, and business law. Fourth, the independence of the local governments can sometimes embarrass and handicap the central government in its foreign relations, as happened when California legislation against Orientals created difficulties for the national government in dealing with China and Japan.

The American federal system. You will remember from your American history that the central government under the Articles of Confederation was not granted sufficient powers to function properly in foreign affairs or even to operate effectively in domestic matters. To save this new union from falling apart, Washington, Madison, Hamilton, and other statesmen of the age gathered in Philadelphia for the purpose of amending the Articles of Confederation in order to strengthen the central government. The result of their deliberations was the Constitution, which provided for an entirely new federal form of government. This federal system, provided for in 1789, is America's great and unique contribution to mankind's political experience.

In the American federal system each state is organized on a *unitary* basis, and they are joined together in a *federal* system. This means that each state creates local political subdivisions, such as counties and municipalities, and it is free to alter these subdivisions, subject only to the state's own constitutional limitations. Within the state, then, the distribution of political power is made by the state government. Within the federal system, however, the distribution of powers between the central and state governments is made by the Constitution, and it can be altered basically only by constitutional amendment.

Distribution of powers. The national government possesses only delegated, "enumerated" powers. Because there seemed some doubt about this fact, the Tenth Amendment, ratified in 1791, stated that "all powers not delegated to the United States by the Constitution, nor prohibited by it to the states, are reserved to the states respectively or to the people." We have seen that the national government does many things undreamed of in the time of the Founding Fathers, but every act, legislative or executive, must find justification somewhere among the powers delegated to the national government.

States, on the other hand, possess powers that are original, inherent, and largely undefined. They possess what may be called "residual powers," or those remaining after the national government has received its grant of specified, delegated powers. It must be emphasized that all government in the American system is limited, state as well as national, and the Ninth Amendment asserts that "the enumeration in the Constitution of certain rights shall not be construed to deny or disparage others retained by the people." The limitations on the national government are in the national Constitution, whereas state governments are limited both by the national Constitution and their respective state constitutions.

Supremacy of national government. Early Supreme Court decisions under Chief Justice Marshall affirmed the supremacy of national power in the areas in which national and state powers overlap or conflict. In many areas the federal government has exclusive powers, as in the conduct of foreign relations and the coining of money. In other areas the states enjoy exclusive jurisdiction, as in education or legislation relating to the maintenance of law and order within the state. In still other areas state and national jurisdictions overlap. Both, for example, may tax citizens. The Constitution, however, was adopted as "the supreme law of the land," in the words of its sixth article. The Supreme Court in *U.S.* v. *Tarble* (1872) explained the doctrine of national supremacy in these words:

There are within the territorial limits of each state two governments restricted in their spheres of action, but independent of each other, and supreme within their respective spheres. Each has its separate departments; each has its distinct laws, and each has its own tribunals for their enforcement. Neither government can intrude within the jurisdiction, or authorize any interference therein by its judicial officers with the action of the other. The two governments in each state stand in their respective spheres of action in the same independent relation to each other, except in one particular, that they would if their authority embraced distinct territorities. That particular consists in the supremacy of the authority of the United States when any conflict arises between the two governments.

Jurisdictional disputes are inevitable in a federal system that distributes power between the national and state governments. These disputes are settled by the Supreme Court. This is much like having a member of one team act as umpire in a ball game, but there seems no better method of settling such disputes. The national supremacy cannot be safeguarded in any other way, and the lessons we learned under the Articles of Confederation proved conclusively that the national government must be superior if it is to fulfill its functions.

Limitations on the national government. Although the national government is supreme, it is by no means unlimited. We have already seen that the Bill of Rights sets up restrictions on the national government. Still other restrictions are to be found in the body of the Constitution, and the Tenth Amendment specifically restricts the national government to the use of its delegated powers.

Limitations on state governments. Although the states possess residual powers, nevertheless they are limited in a number of ways. First, limitations arise from the broad delegation of power to the national government. Specific limitations are found especially in Article I, Section 10, and in the Fourteenth Amendment. The states are excluded from foreign affairs by the express prohibition against entering into any "treaty, alliance, or confederation." Moreover, they are not allowed to enter into interstate compacts except with the express consent of Congress. The courts have interpreted this restriction as applying only to agreements that tend to increase the power of the states or to encroach on the supremacy of the national government. Thus two states can settle a sewage-disposal problem, as New York and New Jersey did, without congressional consent. But the same two states had to obtain the consent of Congress to set up the New York Port Authority.

The states' taxing power is limited in a number of ways. States are not allowed to lay import or export duties or charge duty on tonnage.[1] Taxing power is limited also by the prohibition against depriving any person of property without due process of law, by the prohibition against laws "impairing the obligation of contracts," and by guarantees that "the citizens of each state shall be entitled to all

---

[1] Tonnage duties are taxes levied on a ship on the basis of its carrying capacity or tonnage.

The Supreme Court building in Washington, D.C., houses the highest tribunal in the land. The Supreme Court has limited original jurisdiction, but its appellate jurisdiction has had great influence on the Constitution of the United States. (Standard Oil Co., N.J.)

The Port Authority of New York operates a helicopter on the roof of the Authority's Manhattan building. The bi-state agency, serving New York and New Jersey, supervises tunnels, ferries, and bridges between the two states. (Port of New York Authority)

privileges and immunities of citizens in the several states," and that "no state shall make or enforce any law which shall abridge the privileges or immunities of citizens of the United States." These are general limitations on state powers, of course, and they apply to taxing as well as other powers. State control over commerce is strictly limited (a) to such trade as originates and ends within a single state and (b) is exercised in pursuit of the state's police power. A state may force interstate truck drivers to comply with certain safety requirements, for example, but this is construed as falling within the state's right to protect its inhabitants rather than its right to regulate commerce as such.

Obligations of the national government to the states. The federal system is made stable by certain obligations the national government constitutionally owes to the states. (1) It must respect the identity and the territory of each state. No two states can be joined into one, nor can territory be taken from one state and given to another without the express consent of both states. (2) The national government is obliged to protect every state against invasion and domestic violence. The national authorities do not ordinarily provide forces to put down domestic insurrection or riots unless requested to do so by the proper state authorities. If national laws are violated, however, or national functions (such as carrying of the mail) are interfered with, the national government has the right to interfere on its own initiative. (3) The national government must guarantee to every state a republican form of government. Except during the Reconstruction Era after the Civil War, this provision has operated only a few times in our national history. Congress and the President have the right to decide whether a state has "republican government" and to recognize which of two contesting governments is the rightful one. (4) The national government is obliged to recognize the fundamental equality of the states and to afford them equality of representation in Congress.

Obligations of the states to the national government. Besides the general obligation of fitting into the federal system as devised in the Constitution, each state has the obligation of providing machinery for electing representatives, senators, and the President. Elections are conducted by the several states subject only to such legislations as the national Congress has passed relative to national elections. The states also have the obligation, when occasion arises, of taking the necessary procedural steps to ratify or not to ratify constitutional amendments proposed by Congress.

Obligations of the states to each other. More complicated are the specific obligations that the states owe to each other in our federal system. These are three in number: (1) mutual recognition of legal processes and acts; (2) interstate citizenship; (3) rendition of persons accused of crime. Each of these obligations has been qualified to some extent by experience with concrete cases. Let us therefore look at each of them in more detail.

1. The Constitution requires that "full faith and credit shall be given in each state to the public acts, records, and judicial proceedings of every other state." This apparently simple requirement becomes complicated when we consider such a judicial proceeding as divorce.

Must New York, with its strict divorce laws, recognize the validity of every divorce granted in Nevada, where the only requirement is the establishment of a fictitious residence? The Supreme Court has ruled that a divorce granted by a state enjoying jurisdiction over both spouses is valid and must be recognized in all states. If residence is fictitious or if the divorce is granted by a state in which only one of the spouses is domiciled, then the divorce is not entitled to "full faith and credit" by the other states.

In general, most states habitually give the benefit of doubt to statutes and proceedings of other states. Thus judgments rendered in one state are enforceable in others. If Jones obtained a $500 judgment against Smith in New York, for example, but Smith moved to Indiana before Jones collected, the latter could collect through the Indiana courts simply by presenting the judgment in his favor from the New York court.

2. The purpose of interstate citizenship is to prevent one state from discriminating in favor of its residents against the residents of other states. The Constitution states that "the citizens of each state shall be entitled to all privileges and immunities of citizens in the several states." Obviously, a Kansan moving to California does not take his Kansan privileges and immunities with him. Nor does he automatically receive all the privileges and immunities of California residents. He must meet any reas-

States' Obligations to Each Other

State Line

Interstate Freedom

Rendition of accused persons

Mutual Recognition of Legal acts and processes

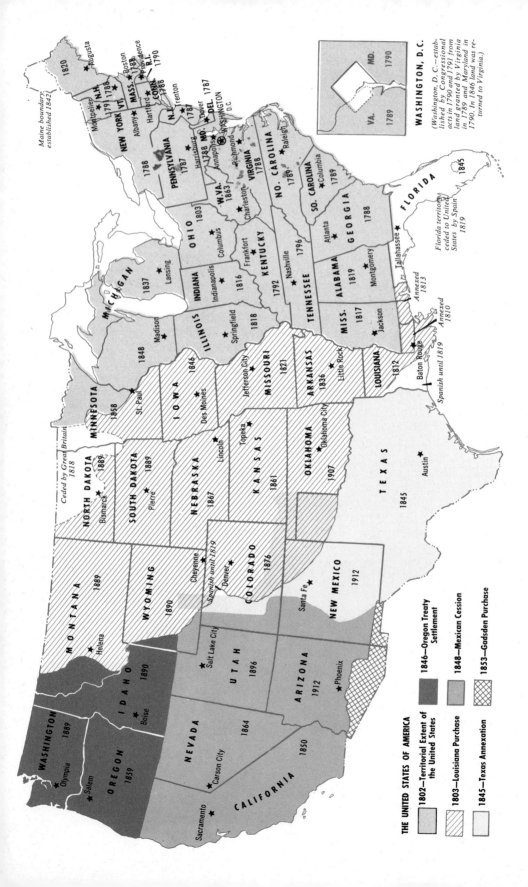

THE UNITED STATES OF AMERICA

1802—Territorial Extent of the United States

1803—Louisiana Purchase

1845—Texas Annexation

1846—Oregon Treaty Settlement

1848—Mexican Cession

1853—Gadsden Purchase

WASHINGTON, D.C.

(Washington, D. C.—established by Congressional acts in 1790 and 1791 from land granted by Virginia in 1789 and Maryland in 1790. In 1846 land was returned to Virginia.)

MD. 1790

VA. 1789

Maine boundary established 1842

1820 ★ Augusta

N.H. 1788 ★ Concord

VT. 1791 ★ Montpelier

MASS. 1788 ★ Boston

R.I. 1790 ★ Providence

CONN. 1788 ★ Hartford

NEW YORK 1788 ★ Albany

N.J. 1787 ★ Trenton

DEL. 1787 ★ Dover

WASHINGTON D.C.

PENNSYLVANIA 1787 ★ Harrisburg

MD. 1788 ★ Annapolis

VIRGINIA 1788 ★ Richmond

W.VA. 1863 ★ Charleston

OHIO 1803 ★ Columbus

NO. CAROLINA 1789 ★ Raleigh

SO. CAROLINA 1788 ★ Columbia

MICHIGAN 1837 ★ Lansing

INDIANA 1816 ★ Indianapolis

KENTUCKY 1792 ★ Frankfort

TENNESSEE 1796 ★ Nashville

GEORGIA 1788 ★ Atlanta

ALABAMA 1819 ★ Montgomery

FLORIDA 1845 ★ Tallahassee

Florida territory ceded to United States by Spain 1819

Annexed 1813

Annexed 1810

Spanish until 1819

★ Baton Rouge

ILLINOIS 1818 ★ Springfield

MISS. 1817 ★ Jackson

LOUISIANA 1812

MINNESOTA 1858 ★ St. Paul

Ceded by Great Britain 1818

IOWA 1846 ★ Des Moines

MISSOURI 1821 ★ Jefferson City

ARKANSAS 1836 ★ Little Rock

NORTH DAKOTA 1889 ★ Bismarck

SOUTH DAKOTA 1889 ★ Pierre

NEBRASKA 1867 ★ Lincoln

KANSAS 1861 ★ Topeka

OKLAHOMA 1907 ★ Oklahoma City

TEXAS 1845 ★ Austin

MONTANA 1889 ★ Helena

WYOMING 1890 ★ Cheyenne

Spanish until 1819

COLORADO 1876 ★ Denver

NEW MEXICO 1912 ★ Santa Fe

IDAHO 1890 ★ Boise

WASHINGTON 1889 ★ Olympia

OREGON 1859 ★ Salem

NEVADA 1864 ★ Carson City

UTAH 1896 ★ Salt Lake City

ARIZONA 1912 ★ Phoenix

CALIFORNIA 1850 ★ Sacramento

onable residence and other requirements to vote, to hold office, or to engage in professional activities such as medicine or law. The guarantee is rather that he will enjoy equal protection of the laws, access to the courts, freedom from discriminatory taxation, and the right to acquire and use property the same way as do residents of the state.

3. States are mutually obliged to render up to each other fugitives accused of a crime. "A person charged in any state with treason, felony, or other crime," the Constitution reads, "who shall flee from justice, and be found in another state, shall, on demand of the executive authority of the state from which he fled, be delivered up, to be removed to the state having jurisdiction of the crime." Ordinarily, writs of extradition, whereby the governor of one state requests the governor of another state to turn over a fugitive prisoner, are honored without question. The mutuality of interest among the states in securing the return of fugitives makes it necessary for them to honor each other's requests. Occasionally, however, the governor of one state will refuse to surrender a fugitive from another state if he believes that the fugitive will not receive fair trial in the state from which he has fled. If the governor refuses to deliver up the fugitive, there is no way of compelling him to abide by the seemingly clear constitutional mandate that he do so. The Supreme Court has ruled that it does not have the power to issue a writ of mandamus against the governor of a state under this constitutional provision.[2]

[2] In *Kentucky* v. *Dennison* (1861), Chief Justice Taney stated: "The words, 'it shall be the duty' were not used as mandatory and compulsory, but as declaratory of the moral duty which this command created, when Congress had provided the mode of carrying it into execution. The act does not provide any means to compel the execution of this duty, nor inflict any punishment for neglect or refusal on the part of the executive of the state; nor is there any clause or provision in the Constitution which arms the government of the United States with this power."

71. ALTERATIONS OF FEDERAL RELATIONS

When the Founding Fathers established our federal government they provided for change in two formal ways: (1) the admission of new states into the federation; (2) constitutional amendment to change the distribution of powers as future needs might dictate. Let us now see how these changes are effected.

The admission of new states. Congress is given power by the Constitution to admit new states subject to two restrictions we have already seen: (1) that it cannot create a state within the jurisdiction of an existing state; (2) that a new state cannot be formed from the junction of two existing states without the consent of both of them. Otherwise Congress is free to set whatever conditions it wishes for the admission of new states.

The usual procedure is for the people of a territory desiring admission to the Union—as Hawaii or Alaska today—to petition for admission as a state. If Congress receives the petition favorably, it passes an "enabling act" authorizing the people of the territory to elect a constitutional convention to draft a constitution. This constitution is then submitted to the people of the territory for approval, and if it is approved in the referendum it is forwarded to Congress. If Congress approves the constitution, it admits the territory to the Union as a new state by joint declaration. However, Congress may suggest or even demand changes in the constitution, and the President may veto the joint resolution of admission if he disapproves of some feature of the constitution.

The people in the territory desiring admission have no recourse except to devise a constitution acceptable to Congress and the President. After once being admitted as a state, however, the constitution may be altered to suit the people of the new state—but this alteration must be within certain limits. The Supreme

Two proposed changes in the flag of the United States of America are shown here: if (left) Hawaii or Alaska is admitted to the Union and (right) if both are admitted. (Designed by Digby W. Chandler)

Court, for example, allowed Oklahoma to change the location of its capital from Guthrie, where Congress insisted it be placed, to the location desired by the Oklahoma government. Again, Arizona was permitted to reinstate a constitutional provision for recall of judges which it had to eliminate from its constitution as a condition of admittance in 1912. In other cases, however, such as provisions concerning public lands in New Mexico and Minnesota, the Supreme Court held that the conditions were permanently binding and contrary action by the states after admission was held unconstitutional.

Method of constitutional amendment. It is noteworthy that despite the revolutionary social and economic changes since 1789 we have had to adopt only twenty-two amendments to the original Constitution. Ten of these were adopted at once as a condition for accepting the Constitution, and for practical purposes they can be considered part of the original document, and the Twenty-first Amendment canceled the Eighteenth.

The statesmen who drew up the Constitution realized that it was not a perfect document to cover all possible contingencies in the future, so they devised a process of amendment that would be neither easy nor impossibly difficult to achieve. The provision for amendment, apart from some temporary provisions, is as follows:

The Congress, whenever two-thirds of both houses shall deem it necessary, shall propose amendments to this constitution, or, on the application of the legislatures of two-thirds of the several states, shall call a convention for proposing amendments, which in either case shall be valid to all intents and purposes as part of this constitution, when ratified by the legislatures of three-fourths of the several states, or by conventions in three-fourths thereof, as the one or the other mode of ratification may be proposed by the Congress.

Two methods of initiative and two methods of ratification are provided. Only one method of initiative has so far been used, since all amendments have been proposed by joint resolution of the two houses of Congress. All amendments except the Twenty-first have been ratified by state legislatures. The Twenty-first Amendment was ratified by state conventions called for that purpose. Some attempts have been made to initiate constitutional revision by a national convention, and occasionally more than two-thirds of the state legislatures forwarded requests to Congress to call such a convention. But as yet the necessary number of requests has not been received in what Congress has considered a reasonable time limit. Moreover, it would seem that if a large number of requests came from the states for a certain amendment, Congress would itself take the initiative, as it did with the Twenty-first Amendment repealing prohibition.

In years past there was some question

as to how long a state legislature could wait before ratifying a proposed amendment. In 1869 the Ohio legislature ratified an amendment proposed eighty years earlier. A child-labor amendment submitted in 1924 was acted on by state legislatures as late as 1937, and in 1939 the Supreme Court recognized it as still pending. At this time the Court suggested that it was up to Congress to decide how long a proposed amendment should remain "alive" for ratification. Beginning with the Eighteenth Amendment, however, Congress adopted the procedure of requiring ratification within seven years. This procedure has been used ever since, except for the Nineteenth (woman suffrage) Amendment, to which no time limit was fixed. As soon as the thirty-sixth state notifies the United States Secretary of State of its ratification, the proposed amendment takes effect as an integral part of the Constitution.

The growth of national power. A marked trend in our national history, especially in the twentieth century, has been the tremendous increase of power and functions of the national government. This trend has been condemned by many Americans as unnecessary encroachment by the central government upon the functions of local government and the private lives of American citizens. It has been reluctantly defended by others as a necessary counterpart of the social and economic developments of the past century. Whether it is necessary or not, it is a trend that Americans should study, evaluate, and, if it seems feasible and prudent, modify or reverse.

To a considerable degree this expansion was inevitable. The addition of thirty-five states to the original thirteen, the growth of population to more than 165,000,000, the building of a complicated industrial economy with a network of transportation lines covering the nation—all these social and economic developments have forced the national government into functions that were formerly reserved to state or local authorities. Moreover, economic changes have created new government functions not thought of a century ago. Finally, the problem of fighting two wars and playing a leading role in world affairs has thrust upon the national government many additional burdens and given it considerable power not habitually employed in our earlier history.

Very little of this growth has been through constitutional amendment. Six amendments have affected the distribution of power between the national and state governments. Two amendments gave the national government increased power. The Sixteenth allowed it to levy income taxes without apportionment. The Eighteenth—repealed by the Twenty-first—empowered it to prohibit the manufacture, sale, or transportation of intoxicating liquors. Four amendments curtailed state powers. The Fourteenth put several restrictions on the states, the

The functions of many departments in the federal government directly benefit the states. The Department of Agriculture conducts tests and surveys, such as this one to determine the amount of snowfall for conservation purposes, in conjunction with state departments. (U.S.D.A. Photo)

United States Air Force troops were called on to combat a 41,000-acre forest fire in New Mexico. Such co-operation between federal and state governments is often necessary in time of disasters. (U. S. Forest Service)

Fifteenth and Nineteenth limited their power to restrict the right to vote, and the Seventeenth provided for the direct election of senators rather than having them chosen by the state legislatures.

Further federal expansion. It is obvious that the tremendous growth of national power cannot be accounted for in terms of formal amendments to the Constitution. Let us therefore list the more important additional methods of federal expansion.

1. *Development of implied powers.* The Constitution gives Congress the power "to make all Laws which shall be necessary and proper for carrying into Execution the foregoing Powers, and all other Powers vested by this Constitution in the Government of the United States, or any Department or Officer thereof." The obligation to attain any objective of government implies the right to use the necessary means to attain it. The liberal interpretation of what "implied powers" constitutes was given classic expression by Chief Justice Marshall in the case of *McCulloch* v. *Maryland.*

The sound construction of the Constitution [the Court stated] must allow to the national legislature that discretion, with respect to the means by which the powers it confers are to be carried into execution, which will enable that body to perform the high duties assigned to it, in the manner most beneficial to the people. Let the end be legitimate, let it be within the scope of the Constitution, and all means which are appropriate, which are plainly adapted to that end, which are not prohibited, but consistent with the letter and spirit of the Constitution, are constitutional.

The power to regulate commerce, to conserve natural resources, to coin and borrow money have all been used to justify the constitutionality of the government's engaging in business on a large scale. The power of national defense implies the power to own and operate munitions plants, engage in scientific research, subsidize universities, and enter into many activities formerly reserved for private citizens.

2. *Judicial interpretation.* It has been remarked that at any given time the Constitution means what the nine judges on the Supreme Court say it means. Although this is not entirely true, inasmuch as tradition, precedent, and current opinion all limit the judges' leeway of interpretation, nevertheless the meaning of any phrase in the Constitution undergoes change according to judicial interpretation. Through the course of a century and a half the Supreme Court has increased the national government's powers by

consistently enlarging the coverage of many phrases. Prominent among these phrases is the "due process" clause of the Fourteenth Amendment, which originally was intended as a protection for the newly enfranchised Negro. Judicial interpretation enlarged its meaning to protect corporate property and civil liberties against arbitrary state regulation. Judicial interpretation of the commerce clause, again, has justified national regulation of wages and hours, and collective bargaining.

3. *Failure of the states to use their powers fully.* We have seen that the states possess "residual power," but in practice it has been difficult to decide just what this power includes and how it is to be used. Problems presented by modern industrial and social developments frequently could not be solved by state action. Either they transcended state boundaries and therefore defied action by any single state, or they involved an outlay of funds and the use of personnel and facilities that the individual state could not provide. Moreover, the states simply failed to accomplish needed reform or take positive action toward ameliorating the Great Depression of the 1930s, and their failure paved the way for New Deal measures which expanded national functions tremendously.

4. *Co-operation between federal and state authorities.* Occasionally federal authorities are employed to enforce state laws, as when federal forest officers are commissioned as state deputy fish and game wardens. More frequently, the national government makes use of state administrative officials to enforce federal law. Thousands of state employees were commissioned to administer the selective service acts of 1917 and 1940. The National Recovery and Agricultural Adjustment Acts, the Pure Food and Drug Act, the Migratory Bird Treaty Act, and a number of other federal laws are administered at least in part by state officials.

Another form of co-operation between national and state governments that expands federal functions is national research as a service to the states. The federal government conducts large-scale investigations by bureaus in the Departments of Agriculture, Labor, and Commerce, and this research cannot easily be duplicated by any of the states. They have therefore come to rely on federal research facilities for information on which to base legislative and administrative reform, as well as to obtain help for private industry and farmers. Finally, there are various other forms of voluntary co-operation between the national and state governments which inevitably extend federal influence and control into state affairs. The TVA, for example, has an agreement with seven states in its area for a joint program of agricultural development and

Federal and state game wardens examine an illegal trap found in a Virginia marsh. Co-operation between the two governments has been extensive in the program to preserve the fish and wildlife of the United States. (Knoblock, Fish and Wildlife Service)

flood control. In the field of crime control there is extensive informal co-operation between state and national officials.

5. *Grants-in-aid.* Federal control over state activity has been very much expanded in the last twenty years through financial grants-in-aid for a wide variety of purposes. Financial assistance from the national government is nothing new in American history. Beginning in 1802, the national government bestowed land on newly admitted states to be used for the development of their schools, and occasionally money was given to the states (in time of surplus revenue) for education, roads, and canals.

In the last two decades, however, a new type of conditional grant has become an important factor in American political life. The grant-in-aid is a device whereby Congress appropriates money for a specific purpose to be achieved by the states. The grant is apportioned among the states on some fixed basis and under the following conditions: that the state spend the money only for the purpose and under the conditions stipulated; that the state match the federal grant, usually in the same amount; that the state accept the regulations and standards set by the national government and allow it to supervise the work done and the results achieved. Grants-in-aid have been made especially for highway construction, public housing, education, health administration, public assistance and welfare, and conservation. Since the depression, the total annual amount of funds granted under these terms to the states has increased substantially. In 1920 they amounted to only $37,600,000, but in 1937 they totaled $582,500,000 and constituted the third largest source of revenue for the states. The amount rose sharply after World War II and has consistently been over two billion dollars a year since 1950.

Grants-in-aid are strongly opposed by those who believe the central government is becoming unwieldy, overburdened, and top-heavy. These critics argue that the national government is less able to take care of its proper functions when it concerns itself with matters that can be handled efficiently enough by state and local agencies. More specifically, the critics have formulated the following general lines of argument: (1) Grants-in-aid are a species of bribery under which the national government purchases the right to control certain state activities. (2) The system coerces the states into overburdening themselves, because no state can "afford" to pass up the "bargain" offered by the central government. (3) They are a means of assuring the party in power of a mass of favorable votes. (4) They tend to destroy the independence of the states and make them rely on handouts from Washington. (5) Grants-in-aid are unjust

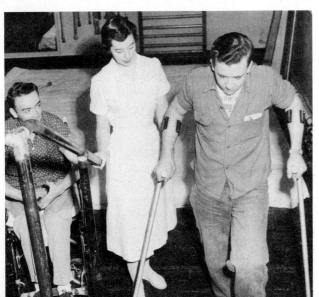

The state-federal program for vocational rehabilitation is a corporate effort to restore the disabled to a self-sufficient life, through medical aid, counseling, training, and job finding. (U. S. Department of Health, Education and Welfare)

Flood control is an example of a problem that is best handled by the states in co-operation with the federal government. Here the Senate Committee on Banking and Currency listens to Governor Harriman of New York at a hearing on proposed disaster risk insurance legislation. (Wide World Photo)

to the richer states, for they must bear a large share of the expense of grants to poorer and more backward states.

Defenders of the system counter by arguing: (1) Grants-in-aid encourage the states to undertake projects they could not otherwise afford. (2) They help the poorer states. (3) They provide for minimum national standards that otherwise would be disregarded in many of the states. (4) Since initiative and responsibility are left to the states, there is no danger of national dictatorship, as the critics of the system seem to imply. However one may feel about grants-in-aid as a policy, there is no doubt that they have become part of our federal system. The Supreme Court has passed on the constitutionality of the system, and opposition to the principle is not as strong as it used to be. Opposition now usually centers around the wisdom of a particular grant-in-aid rather than the general principle.

The problem of centralization. The power and authority of the central government have increased tremendously as compared to the power of state governments. Critics of this trend maintain that, practically speaking, our federal system will eventually end up in unitary government, with the states remaining only as administrative units for nationally determined policies. Advocates of centralization maintain that the United States has been so thoroughly nationalized economically, socially, and in every other way that the old federal system should be abandoned as obsolete.

Critics of the existing federal system point out that the states are ill arranged, that state boundaries are antiquated political lines that do not follow any rational plan and are not adapted to social and economic groupings throughout the country. They point out, for example, that metropolitan New York spills over into three states, and that Chicago should be in the same political unit with Milwaukee and South Bend instead of Cairo and East St. Louis. Some people therefore advocate redrawing the map of the states along more sensible geographic lines. Others advocate replacing the states by regions, such as New England, that would have some kind of social and economic unity. Advocates of these plans insist that their adoption is necessary for the preservation of the federal system, that the states as now constituted cannot function as vital parts of a federal system.

Advocates of such far-reaching alterations in American constitutional life perhaps do not realize that their proposals are revolutionary. Any one of them would transform the states into provinces of a unitary national state instead of members of a federal republic. Thus the essential principle of our Constitution would be lost. Wise political thinkers have ever had an aversion to proposals that would renovate civil society according to schemes of simplified centralization. Complex governments in which power is well distributed have far more security and durability than simple governments in which all power emanates from one central source. France acquired a simple, centralized government through her great revolution in the last years of the eighteenth century and since then has had at least seven revolutionary changes in her government. Our complex federal Republic survived a vast civil war, and its government has never been overturned by violence.

Arresting centralization. Meanwhile more practical steps have been taken in the last twenty years to arrest centralization. A number of the states have set about reforming their own governments in the interest of making them more efficient and effective units of political power. States have also begun to co-operate with each other in order to solve their own problems without appealing for help to the central government. Since 1939 very few additional trade barriers[3] have been erected by one state to discriminate against producers in other states, and a good many barriers have been removed. The Council of State Governments, organized in 1925, has taken a lead in

bringing the states into closer, more harmonious relationship in the last twenty years. Several meetings (such as the Governors' Conference) and associations (such as the National Conference of Commissioners on Uniform State Laws) have promoted co-operation among the states with a view to restoring them to something like their original position in the federal system.

REVIEW

70. The Federal Union and the States

A. Define confederate, federal, and unitary government. Give an example of each.

B. Give several advantages and disadvantages of the federal type of government.

C. How did the Supreme Court explain the doctrine of national supremacy?

D. Explain three ways in which the state governments have been limited by the federal Constitution.

E. What are some of the obligations of the national government to the states; of the states to the national government; of the states to each other?

71. Alterations of Federal Relations

A. Point out two limitations on the admission of new states by Congress. Describe the general procedure by which a new state is admitted to the Union.

B. How is the Constitution amended? What method of amendment has not yet been used?

C. Show how federal government power has expanded through "grants-in-aids."

D. What are some of the problems brought on by the centralization of power in the federal government?

THE CHAPTER IN REVIEW

A. Describe the American system of government. How do the various governments within our system have obligations to each other?

---

[3] Although states are not permitted to levy import duties against goods shipped from other states, they can use their police power—within limits—to put up barriers to interstate commerce. In the interest of the "health" of its citizens, for example, a state can prohibit the importation of certain fruits or vegetables. Such discriminatory legislation usually begets retaliation from the other states, and in the long run it is the citizens of the states who pay the bill for trade barriers.

B. Describe in detail the process for amending the Constitution, including the proposal and ratification of amendments.

C. Briefly describe each of the various ways that the federal government increased its powers and functions since 1789.

SELECTED READINGS

Our distinctive federal system of government can be understood only if one has a thorough knowledge of the Constitution. One of the best books on this subject is Edward S. Corwin, *The Constitution and What It Means Today* (Princeton, N.J.: Princeton University Press, 11th Edition, 1954). A simplified study designed for students is William Kottmeyer, *Our Constitution and What It Means* (St. Louis: Webster Publishing Company, 1949). Other standard and widely used books on the Constitution include: John M. Mathews, *The American Constitutional System* (New York: Mc-Graw-Hill Book Co., 1940); Frank A. Magruder and G. S. Claire, *The Constitution* (New York: McGraw-Hill Book Co., 1930); and Carl B. Swisher, *American Constitutional Development* (Boston: Houghton Mifflin Co., 1943).

The "new Federalism," which is the complexus of relations between the national and state governments developing in the twentieth century, is analyzed in the following studies: R. H. Wells, *American Local Government* (New York: McGraw-Hill Book Co., 1939), which deals largely with federal-state relations; Jane Perry Clark, *The Rise of a New Federalism* (New York: Columbia University Press, 1938); K. C. Wheare, *Federal Government* (New York: Oxford University Press, Inc., 1947); D. Fellman, "Federalism," *American Political Science Review* (December 1947), which gives a good summary of the subject.

The trend toward centralization in the twentieth century is analyzed by George C. S. Benson, *The New Centralization* (New York: Farrar & Rinehart, Inc., 1941). The use of grants-in-aid with consequent increase of national control over local governments is the subject

of Henry J. Bitterman's *State and Federal Grants in Aid* (Chicago: Mentzer, Bush and Company, 1938); E. A. Williams, *Federal Aid for Relief* (New York: Columbia University Press, 1939); and the study sponsored by the Council of State Governments, *Federal Grants in Aid* (Chicago: The Council of State Governments, 1949).

PROJECTS

1. Members of the class could be elected to serve as an amendment committee, to propose an amendment to the Student Council constitution or even the national Constitution. Lively discussion, lobbying by certain interested groups, and the democratic procedures that should be followed will provide the class with an interesting and worth-while activity.

2. A student can make a report on a grant-in-aid made to his state for education, highway construction, or any other project. The report should include the specific purpose of the grant, the extent of federal assistance, and the regulations fixed by the federal government in regard to the supervision of the project. The various state departments (e.g., education, welfare, highways) will be able to supply the necessary information for the report.

PROFILES

ALEXANDER HAMILTON

BORN: Nevis, British West Indies, January 11, 1757
EDUCATION: Provincetown School, N.J.; King's College (Columbia)—1 year
DIED: New York City, July 11, 1804

Hamilton's early years were spent in poverty, but a fortunate connection with Nicholas Cruger, an important New York merchant in the Indies, gave him a chance to prove his business abilities and his capacity for hard work. Through the aid of Cruger and other friends Hamilton was able to come to New York. In New York at the beginning of the Revolution, he joined patriot groups at King's College and rapidly became a leading speaker and pamphleteer in the colonial cause. He left college to command a Continental Army artillery company.

His rise in the army was spectacular: he became Washington's aide-de-camp and concluded his service as colonel commanding a regiment at Yorktown. He served briefly as a civilian member of the Continental Congress in 1782–1783, but more prominently as a key member of the Annapolis Convention in 1786, which paved the way for the Constitutional Convention.

Hamilton attended the Constitutional Convention, where he argued energetically for a very strong central government. Although his ideas were not accepted entirely, he turned his powerful pen to writing more than half *The Federalist* in the fight to ratify the Constitution in New York. In this battle for New York votes, Hamilton formed the nucleus of a political party of like-minded men.

Hamilton served as Washington's Secretary of the Treasury from 1789–1795, rendering his most important service to the nation by establishing the fiscal credit of the United States. His program included the funding of all former debts at face value, including those of the states incurred in the Revolution; as a mark of federal power as well as a source of revenue, he favored the collection of excise taxes, such as the famous whisky tax; and he favored full use of implied powers of the central government to set up a national bank.

During these years Hamilton became the founder of a national political party, the Federalist. It sought to encourage commerce and industrial growth, with a powerful central government under the leadership of men distinguished by birth, education, or wealth. His chief New York opponent, Aaron Burr, led Tammany forces, who were allied with Jefferson. Hamilton persuaded Federalist congressmen not to vote for Burr in the 1800 election, which made Jefferson President. In 1804, Hamilton's attacks on the character of Aaron Burr kept Burr from the New York governorship but led to the duel which cost Hamilton his life.

The most recent readily available biography is *Alexander Hamilton, Nation Builder,* by Nathan Schachner (New York: McGraw-Hill Book Co., 1952). Hamilton's essays in *The Federalist* or his *Report on Manufactures* should be consulted for more direct impressions of his political and economic ideas; both are sampled in the Bowers reference for Jefferson, and printed in full in Henry Cabot Lodge, ed., *Works of Alexander Hamilton,* 12 vols. (New York: G. P. Putnam's Sons, 1904–1906).

HERBERT C. HOOVER

BORN: West Branch, Ia., August 10, 1874
EDUCATION: Stanford University, A.B. in Engineering, 1895

Few men in American history have had such long and distinguished careers as Herbert Hoover's. Herbert Hoover gained recognition here and abroad as an engineer prior to 1917. Hoover administered war relief to the Belgians, and when the United States entered the war in 1917 he was made Food Administrator. He later headed the Russian Relief Commission.

A successful administrator, Hoover was appointed Secretary of Commerce in the cabinet of Harding. He continued as Secretary of Commerce until 1928, when he was chosen as Republican candidate for the presidency. His first year as President was marked by the onset of the Great Depression. It was the first depression in which business did not gradually overcome the hard times and this failure was laid at the door of the White House. Although he had taken some steps toward recovery, such as the Reconstruction Finance Corporation and the Hoover Dam power project, Franklin D. Roosevelt defeated him by a wide margin when he ran for re-election, in 1932.

Feeling was strong against Hoover at the beginning of the New Deal—even the Hoover Dam was popularly referred to as the Boulder Dam until a later Congress changed the name back. A defeated candidate, but far from a defeated man, he remained active in his party and in various positions as adviser to the government. World War II brought him back as a relief administrator, and after the war he was the chairman of the Hoover Commission on the Reorganization of the Executive Branch of the Government. The Commission finished its work in 1955 and many of its recommendations have been adopted.

Recognized as an elder statesman of our country, Herbert Hoover is still active as a consultant on many government matters. His eightieth birthday was the occasion for a warm expression of gratitude from all parts of the United States and from both major parties.

David Hinshaw's *Herbert Hoover: American Quaker* (New York: Farrar, Straus, & Young, Inc., 1950) explains the philosophy and religion of the former President. His own writings, *The Challenge to Liberty* (New York: Charles Scribner's Sons, 1934) and *Problem of Lasting Peace* (New York: Doubleday & Co., Inc., 1942), which was written in collaboration with Hugh Gibson, describe the political faith of Herbert Hoover.

DEBATE

The question: **SHOULD LOBBYING IN CONGRESS BE REGULATED AND LIMITED BY ADDITIONAL FEDERAL LEGISLATION?**

Affirmative presentation

I. Unregulated lobbying is a serious evil in a representative government.
 1. Lobbyists are not necessarily interested in the common good.
  a. Their aim is to secure passage of favorable legislation for their respective interests.
 2. Lobbying, by its nature, puts special interests on an equal footing with public interests.
 3. Unregulated lobbying is an invitation to corrupt practices.
II. Present controls of lobbying are ineffective —they leave lobbies, in effect, unregulated and uncontrolled.

1. Present legislation requires only registration by lobbyists and an accounting of money spent; its sole purpose is to bring lobbying into the open.
2. These provisions do nothing about the amounts of money that can be spent, and little about the ways in which it can be spent.
3. The publicity regulations have proved unenforceable and ineffective.
 a. In 1956 fewer than three hundred lobbyists were registered—but *Congressional Quarterly* estimated four thousand were operating.
 b. Lobbyists do not account for all the money they spend.
  I. In 1950 lobbies reported expenditures of ten million dollars.
  II. In 1955 they reported only four million dollars—but it is common knowledge they spent more than in 1950.
  III. Since several court decisions against the act of 1946, some large lobbies do not bother registering or reporting expenses at all.
4. Big industries spend excessive amounts to influence legislation—and the cost must ultimately be borne by the citizen-consumer.
III. Effective legislation should *really* force lobbying into the open and limit the amount that any lobby may spend.
 1. The people have the right to know the influences brought to bear on their representatives.
 2. Not to limit the amount is to invite government by dollars rather than by men and laws. It gives powerful economic interests an advantage over better government groups.

Negative presentation

I. There is no need for such legislation as the affirmative proposes.
 1. Failure to enforce existing legislation is no argument for additional laws.
 2. Present laws require the registration of all lobbyists seeking to influence legislation. They require information on:
  a. Amount of money spent, by whom furnished, to whom paid.
  b. Name of lobbyist and company or association he represents.

3. If this legislation were enforced, the American people would know what forces are at work lobbying.
4. Laws can accomplish no more—the rest is up to the administration, to Congress, and to the American people.

II. Additional legislation against lobbies would constitute a threat to our system of representative government.
1. Lobbies are a form of petition.
2. Congressmen rely on them to find out how legislation will affect various classes and interests.
3. Through lobbies, the best interests in this country can effect legislation—for example, the NCWC.
4. Lobbies are "watchdogs" to guard against careless legislation or laws inimical to any class in the country. The Chamber of Commerce, the National Association of Manufacturers, the American Medical Association, the AFL-CIO, all watch the interests of their groups. Hence to limit lobbies unnecessarily is to interfere with representative government, for we are all represented by various lobbies.

III. There is serious reason to believe that legislation against lobbies will be unconstitutional.
1. A federal court held in 1952 that the provision of the 1946 act which required the filing of reports was a violation of free speech.
2. Another court held in 1953 that the registration requirement violated the right to petition Congress.
3. More severe limitations will restrict freedom of petition and of speech.

IV. The negative admits that there are abuses in lobbying, as there are in every legitimate activity, but the real solution of this problem is (1) a wide-awake citizenry, and (2) good congressmen.
1. Wide-awake citizens are "lobbyists from afar."
   a. Their protests can overwhelm the influence of any organized lobby.
   b. They can elect congressmen interested in the common good and willing to represent the best interests of their constituencies.
2. Good congressmen are the only effective guarantee that lobbying will be conducted properly and thus perform its proper purpose.

CLASSROOM DISCUSSION: The class should first of all study the Federal Registration of Lobbying Act of 1946 to see exactly what it provides. Then the class members should find out why it was not vigorously enforced (doubtful constitutionality of some provisions? lax administration? general revolt against it by congressmen and lobbyists?). A study of Senator Kennedy's bill to rewrite the act of 1946 and of the 1956 Gore Committee on corrupt practices should acquaint the class with the abuses in lobbying. The next step is to decide whether additional legislation is needed to correct these corrupt practices or whether sufficient legislation already exists. If additional legislation seems necessary, the class should decide whether such laws can be passed without entailing the difficulties and evils the negative has argued will be the result of any such legislation.

SELECTED READINGS

One of the best studies of the basic principles and problems of this subject is the May 1935 issue of the *Annals of the American Academy of Political and Social Science*, edited by H. W. Childs, "Pressure Groups and Propaganda." The *Annals* also contains a good study, "Lobbying," by E. B. Logan (July 1929).

The standard books on this topic are E. Pendleton Herring, *Group Representation before Congress* (Baltimore: The Johns Hopkins Press, 1929); Kenneth G. Crawford, *The Pressure Boys: The Inside Story of Lobbying in America* (New York: J. Messner Co., 1939); Franklin L. Burdette, *Lobbyists in Action* (Manassas, Va.: National Capitol Publishers, 1950); Stuart Chase, *Democracy under Pressure* (New York: The Twentieth Century Fund, 1945); Valdimer O. Key, *Politics, Parties, and Pressure Groups* (New York: Thomas Y. Crowell Co., 1947).

Senior Scholastic has two good studies of the subject: "Lobbies, A Third House of Congress?" (February 18, 1953), and "Lobbying: The Third House behind the Scenes" (February 16, 1955). The articles favorable to lobbies are J. Wilson, "Lobbyists Are Working for Good of All," *Look* (June 2, 1953), and "All God's Chillun Go to Lobbies in Washington," *Saturday Evening Post* (August 13, 1955). Other articles deserving of special notice are: K. Schriftgiesser, "High Pressure Lobbying," *Atlantic Monthly* (October 1951); "Report on Lobbying," *America* (September 5, 1953); "Our Washington Lobbies," *Commonweal* (June 20, 1952); "Lawyers and Lobbyists," *Fortune* (February 1952).

UNIT EIGHT
Problems of Federal, State, and Local Government

Chapter 25. Problems of the Federal Government

72. THE FUNCTION OF CONGRESS

Separation of powers. The framers of the Constitution believed that in all government there should be separation of powers and a system of checks and balances among those powers. Nowhere in the Constitution is there a direct statement of the doctrine of separation of powers, but it is clearly implied in the sentence beginning each of the first three sections.

All legislative powers herein granted shall be vested in a Congress . . .

The executive power shall be vested in a President of the United States of America . . .

The judicial power of the United States shall be vested in one Supreme Court, and in such inferior courts as the Congress may from time to time ordain and establish.

From the beginning, separation of powers has been a basic doctrine in American national government and has been enforced by the courts. You will remember from your American history that the NRA was declared unconstitutional because it gave the President legislative powers belonging to Congress alone. In 1880 the Supreme Court phrased the doctrine of separation of powers in these words:

It is believed to be one of the chief merits of the American system of written constitutional law that all the powers intrusted to government, whether state or national, are divided into the three grand departments, the executive, the legislative, and the judicial; that the functions appropriate to each of these branches of government shall be vested in a separate body of public servants; and that the perfection of the system requires that the lines which separate and divide these departments shall be broadly and clearly defined. It is also essential to the successful working of this system that the persons intrusted with power in any one of these branches shall not be permitted to encroach upon the powers confided to the others, but that each shall by the law of its creation be limited to its own department and no other.

Checks and balances. A second basic principle, which modified the doctrine of separation of powers, is the doctrine of checks and balances. Each of the three great departments of government—legislative, executive, and judicial—checks the others and is checked by them. We shall see that the President has a hand in legislation, the Congress has the right to investigate the executive department's

conduct of government, and the judiciary is within limits a lawmaking and law-enforcing body. Moreover, the President has a check on legislation with his veto power, Congress has a check on the President with its control of the purse, and the Supreme Court has a limited check on both with its power to declare a law unconstitutional and therefore unenforceable.

The mechanics of government, whereby these doctrines are put into practice, are delicately balanced. If any one branch of government grows too strong at the expense of the others, the balance is upset in practice and the constitutional checks fail to operate as the Founding Fathers intended they should. Throughout our history one or another of the branches has occasionally tended to dominate temporarily over the others. One of the continual problems of American national government is to maintain that balance between the legislative and the executive departments without rendering the government ineffective.

The structure of Congress. The Congress under the Articles of Confederation was a one-house body, but the Constitutional Convention that met in Philadelphia provided for a bicameral (two-house) legislature for the new government. The deci-

sion proved to be a wise one, because the issues and policies facing the national government are frequently momentous enough to be weighed by two separate bodies. There is little serious opposition to a bicameral legislature today, although many suggestions are made for changing the composition of either or both houses. The House of Representatives consists of 435 members, a number which some political scientists believe is too large for proper consideration of important measures. The result is that the minority party "railroads" its bills through the lower house by maintaining tight party discipline and foreclosing discussion. The alternative, of course, is endless discussion without action—and this would defeat the purpose of the House.

The House of Representatives represents people; the Senate represents states. Members of the House are elected from single-member districts laid out after each decennial census by the legislature of each state. All of the districts contain roughly equal populations. Two senators are elected from each state. The result is a body of men small enough (96) for serious debate on important measures. Critics of the Senate maintain that it gives too much representation to sparsely populated states like Nevada at the expense of populous states like New York or Pennsylvania. They urge the election of an additional senator for every million people over a certain number. Such a change, however, would enable a few populous states to control both the House and the Senate.

Little fault has been found with the qualifications or—since 1955—with the pay for representatives and senators. A representative must be at least twenty-five, a citizen of the United States for seven years, an inhabitant of the state from which he is elected, and he cannot hold any other office in the national government. The last qualification debars Army and Navy men, as well as those who hold administrative positions in the government. Some political scientists believe that members of the Cabinet should be chosen from the Congress in order to effect closer relationship between the executive and legislative branches of government, or at least should have seats in Congress without the right to vote. Such a change would make our government resemble the British parliamentary system.

Senators have been elected directly by the people since the passage of the Seventeenth Amendment in 1913. They must be at least thirty years old, citizens for nine years, and otherwise have the same qualifications as representatives. Originally members of Congress were given per diem pay, but beginning in 1855 they voted themselves an annual salary, which was fixed in 1955 at $22,500 for both representatives and senators. In addition to salary, each congressman receives money for clerical help and other office expenses, and for travel from his home to Washington and back each session. He also has the franking privilege, or free use of the mails, for official business.

Senators are elected for six-year terms and members of the House for two years. One-third of the Senate in each Congress consists of newly elected men, then, and the entire House is re-elected every two years. A two-year term is a serious handicap for representatives. An individual cannot become a real leader in the House until he has served several terms, and except in districts "safe" for one of the major parties a representative runs the risk of losing office every two years. Many students of government therefore suggest that the representatives' term of office be lengthened, perhaps to four years.

Congressional powers. Congress has powers that are usually classified as (1) concurrent, (2) electoral, (3) executive, (4) judicial, (5) supervisory, (6) investigative, and (7) legislative. Some of these powers raise no particular problem nowadays, and we can dismiss them with a word. *Concurrent power* is shared between Congress and the states, for not a phrase in the Constitution can be amended except by congressional action and the action of thirty-six states. Congress elects the President and the Vice-President in case no one receives a majority of votes in the electoral college. This *electoral power* is conferred on Congress by the Twelfth and Twentieth Amendments. *Judicial power* is vested in Congress in the process of impeachment—rarely used in American history—whereby the House prosecutes a civil official for "treason, bribery, or other high crimes and misdemeanors," and the Senate judges the case.

Executive powers are shared with the President: the confirmation by the Senate of many presidential appointments and the ratification of treaties. Closely associated with executive powers are the *directive and supervisory functions,* which take up a large amount of Congress' time. Congress creates administrative agencies and services, and in so doing it fixes their functions and sets forth policies for their operation. Congress retains the right to scrutinize the work of any agency it has created, criticize it, change its functions, or abolish it altogether.

Investigative powers have been exercised increasingly since the beginning of

Dean Acheson is shown testifying before the Senate Foreign Relations Committee before his appointment to the Cabinet position of Secretary of State was confirmed. (Wide World Photo)

World War II. We have already seen that such power is necessary for good legislation because it is the means of obtaining information on which new laws are based. Moreover, in our American tradition a representative assembly is supposed to inquire into the conduct of the government and make the people aware of its acts. This power, we have already indicated, must be exercised with care so that it is not abused for personal or partisan interests. It is, nevertheless, a power necessary for Congress to possess. In 1927 the Supreme Court observed:

> We are of the opinion that the power of inquiry—with process to enforce it—is an essential and appropriate auxiliary to the legislative function. It was regarded and employed in American legislatures before the Constitution was framed and ratified. Both Houses of Congress took this view of it early in their history . . . and both Houses have employed the power accordingly up to the present time.

Limits to Congress' power of inquiry must be fixed largely by Congress itself. Personal rights, as stated in the Constitution, should not be violated. Another limit is the judgment of the President that certain information possessed by the executive branch should be classified as "confidential" and that—in President Eisenhower's words — "its disclosure would be incompatible with the public interest or jeopardize the safety of the Nation." On these grounds the President directed Secretary of Defense Wilson in 1954 to instruct his employees to refrain from quoting high-level conversations or communications in the Defense Depart-

ment in their testimony before the subcommittee of the Senate Committee on Government Operations. The President added: "I direct this action so as to maintain the proper separation of powers between the executive and legislative branches of the Government in accordance with my responsibilities and duties under the Constitution."

We should remember that Congress' power of inquiry is frequently used in friendly fashion to bring to light the good work done by an agency requesting additional funds or powers. It is usually used fairly and objectively and with sensitive regard both for individuals' rights and for national security. Only occasionally do difficulties arise because of the clash of personalities or ambitions.

Legislative power is the primary power exercised by Congress. Congress is *prohibited* from passing certain kinds of laws, such as bills of attainder or acts creating titles of nobility. If a law violates these constitutional prohibitions, the courts will refuse to enforce it. Congress is also *required* to pass certain kinds of laws, such as reapportioning seats in the House of Representatives after each census. If it fails to fulfill this requirement, as it did after the census of 1920, there is no way to compel it to do so. The sole remedy for Congress' failure to perform its mandatory tasks lies with the electorate, who can choose congressmen who will perform these tasks faithfully. Other grants of legislative power are *permissive*. Congress *may* impose taxes, for example, or borrow money.

Basic and supplementary legislative powers. It is obvious that a body of men in Washington cannot decide every detailed application of every law in the land. But application of the law implies a certain amount of interpretation of what the law means—and in a limited way this implies a certain amount of "on-the-spot" legislation. This leads to the difficult problem of whether Congress can delegate its legislative power. Delegation of legislative power is nowhere prohibited in the Constitution, but the statement that Congress is granted "all legislative powers" seems to imply that Congress alone shall exercise them.

In the last seventy years Congress has adopted the policy of delegating limited and restricted legislative powers to the President and to administrative agencies. When it created the Interstate Commerce Commission in 1887, it prescribed that all rates and services should be reasonable, and then it delegated to the commission the right to determine what rates and services were reasonable. Similar powers have been delegated to a host of other agencies and also to the President, who is given authority, for example, to conclude trade agreements altering tariffs by as much as 50 per cent.

The Supreme Court has passed on the constitutionality of a number of acts delegating legislative power to the President or administrative agencies. Some it has held unconstitutional and some it has held constitutional. The Court has consistently held that *Congress may not delegate basic legislative powers* that involve determination of policy. But after Congress has prescribed the general framework of regulations for an agency or a bureau in the government, it may give that agency the power to fill in administrative details. In other words, Congress alone may exercise basic legislative authority, but *it may delegate supplementary legislative authority* to those whose duty is to administer the law.

73. PROBLEMS INVOLVED IN LAWMAKING

From ten to fifteen thousand bills are introduced in every Congress, and of that number only about one thousand or less eventually become laws. Most of these bills are "special" or "private" bills that apply only to specified persons or places. Many of them are passed without serious consideration by either house. The "public" bills, those of general application, may originate in the White House or with some pressure group, but they must be introduced to Congress by either a senator or a representative. A bill cannot become a law until it has passed both houses in identical form and has been signed by the President or passed over his veto.

To become a law, a bill must be "read" in each house three times. The first reading is by title only. Then the bill is referred to an appropriate committee, which presumably studies its merits and demerits, and then reports it out to the house with a recommendation for its passage or defeat. The second reading takes place after the bill is taken off the calendar. This reading is in full, and normally it is at this time that debate on the bill takes place. If the bill survives this step it is engrossed and read a third time—this last time by title only, when a vote on final passage is taken. This seemingly simple process of passing a law involves a number of serious problems. We shall consider only three of the most important of these problems: (1) How much time is required for adequate debate on a measure? (2) What power over bills entrusted to their consideration should be given to committees? (3) How shall lobbies or pressure groups be controlled in order to obtain information without allowing them undue influence over legislation?

The problem of "time" in Congress. The matter of time presents an especially pressing problem in the House. If each member spoke only ten minutes on each bill, a congressional session could never end in less than two years. In 1841 the House adopted a rule forbidding a member to speak longer than an hour on any one bill, except with unanimous consent. Even this restriction is not sufficient in a house of 435 members. Two additional devices are used to limit debate. The first is advance agreement between party leaders fixing the length of time that discussion on a particular measure can run. The second is the parliamentary maneuver of calling for the "previous question." At any time, except in committee of the whole,[1] any member of the House may "move the previous question." If his motion carries, a quorum being present, discussion is closed and a vote is taken on whatever matter is pending.

The rigorous tactics employed in the House to limit debate have been severely criticized for limiting freedom of discussion and "railroading" bills through the House. But some such devices must be employed in an assembly of 435 men, or the purpose of the House—action on needed legislation—would be frustrated.

There are no limits on the length of speeches in the Senate except by agreement entered into in advance by party leaders in respect to some particular bill. A senator may speak as often as he wishes on any bill, but he may not, without consent, speak more than twice on the same subject in a single day. Occasionally debate in the Senate is limited by "unanimous consent," whereby the members agree to a specified restriction on debate. The freedom of debate in the Senate is occasionally abused by a small number of senators who use the tactics known as "filibustering" to talk a bill to

"The Laws of Moses and the Laws of Today." (Fitzpatrick in the St. Louis Post-Dispatch)

death. Two or more senators can talk for days or weeks and thus force the rest of the Senate to drop the measure or amend it in a way the majority does not desire.

The only device the Senate has adopted to limit filibustering is the closure rule of 1917, adopted after an administration bill for the arming of American ships was defeated by filibuster. The closure device has been used successfully only a few times. It operates when sixteen senators sign a petition to close debate on a specified measure. If two-thirds vote affirmatively on the petition, the measure becomes the "unfinished business" of the Senate until disposed of, and no senator is allowed to speak more than one hour on the measure or its amendments.

The problem of time remains in both the Senate and the House. In considering this problem, however, we should remember that votes are seldom changed by debate on the floor of the House or the Senate. The fate of bills is usually decided in committee sessions or in party caucus,[2]

---

[1] Committee of the whole is a device used for consideration of revenue measures and other public bills because it affords greater freedom of debate. It is the House meeting as a committee rather than as the House formally convened. In committee of the whole, rules governing House procedure do not prevail.

[2] A party caucus is a meeting of party members to decide—usually by polling the members—how all

and debate on the floor is more for the sake of allowing members to put their remarks "on the record" than to influence voting on the measure.

The role of the committee. After a bill's first reading, you will remember, it is referred to the proper committee for study and recommendation. In effect, a committee has the power of life and death over every bill committed to its care. Each committee is composed of Republicans and Democrats in proportion to their strength in the house, and the majority party holds the chairmanship of all committees. The House and the Senate tend to accept or reject bills according to the recommendation of the committee to which they are entrusted. No one in either house can possibly inform himself of the merit of several thousand bills, and he therefore follows the recommendation of the committee.

Committees ordinarily hold hearings on important measures. Interested groups are invited to furnish information about

loyal party members will vote. Party "loyalty" requires all members to abide by the decision of the caucus.

a bill to the committee. The committee has the right to employ research assistants to gather information relating to any proposed bill. After public hearings, the committee usually goes into executive session and reaches its conclusions in private. The committee may send a bill back to the House with the recommendation that it be enacted into law, it may amend a bill in any way it sees fit, or it may substitute a bill of its own authorship. Finally, it may kill a bill by not reporting it out of committee to the House at all.

Committee procedure has been criticized as a system of legislation by small groups of men, with the houses acting only as ratifying agencies. But it is difficult to see how either the House or the Senate could consider every important bill presented for legislative action. Serious consideration must be made by the various committees—which constitute for each house a division of labor on legislation—and their recommendations must ordinarily be followed by the rest of the House. The committee system is subject to abuse, of course, and occasionally bills which a majority of the House

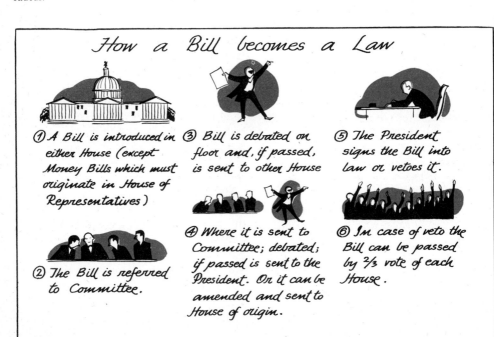

How a Bill becomes a Law

① A Bill is introduced in either House (except Money Bills which must originate in House of Representatives)

② The Bill is referred to Committee.

③ Bill is debated on floor and, if passed, is sent to other House

④ Where it is sent to Committee; debated; if passed is sent to the President. Or it can be amended and sent to House of origin.

⑤ The President signs the Bill into law or vetoes it.

⑥ In case of veto the Bill can be passed by ⅔ vote of each House.

wish to pass are killed or maimed by a hostile committee.

A third serious difficulty in legislation is controlling the influence on legislation of interested parties who "lobby" for bills on their behalf or seek to use undue pressure to kill other bills. More recently pressure groups have attempted to intimidate congressmen by the threat of controlling enough votes to decide their political future.

Legislative Reorganization Act of 1946. Congressmen have been aware of these difficult problems that hamper the legislative process. In 1946 the House and Senate combined to pass the most extensive reorganization act in American history in an effort to improve the legislative process. The provisions of the Legislative Reorganization Act of 1946 can be summarized in this fashion:

Improvement in the committee's role in legislation. In the first place, the number of standing committees, with their attendant overlapping and confusing jurisdiction, was drastically reduced. The forty-eight standing committees in the House were reduced to nineteen, and the thirty-three in the Senate to fifteen. Committee jurisdictions were redefined to eliminate duplication and assign each committee to a definite sphere of activity. With a few exceptions, each representative was restricted to a single committee and each senator to two. Second, all committees are required to fix regular meeting days, keep a complete record of their proceedings, and report promptly all approved measures. Third, each committee may employ a clerical staff of not more than six clerks and four "professional staff members" to assist in research.

Regulation of lobbying. Every person receiving compensation for attempting to secure the passage or defeat of a bill must register with the clerk of the House and the secretary of the Senate. He must indicate by whom he is employed, how much he is paid, and he must render an exact account of all contributions given to him and all the money he has spent in influencing legislation in any way.

Curtailment of private-bill legislation. Private bills, which took a considerable part of congressional time, have been largely relegated to administrative agencies. Bridge-building proposals, for example, are now taken care of by Army officials in the Department of Defense instead of by Congress, and pension claims go to the Veterans Administration.

Consideration of the budget by joint committee. This provision, which is intended to streamline action on the President's budget proposals, will be considered later. It suffices to say here that the provisions of 1946 eliminate confused action on the budget by having the proposals studied and acted on by a joint committee of the House and the Senate.

Strengthening supervision over the administration. All committees are charged with the duty of keeping constant check over the execution of all laws falling within their respective jurisdictions. This provision was adopted in the hope that Congress, which has fallen from its original position as the most powerful branch of the government, would recapture its policy-determining and its supervisory power in the national government.

Additional proposals for improving Congress. The Legislative Reorganization Act of 1946 took several steps toward improving congressional procedure. Some students of government believe that several more steps should be taken to achieve an efficient and effective Congress.

Reduce the size of the House of Representatives. The House is said to be too large for the efficient conduct of legislative business. A smaller number of men could work more efficiently without sacrificing the representative character of the House, and a reduced House need not resort to "railroad" tactics to obtain necessary legislation.

Lengthen the terms of representatives to

four years. It is argued that an election is hardly needed every two years in this age to keep close check on the representatives—and this is the only justification for short terms in office. Many congressmen find themselves compelled to give too much of their attention to the business of getting themselves re-elected.

Introduce joint committees to replace the separate committees which the Senate and the House have on the same subjects. This would eliminate much duplication of effort, with its attendant waste of energy, time, and money. Moreover, it would eliminate or minimize the use of conference committees, which must be formed to resolve differences between the two houses when they do not pass a bill in identical form. Under a system of joint committees most bills will automatically pass both houses in identical form. Conference committees would be needed only to resolve differences that have developed by amendment from the floor of either house—and such instances would be infrequent. On the other hand, however, it is doubtful if this reform would be consistent with the bicameral principle.

Terminate the seniority system for committee chairmanships. The rigid seniority system, whereby committee members achieve rank exclusively on the basis of time served on the committee, minimizes maneuvering for position among committee members. Many students of government think that continuous service is not always the best qualification for committee chairmanship. The only other way of choosing committee chairmen would be by election at the beginning of each new Congress.

Generally improve the parliamentary procedure in both houses. Each house of Congress makes its own rules and is free to change them as it wishes. The members of each house jealously guard this right and do not like criticism of their procedure from any outside source. Changes, however, are made from time to time.

74. THE EXECUTIVE BRANCH OF GOVERNMENT

Only native-born citizens who have attained the age of thirty-five are eligible to be elected President. The presidential term of office is four years, and since the adoption of the Twenty-second Amendment in 1951 no person may be elected to more than two terms. The President's salary is $100,000 a year. In addition, he receives a $50,000 taxable expense account to be spent as he wishes. The President also receives tax-free allowances for entertaining, traveling, and the general upkeep of his office. He pays no rent for his living quarters. He is provided with a private physician, library, movies, and other luxuries at government expense. Altogether, it is estimated that the President's expenses come to about $3,000,000 a year, which is almost five times the total expenses of the national government in Washington's time.

Election of the President. The authors of the Constitution provided a system whereby the President would be selected by a group of men, an electoral college, chosen for that purpose. When the country divided into parties after Washington's election, it was found that the electors did not exercise judgment as they were expected to do, but each voted for the candidate his party had previously selected. The Twelfth Amendment was therefore adopted to govern the procedure of presidential elections. Each state has as many electoral votes as it has senators and representatives in Congress. Thus New York has 45 and Nevada has 3. A total of 266 electoral votes is required for election. If no candidate receives this number, the election is decided in the House of Representatives. This has happened only twice in our history, in 1800 and again in the election of 1824. Because the candidate receives all the votes of each state he carries, it is possible for a candidate receiving a popular

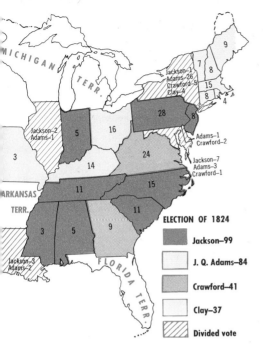

ELECTION OF 1824

Jackson—99

J. Q. Adams—84

Crawford—41

Clay—37

Divided vote

majority of the votes to be defeated by one who has only a minority. Seven minority candidates have been elected in the past, two of them (Cleveland and Wilson) twice.

Critics of the electoral system therefore propose various changes to make the presidential election more democratic. The most radical proposal is to abolish the electoral system altogether and choose the President by a simple majority in the country. Such a system would defy all considerations of state interest and state pride and discriminate against the less populous states. It could hardly be adopted without a uniform national election law—and three-fourths of the states cannot be expected to surrender their constitutional rights to determine voting qualifications and procedures. A second radical proposal is to have each candidate receive a vote for each state he carries by popular vote, and to declare the candidate carrying a majority of the states elected President. This plan offers no substantial advantages over the present plan, and it would give smaller states too much weight at the expense of large

ones. It is manifestly unfair that the 200,000 people in Nevada should count as much as the 15,500,000 in New York.

Other less radical proposals have been introduced from time to time in Congress. One of them is to award each candidate electoral votes from each state in proportion to his popular vote in that state instead of giving all the state's electoral votes to the candidate carrying the state. A second moderate proposal is to count electoral votes on a district instead of a state basis. A candidate would, under this system, receive one electoral vote for each congressional district he carried by a simple plurality. To be elected, one would have to carry 266 such districts. Although there is heated discussion every four years about changing the presidential election system, most of the proposed "improvements" seem little better than the present system. Moreover, some of them involve real disadvantages, and all of them require constitutional amendment, which is not easy to achieve. Finally, it may be said that it is always unwise to amend the Constitution unless clearly recognized necessity requires it.

Functions and responsibilities of the President. The President is charged with responsibilities that would be overwhelming in the mid-twentieth century unless he were helped by a well-organized staff of assistants. He is in charge of foreign relations. He is commander-in-chief of the armed forces. As chief executive he is responsible for the faithful administration of the laws. He must maintain good relations with Congress. He is usually the leader of his party, and he must take a lead in arousing public opinion on various governmental policies. Besides all these important functions, the President must spend an average of two hours a day on such routine business as signing his name to a host of documents.

To help him accomplish his duties, the President makes use of two principal agencies: the Executive Office of the

President, and the Cabinet. The Executive Office of the President includes (1) the White House staff of over a hundred secretaries, clerks, servants, and guards, as well as six executive assistants who relieve the President of much routine work; (2) the Bureau of the Budget; (3) the Council of Economic Advisers; (4) the National Security Council and National Security Resources Board; (5) the Office of Defense Mobilization. These bureaus and councils are concerned chiefly with planning for administration and national defense measures.

The Cabinet consists of the department heads meeting together with the President. The Cabinet is employed at the President's discretion. Some presidents, like Harding, have leaned heavily on their Cabinets; others, like Franklin D. Roosevelt, have acted very independently of them. The Cabinet's sole function is to offer advice to the President. The heads of the ten great departments of administration are in an excellent position, when they come together, to discuss almost any question of policy and to enlighten the President on how any proposed line of action will affect their various departments.

The President's powers can be classified as: (1) control of foreign relations; (2) control of the armed forces; (3) legislative; (4) executive. We shall consider his control of foreign relations and the armed forces later in this volume. Here we are concerned with problems that arise from his sharing with Congress the responsibility for legislation, and from his role as chief executive with its responsibility for conduct of the national administration.

The President as legislator. In the cabinet form of government, such as England and France employ, the executive consists of ministers chosen from the legislature. The Prime Minister and his colleagues are leaders in the legislature, and they hold executive office only as long as they enjoy support from a majority in the legislature. This form of government has the advantage of co-ordinating legislative and executive functions and of fixing responsibility for government policies on a single body of men, the cabinet ministers, who are also the legislative leaders.

Our presidential form of government differs from the parliamentary type in that our executive is outside the legislature, draws his authority from election by the people, is not responsible to the legislature, and he holds office for a definite term of four years. Theoretically, legislative powers are vested in Congress. In practice, the President has had to assume a certain measure of legislative power, and, indeed, the Constitution specifically assigns certain legislative functions to him. Let us discuss these functions briefly.

Messages to Congress. The President is required by the Constitution to report to Congress on "the state of the Union" and to recommend for its consideration "such measures as he shall judge necessary and expedient." Custom and law require the President to transmit three messages to Congress at the opening of each session. One is on the state of the Union; the second is in relation to the budget, which his Bureau of the Budget has prepared; and the third is on his recommendations relative to the country's economy.

The President's role as leader of the majority party—as a rule—and of the nation requires him to formulate a legislative program. There is no constitutional or statutory requirement for Congress to act favorably on the President's proposals or even to give them priority of attention on the legislative calendar, but party leaders ordinarily see to it that presidential recommendations are given a preferred status among proposed bills. Moreover, the prestige of the President's position, together with his control of considerable patronage and his right to appeal to the people for support, makes it wise for practical politicians to entertain his proposals seriously.

The veto power. By refusing to sign a bill the President vetoes it, returning it to the house of its origin with a message stating his objections to the bill. He may also kill a bill, if Congress adjourns within ten days, by letting it lie unsigned on his desk. If he does not sign a bill within ten days after receiving it, the bill automatically becomes law unless Congress adjourns in the meantime.

Hamilton explained in *The Federalist* that the veto "furnishes an additional security against the enactment of improper laws. It establishes a salutary check upon the legislative body, calculated to guard the community against the effects of faction, precipitancy, or of any impulse unfriendly to the public good, which may happen to influence a majority of that body." Presidential veto is not absolute, of course, because Congress can pass a bill over the President's veto by obtaining a two-thirds vote in each house. The threat of veto has frequently been used to kill a bill before it comes out of Congress or, more important, to amend it when Congress learns that the President disapproves of certain of its provisions.

Generally speaking, the veto power of the President has been used in salutary fashion. One improvement, now used in many states, is frequently suggested—as late as 1955 by Senator Byrd of Virginia. This suggested change would give the President the right to veto items of appropriation bills. Under the present arrangement, the President must accept or reject the entire bill as passed by Congress. Congressmen frequently attach "riders" on appropriation bills that could never otherwise get by the President's desk to become law. But because the appropriation bill as a whole is needed, the President is virtually forced to accept the bill with its attached riders. The right to veto items could become a powerful weapon in the hands of an autocratic President, but on the whole the measure might accomplish considerably more good than bad.

The President's executive power. The President's chief function, as set forth in the Constitution and as it has developed down to the present time, is to enforce national legislation. He is bound by constitutional requirement to "take care that

---

MAJOR INDEPENDENT OFFICES AND ESTABLISHMENTS
OF THE EXECUTIVE BRANCH OF THE FEDERAL GOVERNMENT, 1955–1956

ATOMIC ENERGY COMMISSION	NATIONAL ADVISORY COMMITTEE FOR AERONAUTICS
CIVIL AERONAUTICS BOARD	
DISTRICT OF COLUMBIA	NATIONAL LABOR RELATIONS BOARD
EXPORT-IMPORT BANK OF WASHINGTON	NATIONAL MEDIATION BOARD
FEDERAL CIVIL DEFENSE ADMINISTRATION	NATIONAL SCIENCE FOUNDATION
	RAILROAD RETIREMENT BOARD
FEDERAL COMMUNICATIONS COMMISSION	
FEDERAL DEPOSIT INSURANCE CORPORATION	SECURITIES AND EXCHANGE COMMISSION
FEDERAL MEDIATION AND CONCILIATION SERVICE	SELECTIVE SERVICE SYSTEM
	SMALL BUSINESS ADMINISTRATION
FEDERAL POWER COMMISSION	SMITHSONIAN INSTITUTION
FEDERAL RESERVE SYSTEM	TAX COURT OF THE UNITED STATES
FEDERAL TRADE COMMISSION	TENNESSEE VALLEY AUTHORITY
FOREIGN OPERATIONS ADMINISTRATION	UNITED STATES CIVIL SERVICE COMMISSION
GENERAL SERVICES ADMINISTRATION	UNITED STATES INFORMATION AGENCY
HOUSING AND HOME FINANCE AGENCY	UNITED STATES TARIFF COMMISSION
INTERSTATE COMMERCE COMMISSION	VETERANS' ADMINISTRATION

---

the laws be faithfully executed." To achieve this end the President has (1) the power of appointment and removal over all officials in the executive administration, and (2) the power of directing the administration through orders and regulations. Both of these powers have come, through custom and usage, to be exercised in certain ways and surrounded by certain restrictions. Let us therefore discuss each of them briefly.

It would be impossible for the President personally to appoint the several million federal employees. He reserves the right to appoint some of them himself —such as Cabinet officers, judges of the Supreme Court, and ambassadors to foreign countries. The lesser officers and employees of the government are appointed by department heads and other officials in the administration, but ultimate responsibility for these appointments rests with the President as chief executive. Appointments are limited in two principal ways. (1) Most federal positions are filled subject to the requirements of a merit system, which we shall see in Chapter 28. (2) Presidential nominations are made "by and with the advice and consent of the Senate." Senatorial consent is frequently given automatically, but the President must always take it into consideration and make sure in advance that he has chosen a man acceptable to the senators from the state in which the appointment is made.

The power of directing his subordinates in the national administration is implied in the President's obligation to enforce the laws faithfully. The direction of administration requires rules and regulations governing procedure and operation of all the different departments and branches. Thus there are Consular Regulations and Civil Service rules, regulations for the Patent Office and for the Internal Revenue services. These rules or ordinances are promulgated by the President, although they are normally drawn up by a department head or someone under his supervision. We saw earlier in this chapter that "administrative lawmaking" is limited to the filling in of details on ways and means of accomplishing the objective set down by Congress. It is supplementary, not basic legislation.

Finally, as chief executive the President exercises powers of pardon, reprieve, and amnesty. In exercising the power of pardon he acts in complete independence of Congress and of the courts. In practice, the President usually follows the recommendations of the Attorney General. Every application for

President Dwight D. Eisenhower is shown meeting with his Cabinet and other policy-making members of the government at Camp David, Md. Reliance on the Cabinet has varied with different administrations, but President Eisenhower customarily invites such officials as the Civil Service Commissioner, Defense Mobilization Director, Budget Director, and his presidential assistants to his Cabinet meetings. (The New York Times)

pardon is investigated by the pardon attorney in the Department of Justice, and his report is used by the Attorney General in his recommendation to the President. Reprieve is simply a stay of execution, and it is granted only on the supposition that the defense can produce new evidence to warrant another trial and a change of sentence. Amnesty is a kind of blanket pardon granted to a number of people who have not been convicted individually but have violated some federal law, as, for example, by engaging in rebellion. Amnesty can be granted by act of Congress, but the usual method has been that of presidential proclamation.

Administrative reorganization. Hamilton observed in *The Federalist* that "the true test of good government is its aptitude and tendency to produce a good administration." The importance of administration is readily seen when we remember that it is the process of putting law into effect. Without sound administration, the best conceivable policies are only nice-sounding words. The entire nature of a good government can be changed, in the way it affects our daily lives, by an unco-operative administration or by one that frustrates the intent of legislators.

Most of the administration—though not the whole—is conducted by the ten big departments: (1) State, (2) Treasury, (3) Defense, (4) Justice, (5) Post Office, (6) Interior, (7) Agriculture, (8) Commerce, (9) Labor, and (10) Health, Education and Welfare. The Department of Defense consists of the former War and Navy Departments and a new Air Department. Each of these departments has its own status in many respects, but the three are unified for the sake of closer coordination of the various military units, and only the Secretary of the Department of Defense is a cabinet member.

Each department of government is headed by an officer of Cabinet rank. These are political appointees, quite properly, because they are policy-forming officials. Most departments also have undersecretaries, also politically appointed, who serve as department heads in the absence or incapacity of the chief. Under the two top men are a number of assistant secretaries, usually political appointees, who serve as advisers in specialized areas. The work of the department is accomplished by bureaus, divisions, offices, and services, generally headed by career men who stay in office through changes in the top administration.

Outside the department arrangement are various kinds of independent establishments. Some of the most important of these are the independent regulatory commissions, such as the Interstate Commerce Commission and the Federal Trade Commission. Their work is as much legislative and judicial as it is administrative. Whereas the departments are headed by single administrators, the commissions are headed by boards of three to eleven persons—a device well suited for legislative functions but poorly suited for efficient administration. Besides the regulatory commissions are the many government corporations, like the St. Lawrence Seaway Corporation, the Home Owners Loan Corporation, and the Tennessee Valley Authority. Outside departmental organization are also many other independent establishments that defy classification, such as the Veterans Administration.

Confusion of government agencies and services came about partly because services and bureaus were thrown into departments without any functional reason. Secret Service men, for example, are in the Treasury Department. A second reason for confusion was that lines of responsibility were not clearly established as new agencies were created. That is why President Roosevelt's Committee on Administrative Management said that there had grown up "a headless fourth branch of government, responsible to no one, and impossible of coordination with the general policies and work of the government as determined by the people through their duly elected representatives."

Principles underlying sound organization. For many years reorganization was urged, and experts agreed that the following general principles must underlie any sound administration. (1) Activities should be grouped by their nature or function into a small number of large departments. (2) Every agency and every individual should stand in some definite relationship to a superior, so that lines of control and responsibility run clearly from top to bottom. (3) Administrative agencies should be headed by a single administrator; boards and commissions are proper for agencies engaged primarily in quasi-judicial or quasi-legislative work. (4) All except the high policy-forming officials should be chosen and retained according to sound merit-system qualifications.

The Hoover Commission. Attempts at reorganization were begun by several Presidents, but the movement made substantial progress only with the appointment in 1947 of the Commission on Organization of the Executive Branch of the Government. Headed by former President Herbert C. Hoover, this commission undertook the most thorough study ever made of the executive branch of the national government, and in 1949 it issued its report. Its recommendations were based on the principles suggested above, together with the general suggestions that executive officials should always be given sufficient staff assistance and that they should have sufficient authority to run their respective agencies in businesslike fashion.

Acting on the Hoover Commission's report, Congress gave President Truman rather broad powers to formulate administrative reorganization plans and to submit them to Congress. If Congress took no action within sixty days, they automatically became law. Six of the first seven proposals Truman submitted were accepted almost without debate. The seventh—to set up a Department of Welfare—was rejected. The Eisenhower administration has carried on the work of administrative reorganization along the general lines recommended by the Hoover Commission, and in 1953 it set up a Department of Health, Education and Welfare.

75. THE SUPREME COURT

The federal judiciary is in many ways the weakest of the three branches of government. It has nevertheless exerted considerable influence on our national development. Men such as John Marshall and Charles Evans Hughes have not played as spectacular a role in American history as many presidents and congressmen, but they have been every bit as influential.

Need of a Supreme Court. The Constitutional Convention provided in Article III that "the judicial power of the United States shall be vested in one Supreme Court, and in such inferior courts as the Congress may from time to time ordain and establish." The need for a federal judiciary headed by a Supreme Court was apparent to those who had lived under the Articles of Confederation. National laws and treaties could not be administered uniformly throughout the several states as "supreme law of the land" by thirteen independent systems of courts. Moreover, since the control of foreign affairs was vested exclusively in the federal government, it was necessary that legal controversies involving representatives of foreign countries should be settled in federal rather than in state courts. Finally, if the federal Constitution and federal laws were to be "supreme," they must be enforced by a federal system of courts rather than by the several states.

The Constitution leaves Congress free to place as many judges as it wishes on the Supreme Court and to create and abolish inferior federal courts as it thinks necessary. The original number of justices on the Supreme Court was fixed by law at six, but since 1869 the number has been nine. Justices are appointed to the Court by the President, subject to confirmation by the Senate. They may resign from office whenever they wish, but they can be removed only by impeachment, for the Constitution guarantees them office for life on condition of "good behavior." The obvious purpose of these provisions is to secure a body of independent judges who will interpret the law objectively and not be swayed by political or private considerations.

The method of appointment for life is perhaps as good a system as can be devised, but critics of the Supreme Court point out that it has not worked perfectly throughout our history. Presidents will obviously select judges who they believe will be favorably inclined toward their interpretation of the Constitution. A President who is in office for a long time can therefore appoint a majority of justices. (This objection loses some of its force since the adoption of the Twenty-second Amendment [1951], which limits the President to two terms.) Justices are

C. K. Berryman's cartoon, "The Ingenious Quarterback," satirized President Roosevelt's request to increase the number of Supreme Court justices. Congress refused the President, believing that the increase would upset the three-way balance of the government. (Library of Congress)

not automatic legal reasoning machines, they are predisposed to interpret the Constitution "liberally" or "conservatively," according to their political philosophy as well as their purely legal reasoning. Defenders of the Court point out, however, that once a man has been nominated to the Court he tends to be independent in his judgments and to "disappoint" the President who expected him to follow the presidential interpretation of the Constitution.

Jurisdiction of the Supreme Court. Some cases originate before the Supreme Court. Over these cases it is said to have *original jurisdiction.* The Constitution specifies that the Supreme Court shall have original jurisdiction: (1) over cases involving ambassadors and other public ministers of foreign countries; (2) over actions of a state against a state; (3) over actions of the United States against a state; and (4) over actions of a state against citizens of another state or against aliens. Congress may not enlarge the original jurisdiction of the Supreme Court, because to do so would be to amend the Constitution in an unauthorized manner.

Most cases reach the Supreme Court through its *appellate jurisdiction.* These are cases which are appealed from inferior federal courts or from the highest state courts when some point of federal law or the federal Constitution is involved. The exercise of its appellate jurisdiction is by far the most important and distinctive feature of the Supreme Court, for in these cases the Court passes on the constitutionality of acts of both Congress and the state legislatures. Thus it serves as guardian of the Constitution and preserver of citizens' constitutional rights.

The Supreme Court refuses to pass on "abstract" cases or to render political decisions. An abstract case would be one in which the Court would pass judgment directly on a law, stating that it was constitutional or not. This would involve the Court in an exercise of legal philosophy, which is repugnant to the Anglo-American tradition. Instead, the Court accepts concrete cases in which the claim is made by one of the parties that a certain law violates the Constitution. The Court renders a decision on the case in hand, but in effect it declares the law either valid or void by passing on its constitutionality.

Political decisions, the Court has held, must be made by Congress or the President. The Court will not decide, for example, whether a given state has a republican form of government or whether its election laws are "un-republican." But it will decide, if a certain election law is challenged, whether a citizen's constitutional rights are violated by the law. Finally, the Supreme Court refuses to render advisory opinions on proposed legislation, as several of the state supreme courts are required to do.

Nowhere in the Constitution is the Supreme Court specifically given the power of judicial review or the power to declare a law unenforceable because it violates the Constitution. It is an old dispute as to whether the framers of the Constitution intended the Supreme Court to have this power, but the historic fact is that the Court began to exercise this power very early in our history (in the *Marbury* v. *Madison Case,* 1803), and it would seem that without it the Court could not function as the framers of the Constitution intended it should.

The consequences of judicial review are very important. The Supreme Court has held only seventy some laws of Congress unconstitutional, but it has invalidated hundreds of state laws. The important fact is that Congress and the state legislatures are denied the right to judge the limits of their own powers, and thus they are forced to exercise care in framing a law so that it conforms to the letter and spirit of the Constitution.

The power of the Court to declare laws unconstitutional has been criticized frequently as an "arbitrary" and "dictatorial" power vested in nine men, whereby five of them can thwart the popular will and prevent government from functioning in "democratic" fashion. Critics of the Court point out that the justices' political and social philosophy plays a considerable part in the decisions they render. The Court can hear only a small fraction of the cases appealed to it. In deciding what are "important" cases, the justices must make political and social decisions. There has been a tendency in recent years, for example, to select civil-rights cases over others. In the second place, critics point out, justices frequently render decisions based as much on their philosophy as on the legal points of the case. If this is not a fact, they ask, how can one account for five judges finding a good part of the New Deal unconstitutional and four other judges finding it constitutional? And how can one account for the fact that new judges, chosen by Roosevelt, found similar New Deal laws perfectly constitutional?

Defenders of judicial review admit that the justices' personal points of view play some part in their decisions, but they

The Supreme Court of the United States. SEATED: *Justice Felix Frankfurter, Justice Hugo L. Black, Chief Justice Earl Warren, Justice Stanley F. Reed, Justice William O. Douglas.* STANDING: *Justice Sherman Minton, Justice Harold H. Burton, Justice Tom C. Clark, Justice John M. Harlan. (Harris & Ewing)*

minimize the amount and point out that some agency must measure the constitutionality of legislation—if the Constitution is to mean anything—and the safest agency is the Supreme Court. If Congress were the judge of its own powers, they insist, in time of emergency and stress congressional power would tend to be unlimited. Moreover, the judiciary is the weakest of the three branches of government. It controls neither the purse nor the sword. It cannot enforce its decisions. Its power results largely from the respect it has earned by using its power of judicial review honestly and objectively. Finally, its defenders maintain, the Supreme Court has never exercised truly arbitrary power to declare laws unconstitutional. Most cases are clearly constitutional or not, and the Court has no choice but to render a legal decisions. (Most decisions handed down by the Court are unanimous.) A narrow lane exists, the Court's defenders admit, in which there is room for disagreement and in which laws can be declared either constitutional or not, depending on the view entertained by the majority of the justices. But this difficulty would remain if any other agency were given the power of review.

Controversy of 1937 over Court reorganization.
All the arguments for and against the Supreme Court came to a head in 1935–1936, when a number of laws passed by Congress as part of the New Deal were declared unconstitutional. Cries went up that "nine old men" were stopping the wheels of progress, that a handful of decrepit, old-fashioned judges were thwarting social justice and protecting vested interests. Critics of the Court maintained that democracy was a mockery when the will of the people, as evidenced in Congress, was nullified by judicial decision.

Others pointed to the Supreme Court as the last valiant defender of constitutional rights against encroachment by a socialistic government. The Court alone, they said, stood between a citizen's rights

and a popular will that recognized no limits to its power and its functions. At any rate, various plans were proposed—and bitterly opposed—to alter the composition or change the power of the Supreme Court. One proposal was to force retirement of judges at the age of seventy—apparently in the belief that older judges were more conservative. Another was to enable Congress to repass any law declared unconstitutional, thus making Congress the final judge of its own powers. A more drastic proposal was to deprive the Supreme Court of any power whatever to pass on the constitutionality of laws passed by Congress.

When President Roosevelt was reelected in 1936 he believed that he had a "mandate" from the people to alter the Court in such a way as to obtain the passage of his New Deal legislation. He therefore proposed a number of reforms of the lower courts in the interest of efficiency—most of which were adopted—and a plan of "packing" the Supreme Court to secure a favorable majority. There was no question of the constitutionality of his proposal, for Congress can increase or decrease the number of justices in the Supreme Court, and Roosevelt's proposal was to add an "associate justice" for each justice who failed to retire at the age of seventy. The maximum number of justices was to be fifteen.

The President's proposal evoked a storm of protest. Backed by popular feeling, Congress refused to "pack" the Court as Roosevelt wished. Eventually, however, a number of the conservative justices either died or retired, and President Roosevelt appointed "liberal" judges to take their places. Thus the Court came to interpret New Deal legislation more favorably. Roosevelt had accomplished his purpose, although not in the manner he proposed. The controversy seems to have made the people respect the Supreme Court more than ever and to have placed it beyond political control.

Problems facing the Supreme Court today.
Chief Justice Hughes once observed: "We are under a Constitution, but the Constitution is what the judges say it is." This is an exaggeration, but it contains a large measure of truth. The Constitution is a living document. It means (1) what the words of the written document evidently mean, (2) what the courts have said it meant in the past, and (3) what the courts say it means today. Thus the Constitution consists of (1) the original written document and its formal amendments, (2) precedent or past interpretations, and (3) current interpretations, based on social and political opinion as well as on constitutional law.

At first this might seem to be a defect in our constitutional system. We might think we would prefer a system that provides for rigid interpretation of the Constitution. Further consideration suggests, however, that the Constitution has worked as well as it has because it is a flexible document designed to meet changing conditions. It can be altered drastically and basically by amendment as provided in Article V of the original document. But amendments are designedly slow and difficult to obtain. The vitality of the Constitution depends on its continual adaptability to slight and gradual changes in American society. This adaptability is provided by judicial interpretation, especially of elastic clauses such as "due process" and "commerce."

The basic problem, then, seems to reduce itself to securing nine justices who are genuinely interested in preserving the Constitution and adapting it to current problems. The justices must keep their personal convictions and their social philosophy as much in the background as possible, and they must judge cases objectively in the light of precedent and the accumulated wisdom of American constitutional law. Generally speaking, the Court has decided cases fairly and wisely. It has maintained more consistently than either other branch of government a reputation of impartiality and of high-mindedness.

REVIEW

72. The Function of Congress
A. Show how the doctrine of separation of powers is implied in the Constitution. Indicate one way in which each branch of the government acts as a check on the others.

B. List the qualifications necessary for one to become a representative; a senator; President; Vice-President.

C. Briefly describe some executive, legislative, and judicial powers of Congress.

73. Problems Involved in Lawmaking
A. What is meant by the "time problem" in Congress? Briefly state how the House and Senate have dealt with this problem.

B. What is the function of a committee in Congress? How did the Reorganization Act of 1946 affect committees? What are lobbies? How are they now registered?

C. Summarize the provisions of the Legislative Reorganization Act of 1946.

74. The Executive Branch of Government
A. Describe several proposals that have been made to change the method of electing a President.

B. List some powers of the President which he exercises alone; some which require senatorial approval. What is the function of the Cabinet? Name the present members of the Cabinet.

C. Discuss several of the legislative functions of the President.

D. Describe some of the executive powers of the President. Show how several agencies of the government have grown in importance in the last three decades. What have been the results of the Hoover Commission's report in 1947 concerning the executive branch of the government?

75. The Supreme Court
A. For how long a term are Supreme Court

justices appointed? How many justices may there be in the Supreme Court?

B. Describe the cases which have original jurisdiction before the Supreme Court; appellate jurisdiction?

C. From what case do we generally note that the Court began to exercise the power of judicial review? Why is the exercise of this power important? Point out several criticisms of the exercise of this power by the Supreme Court.

THE CHAPTER IN REVIEW

A. Describe the structure of Congress and the way its members are elected.

B. Define or describe "committee of the whole"; filibustering; closure rule; party caucus; lobby; seniority system.

C. Describe the main events in the attempt of President Franklin D. Roosevelt to pack the Supreme Court in 1937. What are some of the problems facing the Court today?

SELECTED READINGS

Chapter VII of Father Keller's *Government Is Your Business* is a discussion of what you can do about the national government. The *United States Government Organization Manual,* published annually by the Government Printing Office, supplies all the necessary information on the organization of both the executive department and Congress. Fundamental textbooks to be consulted are: Gosnell, Lancaster, and Rankin, *Fundamentals of American National Government* (New York: Mc-Graw-Hill Book Co., 1955); Swarthout and Bartley, *Principles and Problems of American National Government* (New York: Oxford University Press, Inc., 1955); and Ogg and Ray, *Introduction to American Government* (New York: Appleton-Century-Crofts, Inc., 1952). The work by Ogg and Ray is encyclopedic; it serves as an excellent reference for almost any problem in American government.

Recent studies of congressional procedures in legislation are G. B. Galloway, *The Legislative Process in Congress* (New York: Thomas Y. Crowell Co., 1953); S. K. Bailey and H. D. Samuel, *Congress at Work* (New York: Henry

Holt & Co., Inc., 1952); and Harvey Walker, *The Legislative Process* (New York: The Ronald Press Company, 1948).

The President's role in legislation is objectively analyzed by L. H. Chamberlain, *The President, Congress, and Legislation* (New York: Columbia University Press, 1952); and Wilfred E. Binkley, *The President and Congress* (New York: Alfred A. Knopf, Inc., 1947). Presidential powers and prerogatives are carefully scrutinized by Edward S. Corwin, *The President: Office and Powers, 1787–1948* (New York: Columbia University Press, 1948).

Any study of the problems of national government should take into consideration the recommendations of the (Hoover) Commission on Organization of the Executive Branch of Government. The *Reports* of the Hoover Commission have been published by the Government Printing Office, beginning in 1949.

Histories of the Supreme Court include the following excellent volumes: Charles Warren, *Supreme Court in United States History*, 2 vols. (Boston; Little, Brown, & Co., 1947); Carl B. Swisher, *American Constitutional Development* (Boston: Houghton Mifflin Co., 1943); Alfred H. Kelly and Winfred A. Harbison, *The American Constitution* (New York: W. W. Norton & Company, Inc., 1948).

PROJECTS

1. Elections for the presidency have often hinged on small incidents which later were found to be of great consequence. Some elections were very close. A committee in the class could examine these and report on them to the class. The elections of 1824, 1876, 1884, 1916 would be of great interest in this regard.

2. A major project that would require participation of the entire class would be a study of the President's Cabinet. Each of ten groups in the class could represent one of the departments of the Cabinet. The organization, authority, and function of each should be studied. A spokesman for each group could then make a report to the entire class on the department his group considered.

Chapter 26. Problems of State Government

76. THE STATES AND THEIR LEGISLATURES

The expansion of the national government has led some political scientists to write off the states as obsolete. As far back as 1886 Professor John W. Burgess asserted that "the two natural elements in our system are now the Community and the Nation." He believed that all government functions should be handled either in the local community or from Washington and that the states were "meddlesome intruders" between the two. Complaints are frequently made in our own time that the states have failed and that they no longer perform any vital function.

These complaints, coupled with the growth of federal power, obscure the fact that the states are still very important political units in the American system. They perform more functions by far than they did in the nineteenth century. State governments spent over eleven billion dollars in 1952, sixty times as much as they did fifty years earlier. The state of New York alone has spent more than a billion dollars for a vast range of services such as education, highways, and welfare work during each of the last several years. State governments are responsible for the local agencies of government they create, such as the county and the municipality. States all maintain prisons, mental hospitals, and various other institutions concerned with society. They are responsible for maintaining a system of public highways, for the preservation of law and order, for the promotion of education, for the regulation of business, and for almost any measure that promotes the common welfare.

American citizens should therefore be interested in securing the most efficient state government possible and in solving the problems with which it is confronted. Conditions vary greatly from state to state, and it is difficult to find problems that are of equally acute importance in all forty-eight states. New York has a population of nearly sixteen million, whereas Nevada has only two hundred thousand. Some states, like the Dakotas, are predominantly agricultural, whereas others are predominantly industrial. In other respects the states are similar and have certain problems in common. In this

chapter we shall select some of the more pressing problems common to all or most of the states.

The states are all legally equal. They possess inherent or residual powers. Each has a written constitution that sets up the framework of government that is similar to our national government—a government with separation of powers that check and balance each other, a single chief executive, a representative assembly, and an independent judiciary. Moreover, as we have already seen, each state is a unitary government that has created many subdivisions for local government.

State constitutions. The original states' constitutions were rather brief documents that were confined for the most part to fundamentals. In many respects they were similar to the national Constitution adopted in 1789. Through the nineteenth century, however, state constitutions became longer and more detailed. Thirty-one of the present forty-eight constitutions were drafted in the last half of the nineteenth century. State constitutions became inordinately long for a combination of reasons. First of all, in the latter part of the nineteenth century state legislatures were distrusted and therefore limited constitutionally by minute, detailed restrictions. In the second place,

industrial development presented new problems of regulating railroads, public utilities, and corporate practices, as well as providing needed social legislation. Because constitutional conventions distrusted state legislatures, they put into the constitutions many clauses treating of those subjects which should more properly have been left to legislation. Finally, state constitutions provide for the election of many public officials and prescribe their powers and duties in detail.

Political scientists unanimously criticize excessively long constitutions as harmful to good, efficient government. A long constitution tends to blur the line between a state's fundamental law and ordinary legislation. A long, detailed constitution must be amended frequently—California's has been amended more than three hundred times—because changing conditions make detailed regulations obsolete, whereas fundamental principles like those in the national Constitution remain applicable through judicial interpretation and appropriate legislation. The amending process must therefore be made easy for long constitutions, and the result is frequently legislation by amendment—with its delays and inconveniences—instead of by the state legislature. Another disadvantage of a long constitution

RHODE ISLAND
INDUSTRY'S
IDEAL STATE

WRITE RHODE ISLAND DEVELOPMENT COUNCIL
ROOM 526, STATE HOUSE, PROVIDENCE, R. I.

OPPOSITE: *About 100 years ago the Illinois Central Railroad promoted the development of Illinois in conjunction with the state authorities.* ABOVE: *Today, in order to attract industry, the states maintain development councils to publicize the natural resources, transportation facilities, labor supply, and other features of their area. (U.S.D.A. Photo; R. I. Development Council)*

is that the citizens of a state will never read it or understand its provisions. California and Louisiana have constitutions of more than three hundred pages, for example, and few citizens can be expected to remember all the provisions in such lengthy documents.

Political scientists have suggested that a state constitution should confine itself to fundamentals. It should reduce its bill of rights to a terse summary. It should set up the framework of government, as our national Constitution does, and allow the legislature to fill in the details. A trend toward shorter constitutions developed in the last twenty years. Such new constitutions as Missouri's and New Jersey's, which were adopted since World War II, are shorter than the average state constitution. However, only ten of the forty-eight state constitutions have been drafted in the twentieth century, and most of the remaining constitutions are badly in need of thorough revision.

All constitutions except New Hampshire's provide for revision by piecemeal amendment. These amendments can be initiated in most states by the legislature or by popular petition, and most states require that the proposed amendment be submitted to the electorate before it be-

comes part of the constitution. Piecemeal revision of the constitution by single amendments is generally inadequate. It leads to ever longer constitutions and fails to provide a fundamental framework on which state government can be based. More thorough revision can be accomplished in most states by an appointive constitutional commission or by a constitutional convention. Although the commission procedure has been employed frequently in recent years, the constitutional convention is the usual means by which thorough revision of a state constitution can be accomplished. In some states it is mandatory to submit to the electorate periodically the proposition of electing a constitutional convention. In other states the proposal to elect such a convention is initiated by the legislature or by popular petition. In any case, provision is made everywhere for calling a constitutional convention to revise thoroughly a constitution the people feel is no longer adequate.

Problems of state legislatures. Unlike the national government, state legislatures may do whatever they are not expressly prohibited from doing in the federal or state constitution. In every state, therefore, the legislature has all legislative

IN THE GARDEN STATE OF THE WEST.

THE ILLINOIS CENTRAL RAILROAD CO., HAVE FOR SALE

1,200,000 ACRES OF RICH FARMING LANDS,

In Tracts of Forty Acres and upward on Long Credit and at Low Prices.

THE attention of the enterprising and industrious portion of the community is directed to the following statements and liberal inducements offered them by the

ILLINOIS CENTRAL RAILROAD COMPANY.

which, as they will perceive, will enable them, by proper energy, perseverance and industry, to provide comfortable homes for themselves and families, with, comparatively speaking, very little capital.

LANDS OF ILLINOIS.

No State in the Valley of the Mississippi offers so great an inducement to the settler as the State of Illinois. There is no portion of the world where all the conditions of climate and soil so admirably combine to produce those two great staples, CORN and WHEAT, as the Prairies of Illinois.

EASTERN AND SOUTHERN MARKETS.

These lands are contiguous to a railroad 700 miles in length, which connects with other roads and navigable lakes and rivers, thus affording an unbroken communication with the Eastern and Southern markets.

RAILROAD SYSTEM OF ILLINOIS.

Over $100,000,000 of private capital have been expended on the railroad system of Illinois. Inasmuch as part of the income from several of these works, with a valuable public fund in lands, go to diminish the State expenses ; the TAXES ARE LIGHT, and must consequently every day decrease.

THE STATE DEBT.

The State debt is only $10,106,308 14, and within the last three years has been reduced $2,959,746 80, and we may reasonably expect that in ten years it will become extinct.

PRESENT POPULATION.

The State is rapidly filling up with population ; 868,025 persons having been added since 1850, making the present population 1,723,663, a ratio of 102 per cent. in ten years.

AGRICULTURAL PRODUCTS.

The Agricultural Products of Illinois are greater than those of any other State. The products sent out during the past year exceeded 1,500,000 tons. The wheat crop of 1860 approaches 35,000,000 bushels, while the corn crop yields not less than 140,000,000 bushels.

FERTILITY OF THE SOIL.

Nowhere can the industrious farmer secure such immediate results for his labor as upon these prairie soils, they being composed of a deep rich loam, the fertility of which is unsurpassed by any on the globe.

TO ACTUAL CULTIVATORS.

Since 1854 the Company have sold 1,300,000 acres. They sell only to actual cultivators, and every contract contains an agreement to cultivate. The road has been constructed through these lands at an expense of $30,000,000. In 1850 the population of forty-nine counties, through which it passes, was only 335,598 since which 479,293 have been added ; making the whole population 814,891, a gain of 143 per cent.

EVIDENCES OF PROSPERITY.

As an evidence of the thrift of the people, it may be stated that 600,000 tons of freight, including 8,600,000 bushels of grain, and 250,000 barrels of flour were forwarded over the line last year.

PRICES AND TERMS OF PAYMENT.

The prices of these lands vary from $6 to $25 per acre, according to location, quality, &c. First class farming lands sell for about $10 to $12 per acre ; and the relative expense of subduing prairie land as compared with wood land is in the ratio of 1 to 10 in favor of the former. The terms of sale for the bulk of these lands will be

ONE YEAR'S INTEREST IN ADVANCE,

at six per cent per annum, and six interest notes at six per cent., payable respectively in one, two, three, four, five and six years from date of sale ; and four notes for principal, payable in four, five, six and seven years from date of sale ; the contract stipulating that one-tenth of the tract purchased shall be fenced and cultivated, each and every year, for five years from date of sale, so that at the end of five years one-half shall be fenced and under cultivation.

TWENTY PER CENT. WILL BE DEDUCTED

from the valuation for cash, except the same should be at six dollars per acre, when the cash price will be five dollars

Pamphlets descriptive of the lands, soil, climate, productions, prices, and terms of payment, can be had on application to

J. W. FOSTER, Land Commissioner,
CHICAGO, ILLINOIS

For the name of the Towns, Villages and Cities situated upon the Illinois Central Railroad, see pages 189, 189 and 190 Appleton's Railway Guide.

HOMES FOR THE INDUSTRIOUS
(Advertising cut widely used by the Illinois Central Railroad in 1860 and 1861)

power not granted to the Congress or prohibited to the state. Most important among the residual powers is the so-called "police power," or the power to legislate for the public welfare. This is the power every state legislature possesses "to restrict the individual's freedom of action, or free use of his property, in order to protect the health, safety, morals, good order, convenience, or general welfare of the state."[1] State legislatures are therefore potentially the most important organs in our complex framework of government. They have generally failed to live up to their constitutional possibilities, and in the interest of improving our government we should inquire into the causes of their failure.

Qualifications and salary of state legislators. Early in our history it was believed that competent men could be persuaded to serve in public office without compensation. The term of service in all but administrative positions was short, and good men did accept office out of a sense of public duty. In our time, however, state legislators are required to devote most of their time—in session and out—to legislative problems. Unfortunately they are not adequately paid for the time they must spend in office. Per diem compensation (the pay for each day the legislature remains in session) varies from $5.00 in Kansas to $25 in Kentucky. Other states provide annual compensation, varying from $200 a term in New Hampshire to $5,000 a year in New York.

The pay level has risen in many states in the last two decades, but it is still insufficient to attract competent men as full-time legislators. The results have been unfortunate. Although competent men with a sense of public duty occasionally serve in the state legislature, nevertheless the average legislator in most states is regularly employed in some other occupation—law, insurance, farming, or business—and his legislative work is a part-time occupation. There is, consequently, a rapid turnover in state legislature personnel and a loss of men who have gained experience in legislative procedure. The low pay, moreover, makes it impossible for any competent man to serve unless he can support himself by other means. The result is that incompetent men are frequently elected to state legislatures, and they use the office more for personal advancement than for public service.

Originally the legislatures were clearly stronger than the governors in our American states. But through the nineteenth century the legislatures declined in quality, and governors gained in prestige and power. Americans lost confidence in the state legislatures for a number of reasons. Among them the most important were: (1) widespread inefficiency and corruption; (2) failure to establish control over utilities and corporations; (3) interference with local government; (4) inability to deal with the growing volume of governmental business, much of it highly technical in character. Back of all these failures, of course, was the incompetent personnel serving in the state legislatures, men elected too often to serve special interests rather than the public interest.

Providing adequate compensation for legislators is an inexpensive way to set about getting good state government. The legislature can be considered the generating plant of state and local government. From it come the laws that the executive administers. In it are created the agencies of local government, as well as the state administrative agencies that control education, health, and welfare. The legislature sets the policies of state government and determines the procedures by which they are to be realized. Adequate compensation for the men who perform this service is the first step in obtaining competent legislators.

[1] R. E. Cushman, "The Supreme Court and the Constitution," *Public Affairs Pamphlet*, No. 7 (New York: Public Affairs Committee, 1936), pp. 16–17.

Ohio State University, with an enrollment of over 17,000 in its many colleges, is one of the largest in the United States. Students at state universities who are residents of the state receive this education at nominal costs, the university being largely tax-supported. (Ohio State University)

Size of the state legislature. A good legislative body must be large enough to assure representation to all interests in the state but small enough to deliberate effectively and to legislate without resorting to "steam-roller" tactics. Senates in most states are of better size than the lower houses. The senates vary from 17 in Delaware to 67 in Minnesota. Lower houses vary from 35 in Delaware to 399 in New Hampshire. Over half the states have lower houses of more than 100 members, and the average size of the general session, or the combined houses, is more than 150.

State legislatures have been made needlessly large on the mistaken assumption that there is a direct connection between the size of a body and its representative character—the more men in the legislature, it is assumed, the better the people will be represented. Smaller legislatures operate more efficiently than large ones. They can also operate more economically and thus make possible the payment of better salaries to the individual legislator. Finally, they make it more difficult for the individual legislator to escape responsibility for the body's action. All students of government reform therefore suggest that neither house in a state legislature should exceed about fifty members, and that the senate should be even smaller, twenty to thirty being ideal.

The unwieldy size of state legislatures has led many reformers to favor *unicam-eral state legislatures* as the most efficient, economical, and responsible arrangement for lawmaking on the state level. The unicameral or one-house legislature has been adopted in Nebraska, where it has worked to the satisfaction of both the people and the legislators. The advantages of the unicameral system are obvious. First, it enables the people to focus attention on one house and to find out what happens to proposed bills. In the bicameral system it is easy for the two houses to shuffle bills back and forth until they are lost and no one seems to be blamed. The second advantage of the unicameral system, then, is that it fixes responsibility on one body of men. A third advantage is that the dual committee system is abolished. Finally, the deadlocks and friction between two houses are eliminated, and thus savings in time and money can be effected. Even defenders of the bicameral system in state legislatures have difficulty finding a need for two houses (as there is in our Congress), especially when the great need in the states is for smaller bodies of well-paid, competent men.

77. IMPROVING THE STATE LEGISLATURES

The problem of representation. Representation is usually based on some combination of territory and population. Whatever basis is used, the state legislature almost always lays out the districts, and when population is a factor it redistricts the state after each decennial census. Generally speaking, inclusion of a territorial factor in representation favors rural areas over urban areas. The requirement that each county have one senator, for example, causes almost a million people in Essex County, New Jersey, to have one senator, while Sussex and Cape May counties each have a senator for a population of less than forty thousand.

Since reapportionment of representation can be made by the legislature alone, it is difficult to make any equitable redistricting of a state that runs counter to the interests of the majority party in the legislature. The Illinois constitution, for example, provides for reapportionment of representation after each decennial census, but the legislature has not acted on this constitutional requirement since 1901. The result is that Cook County and Chicago are grossly underrepresented in the Illinois legislature. This is a serious problem throughout the country, because an increasingly large part of legislative business involves urban problems, and this business is too often decided by rural-dominated legislatures. If the majority party in the legislature is not scrupulously fair when the state is redistricted, it can indulge in the partisan practice of *gerrymandering* the state. That is, it can divide the state into legislative districts in such a way as to secure a fairly safe majority for itself in as many districts as possible and crowd the opposition votes into as few districts as possible. This practice of gerrymandering seriously impairs the representative character of the legislature. To offset the evils of this practice, some states have rigid constitutional restrictions to control the redistricting of the state after each decennial census. However, courts are usually reluctant to declare reapportionment acts unconstitutional, for these are political

A new species of *Monster*, which appeared in *Essex South District in*

" *O generation of* VIPERS ! *who hath warned you of the wrath to come ?*"

Gerrymandering is the name given to the practice of rearranging election districts by the party in power to insure their chances of continuing political control. The term is derived from Governor Elbridge Gerry, whose party in 1812 divided Essex County in Massachusetts (forming a dragon-shaped district) to obtain this political advantage. (N.Y.P.L.)

questions which the courts prefer to leave to the legislature's discretion.

Another device proposed for improving the representative quality of the state legislature is *proportional representation.* This is a system of voting whereby minority groups can obtain representation in the legislature in proportion to their strength in the state. A minority group controlling one-tenth the votes in a state, for example, would elect about one-tenth the representatives. No state has yet tried proportional representation, although it is recommended by *The Model State Constitution* and by many political scientists. The plan involves a complicated system of preferential voting, and it is looked on with suspicion by the major parties because it encourages independent candidates to seek office without affiliating with either major party.

Proportional representation would undoubtedly result in a legislature that would more truly reflect the various interests in the state. Under the present system, representatives are elected from single-member districts. The Democrats —or Republicans—might poll only 60 per cent of the vote in the state and still elect almost every representative to the legislature. Such a legislature would not reflect the political make-up of the state. Under proportional representation, on the other hand, the Democrats would elect only about 60 per cent of the representatives, and the other parties would elect the rest according to their numerical strength. Whether proportional representation would encourage the formation of many splinter parties and disorganize the state politically, as its opponents maintain, cannot be known, until it is tried in some one state experimentally. So far, proportional representation has been tried in only a few American municipalities, where it has not worked well.[2]

Direct legislation. A more generally accepted remedy to disproportionate representation in the state legislature has been *direct legislation*. The argument behind this process is that, if the people can legislate directly, lack of adequate representation in the legislature is not as serious an evil as it would otherwise be. Direct legislation takes the form of the initiative or the referendum. The *initiative* is a device whereby a number or a percentage of the voters petition to have a law placed on the ballot for adoption or rejection by the electorate. The *referendum* may take different forms, but in essence it means referring a law directly

---

[2] New York City, Cleveland, and Cincinnati are the largest cities to have tried proportional representation. Toledo, Yonkers, Cambridge (Massachusetts), and several smaller cities have also experimented with it. Courts ruled in some states (Michigan, California, and Rhode Island) that the system was unconstitutional. In other places it was found that it broke up the two-party system and enabled obstreperous minorities to exert undue influence, as was the case with a few Communist members elected in New York City.

How Referendum and Initiative Work

Referendum refers a law directly to the electorate for its approval

Initiative is the petition of a group of voters to have a law placed on ballot

to the electorate for its approval or condemnation. The move for direct legislation began in the Midwest about the turn of the century, and now twenty states make use of initiative and referendum. Since 1918 no new states have adopted direct legislative procedures, and none of the states that had the system at that time has abandoned it.

Experience has shown that direct legislation involves certain disadvantages. (1) It adds to the length of the ballot and puts an additional burden on the voter who would exercise his privilege of voting conscientiously. (2) A great number of voters ignore legislative propositions when they go to the polls because they do not understand them, and thus these propositions are sometimes decided by an interested minority. (3) Since legislative problems are becoming more complex and technical, direct legislation demands more study and more specialized knowledge than the average voter possesses. (4) When special elections are held for such proposals, they add to the voters' burden and to the cost of government. In summary, direct legislation is an ideal that does not work out as well in practice as it appears in theory. Its success depends on the quality of the electorate in any given area.

The problem of lobbies and pressure groups. State legislatures, like the national Congress, are subject to constant pressure from groups desirous of legislation in their own interests. When pressure groups are properly regulated, they perform an important service for legislators. They furnish information and arguments for or against proposed legislation. They let the legislator see how various groups of people throughout the state will react to a proposed bill, and by their various objections they frequently reveal deficiencies in proposed legislation before it is adopted.

States have generally adopted corrupt-practices acts to control pressure groups.

One of the most important responsibilities of the state government is the maintenance of a suitable highway system. State taxes on license plates, gasoline, and tolls collected on the highways help finance this expensive item of the state budget. (Standard Oil Co., N.J.)

These laws enforce: (1) *publicity*, by requiring the lobbyist to register with a proper authority and state what group he represents; (2) *honesty*, by having him list the money he has spent in influencing legislation. Lobbying remains a serious problem in state government, however, because pressure groups can find ways of evading the law, and few states have adopted sufficiently stringent legislation to eliminate all corrupt practices in lobbying.

The problem of planned legislation. A generally recognized defect of the legislative system within our states is that each representative comes to the legislature with one or two pet projects which he wants enacted into law. The result is that the legislature becomes involved with several hundred proposed bills having no relation to one another, many of them contradictory, and few of them in any way connected with the general needs of the state. An average of two hundred laws are passed annually in each state. The need for planned, systematic legislation to achieve the end of good government has therefore long been recognized in the states.

Legislative planning can be done by the governor who, with the advice of a council, can prepare a program of needed legislation and present it to the legislature. Or it can be done by the legislature itself through a legislative council set up for that purpose. *The Model State Constitution* provides for a legislative council of seven to fifteen members. This model constitution provides that "it shall be the duty of the legislative council to collect information concerning the government and general welfare of the state and to report thereon to the legislature."[3] It also states that:

Measures for proposed legislation may be submitted to it at any time, and shall be considered, and reported to the legislature with its recommendations theron. The legislative council may also prepare such legislation and make such recommendations thereon to the legislature, in the form of bills or otherwise, as in its opinion the welfare of the state may require. Other powers and duties may be assigned to the legislative council by law.

Twenty-eight states now have legislative councils of some sort or other. They vary in size from the unwieldy 161 in Oklahoma to three in South Carolina. All existing councils have research divisions with from two to fourteen members employed as impartial, fact-finding experts who furnish the council with information on which intelligent legislation can be based. Some such device as the legislative council, aided by a research staff, seems necessary if state legislatures are to per-

[3] *The Model State Constitution,* Fifth Edition (New York: National Municipal League, 1948), Section 319.

form their functions satisfactorily. If they fail, legislative as well as administrative leadership in the state must fall into the governor's hands.

Recommendations for improving state legislatures. The Committee on Legislative Processes and Procedures of the Council of State Governments has made a number of recommendations for improving state legislatures. Among these recommendations, the following are most important:

1. Reduce the size of the legislatures by establishing the unicameral legislature or drastically reducing the size of each house in most states.
2. Increase the quality of legislators by providing adequate compensation.
3. Increase the representativeness of the legislature by adopting proportional representation.
4 . Provide legislative leadership by creating legislative councils.
5. Reduce the number of committees and their size.
6. Require public hearings on important public measures.
7. Provide adequate technical services, such as legislative reference bureaus, bill-drafting agencies, and research staffs.

78. PROBLEMS OF STATE ADMINISTRATION

The chief executive in each state is the governor. He is elected directly by the people, in most states for a two- or a four-year term. The general qualifications are that he be a citizen of the United States, thirty years old, and a resident in the state in which he is elected for

An important function of the state in promoting the general welfare is to encourage building programs on a private or public basis. This state housing project provides low-rent housing for families whose income is beneath a certain level. (N. Y. State Division of Housing)

The conservation, forest, and police departments are three of the important agencies of the state government. In Wisconsin, the functions of all three departments are the responsibility of the Wisconsin law-enforcement crews that patrol the Great Lakes. (Wisconsin Conservation Dept.)

at least five years. As chief executive, the governor is responsible for the enforcement of law in the state and for the general administration of the government. As we shall see in this section, most states weaken the governor's power over the administration by providing for a number of elective officials whom the governor cannot remove from office, by creating a host of agencies and bureaus that are independent of the governor, and by curtailing his powers with various constitutional restrictions.

The office of governor. In colonial times governors were the object of fear and suspicion by the native population because they represented the English government in the colonies. This fear and suspicion was transferred to the governors of the new states when they won their independence. The early constitutions severely restricted the governor and placed him clearly under the state legislature. The failure of legislatures, as we noted above, put governors in most states in a stronger position. Throughout our history there has been a steady increase, then, in the power and prestige of the governor as compared with the legislature in most states.

The governor's powers can be considered as (1) executive, (2) legislative, and (3) judicial. In addition to these constitutional powers, of course, a governor may exercise considerable power by reason of his personality, his leadership of the party within the state, and his use of his office to mold public opinion and to obtain popular backing for his policies. Let us examine his constitutionally bestowed powers separately.

1. *Executive powers.* The governor ordinarily conducts relations between his state and other states in the Union. Because of the nature of our federal system, however, this is a minor matter. Occasionally, as when an interstate flood-control system is proposed, this power becomes important.

The governor possesses little or no inherent power because he is the chief executive in the state, as the President does in our national government. Whereas the Constitution confers on the President "the executive power," no state constitution bestows similar power on a governor. Executive power in the states is shared by a number of other officers. They, as well as the governor, possess only those powers clearly granted by the state constitution or by some statute. The governor is nevertheless responsible for seeing that the laws are faithfully executed. To do this he must rely on a number of subordinates, many of whom he has not appointed and cannot remove from office. Moreover, he does not have the power to supervise and direct them in the performance of their duties, because the state constitution has detailed regulations governing their conduct in office. The governor, then, "commonly enjoys a very limited power of appointment, a wholly inadequate power of supervision and direction, and a narrowly restricted right of suspension and removal."[4]

Such appointments as the governor can make are usually subject to legislative confirmation. The trend in recent

[4] Ogg and Ray, *Introduction to American Government* (New York: Appleton-Century-Crofts, 1948), p. 929.

state constitutions, such as those of Missouri and New Jersey, has been to strengthen the governor's appointive and removal powers. This is a step toward sound administrative organization, for a superior cannot be held responsible for the conduct of subordinates he does not appoint and cannot control or remove.

As chief executive, the governor also possesses limited military powers. In all states he is commander-in-chief of the state militia or the National Guard, except in time of war. In case of emergency caused by floods, riots, earthquakes, and the like, he may employ these forces to maintain law and order. The governor may also employ the state police and highway patrol for extraordinary purposes of law enforcement in many states, although in some states the highway patrol is limited almost exclusively to highway violations.

2. *Legislative powers.* Like the President, governors have considerable power over legislation. They are required to transmit messages to the legislature, and in these messages they are customarily expected to present a program of legislation. In a loose sense, then, the governor has a certain power of initiating legisla-tion. The governor has also the power to call special sessions of the legislature, and in more than half the states the legislature is limited to consideration of the topics for which it is called. Thus the governor can practically compel the legislature to consider certain matters and put itself on record concerning them.

The governor's most effective control over legislation, however, is his veto power. Every state except North Carolina gives the governor the veto power, and in thirty-nine states he has the power to veto individual items in appropriation bills. This enables him to weed out unnecessary appropriations, and it destroys one of the legislature's most effective clubs over the chief executive. Requirements for the vote necessary to override a gubernatorial veto differ from state to state. The requirements range from a mere majority of the quorum in each house, as in Connecticut, to two-thirds of the full membership of each house, as in twenty-two states. A governor's veto is seldom overridden, and thus it serves as an effective control over legislation.

3. *Judicial powers.* The governor's judicial powers include the right to grant pardons, paroles, and reprieves, to com-

The Ohio National Guard conducts an anti-aircraft drill at Camp Perry during field training. The National Guard, or state militia, is maintained by the states but is subject to call by the federal government in an emergency. (State of Ohio, Adjutant General's Office)

mute sentences and remit fines, and to veto measures for constitutional reasons. Governors of thirty-six states have the power to grant pardons, but in twenty-four of these states advisory boards hear applications and make recommendations to the governor. In the remaining states the power of pardon is reserved to a board, of which the governor is a member. Some states do not allow pardons in the case of certain crimes, such as impeachment or treason, and most states do not allow pardons to be granted before conviction. Reprieve, or stay of execution, is ordinarily granted to permit the defendant to present new evidence. Parole (the release of a prisoner from prison before the expiration of his sentence) is vested in the governor or in a board, and it is usually exercised according to the evidence presented to the governor or the board.

The problem of administrative reorganization. In earlier days state government was a small and simple operation. But economic and social developments necessitated more and more functions by the state. New agencies and boards were created piecemeal, especially after 1900, to meet new demands on state government. State administrations came to be carried on through loose aggregations of depart-

ments, boards, commissions, and other agencies, without a responsible head to co-ordinate their activities. Administrative reorganization became a pressing problem as early as 1911, and it has continued to be one of the serious problems facing all state governments.

Illinois pioneered in this field by adopting a comprehensive plan of administrative reorganization in 1917. By 1938, twenty-six states had reorganized their administrative structures, and within the next ten years thirteen more states adopted comprehensive reorganization plans. The work of the Hoover Commission on Organization of the Executive Branch of the Government gave great impetus to the reorganization movement on the state level, and within two years provision was made in twenty-six states for reorganization surveys.

Here we can only state the general principles of sound administrative organization which all states should adopt—with variations, of course, according to the peculiarities of each state. The Council of State Governments recommends the following principles of administrative organization:[5] (1) group all administrative agencies into a small number of de-

[5] The Council of State Governments, *Reorganizing State Government* (Chicago, 1950), p. 3.

State penitentiaries are expensive to maintain but highly important to the safety of the people. Well-run correctional institutions are partially self-supporting when prison laundries, bakeries, and workshops provide for the inmates and for other public institutions operated by the state. (Department of Corrections, State of Michigan)

The Florida Supreme Court at Tallahassee is the highest court in the state. State courts are generally maintained on four levels, with the Supreme Court having appellate jurisdiction but limited original jurisdiction.

partments; (2) establish clear lines of authority running from the governor down through the entire organization; (3) establish appropriate staff agencies responsible to the governor for planning and advising on policies; (4) eliminate the use of boards and commissions in favor of single directors for administrative work; (5) establish an independent auditor.

The state judiciary: Selection of judges. The most general and most important problems of the state judiciary are two: (1) the selection of competent judges; (2) organization of the state judiciary into a system of courts that operate economically and efficiently in order to administer justice without undue delay or expense to the people of the state.

Although the methods of choosing judges vary from state to state, we can say that most judges in state courts throughout the country are elected. In twenty-one states all judges are elected, and in only six are most of them appointed by the governor. In the remaining states some judges are elected and others are appointed. Election is not the best way to obtain qualified judges. Voters are not able as a rule to evaluate a candidate's technical competency, and the likelihood is that good campaigners rather than good judges will be elected. Moreover, the elective process makes it likely in most states that "party regulars" will win judicial office.

California and Missouri have adopted plans for selecting judges that have attracted nationwide attention and are likely to be adopted by other states. The California plan, adopted in 1934, is a compromise between the appointive and elective systems. Under this plan a supreme court or district court judge may declare himself a candidate to succeed himself before his twelve-year term expires. He then faces the electorate on his record. No one runs against him. The voters decide whether he should stay in office or not. If he is not approved by the electorate, the governor appoints a successor, who must be approved by a commission on qualifications, composed of the chief justice, a presiding judge of one of the district courts of appeal, and the attorney general. The new judge must then face the electorate at the next general election, and he must be approved by a majority of the voters to retain office for the rest of the twelve-year term. The Missouri plan is similar to California's; it differs only in certain details we will not discuss here.

Lawyers, judges, and students of government all agree that the California and Missouri plans have worked well. They have, in the words of the chief justice of the Missouri Supreme Court, "taken the courts out of politics." They save judges the task of campaigning for re-election, which is hard to reconcile with the honor and dignity of the bench. The arrangement is about as good as can be devised for assuring the initial appointment of qualified men to the bench and their remaining in office unless they give cause for widespread dissatisfaction.

Court reorganization. In most states there are four levels of courts: (1) On the lowest level are justices of the peace courts, magistrates' courts, and other courts of limited jurisdiction, which are empowered to hear and dispose of minor criminal cases. (2) Above them in most states are a number of intermediate courts, such as county or municipal courts, which have broader jurisdiction than the lowest tribunals but not general original jurisdiction. In most states the intermediate courts cannot hear cases involving felonies or civil cases involving large amounts of wealth. (3) The third level consists of courts of general jurisdiction —called circuit, district, or superior courts—which hear and dispose of serious criminal and civil cases. (4) At the top is the state supreme court, which has limited original jurisdiction in thirty-seven states and appellate jurisdiction in all states.

Experts on state judicial systems insist that the lack of unified control of the courts causes much waste of time, duplication of effort, and confusion to the litigants in every state. They urge unification of the courts under one general court and such subordinate courts as might be necessary. The chief justice or administrative head of the general court would have power to shift judges to courts where they are needed and to transfer cases to courts properly equipped to handle them. Reformers also suggest that states should all have a judicial council to make recommendations on judicial organization and procedure and to formulate rules for the administration of the courts and rules governing pleading, practice, or procedure.

Conclusion. The growth of national power in the last half century has tended to obscure the many functions still performed by state government, but in the last two decades reformers have centered their attention on state government, and they have achieved many excellent reforms. Reform and improvement are a continuous process, however, and citizens in each state should be vigilant in seeing that their government constantly seeks to improve itself. The forty-eight states constitute forty-eight laboratories where various proposals for better government can be tried. A vigilant citizenry in any one state can study the measures tried in the other forty-seven states and can adopt those that promise to improve the government of their own state. Interest in national and foreign affairs should not obscure the many important functions performed by state and local government, nor should it blind us to the fact that we must constantly seek to improve government on these levels or else we shall have to pay the bill for still more costly federal government.

REVIEW

76. The States and Their Legislatures
A. Why is it difficult to find problems that are equally important to the various states?

B. Why did lengthy state constitutions come into existence? What problems did they create?

C. What are some of the more important residual powers of a state legislature? Show in general how state legislatures vary in size. What are the disadvantages that can result from large lawmaking bodies because of their size?

77. Improving the State Legislatures
A. What problem of representation does geographical districting present? What is gerrymandering?

B. Describe initiative and referendum. What are the drawbacks to these two reforms?

C. How have states generally brought about a regulation of pressure groups? What are the functions of the legislative councils that exist in many of the states?

78. Problems of State Administration
A. Why did early state constitutions greatly restrict the power of the governor?

B. Show how the executive power of the governor is limited. What are some of his important powers in legislation?

C. How are state judges generally chosen? What is the California Plan?

THE CHAPTER IN REVIEW

A. Why did Americans lose confidence in the state legislatures during the nineteenth century? Explain why it is important to have competent state legislators.

B. The problem of having legislatures consider *necessary* legislation has always been a real one. Describe some ways which are being used in order to guide legislatures in passing laws that are desired by the state as a whole.

C. Describe the various types of state court systems. How are they being improved today?

SELECTED READINGS

Chapter VI of Father Keller's *Government Is Your Business* ("State Government Vitally Affects You") is a good and easy-to-read summary of important things everyone should know about state government. The National Municipal League has published a *Model State Constitution,* of which the last edition is 1948, which is basic to any discussion of state government. The Council of State Governments publishes its *Book of the States* biennially and its *State Government* monthly. The *Book of the States* is the best encyclopedic reference work available, and *State Government* discusses problems of current interest to the states. The Council of State Governments also published a volume, *Reorganizing State Government* (Chicago: The Council of State Governments, 1950). The March 1948 issue of the *National Municipal Review* was devoted to "Modernizing State Constitutions."

Among the standard textbooks covering state government problems adequately, the following are important: W. B. Graves, *American State Government* (Boston: D. C. Heath & Company, 1953); Austin F. Macdonald, *American State Government and Administration* (New York: Thomas Y. Crowell Co., 1955); Bates and Field's *State Government,* fourth edition by Pressly S. Sikes and John E. Stoner (New

York: Harper & Brothers, 1954); and Jewell Cass Philipps, *State and Local Government in America* (New York: American Book Company, 1954).

An interesting and readable study of the problems faced by state governments is Richard L. Neuberger, *Adventures in Politics: We Go to the Legislature* (New York: Oxford University Press, Inc., 1954).

Legislative problems are studied in the debaters' handbook edited by Bower Aly, *Unicameral Legislatures* (Columbia, Mo.: Lucas Bros., Publishers, 1950); the pamphlet of A. E. Buck, *Modernizing our State Legislatures* (Philadelphia: American Academy of Political and Social Science, 1936); L. K. Caldwell, "Strengthening State Legislatures," *American Political Science Review* (April 1947); and Harold W. Davey, "The Legislative Council Movement in the United States," *American Political Science Review* (September 1953).

The governor's role in state affairs is studied by Samuel R. Solomon in "The Governor as Legislator," *National Municipal Review* (November 1951), and "United States Governors, 1940–1950," *National Municipal Review* (April 1952).

PROJECTS

1. A class committee can be assigned the task of finding out the salaries of your state legislators, the amount of work they are required to do, and the abilities they should possess to serve the interests of their state. The discussion that follows the committee's report to the class might include the following subjects: salary reforms; qualifications for office; and a program for attracting competent people into the state legislature.

2. A great deal has been said in this chapter concerning proper legislative programs and the importance of planning ahead for needed legislation. Knowing the needs of your own state, a committee of the class could draw up a proposed legislative program for the coming year, stating the need for each bill that is to be introduced.

Chapter 27. Local Government Problems

79. IN THE COUNTIES

The shift of popular attention from local affairs to the national and international scene has had unfortunate effects on local government. Although the individual can exert considerable direct influence on local government, most people tend to neglect it. We should remember, however, that sound local government is an effective means of preserving democracy and restricting the tendency toward centralization that has been at work in America the last thirty years.

Local agencies of government operate such essential services as education, police and fire protection, water supply and sewage disposal, health services, parks and playgrounds, and many other facilities used daily by the average citizen. It is important that such services be furnished efficiently and economically. Local government is important also as a training ground in political life. Finally, it is important because it spends so much of our money. The total expenditures for local government in 1952 were almost eleven billion dollars, almost half of which was spent by the 474 cities with a population of 25,000 or more.

Common features of local government. A nationwide survey of local government suggests at least three features more or less common to all local units.

1. They are all created by the state in which they are located, and they possess only those powers given to them by the state. The inhabitants of most local units exercise a considerable measure of local self-government. But the subdivisions are creatures of the state and they may be abolished or changed by the state government. Reform of local government is therefore frequently dependent on the state legislature or on constitutional amendment.

2. There is a superfluity of local government units. The four principal types of local governments are counties, towns and townships, incorporated places such as villages and cities, and special districts. School districts are the most numerous of this last category, but in recent years there has been a trend toward consolidating small school districts into larger ones. In 1934 the Census Bureau reported 125,627 school districts in the country. In 1942 the number had fallen to 108,579, and by 1952 it was down to 67,346. Many districts maintain a school

for as few as five pupils; most of them have only one teacher, and comparatively few can provide adequate education beyond the primary level. Moreover, the cost of education per pupil becomes excessive in school districts with ten or fewer pupils in school. There is still room for a drastic reduction in the number of school districts. Besides school districts, there are various other special districts in most states created to handle single functions, such as irrigation, or furnishing light or fire protection to an unincorporated area. The number of these special districts can be reduced, chiefly by consolidating various functional districts into a single administrative unit.

Many students of government also urge a drastic reduction in the number of townships or even their complete abolition. The National Municipal League's committee on county government reported some years ago that "the township is no longer a satisfactory organization for the administration of local services," and urged that "steps be taken for its elimination." The notable exceptions to this general condemnation are the 1,429 New England towns and the 61 first-class townships in Pennsylvania. Townships throughout the Midwest are artificial creations, six miles square by the surveyor's chain, and running up the cost of government without performing any service that other units like the county cannot handle adequately.

3. Local units of government have established close relations with the national government in Washington, from which they obtain financial support and therefore considerable direction in handling local affairs. These connections were first established on a strong basis in the 1930s, when local units were unable to handle the relief problems of the depression. The grant-in-aid system maintained and even increased these lines of connection when relief was no longer a pressing problem.

The town meeting is a reflection of one of the earliest democratic institutions in our country. At this Stowe, Vt., meeting, a rural mail carrier speaks his piece. (Standard Oil Co., N.J.)

The Board of Trustees of the village of Northfield, Vt., are shown (left) at their weekly meeting in the municipal building. This board of three men, elected for a three-year term, is the governing body of the village. The governing body in New England towns varies in size. The Board of Civil Authority (right) of Stowe, Vt., counts ballots at a town meeting. (Standard Oil Co. N.J.)

A new and lasting relationship in our federal system thus seems to be permanently established, whereby the national government by-passes the state to co-operate directly with local community undertakings.

Reform of local government. The most important units of local government are the county and the municipality. Before we study these units separately let us list the proposals that have been most frequently made for the general improvement of local government in this country.

1. Drastic reduction should be achieved in the number of local governments. Generally speaking, each citizen should have only one local government to occupy his attention and serve his needs instead of the three or four to which he may be subject.

2. Better personnel can be obtained through businesslike methods of employment and promotion instead of the political preference system generally used at the present time.

3. Functional consolidation of small local units can be achieved in many places, as school districts are doing by the thousands every year.

Number, size, and structure of counties. The county is the one almost universal unit of local government in America. Virtu-

ally all the land area of the country lies within the boundaries of 3,049 counties. Louisiana alone does not have counties, but its 62 parishes are virtually the same as counties. Rhode Island is the only state in which the counties are not units of local self-government; there they serve only as judicial districts. The range in number and size of counties is great. Delaware has only three counties; Texas has 254. The average number of counties per state is about 60. The smallest county in the country, Arlington in Virginia, has only 25 square miles, whereas San Bernardino County in California has an area of 20,131 square miles—more than Maryland, Delaware, and New Jersey combined. Cook County in Illinois has a population of close to five million, whereas Armstrong County, South Dakota, has only 52 inhabitants. Counties average about 40,000 population.

Despite these divergencies of size and population, counties generally have similar organization and perform similar functions of government. County government disregards the traditional division of powers found in national, state, and most municipal government. County courts are part of the state judicial system. Legislative and administrative functions are, for the most part, entrusted to a body known as the county board. This is the agency that exercises most of the county's functions. It levies taxes, makes appropriations for various county purposes, and fixes salaries for minor county officials. In most states outside of New England it is the political unit entrusted by the state with conducting elections. The county board is also responsible for charitable and welfare work and for many miscellaneous activities like issuing liquor or hotel licenses, adopting zoning regulations, and organizing townships and school districts.

Besides the county board, counties in every state except Rhode Island have a number of other officials, all elected and independent of one another. The most important of these are the sheriff and the prosecuting attorney. The sheriff spends most of his time in performance of duties as executive agent of the county courts. He serves writs and other processes in connection with trials, and he carries out the judgment of the courts in civil cases. His police duties are impressive on paper, but in practice they are narrowly limited. There is no county police to support him; the city police and town constables are not under his control. His police functions consist chiefly of keeping the county jail and of making arrests of persons accused of crimes and misdemeanors in unincorporated areas.

Perhaps of greater importance is the prosecuting attorney, known in some states as district attorney, county solicitor, or state's attorney. The prosecuting attorney is elected in most states, although in a few he is appointed by the governor or by the court. The prosecuting attorney is charged with the enforcement of criminal law. The ability and thoroughness with which he performs his duties determine the kind of public order a locality will enjoy. He must investigate crimes that come to his attention, institute proceedings for the arrest and detention of persons suspected of crime, commence criminal proceedings where he believes they are warranted, and conduct the trial of criminal cases. In most states the prosecuting attorney is the legal adviser of county officials, and he conducts the legal business of the county.

Less important county officials include the coroner, the county clerk, the treasurer, the auditor or comptroller, recorder of deeds, and superintendent of county schools. County government is more or less good in each locality accordingly as these officials, especially the prosecuting attorney, are capable, honest men who perform their duties objectively in the public interest. Apart from the quality of personnel, county government suffers from more defects than any other kind of government in the country. Ogg and Ray refer to county government as "a dark continent being gradually explored," because it is only in recent years that serious attention has been given to reforming this unit of government. They conclude:[1]

In general the county has been largely untouched by reform movements which have yielded improvements in city and state; not

[1] Ogg and Ray, *Introduction to American Government,* ninth edition (New York: Appleton-Century-Crofts, 1948), p. 1027.

The shortage of policemen for traffic duty during the school hours has caused some cities to employ women traffic officers on a part-time basis. The plan has worked well, especially in suburban areas. (Police Dept., County of Nassau, N.Y.)

one of the forty-eight states has worked out a genuinely satisfactory system of county government; almost everywhere, cumbersome machinery and antiquated methods persist, along with divided, diffused, and diluted authority and responsibility—defects which, until the depression of a decade or more ago, went practically unchallenged.

Reform of county government. Critics of county government agree on some half dozen principal defects in the system and on remedies they propose to correct these defects:

1. There are too many counties. The large number of counties found in almost every state could be justified in horse-and-buggy days, when travel was slow and difficult. The number of counties remains approximately the same in the present day, when automobile and railway transportation have made distances less formidable than formerly. Moreover, in many places population has shifted drastically, so that some counties have comparatively few inhabitants yet maintain the same form of government as formerly. In most states the number of counties could be reduced by one-third to one-half without inconvenience to the people. This would effect a tremendous saving in local government.

2. Excessive uniformity is required of county government throughout most states. No matter what its size or type of population is, a county must have the same structure of government as every other county in the state. Small or sparsely settled counties are compelled to maintain a government that is too elaborate, cumbersome, and expensive for their purposes. One way to surmount this difficulty is to classify counties and set up a uniform government for all counties within each class. Missouri is empowered by its 1945 constitution to set up four classes of counties and to provide a different form of government for each class. Another solution has been

The Metropolitan Water District of Southern California services an area that extends beyond the city of La Verne, where it is located. Metropolitan districts are often established to co-ordinate the services that might be duplicated by towns and cities on an individual basis. (Pacific Air Industries)

tried by North Dakota: the optional county charter scheme, whereby each county may adopt one of several different standard patterns of government. Still another solution is the home-rule system adopted by seven states. It allows a county charter commission to draft a scheme of government, subject to the provisions of the state constitution and popular acceptance by the voters. All three reforms seem to be improvements.

3. It is generally agreed that county boards are too large and cumbersome. Since their work is chiefly administrative, there is no need for a large number on the board. Three to seven members, elected at large or from very few districts, suffice for a good county board. A larger number cannot act promptly. Its work must be done by committees, which have proved virtually incompetent, but whose work is accepted perfunctorily by the board as a whole.

4. Too many county offices are elective. Only the members of the board and possibly the auditor should be elected. Other officials, like the coroner and the prosecuting attorney, should be appointed on the basis of technical qualifications. Authorities differ on who should make the appointments, but some experts believe the governor should appoint sheriffs and prosecuting attorneys, since their work is to enforce state law within the county. Clerks of the court should be appointed by the courts they serve, and such lesser officials as county treasurers, assessors, surveyors, and superintendents of schools should be appointed by county boards, or by county managers where there are such executive officials.

5. Counties need a chief executive. Because counties do not possess an executive head their governments are little more than a collection of more or less independent and unco-ordinated offices. It has been suggested that counties should copy the example of some seven hundred

cities and appoint a manager to whom they would delegate the supervision of detailed administrative work. He would have control over subordinate officials, together with the power of appointment and removal, subject to Civil Service regulations adopted by the state or the county. Under this system the elective board would be the policy-making body. It would pass on the annual budget and tax levy, enact needed local ordinances, and select a competent county manager to handle the administration.

6. Financial practices in most counties are subject to criticism from the standpoint of being loose, unbusinesslike, and occasionally of doubtful honesty. Some states, such as New York and Nebraska, have taken steps to improve their tangled financial practices. These two states require all counties to use a uniform system of bookkeeping. Other states require uniform budget accounting. In almost every state, however, much still remains to be done in improving financial practices in county government.

80. IN THE MUNICIPALITIES

We saw earlier in this volume that considerably more than half the population live in urban communities. The problem of good city government is therefore an important political problem to most Americans. Even rural people are affected by the general tone of city government throughout the country, and especially by the quality of government in the city near which they live.

The city in the framework of American government. The city owes its existence legally to the state. Every city is a corporation created by state law. As a corporation it can sue at law and conduct business like any other legal person. Its fundamental law, or charter, is drawn up by the legislature in most states, and at any rate depends on some act of the state government. Cities are therefore frequently not free to reorganize or reform their activities or their structure of government until action is taken by the state legislature or by constitutional amendment. One of the great difficulties city government faces in most states is obtaining sufficient freedom from rural-dominated state legislatures.

Close co-operation with the federal government is increasingly important for a city that hopes to accomplish certain municipal undertakings successfully. We saw in an earlier chapter how public housing depends on municipal initiative and federal support. In similar fashion, such other activities as arterial highway projects cannot feasibly be undertaken by most cities except with federal aid.

The fundamental law for each city, we have pointed out, is the charter issued for it by the state. Five methods of obtaining charters are in fairly general use, and each has its advantages and disadvantages.

1. *The special charter system.* This system prevails in New England and in Delaware, Maryland, Georgia, and Tennessee. Each city is granted a charter by a special act of the state legislature. The advantage of this system is that, if the legislature is co-operative, each city can obtain a charter tailored to its own needs. Its chief disadvantage is that the legislature is free to interfere in any city's affairs, and occasionally such interference has been of a particularly meddlesome and partisan nature.

2. *The general charter system.* Legislative interference led to a demand for a system that would correct this abuse. The general charter plan accomplishes this purpose. It provides a state-wide municipal code which serves as the charter for every city in the state. Excessive uniformity has turned out to be a serious defect, because the form of government ideal for a large city like Chicago is not likely to be ideal for Peoria or Mount Vernon.

"Isn't It Time She Had a New Dress" was the title of a cartoon by L. D. Bradley (1904) that awakened Chicago to the need for a new charter.

3. *The classification system.* To correct the evil of excessive uniformity without inviting legislative interference was the aim of this third system of municipal charters. Cities are classified according to population into three or more groups, and the legislature is free to provide for each class whatever form of government it wishes. By ingenious methods of classification, however, some state legislatures —as in Ohio—have managed to create classes into which only one city would fall. It can then legislate for or against the one city without violating the constitutional prohibition against special legislation. Moreover, even when the legislature abides by the spirit of the classification system, it cannot devise a framework of government ideally suited to all cities in the same population range.

4. *The home-rule system.* Almost half the states have adopted constitutional authorization for home rule in at least some classes of cities within the state. The idea behind such authorization is that the people of a city should have the right to draft their own charter, since

they are the ones who will be governed by it. The assumption is that people are interested in local government and politically intelligent enough to devise the best system for their city. Home rule has certain advantages. It enables a city to have the kind of government its people think it needs, and it relieves the legislature from considering local matters throughout the state.

5. *The optional charter system.* Fifteen states have made it possible for cities to select a charter from several standard types that are available. This optional charter system avoids the disadvantages of both a uniform charter and a special charter for each city. At the same time, it avoids any abuse to which the home-rule system might be subject when people are free to devise any type of charter they desire.

Whatever method of granting charters may be employed in a given state, cities obtain a government that falls into one of three categories: (1) the mayor-council type, (2) the commission plan, or (3) the council-manager form.

Mayor-council government. This type of city government was once universal. Despite the trend toward the commission and the council-manager plans, the mayor-council type is still used by more than three-fifths of all cities over 5,000. All cities over 500,000, except Washington, D.C., use it. This type of government applies the basic American principle of division of powers to city government.

Both mayor and council members are elected. The council serves as a municipal legislature. Its principal functions are: to enact local ordinances; to adopt the municipal budget and appropriate funds for various purposes; to grant franchises to public service corporations.

City charters should vary according to the size, location, and business of the cities. These illustrations of the main street in Cushing, Okla. (left); the town of Bedford, Pa. (below left); and the rail yards of Weehawken, N.J., show some of the different characteristics of American cities. (Standard Oil Co., N.J.)

The mayor is the chief executive of the city. In some cases he has little power or authority. He can appoint only a few officials, and the management of municipal services is in the hands of independent individuals, commissions, or boards. The "weak-mayor" plan persists in many cities today, but the trend has been to strengthen the mayor's position and to allow the council to decline. New York, Boston, and Detroit are examples of cities that have adopted the "strong-mayor" plan, under which the mayor's power of appointment and removal is increased, his veto power over council measures is strengthened, and his control over administration is expanded. Since a city's main function is administration rather than legislation, councils have declined considerably in importance throughout the twentieth century.

The mayor-council type of government is criticized as a form proper for national or state government but not for cities. Its diffusion of authority and power in making appointments and in administration makes it difficult for the citizens to fix responsibility on either the mayor or the council. Diffusion of authority also hinders businesslike operation of city affairs —and most city affairs are or should be non-political, business matters such as disposal of garbage and the maintenance of the streets. Some cities have minimized the defects of the mayor-council government by strengthening the mayor's control over appointments, reducing the number of members on the council, providing for non-partisan elections to city office, and providing for popular initiative and referendum on city ordinances. More than 700 cities of 5,000 population and over have discarded the mayor-council type of government altogether in favor of a form not based on the traditional doctrine of separation of powers. These forms are either the commission plan or the council-manager plan.

Commission plan of municipal government. This type of government was first created to meet a crisis, and it proved so successful that it was continued in the city of its origin and adopted in more than 300 cities since 1900. In that year, when a tidal wave devasted the city of Galveston, Texas, the state legislature took the government out of the hands of the mayor and council and vested it in a commission of five businessmen. The results were excellent, and by popular request Galveston retained the commission form of government.

The plan is simple. All legislative and administrative functions are centered in the hands of a commission of five—sometimes three or seven—men elected at large for terms of two or four years. The commission enacts ordinances, fixes tax rates, and makes annual appropriations. Administration is usually organized into five departments, so that one commissioner heads each department and is re-

Government administration in small towns is often on a part-time basis. The mayor of Tomball, Tex., is shown sitting in front of his gas station, where he also maintains an office as a notary public. (Standard Oil Co., N.J.)

Types of Municipal Government

Mayor and Council		Whereby a Mayor and Councilmen are elected to run the city
Commissioner Plan		Whereby a group of commissioners are elected to run the city
Council and Manager		Whereby a group of commissioners are elected and who retain a proffessional city manager

sponsible for its conduct. The commission plan usually includes the initiative and referendum for city ordinances, and the recall[2] for unsatisfactory commissioners.

The commission plan proved especially popular in the first decade of this century because of widespread dissatisfaction with the cumbersome mayor-council government. The commission plan appealed because of its simplicity.

[2] "Recall" is a procedure whereby a petition, signed by a sufficient number of voters, sets forth charges against the incumbent officer and requires him to resign or run again. An election is then held, and if the incumbent does not receive most of the votes he is defeated and must step down in favor of the newly elected officer.

It concentrated power and responsibility in the hands of a small body of men. Moreover, it attracted better candidates for office than the large council had done. But after its initial popularity, the commission plan was found to have defects. No large city has tried it, and a fairly large number of smaller cities have given it up in favor of the council-manager form or they have reverted to the mayor-council government.

The defects of the commission plan can be listed briefly in this fashion. (1) A body of three or five—or even seven—is too small to act as a legislature for a large city. Even if elections are held at large, various groups in the city will be entirely without representation in a body of three or five men who have legislative power in their hands. (2) The commission form is less well adapted for sound administration than the mayor-council type if administrative power in the latter is concentrated in the mayor's hands. The first principle of administrative organization is that authority and responsibility must be concentrated in a single person's hands. Concentration of authority in a board or a commission diffuses responsibility, so that no one can be held responsible for anything. Moreover, commissioners are not elected for technical fitness to head one or another of the city's departments. Experience has shown that policy makers and legislators should be elected, but administrators should be appointed on the grounds of their qualifications for the job.

Council-manager plan. To remedy these defects—which are mainly on the administrative side—more than 700 cities have adopted a modified form of municipal government consisting of an elective

Members of the transportation office of the Board of Education of Richmond, Va., are shown mapping school-bus routes for more economical and efficient service. Each peg represents a bus stop in this carefully designed transportation plan for the city. (Standard Oil Co., N.J.)

council and an appointive manager. Many of these cities are small, but a number of fairly large cities—e.g., Cincinnati, Dayton, Toledo, and Kansas City—have tried the plan with success.

The council in this plan is small, usually consisting of five members but occasionally seven, and in Cincinnati nine. The council is the policy-making and supervisory board. It enacts ordinances, levies taxes, votes appropriations, grants franchises, creates departments, and authorizes borrowing. Its most important function, however, is the selection of a competent manager. The council-manager plan is designed to run the city like a large corporation. The citizens are, in effect, the stockholders who elect a board of directors (the council) which, in turn, chooses a manager to look after the details of administration. The manager is responsible to the council. Theoretically, the council members are not to interfere with the manager's conduct of municipal administration. The council is supposed to have done its work when it sets down broad lines of policy, creates machinery to run the administration, and chooses a competent manager to direct the city's business. In practice, some cities have not accepted the spirit as well as the mechanics of managerial administration, and council members frequently interfere with the management of administrative affairs.

The advantages of the council-manager plan are fairly obvious. Councils under this system do not need to meet frequently—once every two or three weeks —and members can therefore be outstanding citizens who serve on a part-time basis. The success of the system depends entirely on the quality of manager chosen and the freedom he is given in conducting the city's business. The manager is the council's employee, and he must make frequent accounting for his official conduct. A competent manager is a man with executive ability who re-

Twenty-nine pieces of fire-fighting apparatus loaned by the city of New York were rushed to Danbury, Conn., after that city had been ravaged by floods in 1955. Such co-operation between cities is in the finest American tradition of extending aid in times of disaster. (N.Y.C. Fire Dept.)

frains from politics and runs the city in businesslike fashion. He should have power to appoint and remove department heads and other administrative officers. He supervises and, as far as necessary, directs all administrative work.

Some defects of the council-manager plan. With few exceptions, cities trying the council-manager plan have received better, more efficient, and more economical government. The steadily increasing number of cities using the plan testifies

to its worth. But this, like every other form of city government, has certain shortcomings that must be overcome if it is to work successfully. First is the problem of finding a capable manager. Unless an able man is chosen, the managerial plan cannot work well. Second is the problem of confining the council to its proper sphere of policy-making and ultimate supervision. Council members have a propensity to dabble in details of administration, about which they usually know nothing, and to vitiate the system of businesslike conduct of municipal affairs. Third is the problem of resisting politicians and pressure groups who try to obtain special considerations. Fourth is the very real problem of what part the manager should take in civic affairs. Should he, the best-informed individual in the city on most municipal problems, confine himself to the purely administrative role of conducting municipal affairs? Should he refuse to commit himself on questions of policy? Or should he assume a positive role of leadership in civic affairs? It is not easy in practice to draw the line between managerial and council functions when the manager is a forceful, capable man.

Functions of municipal government. From what we have seen so far, it is obvious that party politics have small part in municipal government and administration. Most of a city's business consists in the granting of franchises for such services as transportation or garbage collection;

The larger cities strive to attract visitors and conventions to their areas by regular advertising released through their chambers of commerce and their visitors and news bureaus. The American Legion held its annual convention in the city of Miami, where this photo of the Tennessee float was taken.

the maintenance of city streets and parks; the furnishing of good fire and police protection; the providing of a system of primary and secondary schools—and universities in larger cities; and the collection and disbursement of funds to finance all these activities. These are affairs that should be conducted on businesslike lines once the decision (inevitably of a political nature) is made on such a policy question as whether to have a municipal university or a city-supported swimming pool. Party politics should play no part in *administering* municipal affairs. It is for that reason that many cities have abandoned partisan elections in the choice of councilmen and have made a sincere effort to employ skilled executives to head the various municipal departments.

The efficient conduct of municipal government is a matter of interest to every citizen in the city, because his daily existence will be safe or hazardous depending on the quality of government his city has achieved. Moreover, sound municipal government is a method whereby the people of an urban community can solve the greater part of their problems without calling for more state or federal assistance.

REVIEW

79. In the Counties
A. What three features are more or less common to all local governments?

B. List some of the proposals made most frequently to bring about a reform of local governments.

C. Indicate briefly how counties vary throughout the country. Point out how coun-

ties are generally similar in organization and perform similar functions.

D. List the reforms in county governments that have generally been agreed as necessary.

80. In the Municipalities
A. What are the five ways for a city to obtain a charter? Give an advantage and a disadvantage of each type of charter.

B. Briefly describe the three types of city government that exist in the United States today.

C. What are the main functions of city government?

THE CHAPTER IN REVIEW
A. Describe the organizational structure of a county.

B. How have some of the reforms needed in county government been adopted?

C. What are some advantages of the commission and manager types of city government?

SELECTED READINGS

All of the textbooks included in the reading list for the previous chapter have sections on local government. The *National Municipal Review* frequently carries articles dealing with county and municipal government, and *American City* is devoted entirely to problems of urban government.

Books dealing with local government in general include the following: J. E. Pate, *Local Government and Administration* (New York: American Book Company, 1954); R. H. Wells, *American Local Government* (New York: McGraw-Hill Book Co., 1939); and Herman G. James, *Local Government in the United States* (New York: D. Appleton & Company, 1921).

County government, long a neglected area in this country, has received considerable attention recently. An informative volume on the subject is *County Government across the Nation,* edited by Paul W. Wager (Chapel Hill, N.C.: University of North Carolina Press, 1950). Also useful and informative is Lane W. Lancaster, *Government in Rural America* (New York: D.

Van Nostrand Co., Inc., 1952). The National Municipal League has published the following pamphlets on county government: Edward W. Weidner, *The American County-Patchwork of Boards* (1946); *The County Manager Plan* (1950); and *Principles of a Model County Government*, the last appearing in the *National Municipal Review* (September 1933).

Chapter V of Father Keller's *Government Is Your Business* is entitled "City Government Depends on You." Austin F. Macdonald, *American City Government and Administration* (New York: Thomas Y. Crowell Co., 1951), continues to be the standard textbook on the subject. Also widely used are Harold Zink, *Government of Cities in the United States* (New York: The Macmillan Co., 1948); Arthur W. Bromage, *Introduction to Municipal Government and Administration* (New York: Appleton-Century-Crofts, Inc., 1950); and E. B. Schultz, *American City Government* (Harrisburg, Pa.: Stackpole & Heck, Inc., 1949). Types of municipal governments are discussed in a pamphlet by R. L. Mott, *Home Rule for American Cities* (Chicago: American Municipal Association, 1949), and by Cornelius P. Hurley, S.J., "Trend Toward City Manager," *Social Order* (May 1955).

PROJECTS

1. It has been said that the business of the city government calls "not primarily for operations of *government* in the stricter sense, but for *management,* very much as if the city were, and indeed it truly is, a corporate business enterprise." Examine the functions of your city government and report to the class on the businesslike aspects of its operations.

2. It is important for you to be familiar with the organization of your city or town government. Examine the structure of your local government and compare it with the types of government discussed in this chapter. Try to determine the reasons for the type of government that you have and present your conclusions to the class for discussion.

3. The question of protection for a community varies in different localities. Two or three members of the class can examine the needs of the community and report to the class on the work of the police, sanitation, and fire departments. It may be of additional interest to have a representative of one of these departments (or from the housing, hospital, welfare, or public works department) visit the school and explain to the class the problems peculiar to your community. This information may be obtained by letters and then written into the report of the committee.

PROFILES

JOHN MARSHALL

BORN: Germantown, Va., September 24, 1755
EDUCATION: Private tutors; College of William and Mary (no degree—1780)
DIED: Philadelphia, July 6, 1835

Marshall received a captain's commission during service in the Revolutionary War that included the winter at Valley Forge. The weaknesses of the central government during the war convinced him that a powerful central government should exist, and he rapidly moved into Hamilton's party after the Constitution was adopted.

After he achieved prominence as an attorney, Marshall served in the Virginia legislature. Until 1797 he did not accept federal appointments, although Washington had offered him the post of Attorney General. He served briefly overseas as a commissioner to France in the XYZ crisis, then entered Congress as a Federalist. President Adams turned to Marshall in June 1800, after Hamilton's personal followers had withdrawn their support from the President. Marshall served as Secretary of State until February 1801, when he was sworn in as Chief Justice of the United States.

The Supreme Court was regarded as a rather

unimportant part of the government at the time, and it was Marshall's contribution to the country that established both the power and prestige of the Court as a force in the nation. Although many of his colleagues and predecessors on the Court regarded its duties as onerous, Marshall devoted himself to the Court as his career. Marshall himself prepared the formal opinions of the Court on the most important cases to arise during his thirty-four years as Chief Justice.

Marshall's first important decision, in the case of *Marbury* v. *Madison,* was precedent-setting in that it was the first case in which an act of Congress was declared unconstitutional and therefore non-enforceable. Among the major decisions made by the Court in Marshall's time, the doctrine of implied powers was upheld in the interest of the Bank of the United States, and the powers of the federal government over interstate commerce were extended to prevent monopolies of transport systems. Decisions involving the taxing powers of state governments and interpretations of the clauses of the Constitution which affect contracts were of long-lasting importance. Marshall's support of the federal government, his careful and clearly reasoned judgments, and his model of industrious application to the work of the Court combined to make him unquestionably the most important justice in American history.

Although not wholly up to date (recent isolated studies tend to discount some of Beveridge's opinions), the best generally available biography is Albert J. Beveridge, *The Life of John Marshall* (Boston: Houghton Mifflin Company, 1924). His impact on American constitutional history should be studied through a special textbook on the subject such as *The American Constitution,* by Alfred Kelly and Winfred Harbison (New York: W. W. Norton & Company, Inc., 1948).

SAM HOUSTON

BORN: near Lexington, Va., March 2, 1793
EDUCATION: A few terms in elementary school
DIED: San Antonio, Tex., July 26, 1863

Although he is immediately associated with Texas, Sam Houston, one of the most colorful figures of the nineteenth century, spent his first thirty-nine years in Virginia and Tennessee.

As a youth Houston lived with the Cherokee

Indians. He taught school for a brief time, leaving to join the Army and fight under Andrew Jackson in the War of 1812. Having resigned from the Army, he studied law and was admitted to the bar in Tennessee. His legal work carried him into politics and he served as congressman from Tennessee (1823–1827) and as governor of that state (1827–1829).

In 1832, at the request of Andrew Jackson, he negotiated a treaty with the Indians. The following year he was a delegate to the San Felipe constitutional convention which petitioned for the separation of Texas from Mexico. With the outbreak of the war for Texan independence Houston was named commander in chief of the Texan army. He established the independence of Texas by routing Santa Anna and was chosen first president of the new republic (1836–1838). Re-elected to the presidency, Houston obtained recognition of the republic by the United States, and when the state was annexed to the Union he became one of its first two senators (1846–1859).

Houston's strong conviction that the federal government was supreme caused him as governor of Texas to oppose bitterly the secession movement that followed the election of Lincoln as President in 1860. His influence, however, was waning and Texas was one of the seven states to form the Confederacy before Lincoln was inaugurated. He relinquished his office on March 18, 1861, and retired from public life.

An interesting and accurate account of the life of Samuel Houston is *The Raven* (Indianapolis: Bobbs-Merrill Co., Inc., 1937), by Marquis James. The *Dictionary of American Biography* contains a good brief sketch of Houston, and an imaginative account of the Texan revolution under Houston is *Remember the Alamo* (New York: Dodd, Mead & Co., 1927), by A. E. Barr.

ROBERT A. TAFT

BORN: Cincinnati, Ohio, September 8, 1889
EDUCATION: Yale University (B.A., 1910); Harvard Law School (LL.B., 1913)
DIED: New York, July 31, 1953

Robert A. Taft, the eldest son of President William Howard Taft, received the finest academic and practical education his family could provide for a career in law. His legal training was ably put to use during World War I when he served as legal counsel to wartime government agencies, and after the war to the American Relief Administration.

A profitable law business in Ohio was interrupted by periods of service in the Ohio legislature and by regular allotments of time to Republican party affairs. Taft was first elected to the United States Senate in 1938, at the midpoint of Franklin Roosevelt's second term.

Probably his chief service to the country lay in revitalizing the demoralized Republican minority in the Senate: his own election, coming so soon after Roosevelt's almost unprecedented victory in 1936, was an indication that the two-party system was not dead. Taft's actions and speeches aroused fellow Republicans from their defeatist attitudes and revived his party's spirit.

Clear and forceful thinking and emphatic but not spectacular speeches brought Taft the position of chief spokesman for his party. He criticized many features of the New Deal domestic policy, and he opposed with equal vigor and competence what he considered rash, rather than prudent, idealism in international policy. His reputation grew to the extent that members of both parties nicknamed him "Mr. Republican" and turned to him for authoritative and intelligent statements of his party's principles. When Republicans won majorities in the Senate, Taft was their leader. During a period of Republican supremacy in the Senate, the much-debated Taft-Hartley Labor Relations Act was passed. Later he vigorously opposed Truman's Far Eastern policies, which he considered ill advised and dangerous, criticizing the refusal to use Nationalist Chinese troops during the Korean War.

Taft sought the Republican nomination three times, in 1940, 1948, and 1952. The last time, after a hard campaign, he lost to Dwight D. Eisenhower, whom he then supported in the general election. His final legislative services, performed under the physical strain and eventually the realization of his impending death from cancer, were devoted to establishing the first Republican administration in twenty years on a firm footing and making up for the comparative inexperience of many Republican leaders in national politics.

For a brilliant and readable estimate and interpretation of Taft, see W. S. White, *The Taft Story* (New York: Harper & Brothers, 1954). Caroline T. Harnesberger's *A Man of Courage, Robert A. Taft* (Chicago: Wilcox and Follett Company, 1952) includes liberal quotations from Taft's speeches. His own *A Foreign Policy for Americans* (New York: Doubleday & Company, Inc., 1951) gives Taft's ideas on proper principles and courses of diplomatic action for the United States.

DEBATE

The question: **SHOULD CONGRESSIONAL INVESTIGATION COMMITTEES BE LIMITED TO FACT-FINDING CONNECTED WITH PROPOSED LEGISLATION?**

Affirmative presentation

I. Americans are in serious need of protection from irresponsible congressional investigation committees.

  1. *Personally:* Many Americans have suffered defamation of character at the hands of such committees.

    a. Under the law, they have no recourse from such action.

    b. They enjoy no procedural rights, as before a judicial court.

    c. Some congressmen show no respect for human rights—and there is no protection against them.

  2. *As Citizens:* Americans have a right to expect their congressmen to tend to legislative business and protect the interests of their constituencies.

    a. Investigation committees often become circuses. They are a way of attracting interest and getting votes.

    b. They are sometimes used to hurt a committee chairman's political enemies or to obtain revenge for past actions.

    c. They frequently interfere with the normal conduct of government. They take up months of an official's time. They frighten many competent men out of government employ.

II. These committees frequently conduct "investigations" for which there is no need.

  1. Congress is a law-making body.

  2. It has a right to information connected with proposed legislation.

  3. Investigations for other purposes are

outside Congress' competence and are almost sure to be abused for ulterior purposes.

Affirmative conclusion: Investigation committees can perform their work well if limited to fact-finding connected with proposed legislation; and at the same time they will be limited in their power to inflict harm.

Negative presentation

I. The negative concedes that congressional investigation committees have a wide range of powers.
   1. Occasionally these powers have been abused—but very infrequently.
   2. Congress needs these powers if it is to obtain information.
      a. Investigation cannot be channeled by procedures, as can a judicial trial.
      b. Many "suspected" persons clear themselves from suspicion as a result of investigations.
      c. Most investigation committees do excellent work, in a considerate way, and they are appreciated by the government.
   3. Congress is more than a lawmaking body—it is our "watchdog." Under the proposal, Congress would be robbed of watchdog functions.
II. The alleged abuses can be corrected without rendering Congress impotent.
   1. Voters should elect the kind of congressmen who will not abuse powers.
   2. Strongly voiced, intelligent public opinion will prevent any committee from committing these abuses.
   3. Irresponsible committees put on "circuses" only if the public seems to demand them.

Negative conclusion: There is no need to adopt this proposal to protect ourselves from irresponsible committees—and there is positive danger in tying all committees' hands so that they cannot perform their proper work.

CLASSROOM DISCUSSION: The class should try to arrive at a decision on this proposal by settling two questions: (1) Can Congress perform its proper functions if the proposal advocated by the affirmative is adopted? (2) If not, is there reason to believe that the negative's counter-proposal is realistic and has any chance of adoption in the current political scene?

SELECTED READINGS

This topic is so phrased that the student will not find articles or books taking a simple stand for or against the proposal. The literature on the subject breaks down into general information on the problem, and proposed reforms. A good collection of articles on the subject is the Reference Shelf volume compiled by Julia E. Johnsen, *The Investigating Powers of Congress* (New York: H. W. Wilson Co., 1951).

Articles that are chiefly informational are the following: George B. Galloway, "The Investigative Function of Congress," *American Political Science Review* (February 1927); Robert W. Atwood, "The Senate Investigates," *Saturday Evening Post* (July 11, 1936); Scott W. Lucas (former senator from Illinois), "Congressional Hearings," *New York Times Magazine* (March 19, 1950); M. Nelson McGeary, "The Congressional Power of Investigation," *Nebraska Law Review* (May 1949); James A. Perkins, "Congressional Investigations of Matters of International Import," *American Political Science Review* (April 1940); Edward Martin (senator from Pennsylvania), "Investigation of Organized Crime," *Congressional Record* (July 10, 1950); M. D. Conway, "Congressional Commmmittee in Operation," *Catholic World* (December 1954); Jerome G. Kerwin, "Congressional Committees," *Commonweal* (March 26, 1954); Joseph R. McCarthy (senator from Wisconsin), "Investigating-Committee Methods," *U. S. News and World Report* (August 6, 1954); J. Rorty, "Storm over Investigating Committees," *Commentary* (February 1955).

Various proposals are made in: Robert K. Carr, "How to Improve Congressional Inquiries," *New York Times Magazine* (August 29, 1948); Estes Kefauver (senator from Tennessee), "Congressional Reorganization," *Journal of Politics* (February 1947); Estes Kefauver, "Fair Conduct Code for Congress: Congressional Investigations," *New Republic* (March 16, 1953); Edwin H. Goldberger, "Protection from Defamation in Congressional Hearings," *University of Chicago Law Review* (Spring 1949); Charles E. Wyzanski, Jr. (U. S. District Court judge), "Some Practical Reforms," *Fortune* (November 1948); Irving M. Ives (senator from New York), "In Place of Congressional Circuses," *New York Times Magazine* (August 27, 1950); George Meador, "Limitations on Congressional Investigation," *Michigan Law Review* (April 1949); K. B. Keating, "Code for Congressional Inquiries," *New York Times Magazine* (April 5, 1953).

UNIT NINE
The Size, Cost, and
Services of Government

Chapter 28. The Government As Employer

81. FROM THE SPOILS SYSTEM TO THE CIVIL SERVICE

The national government is the largest single employer in the country. It employs almost two and a half million persons. State and local governments hire many millions more. Government employees perform many more functions than the filing and typing tasks that are popularly associated with Civil Service work. They are foresters, physicians, and dentists. They watch the weather and test the water. They inspect weights and they arrest criminals. Their tasks are manifold, and it is no easy job to utilize efficiently the several million persons doing so many things for the federal and local governments. One of the difficult and continual problems facing government, then, is the problem of personnel management, of obtaining efficient job performance from these many and varied employees who are likely to be lost sight of because of the vast size of the organization for which they work.

The central problem of efficient civil service can be stated simply, because it is the same problem facing any big business

—the problem of obtaining and keeping employees capable of carrying on the many tasks the business must perform. The Hoover Commission reported in 1949 that personnel policies should be subjected "to just one test: namely, their ability to provide the United States Government, particularly in our scientific, administrative, technical, and professional jobs, with men and women of unquestioned ability, integrity, and devotion to the common good. We cannot entrust the government of today to second-rate men and women."

The record of the government as an employer is not a particularly good one. Although a great deal has been accomplished toward bringing most positions under Civil Service, as we shall see, the government fails to obtain as many first-rate employees as it needs and to keep those it obtains. In recent years about a half a million employees have been leaving the federal service annually: a turnover of almost 25 per cent, which would be enough to disrupt any private business

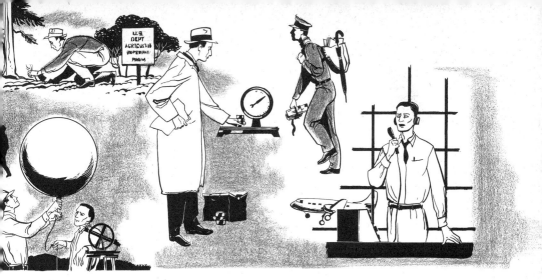

and cause a shakeup in the personnel department. We are interested in seeing what problems confront the government as an employer, what steps have been taken to solve these problems, and what further steps can be taken.

Before we look at these problems, let us state a few general principles about government employment that must be agreed upon at the beginning. First, there are some government positions—the Civil Service Commission listed 1,078 out of 2,346,710 in 1954—that are *policy-forming* and must therefore be filled by political appointment. A policy-forming position is one that involves making political decisions whereby the government's announced policies are put into effect. Department heads are policy formers. Such officials cannot hold office for life; when a new administration with new policies comes in, new policy-forming officials must be installed in office.

The principles governing the vast majority of government positions are roughly the same as those governing any sound business enterprise. Provision must be made for obtaining and keeping competent, loyal employees. This involves problems of recruitment, promotion, pay, working conditions, and retirement —for all of these problems are involved in keeping employees in the service. Competency means fitness (technical fitness) for the particular position an employee holds and also a general sort of fitness for working with other people (social and intellectual fitness). Like any other business, the government must obtain employees who are morally as well as technically fit, who are sober, industrious, and trustworthy. Loyalty is an even more important consideration with the government than with other employers, because disloyalty can be so costly to the government welfare and to national defense— which are the objectives of government business.

This drawing by C. H. Broughton was titled, "The Office-Seekers' Invasion of the White House." As a result of Civil Service reform within the past one hundred years, only about 15 per cent of government positions are classified as "policy-forming" and filled by political appointment. (Library of Congress)

CIVILIAN EMPLOYMENT OF THE
FEDERAL GOVERNMENT
(JUNE 30, 1955)

	TOTAL	PART-TIME
LEGISLATIVE BRANCH		
Congress	5,629	—
Architect of the Capital	1,034	—
Botanic Garden	52	5
Accounting Office	5,764	6
Govt. Printing Office	6,723	69
Library of Congress	2,476	146
Comm. on Organization of the Exec. Branch	33	—
TOTAL LEGISLATIVE BRANCH	21,711	226
JUDICIAL BRANCH	4,136	307
EXECUTIVE BRANCH		
Executive Offices of the President:		
White House office	290	7
Bureau of the Budget	444	8
Council of Economic Advisors	35	4
Executive Mansion	70	—
National Security Council	28	—
Defense Mobilization	272	31
President's Advisory Comm.	5	—
President's Commission on Veterans' Pensions	23	6
TOTAL EXECUTIVE OFFICES	1,167	56
Executive Departments:		
State	20,969	51
Treasury	79,180	767
Defense	1,186,580	2,376
Justice	30,686	273
Post Office	511,613	72,845
Interior	55,107	3,191
Agriculture	85,503	18,927
Commerce	46,038	4,986
Labor	5,051	315
Health Education & Welfare	40,405	468
TOTAL EXECUTIVE DEPARTMENTS	2,061,132	104,199
Independent Agencies (47):	309,122	20,650
TOTAL EXECUTIVE BRANCH	2,371,421	124,905
TOTAL ALL BRANCHES	2,397,268	125,438

Civil Service of the United States (total as of June 30): (1935) 757,543; (1940) 1,042,780; (1945) 3,816,310; (1950) 1,960,708. For security reasons, the total number of employees of the Central Intelligence Agency has not been included for any years.

The problem of ending the "spoils system." The original problem facing the government as an employer was to end the "spoils system" and to base employment and promotion on merit. You will remember from your American history that as early as Jefferson's time party loyalty was accepted as the first qualification for obtaining a government job. By Andrew Jackson's time the principle was well established that "to the victors belong the spoils." Advocates of the spoils system believed that any normal person could do the work required by any government job. Everyone was qualified, as far as merit was concerned, for almost any job. Moreover, the spoils system was a way of building up party strength.

The spoils system was unchecked from 1829 until after the Civil War. Its bad effects were apparent even in an age when the government performed comparatively few functions. A career in the federal government administrative service was impossible, because each change of administration meant a turnover in personnel in almost all positions. A complete change-over was devastating to government efficiency. Employees picked for party loyalty were seldom qualified for the positions they received. Critics of the system pointed out their defects and made the public generally aware of them. They held forth the model of the recently reformed British civil service. Various civil service associations were formed in this country to promote the cause. Magazines like *Harper's Weekly* and *The Nation* took up the campaign, and every congressional session after 1865 debated civil service reform.

Congressmen were naturally reluctant

The assassination of President Garfield in 1881 by a disappointed office-seeker moved Congress to enact laws to reform the Civil Service. In 1883, it passed the Pendleton Act, the first in a series of laws to regulate the Civil Service. (Library of Congress)

to surrender the juicy plum of thousands of jobs to which they could have their friends appointed. So nothing was accomplished in Congress for almost twenty years. But when President Garfield was shot in 1881 by a disappointed office seeker, the nation was shocked and Congress was galvanized into action. In 1883 it passed the Pendleton Act, which still serves as the basis of our federal Civil Service system. The early problem which the Pendleton Act attempted to solve without completely antagonizing politicians was how to bring as many federal positions as possible into the Civil Service system. The act placed certain positions in the Treasury and Post Office Departments in the system and provided that other positions should be put in by presidential directive.

Progress was slow. In the first year about 14,000 positions out of a total of 110,000 were put in the federal Civil Service system. Presidents have generally been willing to extend Civil Service coverage because it relieves them of the thankless task of passing out jobs down to the lowest levels of federal employment. Congressmen have been less enthusiastic about the Civil Service. Some of them have been its most ardent champions, but there is a general reluctance among congressmen to surrender any means of rewarding their friends. Many congressmen — and others — are convinced that intelligent use of the spoils system gives better results than rigid Civil Service procedure. As late as 1937 one of them put it this way on the floor of Congress: "I would like to know what is the matter with the so-called spoils system. . . . I say, as does the gentleman from Mississippi, that I am better qualified to select a man to be postmaster in any of my towns than any member of the Civil Service Commission."

The pressure of public opinion and of interested legislators and reformers through the years caused the Civil Service system to increase its coverage of federal jobs. At the time Franklin D. Roosevelt became President in 1933, more than 450,000 jobs were covered by Civil Service. The number covered now is about two million, or 85 per cent of the positions in federal service. The first problem, then, of substituting employment on the basis of merit for the spoils system is largely—though not completely—solved. Experience in the last twenty years has shown that it cannot be permanently solved, because job-hungry political parties try to force declassification (taking jobs out of Civil Service) by the President when a new administration comes to power. In each administration there have been gains and losses all along the line, but in the long run the gains have outweighed the losses by a large margin. Now we must inquire whether the Civil

Service gives us better administration than the spoils system.

The Pendleton Act has been amended and amplified in various ways to provide the largest employment agency in the world today. The original act created a Civil Service Commission to administer the merit system. The commission consists of three members, not more than two of them from any one party. The Pendleton Act divided jobs in the administration into two categories: those in the unclassified service, and those in the classified. Certain positions are specifically exempted from the classified service by act of Congress when the positions are created. Others are exempt because they are positions filled by presidential appointment with the advice and confirmation of the Senate. Power to determine in which category to place the other positions was granted to the President. The successful accomplishment of the Pendleton Act's purpose therefore depends largely on the presidents.

The act provided that admission to the classified service be based on competitive examinations administered by the Civil Service Commission. The act required that the examinations be "practical" in character, as distinguished from the general examination given in the British civil service system. Those passing the examination are placed on a register of persons eligible for appointment, and when a vacancy occurs appointment is made from among the top names on the register, usually from the top three. The Civil Service Commission does not make the appointment. It certifies the names on the register to the agency involved, and the person with appointive power in the agency selects the candidate he wants from among the top names. The employee serves a six-month probationary period, after which he assumes permanent Civil Service status, with the security it is supposed to confer.

The Pendleton Act attempted to take the civil service out of politics. It forbade employees in the classified service to take an active part in politics, and congressmen were not allowed to influence the Civil Service Commission in regard to the employment of any individual. Two provisions were adopted that were politically expedient but harmful to sound employment practices. The first, which resulted from persistent and powerful lobbying by the Grand Army of the Republic, gave preference to Civil War veterans by adding five points to their examination scores and ten points if they were disabled. This recognition of veterans' sacrifice for the Union was politically generous, but it weakened the merit system by often passing over the fittest candidates. In the second place, provision was made that appointments were to be distributed as far as possible on a geographic basis. The ratio of appointees from each state was to be roughly the same as the ratio of the state's population to the national total. Again, this weakened the merit system because the fittest candidates frequently had to be passed over to find one from a state lagging behind in its quota of appointments.

The Ramspeck Act of 1940 authorized the President to include in the classified

A blind candidate for a Civil Service position takes a test especially constructed to measure in physically handicapped applicants the same qualification that the regular tests measure in the non-handicapped. (U. S. Civil Service Commission)

service all remaining exempt positions except those requiring senatorial confirmation and a few other limited groups. This act made it possible for the President to classify thousands of positions that Congress had specifically exempted from the Civil Service when it created them. In the following year President Roosevelt put an additional 182,000 positions in the service by a single order.

The Hoover Commission devoted considerable study to the Civil Service system to find out why the turnover (25 per cent a year) was so high. The commission recommended in its report in 1949 that the Civil Service be put under the control of a single administrator responsible to the President, and that this officer act as presidential adviser on all matters relating to classified federal employment. It recommended, in the second place, that each major department or agency in the government set up an employment unit to examine, employ, dismiss, and promote its own employees, subject to regulations set by the Civil Service Commission. Such a system, which has been adopted, was designed to replace the centralized control of all examinations, dismissal and promotion procedures by the Civil Service Commission. The Hoover Commission also recommended warmly that pay scales be raised and equitably adjusted, and efforts be made to secure employment of able young persons who will make a career of federal service.

Acting on the Hoover Commission's recommendations, President Truman reorganized the service by putting the chairman of the commission in charge of all executive and administrative functions. He thus becomes the single administrative head called for by the Hoover Commission's report. On the basis of the report, moreover, pay scales have been raised and equalized by an entirely new classification system. A number of small increases in pay have been made since the basic reorganization of 1949.

82. PROBLEMS OF THE FEDERAL CIVIL SERVICE

The first basic problem of the Civil Service—to cover every non-policy-forming position in the federal service—has been fairly well accomplished. The problem today seems rather to obtain and keep good employees. This is a very difficult problem, for by the nature of things a government employee does not enjoy the same security from investigation and from loyalty requirements that he would enjoy in private employment. Inducements to work for the government are not always financially and psychologically attractive. The problem faced by the Civil Service is to overcome these obstacles in order to obtain and keep about two million capable employees. Let us break this problem down into its parts.

Classification and pay. An effective personnel program requires that jobs be broken down into classes on the basis of work performed. Each job must be described in terms of duties and qualifications, and those requiring similar qualifications must be placed in the same category. Otherwise employees will be dissatisfied, and morale will deteriorate.

The Pendleton Act made no provision for classification of jobs in the Civil Service. Although there was long agitation for some kind of classification, it was not accomplished until 1923, when the Federal Classification Act broke the Civil Service into five sub-services. These were replaced by the Classification Act of 1949, which divided the services into two groups: (1) the General Schedule employees, including professional, clerical-administrative-fiscal, and sub-professional classes; (2) the Crafts, Protective, and Custodial Schedule employees—carpenters, guards, janitors, and the like. Eighteen grades of General Schedule employees were created, and ten grades of Crafts, Protective, and Custodial positions. A minimum and maximum pay scale, dependent on length

Uncle Sam's Personnel Problems

of service and other factors, was fixed for each grade. Most federal employees now find themselves in one or another of the General Schedule (GS) categories.

The pay scale within the Civil Service has traditionally been low. A person qualified to earn five thousand dollars in the federal service, for example, can find a position elsewhere at considerably higher pay. Civil Service can compete successfully with private business in attracting capable personnel in either or both of two ways. It can increase its pay schedule or it can offer other inducements that compensate for lower salaries and wages. The Civil Service Commission has tried to do both things, but congressional action is required for such changes.

The difference between adequate and inadequate pay for Civil Service employees would be only a small fraction of the annual budget. In terms of efficient administration, however, it is the difference between a well-run business and a bungling enterprise. In the last decade

Congress has become more liberal in adjusting pay schedules upward to meet inflated living costs and the competition of private business for capable employees. A fairly comprehensive pay-adjustment act in 1954 abolished the pay schedule for the Crafts, Protective, and Custodial (CPC) services and transferred those employees to a pay system based on local prevailing wage rates. The same act provided for more liberal overtime pay, for additional positions in the higher-salaried categories (GS-16, 17, 18), for a liberalized incentive-award program, and for a number of other provisions that enabled the Civil Service Commission to offer more attractive pay especially to those earning more than five thousand dollars —the class of employee the government finds hardest to keep in the Civil Service. In 1955 Congress, at President Eisenhower's request, voted a comprehensive pay increase of 7½ per cent for all government employees.

The second way of handling the low

salary problem is to increase other benefits to compensate for low pay. Security checks continually made in the last ten years, together with the widespread coverage of this necessary program by the more sensational newspapers, has made it considerably more difficult for the Civil Service Commission to convince prospective employees that federal jobs offer lifetime security. A close study of the problem shows that federal employment is more secure than comparable employment in private business, but the impression has been created that no federal employee is safe from sudden dismissal for reasons unknown. Such an impression has been detrimental to the recruitment of capable personnel.

Another inducement to employment in the Civil Service is the retirement plan, which has been made more generous by congressional action in the last few years. Retirement age is now seventy, although persons are eligible to retire at sixty if they have worked for thirty years in the service, and at sixty-two if they have worked fifteen years. Each employee puts 5 per cent of his salary into the retirement fund, and he draws benefits according to his length of time in the service and his salary at retirement. In addition to pension provisions, the Civil Service employee is also protected by a workman's compensation plan of payments for death or injuries arising out of federal employment. Employees in the Civil Service are also eligible to participate in a group-insurance plan that offers life insurance at low rates.

Entry into Civil Service. Private businesses have developed intensive recruitment campaigns to obtain capable young employees. Very much like major-league baseball teams, big corporations send their "scouts" to college campuses to interview promising young people. The Civil Service Commission has traditionally followed the more prosaic procedure of announcing competitive examinations for certain ratings in the service. The time and place of examinations are posted in public buildings, and occasionally noted in newspaper advertisements.

Entry into the service is by competitive examination. The Pendleton Act required that "examinations shall be practical in their character, and so far as may be shall relate to those matters which will fairly test the relative capacity and fitness of the persons examined to discharge the duties of the service into which they seek to be appointed." Although there has been a tendency to require something more in the way of general knowledge and ability, the practical character of examination required by the Pendleton Act still prevails.

There are certain advantages and disadvantages to practical examinations. They indicate the fitness of the candidate to fill the job he has applied for, such as filing clerk or perhaps clerical employee in a consular office in France. But they do not test the candidate's ability to fit into the service and to advance to more responsible positions. The result is that the federal service has been filled in its lower ranks with mediocre employees. The attempt to fill higher positions by promotion from the ranks runs into the difficulty of not finding potential administrators in the lower ranks.

In the lower GS (General Schedule) ratings of Civil Service, emphasis is placed on specialized techniques rather than general knowledge and native ability. Pictured here is a civil-service examination for typists, measuring speed, accuracy, and efficiency. (U. S. Civil Service Commission)

Candidates for Civil Service positions in management internship are shown taking a group oral examination. Candidates discuss freely an assigned subject. Examining officials observe but do not participate in the discussion. (U. S. Civil Service Commission)

The trend in recent years has been toward somewhat more general examinations. Here the Civil Service Commission is following the practice of large corporations in this country. Experience shows that a young person with native ability and with a good general education is usually capable of acquiring the technical knowledge needed for most positions and that he is capable of developing into a good administrator. The contrast between the American and British systems, between practical and general examinations, is summed up by Professor Ogg:[1]

There is something to be said, of course, for both systems. The American is more democratic; it exacts little of the beginner in the way of general knowledge, and it affords a haven for men and women of all ages who are attracted by its pecuniary rewards, modest though they are. This, however, is about all that can be said for it. The British system is less democratic. But it attracts to the public service men and women who, on the average, not only are younger and more energetic than American appointees, but better fitted by education, and probably native capacity as well, to become increasingly able, useful, and responsible officials.

If federal service is to be made a career attracting capable people, it would seem that entry into it should be based on examinations designed to test ability,

[1] F. A. Ogg, *English Government and Politics,* second edition (New York: The Macmillan Co., 1936), pp. 231–232.

adaptability, and breadth of outlook. Practical examinations seem the best kind for recruiting typists, filing clerks, and others who ordinarily work only a few years and do not expect to make a career of the service. Practical examinations should also be given to tradesmen, janitors, and the like. A "pass" examination proving they have adequate technical knowledge for the job is sufficient for these categories. The others, however, should be recruited on the basis of general ability. Such recruitment, with adequate pay and a sound system of promotions, would do much to make the federal service attractive to capable people.

Promotion in Civil Service. Experience in government employment and in private business has shown that employee efficiency and morale depend largely on the system of promotions followed by an organization. Employees who know that they will be promoted if they prove themselves capable will ordinarily work hard and efficiently. If they know that promotion is based instead on "knowing the right people" or on a hit-and-miss system, there is little inducement for them to do more than perform their tasks.

The Pendleton Act provided for promotion from one category to another on the basis of competitive examinations. With certain modifications, this procedure is still employed. It is a difficult personnel problem to decide whether competitive examinations are as good procedure as "pass" examinations given to those whose service records indicate they are qualified for higher positions. An attempt has been made in recent decades to have administrators rate their employees on the quality of their service. Superiors fill out standard rating scales so that each employee can be rated in comparison with his fellows. Such rating is not very reliable because one man might rate an employee "fair" for work that another would label "good" or even "excellent." Personnel experts have spent much time trying to devise a more objective method for rating performance.

Whatever difficulties the problem of a good promotion system involves—and every big corporation faces this same problem—the principles remain clear. The system should allow every employee, no matter where he starts in the service, to advance to the top through a series of promotions based on his past performance and his likelihood of success on the next level. Whatever standards are adopted to measure these qualities, they should be applied objectively.

Discipline and removal. A peculiar notion persists with some Americans that once a person gets a Civil Service position he cannot be fired for anything except treason or disloyalty. The Pendleton Act and its amendments do not seek to offer federal employees any such protection. The aim of the Civil Service is to protect employees from removal for political reasons. It must and does provide for removal for incompetence, disloyalty, or unfitness. Removal is a somewhat more delicate problem in government service than in private business. If it is too easy, political partisanship can enter under the guise of "the good of the service." If removal is made too difficult, the Civil Service will come to harbor many incompetent and lazy employees.

A sincere attempt is made to steer a middle course between the two extremes. The basic provisions governing removal from the service are stated in the Lloyd-La Follette Act of 1912:

No persons in the classified civil service of the United States shall be removed therefrom except for such cause as will promote the efficiency of said service and for reasons given in writing, and the person whose removal is sought shall have notice of the same and of any charges preferred against him, and be furnished with a copy thereof, and also be allowed a reasonable time for personally answering the same in writing.

The individual to be discharged is thus guaranteed a copy of the charges against him and an opportunity to answer the charges in writing. If the employee alleges that he is being dismissed because of political or religious prejudice, or that the proper procedure has not been followed, or that other cases have not been handled with the same severity, then the Civil Service Commission may investigate the case. The Hoover Commission found that the dismissal of one incompetent stenographer was delayed for seventeen months. This is an indication that the removal procedure is perhaps made too difficult in the interest of protecting employees.

Employees may be dismissed for incompetency or inefficiency. Sometimes the charge of "general incompetence" is hard to prove, even though the employee may be a troublemaker and a thoroughly disruptive force in the agency. Criminal or immoral conduct is another ground for removal. The Hatch Acts of 1939 and 1940 make political activity another cause for dismissal, but it is not easy to draw the line between a federal employee's private expression of his political views—to which he has a right—and his becoming active politically.

In the last decade disloyalty has become an important reason for dismissal. No one can quarrel with the principle that disloyal employees should be dismissed from the federal service, just as any private business has the right to dismiss employees for disloyalty to the firm

Not all Civil Service positions are desk jobs. Here a government soil conservation agent and a farmer examine a gully to determine how best to reclaim the ruined land. (Standard Oil Co., N.J.)

that employs them. Communists and fellow travelers are obviously disloyal, but it is not easy, in many concrete cases, to decide where to draw the line between loyal and disloyal employees. Like so many other personnel problems, this one is difficult to solve, even though the principles governing removal for disloyalty are easy to state.

The problem of unions in the Civil Service. It was a natural development for the federal government, the largest employer in the country, to be faced with the problem of its employees organizing to bargain collectively for higher pay and better working conditions. It was also natural for organization to begin among employees of the post office, where pay was inadequate, hours long, and working conditions bad. Letter carriers organized nationally in 1889, post-office clerks in 1890, railway mail clerks in 1891, and rural letter carriers in 1903. Since these early unions were mostly fraternal in character, they were encouraged by officers in the Post Office Department.

Beginning about 1898, however, the postal employees lobbied in Congress for better pay. In 1902, President Theodore Roosevelt issued an executive order forbidding all federal employees to lobby for higher wages or any other benefits. Reaction to this "gag rule" was strong enough to push Congress into passing a law in 1912 that guaranteed federal employees the right to lobby for improvement of working conditions and to affiliate with labor unions outside the federal service. The only restriction was that federal employees were not allowed to engage or assist in "a strike against the United States."

The law of 1912 stated the attitude still maintained toward unions by the federal government in its capacity as an employer. Federal employees cannot be dismissed from the Civil Service for union membership. They are free, individually and collectively, to lobby for higher pay

scales, better pension systems, shorter hours, and better working conditions. The Taft-Hartley Act of 1947 specifically forbade them to strike. This is the principal limitation on union activity of federal employees. The nature of Civil Service, with employment by competitive examination, makes the closed shop or even the union shop impossible. Nevertheless, union organizers have persuaded the vast majority of federal employees to join one or another of the unions to which they are eligible.

Conclusion. A century ago the federal government functioned worse as an employer than in almost any other respect. Federal employees were mostly political "hangers-on" and were cleaned out after each change of administration to make room for another crew. Some of them were capable employees, to be sure, but their capability was seldom the cause of their employment. In the last seventy years a great deal has been accomplished to make the federal government a better employer. The struggle to take federal jobs out of politics has been largely, though not completely, won. The extension of federal accomplishments to state and local government positions is perhaps the biggest task facing Civil Service reformers, for the merit system has made little headway in these areas of government.

REVIEW

81. From the Spoils System to the Civil Service

A. What is the central problem of efficient civil service today?

B. State a few general principles pertaining to government employment that must be borne in mind. What is meant by the "spoils system"? What were the bad effects of this system?

C. What was the purpose of the Pendleton Act of 1883? How are government positions filled under this act?

D. What recommendations in regard to civil service were made by the Hoover Commission?

82. Problems of the Federal Civil Service

A. What are the inducements to employment in the federal civil service?

B. What improvements have been made in the examination system of the civil service?

C. How is promotion in the civil service generally achieved? What principles should be used in promotion? What are some of the reasons for dismissal?

D. Trace the development of "unions" in federal service.

THE CHAPTER IN REVIEW

A. What are some of the serious problems facing federal civil service today? What solutions have been offered for these problems?

B. Discuss the extension of civil service in the federal government from the Pendleton Act to the present day.

C. Discuss the major arguments for and against the "spoils system."

SELECTED READINGS

The problem of the government as an employer should be studied in two reports of presidential committees appointed to study this and similar problems. The first is the President's Committee on Administrative Management, *Personnel Administration in the Federal Service* (Washington: Government Printing Office, 1937), and the second is the Commission on Organization of the Executive Branch of the Government, Herbert Hoover, Chairman, "Personnel Management," *Report* (Washington: Government Printing Office, 1949).

Good standard studies of the subject include: Sterling D. Spero, *Government as Employer* (New York: Remsen Press, 1948); Fran-

ces T. Cahn, *Federal Employees in War and Peace* (Washington: The Brookings Institution, 1949); and W. G. Torpey, *Public Personnel Management* (New York: D. Van Nostrand Co., Inc., 1953). Chapter VIII of Father Keller's *Government Is Your Business* is entitled "What Everybody Should Know about Civil Service."

Two good books on problems that come about from bigness in government are: Paul H. Appleby, *Big Democracy* (New York: Alfred A. Knopf, Inc., 1945), in which the author maintains that reduction in size of government is not as much the solution as are more efficient procedures; and John H. Crider, *The Bureaucrat* (Philadelphia: J. B. Lippincott Co., 1944), in which the author points out the danger of bureaucratic expansion and attacks bureaucratic methods.

Two books that deal with Civil Service jobs from the standpoint of their requirements and how you go about getting them are: Sterling D. Spero, *Government Jobs and How to Get Them* (Philadelphia: J. B. Lippincott Co., 1945), and James C. O'Brien and P. P. Marenberg, *Your Federal Civil Service* (New York: Funk & Wagnalls Co., 1940).

PROJECTS

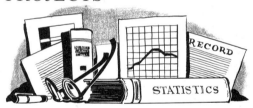

1. It would be of value to the entire class to know the many opportunities of employment in the federal civil service system. A class committee could write to the Civil Service Commission in Washington, D.C., to inquire about the requirements and the salaries for these positions. Information concerning the availability and location of various jobs might also be obtained.

2. A clearer picture of the federal employment program may be seen from charts that show the total number of federal employees and those who have civil service status. The change in this percentage over the past fifty years should be noted. A worth-while project then would be the making of a chart that contained information tracing this development in ten-year periods since 1900.

Chapter 29. The Cost of Government

83. FEDERAL EXPENDITURES

We have seen that the federal government is the largest single employer in the country. It is also the heaviest spender, and it has the largest income. In 1953 the federal government spent $74,300,000,-000, and its receipts were $64,800,000,-000. In 1954 and 1955 economies in the national defense program enabled the government to cut its expenditures to $67,600,000,000 in the former year and to an estimated $64,000,000,000 for 1955. Tax reductions cut its receipts for those years to $64,600,000,000 and $59,300,-000,000, respectively. These figures can be better understood if we realize that the federal government spends every fifth dollar spent in this country and that its revenue is roughly one-fifth the total national income in any given year.

The primary reason for these heavy expenditures is to maintain the national defense and to promote the general welfare as interpreted by the administration. And the primary reason for taxes is to obtain the money with which to pay government expenses. We can consider the problem of government finances as a problem of the cost of government, how to spend wisely and how to get the money to pay the bills. This involves problems of economy, of course, and more intricate problems of how best to finance certain items of expense. It also involves many problems of how to raise the money without doing injustice to individuals and without hurting the American economy.

But government finance is not as simple as a family budget, where expenses must be considered carefully in order to be kept down to the family income. Government finance cannot ignore secondary aspects involved in obtaining and spending billions of dollars annually by the federal government. Heavy spending by the government, for example, tends to inflate prices and to promote both capital investment and employment in certain industries. Curtailment of government spending has the opposite effect. Thus government spending policies have a great and important effect on the national economy. The point we want to remember is that government expenses are incurred primarily to perform the business

of government, but in setting forth a program of expenditures for any year the administration must take many other things into consideration. Because the federal government is by far the biggest spender in the country, what it does with its money in any given year has considerable influence on the business cycle.

The principal object of taxes is to pay the expenses of government. But a tax program is never devised with only this primary objective in mind. Taxes are devices for encouraging or discouraging investment or saving, rewarding certain kinds of enterprise and punishing others. The social and economic consequence of various tax programs is a very involved subject, and we shall not attempt to discuss it in this volume. It is sufficient for us to realize that the problem exists and that the administration must pay attention to these secondary effects of its financial program when it draws up its annual budget.

The tremendous growth of federal expenses can be appreciated when we remember that they were about $11,000,000 in 1800, about $40,000,000 in 1850, and about $520,000,000 in 1900. In this century, of course, the country had increased tremendously in population and in area. However, there was also a considerable growth of government services and functions into areas previously neglected or left to individual enterprise.

Budgets since the outbreak of the Korean War have been in the neighborhood of seventy billion dollars, although the end of the Korean War and other international developments convinced the Eisenhower administration that it could reduce government expenditures to about sixty-four billion in 1955. Most of this huge sum is spent for national defense or the payment of previous wars. Only about five billion dollars are spent on what can be considered regular government expenses. This compares with about three and a half billion spent in 1930. Since there has been gradual inflation since the 1930s, it is hard to see how great savings can be made in the area of regular government expenses. Big savings can be effected with safety only if there is some security for world peace and a reduction of armaments. Because this is unlikely to occur in the foreseeable future, we must expect to have gigantic federal budgets for many years to come.

Added to federal expenditures, of course, are those of the state and local governments. State governments spend about fourteen billion dollars a year, part of which they return to local agencies of

On an average, about nineteen postal employees process each letter mailed in this country. The huge Post Office Building in Washington is the hub of this complex organization. The rural post office (right) presents a contrast in everything but service, as uniform postal rates apply throughout the country and the world's largest postal system manages to give personal attention throughout its departments. (U. S. Post Office; Standard Oil Co. N.J.)

government for highways, schools, and public welfare work. Local governments spend somewhere around nine billion a year. When these sums are added together, we see that the total cost of government in the United States for 1955 was more than eighty-seven billion dollars. This is a charge of considerably more than five hundred dollars a person in the country: the price for national defense and for the various protective and welfare functions the government performs for us, for parks and playgrounds, for police protection, for slum clearance and public housing and all the other services performed by local, state, and national government.

Let us see more specifically how the federal government spends its money. The largest single item, of course, is national defense. In the last "peace budget" before the Korean War it took $13,500,-000,000, or 32 per cent of the budget. In 1955, after reductions from the previous two years, it amounted to $41,900,000,-000, or 66 per cent of the budget. This national defense item includes: (1) the military functions of the Department of Defense, or the operational expenses of the armed forces; (2) the mutual security military program, or our contributions to

European and Asian defense systems against Communist imperialism; (3) the atomic energy program, which involves huge outlays for research and experimentation; (4) the stockpiling of strategic and critical materials.

About 23 per cent of the 1955 budget, almost $15,000,000,000, was for charges fixed by law. The largest items in this category are interest on the national debt and payments to veterans. Other large items are grants-in-aid to the states and agricultural price supports. Expenditures for all remaining federal programs in 1955 were estimated at $7,200,000,000, or 11 per cent of the total budget. Included in this third category are such diverse items as foreign economic aid, operation of the Selective Service system, the collection of taxes, federal public works, and law enforcement. A breakdown of federal expenditures shows us that regular expenses of government have increased greatly in the last twenty-five years because the government has assumed many new functions. But the principal cause of the tremendous increase in expenditures has been the two world wars and the maintenance of large military forces since the end of the Korean War. Undoubtedly some economy can be effected by eliminating wasteful spending, but large savings can be achieved in the present international situation only at the risk of national security.

Constitutional limitations. The Constitution says more about raising revenue than about spending it. It does empower Congress to "pay the debts and provide for the common defense and general welfare of the United States." Moreover, the power to collect taxes and to borrow implies the power to spend. The restrictions on this spending power are relatively few. (1) Congress cannot appropriate funds for the military forces for a period longer than two years. The obvious reason for this proposal was to give Congress close check on the executive and the military force at his disposal. (2) Regular statements of receipts and expenditure of public money must be made "from time to time." (3) No money can be spent except "in consequence of appropriations made by law." This is a safeguard erected against the chief executive and his subordinates in the administration. It prevents them from spending money appropriated for one purpose on another object of their own choosing. Money appropriated to build veterans' hospitals, for example, can be used for no other purpose. And no money can be spent on the veterans' hospital except what Congress appropriates for that purpose.

The appropriation arrangement has always been Congress' most powerful weapon in dealing with the administration. It gives individual congressmen on the Appropriations Committee control over administrative agencies, for they have the power to cut any agency's requested appropriations or even to leave the agency without any funds at all. The threatened use of this power is occasionally abused by congressmen to get jobs for friends or to have enemies fired, but the appropriations system is a necessary device for holding the administration accountable to Congress.

Constitutional limitations on the government's spending power are restrictions on spending procedure, not on the amount the government may spend. Congress and the Supreme Court have taken

Our national defense budget includes many unique expenses. From a frozen plain near the edge of the ice cap in northern Greenland, engineers have carved out Thule Air Base. (Air Force Photo)

Two drag parachutes are standard equipment on the Boeing B-47 Stratojets. Although not the largest bomber, it is one of the fastest, attaining speeds of over six hundred miles per hour. The 200,000 pound aircraft is an essential but expensive item in our defense budget. (Official U. S. Air Force Photo)

a broad view of the spending power, and the Court has stated that Congress' power to spend "is not limited by the direct grants of power found in the Constitution." Attempts were made to contest government spending through grants-in-aid, and again a test case was brought into the courts to challenge federal support of slum clearance and housing projects. In each case the Supreme Court made it abundantly clear that Congress is free to appropriate whatever money it wants for any purpose comprehended within the common defense and the general welfare.

Preparation and adoption of the budget. Until 1921 appropriations were made by Congress in rather unbusinesslike fashion. House and Senate committees drafted different appropriations for various purposes without any relation to each other and without much consideration of revenue. Although such a loose system was not businesslike, it did not entail serious difficulties when expenditures were comparatively small and revenue easy to obtain. The defectiveness of these loose methods was revealed by the heavy expenditures of World War I, and in 1921 the Budget and Accounting Act was passed. This act remains the foundation on which our present budget system operates.

The Budget and Accounting Act of 1921 provides for an executive budget which is submitted to Congress annually. It created the Bureau of the Budget to prepare the annual request for expected expenditures. This Bureau, now attached to the Executive Office of the President, receives estimates from the various governmental agencies. It has power to revise, reduce, or increase these estimates. It draws them together into a single document, which is submitted by the President to Congress early in January of each year. The act also created the General Accounting Office, headed by the Comptroller General, whose function is to supervise and audit the accounts of the government to ensure that all expenditures have been made according to congressional specifications.

The Bureau of the Budget has become an important arm of the executive branch of the government. Through it the administration's financial policy is put into effect. It begins the budgetary process by sending letters to the various department and independent agency heads in which

U.S.S. Coral Sea and a flight of Banshees are shown on maneuvers at sea. The cost of our defense program in 1955, a non-war year, was staggering—consuming over 65 per cent of the tax dollar. (Official U. S. Navy Photograph)

it outlines the general financial policy of the administration—whether to retrench or to spend more, what functions and services are to be promoted and which ones curtailed, and other such general statements. Each government agency then prepares a list of estimated expenses in detail. The Bureau of the Budget receives these estimates, studies them carefully, and makes such alterations as it thinks necessary. The budget is then prepared as a single document containing an integrated plan for government expenditure. The total budget must be co-ordinated with expected revenues, a schedule of which is prepared by the Treasury Department.

The budget is transmitted by the President to Congress, together with his annual budget message, shortly after the opening of the session in January. The budget is a book-length document. It is referred to the House Committee on Appropriations, which breaks itself down into a number of sub-committees to study various parts of the budgetary requests. Heads of the various departments are called before the committee to support their requests by oral testimony. It is at this point that department heads who have offended members of the Appropriations Committee find themselves in for a difficult time—and frequently their requests are denied.

Until 1950 the Appropriations Committee reported back to the House the appropriation measures it wished to recommend, usually about a dozen measures in all. After these measures were passed by the House they went through the same procedure of committee examination and final passage in the Senate. The Legislative Reorganization Act of 1946 attempted to bring together the House and Senate committees in charge of revenue and appropriations in order to draw up a legislative estimate of maximum total revenues and appropriations to be used as a guide in studying the

While a Public Health Service medical officer stands by, a sick merchant seaman is removed from the quarantine boat. This service is under the direction of the Department of Health, Education and Welfare. (U.S.P.H.S.)

President's budget proposals. The House Ways and Means Committee (in charge of revenue bills in the House), the House Appropriations Committee, the Senate Finance Committee, and the Senate Appropriations Committee now meet jointly for this purpose. Moreover, Congress now passes one major appropriations act and whatever supplementary acts are necessary, instead of a dozen or more separate acts.

The chief weakness of the budgetary process continues to be congressional padding of the executive budget. The Senate voluntarily restricted itself somewhat in this respect in 1946, but senators as well as representatives are still free to add millions of dollars to administrative requests. Critics of the system urge that Congress restrict itself, as the British Parliament has done, from voting money for any purposes or in any amounts not requested by the administration. The other solution, as we have already suggested, is to enable the President to veto single items of appropriations bills while ac-

THE LAST ROLL.

Tom Nast's cartoon in Harper's Weekly *(1886) depicts President Cleveland's war on the congressional practice of logrolling. Cleveland's reforms included such matters of government as the administration of public lands, the Navy, and pensions. (Library of Congress)*

cepting others. This would limit Congress to accepting, rejecting, or cutting down the various appropriations requested by the administration. It would minimize the evils of "logrolling" and "pork-barrel" legislation,[1] which are not as bad as formerly but still consume much congressional time and millions of the taxpayers' dollars.

Spending the appropriations. The spending of government money is subject to very careful control. Most funds must be disbursed through the Treasury Department or through officers it designates for that purpose. Disbursing officers must give bond for the performance of their duties, and every dollar must be accounted for on proper forms. Control of spending rests with the General Accounting Office, an agency independent of the executive and headed by the Comptroller General,

---

[1] These terms describe the practice whereby one legislator votes favorably on another's pet bill in return for support on his own. The attempt to satisfy greedy constituents lies back of this unhealthy practice.

appointed for a fifteen-year term. He can be removed only by Congress.

The Comptroller General makes a "post-audit" or a review of expenditures for their legality and the availability of appropriated funds. If the disbursement has been improperly made or if funds are not available, the Comptroller General disallows the expenditure and the disbursing officer must repay the government. The Comptroller General also makes a "pre-audit" at the request of an agency head who wants the validity of a disbursement passed on before it is made. The General Accounting Office makes still another kind of audit, a "business-type" audit of the accounts of such government corporations as the Tennessee Valley Authority and the Home Owners Loan Corporation.

The Comptroller General has considerable discretionary power, as was illustrated by the incumbent during the time of the New Deal. John J. McCarl, Comptroller General at the time, was personally hostile to some New Deal measures, and he held up many payments of New Deal agencies because they lacked proper authorization in congressional appropriations. It was not surprising, then, that the President's Committee on Administrative Management suggested the abolition of the office and the creation of a new office of auditor general who would make only post-audits. The function of making pre-audits would be transferred to the Treasury Department. The requested change was not made. The present Comptroller General, Joseph Campbell, has worked more closely and harmoniously with the executive branch, and there has been little criticism of the office recently.

84. FEDERAL REVENUES

Taxes are the principal but by no means the only source of federal revenue.

The increasing number of older persons in our country requires new appraisals of our social security system from time to time. Since a majority of Americans are dependent on wages and salaries (and are not self-sufficient without them), provisions must be made for their security when they can no longer be gainfully employed. (Standard Oil Co., N.J.)

The National Recovery Act of 1933 was the initial effort of the federal government to allay the crippling effects of the Great Depression. Its provisions provided the groundwork for the social security laws in effect today. (National Archives)

Borrowing is a means of meeting unusual expenditures, but a loan is not properly revenue because it must be paid back with interest out of revenue. Borrowing is a means of living off expected future revenue. Other sources of government revenue add up to about a billion and a half dollars annually. They can be listed as: (1) receipts from various government businesses, such as the post office, the Panama Canal, the Tennessee Valley Authority, and the Inland Waterways Corporation; (2) fees charged for services, as for issuing patents; (3) fines and forfeitures levied in federal courts; (4) income from sale of public lands, rental of grazing land, interest on loans to farmers and home owners; and (5) gifts, such as the National Gallery of Art in Washington.

Although these sources add up to a considerable amount, the federal government finances its operations principally from taxes. No one contests the wisdom of the Founding Fathers in empowering the federal government to reach past the states and to tax citizens directly. Under the Articles of Confederation the central government had been rendered impotent by having to depend on requisitions from states that were reluctant or negligent in making their contributions. The power to tax is an essential right of a sovereign government. But the power to tax without limit is the power to destroy. That is why the Founding Fathers wrote into the Constitution a number of restrictions on the federal government's taxing power.

Constitutional basis and restrictions on taxation. In the eighth section of the first article of the Constitution, Congress is given the power "to lay and collect taxes, duties, imposts, and excises." These terms all meant something specific when they were employed by the framers of the Constitution. Taxes are levies on persons or property, like poll taxes or land taxes, which cannot be shifted to other people's shoulders. Duties and imposts are levies on imports and exports. Excises are indi-

SAFE AS AMERICA

U.S. SAVINGS BONDS

PAYROLL SAVINGS PLAN

National campaigns are conducted to encourage the purchase of government bonds. The income from these bonds, which earn a high rate of interest, enables the government to provide for the enormous cost of our national defense. (Advertising Council)

The individual's tax problem is discussed by experts of the Internal Revenue Bureau prior to the April 15 tax deadline. Income taxes are the chief source of our country's revenues. (Bureau of Internal Revenue)

rect taxes; that is, levies on the production, distribution, or use of commodities. An excise tax can be passed on to the consumer in the form of higher prices, so that it becomes, in effect, a "hidden" tax he does not ordinarily know he is paying.

Congress is limited to levying taxes only "to pay the debts and provide for the common defense and general welfare of the United States." What this seems to mean is that Congress can levy taxes for anything it is empowered to do by the Constitution. Limitation as to purpose, then, is more theoretical than practical.

The second restriction is that "all duties, imposts and excises shall be uniform throughout the United States." The requirement of uniformity for indirect taxes does not forbid such a tax as one on tobacco or alcohol which falls only on districts growing tobacco or manufacturing alcoholic beverages. It only requires that tobacco or alcohol be taxed at the same rate everywhere in the country.

Uniformity of import duties used to mean that the same tariff had to be charged on the same class of goods at all ports in the country. Since 1901 the Supreme Court has allowed different duties to be charged on the same goods, depending on the country from which they are imported. In other words, the federal government is left free to make trade arrangements that will give one country preferred tariff arrangements over another. Thus wine shipped from France need not have the same import duty as the same kind of wine from Portugal. The only constitutional requirement is that the tariff on the wine from each country be uniform at all ports. Congress is forbidden to levy export duties at all, although it is otherwise free to regulate foreign trade.

Finally, the Constitution requires that direct taxes must be apportioned among the states according to population. The difficulty of conforming to this requirement prevented Congress prior to 1913 from resorting to direct taxes as an ordinary means of raising revenue. Only four times in history, the last in 1861, has Congress resorted to a direct tax on persons or land. The one notable possible exception is the income tax, which the courts have held both to be and not to be a direct tax. To avoid any question of validity, the Sixteenth Amendment (1913) simply authorizes Congress to lay and collect taxes on incomes without apportioning them among the states.

Nature and types of taxes. Normally a tax is a levy imposed to raise money for public purposes. It has been defined by the Supreme Court as "an exaction for the support of the government." There is no relation between the taxes an individual pays and the benefits he receives from the government. Taxes are compulsory exactions. They are of different kinds. We have seen that they can be classified as direct and indirect. They can also be classified as proportional, progressive, or regressive. A proportional tax is one that is a certain percentage of the value of the taxed item, no matter what the amount might be. The city earnings tax in St. Louis, for example, is proportional because it is one-half of 1 per cent of every dollar a St. Louisan earns. The federal income tax is progressive because the tax rate increases as the amount of income becomes larger. A person pays roughly 20 per cent on his first thousand dollars of taxable income, and about 85 per cent on everything over a million dollars. A regressive tax works in opposite fashion. It decreases as the amount of taxable property becomes larger. Property taxes are frequently regressive. A sales tax is regressive in a general way, because poor people spend almost all their income on items covered by the sales tax, whereas wealthy people spend only a small proportion of their income in the same way. Therefore, a poor person spends a greater proportion of his income on the sales tax than does the wealthy person.

Tractors and other pieces of farm equipment are loaded on a Danish ship for delivery to our overseas customers. Without export duties, foreign trade has kept up with the growth of the production capacity of our country.

485

This is one of the larger Pentagon office areas where hundreds of enlisted men sort and file Army personnel records. Most of the inactive Armed Forces files are stored outside Washington to make room for the active information. Civilian employees (right) sort queries in the Pentagon's huge Personnel Information Office. (Official Department of Defense Photo; U. S. Army Photograph)

Justice dictates that taxes should be based on many considerations. Among them, the following are important. (1) All people should pay some taxes, because everyone benefits from governmental protection and should pay at least something for this important service. (2) Taxes should be based on ability to pay. This means that wealthy people should pay proportionately more than poor people. (3) Taxes should be levied in such fashion that they can be efficiently and economically collected. (4) They should also be certain; that is, not easy to evade.

Taxes are sometimes used for other purposes than to raise revenue. Tariffs have been employed to protect domestic industries by making the importation of certain goods prohibitively high. Steeply progressive income taxes aim at preventing the accumulation of large fortunes in single individuals' hands. Any such progressive tax tends, intentionally or not, to alter the distribution of wealth to some extent. Taxes can be used to encourage or discourage investment or spending, and this is frequently a consideration in a revenue-raising measure. Heavy taxes on alcoholic beverages or on cigarettes are partly to discourage consumption of these items and partly to raise revenue by taxing items of luxurious expense.

The taxing power presents few moral problems when it is used strictly for revenue purposes. The only requirements are that taxes be levied equitably and in proportion to ability to pay. When it is used as a regulatory device, however, many moral problems are raised. For many years people had to pay a tax of ten cents a pound for colored oleomargarine (in areas where it was available), not to furnish money for the government, but to persuade them to buy butter instead. Is such a means proper to defend the dairy industry, or should butter have to compete in the open market with oleomargarine? It is obvious that each use of the taxing power as a regulatory device requires careful consideration of the moral and political issues involved. No general statement can be made condemning or endorsing the use of taxing power for other than revenue-raising purposes.

A final general consideration is the problem of multiple taxation. Each of us is subject to taxation from at least three units of government, and many of us from four or five. The national, state, and local governments all derive their revenue from the same people. If all governments tax the same kind of property or source of wealth, the cumulative effect would be disastrous not only to the individual but to the country's economy. There has been a general tendency for each level of government to concentrate on a different kind of tax. The federal government derives most of its revenue, as we shall see, from income taxes. The state governments have come to rely more and more on sales taxes and such excises as the gasoline tax. Local governments rely largely on personal and real property assessments. Despite these general trends, there is still considerable overlapping by federal, state, and local governments. St. Louisans, for example, pay three taxes on their income: one to the city of St. Louis, one to the state of Missouri, and one to the federal government. In many localities people pay three taxes on cigarettes and alcoholic beverages. Co-operation by state and local governments with the fairly well-established federal tax pattern would eliminate many of the inequalities that develop from multiple taxation.

Continuing problems in federal finance. Taxes on individual and corporate incomes account for the greater part, over three-fourths, of the total federal revenue. In 1955 about $27,700,000,000 came from individual incomes, and about $18,300,000,000 from corporation income taxes. The remainder of the federal income is made up of excise taxes, various fees for federal services, and such miscellaneous taxes as those on gifts and estates.

General agreement seems to be established that the federal government should rely chiefly on income taxes for its revenue and that other taxes, like excise and gift taxes, should be used only to supplement the basic sum obtained from the tax on incomes. There is serious difference of opinion, though, on how the income-tax burden should be distributed. During the Eisenhower administration

Democrats insisted on tax relief for the small income earner, whereas Republicans believed that relief should be extended to corporations and to larger income earners, who, they contended, were already paying more than their just share of taxes.

This difference of opinion as to how the tax burden should be distributed is basic. Compromise between the two points of view usually results in a distribution of the tax burden that most experts regard as fairly equitable. Very few employed persons escape paying income taxes altogether, but those on the lower rungs of the income scale—whose income is used up for the necessities of life —do not pay nearly the same rate as do persons with large incomes. Whether the exemption for dependents should be $600 or $1,000 is an issue that cannot be easily decided. It not only depends on government revenue needs but involves intricate problems of releasing additional purchasing power or encouraging investment, the simple problem of winning votes, and the basic problem of whether to "soak the rich" or "make the poor man pay." The present pattern of exemptions does not favor large families. It tends, rather, to discourage them.

The unbalanced budget. A second continuing problem of federal finance is that of balancing the national budget. A balanced budget is one in which expenditures and receipts are equal. At certain times in the nineteenth century the federal government was embarrassed with the problem of how to spend excess revenue. Two world wars and the depression expanded government functions and expenses so tremendously that even the higher taxes we now pay are not enough to balance the budget. When the budget is unbalanced year after year, the national debt grows larger, monetary inflation continues, and an ever larger part of the annual revenue must be used in paying interest on the debt.

RECEIPTS

INTERNAL REVENUE:

Individual income taxes withheld and other	$31,649,497,897
Corporation income taxes	18,264,716,487
Excise taxes	9,193,766,080
Estate and gift taxes	936,267,445
Taxes not otherwise classified	7,350,547

Employment taxes:

Federal Insurance Contributions Act and taxes on self employed individuals	5,339,572,594
Taxes on carriers and their employees	601,217,108
Taxes on employers of 8 or more	278,809,999

CUSTOMS	606,396,634

MISCELLANEOUS RECEIPTS:

Proceeds from government-owned securities	298,345,641
Seigniorage	28,979,571
Surplus property disposal	147,229,527
Other	2,016,009,268

TOTAL BUDGET RECEIPTS	$69,368,158,804

DEDUCT:

Appropriations to Federal old-age and survivors insurance trust fund	$5,039,572,594
Appropriations to Railroad Retirement account	599,999,051

Refunds of receipts:

Internal revenue	3,399,977,898
Customs	21,619,848
Other	4,485,803

TOTAL DEDUCTIONS	$9,065,655,196

NET BUDGET RECEIPTS	$60,302,503,608

EXPENDITURES

Legislative Branch	$68,116,794
The Judiciary	30,427,149
Executive Office of the President	8,534,506
Funds appropriated to the President for mutual security	3,971,770,268
Independent Offices	6,787,469,431
General Services Administration	973,042,630
Housing and Home Finance Agency	127,020,187
Agriculture Department	4,633,529,573
Commerce Department	1,076,600,958
Defense Department:	
Military functions	35,729,611,014
Civil functions	548,189,219
Undistributed (foreign disbursements)	117,846,475
Health, Education and Welfare Department	1,992,539,310
Interior Department	514,986,201
Justice Department	181,549,698
Labor Department	393,783,666
Post Office Department	365,562,827
State Department	134,130,080
Treasury Department	6,817,475,563
District of Columbia— Federal contributions and loans	21,890,000

TOTAL BUDGET EXPENDITURES	$64,494,075,559
BUDGET DEFICIT	$4,191,571,951

One of the most widely used of the veterans' benefits is the G.I. home loan. Here Veterans Administration fee appraisers are inspecting new homes before allowing the veterans' government insured mortgages, thereby protecting the interests of both the veterans and the government. (*Veterans Administration*)

In 1932 the national debt was only $20,000,000,000, but the economic policies of the government during the depression caused it to double by 1940, and the tremendous expenses of World War II raised the debt to $275,000,000,000. This was reduced slightly in the years after the war, but the Korean War and the need of large outlays for national defense made further reduction difficult if not impossible. At the present time we are paying about $6,000,000,000 a year interest on the debt, which is a bigger figure than the total budget in the early 1920s. When the budget is unbalanced in any one year, the deficit—the difference between expenditures and revenue—must be made up by borrowing. Continual borrowing is imprudent for a government, just as it is for an individual, because it merely post-

Ownership of Gross Public Debt 1954

$271,500,000,000.00

49½	Government Investment Accounts
64½	Individuals
26½	Institutions
17	Corporations
25½	All Others
63½	Commercial Banks
25	Federal Reserve Banks

pones the date of payment and it raises the cost of government by adding on interest charges. It also raises the price of everything else by inflation. A continual deficit throws the burden of paying for one generation's expenditures on later generations.

A third continuing problem of national finance is the reduction of federal expenditures. This is a more difficult problem than it appears to be at first sight. We have seen that the principal items of federal expense are those connected with national defense and with paying off the cost of past wars in the form of veterans' payments and interest on the debt. These items cannot be eliminated from the budget, but economies can undoubtedly be effected in their administration. Rigid economy in other fields, such as in grants-in-aid to the states or foreign-aid appropriations, can save some money. But economy must be practiced in additional areas if the national debt is to be reduced appreciably.

The government seems faced with the unpopular choice of continuing high taxes if it is to effect any substantial reduction in the national debt, or even to prevent further increase. Popular demand for tax reduction makes it difficult for either the administration or Congress to maintain a high tax schedule. Even the Eisenhower administration, which has stressed the need of a sounder financial program, was willing to add about $5,000,000,000 to the national debt by cutting taxes an estimated $7,400,000,000. Relief from taxation is likely to make the burden for future generations heavier.

The problem of an unbalanced budget and a large national debt is not likely to be solved unless the American voters realize that lower taxes are not wise unless the cost of government is also lowered. This is not to say that the citizens alive today should load themselves with the obligation to pay off the national debt in a few years. That would be

neither possible nor just. The great debt was incurred to meet the gigantic national and world crises of the twentieth century: two large and costly wars, an economic catastrophe in the 1930s, and the necessity of enlarging government to serve the needs of a vast industrialized society. No one generation could pay this debt; it must be spread over a number of generations. The important thing now is that the increase of debt be stopped and that the interest be paid while maintaining a balance between government revenues and expenditures. Then, if there are no new wars, the natural and continuous increase in the wealth of the country will produce sufficient surpluses to reduce the debt to safe and manageable dimensions. That debt, it must be remembered, is not only an obligation of the government but an investment by the people in the future of their country.

REVIEW

83. Federal Expenditures
   A. Briefly describe the effect of government spending on business economy.
   B. What are the major items that are included in the budget for the fiscal year?
   C. List the constitutional limitations on raising and spending revenue.
   D. Describe some of the chief weaknesses of the present budgetary process.

84. Federal Revenues
   A. What are the main sources of federal revenue?
   B. List the constitutional restrictions on taxation.
   C. Define a direct tax, excise tax, proportional tax, progressive tax.
   D. What are some of the problems of multiple taxation?

THE CHAPTER IN REVIEW

A. Describe the methods for the preparation and adoption of the budget that are in use at the present time.

B. List the principles of taxation that are dictated by justice and should be considered by the government. What are some of the purposes of taxation?

C. Describe some of the problems faced by the government in regard to the distribution of the income tax burden.

SELECTED READINGS

All the standard textbooks on American government have a chapter on government finance. More specialized treatments of this general problem can be grouped into those (1) on government finance, (2) on the national debt, (3) on budgetary problems, and (4) on taxes, although all these subjects overlap.

1. The following are good analyses of government finance problems: Paul H. Douglas, *Economy in the National Government* (Chicago: University of Chicago Press, 1952); Harold M. Groves, *Financing Government* (New York: Henry Holt & Co., Inc., 1954); Alfred G. Buehler, *Public Finance* (New York: McGraw-Hill Book Co., 1948); and Stuart Chase, *Where's the Money Coming From?* (New York: The Twentieth Century Fund, 1943). The study of public finance of defense measures is the subject of Albert G. Hart and E. Cary Brown, *Financing Defense* (New York: The Twentieth Century Fund, 1951), and Maxwell S. Stewart, *How Can We Pay for Defense?* (New York: Public Affairs Committee, 1951).

2. The Committee on Debt Policy published a study under the title *Our National Debt* (New York: Harcourt, Brace & Co., 1949), and an excellent study of the problem is that of Charles Cortez Abbott, *The Federal Debt, Structure and Impact* (New York: The Twentieth Century Fund, 1953). Other books on this subject are Seymour E. Harris, *The National Debt and the New Economics* (New York: McGraw-Hill Book Co., 1947), and William Withens, *The Public Debt* (New York: The John Day Co.,

1945). A good article, which simplifies the subject, is Rev. Charles A. Frankenhoff, S.J., "You and the National Debt," *Social Order* (March 1955).

3. The Hoover Commission's *Report* published a section on "Budgeting and Accounting" (Washington: Government Printing Office, 1949). Good studies on the subject are V. J. Browne, *Control of the Public Budget* (New York: Public Affairs Press, 1949), and J. R. Hicks, *Problem of Budgetary Reform* (New York: Oxford University Press, Inc., 1949).

4. A simplified explanation of a complex subject is Francis J. Corrigan, "Budgets and Taxes," *Social Order* (December 1953). The Chamber of Commerce of the United States (New York) published two pamphlets on taxes in 1953: *Spending and Taxing,* and *Taxing, Spending, and Debt Management.* An attempt to put these problems simply is "Uncle Sam's Twin Headache: Taxes and Spending," *Senior Scholastic* (March 8, 1950).

In general, *United States News and World Report* and other news magazines carry timely articles on government spending, debts, and finances. These periodicals often contain charts and tables that sum up clearly the complex spending program of the government.

PROJECTS

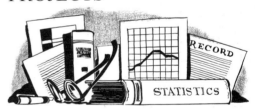

1. The business of paying one's income tax is frequently a complicated matter. The government, therefore, publishes a booklet to assist the taxpayer in making out his return. A committee could study this booklet and report to the class on the levels of taxable incomes, exemptions and the way in which they are computed, and the many other features of the publication.

2. Examples of multiple taxation are easily located. Individuals in the class can analyze those taxes on furs and luxuries, cigarettes and tobacco, gasoline and oil, and others. Large producers of these items take definite stands on taxes. The students can write to these people and then present evidence to the class to support a particular side of the issue.

Chapter 30. Social Security and the Welfare State

85. GOVERNMENT, INDUSTRIAL SOCIETY, AND SOCIAL INSURANCE

The progress of industrialism in Europe created a serious social and political problem by the end of the nineteenth century. Millions of workers had been made dependent on their jobs alone. They owned no property except such personal possessions as clothes and furniture. If they were suddenly thrown out of work, they had little or no savings on which to draw until they could find work again. When they reached advanced age and were no longer employable, they had to find some kind of public or private charity. In other words, they had no financial security.

To solve this problem, the various governments of Europe passed "social security laws" such as old-age pensions and unemployment compensation. Critics of this tendency warned that it would eventually produce a "paternalistic" state in which most people would become state wards. Financially dependent on the state, critics said, the mass of citizens would lose their personal independence as well as their economic freedom. Even-

tually the problem of social security became acute in this country, and the government undertook many new functions to alleviate the difficulties created by the depression of the 1930s.

This social and political trend caused by industrial development is described by Ogg and Ray:[1]

Time was when the functions of the state hardly extended beyond police, taxation, diplomacy, and defense. To these were gradually added a wide variety of controls applying to industrial production, agriculture, trade, transportation, communications, banking, insurance, and what not; and thus to the police state succeeded the regulatory state. To the regulatory state, however, has now succeeded the *service* state, based on a conception of government as existing not merely to keep the peace and provide defense, nor yet merely (in addition to these things) to order or control economic life in the interest of fairness and opportunity, but to take systematic and continuous measures to promote and protect the education, health, comfort, security, and general well-being of the mass of the people. . . .

The concept of the welfare state. As the government assumed these new functions,

---

[1] Frederick A. Ogg and P. Orman Ray, *Introduction to American Government*, ninth edition (New York: Appleton-Century-Crofts, 1948), pp. 5–6.

there developed in the minds of many people a new concept of the state—the concept of a service or a welfare state. This concept is of a state that provides directly for the material and cultural needs of the people and supplies them with everything necessary for every contingency in life. Many people advocate a modified form of the service or welfare state that would furnish such social security only for people unable to attain security for themselves or through other institutions. At any rate, the term "welfare state" is popularly used to describe any state that has embraced a comprehensive social security program and has therefore assumed a large number of positive functions in addition to the protective functions of former days.

The welfare state would be incomprehensible except in an industrialized society in which most persons are completely dependent on their jobs for the necessities of life. They have no other means of income and little or no chance to acquire productive property. Savings from wages can rarely supply the means of providing security to tide them over times of illness or unemployment or crippling injury. Such persons provide an income for themselves after they are forced to retire only by buying annuities or ob-

taining pensions. More than any other single development in American history, the Great Depression of twenty-five years ago made Americans security-minded. It is the Great Depression that lies back of our social security system, which is now an accepted feature of American civil life. This point is well made in the following paragraph:[2]

It is difficult to convey the spirit of insecurity, of doubt, and of dismay that characterized a large portion of the American population in the early thirties. Their marvelous system had broken down and, paradoxically enough, it would not get going again until the demands for war material to fight another world war finally started the wheels of industry rolling smoothly once again. It is not surprising that in this atmosphere of disillusionment there should again be "thunder on the left" and "lightening on the right." . . . Among the legislators in the country two approaches were finally outlined. The first was an *ad hoc* solution for the immediate needs of the people. Federal aid had to be supplied at once and in various forms to alleviate the wants of the people and to get the wheels of industry rolling once again. The second approach was to fashion a long-range program of social security so that the country might never again face a depression so utterly

[2] Rev. John L. Thomas, S.J., "Economic Insecurity and the Welfare State," in Land, Thomas, and Gavin, *Democratic Living* (Chicago: Loyola University Press, 1952), II, pp. 348–349.

unprepared. In actual practice, this second approach went much further. A system of social security was established which was designed not only to protect the members of society from the dire effects of a future possible depression, but also, as a result of the ferment of social reform which had long been working in the minds of many, programs were proposed which would mitigate the hardships of those in need and guarantee some measure of security to those dependent on their job for their livelihood.

State and local governments proved unwilling or unable to finance social security plans. Beginning in 1933 the federal government undertook to provide both relief to those who needed it and certain kinds of social insurance to those who participated in the plan for a minimum length of time. The basic act putting this system into effect was the Social Security Act of 1935. Its extension in 1950, together with a number of other pieces of "welfare legislation" since World War II, shows that as a nation we have committed ourselves to a federally sponsored and directed social security system. As we shall see, the system works in part through the several states, and in part it is administered directly by the national government. In part it is direct relief to those who qualify as needy, and in part it is insurance to those whose contributions qualify them to obtain benefits. Contributions come partly from employers and partly from employees, and they are supposed to be based on sound actuarial principles used by private insurance companies.

The American social security system. During the first two years of the Roosevelt administration federal outlays to the states and in the form of direct relief amounted to billions of dollars. This early program consisted of temporary measures which the national government adopted in its efforts to turn the tide of the depression. The Social Security Act of 1935, on the other hand, aimed at tapering off the federal government's role and putting relief and welfare activity back into the hands of the states. The act sets up eight distinct programs. Two of them are unemployment insurance and old age and survivors' insurance. Three provide public assistance to the aged, to the needy blind, to dependent children, and to the permanently and totally disabled. Three other programs provide maternal and child-health services, services for crippled children, and child-welfare services.

The federal government operates only the old-age and survivors' insurance program. This program is administered by the Social Security Administration, which was placed under the Department of Health, Education and Welfare when the latter was established in 1953. The Social Security Administration participates in the administration of the other programs by examining individual state programs to see if they conform to the standards set up by the federal law. If they do, the Social Security Administration certifies them for receiving federal grants as provided by the law.

Unemployment compensation. The Social

Over 12,000 "hunger marchers" traveled from Pittsburgh, Pa., to Washington, D.C., in January of 1932. Two of their members died from exposure on the trek to present their relief demands to the government. (Acme)

Surplus apples and price signs were distributed free to unemployed men during the 1930s to provide them with a temporary means of livelihood. (International News Photo)

Security Act of 1935 aims at cushioning the effect of temporary unemployment on the individual worker. It is not designed to support millions of unemployed during a long depression. The unemployment plan is financed by the federal government's taxing the payroll of all employers of eight or more persons. The tax is 3 per cent of each employee's wages up to $4,200. Originally the amount was $3,000; in 1950 it was raised to $3,600, and in 1955 to the present amount of $4,200. A rebate of up to 90 per cent is granted to any employer who pays a comparable tax to his state for the support of a state unemployment compensation program. Thus the states were virtually forced to set up state programs, and all of them have done it. The states technically collect the funds, which they deposit in the federal treasury and on which they draw as needed to make payments to the unemployed.

The law of each state specifies how workers qualify for compensation, how much they may receive, for what length of time, and other such matters. State laws differ considerably, but the following general statements can be made: The beneficiary must register for work at a public employment office, and he must file his claim for benefits. He must be able to work and be willing to accept a job comparable to the one he has lost. He must have worked long enough to build up a certain amount of "wage credits" entitling him to compensation. Compensation is limited as to amount and as to the length of time the unemployed worker may receive it.

During the year ending June 30, 1954, more than 6,000,000 persons drew one or more checks under the unemployment compensation plan. The average beneficiary drew 11 checks for an average amount of almost $25 a week. The total amount paid to unemployed workers during this fiscal year was $1,600,000,000 for 67,500,000 weeks of unemployment.

Old-age and survivors insurance. This is the only part of the national security system operated completely by the federal government. Originally this section of the Social Security Act covered approximately the same persons as did the unemployment compensation section, workers in commerce and industry. In 1950, however, farm laborers, household employees, and many self-employed persons were added to the rolls covered by old-age insurance. Amendments in 1954 added about 9,000,000 more employees to the program, so that by 1955 approximately nine out of every ten workers in the country were participants, an estimated total of more than 69 million persons.

Contributions are made in equal amounts by employee and employer. Each pays 2 per cent of the annual wage up to $4,200. This payment is scheduled to rise to 2½ per cent in 1960, to 3 per cent in 1965, to 3½ per cent in 1970, and finally to 4 per cent in 1975 and thereafter. These contributions are placed in the Old Age and Survivors Trust Fund in the Treasury, and they are invested in government bonds. Assets in the fund at the beginning of 1955 were about $20,500,000,000.

Insured workers are entitled to receive monthly payments upon retirement at the age of 65 or later. The amount of an individual's monthly benefit depends on a number of items: whether he is married or single, whether he has dependent children, whether he has made the required number of payments for maximum coverage, and whether he has been retired from full-time employment. Amendments to the act in 1954 raised the minimum monthly payment from $25 to $30 and the maximum from $85 to $98.50. In September 1954—the first month under the increased benefits plan—about $326,000,000 was paid out to nearly 6,700,000 beneficiaries.

Critics of the old-age insurance provisions of the Social Security Act point out a number of deficiencies in the plan. Although the plan was to be self-supporting, Congress froze the original 1 per cent contribution of workers and employers for so long that the reserve was not being built up to handle the benefits that will come due in the future. Large appropriations will be necessary, critics say, to support the program. Consistent criticism has been made that the program was not truly national because many workers were excluded. Extension of the coverage by amendments in 1950 and 1954 minimizes the importance of this criticism. Critics point out also that benefits received are not adequate for any sound old-age insurance program. A person can obtain more relief under the public assistance program, for which he makes no contribution whatsoever. As a matter of fact, large numbers of those drawing old-age insurance benefits have also had to apply for old-age assistance in order to make ends meet.

Public assistance. The Social Security Act of 1935 and its amendments provide pub-

An important duty of the Social Security Administration is to educate its "policy-holders" concerning their entitlements. When the insured deceased worker leaves no widow or children, monthly insurance benefits may be paid to an aged dependent parent. (U. S. Department of Health, Education and Welfare)

lic assistance to four classes of needy dependents: the aged, the blind, dependent children, and the permanently and totally disabled. All four types of assistance are accomplished through the grant-in-aid, whereby the national government matches state assistance up to certain amounts set down in the law. The various states are practically forced to set up programs that meet minimum requirements of the Social Security Administration. Such assistance is denied to people living in public institutions, since one of its aims is to help them live at home. Federal law further requires that assistance be given in relation to the need in each case, but the administration of the program remains in state officials' hands.

At the beginning of 1955 more than 2,500,000 needy aged persons were receiving assistance. The average monthly payment was $51.77. An average of $56.06 was paid monthly to 101,800 needy blind, and an average of $85.52 to almost 600,000 families with more than 1,500,000 children. Finally, average monthly payments to 219,800 disabled persons were $53.72. These payments came to a total of $2,500,000,000, of which the federal government furnished slightly more than half.

Maternity, child-health, and child-welfare services. The Social Security Act makes similar provisions for maternity services and health and welfare services for children. It gives funds to the states in the form of grants-in-aid for all these services, which are administered by the states. During the fiscal year ending in mid-1954 the federal government paid out about $17,-800,000 for maternity and child-health services and about $6,800,000 for child-welfare services.

The aim of the program is to strengthen family life. The extent to which this objective is accomplished cannot be easily determined, but it does seem that fatalities incurred in childbirth and early childhood have been reduced by the program. In 1935 only 37 per cent of the births in the country were delivered in hospitals; by 1949 the figure had risen to 87 per cent. In 1935 the maternal mortality rate was 58 per 10,000 births, and by 1950 the figure had dropped to less than 10 per 10,000. Moreover, in many sections of the country the figure had dropped to less than 5 per 10,000 births. Various factors contributed to this improvement in maternal mortality, but among them the program inaugurated by the Social Security Act of 1935 played a considerable role.

86. OTHER GOVERNMENT WELFARE ACTIVITIES

In addition to the insurance and assistance programs set up by the Social Security Act of 1935, the national government makes a number of other direct contributions to the "welfare" conditions of its citizens. Here we shall summarize only the most important of these contributions.

Aid to veterans. Various payments to veterans have been among the largest items of federal expense since the Civil War. These payments averaged around six to seven billion dollars a year after World War II, but in the last few years they have decreased considerably in amount. Benefits given to veterans include medical care for any disease or disability incurred in the service, extended unemployment compensation, and general assistance for education or vocational training. The G.I. Bill of Rights, passed in 1944, also guaranteed certain loans to veterans for the purchase of homes, farms, or business enterprises. Most of these benefits have been extended to veterans of the Korean War and to all those who served in the armed forces since that time and have been honorably discharged. It seems that the principle has been established that anyone who interrupts his lifework for a "hitch" in the armed services is entitled to certain welfare benefits enabling him to readjust without loss of time to his civilian career.

Public housing. In addition to the aid given to home owners through easy credit facilities supplied by the Home Owners Loan Corporation, the Federal Housing Administration, and the Federal Home Loan Bank System, the national government has undertaken many public housing and slum-clearance projects throughout the country. These are financed by the grant-in-aid and by loans made to local governments by the Public Housing Administration. To permit below-cost rents for low-income groups, the national government subsidizes local housing authorities.

Medical care. We have already seen that the American people have given serious consideration to a nationally supported health-insurance scheme such as England has, and they have rejected it in favor of various other means of providing adequate medical and hospital care. Nevertheless, the federal government does provide a good deal of direct med-

The huge Library of Congress is maintained at government expense as an important source of reference materials and educational services to libraries and schools. The Library maintains a most thorough catalogue which includes reference cards for textbooks such as this. (Library of Congress)

ical care to certain special groups in the country. It also finances and conducts a large health research program.

About twenty-four million people obtain varying degrees of medical service from federal agencies. Among these are the members of the armed forces and their dependents, veterans, government employees, and inmates of federal prisons. The government also maintains hospitals and dispensaries for longshoremen, harbor workers, and others covered by national workmen's compensation laws. It also helps the public health programs of all forty-eight states to do such things as maintain free clinics, build additional hospitals, and train competent personnel.

Education. The federal government maintains and operates academies to train officer personnel for the armed forces at West Point, Annapolis, and Colorado Springs. It also operates a number of Indian schools and colleges, and Howard University for Negroes. It maintains several museums and observatories, and the Library of Congress is a most important source of reference materials and educational services to local libraries and schools.

In addition to these institutions, the federal government promotes education through grants-in-aid to the states, through research conducted by the Office of Education, and through direct support of veterans who wish to take advantage of the education provisions of the G.I. Bill. In 1956, President Eisenhower asked Congress to authorize $1,250,000,000 in federal aid for school construction and education research in the following five years. This request is for an annual expenditure for education almost as large as the total budget in 1900.

Department of Health, Education and Welfare. Most of the welfare functions we have been discussing were commonly considered "Democratic" measures because they were introduced when the Democrats were in office (1932–1952) and have generally been sponsored more enthusiastically by Democrats than by Republicans. Congress refused President Truman's request that these welfare functions

Education of our youth as an adjunct to our defense program has long been a function of the government. A cadet receives his initial issue of textbooks for the first academic year at the U. S. Air Force Academy in Denver, Colorado. The stack weighs sixty-five pounds and costs $84.43. (U. S. Air Force Photo)

be assembled into a single department to be created for that purpose. The same request was made by President Eisenhower when he took office, and in 1953 the Republican Congress created the Department of Health, Education and Welfare and assigned Cabinet rank to its head. The fact that both parties desired to create the department indicates they agree that the national government is permanently committed to welfare functions. Moreover, it is noteworthy that when the Republicans came to power in 1953 they made no attempt to discontinue or even to reduce substantially the welfare functions inaugurated under the Democrats' sponsorship.

The ramified programs of the Federal Security Agency have been placed within the new Department of Health, Education and Welfare. Also included in the department are the Office of Education, the Public Health Service, the Food and Drug Administration, and the Bureau of Federal Credit Unions. The total number of employees in the department in 1955 was 36,656, as compared with 21,000 in the Department of State and 43,460 in the Commerce Department.

The issue of the welfare state. The measures we have discussed do not create a complete welfare state as that term is generally understood: that is, a state that provides for our medical, educational, social, and financial welfare, and in so doing makes us all more or less dependent on the national state. We have seen that in most respects the federal government leaves the direction of the program in the states' hands. But at the same time the long-term implications of the program are unmistakable. The national government does things it never thought of doing in days past. It takes part of our wages to support us in old age. If the insurance is insufficient, it gives us money for our groceries and our rent. If we are needy and blind, it is to the federal government that we turn for support. One-sixth of us have our doctor bills taken care of by the national government. It takes a goodly share of our income, no matter who we are, and it gives back to many of us various services that were formerly taken care of by individuals themselves.

The question is whether public policy is to aid private initiative or supplant it. Is the government assuming tasks that

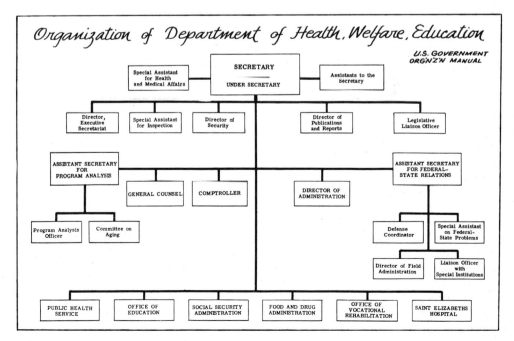

could be better performed by private individuals or groups? Are the programs we have discussed above starting America on "the road to serfdom," toward a "welfare state" from which there is no return? If this is so, is it inevitable? Or have we freedom to go in some other direction?

Most Americans will not condemn any one of the social security programs we have outlined, but almost every American will condemn the totality of them. Some persons representing large groups like the CIO and the National Farmers' Union urge that social security be extended and expanded to include everyone in the country, and in much larger amounts. Other people express fear that we have already gone too far and that we have purchased security at the price of freedom; in other words, that our measures already add up to a "servile state."

When we look at the problem closely, we see that the controversy is really

The federal government as a benevolent but foolish Santa Claus is mocked in this newspaper cartoon depicting the attitudes which an overwilling welfare state would encourage. (Dowling in the New York Herald Tribune)

You Don't Have To Be Good Any More

about means rather than ends. This is a philosophical way of stating that Americans agree that social security is a good thing and that somehow it must be provided in our modern society. What they disagree on is whether the state should play the large role it does in providing this security. In other words, are we using the wisest means to achieve the end of social security?

When the question is put this way, we see that we must invoke the principle we have referred to frequently in this volume, the principle of subsidiarity, which holds that the national state should not assume any function that can be adequately performed by individuals or by a smaller political unit. When such functions cannot be adequately performed by smaller groups and when they are necessary to the welfare of the community, then the national state has the obligation to intervene. More specifically, four conditions are necessary to justify intervention by the national government.

1. Refusal of federal intervention must result in some harm to the essential rights or interests of the whole community or one of its groups. It cannot intervene in the interests of mere efficiency, convenience, or for some other relatively slight reason.

2. The damage must have already occurred or be imminent. In other words, there must be compelling and immediate reason for federal intervention.

3. It must be eminently clear that individuals or local communities cannot remedy the harm threatening the common good of the nation. Federal intervention must be considered as a last resort.

4. The amount of state intervention is limited by the social injury to be corrected. This last condition is the one most frequently violated, for there is a tendency to use an emergency to justify state intervention and then to discover all sorts of excuses and causes for perpetuating and

extending the services of the agency originally created. It is a political truism that when the state once intervenes it almost never relinquishes its functions, but rather extends them into wider and wider areas of activity. The conclusion, then, is that we must examine carefully every program proposed to give us social security, and we must adopt only those that clearly meet the conditions outlined above.

REVIEW

85. Government, Industrial Society, and Social Insurance

A. How do the functions of the regulatory state differ from those of the police state? Why is it said that there is a need today for some type of welfare state?

B. When did the American people become security-conscious? Trace the development of the federal government's social security program.

C. Describe briefly the program for unemployment compensation.

D. Show how the groups included in the old-age insurance program have been enlarged since 1935. Briefly describe the operation of this program.

86. Other Government Welfare Activities

A. Describe the benefits which have been given to veterans by the federal government.

B. How does the government grant aid in the fields of medicine and education?

C. How does the principle of subsidiarity pertain to welfare programs? What conditions must be present to justify intervention by the federal government?

THE CHAPTER IN REVIEW

A. Briefly summarize the historical facts that have brought about the intervention of the federal government in social security programs.

B. What types of programs were set up by the Social Security Act of 1935? Briefly explain how each is administered.

C. Summarize some of the aid programs of the government at the present time, pointing out some benefits and dangers of these programs.

SELECTED READINGS

The complex moral and political problems involved in the trend toward the welfare state are well handled by Rev. John L. Thomas, S.J., in Section IV of *Democratic Living* (Chicago: Loyola University Press, 1952).The following books are concerned mainly with analyzing and explaining the social security system adopted in this country in the 1930s: E. M. Burns, *The American Social Security System* (Boston: Houghton Mifflin Co., 1949); Grace Abbott, *From Relief to Social Security* (Chicago: University of Chicago Press, 1942), a historical treatment of social security legislation; Paul H. Douglas, *Social Security in the United States* (New York: Whittlesey House, 1939); and William Haber and Wilbur Cohen, *Readings in Social Security* (New York: Prentice-Hall, Inc., 1948).

The Social Security Administration publishes a monthly journal, *Social Security Bulletin,* and an annual, *Social Security Yearbook.*

The well-known Australian economist, Colin Clark, published a scholarly criticism of the British experiment in welfare legislation. This study is analyzed by Rev. Philip S. Land, S.J., "Colin Clark on the Welfare State," *Social Order* (October 1954). The Reference Shelf volume edited by Herbert L. Marx, Jr., *The Welfare State* (New York: H. W. Wilson Co., 1950), contains the usual collection of articles for and against the subject for debaters. A similar collection is edited by Bower Aly, *The Welfare State* (Columbia, Mo.: Lucas Bros., Publishers, 1950). A series of lectures on the subject under the auspices of the Social Science Research Center of the Graduate School of the University of Minnesota is published under the title *The Welfare State—Menace or Millennium?* (Minneapolis: University of Minnesota Press, 1950). Briefer treatments of the issue are to be found in V. A. Demant, "Christian Ethics and the Welfare State," *Cross Currents* (Fall, 1952; Eugene J. McCarthy, "Welfare State," *Commonweal* (November 7, 1952); and H. Sommerville, "What Is the Welfare State?", *Catholic Mind* (November 1953).

PROJECTS

1. A group in the class could contrast the government benefits which the school and school children receive today with the aid program of twenty-five years ago. A report to the class on the differences could include the benefits received from federal, state, and local governments.

2. A group in the class could find out about the unemployment compensation law in your state. They could report to the class on the procedure that must be gone through in order to obtain the benefits, outlining the requirements for eligibility in the program. It may prove helpful to illustrate this with imaginary cases.

3. A member of the class could write to the Department of Health, Education and Welfare to obtain information on the activities of a specific division of this organization such as the Public Health Service or the Food and Drug Administration. An illustrated chart could be made of this information and added to as information on the other divisions is gathered by the students later.

PROFILES

THEODORE ROOSEVELT

BORN: New York City, October 27, 1858

EDUCATION: Harvard University, class of 1880
DIED: Oyster Bay, N. Y., January 6, 1919

The dynamic President who gave his name to one feature of American foreign policy and his nickname to every child's favorite toy turned to politics while still a student. Two years after graduation from Harvard, he served in the New York State Assembly, as the nominee of a group of the Reform Republicans.

Poor health caused him to live from 1884 to 1886 in North Dakota, where his love of the outdoors was given full rein. Shortly after his return to New York he re-entered the public service as a member of the United States Civil Service Commission and as New York City's Police Commissioner. In both capacities he demonstrated a willingness to risk his own position with politically powerful people whose actions he condemned. His reputation was further enhanced by his brief service as Assistant Secretary of the Navy.

The war with Spain brought Roosevelt national prominence as lieutenant colonel of the 1st United States Volunteer Cavalry, the famous "Rough Riders," who performed sensationally, if not overefficiently, in Cuba. His hero's reputation gained in the short and victorious war helped him in his campaign for the governorship of New York, despite the disapproval of the Republican party machine leader, Thomas C. Platt. To get Roosevelt out of New York, Platt arranged for him to be nominated for the vice-presidency in the 1900 election. An assassin's bullet killed McKinley, and the bespectacled reformer became President of the United States.

As President, Theodore Roosevelt instituted several notable changes: he enthusiastically backed measures to conserve our natural resources, to require inspection and proper labeling of food and drugs sold to the public, and to develop the Panama Canal as an American enterprise. He took the unprecedented step of intervening in a labor dispute, the coal strike of 1902, on a neutral basis. His foreign policy was noteworthy for the Roosevelt Corollary to the Monroe Doctrine, backed by his famous "big stick"—a heavily reinforced modern navy. His efforts in bringing about peace between Russia and Japan brought him a Nobel Peace Prize.

Roosevelt broke with the Republican party in 1912, introducing his "Bull Moose" party, which was defeated. Even so, his party helped make 1912 the high point in the "progressive" movement in national politics.

For a complete biography of Theodore Roosevelt, H. C. Pringle's *Theodore Roosevelt* (New York: Harcourt, Brace & Co., 1931) is highly recommended. Roosevelt's *Autobiography* (New York: The Macmillan Company, 1913) contains his own estimate of his greatest achievements.

FRANKLIN D. ROOSEVELT

BORN: Hyde Park, N.Y., January 30, 1882
EDUCATION: Harvard College, B.A., 1904; Columbia University Law School
DIED: Warm Springs, Ga., April 12, 1945

Heir to a considerable fortune, young Roosevelt entered politics as a Democrat after commencing his career as a lawyer. An admirer of Woodrow Wilson, he was named Assistant Secretary of the Navy in 1913, where he was closely concerned in the administration of fleet affairs in World War I. This experience, plus the magic of the Roosevelt name, gained for him the vice-presidential nomination in 1920, when the Republicans won a landslide victory. Roosevelt's career seemed ended in 1921, when poliomyelitis left him partially paralyzed. Promoting medical aid programs for infantile paralysis victims became his chief non-political activity, but he re-entered party politics shortly after his recovery.

Roosevelt made the nominating speeches for Alfred E. Smith at both the 1924 and 1928 Democratic conventions, then was prevailed upon by Smith to run for the New York governorship in 1928. His victory that year and in 1930 made him the logical candidate for the presidency in 1932. His experience as a depression governor and his ideas for recovery, expressed in dynamic speeches, aided him in easily defeating Hoover for the first of four presidential election victories.

Roosevelt attacked depression problems with great enthusiasm. He surrounded himself with experts in various fields, known as the "Brain Trust," and began a vast program of relief activity. This was coupled with experiments in changing the gold content of the dollar and in controlling wages and production in industry and agriculture. His program of direct government action to encourage or regulate aspects of banking, farming, labor relations, and public utilities led to enormous new public agencies that employed thousands of people and increased the public debt.

In foreign relations Roosevelt fostered reciprocal trade agreements and denounced aggression by dictator states. After 1939 he made American aid available to Great Britain and her allies. During the war he headed the largest government organization in history, directed over-all strategy after conferences with the heads of Allied governments, and laid the foundations for the United Nations organization. His death, shortly after his return from the Yalta meeting with Stalin and Churchill, came when American forces were within sight of victory in the war.

Probably no person in modern times has been written about so much by former associates. In the dual study, *Roosevelt and Hopkins* (New York: Harper & Brothers, 1948), F.D.R.'s speech writer, Robert E. Sherwood, describes much of the organization of the government under Roosevelt. Selections from his presidential speeches are included in *Nothing to Fear*, edited by B. D. Zevin (Boston: Houghton Mifflin Co., 1946). Personal materials are being made available regularly. Among these, *F.D.R., His Personal Letters* (New York: Duell, Sloan & Pearce, 3 vols., 1947–1950), edited by Elliott Roosevelt, includes a considerable amount of material for personality and character study.

GEORGE W. NORRIS

BORN: Sandusky County, Ohio, July 11, 1861
EDUCATION: Law degree from Northern Indiana Normal School (Valparaiso University)
DIED: McCook, Neb., September 2, 1944

Ohio-born George W. Norris served the state of Nebraska in the House of Representatives and later in the Senate from 1903 to 1942.

One of the Progressives active in the early part of the twentieth century, Norris came to national attention during the famous Bull Moose campaign of Theodore Roosevelt in 1912. He was an outspoken opponent of this nation's entry into World War I and the League of Nations. He was later to change his isolationist views, advocating the participation of the United States in World War II.

Norris was a strong leader in Congress and distinguished himself in three important fields: federal service, labor, and government control in projects of the TVA type. He was co-sponsor with Fiorello La Guardia of the Anti-Injunction Act of 1932, which declared that "yellow-dog" contracts were invalid and also prohibited the issuance of injunctions to prevent picketing and strikes.

He was responsible for reducing the authority of the Speaker of the House, who in 1910 (Joseph Cannon was the Speaker) acted in the manner of a dictator. By mustering the backing of both parties Norris was able to break the control of the Speaker over House legislative procedures.

His fight for many years to end the lame-duck sessions of Congress finally was successful in 1933 with the addition of the Twentieth Amendment to the Constitution.

Norris envisioned government-owned projects for flood control, water power, and cheap electricity. His efforts for the adoption of such notions were rewarded in 1933 with the establishment of TVA. Other multipurpose projects of a similar nature followed the Supreme Court's decision upholding the TVA as constitutional.

From his earliest days in the House, when he sponsored bills that proved to be a preview of the later New Deal labor legislation, to the close of his nearly forty years of public service, Norris was an independent thinker and a courageous and relentless fighter for what he believed would benefit the United States as a whole.

An interesting account of the life of George Norris is his own story, *Fighting Liberal, Autobiography* (New York: The Macmillan Co., 1945), edited by James E. Lawrence. Important references to his life appeared in many articles that dealt with the TVA and the Twentieth Amendment, and are indexed under those titles in the *Guide to Periodical Literature.*

DEBATE

The question: **SHOULD THE UNITED STATES ADOPT A PROGRAM OF FEDERAL COMPULSORY HEALTH INSURANCE?**

At the outset, this question seems to involve two conflicting principles, both of which are sound: (1) the principle that the federal government should promote the health and welfare of the American people; (2) the principle of "subsidiarity," that people should take care of such matters as health themselves. The problem, then, seems to be to determine which of these principles should prevail in America at this time.

Affirmative presentation

I. There is a serious need for additional health care, which no one denies.
  1. Health is a national resource and is of vital importance to the welfare of America.
     a. Health is personally important for each one of us: illness is the loan shark's friend; it impoverishes families; it breaks up homes.
     b. Health is nationally important, for healthy people are our greatest national asset.
     c. Health is economically important, for more work-time is lost because of sickness than for any other reason.
  2. Large numbers of people are not adequately cared for today.
     a. Only the wealthy can afford adequate private care.
     b. Very few spend money for preventive care.

II. Needed additional health care must be provided by federal compulsory health insurance.
  1. Private medicine cannot provide for additional health care.
     a. Medicine is a commodity, and only the wealthy can afford it.
     b. Care is given in clinics and through charity to only a small proportion: only to those in larger cities; only to the poverty-stricken, which eliminates the middle class.
  2. Voluntary medicine and insurance plans give inadequate coverage.
     a. These plans cover only those in populous areas.
     b. These plans cover only those in certain occupations or large industries.

III. Federal compulsory health insurance is a sound American solution to a serious problem.

1. It is a serious aspect of the common welfare, which the government is to promote.
2. It is similar to other social security legislation, which is now considered part of the American system (e.g., unemployment compensation, old-age insurance, benefits for the blind).
3. These measures have not resulted in "socialism" or made us a "nation of serfs," as their opponents charged they would.
4. Compulsory health insurance would work on the principles already established for other social security legislation. (Here the affirmative should present the concrete plan they propose. The affirmative team should have devised a plan that falls within the meaning of the question and one that seems practical.)

Affirmative conclusion: Private medicine and group plans are good, but they leave a sizable part of the population that can be covered only by compulsory health insurance on a national scale. Some other effective way to care for the health of *all* Americans must be proposed *if* it can be shown that our plan is worse than the evil that the affirmative proposes to cure.

Negative presentation

I. Private medicine has done wonderful work in caring for Americans' health.
 1. Technically private medicine has made progress unparalleled in history (e.g., the checking of polio and infectious diseases).
 2. Private medicine has extended coverage to more and more Americans every year.
 3. Voluntary insurance groups have insured millions of Americans and continue to insure more millions each year.
 4. The United States as a nation has the best medical care in the world.
II. The affirmative asks us to scrap this system for one of dubious value.
 1. Socialized medicine has not worked out well in England.
 2. Other countries with compulsory health insurance (e.g., Sweden, France, Italy) do not compare favorably with the United States, health-wise.

III. Compulsory health insurance is a step toward socialized medicine.
 1. The government will control the funds, collect and disperse them.
 2. It is a small step to assign doctors to patients to simplify administration of this vast program, and in time to control American medical practice.
 3. This amounts to ending our voluntary system—similar to putting everyone in the Army.

Negative conclusion: Our present system is better than the affirmative's proposal; and, given time and freedom, it will cover all Americans adequately. Comparisons show that our present system is superior to what the affirmative proposes. The affirmative proposal entails almost certain dangers in exchange for dubious gains.

Affirmative rebuttal

The negative arguments boil down to two: (1) Americans are doing pretty well now; (2) the affirmative proposal is dangerous.
I. The affirmative admits Americans are doing "pretty well," but let us do a "little better."
 1. Complacency is dangerous and inhumane, since millions need health care today.
 2. Americans have never been satisfied with "pretty well."
II. The affirmative denies that its proposal is dangerous.
 1. Comparisons with England and other countries are irrelevant and meaningless.
 2. The negative has not condemned compulsory health insurance, but has condemned what they tell us *will come later.*
 3. The affirmative proposes a good system and suggests that the debate be centered on it.
  a. This is extension of group insurance to all, and the negative favors this kind of insurance.
  b. It amounts to a nationwide Blue Cross and Blue Shield plan to which all must subscribe: you can still pick your doctor and your hospital; you can still avoid seeing a doctor if you prefer. The difference is that the government pays for your medical expenses because you are insured.

Negative rebuttal

The difference of opinion seems to reduce itself to the affirmative taking a short-range point of view and the negative taking a long-range point of view.

I. Rational people talk of consequences of a measure or an action.
    1. In the long run, private medicine has done a wonderful job.
    2. In the long run, governments do not belong in medicine, and harm comes when they enter the field.
II. The cure is definitely worse than the disease.
    1. Federal compulsory health insurance will not eliminate disease. It is only a new procedure for taking care of it.
    2. This procedure is to turn health administration and insurance over to the national government.

CLASSROOM DISCUSSION: The class should decide: (1) whether the government has a legitimate interest and right to act in the field of health. If it has, then discussion should be guided by the principle of subsidiarity discussed in Chapter 22, to decide whether the problem of national health care can be handled adequately by other groups, private or on a lower governmental level.

SELECTED READINGS

It is difficult to find any truly objective writing on national compulsory health insurance. In a general way, labor tends to favor it; medical men generally oppose it, as do management and most business people; other professional people are divided on this question.

Readings that are mainly informational include: "Uncle Sam's Health Problems," *Senior Scholastic* (May 4, 1955); "Foreign Governments Health Programs," *Congressional Digest* (March 1955); G. W. Bachman and Lewis Meriam, *Issue of Compulsory Health Insurance* (Washington: Brookings Institution, 1948); M. M. Davis, *Medical Care for Tomorrow* (New York: Harper & Brothers, 1955); Julius Manson, *British Health Service* (New York: League for Industrial Democracy, 1952); O. N. Servein,

Jr., *Paying for Medical Care in the United States* (New York: Columbia University Press, 1954); Howard Whitman, "Doctors in an Uproar," *Collier's* (May 21, 1949); Peter Wyden, "Newest Kind of Medical Insurance," *Coronet* (September 1954); Max Seham, "Government in Medicine," *Reporter* (September 18, 1951); Marion Robinson, "What Kind of Health Law?", *Survey* (April 1949); D. V. Whipple, "Health Care—England and U.S.A.," *Survey* (September 1950).

Arguments for and against the proposal are presented in the following: the Reference Shelf volume edited by Poyntz Tyler, *Social Welfare in the United States* (New York: H. W. Wilson Co., 1955); "Health Reinsurance Proposal," *Congressional Digest* (March 1955); "A.M.A. and National Health Insurance," *Consumer Reports* (April 1949); Rebecca West, "Can a Nation Afford Health for All It's People?" *Ladies' Home Journal* (September 1950); R. W. Campbell and W. G. Campbell, "Compulsory Health Insurance," *Quarterly Journal of Economics* (February 1952).

Arguments in favor of compulsory health insurance are included in: O. R. Ewing, *Nation's Health: A Report to the President* (Washington: Superintendent of Documents, 1948); S. E. Harris, *National Health Insurance and Alternative Plans for Financing Health* (New York: League for Industrial Democracy, 1953); William Green, "National Health Program for a Stronger America," *American Federationist* (February 1952); Franz Goldman, "Labor's Attitude toward Health Insurance," *Industrial and Labor Review* (October 1948).

Arguments against the proposal are included in: Dave Beck, *Government Medicine—Danger Ahead!* (Chicago: American Medical Association, 1951); *National Compulsory Health Insurance Is Not the Answer* (New York: Chamber of Commerce of the State of New York, 1950); *You and Socialized Medicine* (Washington: Chamber of Commerce of the United States, 1949); F. E. Robin and G. H. Shafter, "National Health Insurance," *American Journal of Nursing* (September 1950); "Brookings Report on Compulsory Health Insurance," *American Medical Association Journal* (June 5, 1948); E. J. Faulkner, "Why Federal Health Reinsurance Is Not the Answer," *American Medical Association Journal* (December 18, 1954); Benson Ford, "Health Policies—A Business Man's View," *Hospitals* (December 1954); E. L. Henderson, "Here's Health the Voluntary Way," *Reader's Digest* (May 1950).

UNIT TEN
The Foreign Policy of the
United States

Chapter 31. Principles and Factors in Foreign Policy

87. NATURE AND IMPORTANCE OF THE SUBJECT

The problems we have discussed so far can be considered domestic problems. Some of these problems—like immigration and race relations—have international consequences; but even these are domestic problems to be solved as the nation wishes. In the rest of this book we shall be concerned with international problems. These are problems over which we Americans do not have full control because they involve our relationships with peoples under other sovereign jurisdictions—that is, peoples who owe allegiance to other governments, who obey different laws, who belong to other cultures and have other sets of values. We cannot deal with these peoples by legislation. We must negotiate to solve problems we hold in common with them.

A wise foreign policy has been one of the principal protective duties of the state all through recorded history. We have seen that political society is established to make it possible for men to live the good life and that the purpose of government is to preserve law and order in the community so that men can pursue both the natural and supernatural ends for which they have been created by God. No government can perform this essential protective service if it fails to maintain such relations with other governments as will effectively safeguard the national security and the national interests.

The law of nations. For many centuries prior to the French Revolution, the nations of the European international community recognized that there was a law of nations founded on the universal natural moral law. The great political thinker, Montesquieu, in the eighteenth century defined the essential principle of the law of nations in these words:

> The law of nations is genuinely based on this principle, that the divers nations should do each other the most good during peacetime and the least harm during wartime without harming their true interests.

Although the world in our times seems to know little about the old law of nations,

it is evident that necessity is hastening a restoration of this concept.

No country's foreign policy consists of a simple application of general principles to international relations. Such principles do not show precisely what must be done to solve a particular problem that arises in a certain quarter of the globe. The foreign policy of this country is not the result of abstract ideas. It is not to be found in any single document or declaration of intention by our government. It derives from a series of congressional and presidential statements and decisions about specific problems throughout the world. Of necessity our foreign policy is constantly changing. As new problems arise or old problems change, new formulations of foreign policy must be made. The basic objectives of a sound foreign policy—the promotion of our legitimate national interests throughout the world—remain the same. The means to achieve these objectives change as a fluid world situation alters, as the grouping of other nations shifts, as new economic, political, and ideological factors assert themselves.

The discussion of whether we should follow a "realistic" or an "idealistic" foreign policy therefore misses the point at issue. The choice confronting Americans —if we are to remain true to our heritage —is not between a so-called "realistic" policy, divorced from morality and based on power alone, and a so-called "idealistic" policy that pays no attention to the realities of power. There is another alternative, a foreign policy guided by moral principles but acknowledging that factors of military power, economic needs, and geographic possibilities must all be taken into consideration in making foreign policy decisions.

History teaches that it is dangerous for a nation to ignore the realities of power in the conduct of its foreign relations. History also teaches that it is both immoral and unwise to use power recklessly. The possession of power imposes the obligation that it be used well, an obligation that rests more heavily on the American nation today than at any time in the past because of the magnitude of the power it now possesses.

The significance of power in foreign relations. Let us see briefly under what conditions power can be used justly. Generally speaking, the use of force is justified for two reasons: to defend the essential right of a nation, as for example its territorial integrity or its independence; and to support another country that is justifiably defending such a right. This is another way of saying that under certain conditions defensive war is justifiable. These conditions are generally listed as two-fold: (1) the importance of the cause must be proportionate to the seriousness of the evils that will result from the prospective conflict; (2) all other means to accomplish redress of the grievance must have been tried without success.

The first of these two conditions means that war over trifling causes is unjust. The problem of proportion between the cause to be defended and the destructiveness of modern war is a problem for the moral and political leaders in the country. The second of these conditions, again, is one that must be decided by the leaders of the nation. The average citizen is not in a position to decide whether the President and his associates have exhausted every peaceful means of protecting our national interests before having recourse to war. It is enough for the average citizen to realize that the employment of force and coercion is a last resort in foreign relations. The highest goal to which our foreign policy can aspire in the mid-twentieth century is to unite might with right in international relations.

88. MEANS AND USE OF POWER

The power of any nation depends primarily on four elements: population, material resources, geography, and intelligent leadership. To become great, any nation must possess an adequate population, an abundant supply of material resources, and a large territory offering an advantageous situation for conducting a successful war strategy. Lastly, the wisdom and sagacity of the nation's statesmen is of the highest importance. Other factors, such as the nation's economic system, government, education, and technology, all go to determine what use it will make of the factors of population, resources, and geographic location. The United States is richly endowed with all the material ingredients of power. Several countries are comparable in area to this country, and the Soviet Union is almost three times larger. Our population of more than 160,000,000 is exceeded by that of China, India, and the Soviet Union. But no country surpasses us in combination of the basic material factors, together with such advantages as a highly developed technology, which enable us to make the most of our population and our material resources. Whether the sagacity of our statesmen measures up to these other advantages is, of course, a question to which no certain answer can be given.

The geographic location of a country is perhaps the most important single factor in determining its vital interests in international relations and in shaping its foreign policy. The United States enjoys a singularly favorable location for a great power. Our long coast lines on the Atlantic and Pacific oceans provide us with excellent ports, placed at the crossroads of international commerce, and thus give us ready access to sources of raw materials and to markets throughout the world. The coming of long-range bombers and of remotely controlled weapons has altered the nature of our geographic advantage. Instead of merely patrolling our coast line to secure the country against attack by sea, we now must also maintain a radar screen near the Arctic Circle to intercept air attack over the world's northern ice cap. But the basic advantages we enjoy from our geographic location have not been lost; and indeed the new methods of warfare have served rather to augment our power in the world than to weaken our national defense. As the great power of the Western Hemisphere, we are *comparatively* safe from attack. The countries on the Eurasian land mass, on the other hand, must concern themselves with potential enemies in much nearer striking distance.

The factor of climate is so much taken

for granted that it is frequently overlooked in assessing the power potential of a country. The natural wealth of a country, in terms of food, clothing, shelter, and industrial production, is largely the result of its climate. It is for this reason that the most powerful nations of the world have been situated in the temperate zones of the world. The United States occupies a larger temperate zone than any other country with the exception of the U.S.S.R. A fairly large part of the region occupied by the Soviet Union is dry tundra area that must be rendered fertile by artificial means. No nation has yet populated and developed a fertile region as large as that of the United States.

Prudence in the use of power. American foreign policy must be realistic in the right sense of the word. Nothing is more unrealistic than to ignore moral principle in foreign policy, just as nothing is more harmful to attaining ideals than to ignore the concrete reality of ways and means of attaining them. We must therefore emphasize the fact that foreign policy consists in more than determining the objectives we seek. It must also determine what particular conditions are to be encouraged or discouraged in each region in order to attain our purposes, and it must find out what means or measures will secure these ends. The conduct of foreign policy involves decisions as to what specific commitments this nation is willing to enter and maintain.

Commitment is an obligation which, in the last resort, may have to be backed up with armed force. It is more than a mere declaration to act or not to act in a prescribed manner or to take a certain attitude about other nations' policies. It is an assumption of responsibility outside the territory of the United States to act in a certain way under given conditions. Commitments may be incorporated into alliances or other international agreements. Or they may be extended by a powerful nation like the United States to

This is a view of the council chamber at the Palais des Nations in Geneva as the heads of government of the U.S.S.R., France, England, and the United States met at the summit conference in July 1955. (United Nations)

weaker nations unilaterally; that is, without any tangible return from the weaker country except willingness to "be on our side." No nation should make commitments that are not necessary for its own welfare or for the general welfare of the international community. Moreover, a sound foreign policy must do more than determine what commitments are prudent for a nation's welfare in the world. It must also adopt the measures necessary for backing up these commitments.

The backing up of commitments involves a nation in the difficult problem of the relationship between foreign commitments and military power. A nation cannot prudently make commitments beyond its strength. Military power and foreign commitments must be commensurate. The close relationship between power and foreign commitments has led some political thinkers into the fallacy of advocating what they wrongly term a "realistic foreign policy," or a policy that has regard only for power and not for moral principles. A foreign policy based on considerations of power alone, without regard for right and wrong, is morally insane and will infallibly produce an international coalition against the nation that resorts to such a policy.

Power is essential to back up sound foreign policies, but it is not a substitute for policy itself. Force alone cannot maintain sound international relationships. A sound foreign policy, then, is necessary for maintaining a durable peace, and our military and diplomatic activity should be subordinate to this end. Power adequate to back up national commitments is necessary to show that our diplomatic negotiations are serious and that our commitments are made with a view to being kept.

The prevailing opinion in the government and throughout the country is that since World War II our security depends not only upon the extent of our military preparedness at home but also upon the success of our diplomacy in securing friendly relations with other states whose power might otherwise become aligned with an enemy. Since 1942 our government has operated on the assumption that we must establish dependable alliances with nations who can reinforce and assist us in time of war and that we must strengthen our friends and allies abroad.

America's present program of alliances, military subsidies, and economic assistance is designed primarily to promote our own defense and security. The commitment to such measures reflects one of the gravest problems confronting our foreign policy. That is the problem of how to form and maintain a power combination stronger than the combination that threatens us.

89. AGENTS CONDUCTING OUR FOREIGN RELATIONS

The control of foreign affairs is implied in the very nature of sovereignty and is therefore lodged in the national govern-

John Foster Dulles, Secretary of State under President Eisenhower, has served his country in international affairs since 1907 when, as a young man, he was secretary to the Hague Peace Conference. (National Archives)

ment. The Constitution, however, does not charge either the executive or the legislature with control of foreign affairs. Neither has exclusive control of them. The Constitution authorizes the President to appoint ambassadors and consuls, to receive the representatives of other countries, and to make treaties. It gives the Senate a check on presidential power by making its advice and consent necessary for appointments and treaties. It confers on Congress the right to regulate foreign commerce, and it also gives Congress the right to declare war.

Custom and necessity have placed the immediate conduct of foreign affairs chiefly in the President's hands for two main reasons. (1) He is given power to appoint ambassadors and military personnel, to negotiate with foreign countries, and to receive their representatives. Such powers are essential to the conduct of foreign relations. (2) As John Jay pointed out in *The Federalist,* the President's office enjoys the capacity for secrecy of dispatch, continuity, and administrative unity which make it the natural custodian of diplomatic relations. In the immediate conduct of American foreign relations, then, the President has a very free hand. In determining policies to be followed, he shares powers with the Senate alone and with Congress as a whole.

Department of State and the foreign service. Some presidents, such as Woodrow Wilson and Franklin D. Roosevelt, took an active personal role in the conduct of foreign affairs. Others, like President Eisenhower, work through the Secretary of State, with whom they consult frequently to arrive at full agreement on the policies to be pursued and the ways and means of achieving them. The Department of State is entrusted with a number of "home functions," such as promulgating the laws of Congress, but its main function is to carry on the official transactions of this country with foreign governments. The Political Affairs Division of the Department of State is subdivided on a geographic basis, with each subdivision staffed by men specially trained in the problems of that area of the world.

Daily contact is maintained with other countries through their officially accredited representatives in Washington and through our representatives abroad. The diplomatic functions of our foreign service—as distinct from consular functions—can be summed up this way: (1) to convey messages and inquiries from Washington to the foreign government to which they are accredited, and transmit messages and information in return; (2) to develop friendly relations with the foreign government and to be available to settle minor controversies promptly and amicably; (3) to negotiate treaties and other formal agreements under directions from the State Department; (4) to keep Washington informed of developments in the foreign country that might affect our relations in any way; (5) to watch legislation and other domestic developments in the foreign country in order to see that American interests or rights are not threatened, and to lodge due complaint if they are.

Top positions in the Department of State are filled by presidential appointment because they are considered policy-forming positions. The thousands of lesser positions are filled by competitive examination. They are staffed by career foreign service men who are ordinarily thought of as carrying out policies formulated by the President and by officers in the higher positions. The career diplomats, however, play a considerable part in formulating foreign policy through their reports and recommendations as well as through their daily conduct of foreign affairs—for policy is formulated to some extent in the way foreign relations are conducted from day to day.

The role of the President and Congress. The President plays the chief role in initiating and carrying on our dealings with foreign countries. By reason of his office he is official spokesman for the nation on ceremonial occasions. He receives foreign ambassadors and ministers. The power of recognizing one government or another has traditionally been assumed by the President. Thus the recognition of

President Eisenhower strolls with Guatemalan President Carlos Castillo Armas at Fitzsimmons Army Hospital in Denver, where the Chief Executive recuperated after his heart attack in 1955. The Armas government was established after the unsuccessful Communist attempt to gain control of a Western Hemisphere country. (United Press)

Senator John W. Bricker (R., Ohio) is the author of the controversial amendment to curb the President's power regarding treaties and "executive agreements." (United Press)

either Communist or Nationalist China is a presidential rather than a congressional function, although it is subject to the Senate's power to confirm diplomatic appointments and Congress' power to appropriate funds for the foreign service.

The Constitution provides that the President "shall have power, by and with the consent of the Senate, to make treaties, provided two-thirds of the senators present concur." The language of the Constitution seems to associate the Senate with the President throughout the entire process of negotiations. But experience proved that it was better for the President to initiate and complete negotiations and to present the treaty to the Senate for its "advice and consent," or ratification. In recent decades the President has found it advisable to consult certain senators in advance, especially those on the Foreign Relations Committee, to obtain their advice and their agreement to the arrangements he hopes to make. Either house of Congress has the right to pass a resolution requesting the President to negotiate a treaty, but this procedure has seldom been used in American history.

Not all agreements entered into by the President with foreign governments are treaties. Minor matters are taken care of by "executive agreements," for which senatorial consent is not required. The Supreme Court has held that executive agreements are part of the supreme law of the land. Because the Constitution nowhere defines limits between treaties and executive agreements, the President can evade obtaining senatorial consent—at least temporarily—by labeling his contract with a foreign country an executive agreement instead of a treaty. The presumption is that executive agreements deal with minor matters and treaties with major concerns, but there is still no clear line of demarcation between the two.

Controversy over treaty-making procedures. Dissatisfaction with our treaty-making arrangements has been voiced from time to time. The need of a two-thirds instead of a simple majority is said to make it too easy for special interests to hold up or defeat a treaty. It has therefore been proposed that both houses share in treaty-making by requiring a simple majority of each house for ratification. It has also been proposed that the Senate alone have the power of ratification, but that it be made by simple majority instead of a two-thirds vote. No change can be made in the process, of course, except by constitutional amendment.

There is some doubt as to the constitutional position of treaties. The Constitution makes them, with the Constitution and federal legislation consistent with it, "the supreme law of the land." Supreme Court decisions in the 1920s have led some people to fear that a treaty may enable the federal government to accomplish objectives that would otherwise be unconstitutional. For that reason Senator Bricker of Ohio and sixty-one other senators introduced a proposed constitutional amendment in the Eighty-third Congress (1953–1954) providing: (1) that any treaty conflicting with the Constitution would be of no effect; (2) that legislation making a treaty effective as domestic law would be null and void unless it would be constitutional even if no treaty had been made; (3) that Congress should have the power to regulate executive agreements in the way that it regulates treaties. Most experts in constitutional law declared that the so-called Bricker Amendment was unnecessary and that it would seriously hamper the President in his treaty-making negotiations.

Senator Bricker reintroduced his amendment in slightly modified form in 1955. Most constitutional lawyers continued to maintain, however, that even the modified version would handicap the President and the State Department in negotiating with foreign countries. The amendment would obviously prevent the President from evading the constitutional requirement of senatorial consent for treaties by calling commitments to foreign countries "executive agreements." But at the same time it raises the serious problem whether the executive or the legislature is to play the determining role in the conduct of foreign relations.

Although the President plays the chief role in making foreign policy, he does not by any means play a lone hand. Congress plays a large part in formulating national policies that have important consequences in foreign affairs. It was a zealous Congress that forced the War of 1812 on a reluctant President, and it was an unconvinced Senate that prevented this country from adhering to the League of Nations. One of the most important committees in each house is the committee on foreign relations. In their sessions, problems of foreign policy are extensively discussed. Members of these committees consider themselves the people's "watchdog" on foreign policy.

Relations with other countries can be carried out, of course, only with funds appropriated by Congress. This gives Congress considerable influence over the President and the Department of State. Moreover, Congress has some legislative control over foreign affairs, as the Presi-

dent has executive control. Congress passes laws regulating immigration, for example, and other laws relating to our foreign relations. The President is obliged to enforce these laws. Finally, Congress can force decisions and policies on the President by joint resolution. In this fashion it annexed Texas and Hawaii and ended World War I against Germany and Austria. By legislation it can render the provisions of treaties null and void. It can set up special committees to investigate any aspect of foreign relations. The President therefore conducts foreign policy in a framework of regulations set down by Congress. Which branch of the government is to be dominant in foreign affairs at any given time depends pretty much on the relative strength of congressional and executive leaders at the time.

Limits to freedom of action in foreign relations. Sometimes critics of American foreign policy overlook two serious limitations under which foreign relations must be conducted. In the first place, they are conducted with other independent nations. It is obvious that our government has no right to dictate to other countries what laws they must enact, what products they may exchange, what agreements they may establish with other nations, and what policies they may pursue.

The second limitation on freedom in conducting foreign relations arises from the fact that they cannot be conducted independently of domestic affairs. There is strong mutual relationship between domestic and foreign policy. Indeed, it is scarcely possible to understand many of our national problems or devise workable means of regulating them unless they are seen in perspective with the problems of our foreign policy. Foreign affairs have influenced our national life profoundly. About 85 per cent of our national budget is devoted to defense measures or to the payment of past wars. This means that 85 cents out of every dollar paid in taxes is used to support our foreign policy.

This, in turn, affects our economy, our standard of living, and the things that each family in the country is able to do. Our foreign commitments require that most young men in the country interrupt their education for about two years to serve in the armed forces. The requirements of an adequate defense program limit the freedom of every American. The possibility of air attack in the future plays some part in the planning of cities and the relocation of industrial plants. It gives rise to such local difficulties as the denial to the city of Los Angeles of additional government contracts for airplane construction on the grounds that such industry must be dispersed throughout the country and not concentrated on either coast. In these and many additional ways, then, foreign policy has an important effect on domestic affairs.

In similar fashion, domestic problems influence foreign affairs. Tariff struggles between agricultural and industrial groups in this country have played a large part in determining our trade policies and our relations with other nations of the world. Unemployment problems have been solved—whether intentionally or not—by enlarging our military forces. Surplus products have been absorbed by foreign-aid programs. The connection between domestic problems and foreign policy has caused certain lobby groups in this country to speak out on foreign relations.

No foreign policy could be maintained for any length of time if it were solidly and vehemently opposed by a large majority in the country—unless our democratic system of government broke down —because Congress would soon reflect the majority's will and force it upon the executive. Successful foreign policy must receive at least the passive support of the people in this country. There has been a great increase of popular interest and information regarding foreign policy since World War II, but there is reason

To halt the spread of communism in Europe, the Crusade for Freedom was organized in the United States. It sponsors such programs as Radio Free Europe and employs propaganda techniques, such as the releasing of balloons containing factual information about the free world, across the Iron Curtain. (Advertising Council)

to doubt whether the public is yet in a position to understand the issues of foreign affairs well enough to pass considered judgment on them.

We must remember that international relations have been conducted in a rather novel fashion in the last two decades. The old system of negotiations between the governments' accredited representatives —negotiations carried on quietly and secretly—have been replaced by a system that mixes threats and propaganda barrages, foreign-beamed radio programs and rumor campaigns with negotiations carried on under Klieg lights and before microphones. Even an intelligent and interested public has an almost impossible task disentangling truth from error and arriving at prudent decisions under such conditions.

90. THE PATTERN
OF AMERICAN INTERESTS

To understand our stakes in the world, however, let us first summarize our interests in each of the four broad geographic areas into which the Department of State divides its interests in international political affairs. It is important for us to do this because the bulk of our foreign relations problems are connected with the regions in which they arise. These regions are: the Western Hemisphere, Europe, the Middle East and Africa, and Asia.

America's interest in the Western Hemisphere. Since 1945 our attention in foreign relations has been chiefly upon Europe and Asia, but this should not obscure the fact that our primary interests still center in the Western Hemisphere. For purposes of discussion, these interests may be divided into three areas: North America, the Caribbean, and South America.

North America. The United States possesses an overwhelming preponderance of power on the North American continent. Moreover, our relations with Canada and more recently with Mexico have been friendly. The result of these combined factors is that we have no reason to fear inimical action by either of our contiguous neighbors. Our own security and our friendly interest in these two countries, however, give us a permanent strategic interest in seeing that neither country is seized by a potential enemy who could use it as a base for an invasion of this country.

Our defense interest in Canada has increased with the coming of the long-range bomber. The most likely direction for air attacks on this country is from the polar region across Canada. This is the shortest air route from the U.S.S.R. For this reason we have entered into a military alliance with Canada, and both nations have become members of the North Atlantic Treaty Organization (NATO), which we shall discuss in the next chapter. In the interest of mutual security, the two nations jointly maintain a growing system of defense bases on Canadian soil, and we have stretched a radar warning screen across northern Canada.

The defense of Mexico does not seem to pose the same immediate problem at the present time because it is unlikely that a full-scale attack on this country would be launched from the south. We continue to maintain an interest in the political and military security of Mexico, however, and we shall continue an interest in friendly relations with that country.

The United States also has economic interests in its two neighboring nations. Trade with both of them plays an important part both in our economic prosperity and in our defense measures. From Canada we obtain large supplies of wood pulp, asbestos, nickel, cadmium, uranium, and other minerals. From Mexico we obtain copper, zinc, lead, and smaller supplies of other metals. We must therefore guarantee security of access to these raw materials in time of war. Finally, we are concerned with maintaining good trade relations with both countries because they are among the largest export markets for our manufactured goods.

The outstanding problems in our relations with these countries have been (1) the St. Lawrence River development project and (2) the illegal entrance of Mexican laborers into this country. The St. Lawrence River connects the Great Lakes with the Atlantic Ocean, and rendering it navigable by ocean liners will make Great Lake ports accessible to ocean-going traffic. It will also secure an adequate wartime supply of iron ore from the Great Lakes region. It will enhance the economic value of the region considerably and serve as a valuable source of hydroelectric power to both countries. Because the St. Lawrence is the frontier between the two countries along part of its course, it cannot be efficiently developed by either country alone.

Both Canadians and Americans have long recognized the importance of developing the St. Lawrence for ocean shipping. For various reasons this country long postponed taking final action on pending agreements with Canada on the St. Lawrence River project. After thirty-five years Congress finally took the first step toward joint development of the project when it created the St. Lawrence Seaway Development Corporation in 1954. The corporation is to construct the locks, canals, and channels on the American side of the border, which are to be operated in co-operation with a similar Canadian group. One hundred five million dollars were appropriated for the project, which is expected to be finished in six years.

The illegal entry into this country of migrant workers from Mexico has created an annoying problem of border control between the two countries. Much of the Rio Grande border lies in sparsely populated desert or range land. Through most of the year the river can be crossed by wading. These two factors make it al-most impossible to prevent large numbers of "wetbacks" from entering the country illegally in the hope of seasonal farm employment. The Mexican and American governments have co-operated in trying to solve this problem. It will probably exist, at least to some degree, as long as migrant farm labor persists in this country and unemployment and poverty exist among the Mexican farming population.

The Caribbean area. This area is one of the most important communications crossroads in the world. Through it pass lines of communication between North and South America, between Europe and Hispanic America, and between the Atlantic and Pacific oceans. Our political and strategic interests in this area have been paramount from the earliest period of our national history. The construction of the Panama Canal early in this century enhanced these strategic interests. Moreover, we are tied to this region economically. From it we obtain a large number of tropical and semi-tropical products. It supplies us also with iron ore, bauxite, and oil. Its islands are important links in

Initial work on the construction of locks, canals, and channels of the St. Lawrence Seaway was begun in 1954. It is expected that Great Lakes ports will be accessible to ocean-going traffic by 1960. (Power Authority of the State of New York)

Illustrative of the Good Neighbor Policy is the co-operative agricultural program between Peru and the United States. American technicians have taught Peruvians scientific farming to improve their agricultural economy. (I.C.A.)

our system of frontier and canal defenses.

The most important problem in American foreign policy in this area has been to maintain political stability in the various countries of the Caribbean. We have desired to promote the prosperity and stability of the area because we believe our own security is affected by recurrent disorders there. In past times the impolitic way in which we safeguard our interests in this area led to suspicion and mistrust of the "Yankees" among the natives of the Caribbean countries, but this feeling has been dissipated to some extent by our changed methods in the last twenty-five years.

South America. Our interests in the South American countries are not as important or as intimate as they are in the Caribbean area. The Caribbean Sea tends to link the nations bordering it to this country, whereas the mountains and jungles of equatorial South America constitute a barrier to closer contacts between the United States and the South American countries. Nevertheless, these countries lie within the Western Hemisphere and we consider them within the orbit of our legitimate influence.

The Monroe Doctrine, which was the foundation stone of our foreign policy in the Western Hemisphere, was used to justify a number of military interventions around the turn of the century. Beginning in 1929 a new approach was used in our relations with the Caribbean and South American countries. Called "the Good Neighbor Policy," it stressed co-operative action for mutual advantage among the American countries. Conferences have been held frequently since the meeting of 1945 at Chapultepec to discuss ways and means of building up hemispheric security. Although suspicion of this country's motives lingers on with many Hispanic Americans as a heritage from the past, it is safe to say that our relations with our neighbors to the south are better than they have been at any previous time in the last century.

When considered from the standpoint of power relations, however, it is evident that the Hispanic nations can make only a limited contribution to the defense of the Western Hemisphere. These nations are not highly industrialized. Their populations are not technically skilled. Widespread poverty and illiteracy, combined

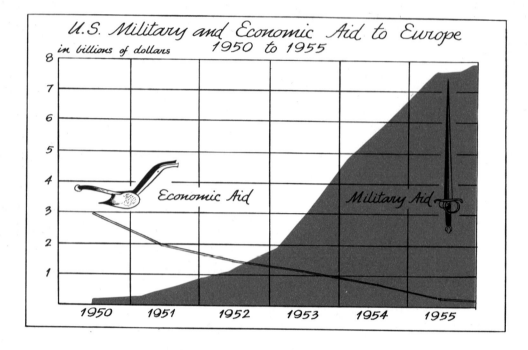

U.S. Military and Economic Aid to Europe
1950 to 1955

in billions of dollars

Economic Aid

Military Aid

1950   1951   1952   1953   1954   1955

with a difficult terrain and a poorly developed transportation system, are obstacles to a unified continental development such as has taken place in North
America. The countries of South America, therefore, do not possess sufficient
military strength to be of much help to
this country. This is one of the reasons

*The imposing United States Embassy in
Grosvenor Square, London, stands on
American ground. Besides being the official residence of the U.S. Ambassador to
Great Britain, the Embassy has offices for
its staff, guest accommodations for American and foreign dignitaries, and is the
scene of brilliant social functions. (Department of State)*

why the United States has sought military alliances in other quarters of the
globe.

America's interest in Europe. The United
States is the only major power with frontiers on both the Atlantic and Pacific
oceans. This creates a problem of "am-
bivalence" in foreign relations. We must
look both ways at once, and we must try
to decide in which direction the greatest
menace to our security lies at a given
time, and which direction should therefore command primary consideration in
foreign relations. Since the end of World
War II members of the State Department
and of our armed forces have not agreed
whether Europe or Asia is of primary importance for our security interests. In the
years immediately after the war Europe
generally received the greatest attention
and the largest amount of American economic and military help. Then, as Communist pressure grew stronger in Asia
and was somewhat relaxed in Europe,
our attention gradually turned to the

Asian theater. In 1955, Foreign Aid Administrator Harold E. Stassen announced that the administration had effected "a basic shift" away from Europe to other "critical areas." Under the new program Europe is to receive no economic aid, but it will continue to receive military help.

The shift of attention from Europe to Asia does not mean that the United States has suddenly decided it has no vital interests in the European theater of operations. It is true that the relative power position of Europe has declined as a result of the revolt of Asian and African nations from European dominance. But Europe remains important strategically, economically, and technologically. If the Soviet Union were to establish control over all the human and material resources of Europe, over its people with their factories and shipyards and air bases, the United States would be faced with the most formidable power combination in the history of the world. We therefore have a serious stake in maintaining the freedom of western Europe.

The combined population of the European nations not under Soviet control is more than three hundred million. Their combined industrial output is greater than that of the U.S.S.R., and it is about equal to that of the United States. The political and cultural influence of Britain, France, Belgium, and the Netherlands is dominant in Africa and significant in the Orient. The western European coast is essential to anything like an "Atlantic community" of nations, where free institutions seem to flourish better than they do anywhere else in the world. Moreover, Europe is strategically situated with respect to the Near East and to North Africa, so that no action can be taken in those areas without reckoning with European interests.

Our economic interests in Europe remain important. Our trade with the European nations has always been greater than it has with any other region. Al-

Senator Mike Mansfield (D., Montana) is greeted upon his arrival at Saigon by two members of the Vietnamese Cabinet. Senator Mansfield, a member of the United States Foreign Relations Committee, is recognized as an expert on Vietnamese affairs. (Department of State)

though it is a highly industrialized area, Europe has traded more with us than have agricultural countries such as Argentina. It is still the largest consumer of our exports, and it sends more goods to this country than does any other area.

The comparatively small size of Europe creates serious problems of defense. It contains the greatest concentration of industry and skills in the world, but its limited area exposes it to the greatest dangers in this age of air attack, atomic bombs, and mechanized warfare. Military experts agree that Europe must be heavily armed to protect itself against Soviet forces. A Soviet conquest of Europe would cost us a power potential almost equal to our own, and it is hard to see how such losses would not work irreparable damage to our defense position.

American interests in the Middle East and Africa. The "Middle East" refers to the lands of western Asia between the Mediterranean and the Indian Ocean. These countries include Iran, Iraq, Syria, Saudi Arabia, Lebanon, Trans-Jordan, and Israel. The peoples of this region are principally agricultural and pastoral in occupation, Islamic in religion and culture, and backward in industrial technique. The area is important economically as the principal source of oil for Europe. It is important strategically because it controls the passages to the Far East and because any power in control of this region could menace Europe, Africa, and Asia. Great Britain formerly held a position of great influence in the Middle East, but the decline of British power and America's increasing interest in the security of the non-Communist areas of the world have thrust on us a major portion of the burden of maintaining the security of this area.

Africa is the second largest continent in the world. Most of this land mass is located in the equatorial regions. It is sparsely populated and economically undeveloped. Prior to World War II the United States had rather few interests in Africa. Recently we have come to appreciate the strategic importance of the North African area, and we have begun to import increasingly large quantities of mineral products from middle and southern Africa. It is the principal source of our uranium supply, and it promises to furnish large quantities of copper, cobalt, and other minerals. The potential resources of raw materials are a guarantee that Africa will become immensely important in the future world economy.

Our strategic interests in Africa have also increased since the beginning of our participation in World War II. The Atlantic bulge of western Africa could be used as a base for attack on the Western Hemisphere, and in enemy hands it would menace the Atlantic sea routes. We are therefore anxious that this area not fall into a potential enemy's hands. The strategic importance of the North African coast is obvious, for it borders on the Mediterranean and looks across the water at southern Europe. Our defense strategy is based partly on American air bases constructed in Morocco and the inclusion of part of northwestern Africa in the area we are committed to defend under the North Atlantic Treaty.

Our strategic interests in the southern and equatorial regions of Africa are comparatively small. Tensions between the native populations and the dominant European minorities in these areas are potential causes of world unrest, however, and we have applied the Point Four program to this part of Africa, as we shall see later, to help develop it and to eliminate poverty and discontent.

American interests in Asia. Facing us across the wide Pacific Ocean is the largest and most populous continent in the world. Asia contains more than a billion people, about half the world population. China has a population of between five and six hundred million, and it occupies a dom-

The cruiser U.S.S. Toledo is shown docked at the port of Ras Tanura in Saudi Arabia. Saudi Arabia's oil resources and strategic location at the gateway to the Far East have become important concerns of the United States. (Standard Oil Co., N.J.)

The mutual interests of Libya and the United States are protected by American military installations in northern Africa. Libyan labor is introduced to American technology as they are employed in building airstrips. (U. S. Army Photograph)

inant position on the mainland of Asia. India and Pakistan, with a combined population of about four hundred million, occupy the greater part of South Asia. These two regions are separated by the Himalaya Mountain ranges, the broadest, highest, and most formidable physical barrier in the world.

The smaller nations of Southeast Asia include some two hundred million people living on the continent and on the island archipelagoes jutting out from the mainland. Japan, with a population of some eighty million, occupies a small island area lying about six hundred miles off the coast of North China and Korea. The Soviet Union must also be counted among the Asian nations, for more than half its territory is situated in central and northern Asia, although its greatest concentration of population and industrial power is in the European area. In recent years the Soviet Union has moved a considerable amount of its industry and at least some of its population into Asian U.S.S.R.

In the past the United States had fewer and less intimate contacts with Asia than it had with Europe or Latin America. During most of our national history the peoples of Asia did not present any threat to our security, nor did they seem

necessary to our prosperity. In recent years they have made considerable progress in acquiring industrial skills and in achieving something like political independence. With their teeming numbers and their deep-seated resentment against the nations of Western Christendom; with their acquisition of industrial efficiency and their drive for a position in the world, they are rapidly becoming crucial to world power and world peace.

Until 1945 Japan seemed to be the only grave threat to international peace and security in the Asian area. The defeat and disarmament of Japan, coupled with the Communist revolution in China and the alliance of that country with the U.S.S.R., created a new and powerful menace to peace and order in Asia. India and Pakistan have become independent nations. India is jealous of its independence and suspicious of any attempt to align it with the Western powers against Communist aggression. The Indian Government maintains an attitude of official neutrality in the opposition of the Soviet and non-Soviet power blocs in the world.

The changed power situation in Asia presents us with some of the most difficult problems in the history of our foreign policy. Native populations everywhere are caught between the longing for economic security and the desire for absolute political independence. Problems of military defense and of economic aid present themselves to each country resisting Communist attack or infiltration. We shall see that American interests in Asia can be understood only when they are studied in connection with the expansion of Soviet-directed communism in that area. Our interests are protected and promoted by military measures, by cultivating the good will of the Asian peoples, and by economic aid designed both to prevent the further spread of communism and to help the Asian peoples grow strong enough to defend themselves.

REVIEW

87. Nature and Importance of the Subject

A. Why is a wise foreign policy a principal protective duty of the state?

B. What is meant by the law of nations? Why are the means for achieving the basic objectives of a sound foreign policy subject to change?

C. Describe the conditions that must be present to make a defensive war justifiable.

88. Means and use of Power

A. Name the four major elements upon which the power of a nation depends. Show how the United States possesses these elements.

B. What is meant by prudence in the use of power? What is meant by the term "commitment"?

C. Why is a foreign policy based solely on power wrong? What should be the proper position of military power in our foreign policy?

89. Agents conducting our Foreign Relations

A. What does the Constitution say concerning the control of foreign affairs? How has custom altered this?

B. How are treaties negotiated and ratified in the United States? In what way have the presidents avoided senatorial consent in this matter?

C. What are the provisions of the Bricker Amendment?

D. Indicate several ways by which Congress, as a whole, can exercise control over foreign affairs.

90. The Pattern of American Interests

A. Summarize briefly the interests of the United States in the affairs of North America.

B. Why are our interests in the Caribbean area more important than our interests in South America?

C. Describe the strategic, cultural, and economic importance of Europe to the United States.

D. What is the primary economic and strategic importance of the Middle East to the free world? Why has Africa become an important center of interest since World War II?

THE CHAPTER IN REVIEW

A. Discuss some of the aims and purposes which must be present in the foreign policy of any country.

B. Describe the roles played by the President, Congress, and the Department of State in the shaping of our foreign policy.

C. Account for the increased interest of the United States in the countries of Asia. What is the United States foreign policy in regard to these countries?

SELECTED READINGS

An adequate understanding of American foreign policy can be obtained only by seeing how our present policy evolved historically. Two of the most widely used histories of American foreign policy are Samuel F. Bemis, *A Diplomatic History of the United States* (New York: Henry Holt & Co., Inc., 1950), and the more popularly written Thomas A. Bailey, *A Diplomatic History of the American People* (New York: Appleton-Century-Crofts, Inc., 1950).

The history of foreign policy is brought up to date and the revolution which it underwent after World War II carefully analyzed by William G. Carleton, *The Revolution in American Foreign Policy* (Garden City, N.Y.: Doubleday & Company, Inc., 1955), one of the Doubleday Short Studies in Political Science.

Analyses of American foreign policy since 1945 are made in the following works: Charles B. Marshall, *The Limits of Foreign Policy* (New York: Henry Holt & Co., Inc., 1954), which is condensed by the author in "Foreign Policy Illusions," *Commonweal* (October 1, 1954), in which the author points out that the administration is not free to do exactly as it would like in foreign relations; Morton Gordon and Kenneth N. Vines, *Theory and Practice of American Foreign Policy* (New York: Thomas Y. Crowell Co., 1955); a thorough and basic work by William Yandel Elliott and Associates, *United States Foreign Policy: Its Organization and Control* (New York: Columbia University Press, 1952), a condensation of which appeared as a pamphlet edited by Maxwell S. Stewart, *Strengthening Our Foreign Policy* (Washington: Public Affairs Committee, 1952); R. J. Bartlett (editor), *The Record of American Diplomacy* (New York: Alfred A. Knopf, Inc., 1954), which contains documents and readings of official papers; five excellent essays on various aspects of morality and power in foreign policy edited by Alfred H. Kelly, *American Foreign Policy and American Democracy* (Detroit: Wayne University Press, 1954); Julius A. Pratt, *A History of United States Foreign Policy* (New York: Prentice-Hall, Inc., 1955), which reviews the principles of our foreign policy from 1775 to 1954; and the penetrating little book by Feliks Gross, *Foreign Policy Analysis* (New York: Philosophical Library, Inc., 1954).

In addition to these works, note should be made especially of *Major Problems of United States Foreign Policy,* published each year by The Brookings Institution of Washington, D.C. These volumes are designed primarily for college and university students, but they can be understood by the interested senior in high school. Basic problems of American foreign policy are considered by Hollis W. Barber, *Foreign Policies of the United States* (New York: The Dryden Press, Inc., 1953), and the Reference Shelf volume for debaters edited by Robert E. Summers, *The United States and International Organizations* (New York: H. W. Wilson Co., 1952). A summary of contemporary alternatives and problems is given by Rev.

Robert C. Hartnett, S.J., "U. S. Foreign Policy," *Catholic Mind* (May 1955).

The foreign-policy responsibilities of this country as a mature nation are discussed from the moral and political point of view by Martin F. Hasting, S.J., "With Man's Estate," *Social Order* (February 1956). The same issue contains a good critical bibliography on "National Interest in Foreign Policy."

PROJECTS

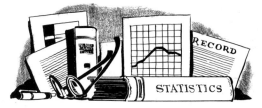

1. A career in foreign service might be an appealing one to many in high school. A committee could write to the State Department for literature on the many and varied types of positions offered and the educational requirements needed for each. They could then write to Georgetown University (School of Foreign Service) or another university for a bulletin describing such training. The day that this information is displayed on the bulletin board, the committee could stay after school to help answer the questions of those students who are interested in this field.

2. Although the law of nations is more readily applied to the countries of Europe, the principle underlying it has always guided the United States foreign policy. Write a newspaper editorial on the need for the application of the law of nations in the world today. Confine your remarks to the United States and its relations with countries of Europe. Another student might write on the relations of the United States with the countries of Asia. A clear understanding of the present foreign policy of our country is necessary before you can offer constructive criticism of it.

3. Consult the North American Defense map that appears in the text and prepare a talk to be given before the class on the importance of the Caribbean area to the defense system of the United States. Include in your remarks the political and economic interests of the United States in this area. A committee could prepare similar reports for Europe and Asia, consulting these maps in the text.

Chapter 32. Our System of Alliances

91. HISTORIC OPPOSITION TO PERMANENT AND ENTANGLING ALLIANCES

From what has been said about the meaning and importance of foreign policy, it is evident that there is no quick or easy method to gain an adequate knowledge and understanding of the problems of American foreign policy. It is necessary that we know something of the historical background of today's foreign policy, for then we shall know how our present problems grew and how our present attitudes toward world relations developed.

It is a commonplace that this country had a foreign policy before it had a constitution. You will remember from American history that the alliance with France (1778) played a considerable part in winning our War of Independence. This alliance was made for the specific purpose of defeating Great Britain—the supreme object of foreign policy for both France and the American colonies in 1778. It provided for combined war effort by the two countries until the independence of this country was assured. It therefore provided that neither country should make a separate peace. You will remember from American history also that, in his Farewell Address, Washington warned the young nation against making "permanent alliances with any portion of the foreign world." Our first President feared that such alliances would open the door to foreign influence in the country and perhaps subvert the young Republic. "If we remain one People, under an efficient government," he said, "the period is not far off, when we may defy material injury from external annoyance; when we may take such an attitude as will cause the neutrality we may at any time resolve upon to be scrupulously respected." Washington did not, however, rule out occasional temporary alliances, since his counsel included the following: "Taking care always to keep ourselves, by suitable establishments, on a defensive posture, we may safely trust to temporary alliances for extraordinary emergencies." Washington's words—and also those of Jefferson, who cautioned against "entangling alliances"—exerted such a strong influence on American minds that our country made no alliances until the twentieth century.

It was not alone the words of these great Americans but also historical and geographical circumstance that kept our government aloof from forming alliances of any kind. Through the nineteenth century we were able to achieve our foreign policy objectives independently.

Early objectives of American foreign policy. The first of these objectives was to attain territory stretching to the Pacific Ocean. It was comparatively easy for us to obtain this territory by purchase, by peaceful and unchallenged annexation, and by war. We could do this because no great power considered the territory we wanted essential to its interests and because our statesmen were both visionary enough and realistic enough to take advantage of each favorable international situation— as when Jefferson purchased the Lousiana Territory from a Napoleon who could not defend it and who feared it would fall into British hands.

The second of these objectives was security against any major European power. This policy was expressed in the Monroe Doctrine, which contained three principal propositions: (1) that the American continents were no longer to be considered areas for colonization by any European powers; (2) that the United States would consider any attempt by Euro-

pean powers "to extend their system to any portion of this hemisphere as dangerous to our peace and safety"; (3) that we would consider interference in the sovereignty of any American nation a manifestation of an unfriendly disposition toward the United States.

The basic foreign policy of the Monroe Doctrine was maintained for well over a century because of a combination of favorable factors: capable American statesmanship and growing American power, especially after the Civil War; a strong British navy backing up a British foreign policy in sympathy with the Monroe Doctrine's principal provisions; a concern by most of the potentially interested governments with other more pressing matters. At any rate, we were able to maintain the Monroe Doctrine without either alliances or formal commitments to other powers. It was a declaration of attitude, an announcement to the world of how we would react under certain conditions. The comparative ease with which the Monroe Doctrine was maintained did not prepare us well for the more complicated diplomatic life of the twentieth century.

You will remember from American history how the Spanish-American War of 1898 marked a decisive turning point in our foreign relations. We became a great power with interests as far removed as the Philippine Islands. Our acquisition of new territories in the Pacific area served to emphasize the need for better sea communications between the east and west coasts of our country. An inter-oceanic canal would serve as a commercial highway and, even more important, as a means of quickly shifting our naval forces from the Atlantic to the Pacific or back again as the need for defense might require. For these reasons we secured control of a strip of territory through the Central American republic of Panama and built a canal (opened in 1914) linking the two oceans. Determination to keep this life line safe led us to oppose with utmost vigilance any interest by European powers in the Caribbean area, and it led us to foreign intervention on our own part to maintain or restore order in the area.

American foreign policy and World War I. By 1914, when World War I began, the United States was one of the world's so-called Great Powers. The others were Great Britain, France, the Russian Empire, Germany, Austria-Hungary, Italy, and Japan. The war completely changed the order of power in the world. The Russian Empire succumbed to military defeat and Communist revolution; Germany was defeated, forced to cede territory and accept certain international controls designed to prevent her from making war again; Austria-Hungary was dissolved. Great Britain, although somewhat weakened, remained a very great power. France and Italy augmented their territory and became even more influential in the world. Japan expanded in the Far East.

The United States in that war demonstrated itself to be, potentially, the greatest of the Great Powers. Our entry into the war in 1917 proved to be the decisive factor in Germany's defeat and led inevitably to our playing an important role in attempting to establish conditions of a stable peace. Although the United States made no alliances and fought as an "associated" power rather than as one of the Allies, President Wilson acted as spokesman for the Allied Powers in the last months of the war. The supreme aim of his policy was the creation of the League of Nations to enforce the peace terms and to safeguard the future peace of the world. This ideal for a time was enthusiastically supported by the American people.

The Treaty of Versailles, of which the Covenant of the League of Nations was made an integral part, soon took on the appearance of a "permanent" and "entangling" alliance. The Senate, with apparent approval by the nation, refused to ratify it and bring the United States into the League of Nations. Thereafter the American government refused to assume any responsibility to maintain the peace of the international world through the instrument of alliances. We furnished skilled technicians and a great deal of economic aid to solve certain pressing problems arising out of the distress and chaos of post-war Europe. We made several attempts to induce other powers to reduce armaments. But we would assume no international treaty commitments for the maintenance of peace by the use of our power.

Realignment of powers after World War I. During the twenty years that elapsed between the Peace of Paris in 1919 and the outbreak of World War II in 1939, great changes took place in the distribution of power in the international world. Germany rose again under Hitler, Italy expanded under Mussolini, and the Soviet Union became a mighty force under the dictatorship of Stalin; but the great position of France was undermined, and many signs indicated that Great Britain's power in the world was diminishing. Japan, which had come out of the first war considerably aggrandized, undertook to dominate China and became a very great power. As the world drifted toward a new war, the dominant impulse of the United States was to keep from being involved in it. A belief had spread that our entrance into war in 1917 had been a mistake. A popular opinion held that American diplomats were "innocents abroad" who had been trapped into fighting other nations' wars and that they were the dupes of munitions makers and other industrialists who stood to gain from war contracts.

This belief inspired the neutrality acts of the 1930s, which were popularly supported and were passed with little debate. These acts aimed at prohibiting American involvement in any future wars by renouncing many of the neutral rights we had insisted upon in 1914. The sale of munitions and implements of war to belligerents was prohibited. The entrance of American ships into war zones was forbidden.

Our government was powerless to halt the dangerous drift to war, partly because of our foreign policy of impartiality to the doings of other nations and partly because many of these events were outside the ambit of our power even if we had desired to interfere. The Soviet Union in these years was hostile to the "capitalistic world" and ready to promote whatever measures would weaken European or American governments. Italy had proclaimed a vigorous foreign policy which, Mussolini announced, would disturb the existing order of powers in the world. His march into Ethiopia in 1935 was not opposed with strong measures by the League of Nations partly because American co-operation could not be counted upon. Germany began a systematic program to dominate a large part of Europe. By 1936 Hitler and Mussolini found that they could synchronize their moves to their mutual advantage, and in 1938 they entered into a formal alliance called the Axis. Japan had meanwhile defied the League and the United States by moving into Manchuria. The Japanese Government began to collaborate with the Axis powers in 1938, and later formally entered into the Axis alliance.

By 1938 the combined military power of Germany and Italy surpassed that of Britain and France, who earnestly desired to preserve peace. Axis power was also evidently superior to that of the Soviet Union, against which that alliance pretended to be mainly directed. So long as this country continued to adhere to its announced determination not to take sides in any conflict, the ability of Britain and France to curb the Axis powers seemed to depend on an alliance with the Soviet Union. The ambiguity of the U.S.S.R.'s foreign policy—which aimed at checking the Axis but also at the eventual overthrow of the "capitalistic democracies"—combined with divided opinions in France and Britain to prevent any coalition against Axis aggression. Even though the Soviet Union appeared willing to work with any power for the limited objective of containing or defeating the Axis powers, it was fundamentally hostile to every power that opposed the spread of world communism. In August 1939 the Soviet dictator, Stalin, came to an agreement with Hitler, who was poised for war against Poland. In return for a generous portion of Polish territory the Soviet Union agreed to maintain benevolent neutrality if Britain and France, who were allied with Poland, went to war against Germany. The German attack on Poland precipitated World War II.

The United States maintained a policy of neutrality until, in the spring of 1940, the Germans overran Denmark, Norway, Belgium, Holland, completely defeated the French armies, and drove the British from Europe. It was evident then that if Britain were conquered by Germany, an immense peril to the United States would appear. Dominant in Europe and the British Isles, the Germans would control the Atlantic approaches to North and

South America. President Roosevelt resolved to help the British beat off the impending German attack.

92. IMPACT OF WORLD WAR II
AND THE MENACE OF SOVIET COMMUNISM

Opinion in both parties came to favor President Roosevelt's policy of helping Britain. The Republican presidential convention of 1940 was swept by a well-organized and vocal public opinion in favor of Wendell Willkie, who in principle favored Roosevelt's foreign policy. Soon after Roosevelt's election to an unprecedented third term Congress passed the Lend-Lease Act in order to extend material support to Great Britain and to all governments who "were resisting aggression and thereby keeping war away from our hemisphere." The Lend-Lease Act empowered the President to provide "the democracies" with arms and other supplies needed to fight the Axis powers. Most Americans still hoped to avoid armed involvement in war, but at the same time they were committed to the eventual defeat of Germany and its allies.

United States strategy in World War II. Eventually this country entered the war (in 1941) and became the leading power in carrying on the struggle against Germany and Italy in Europe and against Japan in the Pacific. By that time the Soviet Union had been attacked by the Axis powers, and thus it became a military ally of this country and the other nations fighting against the Axis powers. The U.S.S.R. played an indispensable part in defeating Germany, partly because of its geographic position and demographic resources and partly because of the war supplies shipped into Soviet territory by the United States and Great Britain.

A major feature of our strategy was to deliver vast quantities of all kinds of war supplies to the Soviet authorities, in order to keep the Germans heavily engaged on the Russian front until we and the British were ready to strike a massive blow against them in western Europe. Since President Roosevelt and Prime Minister Churchill were determined to force the enemy to an "unconditional surrender," and they could not accomplish that purpose without the Red Army, this strategy was militarily sound. But for the successes of the Soviet forces against the Germans, the Americans and British could not have compelled the Germans to surrender. Unfortunately, however, this strategy resulted in bringing the Red Army to the heart of Europe and delivering the greater part of central-eastern Europe into the hands of the Communists.

President Roosevelt and his advisers hoped that our military alliance with the Soviet Union would lead to friendly co-operation in obtaining and securing world peace in a new international order. The President made two long trips, to Teheran in Iran in 1943 and to Yalta in the Soviet Union in 1945, in order to confer with Stalin and pin him down to agreements. The Soviet dictator was a hard bargainer; he exacted numerous valuable concessions and in due course broke all the promises given in return for the concessions made to him. By the end of the war in Europe (May 1945) it was evident that a spirit of mutual suspicion and hostility was entering into American-Soviet relations. Although the Soviet Union helped to form the United Nations and promised to co-operate with the other victorious nations in securing the peace, it was evident that a militant communism had again become the controlling principle of Soviet policy.

Foreign policy and the cold war. All efforts to maintain at Berlin a united provisional administration of defeated Germany failed. The Soviet authorities not only annexed much territory in Europe but established a system of satellite states in Poland, Hungary, Rumania, Bulgaria, Yugoslavia, Albania, and eventually in

The importance of the Near East to American economic and defense interests was realized as early as 1945 when President Roosevelt met with King Ibn Saud of Saudi Arabia aboard the U.S.S. Quincy *off the coast of Egypt. (U. S. Army Photograph)*

their zone of occupied Germany. They supported a Communist effort to gain control of Greece but did not succeed, and made a similar and equally unsuccessful effort to hold Iran. In 1948 Czechoslovakia fell under their domination. Later in the same year the Soviet authorities in East Germany attempted to force the Western powers from Berlin by shutting off all land communication between that city and the western zones of military occupation. A spectacular airlift, whereby American planes supplied all the physical needs of the city from the summer of 1948 to the spring of 1949, defeated this Soviet maneuver.

Meanwhile measures of the highest importance had been taken by the United States to counter Soviet aggression in Europe. If we were slow in reacting against this new peril, it was because it was hard for President Truman and his advisers to realize that the great beneficence and

The Potsdam Conference held in 1945 was the scene of this meeting of President Truman with Prime Minister Churchill and Premier Stalin, when illusory hopes of real co-operation with the Soviet were held by many. As in the meetings before (Teheran and Yalta), the Soviet dictator was a hard bargainer. (U. S. Army Photograph)

good will shown by our country to Soviet Russia during the war had actually been wasted. Some Americans, even in high places, believed that a little more patience and friendly concession would produce a salutary effect on the Soviet rulers.

When our leaders were finally convinced that strong measures against Soviet ambitions were required, they proceeded to help European states resist this new danger. Our aim was partly altruistic —to save additional nations from falling under Soviet domination. But our prime purpose was to promote American national security. Our first step to strengthen the European bastion was to give direct military assistance to Greece and Turkey.

Greece was then torn by civil war. Native Communist guerrillas were aided by the governments of Albania, Bulgaria, Yugoslavia, and the Soviet Union. Turkey was in better shape than Greece, domestically, but it was unable, alone, to set up defenses strong enough to resist Soviet aggression if the U.S.S.R., as seemed likely, should seize a pretext to march into Turkey. President Truman therefore appeared before a joint session of Congress on March 12, 1947, to request military aid for these two countries. In what remains a historic landmark in American foreign policy, the President distinguished between totalitarian and "free countries." Giving aid to Greece and Turkey would put into force a policy of aiding anti-Communist or "free" countries endangered by Soviet aggression.

The Truman Doctrine achieved its immediate objective. Within three years the Greek Communists were beaten and had

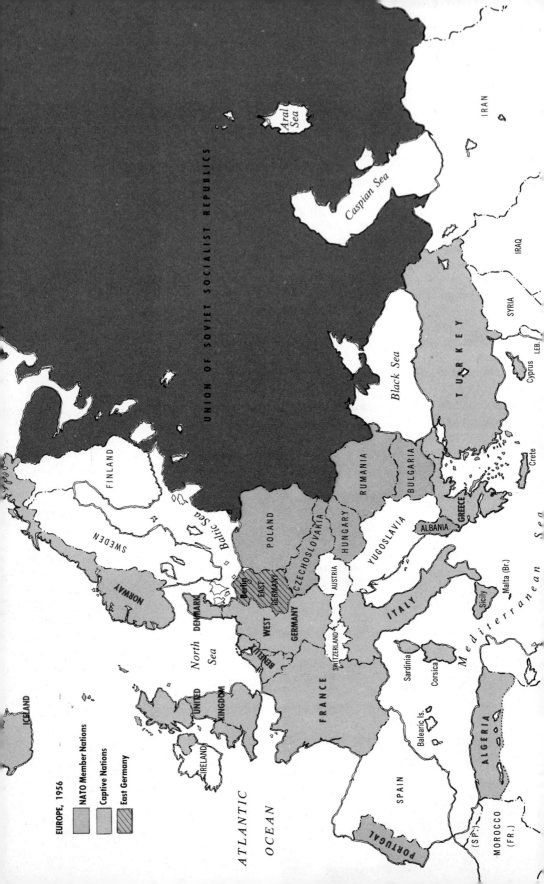

EUROPE, 1956

NATO Member Nations
Captive Nations
East Germany

ATLANTIC OCEAN

ICELAND

IRELAND

UNITED KINGDOM

NORWAY

SWEDEN

FINLAND

Baltic Sea

North Sea

DENMARK

BENELUX

WEST GERMANY

EAST GERMANY

Berlin

POLAND

CZECHOSLOVAKIA

FRANCE

SWITZERLAND

AUSTRIA

HUNGARY

RUMANIA

YUGOSLAVIA

BULGARIA

ITALY

ALBANIA

GREECE

UNION OF SOVIET SOCIALIST REPUBLICS

Aral Sea

Caspian Sea

Black Sea

TURKEY

IRAN

IRAQ

SYRIA

LEB.

Cyprus

Crete

Mediterranean Sea

Malta (Br.)

Sicily

Sardinia

Corsica

Balearic Is.

SPAIN

PORTUGAL

(SP.)

MOROCCO (FR.)

ALGERIA

vanished. The country achieved domestic peace and was set on the road to recovery. Three years of military assistance also enabled Turkey to strengthen its military position effectively. Soviet pressure on these sensitive areas was relaxed. This success was achieved at the cost of $1,800,000,000, somewhat less than 1 per cent of our national income for 1950. The Truman Doctrine, then, halted Soviet aggression at this point. It also committed us implicitly to aiding other countries that were similarly menaced.

The Marshall Plan. Our next step in strengthening Europe took shape as the Marshall Plan. We shall discuss this in more detail in Chapter 34. This plan differed from the Truman Doctrine in several respects. First, it was not aimed directly at the U.S.S.R. but, in Secretary of State Marshall's words, at "hunger, poverty, desperation and chaos." Second, military aid was not given. Third, it required co-operation among the participating countries as a condition of American aid. Finally, all European nations were invited to participate. The Soviet Union refused to co-operate, and its European satellite nations were ordered to boycott the plan. As a result, the co-operating nations turned out to be chiefly those from western Europe.

The Marshall Plan was designed as a cure rather than a relief measure for Europe's distress. In four years, it was proposed, American aid would help European nations clear away war-created debris, rebuild their industrial plants, and recover a working economy. In the first three years of the plan we spent slightly more than twelve billion dollars, and then the outbreak of the Korean War interrupted the Marshall Plan timetable. American contributions were about one-fourth the total cost of European recovery. This plan, again, was successful in accomplishing its immediate purpose of promoting European economic recovery.

The United States did more than adopt a policy of large-scale assistance in the economic and social reconstruction of the independent European nations. We also assumed a leading role in promoting closer political and military co-operation and unity among these nations. The most important step in this regard was the development of the North Atlantic Treaty Organization. Our decision to participate in the peacetime defense system of western Europe committed us for the first time in our history to a long-term alliance during times of peace.

93. NATO, KOREA, FORMOSA

The North Atlantic Treaty Organization (NATO) was created in 1949 for the stated purpose of defending member nations against the increasing threat of Soviet aggression. The signatory powers pledged themselves to consider an armed attack on one member as an armed attack on all. They also pledged themselves to "maintain and develop their individual and collective capacity to resist attack" by self-help and mutual aid. The original members of this alliance were the United States and Canada; Belgium and the Netherlands; Denmark, Iceland, and Norway; France, Luxembourg, and Italy; Great Britain and Portugal. Later, Greece and Turkey were added. The term of the alliance is twenty years. Spain is not a member of NATO, but it has entered an alliance with the United States and it provides this country with naval and air bases. Yugoslavia, which threw off Soviet domination in 1948, is not a member of NATO, but it has received military and other supplies for the same purposes and it has formed a supplementary regional alliance with two member nations, Greece and Turkey.

NATO is primarily a military alliance against the Soviet bloc of nations. Its founders regarded it as also the first step toward some kind of united European

On July 27, 1953, General Mark W. Clark, commander-in-chief of the UN Command in the Korean War, signed the armistice agreement in Munsan-Ni, Korea. Peace overtures had been made by the Communists as early as June 1951, but their unreasonable terms (the withdrawal of all foreign troops from Korea before armistice talks) and their subsequent manifestations of bad faith caused the war to drag on. (U. S. Navy Photograph)

This newsreel photograph shows how Communist-inspired riots in Tokyo attracted students to take part in the May Day demonstrations. The extent of Communist gains in the East became more serious when Japan, recovering after the war under the direction of the United States, was also affected. (International Motion Pictures, Inc.)

political arrangement. Article 2 of the North Atlantic treaty states:

The Parties will contribute toward the further development of peaceful and friendly international relations by strengthening their free institutions, by bringing about a better understanding of the principles upon which these institutions are founded, and by promoting conditions of stability and well-being. They will seek to eliminate conflict in their international economic policies and will encourage economic collaboration between any or all of them.

After the formation of NATO, Soviet policy in Europe gradually became more cautious and defensive. In Asia, however, the opposite happened.

Communism in Asia. Communism made greater gains in Asia than anywhere else in the world after World War II, and conditions in that area are such that it seems more likely to make additional gains there than anywhere else. The problem of communism is complicated in Asia by a completely different historical background from that of European and American countries. A long period of aggressive imperialism in Asia by the Western powers left a heritage of bitterness among the native peoples. Their opportunity for independence was precipitated by the defeat of Japan and by the decline of Great Britain and France as world powers. Communist leaders cleverly endorsed the nationalist aspirations of the Asian peoples. They identified Communist goals with Asian nationalist aspirations, and they also posed as social reformers who would end poverty in Asia and bring the natives a measure of prosperity and social justice. The greatest Communist achievement was a victorious revolution in China (1946–1949) and the creation of a warlike Communist state embracing perhaps six hundred million people. The Chinese Communists, materially aided by the Soviet Union, drove the former government of China, headed by Chiang Kai-shek, to take refuge on the island of Formosa.

The United States and the European powers failed to take effective measures to check the spread of communism in Asia, primarily because they were preoccupied with the danger in Europe and also because they greatly miscalculated the strength of the Chinese Communists.

The Korean War and its aftermath. The inability of the United States and the Soviet Union to come to any agreement after 1945 for creating a government for the former Japanese-dominated country of Korea led to the creation of two rival republics. In North Korea there arose a regime trained and manipulated by the U.S.S.R.; in the south there came into being a new state sponsored by the United States and the United Nations. In June 1950 the North Korean Army invaded South Korea, thus starting a civil war between two rival governments, each claiming to be the rightful government of the whole of Korea. President Truman ordered American forces to go to the help of the South Koreans and appealed to the United Nations to join in the rescue action. The North Koreans were completely defeated in a few months, but then the Chinese Communists intervened. The result was a war lasting until the summer of 1953, when a truce was made which left Korea divided almost exactly as it had been before the war started.

The United States Government followed a policy of keeping this conflict strictly limited and not striving for a decisive victory, lest the Soviet Union enter the war. This curious and little-understood policy was due to the fear that the Russians might overrun Europe if we became involved in a general war against Communist China. In 1949 the Soviet Union had exploded its first atomic bomb, which had struck terror in Britain and western Europe. The British Government, which had recognized the new regime in Communist China, exerted every influence to persuade the United States to the policy that we adopted. The result was a heavy loss of prestige for us in Asia and what wore the appearance of a triumph for the Chinese Communists. They have since shown scant respect for the truce of 1953 and have even aided a successful Communist revolution in a part of what formerly was French Indo-China.

The Formosa question. The Communist government of China has publicly declared its determination to seize the large strategic island of Formosa, seat of the Nationalist regime of Chiang Kai-shek. In 1954, however, the United States negotiated a mutual security treaty of alliance with this government, and early in 1955 President Eisenhower dramatically requested the Senate to endorse his determination to prevent the Communist capture of Formosa. The request was

Generalissimo Chiang Kai-shek, President of Nationalist China, is shown delivering an address at a military function on Formosa in June 1955. Behind him stand Karl Rankin, United States Ambassador to Formosa, General Maxwell D. Taylor, Army Chief of Staff, and Yu Ta-Wei, Minister of National Defense, Nationalist China. (U. S. Army Photograph)

535

TRUCE LINES

KOREA 1953

NORTH KOREA / SOUTH KOREA
38°
Seoul

INDO-CHINA 1954

NORTH VIETNAM / REPUBLIC OF VIETNAM
17°
Hanoi
LAOS
Saigon
CAMBODIA

ALEUTIAN IS.

HAWAIIAN IS.

PACIFIC OCEAN

MARSHALL ISLANDS

NEW CALEDONIA

Coral Sea

SOLOMON IS.

NEW GUINEA (NETH)

Guam

TIMOR

AUSTRALIA

KURILE IS.

MANCHURIA

N. KOREA

S. KOREA

Tokyo

N

JAPAN

TAIWAN (FORMOSA)

PHILIPPINES

Manila

CELEBES

NORTH BORNEO

SARAWAK

BORNEO

MALAYA

Singapore

REPUBLIC OF INDONESIA

Peiping

Shanghai

Hongkong

INDO-CHINA

THAILAND

Rangoon

BURMA

OUTER MONGOLIA

SINKIANG

CHINA

TIBET

BHUTAN

NEPAL

PAK

Calcutta

INDIA

New Delhi

GOA

CEYLON

INDIAN OCEAN

U. S. S. R.

AFGHANISTAN

PAKISTAN

IRAN

IRAQ

SAUDI ARABIA

MADAGASCAR

ASIA, 1956

Communist Bloc

U.S. Mutual Defense Treaties

Manila Treaty

Anzus Treaty

Japanese Treaty

South Korean Treaty

granted by overwhelming vote. If Formosa should fall to the Chinese Communists, our Far Eastern Pacific defenses would be breached.

The position of the Nationalist government of China on this island is anomalous. Prior to 1895 Formosa was part of China; it then was taken by Japan and held as an important strategic part of the Japanese Empire until 1945. During World War II it became the publicly declared policy of the United States and Great Britain to force Japan to return it to China. At the end of the war the Nationalist government of China—then still the actual government of China—occupied Formosa. Not until 1951, however, did the United States and its allies sign a treaty of peace with Japan; by that time mainland China proper was under Communist control. Since the United States did not recognize the Communist regime as the lawful government of China and was then fighting against Chinese Communist armies in Korea, there could be no thought of allowing Formosa to go under *that* Chinese government. On the other hand, the British and several other states objected to the Chiang Kai-shek government, which they did not recognize as the government of China. Hence the international legal status of Formosa remains undetermined, although it is ruled by the Nationalist government and probably will continue for a long time under that rule if the United States remains firm in its present commitment. We have sent large supplies of military equipment to Formosa, and our naval and air forces protect it against invasion.

Our Pacific defenses against Asian communism are good. We have an extensive chain of bases reaching from Alaska to the Philippines. Our naval power is unchallenged. We possess adequate air strength and atomic weapons of great variety. Japan is our ally and with our help has begun to restore its military

"Chiang's Drifting Island" (Justus in the Minneapolis *Star)*

power. Our South Korean allies have proved themselves to be patriotic, capable, and loyal to their alliance with us. In 1954 we took the lead in organizing the Southeast Asia Treaty Organization (SEATO) somewhat along the lines of NATO. The other nations in this alliance are Great Britain, France, Australia, New Zealand, Pakistan, Thailand, and the Philippine Republic. The purpose of SEATO is to protect Southeast Asia against further Communist aggression. All of these developments appear to have had a sobering influence on the Chinese Communist leaders.

NATO since 1949. The alliance of the United States and Canada with Great Britain and the nations of western Europe, Italy, Greece, and Turkey has gradually come to be the most important feature of our new alliance system. At the time of its adoption the intention was to form within NATO a single western European defense system, aided and supported by the United States and Great Britain. That is to say, a European Defense Community (EDC) was to be formed in which the western European members of NATO would combine their armed forces under a united command. To this system Western Germany, still under Allied occupation in 1949, would be admitted. Both the American and British governments were convinced that Western German military forces were

General Alfred M. Gruenther, Supreme Allied Commander in Europe of forces contributed by NATO nations to the defense of Europe, stressed in 1954 the importance of NATO to free world security. (Advertising Council)

necessary to make the European Defense Community able to meet its responsibilities.

Before the EDC was formed the Soviet dictator, Stalin, died (March 1953), and a period of crisis opened for the U.S.S.R. Riots and uprisings took place in Communist East Germany, and it became evident that serious difficulties faced the small group of leaders who succeeded Stalin in the Soviet administration.

In this situation France rejected the EDC treaty, seeing less need for it and fearing that it would compromise her independence. She also renewed her opposition to the restoration of German military forces. In 1954, however, a revised arrangement was negotiated by the NATO powers. It provided for the admission of Western Germany as a sovereign power to membership in NATO with the right to rearm. France was won over by the British promise to maintain armed forces permanently on the European continent, and President Eisenhower indicated that a large body of American troops would remain indefinitely in Germany. This new agreement was ratified by all the NATO powers and came into operation in 1955, in spite of vigorous Soviet diplomatic efforts to prevent it. Thus Western Germany was added to the American alliance system.

This whole development has proved a signal diplomatic defeat for Soviet policy, and the fact appears to have been recognized by the Moscow government. Since the death of Stalin and the Korean truce in 1953 a more conciliatory note has crept into official Soviet utterances, and greater caution has marked Soviet policy. Moreover, there have been reports and rumors of serious economic difficulties in the Communist empire. Early in 1955 Moscow agreed to a treaty for the evacuation of Austria, which had been under joint occupation by British, American, French, and Soviet forces since 1945. For a long time the Western powers had pressed for an agreement to remove all foreign troops from this small country, and the Communists had refused to negotiate such a treaty. Now it was done. It marked the first retreat of the Red Army from a European position since the end of World War II.

Prospects for the American alliance system. The distribution of power in the world has undergone considerable change since 1945, when the United States, Great Britain, and Soviet Russia (the "Big Three") appeared to be able to settle among themselves the arrangement of the world. Britain seemed for a time to go downhill as a great power, leaving the field to the two "super-powers"; but in the last five years her recovery has been notable. She has a large navy, atomic weapons, a very considerable empire, and important political and economic connections with Canada, South Africa, Australia, New Zealand, and Pakistan, all of whom acknowledge the British monarchy. The recovery of France as a power has been less impressive, but real. Communist China has risen to be a major force in world politics and has perhaps excited some jealousy and alarm in Moscow. India, still British in 1945, has become an independent state with the opportunity to play a skillful diplomatic role between the Communist and "free" worlds. Both Germany and Japan have gained a measure of freedom in conducting their foreign relations. Spain is a greater force in the world than she has been since before the Spanish-American War. In the United Nations every member has an opportunity to make its voice heard and to assert its rights and interests. The United States and the Soviet Union are no longer the sole possessors of atomic and nuclear weapons of war. Political power is more widely distributed than it was at the end of World War II.

If this trend continues and world peace is preserved, it is likely that the costly burden of our alliances (which almost everywhere involve some degree of military or economic aid) will diminish. Some of them may be allowed to lapse, and if the grip of communism on Russia and China should be loosened, we probably would give up or dismantle many of the far-flung military, naval, and air bases which we have acquired over a great part of the world. As long, however, as the threat of aggression by the Communist powers continues, it seems likely that the United States will continue to maintain its defensive alliances. None of these is a permanent alliance; all are conceived of as long-term alliances to meet a prolonged emergency.

"Co-existence" of communism and the free nations. Although communism is by nature aggressive and animated by the purpose of promoting revolution throughout the world, the rulers of the Soviet Union have from time to time declared peaceful intentions. They have propagated the doctrine that "peaceful co-existence" between the Communist bloc of states and the United States and its allies is both possible and desirable. Utterances of this sort have in the past appeared to mean that the Soviet Union wished only for a breathing spell to consolidate revolutionary gains or to disarm the suspicions of other states. Since the death of Stalin and the successful checking of Communist aims in various parts of the world, the doctrine of "co-existence" has been monotonously repeated in Soviet propaganda. Much practical consideration has been given to this doctrine by political leaders in the United States, Great Britain, and other countries.

It should be obvious that there can be no peaceful co-existence between independent nations and a power dedicated to their overturn. Only if the Communists abandon their goal of world revolution, liberate the peoples of Europe over whom they now tyrannize, and choose to abide by treaties and the law of nations can there be true peace between the Soviet Union and the rest of the world. The same may be said of Communist China. Of course if such a transformation in the character of these lawless powers were to take place, they would have ceased in effect to be Communist. It would be unrealistic to the point of insanity to imagine that Communist leaders in Russia and China are likely to reform themselves in this manner voluntarily. They appear, however, to be practical men who can be forced to face facts and govern their conduct according to the realities of power. If the United States and its allies can manage to impose checks and inflict diplomatic defeats on them, they may decide to adjust themselves to the world instead of trying to conquer it. Then their

"International Salesman" (Justus in the Minneapolis Star)

tyrannical systems would disintegrate, since a political movement that is by nature expansionist must either expand or fail.

In his Christmas Eve address of 1954, Pope Pius examined the problem of "co-existence" with judicious care. After declaring that "co-existence" was better than "cold war," he went on to point out that any co-existence based on fear and distrust was not to be confused with true peace. It is, he said, "only a provisional calm whose duration is conditioned upon the changeable sensation of fear and upon the varying calculation of present strength." The Pope, however, saw cause for reserved optimism and cautious hope.

REVIEW

91. Historic Opposition to Permanent and Entangling Alliances

A. What were views of Washington as expressed in his Farewell Address on alliances with foreign powers?

B. What were the objectives of American foreign policy during the nineteenth century?

C. What was the nature of our acting with other powers during World War I? What was the foreign policy of the United States during the '20s and '30s?

92. Impact of World War II and the Menace of Soviet Communism

A. What was accomplished by the Lend-Lease Act of 1940? Briefly show why Allied relations were breaking toward the close of World War II.

B. Briefly trace the action of the USSR after the end of World War II that brought on the "cold war."

C. What was the purpose of the Truman Doctrine? How was this purpose accomplished?

D. How did the Marshall Plan differ from the Truman Doctrine?

93. NATO, Korea, Formosa

A. Describe the pledges taken by member nations of NATO.

B. Briefly explain the reason for the spread of communism in Asia after 1945. What have been the unfortunate effects on the prestige of the United States as a result of the Korean War and the truce that followed?

C. What problem concerning Formosa arose after World War II? What is the United States policy with respect to Formosa?

D. Describe the negotiations that brought about the inclusion of West Germany in the NATO system. Show one way in which the USSR "retreated" in Europe in 1955.

E. What is meant by the term "co-existence"? What did Pope Pius XII say concerning this idea?

THE CHAPTER IN REVIEW

A. Briefly summarize the foreign policy of the United States from 1790 to 1917.

B. Point out how the Truman Doctrine, the Marshall Plan, and NATO were effective answers to Soviet post-war aggressiveness.

C. Point out events in Asia since 1945 that have made that area a real danger to the United States and the free world today: Briefly indicate two problems that the Far East presents to the free world.

SELECTED READINGS

Items in the reading lists of the previous chapter should be consulted for this chapter. In addition to these, the following works will supply additional knowledge about Soviet power and the strength of the Soviet Union in foreign relations: George B. Cressey, *How Strong Is Russia? A Geographic Appraisal* (Syracuse, N.Y.: Syracuse University Press, 1954); and George B. de Huszar and Associates, *Soviet Power and Policy* (New York: Thomas Y. Crowell Co., 1955).

William Henry Chamberlain, *Beyond Containment* (Chicago: Henry Regnery Co., 1953), admits that the policy of containment is better than that of appeasement, but he condemns our policy toward the Soviet Union since World War II.

The problem of "co-existence" with the Soviet Union is analyzed in careful fashion by James Hogan, "Prospects of Co-existence with Communism," in the *Irish Esslesiastical Record* (February, March, and April 1955). This is a sober approach to a difficult problem, and it reviews Soviet foreign policy since 1919. Briefer and more popular treatments are to be found in Msgr. J. Kozi Hovath, "Is Peaceful Co-existence Possible?", *Catholic Mind* (March 1955); David J. Dallin, "What's Peaceful Co-existence?", *The Sign* (January 1955); and the article by Anthony J. Bouscaren, "Co-existence: Soviet Victory Weapon," *Social Order* (May 1955).

Pope Pius XII's Christmas message for 1954 was on the problem of co-existence. It is printed in the March 1955 issue of *Catholic Mind* and also in *The Pope Speaks,* a magazine devoted exclusively to publishing in English all papal pronouncements (Vol. I, 1955).

PROJECTS

1. An interesting history project that will aid the class in interpreting correctly the idea that Europe's misfortunes benefited the United States in her territorial expansions would begin with a reference to the map of the United States that appears in this book. On a corresponding time chart the wars and other significant events occurring in Europe during the period of expansion should be noted.

2. A student interested in statistics could report to the class on the extent of economic aid granted by the United States to the countries of the world since World War II. The total compound to the national income, and other interesting figures (e.g., amount of exports of food, manufactured products, and raw materials), should help explain the many reasons for extending this aid.

3. A better understanding of the history of the diplomatic relations of the United States may be gained from an examination of a selection of important documents. Of the various collections, *The Record of American Diplomacy: Documents and Readings in the History of American Foreign Relations,* edited by Ruhl J. Bartlett, is recommended. The selection, of course, is not complete, but it is highly representative. An interesting report can be made to the class if a single problem is traced from the first exchange of diplomatic notes to the final resolution of the problem. Examples of this are numerous — the slave trade, boundaries, intervention of foreign powers in South America, to name a few.

PROFILES

JOHN QUINCY ADAMS

BORN: Quincy (Braintree), Mass., July 11, 1767
EDUCATION: Attended the University of Leyden, Holland; Harvard, 1787
DIED: Washington, D.C., February 23, 1848

The eldest son of John Adams, John Quincy Adams was a student and part-time diplomatic secretary in Europe during the Revolutionary War, when he worked in Russia and England as well as France and the Netherlands. Diplomatic assignments were given him later by Washington and by his own father, and he returned to this country in 1801 to enter domestic politics. Elected senator from Massachusetts in 1803, he sacrificed his home-state popularity by supporting Jefferson's Embargo Act in 1807, resigned his Senate seat, and turned briefly to a teaching career.

The Republican administrations, however, recalled Adams to the foreign service, sending him to Russia in 1809–1814, where he worked with the Czar to settle the War of 1812; he headed the American delegation that negotiated the Treaty of Ghent, then moved to the most important post in the American diplomatic service, that of Minister to Great Britain.

President Monroe recalled Adams in 1817, and appointed him Secretary of State. His outstanding contribution was the Adams-Onís Treaty, which annexed Florida to the United States, set the southern boundary of the Louisiana Purchase, and established a new American claim on Oregon. In the years 1822–1823 he handled the background work for the Monroe Doctrine, which had been suggested as a joint Anglo-American declaration. Adams insisted on a separate United States statement and helped Monroe draft the statement of the "doctrine."

Adams was elected President by the House of Representatives after the indecisive electoral race of 1824: he edged Jackson out through Clay's support in the House. As President, he was noteworthy for not building up a personal political machine and for his efforts to build a network of internal improvements. Jackson defeated him in the election of 1828, the year in which the splintering of the old Republican party was made permanent.

Adams returned to Washington as a representative, the only ex-President to serve in Congress. He distinguished himself in the years 1830–1848 by his strong but non-inflammatory opposition to the extension of slavery and by his defense of the right of petition.

The influence of this Secretary of State and President is well presented in *John Quincy Adams and the Foundations of American Foreign Policy,* by Samuel F. Bemis (New York: Alfred A. Knopf, 1949). His own writings, published in one edition by W. C. Ford (*Writings of John Quincy Adams,* which are very old and rather spotty in content), are now being edited, together with other Adams family papers, for publication in the near future.

WILLIAM E. BORAH

BORN: Fairfield, Ill., June 29, 1865
EDUCATION: University of Kansas
DIED: Washington, D.C., January 19, 1940

After completing legal studies, the young Borah spent a year practicing in Kansas, then moved to the boom town of Boise, Idaho. There his skill as a lawyer and his flair for dramatic speeches (a holdover from boyhood ambitions to be an actor) made him the most successful trial lawyer in the state. He held a number of minor political positions, eventually becoming secretary to the governor, whose daughter he married. He later became state prosecutor, and in that capacity he opposed the nationally famous Clarence Darrow, who praised Borah's presentation of the famous Haywood case in which the leader of the IWW was accused of the murder of Idaho Governor Steunenberg.

Borah was elected U. S. senator in 1907, beginning a tenure which lasted until he died. This long term did not indicate party "regularity": Republican leaders found Borah hard to handle, and he opposed party policy on issues such as the eight-hour day and the income tax, both of which he favored. Borah ignored frequent attacks on his record or personality.

In the field of foreign policy Borah became the unquestioned leader of a nationalist, even isolationist, group of senators after World War I. His speech had decisive effect in the debate on the Versailles Treaty, and despite their defeat his opponents praised it as an objective approach to the issues.

During the twenties and thirties he continued to argue for his own concept of proper American policy: he favored recognition of governments such as that of the Soviet Union, but demanded an independent course for American policy, which would be determined primarily by the domestic situation and needs of the United States. Thus, when war came again (1939), he opposed relaxing the Neutrality Act to permit shipment of arms to France and England just as vigorously as he had opposed American participation in the League of Nations. His was the chief voice of the nationalist wing in the Senate foreign policy debates during the immediate pre-war years, but at his death President Roosevelt, whose policies he had scathingly criticized, publicly regretted the passing of this analytic and forceful contributor to the discussion of American foreign policy.

Borah's career is detailed in *Borah of Idaho,* by Claudius O. Johnson (New York: Longmans, Green & Co., 1936), a hastily prepared campaign biography, published when he was candidate for the Republican presidential nomination. Background for his more important foreign policy activities may be found in *The Road to War* (Boston: Houghton Mifflin Company, 1935), by Walter Millis, and in Denna F. Fleming's *The Treaty Veto of the*

American Senate (New York: G. P. Putnam's Sons, 1930).

JOHN FOSTER DULLES

BORN: Washington, D.C., February 25, 1888
EDUCATION: Princeton, B.A., 1908; Sorbonne, Paris

John Foster Dulles, the fifty-first Secretary of State, has held a variety of positions with the United States Government, almost all of which have dealt with international affairs. Dulles began the practice of law in 1911 in New York City, but from 1907, when he served as secretary to the Hague Peace Conference, to his appointment as Secretary of State by President Eisenhower in 1953, his activities have carried him to the four corners of the world.

In 1917 Dulles was a representative at the Second Pan-American Scientific Congress and a special agent of the Department of State in Central America. He served as counsel to the American Commission to Negotiate Peace and as a member of the Reparations Commission in 1919. He also served as a legal adviser to various commissions set up to aid the economic recovery of Europe and the settlement of war debts. His extensive background as a United States representative in international affairs led to his appointment in 1945 as a member of the American delegation to the San Francisco Conference on World Organization and as delegate to the United Nations General Assembly in 1946, 1947, 1948, and 1950.

Before his appointment as Secretary of State by a Republican administration Dulles had served during Democratic administrations as an adviser to the Secretary of State at the meetings of the Council of Foreign Ministers from 1945 to 1949. In 1951, with the rank of Ambassador, he negotiated the Japanese Peace Treaty as well as security treaties with other nations.

Achievements of the State Department since his appointment as its head include a number of treaties and pacts that have fortified the military position of this country and also helped to maintain peace in the world. NATO and SEATO have been strengthened by his personal attention to these groups; the recognition of West Germany and the ending of the fighting in Korea came to pass during his tenure.

The following publications of the State Department will acquaint the student with the foreign policy of the United States and Dulles' role in its formulation: *The United States and Germany, 1945–1955* (1955); *Making the Peace Treaty 1941–1947* (1947); *The Occupation of Japan, Policy and Progress* (no date)—all published by the Government Printing Office, Washington, D.C. Also recommended are *War or Peace* (New York: The Macmillan Company, 1950), by John Foster Dulles, and the annuals published by Harper & Bros., New York, entitled *The United States and World Affairs*. No full-length biography of Dulles has been published, but *Current Biography* (New York: H. W. Wilson Co., 1953) contains an interesting sketch of his life.

DEBATE

The question: **SHOULD THE PROPOSED BRICKER AMENDMENT OF THE CONSTITUTION BE ADOPTED?**

Affirmative presentation

I. An examination of the treaty-making power will show that this amendment should be adopted.
  1. Presidential treaty-making powers are extensive.
  2. The existing limits on these powers are not sufficient.
II. The purpose of the Bricker Amendment is two-fold.
  1. It prevents the President from amending the Constitution by treaty.
  2. It prevents him from dodging the constitutional requirement of ratification by calling a treaty by another name.
III. This amendment places checks on the President in the conduct of foreign relations.
  1. Should the President be allowed to violate the Constitution merely to have a free hand in foreign affairs?
  2. Our whole system of government is one of checking and restraining the various agencies so they can do only what they are supposed to do.
  3. The President is not supposed to be free

to give our rights away by treaty.
  a. Is the President above the Constitution?
  b. Is he subject to it or can he amend it as he wishes?

Negative presentation

I. An examination of the treaty-making provisions in the Constitution will show that the President's power is limited.
  1. The President is sufficiently limited to protect our rights.
    a. Ratification is necessary for treaties, and no President has ever tried to call a major treaty anything else.
    b. Appropriations are necessary to put treaty provisions into operation.
    c. There is the ultimate check of public opinion.
  2. The President is elected by the American people as a body.
II. The negative believes the basic issue is whether the President or Congress is to conduct foreign affairs.
  1. An examination of constitutional provisions and American history will show that the President has this function.
  2. The Bricker Amendment violates the spirit of the Constitution and misunderstands the facts of American history.
III. The Bricker Amendment is especially dangerous at this time.
  1. The President needs the confidence of foreign powers in his ability to speak for this country.
  2. The Bricker Amendment would weaken his bargaining position.

CLASSROOM DISCUSSION: Let us see if we can agree: (1) That the President should conduct foreign relations; (2) that he should have the power and means necessary to accomplish this task; (3) that he should not be given *carte blanche* to make any kind of treaty he wants. Then we would seem to settle on two questions: (1) Are the present checks on his conduct of foreign relations sufficient? (2) Would the President be sufficiently free under the Bricker Amendment to conduct foreign affairs effectively and efficiently?

SELECTED READINGS

Senator Bricker has defended his proposed amendment in the following interviews and articles: "Bricker Amendment," *Time* (August 3, 1953); "Bricker on the New Fight for His Amendment: An Interview," *Newsweek* (January 10, 1955); "Shall the United Nations Make Our Laws?", *American Mercury* (October 1953); "Curtail the Treaty-Making Power," *Foreign Policy Bulletin* (May 15, 1953).

Strong support is given to the Bricker Amendment in a series of editorials in the *Saturday Evening Post.* They can be found in the following issues: May 16, 1953; November 21, 1953; January 23, 1954; March 6, 1954; May 15, 1954.

The pro and con of the issue are presented in the following: "Should the President's Treaty Power Be Limited?", *Senior Scholastic* (April 29, 1953); "Treaty Powers Debate," *Senior Scholastic* (March 3, 1954); "Bricker Treaty Power Amendment: Background Material and Pro and Con Discussion," *Congressional Digest* (October 1955).

Good arguments for and against the amendment can be found in the following speeches in *Vital Speeches of the Day:* T. H. Kuchel, "Let Our Constitution Be Supreme" (August 1, 1953); F. E. Holman, "Great Threat to our American Heritage: Bricker Amendment" (September 15, 1953); H. Butler, "Bricker Amendment" (February 15, 1954); H. A. Smith, "Treaty Amendment Not Necessary; Edward S. Corwin Memorandum" (February 15, 1954); J. T. Brand, "In Defense of the Constitution: Bricker Amendment" (March 15, 1954).

America has been critical of the Bricker Amendment in editorials in the following issues: March 7, 1953; April 4, 1953; April 18, 1953; June 27, 1953; July 4, 1953; January 9, 1954; January 30, 1954; February 6, 1954; March 13, 1954. It has carried also the following articles by a staff member: Edward A. Conway, S.J., "Darling Daughter Amendment" (February 15, 1954) and "Strait-Jacketing the Treaty Power" (March 14, 1953).

The following are more or less objective and factual in their treatment of the subject: A. H. Dean, "Bricker Amendment and Authority over Foreign Affairs," *Foreign Affairs* (October 1953); "ABC's of the Bricker Amendment," *Senior Scholastic* (February 3, 1954); "ABC's of Bricker Amendment," *U.S. News and World Report* (January 22, 1954); "Why a Loyal Republican Wants to Limit Ike's Power: Bricker Amendment," *U.S. News and World Report* (January 29, 1954); N. Stanford, "ABA, or Bricker Amendment," *Foreign Policy Bulletin* (June 1, 1955).

UNIT ELEVEN
Foreign Trade, Aid, and Procurement

Chapter 33. Foreign Trade Relations

94. IMPORTANCE OF OUR FOREIGN TRADE

Foreign trade has been a most important item in the American economy since colonial times. Rich natural resources in this country and the colonists' need for manufactured goods combined to make commerce with the mother country a big factor in colonial economic life. The attaining of political independence did not change the economic position of the new country. The American government therefore promoted foreign trade from the very beginning. It can even be said that we had foreign commercial relations before we achieved the status of a nation.

As the American nation grew in population and wealth, its foreign commerce expanded rapidly and steadily. The balance of trade shifted as we became an industrialized nation that exported more than it imported, but the volume of foreign trade nevertheless continued to grow until American foreign trade has become the most important single factor in the international commerce of the world. The volume and value of our foreign trade increased tremendously during and after

World War II. In 1940 it was about three billion dollars, and in 1954 it was fifteen billion. This is more than twice the amount of Great Britain's and more than triple the volume of any other country's foreign trade.

American prosperity is closely dependent upon foreign trade. Although the development of American industry diminished the number of finished products we had to import from abroad, a high level of prosperity still requires the importation of some finished products. More important now is our need for raw materials from abroad. Today we consume about 10 per cent more raw materials than we produce. Our increasing population will consume a greater amount of raw materials annually, and our domestic production of many of these goods will decrease or cease altogether.

This country is dependent also on foreign markets. A good part of our agriculture and many of our industries are geared to an export market as well as a domestic market, and the loss of foreign markets would bankrupt many producers in this country. A large percentage of basic agricultural products are sold

abroad: more than one-third of our wheat and cotton; over one-quarter of our sorghum and tobacco; about one-fifth of our soybeans.

Even more important for the American economy is the exportation of industrial products. In 1954 we exported $1,500,-000,000 worth of industrial machinery, $2,700,000,000 worth of automobiles and other vehicles, and over $1,000,000,000 worth of chemical products. Exports account for a fairly large percentage of our industrial production: about one-fifth to one-fourth of textile machinery, tractors, and machine tools; about 10 to 15 per cent of our agricultural machinery, motor trucks, and Diesel engines. By 1954 we were exporting goods worth about $15,-000,000,000, as compared with an annual average of $3,000,000,000 in the period from 1936 to 1940. In this same period imports had increased from $2,400,000-000 to $10,200,000,000.

The importance of foreign trade to the American economy cannot be told in volume alone. The export market is frequently the margin between profit and loss for certain American industries. We are dependent on the importation of certain products that cannot be produced in America and, although they are not large in quantity, they are necessary for indus-

trial efficiency. Such items as commercial or industrial diamonds, chromium, manganese, and tungsten are essential for American industry. We should therefore look upon foreign commerce as an essential and vital part of our American economy, and we should realize that it is to our interest to maintain a large volume of both exports and imports if we wish to maintain economic prosperity.

The nature of foreign trade. Economists explain that foreign trade differs from domestic in only one important respect: the original seller and the ultimate buyer live in different countries. This involves a transaction that carries goods, services, or money over political frontiers. The problem thus becomes as much political as economic. Certain basic economic laws remain in operation, nevertheless, and a government cannot consistently ignore them when it formulates its foreign trade policies.

Trade takes place because of the division of labor and the resultant diversity of occupation that occurs as people advance economically. Many goods that can be produced easily and inexpensively in one country cannot be produced at all or at great expense in others. It is therefore obvious that a certain amount of trade is necessary among nations and that it is mutually advantageous to all nations to engage in a substantial amount of trade with other countries.

Let us examine this principle in more detail. The cost of producing an item in different areas of the world will depend on the advantage of natural resources, of labor supply, and of various other productive factors that one or another area enjoys. Thus Brazil can produce coffee at far lower cost than the United States can. But this country can produce machinery at far lower cost than Brazil can. It is therefore to the mutual interest of both countries to concentrate on what they can do most efficiently and to exchange their "natural" products for those that they can produce only with difficulty and at great comparative cost.

Moreover, even if the United States could produce coffee as cheaply as Brazil can, it would still be advantageous to put American labor and resources into the making of machinery and to import coffee from Brazil. Let us illustrate this principle of "comparative advantage" with arbitrary figures. If coffee could be produced at $1.00 a pound in both countries and a certain machine that cost $100 to make in Brazil could be made here for $75, it would be economically advantageous for Americans to make machines and exchange them for Brazilian coffee rather than produce coffee instead of a certain quantity of machines. For we would enjoy a comparative advantage in making machinery instead of producing coffee. If we were to try to produce everything we consume in this country, we would engage in a considerable amount of inefficient production for which we would pay considerably more than we would for comparable goods imported from countries that enjoy a comparative advantage in their production.

Economists sum up the basic reason for international trade under the term "international division of labor." They show, in theory at least, that just as division of labor within a community and within a single enterprise adds tremendously to the productivity per capita, so too international division of labor enables every country to operate at something closer to full productive capacity. In this sense one can say that international trade is "natural" and that trade barriers *ordinarily* can be justified only on political or other non-economic grounds.

No nation is so self-sufficient that it can achieve a high level of prosperity without foreign trade. Tin is found almost exclusively in Bolivia and Southeast Asia. Chromium comes mostly from Turkey. Diamonds are found mostly in South Africa. The richest sources of uranium are in the Belgian Congo. Specialization has therefore developed naturally among the nations of the world. The British have slight resources of raw materials and very little agriculture in their home islands, but they have developed certain industrial skills to a high degree. Their prosperity is consequently based on the exchange of finished products for food and raw materials. Certain other peoples have developed special skills in which they excel: the Hollanders, for example, excel in cutting and polishing diamonds; the Swiss excel in watchmaking and in producing certain other precision instruments; certain regions in France and Italy specialize in wines, and others in lace and textile goods.

Thus we see that the various countries of the world are economically interdependent, and it is to their advantage to develop foreign commercial relations as extensively as possible. We should also remember that other reasons can occasionally prompt foreign trade. We might want to develop friendly relations with some country in order to have access to a critical raw material, such as manganese or uranium or oil. Again, we might want to extend trade relations with a country in order to bind it more closely to us politically. Or we might develop trade relations with a country primarily to enable it to strengthen itself militarily.

95. CONTROL, CUSTOMS, AND THE BALANCE OF TRADE

The Constitution confers on Congress the power "to regulate commerce with foreign nations." Foreign trade policy is therefore primarily the responsibility of Congress. The term "commerce" has come to include trade in goods, services, money and credit, and all forms of communication with people in foreign countries. Thus a cablegram or a telephone call from Chicago to Paris is foreign commerce from the point of its origin to the point of its termination. A consignment of ladies' hats shipped from Paris to Denver is foreign commerce until such time as the importer has broken the original package and the contents are commingled with the general property of the state in which they have come to rest.

Regulation of foreign commerce by Congress has consisted of three kinds of measures: (1) those designed to promote American shipping and foreign trade; (2) those aimed at restricting or prohibiting trade in certain items; (3) those designed to promote the safety and convenience of persons engaged in foreign trade.

The first kind of measure is typified by the establishment of the Export-Import Bank "to facilitate exports and imports and the exchange of commodities between the United States and other nations." Another measure to promote American trade is the Reciprocal Trade Agreements law of 1934, which we shall discuss later in this chapter. Congress has passed also a number of acts to subsidize the building and operation of a large merchant marine on the grounds that such a fleet is essential to our security.

The second kind of measure consists chiefly of tariff laws designed to protect American industry from competition with foreign producers. Tariff laws have played an important part in our domestic political history and in our relations with the other countries of the world. Occasionally Congress has prohibited trade with certain countries or in certain commodities in order to keep us out of war or as a defense policy in a war in which we were engaged.

The third kind of measure regulating foreign commerce is typified by the navigation or inspection laws passed by the first Congress. These and many subsequent inspection laws are now enforced by a Bureau of Marine Inspection and Navigation in the Department of Commerce. These laws, such as the La Follette Seamen's Act of 1915, seek to safeguard the welfare of seamen, protect the health and safety of passengers, and in general to promote American shipping by enforcing safety measures.

Congress is limited in its power to regulate foreign commerce by the provision that "no tax or duty shall be laid on articles exported from any state." This provision obviously applies to all trade across state boundaries, whether it is domestic interstate trade or foreign commerce. The result of this provision is that we have never had an export tax on American goods shipped abroad. This single limitation on congressional power to regulate foreign commerce leaves Congress a wide scope of action in promoting or restricting our trade with other nations. It is free to subsidize our shipment of goods abroad either by direct payments to the American producer or by payments to the foreign purchaser that enable him to buy American goods. Congress is free to restrict American foreign trade by prohibiting imports and by various "Buy American" requirements for government-supported projects. As we shall see later in this chapter, a limitation of imports into this country will effectually limit exports in the long run. The prohibition against an export duty, then, does not prevent

American banking firms aid our consular service by establishing branches in foreign cities. Here is the Bombay branch of the National City Bank of New York, which serves American businessmen in India. (National City Bank of New York)

Congress from restricting or prohibiting American exports if it so desires.

Federal agencies regulating foreign trade. A large number of civil servants are employed to administer the foreign commerce policies and regulations of this country. One of the major subdivisions of the Department of State, the Consular Service, takes care of some foreign economic affairs. The United States Tariff Commission makes investigations and recommendations in the administration of tariff legislation. The Bureau of Customs, with forty-five geographical districts covering every port of entry into the United States, administers laws relating to imports. A semi-autonomous unit in the Department of State, the International Cooperation Administration, controls the greater part of our foreign-aid activities.

The Consular Service is the principal agency for conducting routine commercial relations in foreign nations. The United States maintains a world-wide network of consulates staffed by foreign-service officers. These officials submit periodic reports on commercial and economic conditions in the countries to which they are accredited. They are instructed to watch for opportunities to promote American trade in their respective areas, to promote conditions favorable to the exportation of American goods, and to furnish information and advice to American businessmen who inquire about economic problems in their localities. Consular duties also include giving assistance to American citizens in

their business affairs abroad, registering births and deaths of Americans abroad, handling immigrant applications, issuing passports and visas, authenticating documents for American citizens, protecting American citizens in foreign countries, and exercising jurisdiction over American vessels and seamen abroad.

The personnel of the consular and diplomatic services have been interchangeable since the passage of the Rogers Act in 1924. But the functions of the two services remain distinct. When a consulate is established in a country in which we do not maintain a diplomatic embassy or mission, however, the consul is empowered to perform many of the normal diplomatic functions as well as his consular functions. Consular officials are part of the executive branch, and they are therefore formally excluded from making foreign economic policy. They are supposed to do no more than carry out the policies and directives laid down by Congress. They play some role, nevertheless, in shaping policy through their studies and recommendations as well as through the way in which they administer national policies and directives.

American customs procedures. The two principal obstacles to a larger volume of imports are our high tariff duties and our complex customs procedures. Most of the laws determining our customs procedures were passed before World War I, and they laid down regulations in such minute detail that customs agents are given little discretion in applying them. These laws—many of which are obsolete—are enforced by the Bureau of Customs of the Treasury Department. The officials of this bureau must classify and appraise imported articles, assess and collect duties, enforce regulations on making invoices, prevent smuggling, and apprehend violators of the customs laws.

Our tariff laws impose *ad valorem* duties (a duty which is a percentage of the value of the imported item) on some items, specific duties on other items, and on still others the higher of the two kinds of duties. The rate and kind of duty in each case depends on how the item is classified. Because the laws governing the classification of imports are so rigidly detailed, customs agents sometimes take several years to pass imported goods completely through customs. Sometimes the final assessment of duties does not take place until long after the imported goods have been sold on the American market, and sometimes the tariff duties turn out to be so unexpectedly high as to wipe out the importer's entire profit. Importing is therefore made a hazardous business because of the uncertainty of what the duty may be and because of the unreasonable delays, unnecessary risks, severe penalties for violation of the customs laws, and the burdensome legal procedures.

A special tribunal, the United States Customs Court, resolves questions of classification and other problems arising under the customs laws. From 1947 to 1953 the number of cases pending before this court involving questions of classification varied from 76,000 to 96,000. Almost as many cases were pending on other questions of evaluation and various customs procedures. The cost of delay and of court procedure becomes an additional item of expense which the American consumer must eventually pay when he purchases imported goods. For these reasons every group that has studied the problem strongly recommends a drastic revision of our customs procedures.

The mechanism of foreign trade. A country must sooner or later strike a balance between its exports and its imports. It is impossible in the long run for any country to export more than it imports unless it makes loans to foreigners which are never repaid, or pays subsidies to exporters to make up for foreigners' lack of ability to pay for the goods they receive. Such practices, of course, are not really trade, but amount to giving away the national products.

Trade is seldom simply a bi-lateral exchange between two countries. It is more often a multi-lateral process in which many countries are involved. Let us take an example to illustrate this point. England might import twenty-five million dollars worth of goods from this country in excess of what she exports to us. This deficit can be made up by an excess of exports over imports with other countries, let us say in this case with France and Italy. In effect, then, the English pay the twenty-five million differential between exports and imports to this country by converting French *francs* and Italian *lire* into American dollars. The point is that the total of English exports and imports, like American, must in the long run strike

Customs inspection of the baggage of newly arrived passengers is shown as the Queen Mary *docks at a New York pier. Trained customs inspectors are alert for any evidence of smuggling. (Standard Oil Co., N.J.)*

a balance. It is not necessary that the exports and imports with any single country equal each other, but rather that the total of each country's imports balance with the total of her exports.

Another complication arises from the fact that services and money or credit enter into the picture. Again let us take a concrete example to illustrate this point. If Italy imports fifty million dollars more from this country than she exports to us, a balance can be struck by Italians rendering various services for which they receive American dollars. Let us suppose that Italian firms insure American shipping at a total premium of ten million dollars, that Italian ships carry more goods in American-Italian trade than American ships do to the extent of ten million dollars in shipping charges, and that American tourists spend thirty mil-

By June 1953, German economy had become stabilized enough to export German-manufactured boats to our country. The American Importer *is shown being loaded at Hamburg with German exports that will help maintain a balance of trade. (United States Lines)*

lion dollars in Italy during the year. These three services balance off the deficit of Italian imports over exports to this country. The balance is eventually struck, then by adding services and goods exchanged among the various countries of the world.

If a balance is still not struck, as has been the case with this country since World War I, then eventually the country whose exports exceed its imports must extend credit to the importing nations so that they can purchase the goods they import. If this imbalance continues year after year, the importing country cannot pay its debts. Either trade relations between the two countries break down or exports are limited to the amount that can be purchased by the importing country; or else the exporting country continues to loan money to the importing country without any expectation that the debt will be paid. In effect, the exporting nation is buying some of its own goods abroad, which it then turns over to the importing nation. It is subsidizing its exporters. This is the policy that the United States followed after World War I until the Great Depression, and resumed again in World War II and still continues.

The effect of protective tariffs. In 1922 Congress passed the Fordney-McCumber Act, which erected higher tariffs on goods imported from abroad. The act was inspired by the fear that the revival of foreign manufactures in countries previously at war would inundate American markets and damage our own manufactures. At that time two circumstances made this law very untimely: First, heavy debts were owing to the United States because of loans made by our government during the war to European states. These loans could be paid back to us only if the European states sent us gold or delivered foreign goods to be sold here and the money was then paid into the United States Treasury; but our debtors did not have enough gold and we did not wish to receive goods that competed with our own manufactures. Second, American businessmen and industrial workers had come to depend greatly on an increased export trade, which required a larger import trade if foreign countries were to be able to pay for our exports.

The new tariff, however, was designed to check imports. As a result, businessmen and bankers, with the encouragement of the government, undertook an immense extension of loans and credits to foreign countries to help them buy our exports. For a time all went well, but in 1930–1933, the worst years of the Great Depression, most of these loans and credit were simply lost, and we discovered ruefully that during our wonderful prosperity of the 1920s we had really been giving away a great deal of our wealth. The whole situation was made worse by the fact that the Smoot-Hawley Tariff Act of 1930 raised our import duties still higher. This law, passed in the early days of the Great Depression, was inspired by the fear that domestic business conditions, already bad, would be rendered worse by cheap foreign competition.

Other great industrial nations were obsessed by the same kind of fear, and the result everywhere was revival of protective tariffs and drastic restriction of imports. There was also a general cheapening of currencies in an effort to lower the cost of manufacturing and thus compete more successfully in the export trade. But when all nations sought to restrict imports, no nation could have a prosperous export trade. Thus it was that all through the decade of the 1930s foreign trade languished. Everywhere surpluses of goods, both manufactures and agricultural products, accumulated but could not be profitably exchanged.

Then came World War II, during which the United States vastly expanded its production of food and manufactures not only to meet the needs of our own war effort but to sustain our allies. Our exports swelled, paid for largely out of our own pockets; and this process continued with costly foreign-aid programs after the war. It still continues. By loans and grants the United States sustains an export trade that annually exceeds our imports by about five billion dollars. How to redress the balance between the wealth going out of the country and that coming in is a major national problem.

96. THE TARIFF PROBLEM IN FOREIGN TRADE RELATIONS

Extending economic assistance to wartorn countries after World War II seriously complicated the problem of balancing American exports and imports. But the basic causes of this imbalance are to be found in our productive power and our tariff policy. For more than thirty-five years Americans have sold more goods abroad than they have purchased from foreign sources. Our productive superiority enables us to supply our needs with a relatively small volume of imports, but at the same time we must export large quantities of goods to maintain a high level of production and employment.

The basic problem in American foreign trade relations, then, is to adopt policies that will bring about a balance between exports and imports. Otherwise the American taxpayer must subsidize both the American farmer and the industrialist who sells goods on foreign markets, or face a grave problem of unemployment of men and capital. Moreover, American foreign trade policy is the most important single factor in the present world economy. In the interests of peaceful and mutually profitable international trade relations we must make whatever adjustments we can in our foreign trade policies.

Such adjustments can be made only by

congressional authorization. Ever since the time of Cleveland, presidents have requested saner trade policies from Congress. As we shall see, they have had some small measure of success since 1934, but the problem of basically revising our trade policies still persists. In 1949 President Truman declared:

If we fail to do our part in putting international [trade] relations on a healthier basis, it is quite likely that some other countries will feel compelled to increase their own controls. Such a development would tend to break the world into trading blocs and could have profound effects upon world politics and the prospects for enduring peace.

In a special message to Congress in 1955 on international trade policies, President Eisenhower pointed out the interconnections between economic, political, and military foreign relations.

From the military standpoint, our national strength has been augmented by the over-all military alliance of the nations constituting the free world. This free world alliance will be most firmly cemented when its association is based on flourishing mutual trade as well as common ideals, interests, and aspirations. Mutually advantageous trade relations are not only more profitable, but they are also more binding and enduring than costly grants and other forms of aid.

Balance of trade can be achieved by increasing imports to equal exports, or by decreasing exports to equal imports. We have followed neither policy in the last seventy-five years. We have consistently encouraged our producers to find additional foreign markets; that is, to increase exports. Meanwhile Congress has refused to encourage an increase of imports, largely through fear of losing votes among laborers, manufacturers, and farmers, all of whom believe they will be hurt individually by foreign competition. It seems obvious that our national welfare requires more imports rather than less exports. American business and agriculture are geared to foreign as well as domestic markets, and any drastic curtailment of exports would be detrimental to the American economy.

Let us examine more carefully the problem of increasing imports to see why economists, experts in the foreign service, and one President after another have insisted that our tariff policy has been fundamentally wrong.

A tariff is a tax or import duty levied by the government on an article produced in a foreign country and brought into this country for sale to an American consumer. Tariffs may be imposed for revenue purposes or to limit or exclude the import of certain goods in order to protect American producers from foreign competition. Experience shows that one purpose tends to defeat the other. High tariffs that limit or prohibit the import of certain goods reduce the revenue, whereas moderate tariffs that permit or encourage imports raise considerably more revenues. During the nineteenth century, when tariff rates were moderate, duties on imported goods were the chief source of revenue for the federal government. In the last seventy-five years, however, when tariffs generally have been very high, they have been a smaller source of revenue.

Protectionism. The dominant trend in tariff laws after the Civil War was toward "protectionism"; that is, the imposition of tariffs high enough to exclude foreign goods from the American market and thus protect American producers from foreign competitors. Some aspects of this problem became acute enough seventy years ago to cause President Cleveland to call the comparatively moderate tariffs then levied an "indefensible extortion and a culpable betrayal of American fairness and justice."

Cleveland urged that our economy would benefit by eliminating or reducing the duty on a large number of articles. He argued that an increase of imports would mean an increase of exports, which would create for American manufacturers "the opportunity of extending their sales be-

"Protectionism" was a major issue in the election of 1884. Protectionists sought to impose high tariffs on foreign goods to protect American producers from foreign competitors. Import duties on some items today practically prohibit their import on a large scale and, in some cases, deny consumers products that are superior to domestic manufacture. (Library of Congress)

yond the limits of home consumption, saving them from depression, interruption of business, and loss caused by a glutted domestic market, and affording their employees more certain and steady labor with its resultant quiet and contentment. . . ." An added injustice of prohibitory tariffs so obvious in our time had not yet become apparent in Cleveland's day—the subsidization of exports by the taxpayer, who is therefore doubly charged by tariff arrangements.

Despite the logic of Cleveland's arguments, the general trend of tariff legislation was to raise duties ever higher. Advocates of higher tariffs defended them on the ground that American industrialists had to be protected from foreign competitors. Otherwise, it was claimed, they would be forced out of business, or else they would have to reduce wages in order to compete with cheap labor abroad. The protectionist argument was made especially for the so-called "infant industries" which needed protection from foreign competitors until they could develop in size and efficiency. The undoubted merit of this argument is somewhat vitiated, however, by the fact that when "infant industries" grow up they lobby to maintain the tariff that was originally granted as a temporary support.

The most popular argument for "protectionism" is that "Buy American" policies protect the American worker and his high living standard. The argument is that when we buy foreign products we give foreigners work, while some Americans remain unemployed. This argument was popular enough to bring about "Buy American" legislation in 1933 which is still in force. The "Buy American" policy forces the United States Government to give special preference and advantage to American suppliers over foreign. Although originally intended as an anti-depression measure in 1933, this act has been kept in force when there has been no need for such measures to maintain employment. Moreover, government purchases of supplies have expanded to a volume that is now about forty times greater in value than it was in 1933.

The general effect of "Buy American" policies has been to increase the cost to our government in its purchases of many items. This increases the already heavy burden of the American taxpayer. It also curtails imports and thus becomes an additional obstacle to balanced foreign trade. Every serious study of American trade policy has recommended substantial modification or outright repeal of the "Buy American" policy. Presidential messages to Congress have repeatedly requested that the "Buy American" act be amended to give the government greater freedom to make advantageous purchases from foreign suppliers.

These arguments for protectionism overlook basic economic laws that govern international trade—the principle of comparative advantage and the principle that exports must eventually equal imports. The most compelling argument for protectionism in our age, however, is the argument that it is essential to national security. The argument holds that, since war is a great danger in the modern world, we should not rely on foreign countries to supply us with anything we can make ourselves. Moreover, we should not rely on foreign markets, for in time of war or depression these markets will be cut off and the American economy will suffer. The decision whether to follow a "protectionist" policy for security reasons, then, must eventually be settled on political and strategic rather than economic grounds.

At any rate, protectionism as a general policy—unrelated to security needs—has been supported by powerful interests and pressure groups, and it has proved difficult to dislodge. Basic tariff legislation since World War I was highly restrictive and on many items absolutely prohibitive. Its aim was not to raise revenue but to limit imports. Significant tariff reductions have been effected by treaties since 1934, but the level of all tariffs is still based upon the Smoot-Hawley Act, which has been characterized as "a virtual declaration of economic war against a world that was deeply in our debt and which we needed desperately to absorb our products." [1] This fundamental policy has been modified, but it has never been repudiated or radically revised.

Tariff revenues now comprise only a

tiny fraction of the total income of the federal government. In the pre-Civil War era tariffs yielded more revenue than the Treasury was authorized to spend. In modern times, when the government seldom manages to raise sufficient revenue to balance its annual budget, our tariff policy not only has neglected but has actually diminished this source of revenue. One of the interesting lessons of American tariff history is the tenacity of protective tariff rates. High tariffs tend to become strongly entrenched because those who oppose them are usually unorganized or inactive, whereas groups that stand to benefit from them are usually well organized and energetic in seeking to maintain a high tariff structure. Each favored group, fearing retaliation, refrains from opposing tariff favors granted to others. Studies of our tariff system show that it is based less upon a concern for the general welfare than upon a logrolling system for the protection of special interests. It has been characterized as a gigantic spoils system with the consumer paying the bill.

The Reciprocal Trade Agreements program. A first step toward balancing our foreign trade was taken in 1934, when Congress passed the Reciprocal Trade Agreements Act. This law authorized the President to negotiate treaties with other countries for mutual tariff reductions. The President was limited in many respects by the original law and by amendments that were added each time the Reciprocal Trade Agreements Act was renewed. No item on the tariff list can be removed to the free list. No reduction can be more than the amount specified in the law—originally 50 per cent of the tariffs in force in 1930. In 1955, when the act was renewed for three years, the President was allowed to negotiate reductions up to 5 per cent of the tariff for each of three succeeding years, or a total of 15 per cent.

Protectionist forces in Congress have all but nullified the Reciprocal Trade

---

[1] C. Grove Haines and Ross J. S. Hoffman, *The Origin and Background of the Second World War* (New York: Oxford University Press, 1947), p. 303.

Agreements Act by adding the "escape clause" and "peril-point" provisions. The President is obliged to include an escape clause in each treaty whereby we can cancel any provision in the treaty that turns out to be "too generous." In other words, the purpose of the act with many congressmen is to increase exports without increasing imports proportionately. Trade with countries with which we enacted reciprocal trade treaties has increased considerably, but the imbalance between imports and exports continues. Our exports to these countries went up 65 per cent, and our imports increased only 27 per cent. The peril-point provision requires the executive to cancel any treaty provisions that allow the importation of items that tend to reduce prices in this country below a certain level considered normal. These provisions have applied chiefly to agricultural products, and they have been forced on the administration by congressmen from the Midwest more than by any other group. Only one significant trade treaty has been negotiated since the escape clause and peril-point provisions were written into the law.

Although the Reciprocal Trade Agree-

REDUCTION OF DUTIES ON IMPORTS (1935 AND 1954 COMPARED)
(*In thousands of dollars*)

	1935			1954		
	Values	Duties	Per-cent	Values	Duties	Per-cent
Chemicals, oils, and paints	66,105	28,205	42.67	174,520	24,690	14.15
Earths, earthenware, and glassware	22,853	11,636	50.92	127,883	31,320	24.50
Metals and manufactures	68,013	23,305	34.27	978,541	117,071	11.96
Wood and manufactures	12,657	2,923	23.09	263,484	15,813	6.00
Sugar, molasses, and manufactures	94,953	39,985	42.11*	354,741	34,748	9.80
Tobacco and manufactures	25,974	21,958	84.54	84,845	17,161	20.23
Agricultural products and provisions	219,133	87,559	39.96	692,687	63,608	9.18
Spirits, wines, and other beverages	42,384	39,326	92.79	155,995	36,493	23.39
Cotton manufactures	27,136	10,852	39.99	60,426	12,783	21.15
Flax, hemp, jute, and manufactures	62,430	15,083	24.16	115,263	8,215	7.13
Wool and manufactures	28,857	23,510	81.47	266,219	56,636	21.27
Silk and manufactures	6,039	3,557	58.90	26,203	7,885	30.09
Rayon and other synthetic textiles, manufactures	1,730	831	48.03	27,054	5,983	22.12
Pulp, paper, and books	11,118	2,697	24.26	48,633	4,701	9.67
Sundries	11,030	36,172	32.58	306,074	61,308	20.03

ments Act was the first step in revising our protectionist foreign trade policy, it cannot by itself bring about any large-scale improvement of international trade. The amount of tariff reduction is rigidly limited; the number and kinds of items that can be put on the free list are also limited. Moreover, Congress must renew the act every three years or less. Each time it comes up for renewal the act is subjected to additional crippling amendments pushed by various groups, each interested in maintaining a high tariff on its own product. Trade experts predicted when the act was passed in 1955 that its net effect would be to keep tariffs about the same for the following three years.

Let us conclude our discussion of these problems by summarizing the recommendations of various commissions and experts who have studied our foreign trade problems in recent years. (1) The President should be granted broader powers under the Reciprocal Trade Agreements Act to reduce American tariffs substantially by multi-lateral as well as bi-lateral negotiations. (2) The instability and uncertainty of our foreign trade policy, which make negotiations with other nations difficult, should be corrected by the elimination of escape clauses and peril-point provisions and by not requiring a renewal of tariff legislation every three years or less. (3) Drastic revision of our customs procedures should be accomplished with the general aim of safeguarding the welfare of Americans rather than making it difficult or impossible to import goods into this country.

The object of a sound foreign trade policy is to strengthen the national economy, to increase domestic production, and to raise the general standard of living in this country. Legislation should therefore aim at promoting the national interest rather than the interest of any small group of producers of some article or other. Certain industries should be pro-

tected for military and political reasons, of course, because this is in the national interest. American producers should also be protected from unfair competition from foreign producers who are subsidized by their governments or who would sell their products below cost in this country to get rid of a surplus.

REVIEW

94. Importance of Our Foreign Trade

A. What were the circumstances that contributed to the important position of foreign trade in the pattern of colonial life in this country?

B. Indicate how American prosperity today is quite dependent on foreign markets. Point out the part imports play in our economy.

C. Describe the political factors that differentiate foreign trade from domestic trade.

D. Explain why trade between countries is of advantage to all. What is meant by the term "international division of labor"?

95. Control, Customs, and the Balance of Trade

A. What forms of trade does the term "foreign commerce" encompass?

B. What kinds of regulations has Congress enacted concerning foreign commerce? Give an example of each type.

C. What is the single limitation that binds Congress in its regulation of foreign commerce?

D. Describe the work of the Consular Service in administering the foreign trade policies of this country.

E. What are the two principal obstacles to an increased volume of imports into this country?

F. Explain briefly the foreign trade policy of the United States with a country whose imports exceed its exports.

96. The Tariff Problem in Foreign Trade Relations

A. What is the basic problem in American foreign trade relations today?

B. Define a tariff. What can be the twofold purpose of a tariff?

C. What was the value of the "infant industries argument"? How has it become obsolete? What has been the general effect of the "Buy American" trade policies?

D. Describe the purpose of the Reciprocal Trade Agreement Act of 1934. What provisions of the act have all but nullified the ideal of the Reciprocal Act?

THE CHAPTER IN REVIEW

A. Explain why foreign trade has been and is important to the American economy.

B. Contrast the value of tariff revenues to our national income between the pre-Civil War period and the present day.

C. Summarize American tariff history since World War I, pointing out how most of these laws have been unrealistic or have been badly applied.

D. Summarize the recommendations of the various commissions who have studied our foreign trade problems in recent years.

SELECTED READINGS

Two books on foreign trade, which discuss the arguments in favor of protection but conclude that lower tariffs are necessary, appeared shortly after the end of World War II. Nevertheless, they are still of considerable value for their discussion of basic arguments about the tariff. They are Michael A. Helperin, *The Trade of Nations* (New York: Alfred A. Knopf, Inc., 1947), and Norman S. Buchanan and Friedrich A. Lutz, *Rebuilding the World Economy* (New York: The Twentieth Century Fund, 1947). More recent studies are Howard S. Piquet, *Aid, Trade, and the Tariff* (New York: Thomas Y. Crowell Co., 1953), and Clarence B. Randall, *A Foreign Economic Policy for the United States* (Chicago: University of Chicago Press, 1954). The Reference Shelf book for debaters, *Aid, Trade, and Tariffs*, edited by Clifton H. Kreps, Jr., and Juanita Morris Kreps (New York: H. W. Wilson Co., 1953), has good articles on both sides of the question.

The Catholic Association for International Peace has published the pamphlet, *Tariffs and World Peace,* by Rev. Thomas F. Divine, S.J. (Washington: C.A.I.P.), and another by Sister M. Thomasine, O.P., *The International Trade Organization* (Washington: C.A.I.P.). Essential for any discussion of this subject is the report to the President by the Public Advisory Board for Mutual Security, *A Trade and Tariff Policy in the National Interest* (Washington: Government Printing Office, 1953). Government publications all favor freer trade as the policy the administration has tried to promote in Congress for many years. Important among these publications are: *What the International Bank Means to You* (Washington: International Bank for Reconstruction and Development, 1947); and *Together We Are Strong* (Washington: Government Printing Office, 1952). Private organizations favoring reform of tariff policy have published the following pamphlets: *The Citizen and International Trade* (Washington: League of Women Voters, 1952); J. B. Condliffe, *International Trade and Economic Nationalism* (Washington: Carnegie Endowment for International Peace, 1951); and Beatrice Pitney Lamb, *Trade—and Aid* (Washington: Public Affairs Press, 1953).

PROJECTS

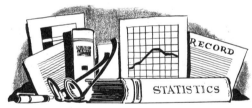

1. Make up a chart showing the principal exports and imports of the United States during the past five years. This will give us a better idea of what we have produced for the foreign market and what we need from other countries.

2. Try to envision what ordinary daily life would be like without any imports. A group could draw up a list of items which we would not have except for imports. They could then show what effect the lack of these items might have on the standard of living.

3. Make a list of the important tariffs in American history, noting the date, the name of the tariff, its purpose, who was President, and what it might have accomplished. This will give you a clear picture of our past tariff history.

Chapter 34. American Foreign Aid
and Procurement Programs

97. REASONS FOR EXTENDING FOREIGN AID

The destruction of World War II was without parallel in history. Not only were millions of lives and billions of dollars' worth of property destroyed, but trade relations, production, and anything like a stabilized economy were disrupted everywhere. The bombings in Europe left many cities little more than heaps of rubble. Transportation facilities were disrupted. Factories were destroyed or damaged in most parts of Europe. As a result, the peoples of Europe were unable to supply the goods and services needed to keep themselves alive. They depended on other parts of the world that had not been seriously damaged to supply them with food and other basic requirements.

The most important producing area in the world at the end of World War II was the United States. Its productive power had expanded enormously during the war. It was therefore natural for American industrialists and farmers, having expanded their productive capacity, to look for foreign markets to absorb their sur-

pluses. It was natural also for Europeans to look to America for the goods they needed. The basic problem in such a natural trade arrangement was this: How were Europeans, who could not produce anything for export, to pay for the goods they imported from this country? Immediate relief did not present a serious, lasting problem. Americans were willing to write off relief measures as unrecoverable expenditures designed to keep starving people alive and warm. Within a short time, however, it became apparent that relief measures were not enough. Relief alone would never bring about a recovery of the European economy.

The problem of rebuilding Europe's economy was made more difficult and its solution was needed urgently because of Soviet exploitation of want and distress in the war-torn areas of Europe. The Soviet Union seized control of eastern Europe, as we have seen, and it did not allow its satellite countries to participate in any trade arrangements with western Europe. The Soviet Union integrated the economy of central-eastern Europe into its own, and thus it made more difficult

any general economic recovery of the remaining states of Europe. Moreover, failure by the western countries to solve their economic problems increased their fear of Soviet expansion across their borders. A solution to the problem of recovery from the damages and the disruption of the war therefore became urgent for the western European countries.

Economic recovery in Europe. It is probable that European recovery could not have been accomplished in less than a generation without American aid. Europe is economically a deficit area that must import raw materials to maintain its industry and its population. For several decades it had faced increasing difficulty in selling abroad because of its obsolescent equipment, because America had been producing so efficiently and cheaply, and because of high tariffs in this and other countries. Moreover, the increasing industrialization of the rest of the world decreased the demand for European goods and utilized more of the world's supply of raw materials. All these factors militated against a substantial recovery of the European economy.

Economic recovery in Europe occupied a high place in American foreign policy. Europe has always been the largest market for American exports. We saw in the previous chapter that sound trade relations can be maintained only if there is a balance between exports and imports and that our trade with Europe was conducted in the decades before World War II only through large American loans. It was in America's interest to eliminate or reduce the huge deficit in our trade with Europe, and this could not be done until, among other things, Europe recovered economically. Even more important, durable peace could not be established until Europe's economy operated productively again. Finally, in the years after the war it seemed probable that if European economic recovery did not take place quickly communism or some other radical solution would be tried by the desperate peoples of western Europe.

The United States was the only nation able to assist Europe in solving its economic problems, for this country alone had the resources and the political interest to invest billions of dollars in European recovery. Since the end of the war we have spent about fifty billion dollars in foreign-assistance programs, and the greater part of this aid has been expended in the European area. In the first few years after the war most of these grants were for direct relief of populations uprooted and impoverished by the

CARE, a non-profit organization that is supported by the generosity of individuals, has shipped supplies to needy peoples all over the world. This display of the genuine interest of Americans in the welfare of the less fortunate helps the world to understand that Christian democracy means a love for all people. (Advertising Council)

war. The programs developed in piecemeal fashion at first, apparently on the assumption that they were emergency measures that would be needed for only a short time. Generally speaking, they were successful in accomplishing their immediate purposes of furnishing food and shelter to homeless people, rehabilitating millions of refugees, and restoring the European economy to a high level of production again.

But in the decade after the war American foreign-aid programs assumed a permanent character. Unless there is a sudden and surprising reversal of our foreign policy, they will be part of our foreign relations for many years to come.

Administering the Marshall Plan. In the two years after the conclusion of war we had advanced more than sixteen billion dollars in aid to Europe, but it was clear that normal economic conditions were still far from established. Secretary of State Marshall stated that further American assistance "should provide a cure rather than a mere palliative." In his famous Harvard University commencement address, Marshall went on to define the problem in these terms:

Europe's requirements for the next three or four years of foreign foods and other essential products—principally from America—are so much greater than her present ability to pay that she must have substantial additional help or face economic, social, and political deterioration of a very grave character.

Before, however, the United States can proceed much further in its efforts to alleviate the situation and help start the European world on its way to recovery, there must be some agreement among the countries of Europe as to whatever action might be undertaken by this Government.

It would be neither fitting nor efficacious for the Government to draw up unilaterally a program designed to place Europe on its feet economically. . . . ·The initiative . . . must come from Europe.

An invitation to participate in the plan was extended to all the countries of Europe, including the Soviet Union and her satellites. Eventually sixteen countries took part in the Marshall Plan. Representatives from these countries pledged themselves to do everything possible to balance their budgets, combat inflation, and stabilize their currencies. They also planned to abolish abnormal trade restrictions and to create a sound multilateral trading system among the participating nations. The sixteen nations outlined a plan for economic recovery to be completed by 1951. It involved modernization of equipment and the dovetailing of the various countries' economies to create an integrated economy among the countries of western Europe.

The plans called for somewhat more than nineteen billion dollars from the United States. These funds were to be furnished in the form of grants rather than loans. In return, the United States was to exercise a measure of control over the participating countries' budgets. A large part of the supplies and technical assistance would be furnished by Americans, of course, and thus a goodly share of the expenditures for European recovery would ultimately be spent in this country. Emphasis was to be laid at first on getting food, fertilizers, fuel, and agricultural equipment, as well as such important basic materials as iron and steel. Later the emphasis was to be on machinery and improved industrial technique.

President Truman requested Congress to appropriate seventeen billion dollars for the European Recovery Program, to be spent over a four-year period beginning in 1948. Although there was considerable opposition to the request, it was ultimately passed by Congress with certain modifications. Congress cut Truman's first-year request from $6,800,-000,000 to five billion, made one-fifth of it a loan instead of a grant, required half the goods to be shipped at higher rates in American vessels, added a subsidy-to-American-agriculture clause, and required the participants to help furnish stockpiles of strategic materials to us.

The European Recovery Program worked more successfully than either its critics or its advocates anticipated. Within a year industrial production in the ERP countries increased 14 per cent and agricultural production was up 20 per cent. By 1950 industrial production was 20 per cent above the pre-war level, and intra-European trade had increased 14 per cent over the amount in 1938. The European balance of exports and imports had improved from an eight-billion-dollar deficit in 1947 to a one-billion-dollar deficit in 1950. The plan had worked so well that in 1951 four countries (Great Britain, Ireland, Portugal,

General George C. Marshall, who as Secretary of State was the author of the Marshall Plan, believed that aid for Europe should not merely relieve the pain of a disrupted economy but should do all that is possible toward effecting a real cure. (National Archives)

and Sweden) announced they no longer required ERP assistance.

Military aid to Europe. The original plan was to accomplish the economic reconstruction and recovery of Europe within four years. Before the program was completed, however, the Korean War broke out and the United States had to revise its foreign program drastically. European economic aid was reduced as direct military aid took precedence over economic measures. Meanwhile the increased pressure of communism in the Asian area caused us to concentrate on the economic rehabilitation of the underdeveloped areas of the world rather than on Europe. Although the ERP was cut short, nevertheless it can be pronounced a success as far as achieving its immediate objective is concerned. The American contribution to this program, apart from the initiative and supervision we furnished, amounted to about one-fourth the total cost. The rest was furnished by the European taxpayers.

After 1951, American assistance assumed a distinctly military character. Under the Mutual Defense Assistance Program the United States subsidizes the construction of defense facilities for our own forces and those of the Allied countries abroad. The Direct Forces Support Program subsidizes the manufacture of arms and other military equipment in foreign plants for Allied or NATO military forces. The aim of our economic aid to Europe has been increasingly narrowed to military purposes. This has

been done in the belief that the European economy is now fairly healthy and that help is needed more urgently in other areas.

The Point Four program. Economic aid is by no means confined to Europe. By 1955 various foreign-aid programs were being carried out in the Near East and Africa, in the Far East and Latin America, as well as in Europe. The European area seemed to be the most important to strengthen in the years immediately after the war, and we have seen that it continues to receive military aid. But the course of events has shifted our emphasis in foreign policy to the Asian area as the place where Communist pressure has become the greatest. The Communist military triumph in China, the Korean War, and the threat of additional violent aggression in Indo-China combined to bring about this changed emphasis.

Aid in this area differs in many ways from help to the highly developed economies of western Europe. The underdeveloped areas of the world present an even more difficult problem to this country. They present a fertile ground for Communist activity because of their poverty and their revolt against Western imperialism. Any successful foreign policy in this area involves raising the native peoples from their condition of abject poverty and resentment against the Western countries. In the contest that has unfortunately developed between the Soviet Union and this country the vast areas of the globe that are underdeveloped and impoverished economically can ally themselves either with the Soviet-dominated bloc of countries or with the nations clustering around the United States. Which way they will go depends to a great extent on the help we afford them in developing their economies in order to diminish the poverty in which their populations live.

Economic development in most of the Asian area cannot advance without extensive foreign help. Such development can be accomplished only when there is a combination of two important ingredients: (1) technological skill or "know-how," such as has been developed so intensively in this country and in western Europe; (2) capital, or the machinery, tools, fertilizers, equipment, transportation facilities, and other material means to increase the productivity of the land and of labor in these areas.

Most of the communities in Asia are hardly able even to sustain life, let alone lay aside a surplus for capital investment with which to develop their economies. Even with foreign help they cannot reasonably develop the necessary skills and capital for economic prosperity without first reducing the illiteracy, malnutrition, and disease which prevent them from efficiently utilizing their large labor supply. For these reasons, problems of education, health, and nutrition become important aspects of the general problem of economic development in the impoverished areas of Asia.

The United States took official recognition of the problem of underdeveloped

Aid to Europe after World War II changed from economic to military when recovery in the stricken countries was in evidence. Aid to Austria had included materials and technical advice to build dams and power plants, such as this one near Vienna. (ICA)

President Truman added a fourth point to our foreign policy when he stated that we should embark on a program to make known the technical and scientific advances of this nation to the backward countries of the world.

areas and of our interest in promoting their development by means of technical assistance and capital investment when President Truman proclaimed the so-called Point Four policy in 1949. In his inaugural message of that year he assured the world that we would support the United Nations, we would continue our program for world recovery, and we would strengthen Allied and friendly nations against the danger of Soviet-backed aggression. Then he added a fourth point to our foreign policy in these words:

> We must embark on a bold new program for making the benefits of our scientific advances and industrial progress available for the improvement and growth of underdeveloped areas. . . . We should make available to peace-loving peoples the benefits of our store of technical knowledge in order to help them realize their aspirations for a better life. And, in cooperation with other nations, we should foster capital investment in areas needing development. Our own aim should be to help the free peoples of the world through their own efforts, to produce more food, more clothing, more materials for housing, and more mechanical power to lighten their burdens.

The United States was not alone in recognizing the need of technical assistance and capital investment to promote the economic development of the retarded areas of the world. The United Nations had previously started programs of technical assistance and economic development for these areas, and the problem immediately arose as to whether American aid should be channeled exclusively through the UN or whether a large part of it should be extended independently by this country.

Objectives and problems of Point Four. President Truman's Point Four program ran into difficulties in Congress. It was implemented, over vigorous objection by some congressmen, by the Act for International Development in 1950 and by several subsequent laws. In the first year only $34,500,000 was allotted to the program. Of this amount twelve million went to the United Nations technical assistance program. Only two million dollars was set aside for the Far East. As the problem became clearer with Communist pressure increasing in Asia, however, a larger proportion of Point Four funds was given to the Far East, and funds in the other areas of the world were proportionately reduced. In 1955 the Eisenhower administration requested $1,500,-000,000 for economic aid in the Far East and nothing at all for European economic aid.

The problem of developing economically retarded areas cannot easily or quickly be solved. Technical skills are not quickly acquired, and capital investment frequently does not show appreciable returns for many years. Nevertheless, a considerable degree of success can be claimed for the first years of operation of the Point Four program. Assistance is given only upon specific request from an underdeveloped country. American technicians then work with native experts to map out plans for economic development and to draw up a list of intermediate objectives. In the first three years of its operation Point Four cost this country

$156,000,000—less than the price of one battleship. Concrete results were obtained in that time. The potato yield in one area of India was increased from 119 bushels an acre to 235, for example, and the farm families in one area of Liberia increased their cash incomes from $50 a year to $300.

Continuance of foreign-aid programs as a feature of our foreign policy involves many difficulties and problems. Here let us discuss some of the technical problems of the ways and means of giving assistance, and postpone until later our discussion of the basic question whether any such assistance should be given. The major part of the burden of technical and economic assistance for the underdeveloped areas falls upon the United States, because we have more capital available for investment than any other country and we also have available a larger supply of technical skills.

There is a question—as yet not resolved—whether capital investment is primarily a matter for private enterprise, with the government's role limited to securing conditions abroad that will attract private capital. This consideration played a large part in prompting Congress to stress technical assistance and minimize capital investment in making Point Four appropriations.

A second problem arises when there are many demands throughout the world for our capital and our manpower in defense armaments. What proportion of our aid and our skills should we allot to the economic development of retarded areas? This question must be weighed carefully because even our rich resources are limited in amount and they are far from adequate to take care of all the demands upon them.

A third problem is whether foreign-aid programs can best be carried out by individual governments or through the United Nations. Congress is naturally reluctant to appropriate funds over which this government has not complete control. On the other hand, insistence on administering our own foreign-aid programs leaves us open to the charge of American economic imperialism — a charge which the Communists exploit fully with the sensitive peoples of Asia. At present we straddle this problem by implementing the Point Four policy both

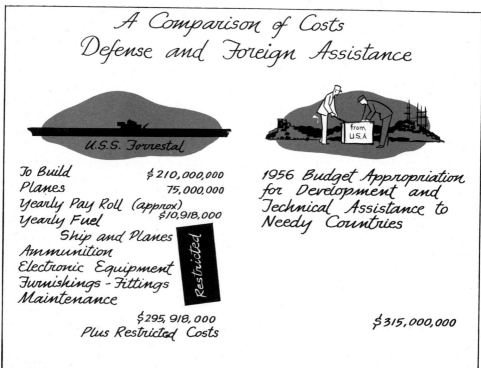

A Comparison of Costs
Defense and Foreign Assistance

U.S.S. Forrestal

To Build	$210,000,000
Planes	75,000,000
Yearly Pay Roll (approx)	
Yearly Fuel	$10,918,000
Ship and Planes	
Ammunition	
Electronic Equipment	*Restricted*
Furnishings - Fittings	
Maintenance	

$295,918,000
Plus Restricted Costs

1956 Budget Appropriation for Development and Technical Assistance to Needy Countries

$315,000,000

through programs we administer ourselves and through contributions to UN agencies engaged in this work.

98. THE BASIC PROBLEM OF FOREIGN AID

There is considerable difference of opinion among Americans on the part that foreign aid should play in our foreign policy. Some believe that the Point Four program has not been sufficiently emphasized, and others believe that foreign aid should be limited strictly to military measures necessary for our defense. Any general increase of economic and humanitarian aid to underdeveloped countries will obviously depend on problems of military preparedness in the future, because we do not have the resources or the manpower to back up far-flung military commitments and promote extensive economic development throughout the world at the same time.

But the basic problem remains: Should this country, when it is able, undertake large-scale economic-development programs in the retarded areas of the world? Many Americans point to the fact that foreign-aid programs have become so important in American life that a separate agency—Foreign Operations Administration—was created to direct and co-ordinate the programs. The FOA expired on June 30, 1955, and its place was taken by the International Cooperation Administration, which was set up as a semi-autonomous unit in the State Department to supervise the economic phase of all foreign-aid programs.

Advocates of the program argue that foreign aid contributes to international stability and justice and that, in view of the dangers of Soviet and Chinese communism, it is a good method for augmenting our national security. Critics answer this contention by insisting that foreign-aid programs tend to become permanent, and they must be judged not as temporary measures but as a permanent policy that will drain a substantial part of American wealth.

Principles governing the foreign-aid program. Since our resources are not limitless and since the need for aid is widespread, our resources must be put into programs prudently and in such a way as to accomplish the best results. Another guiding principle is that foreign aid should not take the place of self-help. It should be so devised and administered that it develops the resources and skills of the retarded peoples as thoroughly and quickly as possible. It fails if it keeps the retarded population permanently dependent on the helping nation.

In 1955 eighty-eight religious leaders (thirty-three of them Catholics, including four bishops) issued a statement entitled "American Abundance and World Need." The statement adverted to American wealth and to the responsibilities such wealth enjoins upon us. "In a moral universe, the continued prosperity of one nation can only be justified by its faithful and courageous efforts to make comparable abundance available to all nations. . . . In the international sphere, America's goal should be greatly expanded sharing of our material abundance, our technical skills and the dynamic spirit of a free society."

The statement went on to advocate a number of specific policies and programs. Among them the following are pertinent to our discussion:

1. Expanded programs of technical assistance in the fundamental work of world economic and social development.

2. International trade and monetary policies designed to facilitate and expand the international flow of goods and services. Appropriate public aid should be provided to agricultural and industrial enterprises facing adjustments as trade barriers are progressively removed.

3. Foreign economic aid programs geared to meet situations of emergency and long-time need. For this purpose both the offices of gov-

ernment and of the voluntary and religious agencies should be used.

The religious leaders asked for the full utilization of private agencies in trade, aid, and technical assistance programs, and for use of the already existing specialized agencies in the United Nations.

If this appears as a dangerous departure from American tradition, we may recall with some reassurance the words of George Washington, in his Farewell Address:

> It will be worthy of a free, enlightened, and, at no distant period, a great nation, to give to mankind the magnanimous and too novel example of a People always guided by an exalted justice and benevolence. Who can doubt that in the course of time and things, the fruits of such a plan would richly repay any temporary advantages, which might be lost by a steady adherence to it? Can it be that Providence has not connected the permanent felicity of a Nation with its virtue?

99. THE RAW-MATERIALS PROBLEM

We have already seen that raw materials are essential for industrial production. They are required in great abundance for the maintenance of a high level of production and a high standard of living. They are also essential for military power. The growth of population throughout the world, combined with increasing industrialization in most areas, has greatly increased the annual consumption of raw materials. Military demands in the two world wars have done much to deplete many convenient sources of supply. All these factors have combined to create a problem of obtaining and using wisely the raw-material resources of the world. The nature of this problem can be better appreciated if we remember that since 1914 the United States alone has consumed more metals and mineral fuels than had been used by the entire world in the previous recorded span of history.

Imported raw materials are coming to play a more important part in our economic and political life every year. In the 1936–1940 period, for example, we imported an average of $261,000,000 worth of wood and paper. In 1954 the figure had risen to $1,300,000,000. Imports of metallic ores increased more than six times in the same period, and imports of other minerals increased fourfold. In 1954 we imported 11 per cent of the raw materials used in this country, and estimates were that the percentage would increase to 20 or more within a decade. Discussion of our raw-materials procurement problems must therefore assume that we shall have to secure about one-fifth of our supply from abroad. This is a new problem for the United States, because throughout most of our history we were a net exporter of raw materials.

Our most serious problems in this field are not with agricultural products but with mineral resources. Coal, iron ore,

America's abundance and the world's needs should both be considered in a foreign-aid program. The first ten thousand of two million tons of wheat that were shipped to India after World War II are being loaded aboard a United States liberty ship in this photograph. Madame Pandit, Ambassador from India to the United States, remarked at this time, "Never once did I doubt that the United States would come to the aid of India." (ICA)

An engineer from an American company demonstrates a photo-off-set press to trainees in Punjab, India. The technical assistance given under Point Four was far-reaching as the trainees returned to their individual states to produce agricultural pamphlets, newsletters, and the like, on American machines. (ICA)

and petroleum are the most important of the minerals. Then come aluminum, copper, tin, and zinc. Finally, there are a number of metals, such as tungsten and manganese, important in making various forms of steel. They are needed only in small quantity but are of the utmost importance in our industrial economy. Our coal reserves are practically inexhaustible, but we are not so well off with regard to future domestic supplies of iron ore and petroleum. At the present time we depend on imports of high-grade iron ores to supplement diminishing and poorer-grade domestic ores. From the rate at which we continue to consume iron supplies we have every reason to expect imports of this commodity to increase. Our average annual imports of iron ore in the 1936–1945 decade were about $4,000,000 in value. In 1950 they were eleven times that amount, and in 1954 they totaled more than $119,000,-000. Canada and South America are the most important sources for iron ore imported by this country.

Although we are the largest oil producer in the world, since 1947 we have had to import increasingly large quantities of this commodity. In the five-year period from 1936 through 1940 our average annual imports of oil were valued at $47,600,000. The annual average had increased to $379,000,000 for the five-year period of 1946–1950. It was $691,000,000 in 1952 and $828,000,000 in 1954. Venezuela has been our principal foreign source of oil. Large petroleum resources are found in Iran, Iraq, and Saudi Arabia, but our friendly relations with the European world seem to dictate that we should not compete with western European countries in the procurement of these oil resources on which they are vitally dependent for domestic prosperity and military preparedness. Our over-all interests require us to encourage the expansion of oil production in other likely places in the world, especially in Hispanic America, and perhaps that we develop synthetic oil production at home.

Aluminum ore is another important import. This metal is light in weight, strong, and capable of being alloyed with many other metals. It is the basis of our aircraft industry, and it is used extensively for railway cars, automobiles, the shipbuilding industry, construction materials, and household goods. Aluminum has supplanted steel for many uses and, unless it becomes scarce, it will likely continue to supplant it in many additional respects. It is relatively cheap and easy to handle. Most of our aluminum ore is imported from Dutch Guiana.

The maintenance of our present high level of production depends on large-scale imports of many other raw materials. Imports of nonferrous metals used in American industry increased from an annual average of $183,000,000 before the last World War to nearly $1,500,-000,000 in each of the last four years. In this period copper imports increased from an average of 87,680 short tons a year to 671,548 in 1953. A comparable increase took place in zinc, tin, lead, nickel, manganese, chrome, tungsten, cobalt, and other metals. We now import about 40 per cent of our copper and almost all of our tin, nickel, antimony, chrome, and several other metals. Many of these are used in small quantity, but they are nevertheless essential for industrial and military purposes.

It is possible to substitute synthetic production of some of these materials, notably oil and rubber. Generally, synthetic products are more expensive than imported natural products. Large-scale production of synthetic substitutes absorbs considerable manpower and capital and thus lowers our standard of living to some extent. It is also possible to increase domestic production of some raw materials by discovering and utilizing hitherto unknown or unworked sources. Sufficient deposits of uranium-bearing ores may be found within our boundaries, for example, and there are still unexplored possibilities of additional oil fields in the country. But it is extremely unlikely that workable sources of some ores, such as tin or chrome, will ever be found in the United States.

It is therefore evident that we shall be increasingly dependent on the procurement of certain raw materials from abroad. We saw in an earlier chapter that we must use and conserve our natural resources wisely, but conservation of raw materials will not solve the problem by itself. It is evident that we must take diplomatic action to procure certain needed raw materials. The most obvious way to do this is to authorize the President to negotiate reciprocal trade agreements with countries possessing large supplies of the raw materials we desire.

Our military needs. The procurement of raw materials is complicated by military considerations. Not only do military requirements use up many raw materials, but they also limit the sources on which we can safely depend in time of war and, to some extent, in time of "cold peace." Military security requires us to rely on sources over which we can reasonably maintain control in time of war. This requires us to develop sources abroad that may not be the best from the standpoint of economy or efficiency. China is the best source of tungsten, for example, but military considerations require us to develop less economical but more secure sources in other parts of the world.

Military security introduces another complicated problem in procurement

This colorful ceremony was held on a wharf in Karachi in 1953 after the arrival of the first consignment of American wheat for Pakistan. (ICA)

programs: the problem of stockpiling certain strategic materials. Ordinarily it is unbusinesslike to store up a larger supply of materials than is necessary to keep production moving smoothly. Accumulated stocks cost money for which there is no return. They take up space, they must be insured and watched, and most stocks deteriorate in time. This is also true of raw materials imported for use in this country. The possibility that we may be cut off from normal supplies of certain materials used in war industry modifies normal business considerations. It seems advisable to store up or "stockpile" a quantity of each of these strategic materials. Pursuant to the Strategic and Critical Materials Stockpiling Act of 1946 we have accumulated strategic materials worth more than $7,500,000,000. About four-fifths of these supplies are of goods obtained abroad.

Stockpiling has been abused to some extent in the past and it has been an unnecessarily heavy burden on the taxpayer. Since it is sometimes necessary as a security device, let us see briefly what rules should govern stockpiling in the future. (1) It should be accomplished in advance of the emergency for which the reserve materials are needed. (2) It should be accomplished gradually in order not to create unnecessary shortages in the commodity and thus run up its price. (3) Only those materials should be stockpiled that cannot be produced at home or secured from countries with which we can expect to trade in time of war, such as Canada or Venezuela or Mexico. (4) Only such quantities as are needed should be laid aside for emergency use. Stockpiles represent a large investment of capital that remains idle until used. They are therefore a drain on the American economy and should be kept at the minimum necessary for security.

Because stockpiling is a costly way to achieve security in strategic materials, many experts suggest that it is better to develop the resources of neighboring friendly countries on which we can rely in time of emergency or war. They maintain that stockpiles are necessary for only a few materials located in only one or two places in the world. Most other materials are produced naturally in areas we can develop with American capital more economically than we can stockpile the same quantity in this country.

Conclusion. We have seen in this chapter that this country has developed a set of foreign economic relations profoundly different from anything we experienced in the past. Since World War II we have assumed serious economic as well as military commitments in Africa, South America, Europe, and Asia. These commitments have cost us billions of dollars. They have been made on the assumption that they defend and promote legitimate American interests in the world. Originally designed as temporary measures, they have become permanent in nature, and there is no reason to believe they will be abandoned in the foreseeable future. These economic commitments are an essential part of our present foreign policy, which we have been studying in these last four chapters.

REVIEW

97. Reasons for Extending Foreign Aid

A. Why was there a need on the part of the United States to extend foreign aid at the end of World War II? What was the main problem in the task of rebuilding Europe's economy?

B. How was the Marshall Plan developed and handled? What were some of the results of the Marshall Plan?

C. What has been the purpose of American military aid to Europe?

D. Describe what the Point Four program means. Indicate the three main problems the program is confronted with.

98. The Basic Problem of Foreign Aid

A. Comment briefly on this question: Should this country, when it is able, undertake large-scale economic development programs in the retarded areas of the world?

B. What are some other necessary considerations we should bear in mind in considering foreign aid programs?

C. What did religious leaders in 1955 urge concerning foreign aid programs?

99. The Raw-materials Problem

A. Why are imported raw materials playing a more important part in our economic and political life every year?

B. Indicate the needs of the United States in regard to the importing of raw materials of a mineral nature.

C. Point out how our military needs have added to the necessity of importing raw materials. What should govern our methods of stockpiling of critical and strategic materials?

THE CHAPTER IN REVIEW

A. Describe the need for aid after World War II. Why was the United States required to play such a prominent part in the foreign aid program?

B. Point out the origins of the Point Four program and indicate the need for it. Explain why it is an important part of our foreign policy today.

C. Outline the needs of the United States for raw materials. Indicate the steps we have taken to provide ourselves with a sufficient amount of raw materials.

SELECTED READINGS

In addition to the readings given at the end of the previous chapter, the following will be found helpful for the general subject of foreign-aid programs:

An enthusiastic analysis of the Point Four program by a former deputy administrator is Jonathan B. Bingham's *Shirt-Sleeve Diplomacy* (New York: The John Day Co., 1954). A more scholarly but still approving study of this subject is Sister M. Florian Volkerding, "An Appraisal of the Truman Doctrine, Marshall Plan and Point Four," *The Historical Bulletin* (January 1955). Rather objective accounts of what was done, the difficulties involved, and the general working out of American programs can be found in Carl F. Taeusch, "Foreign Aid Policies and Achievements," *Social Order* (February 1954); William Adams Brown, Jr., and Redvers Opie, *American Foreign Assistance* (Washington: The Brookings Institution, 1953).

Two Reference Shelf volumes giving articles for and against the Marshall Plan and the Point Four program are Robert E. Summers (editor), *Economic Aid to Europe: The Marshall Plan* (New York: H. W. Wilson Co., 1948), and Walter M. Daniels (editor), *The Point Four Program* (New York: H. W. Wilson, Co., 1951).

The Catholic Association for International Peace, located in Washington, has published three pamphlets that deal with the subject matter of this chapter: Rev. Edgar Schmiedeler, O.S.B., *Agriculture and International Life;* Helen C. Potter, *The Marshall Plan;* and Clarence Enzler, *Can the World Feed Itself?* Other pamphlets worth consulting are: J B. Condliffe and Harold H. Hutcheson, *Point 4 and the World Economy* (Washington: Foreign Policy Association, 1950); *United Nations Technical Assistance* (New York: United Nations, 1953); and *The Story of F.A.O.* (Washington: Food and Agriculture Organization of the United Nations, 1951).

PROJECTS

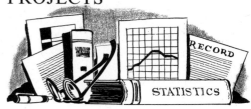

1. The Point Four program has become an important part of our foreign policy. Have a committee write to the International Cooperation Administration in Washington, D.C., to obtain specific information on what this program has accomplished so far. A report can then be made to the class.

2. Draw a map of Europe and indicate on it the value of goods these countries received under the Marshall Plan. Note in another color the total aid these countries have received from all sources since 1945.

3. Examine copies of three news magazines for the last three months to note developments in new products and discoveries of new sources of raw materials that will aid the United States should our present sources be cut off. Prepare a display of this information on the class bulletin board and explain your findings to the class.

4. Write an essay on the moral obligations of the United States to aid the less privileged peoples of the world. Bear in mind that, in justice, the federal government's first concern is our own people. You might include mention of the role that private philanthropy and individual charities should play in this work.

PROFILES

GROVER CLEVELAND

BORN: Caldwell, N.J., March 18, 1837
EDUCATION: Self-educated in law; admitted to New York bar, 1859
DIED: Princeton, N.J., June 24, 1908

One of many children of a Presbyterian minister, Grover Cleveland became a self-educated lawyer whose professional career started as a clerk in a Buffalo law office. He showed an interest in politics while practicing law in Erie County, N.Y., where he was appointed assistant district attorney in 1863 and became sheriff of the county six years later. Grover Cleveland was a staunch supporter of the Democratic party, and his political rise was meteoric. He was elected mayor of Buffalo in 1881, governor of New York State in 1882, and President of the United States in 1884, being the first Democratic candidate to win the presidency in nearly thirty years.

Believing that high tariffs actually raised the cost of living for all, and recognizing no need for the surplus moneys accumulating in the United States Treasury, Cleveland vetoed proposals for increased tariffs. His tariff policy, his sympathetic attitude toward the South, and his veto record (over two-thirds of the bills submitted) cost him defeat in the 1888 election. He was elected President again in 1892, becoming the only President to serve two discontinuous terms of office.

His effort during his second term to get passage in the House of an act to lower tariffs failed because Senator Gorman added so many increases to it that the Wilson-Gorman tariff was only slightly different from the high McKinley tariff of 1890.

Other important measures marked the two administrations of Cleveland. The Interstate Commerce Commission, established in 1887, was the first attempt of the federal government to regulate railroads. His firm stand in support of "hard money" resulted in the repeal of the Sherman Silver Purchase Act, which he had seen as a "dangerous and reckless experiment of free, unlimited, and independent coinage." The Monroe Doctrine was tested by the Venezuelan boundary dispute, and Cleveland's clear statement to the British of the American position in this case brought about a settlement of the question that was favorable to American interests.

Grover Cleveland, who had made the statement that "public officials are the trustees of the people" and heard it echoed as "a public office is a public trust," lived up to this principle as he extended the lists of classified positions in the Civil Service despite the number of positions that had to be granted to Democratic office seekers if he was to retain the lead of his party.

An excellent biography of Cleveland was written by Allan Nevins, *Grover Cleveland, A Study in Courage* (New York: Dodd, Mead & Co., 1933). *The Cleveland Era* (New Haven: Yale University Press, 1921), by H. J. Ford, is an older book in the Chronicles of America series, but valuable for a study of the times.

CORDELL HULL

BORN: Pickett, Tenn., October 2, 1871
EDUCATION: Cumberland University, B.L., 1891
DIED: Washington, D.C., July 23, 1955

Hull's legal training and interest in politics enabled him to enter the Tennessee House of Representatives (1893) where he served until

1897. His patriotic spirit caused him to abandon his law practice briefly and serve as captain of a Tennessee volunteer infantry company during the Spanish-American War.

He was elected circuit judge in 1903, and it was not until 1906 that he entered national politics, winning a seat in the House of Representatives. He continued in Congress until 1931, with the single exception of the Republican landslide in 1920. Winning a Senate seat in 1930, he remained there until 1933. Hull had a distinguished record in Congress as a careful analyst of treaty and statute law, being chiefly known as the author of the first income tax law.

F.D.R. appointed Hull Secretary of State, an office which he occupied for eleven years, the longest term of any American Secretary of State. It is difficult to distinguish the Hull from the Roosevelt ideas in foreign policy, for the Secretary directed affairs as unostentatiously as possible. Certainly, however, his skill in drawing up and concluding reciprocal trade agreements with other nations testifies to his great personal interest in this program of tariff reductions. Also, his success in implementing the "Good Neighbor" policy of Roosevelt was very effective in diminishing the suspicions of Yankee motives that were entertained in Latin America.

The field of international co-operation and the development of the apparatus for joint action with other nations occupied a great portion of Hull's time during the later years of his official life. The behind-the-scenes organization of wartime conferences among the heads of states was largely Hull's responsibility; he carried out the foreign policy of the Roosevelt administration, organized the multitude of agencies to carry it out, and supervised the execution of it. Laying the foundation for the United Nations through the Bretton Woods and Dumbarton Oaks conferences was his last major work before the President accepted his resignation for reasons of health in 1944.

Special aspects of Hull's activity are treated in *The Reciprocal Trade Policy of the United States*, by H. J. Tasca (Philadelphia: The University of Pennsylvania Press, 1938), and in the "white paper" collection of official documents called *Peace and War: United States Foreign Policy, 1931–1941* (Washington: Government Printing Office, 1943). The Secretary's own story of his years of service is told in *The Memoirs of Cordell Hull*, 2 vols. (New York: The Macmillan Company, 1948).

HARRY S. TRUMAN

BORN: Lamar, Mo., May 8, 1884
EDUCATION: Public schools, Independence, Mo.; Kansas City Law School, 1925

Truman's education was interrupted for a number of years by his work on the family farm. He served in the army in World War I, during which he rose to the rank of captain in the field artillery. Business experience in Kansas City, coupled with evening study of law, completed his education. While still a law student he became very interested in Democratic party politics in Kansas City and was the regular party nominee for a number of judgeships (judge of Jackson County Court, 1922–1924; presiding judge, 1926–1934) and finally for United States senator, being elected in 1934 and 1940.

As a senator, Truman attracted national attention for his handling of the committee investigating the defense program, and he was accepted by the 1944 national Democratic convention as the replacement for the controversial Henry Wallace as vice-presidential nominee. Roosevelt's death placed Truman in the White House, with the task of completing the war effort and directing the United States efforts to build a lasting peace settlement.

Truman's domestic policy, which continued the "New Deal," encountered severe opposition from a Republican-controlled Congress in 1946. His insistence on a civil-rights program in 1948 led southern Democrats to repudiate him, and he was almost universally expected to lose the presidency. His victory was due largely to his own forceful and effective speeches in dozens of small "whistle-stop" towns and cities.

Truman's foreign policy was marked by several new developments. His Point Four program sought to place American technical knowledge at the disposal of less skilled peoples so that their natural resources might be better used and their living standards raised. Convinced that the U.S.S.R. must be curbed, he announced the Truman Doctrine, under which the United States would help friendly governments to resist Communist revolution; this aid was credited with saving Greece and Turkey from Red rule. He approved the Marshall Plan to send American economic aid to European nations struggling to rebuild war-damaged production systems. Finally, Truman sent American forces into a limited military action against the invasion of the Republic of Korea by Communist forces. He set as new American foreign policy objectives the assistance of underdeveloped or undefended nations and the containment of Communist rule.

No full-length biography of Truman including his full term as President yet exists. His own writings are available and include his *Memoirs,* in two volumes (New York: Doubleday & Co., Inc., 1955–1956). Also recommended is *Mr. President,* by William Hillman (Farrar, Straus & Young, 1952).

DEBATE

The question: **SHOULD THE UNITED STATES ADOPT A PERMANENT POLICY OF FOREIGN AID, AS EXEMPLIFIED IN THE POINT FOUR PROGRAM?**

The class must realize that this is a very complicated problem that involves questions of foreign policy, American productive power, the allotment of our limited resources, and a general political and economic philosophy. All these aspects of the question should be weighed, and then a prudential decision should be made. The class will realize that in such decisions one expects to find benefits and liabilities on both sides, and the prudent decision is that which adopts the greatest measures of good and the least of inconveniences and shortcomings.

Affirmative presentation

I. There are several compelling reasons for adopting this policy:
  1. To aid the economically underdeveloped areas of the world.
    a. This is humane action—for which Americans are well known.
    b. It is politically expedient, for it removes one of the causes of Communist revolution, and it wins us friends among the hitherto underprivileged peoples.

  2. To maintain a full economy at home.
    a. Keeps our skills and our capital employed.
    b. Increases our wealth in the long run, for return on American labor and capital spent here and trade with underdeveloped areas will increase.
II. A permanent policy of foreign aid will benefit American prestige and power.
  1. It can be used to strengthen our allies.
  2. It will win us good will abroad and will prove a refutation of Communist propaganda among the backward peoples.
  3. It will ultimately relieve us of the burden of protecting these peoples.
III. The Point Four program has worked to our benefit, and it substantiates the arguments outlined above.
  1. It has produced wonderful results technically and materially.
  2. It has been opposed only by the Soviet-dominated nations.
  3. It has not involved us in dangers originally alleged against it.
    a. The amount of money spent on such aid is proportionately small.
    b. It has not created a class of "bureaucrats" or a "vested interest" of any kind.
    c. It is subject to congressional review at every appropriation time.

Negative presentation

Introduction: We concede that the Marshall Plan and Point Four program accomplished a certain amount of good and that they were needed as temporary measures after the war. But the question here is whether to adopt a *permanent policy of foreign aid.*
I. Such a policy is contrary to sound government.
  1. It is a global "giveaway" program.
  2. We are opposed to "giveaway" programs on even national and local levels.
    a. They destroy the independence of those receiving them.
    b. They put them under our permanent control.
    c. They increase American liabilities throughout the world by making backward peoples permanently dependent on us.
II. As a permanent policy, foreign aid is deceptive and it is harmful to America.

1. Who pays for awards on "giveaway" programs on radio or television?
   a. Not the advertiser, but the user of his product pays.
   b. Similarly the American taxpayer pays the bill for foreign aid.
2. The American taxpayer is already overburdened.
   a. Additional taxes will involve real hardships for taxpayers.
   b. It will also drain money out of productive employment.
3. A world economy is not healthy if one nation must permanently aid others.

CLASSROOM DISCUSSION: The class should try to determine (1) what the extent of foreign aid is likely to be; (2) how that compares to our annual domestic and defense expenses; (3) whether foreign aid might effect reductions in expenses of foreign defense commitments; (4) whether it can be expected to produce some offsetting good results economically.

If these questions are answered so as to suggest that foreign aid is within our means, then the class should decide whether it is morally and politically prudent to make it a permanent policy. (Some agreement should be reached on the meaning of "permanent," because no policy can be considered as desirable for centuries.) Apparently conflicting principles of "subsidiarity" and of "helping one's neighbors" should be discussed in arriving at a decision on this complicated problem.

SELECTED READINGS

The following deal with the Point Four program, which is taken as the model for the type of foreign aid advocated in this debate: the Reference Shelf volume edited by Walter M. Daniels, *The Point Four Program* (New York: H. W. Wilson Co., 1951); the pamphlet published by the Chamber of Commerce of the United States, *Point Four Program* (Washington: the Chamber, 1949); a pamphlet by Henry Hazlitt, *Illusions of Point Four* (Irvington-on-Hudson: Foundation for Economic Education, 1950); H. L. Hoskins (ed.), "Aiding Underdeveloped Areas Abroad," *Annals of the American Academy of Political and Social Science* (July 1950); "Congress Takes a Look at the President's Point Four Program," *Congressional Digest* (May 1950); "Helping the World Help Itself: Point Four," *Senior Scholastic* (April 2, 1952).

The problem of foreign aid as related to our general foreign policy is considered in the following: Dwight D. Eisenhower, "Recommendations Concerning U.S. Foreign Economic Policy" (a message to Congress), *Vital Speeches of the Day* (May 15, 1954); Gordon Gray, *Report to the President on Foreign Economic Policies* (Washington: Superintendent of Documents, 1950); Nelson Rockefeller, "Widening Boundaries of National Interest," *Foreign Affairs* (July 1951); F. Altschul, "America's New Economic Role," *Foreign Affairs* (April 1953); Henry Ford, "Free World Can't Trade on a One-Way Street," *Vital Speeches of the Day* (March 15, 1953); A. Sproul, "New Opportunities for a Liberal Foreign Trade Policy," *Vital Speeches of the Day* (January 1, 1955); "Question of U.S. Foreign Economic Policy," *Congressional Digest* (August 1954); "Question of U.S. Foreign Trade Policy," *Congressional Digest* (January 1954); W.W. Aldrich, "Basis for a New Foreign Economic Policy," *Vital Speeches of the Day* (January 15, 1953); A. Johnson, *Breaking the Barriers to Capital Investment Abroad* (Washington: U. S. Department of State Bulletin, October 6, 1952); Chamber of Commerce of the United States, *What the Chamber Stands for in World Affairs* (Washington: the Chamber, 1952); Chamber of Commerce of the United States, *International Trade Policy Issues* (Washington: the Chamber, 1953); H. S. Piquet, *Aid, Trade and the Tariff* (New York: Thomas Y. Crowell, 1953); J. H. Williams, *Trade not Aid: A Program for World Stability* (Cambridge, Mass.: Harvard University Press, 1953).

The problem of foreign aid is more specifically discussed in: Brookings Institution, *Current Issues in Foreign Economic Assistance* (Washington: the Institution, 1951); *Administration of Foreign Aid* (U. S. Department of State Bulletin, August 24, 1953); *Reorganization of Foreign Aid and Information Programs* (U. S. Department of State Bulletin, June 15, 1953); P. Hotchkiss, *U.S. Economic Policy toward Underdeveloped Countries* (U. S. Department of State Bulletin, May 10, 1954); I. Lubin, *Answer to Soviet Attacks on U.S. Policy toward Underdeveloped Areas* (U. S. Department of State Bulletin, December 1, 1952); "We're Not in Foreign Aid for Profit," *Saturday Evening Post* (February 5, 1955); *Foreign Aid by the United States Government* (Washington: Department of Commerce, 1953); and in R. M. Bissell, Jr., "Foreign Aid: What Sort? How Much? How Long?" *Foreign Affairs* (October 1952).

UNIT TWELVE
International Organization
for Peace

Chapter 35. The United States and the United Nations

100. HISTORICAL BACKGROUND

The ideal of bringing all nations together in a system or organization for the maintenance of international peace and co-operation in the general interest of all mankind is very old. In the European Middle Ages, when the greater part of the world was still unknown to the people of Europe, it was assumed that there existed an international community which men called Christendom. All Christian rulers acknowledged, in theory at least, that the political head of Christendom was the Holy Roman Emperor; and no Christian doubted that the Pope was the religious head. The ancient Roman imperial tradition, the Catholic religion, and the periodic conflicts between the Christian world and the Mohammedan world nourished this sense of a Christian international community.

Between 1250 and 1650, momentous developments came close to obliterating this sense of community. The kings and princes of Europe acted in complete independence of the Holy Roman Emperor, who was reduced to being little more than the nominal monarch of Germany. The churches in much of eastern Europe rejected the authority of the Pope. The Protestant revolution changed the whole character of religion throughout large regions of northern and western Europe. Thus the old unity of Christendom was shattered just as the nations had begun to expand, colonize, and found overseas dependencies. By the mid-seventeenth century an era was opened in which the European states (some of them now having strong armies, navies, and colonies) acted as if there were no international community. Frequent wars occurred, arising from dynastic, colonial, and trading rivalries. Some philosophical thinkers continued to remind Europe that it was still fundamentally a sort of great Christian republic or commonwealth of nations. Other thinkers drew up plans or proposals for leaguing the states into a collective security system in which the governments would unite to maintain peace instead of seeking their own interests at the cost of frequent wars.

The balance of power. The most practical idea in this disunited world of the seventeenth and eighteenth centuries was that of trying to maintain a balance of power among the principal states. It was recognized that excessive power was always abused, and therefore statesmen tried to maintain a fairly balanced distribution of it. If one power grew too great it menaced the other powers, and they tended to combine against it. If this principle did not prevent all war, it certainly prevented some wars and moderated the ambitions of rulers. Each major power knew that if it went too far it was likely to provoke a combination of powers against it. All enlightened diplomacy respected this balance of power. Another check against unrestrained national or princely ambition was the generally prevalent respect for the law of nations. The idea of the balance of power and the law of nations operated with great force and effect in making treaties of peace after wars. Efforts to annihilate defeated states or to impose on them terms of "unconditional surrender" were not compatible with accepted international principles.

The principle of the balance of power may be said to be of permanent necessity in international society. It is in no way opposed to the principle of international organization for collective security. Nations can never combine their forces to maintain peace by preventing aggression unless each is sure that such action will not lead to a violation of its interests or impose on it an unjust share of the burden. Great powers have often abused the principle of the balance of power and thus brought discredit upon it, but wise men have always regarded it as necessary for international peace.

The great era of war and revolution which opened with the American struggle for independence from Great Britain and continued until 1815, when Napoleon was finally defeated, convinced the leaders of Europe that some new form of international organization was necessary. The Czar of Russia sponsored the "Holy Alliance," which almost all the Christian states of Europe joined. It proved unworkable because the Russian and Austrian governments tried to convert it into a league for maintaining despotic government. Much more practical was the Concert of Europe, which was formed at the same time. The principle of the Concert was that the great powers of Europe should meet from time to time to negotiate on matters of common interest and to maintain the balance which they had to restore after Napoleon had overturned it.

The Concert of Europe could not, however, meet the needs of the international world as an instrument of peace and co-operation. Too often it was divided and unable to act effectively. Moreover, it was merely European. By the twentieth century the United States and Japan had become great powers, so that a much broader international instrument was needed.

The League of Nations. World War I persuaded people all over the world that the old European balance-of-power principle was no longer workable and that some kind of league or international federation should be formed on a universal scale. Such an organization, it was felt, should be able to provide a general collective security for all nations. Sir Edward Grey, British Foreign Secretary, expressed the idea in these words in 1915: "The pearl of great price, if it can be found, would be some League of Nations that could be relied on to insist that disputes between any two nations must be settled by arbitration, mediation, or conference of others. International law has hitherto had no sanction. The lesson of this war is that the Powers must bind themselves to give it a sanction."

President Wilson included this idea in his Fourteen Points, which he delivered to the world on January 8, 1918, as the war aims of the United States. The fourteenth point stated: "A general association of nations must be formed under specific covenants for the purpose of affording mutual guarantees of political independence and territorial integrity to great and small states alike." The victorious powers created the League of Nations when the war was over. It was a loose confederation of sovereign states that joined together for the twofold purpose of preventing war and promoting peace and security among nations.

The League described itself as "a free association of states which undertake to pursue certain common aims; the individual states which belong to it do not thereby renounce their national sovereignty, nor, consequently, their *liberum veto.*" What this means is that the League was free to formulate and propose solutions to various problems, but it remained for the individual states to act or not to act, as they pleased. All member states belonged to the *Assembly,* where they met on ground of theoretical equality, since each state had one vote. The Assembly set general policies for the League by resolution.

The *Council* of the League originally was to have nine members. Five permanent members were to have been the United States, Great Britain, France, Italy, and Japan. The four remaining members were to be elected by the Assembly. More non-permanent members were admitted to the Council, until by 1938 there were ten such members. The Council, like the Assembly, was designed to formulate plans and propose solutions for international problems. It was specifically charged with the task of devising plans for disarmament, for protecting member states in time of aggression, and for mediation in international disputes.

The *Secretariat* was to be the permanent organ of the league. Consisting of a secretary general and a staff of several hundred persons, the Secretariat dealt with the League's day-to-day business. It prepared business for the Assembly and the Council meetings, carried out the decisions reached by these bodies, and handled the vast amount of business connected with non-political activity entrusted to the League. Its seat was at Geneva.

The League was organized primarily to prevent war and to settle problems that might eventually lead to war. Its failure to achieve this primary objective means that it did not accomplish its main purpose, even though it did excellent work in such technical fields as administering certain internationalized territories, conducting economic conferences, and obtaining co-operation in such fields as labor and narcotics traffic.

The member states assumed the obligation, in joining the League, to establish "the understandings of international law as the actual rule of conduct among governments" and to "respect all treaty obligations." They further agreed to reduce their armaments "to the lowest point consistent with national safety," to a frank interchange of information on armaments, and to regulate the private manufacture of armaments within their borders. Finally, all members agreed to respect and to preserve against aggression the territorial integrity of all member states. If these agreements were faithfully observed, war would have been virtually impossible among the states belonging to the League.

Weakness of the League. If war did break out, the Council was to advise on what steps should be taken; whether, for example, an economic boycott should be imposed, or whether armed action should be taken by the members of the League against the aggressor. The League Covenant simply stated that war or the threat of war was a common concern of all states and that "the League shall take any action that may be deemed wise and effectual to safeguard the peace of nations." Provision was made for arbitration or judicial decision of disputes between members, but war was not renounced as a final recourse in such disputes. Moreover, each sovereign state was left free to follow or not follow the League's recommendation for action.

The League therefore could make suggestions, but it had no power to enforce its will upon the member nations. This was its inherent weakness: it depended upon unanimity of decision and action among the major powers who were members. But such unanimity was never forthcoming. Therefore, the League tried to evade issues that involved major powers.

It failed to take a strong stand when Italy bombed the island of Corfu in 1923, for example, or again when Italy attacked Ethiopia in 1935 in obvious violation of the League Covenant. It failed in similar fashion to take action against Japan when it invaded Manchuria in 1931.

We can see that the League was inherently weak and unable to accomplish the purpose for which it was created. We should also remember that its rejection by this country—the wealthiest and most powerful country in the world—was a crippling blow at the time of its birth after World War I. The League probably could not have operated successfully even with American participation—no one can say for sure—but our failure to participate contributed to the League's failure. The result of the League's failure was to divide public opinion even more sharply on the subject of an international organization when we entered World War II. Some believed that the League of Nations not only had failed to maintain peace but that it was a meddlesome organization that helped bring on the war. Others—an increasing number—felt that the League was too weak to accomplish its purpose and that world peace could be secured only by a stronger international organization. Out of these considerations came the United Nations in 1945, which countless millions of people hoped fervently would be able to accomplish the difficult task of maintaining peace in the troubled world of the mid-twentieth century.

101. NATURE OF THE UN

From the very beginning of our participation in World War II, Americans gave thought to making a peace that would be just and lasting. They differed among themselves on what constituted a just and lasting peace, but they all agreed that the Peace of Versailles in 1919 had

The educational program of UNESCO reaches to all countries. This picture, taken at the Fundamental Education Center at Patzcuaro, Mexico, shows an expert explaining to a Tarascan farmer how to build a granary on stilts so that rodents will not destroy his corn. (United Nations)

been a failure and that the League of Nations did not accomplish its avowed purpose of preventing war. A majority of Americans seemed to believe that a more effective organization than the League was needed to prevent war and that the United States must play a leading part in creating such an institution.

In October 1943, Secretary of State Cordell Hull presented proposals for a new world organization to the representatives of the English, Soviet, and Chinese governments, gathered at Moscow. The four powers then stated to the world their belief in the need of a general international organization. In 1944 representatives of these powers met at Dumbarton Oaks to work out concrete proposals for an international organization. In the name of all four powers the United States invited the governments of the other nations at war with Germany and Japan to meet at San Francisco on April 25, 1945, to create an international organization. Fifty states sent representatives to the San Francisco conference, where they drafted the Charter of the United Nations. The Charter went into

force on October 24, when it received the necessary number of ratifications.

The United Nations: purpose and structure. The United Nations was organized to achieve four stated objectives: (1) to maintain international peace and security; (2) to develop friendly relations among nations, based on the principle of equal rights and self-determination of all peoples; (3) to solve international problems of an economic, social, cultural, or humanitarian character by international co-operation; (4) to promote and encourage respect for human rights and human freedoms.

To attain these ends the United Nations created institutions which they modeled after the League of Nations but which they hoped would be strong enough to achieve the objectives they had in view. There are six principal organs in the UN: (1) a General Assembly; (2) a Security Council; (3) an Economic and Social Council; (4) a Trusteeship Council; (5) an International Court of Justice; (6) a Secretariat.

The General Assembly. The General Assembly consists of all member states, theoretically equal. The Assembly, according to the Charter, may discuss "any questions relating to the maintenance of international peace and security" brought before it, and it may "initiate studies and make recommendations" to promote international co-operation in the interests of peace and social-economic accomplishments. No binding decisions are made by the Assembly, since each nation reserves the right to ignore the Assembly's recommendations. The General Assembly is essentially a "world forum" where powers that have no other means for discussing their problems can talk things over and sometimes come closer to agreement.

The Security Council. Five of the eleven members of the Security Council are permanent members: the United States, the Soviet Union, Great Britain, France, and

China. Six others are elected by the Assembly for two-year terms. Each member state has one vote. The Security Council functions continuously, unlike the Assembly, which ordinarily meets once a year. The Council is charged with the "primary responsibility for the maintenance of international peace and security," and it is therefore supposed to keep constant watch on disputes or situations that may threaten the peace of the world. Whenever the Council decides that peace is threatened it has the authority to "determine the existence of any threat to the peace, breach of the peace, or act of aggression," and it is empowered to take such action "as may be necessary to maintain or restore international peace and security."

Thus the Security Council, acting for the UN, is given power to enforce its decisions. The application of both peaceful sanctions (such as economic boycott)

and armed force, or the decision on any other question that is not merely procedural, depends upon unanimity of the Big Five. That is to say, any one of the *permanent* members can prevent any action by the Council. Hence, under the Charter no one of the major powers can be made subject, against its will, to any act of the Council. The "veto power" works in this way: decisions of the Security Council on procedural matters are reached by the vote of any seven members; decisions on other matters (such, for example, as taking armed action against a transgressor state) require seven affirmative votes, including *all five* of the permanent members.

The great powers have thus reserved to themselves decisions on the important questions affecting war and peace. The Assembly is allowed to discuss such questions and make recommendations, but the decision to take action or not to

This aerial view of the headquarters of the United Nations in New York shows the Secretariat, Conference, and General Assembly buildings, with the East River in the foreground and, in the back, the buildings of Manhattan. (United Nations)

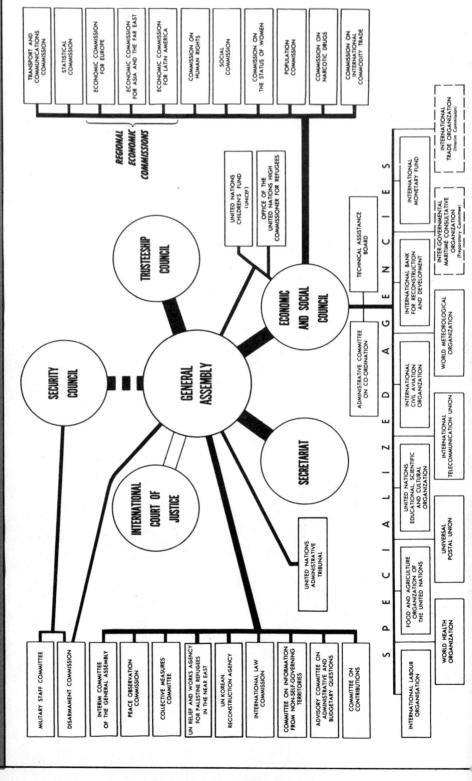

United Nations Organization

TRANSPORT AND COMMUNICATIONS COMMISSION
STATISTICAL COMMISSION
ECONOMIC COMMISSION FOR EUROPE
ECONOMIC COMMISSION FOR ASIA AND THE FAR EAST
ECONOMIC COMMISSION FOR LATIN AMERICA
COMMISSION ON HUMAN RIGHTS
SOCIAL COMMISSION
COMMISSION ON THE STATUS OF WOMEN
POPULATION COMMISSION
COMMISSION ON NARCOTIC DRUGS
COMMISSION ON INTERNATIONAL COMMODITY TRADE

REGIONAL ECONOMIC COMMISSIONS

TRUSTEESHIP COUNCIL

SECURITY COUNCIL

GENERAL ASSEMBLY

INTERNATIONAL COURT OF JUSTICE

SECRETARIAT

ECONOMIC AND SOCIAL COUNCIL

UNITED NATIONS CHILDREN'S FUND (UNICEF)
OFFICE OF THE UNITED NATIONS HIGH COMMISSIONER FOR REFUGEES

TECHNICAL ASSISTANCE BOARD

ADMINISTRATIVE COMMITTEE ON CO-ORDINATION

UNITED NATIONS ADMINISTRATIVE TRIBUNAL

MILITARY STAFF COMMITTEE
DISARMAMENT COMMISSION
INTERIM COMMITTEE OF THE GENERAL ASSEMBLY
PEACE OBSERVATION COMMISSION
COLLECTIVE MEASURES COMMITTEE
UN RELIEF AND WORKS AGENCY FOR PALESTINE REFUGEES IN THE NEAR EAST
UN KOREAN RECONSTRUCTION AGENCY
INTERNATIONAL LAW COMMISSION
COMMITTEE ON INFORMATION FROM NON-SELF-GOVERNING TERRITORIES
ADVISORY COMMITTEE ON ADMINISTRATIVE AND BUDGETARY QUESTIONS
COMMITTEE ON CONTRIBUTIONS

S P E C I A L I Z E D   A G E N C I E S

INTERNATIONAL LABOUR ORGANISATION
WORLD HEALTH ORGANIZATION
FOOD AND AGRICULTURE ORGANIZATION OF THE UNITED NATIONS
UNIVERSAL POSTAL UNION
UNITED NATIONS EDUCATIONAL, SCIENTIFIC AND CULTURAL ORGANIZATION
INTERNATIONAL TELECOMMUNICATION UNION
INTERNATIONAL CIVIL AVIATION ORGANIZATION
WORLD METEOROLOGICAL ORGANIZATION
INTERNATIONAL BANK FOR RECONSTRUCTION AND DEVELOPMENT
INTER-GOVERNMENTAL MARITIME CONSULTATIVE ORGANIZATION (Preparatory Committee)
INTERNATIONAL MONETARY FUND
INTERNATIONAL TRADE ORGANIZATION (Interim Commission)

take it remains with the Security Council. This arrangement is subject to abuse, of course, and it has been abused by the Soviet Union. Its justification originally lay in the fact that the great powers would bear the brunt of any general war, and they thought it necessary to protect themselves from being pushed into such a situation by the affirmative vote of small powers. They also realized that without unanimity of action among the great powers a decision for action by the Security Council would break up the Council and probably lead to war.

The UN Charter allowed for the use of armed force by the Security Council. It authorized a Military Staff Committee composed of the chiefs of staff of the permanent members of the Security Council. This committee was to advise on all military matters and to have control of any armed forces placed at the disposal of the Security Council. The provision for UN armed forces, however, was not thought of as a replacement of national armies. Individual states retain the right of self-defense and therefore the right to take whatever measures are necessary to prepare for self-defense.

The Economic and Social Council. This Council was organized because the UN realized the intimate connection between international peace on the one hand and economic and social well-being on the other. It therefore sought to create "conditions of stability and well-being which are necessary for peaceful and friendly relations among nations," and to promote higher standards of living, solutions of international economic, social, and health problems, and respect for human rights and freedoms. The general direction of these matters was entrusted to the Economic and Social Council. It co-ordinates the activity of specialized agencies dealing in these matters, initiates studies and reports on such subjects, and makes recommendations for accomplishing these objectives. The Economic and So-

cial Council consists of eighteen members elected for three-year terms by the Assembly. Each member state has one vote, and a majority vote is sufficient for action by the Council. The Economic and Social Council must rely on the co-operation of individual states to carry its recommendations into effect.

The Trusteeship Council. Like the Economic and Social Council, the Trusteeship Council was devised to meet a need not adequately met by the League of Nations. Members of the UN which administer territories where the people have not attained self-government promise that they will not abuse their trust, that they will respect the culture of the native peoples, and that they will promote such developments as will make the territories self-governing in time. The Trusteeship Council has some supervisory authority over these trusts in non-strategic areas. But in strategic areas, as in the Pacific islands taken as trusts by the United States after overcoming the Japanese, the Council has no effective right of interference. The general aim of the trustee system is to promote the social, economic,

Student groups in the United States and the United Kingdom purchased six hundred dollars' worth of coupons to provide lathes for a woodworking class in a Korean school. The gift-coupon program is sponsored by UNESCO. (United Nations)

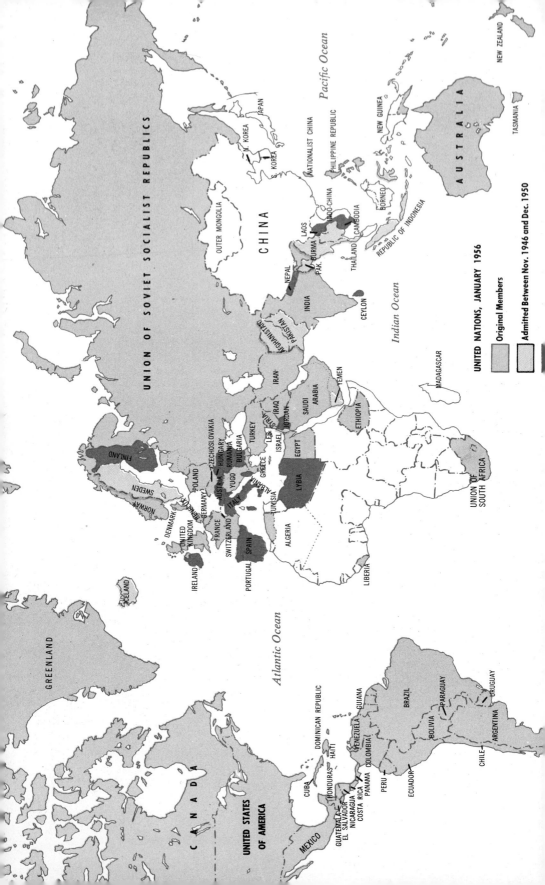

UNITED NATIONS, JANUARY 1956

Original Members

Admitted Between Nov. 1946 and Dec. 1950

cultural, and political development of the so-called backward areas of the earth.

The International Court of Justice. Created in 1922, the International Court of Justice was adopted by the UN to handle international disputes that are primarily legal rather than political in character. It handles only disputes between governments, and it settles them on the basis of treaties, international law and custom, and the opinions of accepted scholars in the field. The UN hopes to compile a code of generally accepted international law to govern relations between nations and on the basis of which the International Court can make its decisions. The Court consists of fifteen judges elected by the Assembly and the Security Council. No two judges can come from the same country. They serve a nine-year term of office. The Court is also required to give advisory opinions to the Assembly, the Security Council, and the specialized agencies.

The Secretariat. The large staff needed to handle the administrative work of the UN is called the Secretariat. It is headed by a secretary general, elected for a five-year term by the Assembly on the recommendation of the Security Council. The Secretariat is staffed by persons who are supposed to be "international" in their allegiance, no matter what their native country may be.

Besides these principal organs of the UN there are a large number of other agencies attached in one way or another to the UN organization. Among these are the International Labor Organization (ILO), the Food and Agriculture Organization (FAO), and the United Nations Educational, Scientific and Cultural Organization (UNESCO). Other important organizations are the International Bank for Reconstruction and Development, the Universal Postal Union, the International Civil Aviation Organization, the International Telecommunications Union, the World Meteorological Organization, the World Health Organization, the International Children's Welfare Emergency Fund, and the International Refugee Organization.

102. ACHIEVEMENTS AND FAILURES

UN non-political activity. The UN ideal is popular in the United States, and countless thousands of our citizens visit the headquarters of this institution in New York every year. Much of the work of the subsidiary organizations appeals to the spirit of generosity and benevolence of the American people. The World Health Organization (WHO), for example, attempts to remove the causes of disease, especially in those areas infected by pestilence due to the absence of sanitation and elementary hygiene. Through the work of this agency gains have been made against infectious disease in places such as Egypt, India, China, and the West Indies. In certain areas the death rate has been cut in half. WHO tries to make long-term gains by promoting a knowledge of hygiene and by making available the drugs necessary to combat certain serious diseases such as malaria.

The United Nations International Children's Fund (UNICF) and the International Refugee Organization also have done excellent work. Both were organized as temporary agencies after World War II. The UNICF furnished food, clothing, and medicine to children who suffered from the war. It also set about organizing health and welfare services for children in the underdeveloped areas, and in 1953 it was made a permanent agency of the UN. The International Refugee Organization helped resettle millions of displaced persons after World War II. The IRO's work was later taken over by the Intergovernmental Committee for European Migration and the need is now apparent for some UN agency to care for refugees in Asia.

The Food and Agriculture Organization has taken steps toward improving the production of rice, the principal item of food for people in the Far East, and toward developing new fish resources in the same area. The International Bank has loaned more than a billion dollars for productive enterprises in more than a dozen countries. The International Monetary Fund has assisted countries in the stabilization of their currencies, and it has provided technical advice to governments on their currency and banking problems. The International Civil Aviation Organization has developed a number of regulations to promote safety in international air travel. The United Nations Relief for Palestine Refugees cared for three-quarters of a million refugees who were victims of the hostilities between Israel and the Arab states.

In the social and economic fields, then, agencies associated with the UN have accomplished a considerable amount of good work. Few people criticize this work, although some fear that it tends to turn over to an international agency what the various states should do themselves and thus becomes a "creeping form" of world government. The fact remains, however, that these problems have been international in scope, and in the contemporary world situation it is extremely difficult to get co-operation among nations except through such agencies as those of the UN.

The work of at least two UN agencies has excited much controversy and criticism in the United States. The Commission on Human Rights prepared a treaty containing a list of human rights which the signatories of the treaty pledged themselves to respect. The necessity of trying to accommodate the treaty of some of the tyrannical police states of the world rendered the treaty offensive to a large American opinion, which believed that the United States had nothing to learn about human freedom from the United Nations Commission. The Hu-

man Rights Treaty has never been submitted to the Senate, and if it were submitted it probably would be rejected.

Much criticism, especially from Catholics, has been directed upon the United Nations Educational and Scientific Commission. This body is supposed to promote intercommunication of ideas among peoples of the world by developing student exchanges, the translation of books, establishment of libraries, and promotion of education in "backward" areas. There is, say the critics, nothing objectionable in principle to all this activity, but they have charged that UNESCO is inspired by an unreligious secularism. This criticism was perhaps more justified in the earlier years of UNESCO than it is today. It is worth observing that the Holy See is represented at UNESCO's headquarters in Paris and that the papacy has co-operated in a number of the agency's undertakings.

UN as an instrument for maintaining peace. Much of the criticism of the UN has arisen from a misunderstanding of the political nature of the organization. Some have fancied that it was designed to be a power *above* all nations to force all nations to keep the peace. This is not so. The architects of the organization did not intend to create a world federal state but to establish an institutionalized method of co-operation among free and independent nations. The UN should not be thought of as something existing above or apart from the nations that constitute it; *they are* the UN; that is, the nations that have united to observe the Charter.

It is true that the Security Council as described in the Charter *appears* to be a body authorized to maintain the peace and equipped with power for this purpose. But this body is not set *over* the nations; it is not constituted of persons whose prime interest is in executing the laws of a world legislature. Rather are they there to serve the interests of their own countries. A great deal of close and careful thinking went into the provision that requires the *affirmative* vote of all the permanent members to be among the seven votes necessary for the Council to decide on any positive course of action. By this distribution of power the five permanent members cannot alone dominate the Council; nor can the Council decide any question (that is not merely procedural) against the will of a permanent member.

Repeated use of this veto power by the Soviet Union has virtually paralyzed the Security Council from the start. It has not been able to take any strong action, nor even to obtain agreement for the creation of a military force to be placed at its disposal. This does not mean that the decision to have the veto was unwise and that now the veto should be abolished. No great power would agree to that, because it would thereby lose control over its own foreign policy. Without the veto it is unlikely that the United States would have joined the UN. Certainly the Senate would have been most reluctant to allow our government to be committed, against its will, to undertake a military action at the behest of a Council majority.

In 1950 the Security Council responded to our appeal for support in checking the aggression of the North Korean Communists against the Republic of Korea. That small state, although not a member of the UN, had come into being under the sponsorship of the UN. When the attack on it was launched, President Truman ordered American armed forces based in Japan to go to the aid of the South Koreans *and then* he appealed for support from the Security Council. At that time, the Soviet delegate was absenting himself from the Council because of the refusal of the Council to admit the Chinese Communist government's claim to the Chinese UN membership. Thus the Soviet delegate was not present to veto the decision to support the South Koreans. In a strictly legal sense, the Council had no right to reach this decision without the affirmative vote of the permanent Soviet member; but the other members refused to allow an absent member to paralyze their proceedings. They were compelled to submit to inaction, however, when the Soviet delegate returned.

Then UN action in Korea found its support in the General Assembly. The form that UN military and naval activities took in the Korean War was to name the American commander, General MacArthur, to be also the UN commander. Members of the UN were urged to send forces to co-operate with the American Army and the South Koreans. All, including the United States forces, fought under the flag of the UN. Less than a third of the members of the UN sent armed forces to Korea. Far and above the greater part of the cost of the war, in blood and wealth, was borne by the United States and the Republic of Korea. It may be doubted whether it is strictly correct to describe the defense of South Korea as a UN military action. The So-

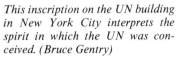

This inscription on the UN building in New York City interprets the spirit in which the UN was conceived. (Bruce Gentry)

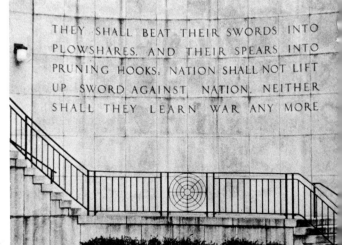

THEY SHALL BEAT THEIR SWORDS INTO PLOWSHARES, AND THEIR SPEARS INTO PRUNING HOOKS, NATION SHALL NOT LIFT UP SWORD AGAINST NATION, NEITHER SHALL THEY LEARN WAR ANY MORE.

viet Union, Communist Poland, and Communist Czechoslovakia—all members of the UN—sided with the North Koreans and the Chinese Communists, even to the length of providing them with arms. The war was almost as much a conflict *within* the UN as it was a struggle between the UN and its enemies. In no sense was it an action to impose restraint upon a member nation.

At the time the UN Charter was drafted there was a widespread hope and expectation that the major powers would co-operate to make the Security Council an effective agency. Soon, however, it appeared that there was too much distrust and hostility between the Western powers and the Soviet Union to allow of such co-operation. If distrust and hostility diminish, the Council may recover its utility and function as it was intended; but it would need some reformation. Nationalist China (Formosa) no longer carries enough weight in world power to entitle it to a permanent membership. The permanent seats will have to be rearranged if the Council is to represent the real forces in the international world. It may have done so in 1945; it does not represent them now. If the UN is to endure, it will before long have to admit Germany and Japan. Italy and Spain, who had long been excluded from membership, were accepted in December 1955, along with fourteen other nations. Japan's entry into the UN was vetoed at this time by the Soviet Union, who had used the veto in the Security Council for the seventy-fourth time. Italy and Spain will in time wish to have an influence equal at least to that of France, which is a permanent member of the Council. When admitted, Germany and Japan will probably seek similar recognition. India may be entitled to the seat in the Council that is likely to be vacated by Nationalist China. Of course if the Chinese Nationalists should reconquer China, the picture would again change importantly.

103. THE CHINA QUESTION AND CHARTER REVISION

No proposal concerning the UN has stirred more public resentment than that of admitting the Communist People's Republic of China. The government of this new revolutionary and aggressive state claims that it is the government of China and hence that it should be allowed to take over the place still held in the UN by the Nationalist Chinese government, which has been confined since 1949 to Formosa and some smaller islands off the coast of mainland China. The United States has refused to recognize the People's Republic, and the UN has so far supported the American position that it ought not be admitted. Since no nation can be admitted to the UN without the approval of the Security Council by a majority including the affirmative votes of the permanent members, the United States has threatened to use its veto power, if necessary, to bar the admission of Red China. However, the question is not really one of *admitting* Communist China but of assenting to its claim to be the government of China and therefore entitled to exercise all the rights and privileges of the existing Chinese UN membership.

There is no article in the UN Charter that prescribes a way of solving this problem. Neither the Security Council nor the Assembly is made the judge of the credentials of its members. Nationalist China cannot be expelled from the UN, because the expulsion of a member requires the affirmative votes of all permanent members of the Council, and the Nationalist government could not be expected to approve its own exclusion. Only by the Council's agreeing to regard this question as "procedural" could a majority of seven members come to a decision against the opposition of the United States. Such an event is extremely unlikely, since the question is one of the most explosive political issues in the world. As long as the United States remains firmly opposed to the seating of Red China, that government is not likely to be admitted.

Neither the United States nor the other members of the UN oppose the seating of Red China because it is Communist, since that could hardly be a bar against entry into an organization that includes the Soviet Union and several of its Communist satellites. The opposition is grounded rather on the fact that Red China intervened in the Korean War against the forces that were fighting under the flag of the UN. For this and many other reasons Red China has not shown a proper disposition to conform to the rules of international society as outlined in the Charter of the UN. In a word, Red China has not been held fit to be a member of the UN. There is, moreover, some doubt as to whether the Chinese Communists have yet proved that their government amounts to anything more than a temporary conquest of mainland China.

Much American opposition to the seating of Red China derives from the Korean War and the malignant hostility that the leaders of that state have not ceased to display toward the United States. Were they to gain their objective in the UN, the event would appear as a great triumph for them and a diplomatic humiliation for us. It would be a triumph, too, for the Soviet Union, which has persistently advocated the seating of Red China, and it would augment the influence of communism in the UN. Many leading Americans, notably the Senate Republican leader, William F. Knowland, advocate the withdrawal of the United States from the UN if Red China should be seated.

This problem is serious and perhaps insoluble. The UN cannot function as it was intended as long as the Security Council is deadlocked and paralyzed; yet

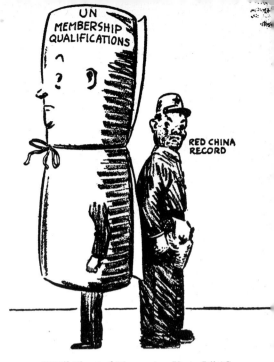

"Still Short of Measuring Up to It" (Carmack in the Christian Science Monitor)

this condition is certain to continue unless some great change is made in the constitution of the Council. If the People's Republic of China endures and shows a genuine will to act according to the law of nations, American opposition to seating it may be abandoned. Even now there is considerable opinion in our country which holds that the best way to "tame" Red China would be to bring it within the UN. Some students of the question see a possible solution in admitting Red China to the UN as a *new* member, removing Nationalist China from permanent membership in the Security Council but not from the UN, and giving the permanent Council seat to India. Thus there would be "two Chinas" and neither would belong to the Council unless elected to a non-permanent seat.

American critics of the UN. The most serious criticism of the UN in our country has come from two different schools of thought. On the one hand are those who expected the UN to be a power capable of enforcing the peace of the world. They

Senator William F. Knowland (R., California) has stated his belief that the United States should withdraw from the United Nations if Red China is admitted. (International News Photo)

conceived it as a supranational force that would be able to "crack down" on aggression anywhere in the world. The UN, however, has never pretended to be a world state, but only an agency for international co-operation and the taking of collective security measures to give effect to prevailing opinion throughout the world of nations. When there is no such prevailing opinion, there can be no agreement on collective security measures. The peace of the world must from the nature of things rest ultimately on justice, good moral behavior of nations, and enlightened opinion.

Some Americans who are disappointed by what they call the "weakness" of the UN agitate for a world federal government with an authority over all nations like the authority of our federal government over the states. This is an absurdly impractical proposal, since no nation would willingly consent to the extinction of its political independence. It is true that the advocates of world government say that it should be limited government; that is, limited to the power of enforcing world peace. But a power great enough to do that would be great enough to do anything. The idea of a world government, however, is impossible. The only way a world state could come into existence is by one nation conquering the world; and no nation is able to do that.

Other critics of the UN's incapacity as an instrument for enforcing peace imagine that the problem could be solved by expelling the Communist nations and then drawing all or a great part of the other members into some kind of federal system. Since no member of the UN can be expelled without the approval of all the permanent members of the Security Council, the Communist nations could not be put out without violating the rule of the Charter. Of course the anti-Communist members could withdraw from the UN and form a new organization, but the fundamental facts of international life would decree that such a new organization could not be a federal state but only another alliance.

A different school of critics attacks the UN for exactly opposite reasons. They fear it is becoming too strong and exerting too much influence on American foreign policy. They charge the UN with having involved us in the Korean War (which it did not) and then for having been a dead weight on our war effort, preventing us from winning a complete victory in Korea. For the latter charge there may be some foundation, although it by no means points to the main reason why we confined ourselves to such a narrowly limited effort. These same critics again and again have voiced a fear that the UN Charter and various treaties made pursuant to our membership in the organization may vitiate our Constitution. Since the Constitution declares treaties to be part of the supreme law of the land, it is feared that UN treaties may lead to the federal government's exercise of powers not granted by the Constitution. For example, the constitutional authority to declare war is reserved to the Congress; yet the country was plunged into the Korean War without congressional authorization, by a President who claimed that it was his duty to uphold the

UN. However, the UN Charter expressly states that nothing contained in it "shall authorize the United Nations to intervene in matters which are essentially within the domestic jurisdiction of any state." And the Supreme Court has repeatedly held that treaties which conflict with the Constitution have no validity.

Another frequently heard criticism of the UN is that it is a "godless" or an "atheist" organization. Such criticism usually seems to be an additional argument offered by persons who are opposed to the UN for other reasons. The criticism stresses the point that the name of God is not found in the UN Charter and that the organization takes no stated cognizance of God's law or His power. Both criticisms could be made just as easily against the American Constitution. The UN is made up of nations and its Secretariat is staffed by people who are Christian and non-Christian, atheist and deist, religious and non-religious. It has tried to follow an official policy of favoring no one religion above others and of being respectful of all religions.

Pope Pius XII has spoken favorably of the UN on several occasions. Pointing out that the UN is not perfect, that it can be improved in many ways, the Pope expressed the hope that it might "become the full and faultless expression of this international solidarity for peace, erasing from its institutions and its statutes every vestige of its origin which was of necessity a solidarity in war."

Revision of UN Charter. An international organization that hopes to fulfill its purposes in the modern world must provide for alteration of its structure and its functions to meet changing world conditions. It must be able to profit from experience and revise itself to become more effective in achieving its aims. The UN Charter provides that amendments can be adopted by a two-thirds vote of the Assembly and a vote of seven members of the Security Council, including all five

"Why Is the Doughnut Less Interesting?"
(Alexander in the Philadelphia Bulletin*)*

permanent members. It provides also that a general conference for revising the Charter can be called by a two-thirds vote of the Assembly and the concurrence of any seven members of the Council. Finally, it provided in 1945 that the calling of a general revision conference would automatically be put on the order of business for 1955, and that the conference would be held if voted for by a majority of the Assembly and any seven members of the Council.

Congressional committees in the United States gave serious attention from 1949 onward to the problem of strengthening the UN. Many different resolutions were introduced into Congress on ways and means of strengthening the UN, but Congress did not find any proposal that seemed to warrant its support. The State Department adopted a policy of trying to make the present UN work rather than sponsor untried schemes of improvement. Various prominent Americans insisted that the need for action was urgent. They assumed that unless the UN is drastically strengthened a new world war will occur—a thermonuclear war that could demolish the world.

Those who advocate revision of the UN Charter stress that the present Charter was written before the first atomic bomb was exploded. Atomic and hydrogen weapons, they insist, have completely outmoded all "pre-atomic" devices for maintaining peace and effecting disarmament. The UN was created in time of war, they point out, and it is more an alliance of partners in war than an institution for maintaining world peace. The alliance, furthermore, was based on the assumption of unity among the Big Five, and the Soviet Union has made this unity impossible. Changes in the UN Charter are necessary, they believe, since new states, such as India, have risen to a position of importance in the world, and former enemy states, e.g. Germany, have become "key states" in their respective regions. Finally, according to some, the Charter should be revised because the UN as now constituted, especially with the veto power as it now works, has shown that it cannot effectively prevent aggression. Advocates of UN revision therefore concentrate on these reforms:

1. Membership open to all states willing to join and able to qualify as "peace-loving" states.

2. Some limitation of the veto, at least in regard to the admission of new states, the amendment process, the peaceful settlement of disputes, and the imposition of sanctions.

3. Greater power to the UN to effect disarmament. This would involve the right of inspection and some amount of control of the manufacture of atomic and thermonuclear weapons.

4. Compulsory jurisdiction over international legal questions for the International Court of Justice.

Not all friends of the UN favor revision of the Charter. The Carnegie Endowment for International Peace conducted a survey of public opinion on Charter revision in representative parts of the world. It concluded, after about a year's study, that demands for revision of the UN Charter are inadvisable. Joseph E. Johnson, president of the Endowment, said that concentration on revision would probably result in public disappointment

"if no new amendments are adopted owing to the application of the veto to amendment proposals, or if amendments are adopted which weaken rather than strengthen the Charter." Mr. Johnson said also that he believed the Charter as it stands "probably represents at least as great an area of agreement upon the role of an international organization as now exists among the governments and peoples of the world."

In similar fashion, the UN Secretariat stated that revision of the UN would more likely result in weakening than in strengthening it. Spokesmen for the Secretariat observed that there was less unanimity among the great powers in 1955 than in 1945, and therefore it was futile to expect agreement on revision.

These judgments proved to be correct. When the projected conference was held in the spring of 1955, there was a chorus of praise for the UN, but no proposals for revising the Charter.

104. VALUE OF THE UN TO THE UNITED STATES

There is at present no prospect for increasing the strength of the organization as a means of enforcing peace among the nations. This is far from meaning, however, that the UN has "failed" and is of no use to the United States. Viewed realistically, it can be seen to have great value. It is essentially a code of right international conduct based on the old principle of the law of nations, which meant that nations should do one another as much good as possible in peacetime. It is also a method of international cooperation and a permanent visible institution that calls the member nations into beneficent community. It works toward strengthening the respect for treaties and broadens the base of international law. It provides a means of expression for international opinion, which no great power can afford to be ignorant of or to disregard. As Secretary of State John Foster Dulles has said, the UN is "a Town Meeting of the World, where . . . differences . . . are talked about and discussed, and where slowly but surely, progress is being made toward finding common denominators of moral judgment and world opinion on which acceptable world law can gradually be built." Between the stated principles of the United Nations and American foreign policy there is no disharmony, and both President Truman and President Eisenhower—charged with responsibility for directing foreign policy—have made UN co-operation an essential feature of our policy.

UN and national sovereignty. Membership in the United Nations in no way violates the sovereignty of the United States but is rather a way of employing sovereign power. Sovereignty does not mean that a nation is a law unto itself; for all nations must obey the law of international society or come to grief sooner or later. Sovereignty means nothing but the ultimate legal and physical power possessed by the state to promote the welfare of all citizens and protect them from aggression. The state must recognize that might can never make right; it must admit that all states, like all human beings, are subject to the moral law; that they have obligations to other states and to the citizens who are subject to their sovereignty.

A closer unity of mankind has always been an ideal of Christian tradition. This closer unity of mankind has been a consistent aim of our tradition because of a number of reasons. The first of these is the unity of the human race, based upon God's creating all men to His image and likeness. Second, as a consequence of this belief we subscribe to the equal dignity of all men in the eyes of the Creator. Third, we know that all men are subject to the same natural law. Catholicism has always seen the human race as one universal society composed of different races and nations which ought to know one another and live in harmony.

States, like individual men, are under moral law, and there should be some arrangement for stating and adjudicating international law in some kind of organized community among the nations of the world. Such a community may be a free association of independent states, if the states voluntarily submit to international law and are willing to have their disputes adjudicated by some tribunal instead of settling them by war.

Conclusion. The UN organization is for our times the only conceivable embodiment of this ideal. Our country had the honor of taking the lead in bringing it into existence, although it came as a response to a universally felt need among the nations of the world. It is likely to endure for long, and no member could wisely withdraw from it. The UN cannot prevent war, but it may tend to diminish some of the causes of war; the Charter is the only treaty that bridges the abyss between the Communist and free nations. So far the most beneficent activities of the UN have been carried on by its subsidiary agencies; while security against war has been sought by our country in armaments and defensive alliances. Politically, the organization has been incapacitated by the division of most of the world into great Communist and anti-Communist alliances, each headed by one of the "super powers" of 1945. Gradually, however, other great nations recover stronger positions; and if the peace is kept, it is likely that power will be rather *distributed* than *divided*. If so, the international world will show something like a balance of power again instead of a division into two hostile armed camps. In that event both the UN Security Council and General Assembly ought to be able to function more effectively and become the main instrument for conducting the foreign policies of all the member nations.

REVIEW

100. Historical Background

A. How was the former unity of Christendom dissolved?

B. What is meant by the "balance of power"? Does this principle oppose the principle of international organization for collective security? Explain.

C. What was the main purpose of the League of Nations?

D. What was the inherent weakness of the League? Cite examples.

101. Nature of the UN

A. State the objectives of the United Nations Organization.

B. Name the six principal organs of the UN.

C. In what way have the permanent members of the Security Council reserved to themselves the important decisions concerning war and peace?

D. Which organ is known as "the Town Meeting of the World"? Which organ was not created by the UN Charter but merely placed under its guidance?

102. Achievements and Failures

A. The United Nations has aided thousands of needy children. Describe the work of four agencies which have participated in this aid to children.

B. Name two UN agencies which have excited much controversy and criticism in this country. Explain briefly.

C. "The United Nations is a power above all nations to force all nations to keep the peace." Is this statement true?

D. Indicate the expansion of UN membership which took place in 1955.

103. The China Question, New Members, Charter Revision

A. What is the basic problem the UN faces concerning the People's Republic of China?

B. Describe the differences of opinion in this country concerning the UN.

C. Describe how the UN Charter can be amended.

D. Cite four proposed reforms of the UN Charter.

104. Value of the UN to the United States

A. Both Presidents Truman and Eisenhower have made UN co-operation an essential feature of our foreign policy. In what ways do the stated principles of the United Nations harmonize with those of our foreign policy?

B. Define sovereignty—what it means and what it does not mean.

C. Describe how the work of the UN can effect *distribution* of power among nations rather than *division* of power.

THE CHAPTER IN REVIEW

A. Indicate five differences between the League of Nations and the UN. Cite three reasons why these differences have helped the UN.

B. Is there a need today for a form of international organization? Explain.

C. Present the problems confronting the UN in the veto power and the China questions. Indicate some possible solutions to these problems.

D. Show how the UN has helped improve world conditions in the past ten years.

E. Cite three ways in which the principles of the UN Charter carry out the Christian traditions of international justice and charity.

SELECTED READINGS

A difficult but invaluable book to serve for the historical background of the discussions in this chapter is John Eppstein, *The Catholic Tradition of the Law of Nations* (London: Burns, Oates & Washbourne, Ltd., 1935). Many books were published toward the end of World War II in which interpretations of Catholic tradition on international affairs were set forth. Among these works the following should be mentioned: Rev. Harry C. Koenig (editor), *Principles for Peace* (Milwaukee: The Bruce Publishing Co., 1943), which is a collection of papal statements relative to peace since the time of Pope Leo XIII; Guido Gonella, *A World to Reconstruct: Pius XII on Peace and*

Reconstruction (Milwaukee: The Bruce Publishing Co., 1944); Thomas P. Neill, *Weapons for Peace* (Milwaukee: The Bruce Publishing Co., 1945); Msgr. Donald MacLean, *A Dynamic World Order* (Milwaukee: The Bruce Publishing Co., 1945).

Papal Christmas messages since 1939 have been concerned with the world community and problems of a peaceful world society in some respect or other. They can be found in *Catholic Mind* and *The Pope Speaks.* Pamphlets bringing papal statements up to date are published from time to time by the Catholic Association for International Peace (Washington: C.A.I.P.). Among these pamphlets are Rev. Harry C. Koenig (editor), *Papal Peace Mosaic*, 1945; Thomas P. Neill (editor), *The Pope Speaks on Peace*, 1949; Catherine Schaefer (editor), *Pius XII and Peace—1939–1944*, 1944.

The following publications by the C.A.I.P. deal with the problem of ethics and the securing of human rights in international society. Msgr. John A. Ryan, *International Ethics*, 1942; and Rev. Wilfrid Parsons, S.J., and Rev. John M. Paul, C.S.P., *Timeless Rights in Modern Times*, 1948. Also valuable for an understanding of this subject are John Eppstein, *Code of International Ethics* (Westminster, Md.: The Newman Press, 1953); and Roger N. Baldwin, *Human Rights—World Declaration and American Practice* (Washington: Public Affairs Committee, 1950).

The relationship of the individual American citizen to world affairs is clearly brought out in the book prepared by the Catholic Association for International Peace, *The Role of the Christian in the World For Peace, A Survey*, 1955, and in a pamphlet prepared by the same organization, *The Obligation of Catholics to Promote Peace and the Rights of the People.* Also good on this subject is Rev. Robert C. Hartnett, *Education for International Understanding* (New York: America Press, 1950).

The United Nations, located in New York City, publishes a yearbook and a monthly journal devoted to information about the UN, *Yearbook of the U.N.*, and *U.N. Review.* The United Nations has also published an elementary handbook explaining the organization. It is entitled *Everyman's U.N.* (New York: United Nations, 1953).

A good explanation of the UN, which is sympathetic to it, is Amry Vandenbosch and Willard N. Hogan, *The United Nations: Background, Organization, Functions, and Activities* (New York: McGraw-Hill Book Co., 1952).

Other basic treatments of the UN are: Abraham H. Feller, *United Nations and World Community* (Boston: Little, Brown & Co., 1952); the enthusiastic pamphlet by Rev. Robert A. Graham, S.J., and others, *Our Way to Peace: A Study of the United Nations Charter* (New York: America Press, 1948); Marie and Louis Zocca, *The United Nations: Action for Peace* (New Brunswick, N.J.: Rutgers University Press, 1953); and A. M. Rosenthal, *The United Nations: Its Record and Prospects* (New York: Carnegie Endowment for International Peace, 1953).

The Catholic Association for International Peace puts out a monthly newsletter, *C.A.I.P. News*, which is devoted in large part to the UN. The Association published a booklet, *The United Nations 1945–1955*, which is scheduled to be the first in its U.N. Series. It has also published a pamphlet, *Peace Agenda for the United Nations*, and has made a number of statements about revision of the UN, which appeared in newspaper articles and in weekly journals through 1955.

PROJECTS

1. If your school is near New York, a visit to the UN can be arranged. If this is not feasible, films and literature describing the functions of the UN can be obtained by writing to their headquarters in New York.

2. Six class groups could be assigned to write to each of the six main agencies of the UN for an account of its chief accomplishments and problems over the past year. Each group could then report to the class on its findings.

3. Postage stamps commemorate noteworthy events and anniversaries in our national history. A display of all the stamps issued, both in this country and abroad, relating to events concerning the United Nations would present a colorful picture of its brief history.

4. The minor agencies of the UN have achieved a high measure of success. With the aid of charts, a report can be made to the class, showing how each one of these agencies is successfully fulfilling its function.

Chapter 36. War and Peace

105. MAGNITUDE OF WAR
IN OUR TIMES

War remains a frightening possibility in the modern world. A major war involving this country and the Soviet Union with its satellites would probably have horrible results, ranging in possibility to the overnight destruction of hundreds of cities and death of millions. Some people, Winston Churchill for one, think our power to kill on such a scale will have the effect of eliminating war as a likelihood in the future. National leaders, they believe, will not resort to war, because even the victorious nations face inevitable vast destruction. In our foreign and domestic policy we cannot ignore the possibility of war, however hard we work to prevent it.

Conditions for a justifiable war. Christian teaching has always held that under certain conditions war is justifiable, perhaps even obligatory. These conditions are:

1. All peaceful means of settling the dispute in question must have been tried before a nation can resort to war. Peaceful means for settling disputes include direct negotiation between the disputing nations, usually with a view to compromising their differences. They also include mediation, or the calling in of a third party, to suggest possible solutions which the disputing nations may or may not be willing to accept. A third form of peaceful negotiations is arbitration, whereby the disputing nations agree beforehand to accept the decision rendered by a third party. Two nations not able to agree on a disputed question can agree to submit it to the International Court of Justice or to the United Nations. These peaceful means of settling international disputes all assume an honest difference of opinion between the disputant states and a willingness to accept the decision of a competent, neutral party.

2. There must be a just cause. Self-defense is the most obvious just cause of a nation's going to war. For a nation, like an individual, has the right to defend itself against attack. Ordinarily the line between defensive and offensive war cannot be as easily drawn as it might seem. The aggressor is not always the nation that fires first, for a nation may be maneuvered into a position in which it is compelled to surrender its independence

if it does not resort to arms. Most wars in the past have broken out not by calculating aggression but because a general international predicament had arisen and the statesmen did not see a peaceful way out of it.

Many people insist that under certain conditions we are justified in fighting a "preventive war"; that is, declaring war against such a potential enemy in order to defeat him before he weakens us or becomes too strong for us to defeat him easily. Bismarck called such a war "suicide in apprehension of death." Preventive war is impossible to justify morally. It assumes a knowledge of the future which no human being possesses. It assumes, moreover, that war is inevitable and the only question is one of timing. In a certain sense preventive war is blasphemous in that human beings arrogate to themselves the powers and the privileges of God Himself.

3. There must be a proportion between the good to be achieved by victory and the evils of suffering and destruction caused by the war. No nation is justified in waging a destructive war for a trivial cause.

4. A final condition necessary to justify war (once it has come) is that no unnecessary destruction of lives or property

be committed and resort is not had to immoral methods of combat. A nation is not justified in continuing to kill soldiers who are trying to surrender, for example, nor may it wantonly and vengefully kill noncombatants in the course of fighting. Only the defense of values that cannot be computed in terms of property and lives —religion, national existence, and freedom—seems adequate justification for war in our time. But even this does not justify the indiscriminate use of weapons of mass destruction. Methods of waging modern war give rise to serious moral problems that leaders in a Christian nation cannot ignore.

War in mid-twentieth century. Thousands of books and articles have been written to describe the almost unimaginable power of atomic and thermonuclear weapons. The bomb dropped on Hiroshima in 1945 demolished four square miles at the center of the city and four more square miles were badly wrecked. This bomb packed the explosive power of twenty thousand tons of TNT. Bombs have been developed since that time that are more than a thousand times as powerful. Scientists have speculated on the probable effects of different kinds of hydrogen bombs, but each day's speculation is outmoded by the next day's technical improvements in manufacturing new weapons of destruction. We are told by those who profess to know that it is now possible to make a hydrogen bomb which, exploded in the harbor at New York City or San Francisco, would destroy the entire city and make it uninhabitable for years to come.

Atomic and hydrogen weapons have also been developed in smaller packages for use by small planes and by infantry forces. Other means of murderous warfare have been perfected at an amazing rate: nerve gases to paralyze the power of resistence; germ weapons which are said to be able to destroy millions of people; various kinds of guided missiles that make the horror stories of pushbutton warfare threaten to become very real. For these reasons some scientists insist that there is no defense against the weapons of the future—except preventing their employment by avoiding war. Their appeals on this score take on a frantic note, but their calculations of damage in terms of "megadeaths" and radioactive "fall-out" and other such new phenomena suggest that their fears are well grounded.

106. THE QUESTION OF NATIONAL DEFENSE

What should our national policy be in the face of a threat of such destructive warfare? Obviously, we must work incessantly for the prevention of war. At the same time, we must prepare what specialists believe is an adequate defense in case war should come about. Our defense measures should be directed at protecting ourselves as well as possible against the devastation of thermonuclear war and at winning the war as quickly as possible by paralyzing the war-making ability of the enemy. Precisely what these measures should be will depend on the latest developments in armaments and in striking power of our own forces and of our potential enemies.

Adequate defense measures are costly and they are seldom popular. About 90 per cent of our national expenses are connected in one way or another with war—either paying for past wars or building defenses and armaments for a possible future war. This means that defense measures lower our standard of living by diverting from peaceful produc-

This is an area of the city of Hiroshima, Japan, where the first atomic bomb fell. Blocks of homes and buildings were wiped out by a destructive force far less powerful than today's hydrogen bomb. (U. S. Army Photograph)

The Air Force's new F-100 "Super Sabre" is the first operational jet fighter to exceed the speed of sound in level flight. This plane, which has a combat radius of over 500 miles, plays an important part in our defense system. (Official Air Force Photo)

"The Honest John" is one of the Army's newest free flight artillery rockets. It is shown here on its tactical "transporter-launcher" at the White Sands Proving Ground in New Mexico. (U. S. Army Photograph)

A Comparison of Strength

	U.S.	Rest of Free World	Soviet Block
Land Area	6%	69%	25%
Population	6%	59%	35%
Steel	43%	35%	22%
Coal	26%	39%	35%
Petroleum	48%	42%	10%
Primary Aluminum	47%	41%	12%
Electric Power	41%	43%	16%
Merchant Fleets	29%	68%	3%

(As of July 1955)

tion a large part of our raw materials and our manpower. They increase our taxes tremendously, raise the national debt, and decrease our purchasing power. They absorb the attention of some of the best minds in the country, and they interrupt the education or the careers of a majority of our young men.

Political leaders are therefore tempted to reduce military expenditures to a dangerously low level. Our military measures must always be sufficient for defense of our homeland from invasion or from air attack. They must be commensurate with our foreign policy commitments. By 1955 we had extended American protection to many quarters of the globe: over our own hemisphere; in western Europe all the way from Turkey and Greece to the Atlantic Ocean; over Iran and Iraq in the Near East; over Canada, Iceland, and Greenland in the north; over large areas of Southeast Asia, including weak

The Air Force's first tactical guided missile, the Martin B-61 Matador, is shown on its portable launcher. A combination of rocket and turbo-jet engine gives the missile great speed with which to overtake and intercept enemy aircraft. (Glenn L. Martin Company)

states like Laos, Cambodia, South Vietnam, Thailand, the Philippines, and Formosa.

Meanwhile our military strength was cut back—perhaps in reliance on the advantage we enjoyed in thermonuclear weapons at the time. Two problems of national defense seem to stand out above others in the second decade after World War II: (1) What kinds of arms and weapons should be given priority—massive hydrogen bombs, smaller atomic weapons, conventional weapons of the past, long-range guided missiles, the navy or the infantry or "push-button" technicians? (2) Is universal military training helpful for national defense, or is it more expeditious for us to put the same energy and money into a small, highly skilled, technically trained army of experts? There are many other problems connected with an adequate national defense, of course, but here we shall analyze these two.

Use of the new weapons in any future war. It would be dangerous to assume that nuclear weapons will not be used in a future war. At the same time, it is dangerous to assume that large numbers of soldiers will be needed, since an enemy might be paralyzed by several hydrogen bombs and we might have no need for an army of millions. This might prove a costly misuse of manpower. A good security program would seem to require continuing research to retain the superior position we hold in the development of nuclear weapons and an adequate defense system. The latter would include: radar screens sufficiently far away to warn American cities of coming attacks; interceptor devices (airplanes, guided missiles, etc.) to destroy bombers before they can strike industrial centers in the country; defense preparations in each urban region to keep loss of life to the minimum in case of successful attack by an enemy; dispersal of industry and of war material in order to prevent crippling ef-

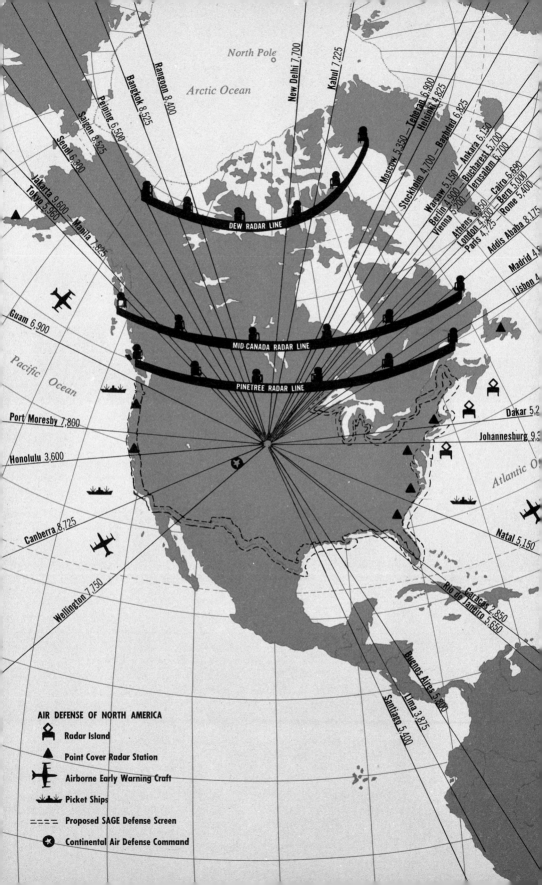

AIR DEFENSE OF NORTH AMERICA

- 🛏 Radar Island
- ▲ Point Cover Radar Station
- ✈ Airborne Early Warning Craft
- ⛴ Picket Ships
- --- Proposed SAGE Defense Screen
- ✪ Continental Air Defense Command

Frenchman's Flat, Nev., was the scene of the first atomic cannon test. Clouds of smoke fill the air as history's first atomic artillery shell is fired from the Army's new 280-mm gun. (U. S. Army Photograph)

The 518th AAA Operations Center at Fort Barry, Cal., maintains a constant radar watch for enemy aircraft. In this photo are the various boards on which are plotted the approach of enemy aircraft and the interceptor activity taken to repel attacks. (U. S. Army Photograph)

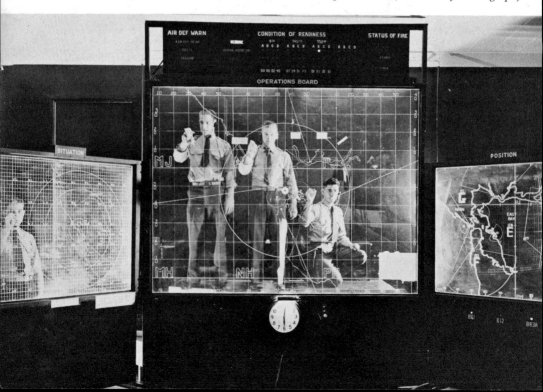

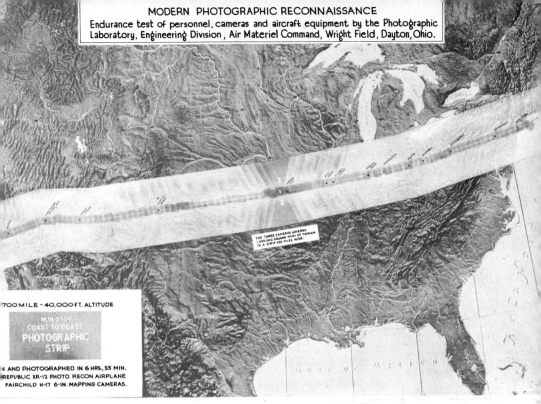

THE THREE CAMERAS COVERED 1,500,000 SQUARE MILES OF TERRAIN IN A STRIP 450 MILES WIDE.

700 MILE - 40,000 FT. ALTITUDE

NON-STOP COAST TO COAST PHOTOGRAPHIC STRIP

N AND PHOTOGRAPHED IN 6 HRS., 55 MIN.
REPUBLIC XR-12 PHOTO RECON AIRPLANE
FAIRCHILD K-17 6-IN. MAPPING CAMERAS.

President Eisenhower's proposal, Mutual Inspection for Peace, to ease world tensions would, if adopted, lead to future reductions in arms. This map shows the path that one airplane can photograph by using three cameras. (Official U. S. Air Force Photo)

fects from single successful bombing missions into this country.

United States offensive strategy seems designed to counterattack instantly in such fashion as to cripple an enemy's ability to wage war against us. Such retaliation must be directed upon military objectives to effect atomic disarmament of the enemy. Unless instantaneous and effective retaliation is accomplished, a future war could well develop into a struggle with nuclear weapons that would render most of the world unfit for habitation. If war cannot be avoided, we are faced with the difficult problem of winning it and still limiting it so that civilization can arise again from its ruins. Any general use of hydrogen bombs, even in the heart of enemy territory, endangers ourselves as well as the rest of the world. These are discouraging prospects, of course, but the ingenuity of man has combined with his perverseness to create weapons of mass destruction which he cannot be trusted not to use when the occasion of war arises. The only sure solution of mankind's future is to prevent war. Although man is ingenious enough to create a hydrogen bomb, he is not wise enough to find sure means of preventing war. And as long as war remains a possibility, the American government is obliged to build defenses against attack and to work out ways and means of winning a possible war with a minimum of damage.

Universal military training. During World War II all men of eligible age and good health were subject to military service. When the war was over, most Americans assumed that we would go back to our traditional policy of maintaining a small army of volunteers, most of whom intend to follow a professional military career.

Rev. Theodore M. Hesburgh, C.S.C., President of Notre Dame, is shown reviewing the school's Naval ROTC units. ROTC units enable American youth to fulfill their UMT obligations without interrupting their education. (University of Notre Dame)

The "cold war" and the Korean War made large military forces necessary, however, and certain groups in the country insisted that we adopt a policy of universal military training. The American Legion and the Veterans of Foreign Wars enthusiastically backed bills for this objective, and a presidential commission on universal military training recommended such training in 1947.

There are three major arguments in favor of universal military training:

1. That it is a matter of military necessity. The selective service system now in force and the reserve system cannot provide us with the pool of trained manpower which may be needed at a moment's notice. Ex-President Truman stated that "universal training represents the most democratic, the most economical, and the most effective method of maintaining the military strength we need." In similar fashion General George C. Marshall said: "It will enable us to face the uncertainties of an explosive international situation with the knowledge that we can be strong militarily without having to imperil our security econom-

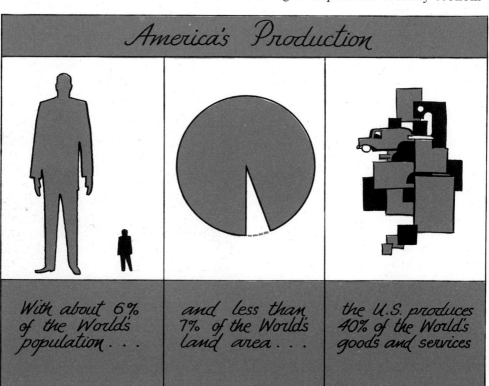

America's Production

With about 6% of the World's population . . . and less than 7% of the World's land area . . . the U.S. produces 40% of the World's goods and services

ically, no matter how long the present world tension may continue."

2. That it is the only way to build up a large body of trained men who can adequately handle the emergencies that would be created in the country by thermonuclear or bacteriological attacks. Without such a force at hand confusion and chaos would result.

3. That it is the only fair way to distribute the burden of defense on all shoulders. For this reason it is a morale-building factor as well as a military requirement. The experience of the Korean War showed that many young men were put in double jeopardy, for many veterans of World War II had to be recalled for service in Korea. Advocates of UMT insist that a pool of trained manpower would have been available for this service if their policy had been adopted.

The following arguments sum up the major objections of those against UMT:

1. That military experience of countries such as Germany and France, both of which had long-established universal military training programs, shows that it is not an effective method of preparing men for military service in time of war.

2. That proposed UMT plans would not produce a pool of trained men. They would have to be recalled to service, re-equipped with the latest weapons, and trained to use them. In effect, they would have to be trained for service like the draftees of World War II, whether they had UMT or not.

3. That UMT, or total peacetime conscription, is the shortest road to the militaristic state because it gives the military control over the minds and bodies of young men at an important period in their lives. It enables the armed forces to mold their wills, control their minds, and affect their thinking to a considerable degree even when they return to civilian life. The arguments of UMT advocates, that it is the best system of promoting democracy and better race relations, be-

trays their view that it is a system of indoctrination. Such procedure is a violent departure from our traditional view of the role of the military in national life.

Universal military training can be justified, of course, if it can be shown that it is necessary for national defense, that it is an efficient means to achieve its objectives, and that it can be conducted in such fashion that it will not reverse the traditional relationship of the military and the civilian branches of government or serve as a school of indoctrination for the youth of America.

107. THE QUEST FOR PEACE

The building of peace is difficult indeed. It requires greater wisdom than does planning for national defense or successful prosecution of war. It requires not only wisdom but also patience and diplomatic skill.

The average American citizen is tempted to relieve himself of the obligation to work for peace on the grounds that he can accomplish nothing to achieve

Dwight D. Eisenhower, President of the United States, has offered the U.S.S.R. a plan of mutual inspection of military installations as a first step toward disarmament. The U.S.S.R. has not accepted the plan because, it is believed, she does not have the technical know-how to make the plan advantageous to her. (Advertising Council)

His Holiness, Pope Pius XII, is shown as he was televised at the Vatican. The Supreme Pontiff has used the latest and most efficient means of bringing his messages of peace and Christian living to the world. (Religious News Service)

it. He sees how he makes a contribution to national defense by serving in the armed forces, by paying taxes, by volunteering for civil defense work, and by other such specific tasks. But it is difficult for him to see any connection between what he might do or say or think on the one hand and the general peace of the world on the other. Whether there will be peace, he is convinced, depends not on what he does but on what the leaders of the great governments of the world do. The fact is that peace depends on this and much more. A little serious reflection will show that one of the most important things that young Americans with a sound sense of values can do is to help create an atmosphere and a public opinion to support policies that in effect tend to secure the peace.

The messages of Pope Pius XII "on peace." Pope Pius XII, on numerous occasions, has analyzed the nature of peace, the moral conditions necessary for its achievement, and the great fundamental obstacles that must be overcome to attain it. His words constitute a remarkable body of Christian moral and political wisdom, and they are studied seriously by many persons who do not belong to the Catholic Church. The Pope insists on "mutual trust and good will" among the nations. Peace is something more than the absence of war. In our Christian tradition it is usually defined as a "tranquil living together in order." Such a condition is possible only when justice is generally

achieved, when each individual, each society and institution, each nation receives what is its due. Such a condition is possible, moreover, only when each is content with his due and is willing to make his contribution to the general good of the human race.

In his various analyses of peace, the Holy Father repeatedly reminds us that the problems of peace can be studied on three levels: on the international level, to establish peace among nations; on the national level, to establish social peace among the people of a country; on the individual level, to establish peace of conscience and tranquillity of mind. These three levels of peace are intimately related, and when you promote any one of them you automatically promote the others to some extent.

In his 1940 Christmas Eve message the Holy Father laid down certain prerequisites without which peace cannot be achieved. These are "victories" which must be won before peace can be established:

"Victory over the hatred which divides nations today and the disappearance of systems and actions which breed this hatred." Here the Pope condemns narrow nationalism, the artificially cultivated and self-righteous belief in the superiority of one's own country and hatred for all others.

"Victory over distrust which exerts a paralyzing pressure on international law and makes all honest understanding impossible. Therefore, return to the principle of mutual trust." Here the Pope focuses attention on the condition that makes treaties and international agreements of any kind impossible or worthless. Unless nations can trust each other to abide by solemnly made promises, nothing can be accomplished toward international security.

"Victory over the dismal principle that utility is the foundation and aim of law, that might can create right. This principle is bound to upset all international relations and is unacceptable to all weaker nations. Therefore, return to honest, serious, and moral international relations." Here the Pope touches on what he calls in other places the root of all our trouble —the rejection of morality and the acceptance of the rule that whatever is useful is good. This latter standard justifies any conduct as long as it is successful. It is by nature destructive of peace and of all permanent values.

"Victory over those potential conflicts arising out of the unbalanced state of world economy. Therefore, a new economic order has to be gradually evolved which gives all nations the means to secure for their citizens an appropriate standard of life." Here the Pope condemns the attempts made in the past by many nations to monopolize world markets and sources of raw materials. As long as there is a serious disproportion in the wealth of "have" and "have-not" nations, he intimates, there will be seeds of war which might grow into armed conflict.

"Victory over the kind of egoism which, relying on its own power, aims at impairing the honor and sovereignty of nations, as well as the sound, just, and ordered liberty of individuals. This egoism has to be replaced by a genuine Christian solidarity of a legal and economic character, and by a brotherly co-operation of the nations, the sovereignty

of which has been duly secured." Here the Pope states a truth of long standing in the Christian tradition, the truth that all persons in the world are members of a single human race, that their interests are common interests which can best be promoted by co-operation instead of by suicidal competition, that while nations constitute legitimate groupings of human society, they are not ultimate and absolute divisions with no common interests.

In 1948 the Holy Father analyzed what he called the "Christian will for peace," which he exhorted not only Catholics but all others of good will to adopt in their work for world peace. The Christian will for peace, he said, comes from God, and its chief weapons are prayer and love. It is not a matter of weakness or resignation. Indeed, the Christian will for peace is strong and it is willing to bear arms against unjust aggression. The Pope also characterized it as practical and realistic, ready to adopt concrete measures that relieve social and economic pressures making for disorder and lack of tranquil living in the world. Finally, the Christian will for peace is not blustering. It does not have quick recourse to the threat of arms, nor does it puff up national pride to make an international crisis out of incidents that can be overlooked in the interest of peace.

The essential elements of a just and lasting peace. Pope Pius XII's discourses on peace have stressed repeatedly the following points as essential to just and lasting peace:

1. Peace must be built on a general acknowledgment of God as Creator and sovereign Master of mankind. For God is the God of all men, whom He has created to His image and destined to the same eternal union with Him. All men and all groups of men, then, are subject to the same moral law, which is God's law as applied to human beings and recognized by human conscience. Just and lasting peace is impossible among man-

kind unless general acknowledgment is made of moral law and unless international relations are based upon this moral law.

2. No peace can be just and lasting unless it respects the dignity of the human being and admits that he possesses God-given, inviolable, natural rights. Such respect for human rights precludes the oppression of minorities and the unfair treatment of backward or colonial peoples. A peace based upon the denial of these rights is not a peace worthy of man. A just and lasting peace, therefore, cannot be established as long as there are tyrannical, aggressive, and totalitarian governments in the world.

3. A just and lasting peace can be established only when economic and social justice prevails among nations and among classes of men within nations. "Within the limits of a new order founded on moral principles," the Pope said in 1941, "there is no place for that cold and calculating egoism which tends to hoard the economic resources and materials destined for the use of all to such an extent that the nations less favored by nature are not permitted access to them."

The 1942 Christmas Eve message was devoted to the conditions of social peace within nations. These conditions were grouped in the following manner: (1) respect for man and his right to bodily, mental, and moral development, especially his rights to religious education, to worship of God, to organize for charity, to choose his work in life and his right to use things for his well-being; (2) defense of social unity and respect for the family in its economic, spiritual, moral, and legal rights; (3) respect for the dignity of labor and its right to a family living wage; (4) establishment of a system of law based on the dominion of God, which is just and applicable to all; (5) a state founded on the Christian spirit, dedicated to the common good, to respect for man and his eternal destiny.

Reform of the international political order. Just and durable peace can be established only through reform of the international political order. A sound international order, the Holy Father has suggested many times, respects the right of all nations, large or small, to existence and to the legitimate functions of an independent state. The first fundamental point of just and honorable peace the Pope's 1939 Christmas Eve message stated this way: "A fundamental condition of a just and honorable peace is to assure the right to life and independence of all nations, large and small, strong and weak. One nation's will to live must never be tantamount to a death sentence for another." In 1941 he insisted that "there is no room for the violation of the freedom, integrity and security of other states, no matter what may be their territorial extension or their capacity for defense . . . [Large states must] respect the rights of those smaller states to political freedom, to economic development and to adequate protection, in the case of conflicts between nations, of that neutrality which is theirs according to the natural as well as international law."

The Holy Father recommended the establishment of some kind of international organization with the right to interpret international law in order to settle conflicts between nations, and the power to enforce the decisions arrived at fairly and properly. The Pope does not describe any particular framework as being ideal, nor does he state that the international organization must be a federation, a world government, or any other particular kind of institution. His various statements only lead to the conclusion that some such organization is natural and, given the conditions of the time, necessary to peace. In various places the Pope asserts that functions proper to the national state should not be surrendered to such an international institution, but he implies that functions which the individual states apparently cannot handle adequately—such as preventing war or effecting disarmament—must be undertaken by an international organization.

Pope Pius XII has told us that one of the fundamental conditions of enduring peace is disarmament. It is not the Holy Father's business to tell states how to disarm or to what extent they should reduce their armaments. But it *is* his business to warn of the disastrous results of armament races, of the lost manpower and the lowered standard of living, of the terrible devastation assured for any future war, and of the mutual suspicion and mistrust engendered by armament races.

Conclusion. Just and lasting peace is impossible in the modern world unless a general spiritual renovation is accomplished. In bringing this consideration into all his addresses on peace, the Pope suggests that each person and each nation look into its own heart and conscience to see how it has failed to prepare the way for true peace. A moment's reflection is enough to make us realize that unless mutual distrust and suspicion are dispelled, unless international hatreds and desire of vengeance are removed, unless men of one nation see men of other nations as their brothers, there is no chance for just and lasting peace, for the "tranquil living together in order" which signifies peace in men's hearts, peace among men within nations, and finally peace among nations in the world.

REVIEW

105. Magnitude of War in Our Times
A. Define "preventive war." What did Bismarck call it?

B. Discuss the development of atomic weapons since the first atomic bomb fell on Hiroshima in 1945.

106. The Question of National Defense
A. What are the two major problems of national defense today?

B. Discuss the possible misuse of manpower in any future war.

C. Discuss the major arguments for and against universal military training.

107. The Quest for Peace
A. What can the average citizen do to help achieve the goal of general peace in the world?

B. What is the Christian definition of peace?

C. According to the Holy Father, the problems of peace can be studied on three levels. Name them.

D. What are the five victories which are prerequisites to peace, according to the Pope's Christmas message of 1940?

E. Name the essential elements of a just and lasting peace.

THE CHAPTER IN REVIEW
A. Discuss *how* and *if* the destruction of an atomic war can be reconciled with the conditions necessary to wage a "just war."

B. Why is such a large portion of our national budget devoted to defense expenditures? Explain various defense expenditures.

C. What does Pope Pius XII mean by the "Christian will for peace." Explain briefly.

D. Our Holy Father has told us that one of the fundamental conditions of enduring peace is disarmament. Discuss the part you can do in helping this cause.

SELECTED READINGS

A brief but excellent treatment of modern war, with informed estimates on the destructiveness of thermonuclear bombs, is "Nuclear War," by T. F. Walkowicz and William Pfaff, *Commonweal* (December 10, 1954). David J. Bradley, *No Place to Hide* (Boston: Little, Brown & Co., 1948), is a doctor's account of the effects of atomic energy on people. A good survey of atomic energy for war and peace is Robert Ducharme Potter, *Young People's Book of Atomic Energy* (New York: Dodd, Mead & Co., 1948). A more recent and a briefer study is the pamphlet by John Lewellen, *Primer of Atomic Energy* (Chicago: Science Research Associates, 1952).

The difficult problem of applying Christian principles on war to modern destructive warfare is discussed by F. H. Drinkwater, "The Morality of Nuclear War," *Commonweal* (March 18, 1955), and by Rev. Peter Lumbreras, O.P., "Morality of the A-Bomb," *Catholic Mind* (May 1955). The moral problems involved in pacifism are analyzed by Rev. Cyprian Emanuel, O.F.M., "Morality of Conscientious Objection to War" (Washington: Catholic Association for International Peace, 1943).

Universal military service is advocated by Karl T. Compton, "The Case for National Security Training," *Reader's Digest* (August 1953). The Reference Shelf volume *Peacetime Conscription,* edited by Julia E. Johnsen (New York: H. W. Wilson Co., 1945), gives arguments for and against universal military service as a national policy.

The tradition to which American Catholics are heir can best be seen in the writings of recent Popes and in the statements made by the American bishops. Papal thought on political and social matters is well handled in the following three books: Etienne Gilson (editor), *The Church Speaks to the Modern World* (Garden City, N.Y.: Doubleday & Company, Inc., 1954), an Image Book on the social teachings of Pope Leo XIII; *Fourteen Encyclicals of His Holiness Pope Pius XI* (Washington: National Catholic Welfare Conference, 1937), which includes the most important social writings of Pope Pius XI; Robert C. Pollock (editor), *The Mind of Pius XII* (New York: Crown Publishers, Inc., 1955), which gives a general coverage of social and political problems as handled by Pope Pius XII; the selections are well chosen. Papal political thought since Pope Leo XIII can be followed in Rev. Francis J. Powers, C.S.V., *Papal Pronouncements on the Political Order* (Westminster, Md.: The Newman Press, 1952), and papal thought on international relations is excellently presented by Rev. Harry C. Koenig (editor), *Principles for Peace* (Milwaukee: The Bruce Publishing Co., 1943). Almost every important papal message can be found in *Catholic Mind,* through which the student can bring the above-mentioned works up to date.

A valuable collection of statements by the American bishops is Very Rev. Raphael M. Huber, O.F.M. (editor), *Our Bishops Speak* (Milwaukee: The Bruce Publishing Co., 1952).

Guidance in ways and means of carrying Catholic thought into action can be found in the following works: Father Keller's *You Can Change the World,* especially Chapters X and XIV; Rev. F. Lelotte, S. J., *Fundamental Principles of Catholic Action* (Chicago: Fides Publishers Assn., 1947); Rev. John F. Cronin, S.S., *Catholic Social Action* (Milwaukee: The Bruce Publishing Co., 1948); Rev. Leo R. Ward (editor), *The American Apostolate* (Westminster, Md.: The Newman Press, 1952); Most Rev. Joseph Charbonneau, *Catholic Action* (Chicago: Fides Publishers Assn., 1943); Eugene S. Geissler, *Training of Lay Leaders* (Chicago: Fides Publishers Assn., 1944); Vincent J. Giese, "Opportunity for American Catholics," *Social Order* (January 1954); and James R. Schneid, "Citizens, Principles and the Future City," *Social Order* (March 1955).

PROJECTS

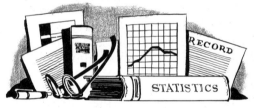

1. A member of the class can be designated to inquire at each of the armed forces' local recruiting stations. A report can be made on the various enlistment possibilities for both men and women.

2. It would be interesting to investigate the cost of each war in which this country has participated. A bulletin-board display can be prepared, showing the losses in manpower and the monetary cost of the Revolutionary War, War of 1812, Civil War, Spanish-American War, World Wars I and II, and the recent Korean conflict.

3. On a world map we might show the areas that are included in the perimeter of our national defense system.

4. The local office of the Civil Defense Authority will be willing to furnish literature concerning the local defense efforts. A member of the CD may possibly be available to speak on this subject.

5. A report on *Hiroshima* by John Hersey will make the class vividly conscious of the unbelievable devastation an atomic bomb can inflict.

DEBATE

The question: **IS THE UNITED NATIONS A SOUND STEP TOWARD ORGANIZATION FOR WORLD ORDER ADVOCATED BY POPE PIUS XII?**

The class has now studied and discussed national problems long enough to know that they are not settled by extremist decisions motivated by emotional animus against a measure or adulation of it. Such extreme decisions are the result of emotion rather than constructive, critical thought. The class will also realize that the United Nations is not a perfect institution. It will therefore be able to weigh its defects and its merits carefully, compare it with past institutions, and decide whether the above question should be answered in the affirmative or the negative.

In this last debate, students should be entirely "on their own" in gathering and evaluating the evidence to be presented on one side or the other. Let us only suggest that the class must (1) find out what the Holy Father has said about organization for world order and how he has been interpreted by competent Catholic authorities; (2) how the United Nations is organized, what its purposes are, how it has operated in the past decade. Then the class is ready to compare the United Nations with papal proposals and to answer the question proposed for discussion. Information on papal teaching can be obtained from the Catholic Association for International Peace, 1312 Massachusetts Ave., N.W, Washington 5, D.C., and from such Catholic magazines as *America, Commonweal,* and *Catholic Mind.* Information about the United Nations can be obtained by writing to UN headquarters in New York City, and critical estimates (pro and con) of the organization can be found in various pamphlets and periodicals.

Affirmative presentation

I. The Holy Father's teaching includes these points:
 1. The unity of the human race and therefore of the nations of the world.
 2. The resulting need of international law and "juridical institutions."
 3. The warning to profit from past mistakes and not to create an unworkable or impotent organization.
II. The United Nations is a new step toward:
 1. Giving political form to world unity.
 2. Establishing true enforceable international law.
 3. Ending international war as a means of settling disputes between nations.

Negative presentation

I. The negative must accept, reject, or modify the presentation of papal teaching on world organization as given by the affirmative.
II. The United Nations does not conform in essentials to the Pope's principles of world organization.
 1. It is not informed by Christian principles—without which there can be no peace.
 2. It is not able to settle disputes between major powers, and these are the occasion of world wars.
 3. The League of Nations, an organization similar to the United Nations, was not able to stop World War II.
III. The United Nations actually obstructs the promotion and preservation of peace.
 1. Its executive arm, the Security Council, is paralyzed by the differences between the Communist and free worlds.
 2. So many disputes are appealed to the UN there is not enough time for them to be heard.
 3. The veto right of the permanent members of the Security Council makes disciplinary measures impossible.

CLASSROOM DISCUSSION: The class should take up the last line of argument advanced by the negative to decide how much truth there is to these three charges against the United Nations. If it is found that the charges are not substantially true, then the class should center its discussion on the extent to which the UN does or does not conform to principles advanced by the Holy Father. This involves arriving at agreement (1) on the Holy Father's principles, and (2) whether the UN is a step in their direction.

Epilogue

The problems we have analyzed in the preceding pages are outstanding American national problems today. Let us recall that problems are part of human existence. There has never been a nation and there has never been an age that did not have many social, political, and economic problems. At all times and in all countries, then, human problems need to be solved. Our study of American problems does not therefore imply that ours is not fundamentally a good society. Critical discussion of our national problems is an assurance that we live in a free society that respects its citizens as responsible persons whose loyalty is above reproach and whose interest in the national welfare is manifest by their concern to analyze and solve their national problems. Our discussion of these problems is therefore witness that America is a noble and free country and that we are loyal citizens interested in making it an even better land, for critical discussion of national problems is the first step toward solving them.

We who are Catholics are fortunate in being at the same time members of another great society. From the Church we receive a long tradition which embraces the wisdom and the experience of many centuries. From it we receive sound moral principles that help us solve the national problems with which we are daily confronted. Catholics are in a peculiarly advantageous position to make a valuable contribution to American national thought on these problems. The Church does not dictate ready-make solutions to us, but it is the supreme teacher of right moral principles in social life. By respecting moral principles in all practical civic and political activity, we can more easily work out our solutions to the national problems we encounter.

There is room for disagreement among Catholics on many of the questions we have described in the preceding pages. On general moral principles Catholics agree, but on working them out in practical life they seldom reach anything like unanimity of opinion. Throughout this book we have discussed such issues as the McCarran-Walter Act governing immigration, our vast foreign-aid programs, the demand for a guaranteed annual wage, "right-to-work" legislation, and similar subjects. The more immediate the moral issue is in each case, the less room for disagreement there is among Catholics. The more the problem is about ways and means of accomplishing a good objective, the more disagreement there is. For when the problem becomes one of effective means to accomplish the end agreed upon, it tends to lose its moral significance and to center on technique.

Let us remember that there is a humanistic value in working at the social problems confronting us. This means that we develop ourselves more perfectly as social persons in the Christian tradition by studying our social problems, by analyzing their profound ramifications, and by proposing just and workable solutions. Such a study could therefore be justified if nothing practical ever came of it, for it helps you develop socially and intellectually.

We must always keep in mind two correlative truths about the principles we find in the Catholic tradition. The first is that, being right principles, they are indispensable for arriving at sound solutions to our national problems. The second is that these principles of themselves solve nothing. The facts relevant to the problem must be carefully gathered. Only after the factual information is complete can principles be intelligently applied.

The Constitution of the United States

PREAMBLE

We the people of the United States, in order to form a more perfect union, establish justice, insure domestic tranquillity, provide for the common defense, promote the general welfare, and secure the blessings of liberty to ourselves and our posterity, do ordain and establish this Constitution for the United States of America.

ARTICLE I: THE LEGISLATURE

Section 1. Establishment of Congress. All legislative powers herein granted shall be vested in a Congress of the United States, which shall consist of a Senate and House of Representatives.

Section 2. House of Representatives. 1. The House of Representatives shall be composed of members chosen every second year by the people of the several States, and the electors in each State shall have the qualifications requisite for electors of the most numerous branch of the State legislature.

2. No person shall be a representative who shall not have attained to the age of twenty-five years, and been seven years a citizen of the United States, and who shall not, when elected, be an inhabitant of that State in which he shall be chosen.

3. Representatives and direct taxes[1] shall be apportioned among the several States which may be included within this Union, according to their respective numbers, which shall be determined by adding to the whole number of free persons, including those bound to service for a term of years, and excluding Indians not taxed, three fifths of all other persons.[2] The actual enumeration shall be made within three years after the first meeting of the Congress of the United States, and within every subsequent term of ten years, in such manner as they shall by law direct. The number of representatives shall not exceed one for every thirty thousand, but each State shall have at least one representative; and until such enumeration shall be made, the State of New Hampshire shall be entitled to choose three, Massachusetts eight, Rhode Island and Providence Plantations one, Connecticut five, New York six, New Jersey four, Pennsylvania eight, Delaware one, Maryland six, Virginia ten, North Carolina five, South Carolina five, and Georgia three.

4. When vacancies happen in the representation from any State, the executive authority thereof shall issue writs of election to fill such vacancies.

5. The House of Representatives shall choose their speaker and other officers; and shall have the sole power of impeachment.

Section 3. Senate. 1. The Senate of the United States shall be composed of two senators from each State, chosen by the legislature thereof,[3] for six years; and each senator shall have one vote.

2. Immediately after they shall be assembled in consequence of the first election, they shall be divided as equally as may be into three classes. The seats of the senators of the first class shall be vacated at the expiration of the second year, of the second class at the expiration of the fourth year, and of the third class at the expiration of the sixth year, so that one third may be chosen every second year; and if vacancies happen by resignation, or otherwise, during the recess of the legislature of any State, the executive thereof may make temporary appointments until the next meeting of the legislature, which shall then fill such vacancies.[4]

3. No person shall be a senator who shall not have attained to the age of thirty years, and been nine years a citizen of the United States, and who shall not, when elected, be an inhabitant of that State for which he shall be chosen.

4. The Vice President of the United States shall be President of the Senate, but shall have no vote, unless they be equally divided.

5. The Senate shall choose their other officers, and also a president pro tempore, in the absence of the Vice President, or when he shall exercise the office of the President of the United States.

---

[1] Revised by the Sixteenth Amendment.
[2] Revised by the Fourteenth Amendment.
[3] Revised by the Seventeenth Amendment.
[4] Revised by the Seventeenth Amendment.

6. The Senate shall have the sole power to try all impeachments. When sitting for that purpose, they shall be on oath or affirmation. When the President of the United States is tried, the chief justice shall preside: and no person shall be convicted without the concurrence of two thirds of the members present.

7. Judgment in cases of impeachment shall not extend further than to removal from office, and disqualifications to hold and enjoy any office of honor, trust or profit under the United States: but the party convicted shall nevertheless be liable and subject to indictment, trial, judgment and punishment, according to law.

Section 4. Election and Meeting of Congress. 1. The times, places, and manner of holding elections for senators and representatives, shall be prescribed in each State by the legislature thereof; but the Congress may at any time by law make or alter such regulations, except as to the places of choosing senators.

2. The Congress shall assemble at least once in every year, and such meeting shall be on the first Monday in December, unless they shall by law appoint a different day.[5]

Section 5. Congressional Organization and Procedure. 1. Each House shall be the judge of the elections, returns and qualifications of its own members, and a majority of each shall constitute a quorum to do business; but a smaller number may adjourn from day to day, and may be authorized to compel the attendance of absent members, in such manner, and under such penalties as each House may provide.

2. Each House may determine the rules of its proceedings, punish its members for disorderly behavior, and, with the concurrence of two thirds, expel a member.

3. Each House shall keep a journal of its proceedings, and from time to time publish the same, excepting such parts as may in their judgment require secrecy; and the yeas and nays of the members of either House on any question shall, at the desire of one fifth of those present, be entered on the journal.

4. Neither House, during the session of Congress, shall, without the consent of the other, adjourn for more than three days, nor to any other place than that in which the two Houses shall be sitting.

---

[5] Revised by the Twentieth Amendment.

Section 6. Compensations, Privileges, and Disabilities of Members. 1. The senators and representatives shall receive a compensation for their services, to be ascertained by law, and paid out of the Treasury of the United States. They shall in all cases, except treason, felony, and breach of the peace, be privileged from arrest during their attendance at the session of their respective Houses, and in going to and returning from the same; and for any speech or debate in either House, they shall not be questioned in any other place.

2. No senator or representative shall, during the time for which he was elected, be appointed to any civil office under the authority of the United States, which shall have been created, or the emoluments whereof shall have been increased during such time; and no person holding any office under the United States shall be a member of either House during his continuance in office.

Section 7. Procedures in Making Laws. 1. All bills for raising revenue shall originate in the House of Representatives; but the Senate may propose or concur with amendments as on other bills.

2. Every bill which shall have passed the House of Representatives and the Senate, shall, before it becomes a law, be presented to the President of the United States; if he approves he shall sign it, but if not he shall return it, with his objections to that House in which it shall have originated, who shall enter the objections at large on their journal, and proceed to reconsider it. If after such reconsideration two thirds of that House shall agree to pass the bill, it shall be sent, together with the objections, to the other House, by which it shall likewise be reconsidered, and if approved by two thirds of that House, it shall become a law. But in all such cases the votes of both Houses shall be determined by yeas and nays, and the names of the persons voting for and against the bill shall be entered on the journal of each House respectively. If any bill shall not be returned by the President within ten days (Sundays excepted) after it shall have been presented to him, the same shall be a law, in like manner as if he had signed it, unless the Congress by their adjournment prevent its return, in which case it shall not be a law.

3. Every order, resolution, or vote to which

the concurrence of the Senate and the House of Representatives may be necessary (except on a question of adjournment) shall be presented to the President of the United States; and before the same shall take effect, shall be approved by him, or being disapproved by him, shall be repassed by two thirds of the Senate and House of Representatives, according to the rules and limitations prescribed in the case of a bill.

Section 8. Powers of Congress. The Congress shall have the power:

1. To lay and collect taxes, duties, imposts, and excises, to pay the debts, and provide for the common defense and general welfare of the United States; but all duties, imports, and excises shall be uniform throughout the United States;

2. To borrow money on the credit of the United States;

3. To regulate commerce with foreign nations, and among the several States, and with the Indian tribes;

4. To establish a uniform rule of naturalization, and uniform laws on the subject of bankruptcies throughout the United States;

5. To coin money, regulate the value thereof, and of foreign coin, and fix the standard of weights and measures;

6. To provide for the punishment of counterfeiting the securities and current coin of the United States;

7. To establish post offices and post roads;

8. To promote the progress of science and useful arts, by securing for limited times to authors and inventors the exclusive right to their respective writings and discoveries;

9. To constitute tribunals inferior to the Supreme Court;

10. To define and punish piracies and felonies committed on the high seas, and offenses against the law of nations;

11. To declare war, grant letters of marque and reprisal, and make rules concerning captures on land and water;

12. To raise and support armies, but no appropriation of money to that use shall be for a longer term than two years;

13. To provide and maintain a navy;

14. To make rules for the government and regulation of the land and naval forces;

15. To provide for calling forth the militia to execute the laws of the Union, suppress insurrections and repel invasions;

16. To provide for organizing, arming, and disciplining the militia, and for governing such part of them as may be employed in the service of the United States, reserving to the States respectively, the appointment of the officers, and the authority of training the militia according to the discipline prescribed by Congress;

17. To exercise exclusive legislation in all cases whatsoever, over such district (not exceeding ten miles square) as may, by cession of particular States, and the acceptance of Congress, become the seat of the government of the United States, and to exercise like authority over all places purchased by the consent of the legislature of the State in which the same shall be, for the erection of forts, magazines, arsenals, dockyards, and other needful buildings; and

18. To make all laws which shall be necessary and proper for carrying into execution the foregoing powers, and all other powers vested by this Constitution in the government of the United States, or in any department or officer thereof.

Section 9. Powers Denied to Congress. 1. The migration or importation of such persons as any of the States now existing shall think proper to admit, shall not be prohibited by the Congress prior to the year one thousand eight hundred and eight, but a tax or duty may be imposed on such importation, not exceeding ten dollars for each person.

2. The privilege of the writ of habeas corpus shall not be suspended, unless when in cases of rebellion or invasion the public safety may require it.

3. No bill of attainder or ex post facto law shall be passed.

4. No capitation, or other direct, tax shall be laid, unless in proportion to the census or enumeration hereinbefore directed to be taken.[6]

5. No tax or duty shall be laid on articles exported from any State.

6. No preference shall be given by any regulation of commerce or revenue to the ports of one State over those of another: nor shall ves-

---

[6] Revised by the Sixteenth Amendment.

sels bound to, or from, one State be obliged to enter, clear, or pay duties in another.

7. No money shall be drawn from the treasury, but in consequence of appropriations made by law; and a regular statement and account of the receipts and expenditures of all public money shall be published from time to time.

8. No title of nobility shall be granted by the United States; and no person holding any office of profit or trust under them, shall, without the consent of the Congress, accept of any present, emolument, office, or title, of any kind whatever, from any king, prince, or foreign State.

Section 10. Powers Denied to the States. 1. No State shall enter into any treaty, alliance, or confederation; grant letters of marque and reprisal; coin money; emit bills of credit; make anything but gold and silver coin a tender in payment of debts; pass any bill of attainder, ex post facto law, or law impairing the obligation of contracts, or grant any title of nobility.

2. No State shall, without the consent of the Congress, lay any imposts or duties on imports or exports, except what may be absolutely necessary for executing its inspection laws: and the net produce of all duties and imposts laid by any State on imports or exports, shall be for the use of the Treasury of the United States; and all such laws shall be subject to the revision and control of the Congress.

3. No State shall, without the consent of the Congress, lay any duty of tonnage, keep troops, or ships of war in time of peace, enter into any agreement or compact with another State, or with a foreign power, or engage in war, unless actually invaded, or in such imminent danger as will not admit of delay.

ARTICLE II: THE EXECUTIVE

Section 1. President and Vice President. 1. The executive power shall be vested in a President of the United States of America. He shall hold his office during the term of four years, and, together with the Vice President, chosen for the same term, be elected as follows:

2. Each State shall appoint, in such manner as the legislature thereof may direct, a number of electors, equal to the whole number of senators and representatives to which the State may be entitled in the Congress: but no sen-

ator or representative, or person holding an office of trust or profit under the United States, shall be appointed an elector.

The electors shall meet in their respective States, and vote by ballot for two persons, of whom one at least shall not be an inhabitant of the same State with themselves. And they shall make a list of all the persons voted for, and of the number of votes for each; which list they shall sign and certify, and transmit sealed to the seat of the government of the United States, directed to the president of the Senate. The president of the Senate shall, in the presence of the Senate and House of Representatives, open all the certificates, and the votes shall then be counted. The person having the greatest number of votes shall be the President, if such number be a majority of the whole number of electors appointed; and if there be more than one who have such majority, and have an equal number of votes, then the House of Representatives shall immediately choose by ballot one of them for President; and if no person have a majority, then from the five highest on the list the said House shall in like manner choose the President. But in choosing the President, the votes shall be taken by States, the representation from each State having one vote; a quorum for this purpose shall consist of a member or members from two thirds of the States, and a majority of all the States shall be necessary to a choice. In every case, after the choice of the President, the person having the greatest number of votes of the electors shall be the Vice President. But if there should remain two or more who have equal votes, the Senate shall choose from them by ballot the Vice President.[7]

3. The Congress may determine the time of choosing the electors, and the day on which they shall give their votes; which day shall be the same throughout the United States.

4. No person except a natural born citizen, or a citizen of the United States, at the time of the adoption of this Constitution, shall be eligible to the office of President; neither shall any person be eligible to that office who shall not have attained to the age of thirty-five years, and been fourteen years a resident within the United States.

---

[7] Repealed by the Twelfth Amendment.

5. In case of the removal of the President from office, or of his death, resignation, or inability to discharge the powers and duties of the said office, the same shall devolve on the Vice President, and the Congress may by law provide for the case of removal, death, resignation, or inability, both of the President and Vice President, declaring what officer then shall act as President, and such officer shall act accordingly, until the disability be removed, or a President shall be elected.

6. The President shall, at stated times, receive for his services a compensation, which shall neither be increased nor diminished during the period for which he shall have been elected, and he shall not receive within that period any other emolument from the United States, or any of them.

7. Before he enter on the execution of his office, he shall take the following oath or affirmation:—"I do solemnly swear (or affirm) that I will faithfully execute the office of President of the United States, and will to the best of my ability, preserve, protect and defend the Constitution of the United States."

Section 2. Powers of the President. 1. The President shall be commander in chief of the army and navy of the United States, and of the militia of the several States, when called into the actual service of the United States; he may require the opinion, in writing, of the principal officer in each of the executive departments, upon any subject relating to the duties of their respective offices, and he shall have power to grant reprieves and pardons for offenses against the United States, except in cases of impeachment.

2. He shall have power, by and with the advice and consent of the Senate, to make treaties, provided two thirds of the senators present concur; and he shall nominate, and by and with the advice and consent of the Senate, shall appoint ambassadors, other public ministers and consuls, judges of the Supreme Court, and all other officers of the United States, whose appointments are not herein otherwise provided for, and which shall be established by law: but the Congress may by law vest the appointment of such inferior officers, as they think proper, in the President alone, in the courts of law, or in the heads of departments.

3. The President shall have power to fill up all vacancies that may happen during the recess of the Senate, by granting commissions which shall expire at the end of their next session.

Section 3. Duties of the President. He shall from time to time give to the Congress information of the state of the Union, and recommend to their consideration such measures as he shall judge necessary and expedient; he may, on extraordinary occasions, convene both Houses, or either of them, and in case of disagreement between them with respect to the time of adjournment, he may adjourn them to such time as he shall think proper; he shall receive ambassadors and other public ministers; he shall take care that the laws be faithfully executed, and shall commission all the officers of the United States.

Section 4. Impeachment. The President, Vice President, and all civil officers of the United States, shall be removed from office on impeachment for, and conviction of, treason, bribery, or other high crimes and misdemeanors.

ARTICLE III: THE JUDICIARY

Section 1. Establishment of Federal Courts. The judicial power of the United States shall be vested in one Supreme Court, and in such inferior courts as the Congress may from time to time ordain and establish. The judges, both of the Supreme and inferior courts, shall hold their offices during good behavior, and shall, at stated times, receive for their services, a compensation, which shall not be diminished during their continuance in office.

Section 2. Jurisdiction of Federal Courts. 1. The judicial power shall extend to all cases, in law and equity, arising under this Constitution, the laws of the United States, and treaties made, or which shall be made, under their authority;—to all cases affecting ambassadors, other public ministers and consuls;—to all cases of admiralty and maritime jurisdiction;—to controversies to which the United States shall be a party;—to controversies between two or more States;—between a State and citizens of another State;[8]—between citizens of different States;—between citizens of the same State

---

[8] Revised by the Eleventh Amendment.

claiming lands under grants of different States, and between a State, or the citizens thereof, and foreign States, citizens or subjects.

2. In all cases affecting ambassadors, other public ministers and consuls, and those in which a State shall be party, the Supreme Court shall have original jurisdiction. In all the other cases before mentioned, the Supreme Court shall have appellate jurisdiction, both as to law and to fact, with such exceptions, and under such regulations as the Congress shall make.

3. The trial of all crimes, except in cases of impeachment, shall be by jury; and such trial shall be held in the State where the said crimes shall have been committed; but when not committed within any State, the trial shall be at such place or places as the Congress may by law have directed.

Section 3. Treason. 1. Treason against the United States shall consist only in levying war against them, or in adhering to their enemies, giving them aid and comfort. No person shall be convicted of treason unless on the testimony of two witnesses to the same overt act, or on confession in open court.

2. The Congress shall have power to declare the punishment of treason, but no attainder of treason shall work corruption of blood, or forfeiture except during the life of the person attained.

ARTICLE IV: THE STATES

Section 1. States Relationships. Full faith and credit shall be given in each State to the public acts, records, and judicial proceedings of every other State. And the Congress may by general laws prescribe the manner in which such acts, records and proceedings shall be proved, and the effect thereof.

Section 2. Duties of States to States. 1. The citizens of each State shall be entitled to all privileges and immunities of citizens in the several States.[9]

2. A person charged in any State with treason, felony, or other crime, who shall flee from justice, and be found in another State, shall on demand of the executive authority of the State from which he fled, be delivered up to be re-

moved to the State having jurisdiction of the crime.

3. No person held to service or labor in one State under the laws thereof, escaping into another, shall, in consequence of any law or regulation therein, be discharged from such service or labor, but shall be delivered up on claim of the party to whom such service or labor may be due.[10]

Section 3. New States and Territories. 1. New States may be admitted by the Congress into this Union; but no new State shall be formed or erected within the jurisdiction of any other State; nor any State be formed by the junction of two or more States, or parts of States, without the consent of the legislatures of the States concerned as well as of the Congress.

2. The Congress shall have power to dispose of and make all needful rules and regulations respecting the territory or other property belonging to the United States; and nothing in this Constitution shall be so construed as to prejudice any claims of the United States, or of any particular State.

Section 4. Protection of the States. The United States shall guarantee to every State in this Union a republican form of government, and shall protect each of them against invasion; and on application of the legislature, or of the executive (when the legislature cannot be convened) against domestic violence.

ARTICLE V: THE PROCESS OF AMENDMENT

The Congress, whenever two thirds of both Houses shall deem it necessary, shall propose amendments to this Constitution, or, on the application of the legislatures of two thirds of the several States, shall call a convention for proposing amendments, which in either case, shall be valid to all intents and purposes, as part of this Constitution when ratified by the legislatures of three fourths of the several States, or by conventions in three fourths thereof, as the one or the other mode of ratification may be proposed by the Congress; Provided that no amendment which may be made prior to the year one thousand eight hundred and eight shall in any manner affect the first and fourth clauses in the ninth section of the first article; and that no State, without its

---

[9] Elaborated by the Fourteenth Amendment, Sec. 1.

[10] See the Thirteenth Amendment.

consent, shall be deprived of its equal suffrage in the Senate.

ARTICLE VI: THE SUPREME LAW OF THE LAND

1. All debts contracted and engagements entered into, before the adoption of this Constitution, shall be as valid against the United States under this Constitution, as under the Confederation.

2. This Constitution, and the laws of the United States which shall be made in pursuance thereof; and all treaties made, or which shall be made, under the authority of the United States, shall be the supreme law of the land; and the Judges in every State shall be bound thereby, anything in the Constitution or laws of any State to the contrary notwithstanding.

3. The senators and representatives before mentioned, and the members of the several State legislatures, and all executive and judicial officers, both of the United States and of the several States, shall be bound by oath or affirmation to support this Constitution; but no religious test shall ever be required as a qualification to any office or public trust under the United States.

ARTICLE VII: RATIFICATION OF THE CONSTITUTION

The ratification of the conventions of nine States shall be sufficient for the establishment of this Constitution between the States so ratifying the same.

Done in Convention by the unanimous consent of the States present the seventeenth day of September in the year of our Lord one thousand seven hundred and eighty-seven, and of the independence of the United States of America the twelfth. In witness whereof we have hereunto subscribed our names.

AMENDMENTS:

First ten amendments (Bill of Rights) proposed by Congress September 25, 1789; ratified by three-fourths of the states December 15, 1791.

Amendment I. Congress shall make no law respecting an establishment of religion, or prohibiting the free exercise thereof; or abridging the freedom of speech, or of the press; or the right of the people peaceably to assemble, and to petition the government for a redress of grievances.

Amendment II. A well regulated militia, being necessary to the security of a free State, the right of the people to keep and bear arms, shall not be infringed.

Amendment III. No soldier shall, in time of peace be quartered in any house, without the consent of the owner, nor in time of war, but in a manner to be prescribed by law.

Amendment IV. The right of the people to be secure in their persons, houses, papers, and effects, against unreasonable searches and seizures, shall not be violated, and no warrants shall issue, but upon probable cause, supported by oath or affirmation, and particularly describing the place to be searched, and the persons or things to be seized.

Amendment V. No person shall be held to answer for a capital, or otherwise infamous crime, unless on a presentment or indictment of a grand jury, except in cases arising in the land or naval forces, or in the militia, when in actual service in time of war or public danger; nor shall any person be subject for the same offense to be twice put in jeopardy of life or limb; nor shall be compelled in any criminal case to be a witness against himself, nor be deprived of life, liberty, or property, without due process of law; nor shall private property be taken for public use without just compensation.

Amendment VI. In all criminal prosecutions, the accused shall enjoy the right to a speedy and public trial, by an impartial jury of the State and district wherein the crime shall have been committed, which district shall have been previously ascertained by law, and to be informed of the nature and cause of the accusation; to be confronted with the witnesses against him; to have compulsory process for obtaining witnesses in his favor, and to have the assistance of counsel for his defense.

Amendment VII. In suits at common law, where the value in controversy shall exceed twenty dollars, the right of trial by jury shall be preserved, and no fact tried by a jury shall be otherwise re-examined in any court of the United States, than according to the rules of the common law.

Amendment VIII. Excessive bail shall not be required, nor excessive fines imposed, nor cruel and unusual punishments inflicted.

Amendment IX. The enumeration in the Constitution of certain rights shall not be construed to deny or disparage others retained by the people.

Amendment X. The powers not delegated to the United States by the Constitution, nor prohibited by it to the States, are reserved to the States respectively, or to the people.

Amendment XI. Proposed by Congress March 5, 1794; ratified January 8, 1798.

The judicial power of the United States shall not be construed to extend to any suit in law or equity, commenced or prosecuted against one of the United States by citizens of another State, or by citizens or subjects of any foreign State.

Amendment XII. Proposed by Congress December 12, 1803; ratified September 25, 1804.

The electors shall meet in their respective States, and vote by ballot for President and Vice President, one of whom, at least, shall not be an inhabitant of the same State with themselves; they shall name in their ballots the person voted for as President, and in distinct ballots, the person voted for as Vice President, and they shall make distinct lists of all persons voted for as President and of all persons voted for as Vice President, and of the number of votes for each, which lists they shall sign and certify, and transmit sealed to the seat of the government of the United States, directed to the President of the Senate;—The President of the Senate shall, in the presence of the Senate and House of Representatives, open all the certificates and the votes shall then be counted;—The person having the greatest number of votes for President, shall be the President, if such number be a majority of the whole number of electors appointed; and if no person have such majority, then from the persons having the highest numbers not exceeding three on the list of those voted for as President, the House of Representatives shall choose immediately, by ballot, the President. But in choosing the President, the votes shall be taken by States, the representation from each State having one vote; a quorum for this pur-

pose shall consist of a member or members from two thirds of the States, and a majority of all the States shall be necessary to a choice. And if the House of Representatives shall not choose a President whenever the right of choice shall devolve upon them, before the fourth day of March next following, then the Vice President shall act as President, as in the case of the death or other constitutional disability of the President. The person having the greatest number of votes as Vice President shall be the Vice President, if such number be a majority of the whole number of electors appointed, and if no person have a majority, then from the two highest numbers on the list, the Senate shall choose the Vice President; a quorum for the purpose shall consist of two thirds of the whole number of Senators, and a majority of the whole number shall be necessary to a choice. But no person constitutionally ineligible to the office of President shall be eligible to that of Vice President of the United States.

Amendment XIII. Proposed by Congress February 1, 1865; ratified December 18, 1865.

Section 1. Neither slavery nor involuntary servitude, except as punishment for crime whereof the party shall have been duly convicted, shall exist within the United States, or any place subject to their jurisdiction.

Section 2. Congress shall have power to enforce this article by appropriate legislation.

Amendment XIV. Proposed by Congress June 16, 1866; ratified July 23, 1868.

Section 1. All persons born or naturalized in the United States, and subject to the jurisdiction thereof, are citizens of the United States and of the State wherein they reside. No State shall make or enforce any law which shall abridge the privileges or immunities of citizens of the United States; nor shall any State deprive any person of life, liberty, or property, without due process of law; nor deny to any person within its jurisdiction the equal protection of the laws.

Section 2. Representatives shall be apportioned among the several States according to their respective numbers, counting the whole number of persons in each State, excluding Indians not taxed. But when the right to vote at any election for the choice of electors for President and Vice President of the United States, representatives in Congress, the executive and judicial officers of a State, or the members of the legislature thereof, is denied to any of the male inhabitants of such State, being twenty-one years of age, and citizens of the United States, or in any way abridged, except for participation in rebellion, or other crime, the basis of representation therein shall be reduced in the proportion which the number of such male citizens shall bear to the whole number of male citizens twenty-one years of age in such State.

Section 3. No person shall be a senator or representative in Congress, or elector of President and Vice President, or hold any office, civil or military, under the United States, or under any State, who having previously taken an oath, as a member of Congress, or as an officer of the United States, or as a member of any State legislature, or as an executive or judicial officer of any State, to support the Constitution of the United States, shall have engaged in insurrection or rebellion against the same, or given aid or comfort to the enemies thereof. But Congress may by a vote of two thirds of each House, remove such disability.

Section 4. The validity of the public debt of the United States, authorized by law, including debts incurred for payment of pensions and bounties for services in suppressing insurrection or rebellion, shall not be questioned. But neither the United States nor any State shall assume or pay any debt or obligation incurred in aid of insurrection or rebellion against the United States, or any claim for the loss or emancipation of any slave; but all such debts, obligations, and claims shall be held illegal and void.

Section 5. The Congress shall have power to enforce, by appropriate legislation, the provisions of this article.

Amendment XV. Proposed by Congress February 26, 1869; ratified March 30, 1870.

Section 1. The right of citizens of the United States to vote shall not be denied or abridged by the United States or by any State on account of race, color, or previous condition of servitude.

Section 2. The Congress shall have power to enforce this article by appropriate legislation.

Amendment XVI. Proposed by Congress July 12, 1909; ratified February 25, 1913.

The Congress shall have power to lay and collect taxes on incomes, from whatever source derived, without apportionment among the several States, and without regard to any census or enumeration.

Amendment XVII. Proposed by Congress May 16, 1912; ratified May 31, 1913.

The Senate of the United States shall be composed of two senators from each state, elected by the people thereof, for six years; and each senator shall have one vote. The electors in each State shall have the qualifications requisite for electors of the most numerous branch of the State legislature.

When vacancies happen in the representation of any State in the Senate, the executive authority of such State shall issue writs of election to fill such vacancies: *Provided,* That the legislature of any State may empower the executive thereof to make temporary appointments until the people fill the vacancies by election as the legislature may direct.

This amendment shall not be so construed as to affect the election or term of any senator chosen before it becomes valid as part of the Constitution.

Amendment XVIII.[11] Proposed by Congress December 18, 1917; ratified January 29, 1919.

After one year from the ratification of this article, the manufacture, sale, or transportation of intoxicating liquors within, the importation thereof into, or the exportation thereof from the United States and all territory subject to the jurisdiction thereof for beverage purposes is hereby prohibited.

The Congress and the several States shall have concurrent power to enforce this article by appropriate legislation.

This article shall be inoperative unless it shall have been ratified as an amendment to the Constitution by the legislatures of the several States, as provided in the Constitution, within seven years from the date of the submission hereof to the states by Congress.

Amendment XIX. Proposed by Congress June 4, 1919; ratified August 26, 1920.

---

[11] Repealed by the Twenty-first Amendment.

The right of citizens of the United States to vote shall not be denied or abridged by the United States or by any State on account of sex.

The Congress shall have power by appropriate legislation to enforce the provisions of this article.

Amendment XX. Proposed by Congress March 3, 1932; ratified February 6, 1933.

Section 1. The terms of the President and Vice President shall end at noon on the 20th day of January, and the terms of Senators and Representatives at noon on the 3d day of January, of the years in which such terms would have ended if this article had not been ratified; and the terms of their successors shall then begin.

Section 2. The Congress shall assemble at least once in every year, and such meeting shall begin at noon on the 3d day of January, unless they shall by law appoint a different day.

Section 3. If, at the time fixed for the beginning of the term of the President, the President-elect shall have died, the Vice President-elect shall become President. If a President shall not have been chosen before the time fixed for the beginning of his term, or if the President-elect shall have failed to qualify, then the Vice President-elect shall act as President until a President shall have qualified; and the Congress may by law provide for the case wherein neither a President-elect nor a Vice President-elect shall have qualified, declaring who shall then act as President, or the manner in which one who is to act shall be selected, and such person shall act accordingly until a President or Vice President shall have qualified.

Section 4. The Congress may by law provide for the case of the death of any of the persons from whom the House of Representatives may choose a President whenever the right of choice shall have devolved upon them, and for the case of the death of any of the persons from whom the Senate may choose a Vice President whenever the right of choice shall have devolved upon them.

Section 5. Sections 1 and 2 shall take effect on the 15th day of October following the ratification of this article.

Section 6. This article shall be inoperative unless it shall have been ratified as an amendment to the Constitution by the legislatures of three-fourths of the several States within seven years from the date of its submission.

Amendment XXI. Proposed by Congress February 20, 1933; ratified December 5, 1933.

Section 1. The Eighteenth Article of amendment to the Constitution of the United States is hereby repealed.

Section 2. The transportation or importation into any State, Territory, or possession of the United States for delivery or use therein of intoxicating liquors in violation of the laws thereof, is hereby prohibited.

Section 3. This article shall be inoperative unless it shall have been ratified as an amendment to the Constitution by conventions in the several States, as provided in the Constitution, within seven years from the date of the submission thereof to the States by the Congress.

Amendment XXII. Proposed by Congress March 12, 1947; ratified February 26, 1951.

No person shall be elected to the office of the President more than twice, and no person who has held the office of President, or acted as President, for more than two years of a term to which some other person was elected President shall be elected to the office of the President more than once.

But this article shall not apply to any person holding the office of President when this article was proposed by the Congress, and shall not prevent any person who may be holding the office of President, or acting as President, during the term within which this article becomes operative from holding the office of President or acting as President during the remainder of such term.

This article shall be inoperative unless it shall have been ratified as an amendment to the Constitution by the legislatures of three-fourths of the several states within seven years from the date of its submission to the States by the Congress.

Index

A page number in italics indicates a page on which there is an illustration of the subject and no other reference. Entries on other pages, however, may be illustrated.

Federal government, U.S.: (cont.)

489; regulatory commissions of, 423; role of as civil-rights protector, 72; role of in maintaining prosperity, 309–310; role of in promoting education, 498; role of in slum-clearance and housing projects, 497; separation of powers a basic doctrine in, 410; social security program of, 494–497; sources of revenue, 482–483; spending policies of and their effect on national economy, 476–477; supremacy of confirmed by Supreme Court, 392–393

Federal Home Loan Bank, established, 269

Federal Housing Authority (FHA), purpose of, 269

Federal Intermediate Credit Act (1923), provisions of, 343

Federal Mediation and Conciliation Board, role of in union disputes, 324

Federal Reserve Act (1913), provisions of, 343

Felony, defined, 209

Feminism, adverse effects of on family, 245–246

Fifteenth Amendment provisions of, 66, 194

Fifth Amendment: "due process of law" clause, 85; provisions of, 83

Filibustering, congressional restrictions on, 415

First Amendment: aim of in respect to religion, 30, 46, 47; rights guaranteed by, 65, 75; Supreme Court decisions concerning, 48–53; Supreme Court doctrine concerning terms of, 76–77

Flag: pledge to, 50; proposed changes for, 398

Floods, control of: allied to soil conservation, 350; federal and state responsibility for, 352; necessity of forests for, 352

Florida: denounces Supreme Court ruling on desegregation, 150; migrant farm workers in, 287; Supreme Court of, 443

Food: importance of to proper function of family, 250; a factor in population trends, 173

Food and Agricultural Organization (FAO), accomplishments of, 587–588

Fordney-McCumber Act (1922), places high tariff on imports, 552

Foreign affairs, U.S.: conduct of, 512–516; control of changed by custom and necessity, 512; limitations on, 515–516. See also Foreign policy

Foreign aid: basic problem of, 567; function of International Cooperation Administration, 567; need for after World War II, 560–561; opinions on role of in U.S. foreign policy, 567; principles concerning sound program of, 567–568

Foreign Operations Administration (FOA), purpose of, 567

Foreign policy (general), a principal duty of state, 508

Foreign policy, U.S.: changing nature of, 509; concerning "cold war," 530–531; commitment, meaning of, 511–512; concerning Korea, 535; conduct of, 511–512; early neutrality policy during World War II, 529; early objectives of, 527–528; Good Neighbor Policy, 519; and European economic recovery, 561; historical background of, 526–527; opinions on role of foreign aid in, 567; proper position of military power in, 512; and problems involving foreign aid, 566; and prudent use of power, 511–512; UN co-operation a feature of, 595; and World War I, 528; between world wars, 529–530

Forests: approved methods of cutting, 353, 354; exploitation of, 352–353; fire protection of, 353; government's role in conservation of, 353; necessary to prevention of soil erosion and floods, 352

Forest Service: on forest exploitation, 353; on lumber needs, 352; work of, 350

Formosa: legal status of, undetermined, 537; objective of Communist China, 535; position of Nationalist government on, 537; strategic importance of to U.S., 537; U.S. policy concerning, 537; U.S. commitments to, 537

Fort Myer, Va., group-study class in history, 144

Fosdick, Raymond, on importance of educational freedom, 142

Foster, William Z., Communist activity of, 329

Fourteenth Amendment: citizenship defined in, 80; provisions of, 66, 68, 194, 393; Supreme Court interpretation of, 67–68

Fourth Amendment, provisions of, 84

France: diminishing power of, 528, 529; family allowance plan in, 252

Frankfurter, Felix, on Minersville v. Gobitis, 50–51

Freedom: correct and wrong notions of, 62–63; historical development of in U.S., 62–72

Freedom, academic: abused by Communists, 147, 148; problems of, 147–150

Front organizations, methods of determining, 108–109

Frost, Robert, 155

General Assembly (UN): function of, 582, 583

Geneva, summit conference at, 511

Geography, importance of to nation's power, 510

Georgia: age requirements for voting in, 372; denounces Supreme Court ruling on desegregation, 150

Geriatrics, origin of, 172; scope of, 236

German Confederation, an example of confederate government, 390

Germany: aggression against Poland, 529; Nazi persecutions a cause of emigration from, 180; pre-Civil War emigration from, 176; a world power, 528, 529

Germany, West, admitted to NATO, 537–538

Gerontology, science of, 236

Gerrymandering, defined, 436

G.I. Bill of Rights, veterans' benefits under, 129

Gitlow v. New York, 67–68

Gompers, Samuel: 320; biography of, 360–361

Goodman, Leo, on immigration and labor, 182

Government (general): basic functions of, 365; common good, the goal of, 366; confederate form of, 390, 391; differences between strong and oppressive, 363–364; federal form of, 390–392, 391; forms of, 390–392, 391; Hamilton on true test of, 423; necessity of, 364; positive and promotional functions of, 366–367; principles of sound organization for, 424; problem of creating adequate, 18; purpose of, 365–367, 508; and trend toward welfare state, 492–494; unitary form of, 390, 391. See also Federal government; and forms listed below.

Government, confederate, nature of, 390

Government, federal: advantages of, 391; American system of, 392; disadvantages of, 391–392; nature of, 390–391

Government, limited, purpose of, 30–31

Government, local: on city level, 451–452; common features of, 446–448; on county level, 448–449; county and municipality important units of, 448; expenditures of, 478; municipal types of, 453–458, 455; reform proposals for, 448; types of, 446

Government, state: constitutional restrictions on, 399–400; expenditures of, 477–478; obligations of to federal government, 395; obligations of federal government to, 394–395;

Government, unitary, nature of, 390

Governor: executive powers of, 440–441; judicial

Law: due process of, Supreme Court statement on, 85; how a bill becomes one, 414, *416*
Law of nations, concept of, 508–509
"Law of population," formulated by Malthus, 172–173
Leadership, importance of to nation's power, 510
League of Nations: creation of, 528; purpose of, 580–581; U.S. Congress' stand on, 528; weakness of, 581
Legislation: direct, as remedy of disproportionate representation in state legislatures, 437–438; planned, problem of in state legislatures, 438–439; "pork-barrel," described, 482n.
Legislative Reorganization Act (1946), provisions of, 417
Legislatures, state: advantages of unicameral system, 435; disadvantages of unwieldy, 435; measures to control lobbies and pressure groups, 438; problem of representation in, 435–437; proposals for improving representative quality of, 436–437; qualifications of legislators, 434, residual powers of, 432, 434; recommendations for improving, 439; varying size of, 435
Leisure, a problem of modern industry, 22
Lend-Lease Act (1940), accomplishments of, 530
L'Enfant, Pierre Charles, biography of, 291
Lenin, Nicolai: and modern strategy of Communist revolution, *111*, 112; as official interpreter of Marxian communism, 113
Leo XIII, Pope, on separation of church and state, 54
Levittown, Pa., housing development at, *26*
Lewis, John L., *322*
Liberalism, meanings of, 42–43
Liberty: associated with productive-property ownership, 36; civil, in conflict with loyalty, 90–93; in relation to civil authority, 74–75; a right safeguarded by Constitution, 30
Library of Congress, *498*
Libya, U.S. military installations in, 523
Life, safeguarded by Constitution, 30
Ligutti, Msgr. Luigi: *276;* and development of Granger Homestead Settlement, 282; on farming as a way of life, 277; on importance of rural community, 275; on need for professional people in rural community, 280
Lincoln, Abraham: biography of, 117–118; and civil liberties during Civil War, 91
Lloyd-La Follette Act (1912), and removal from Civil Service, 473
Lobbies: influence of, 417, 438; regulation of, 417
Lobbying: a form of petitioning, 79; regulated by Legislative Reorganization Act, 417
"Logrolling," described, 482n.
Louisiana, denounces Supreme Court ruling on desegregation, 150
Loyalty: in conflict with civil liberty, 90–93; Eisenhower program, 96; nature of 88–89, 90; present-day problem of, 94–98; questions of in World War II, 92–93; Truman program, 94–96
Lynd, Albert, on Dewey's philosophy, 159

MacArthur, Gen. Douglas, commands UN forces in Korea, 589
McCarran, Sen. Patrick, *97*
McCarran Act (1950). *See* Internal Security Act
McCarran-Walter Act (1952): curbs immigration, 176; debate on, 240; and expulsion of undesirable aliens, 187; opinions concerning, 187–188; opposition to, 180–181; Truman defends veto of, 188
McCulloch v. *Maryland,* 400
McCollum Case: and religious teaching in schools,

McCollum Case: (cont.)
140–141; statement of U.S. bishops on, 56; Supreme Court decision, 52–53
MacCormick, Austin H., on treatment of criminals, 215
McGuffey's Readers, religious references in, 30
McLaurin v. *Oklahoma,* 149
Madison, James: biography of, 59; and religious freedom, 47
Malthus, Thomas, population theory of, 172–173; *173*
Management: artificial "demands" created by, 312–*313;* co-operation of with labor, 311–312, 329–330; obligations of, 310–311, 312; plans of for better relations with labor, 330–331; production problems of, 312; responsibility of toward worker, 330–331; restricted under Wagner Act, 326; role of in large-scale business, 305–306; under Taft-Hartley Act, 327
Mandamus writ, meaning of, 397n.
Manifesto on Rural Life, The on attitude toward rural-life problems, 275; on religious advantage of village community, 280
Mann, Horace, *124*
Manpower, profitable use of, 309
Mansfield, Sen. Mike, *521*
"Man's Relation to the Land," on efficient use of land, 346
Maps: air defense of North America, *603;* Asia, (1956), *538;* election (1824), *419;* election (1932), *383;* election (1952), *383;* Europe (1956), *532;* UN (1956), *586;* U.S., *396*
Marbury v. *Madison,* and Supreme Court's exercise of judicial review, 426
Marine Corps, U.S., and discrimination against Negroes, 81
Marriage: change in concept of, 247; purpose of, 244; and divorce (1940–1953), *248*
Marshall, Gen. George: *563;* on UMT, 606–607; on U.S. aid to Europe, 562. *See also* Marshall Plan
Marshall, John: biography of, 459–460; on interpretation of "implied powers," 400
Marshall Plan: administration of, 562–563; compared with Truman Doctrine, 531; development of, 562; purpose of, 531, 533
Marx, Karl: basic doctrines of communism formulated by, 109, 110, *111;* development of doctrines to present day, 112–113; as practical revolutionist, 112; view of capitalism, 111–112
Marxism: "infallible" doctrine of, 111; revolutionary aspect of, 112
Maryland, accepts Supreme Court ruling on desegregation, 149
Massachusetts: alien population in, 186; religion excluded from public schools, 125
Materialism, dialectical, 109–110
Materials, scarcity of, and economic value, 297. *See also* Raw materials
Maternity, provisions for services under Social Security Act, 497
Meaney, George, president of AFL-CIO, *322*
Medicine: accomplishments of, 225–227; preventive and rehabilitative, 230–232; government's role in, 230. *See also* Socialized medicine
Mental illness, increased incidence of, 233–234
Mentality: rural, 256; secularist, 22
Merger, a form of monopoly, 307
Metals, nonferrous, U.S. imports of, 570
Metropolitan area: and co-operation among component parts of, 260–261; created by decentralization in industry, 261; described, 260; of New York

Property, right to: derivation of, 75–76; necessary regulations of, 76
Proprietorship: advantages of, 303, 304, 305; a form of business, 302–303; tendency toward among small businesses, 304
Prosperity: causes of, 308–309; dependent on foreign trade; government's role in maintaining, 309–310
Protectionism, 555; arguments defending, 555–556; trend toward, 554
Protestant churches, membership in, 200–201
Protestants, views of concerning separation of church and state, 53–54
Protestants and Others United (PAOU), prejudicial aspects of, 201
Proxy, defined, 306n.
Punishment: a deterrent to crime, 208, 213; forms of, 214–215

Quadragesimo Anno (Pope Pius XI), on principle of subsidiarity, 369
Quotas. *See* Immigration

Racial groups: cause of anti-social attitudes in, 193; prejudice against, 192–193; present-day, 190
Radio, a factor in cultural standardization, 23
Railroads: Granger action against, 335; regulation of by ICC, 337
Ramspeck Act (1940), scope of Civil Service increased by, 468–469
Raw materials: importance of, 568–570; stockpiling of, 571; U.S. military needs and importing of, 570–571
Ray, P. Orman: on county government, 449–450; on increased function of state, 492
Recall, defined, 455n.
Reciprocal Trade Agreements Act (1934): effects of protectionists on, 556–557; and promotion of foreign trade, 549; purpose of, 556
Reclamation, Bureau of, function of, 348
Recreation: city's responsibility for, 267; importance of to proper family function, 250
Referendum: defined, 381n.; a form of direct legislation, 437–438; function of, 437
Reform institutions, and juvenile criminals, 220
Refugee Immigration Act (1953), 181
Refugees, UN activity aiding, 588
Regulation of Lobbying Act (1952), 79
Rehabilitation: accomplishments of states in, 232; community responsibility toward, 231; of criminals, 213–214; and disability insurance, 231–232
Religion: a deterrent to crime, 208; essential to attainment of family purposes, 244; excluded from public school curriculum, 125–126; encouraged in school curriculum by Northwest Ordinance, 28–29; and good citizenship, bishops' statement on, 30; importance of in colonial life, 28–30; lack of, a cause of crime, 212; proposals to include in school curriculum, 140; and public schools, 136–141; and released-time programs, 52–53, 140–141; Supreme Court decisions concerning, 48–53; Supreme Court views on government support of, 51–53
Religion, freedom of: guaranteed by Constitution, 30, 46–51, 65; and need for national unity, 22; part of American ideal, 33
Religious groups, prejudice against, 192; present-day, 190–191; relations among, 200–202
Rent control: during and after World War II, 270, 271; a factor in home-building lag, 270; problems created by, 271

Reorganization Act. *See* Legislative Reorganization Act
Representatives: length of term, 412; method of election, 411; requirements for eligibility, 412
Republican party: election expenditures of, 384; type of membership in, 378
Resources, material, importance of to nation's power, 510
Resources, natural. *See* Natural Resources
Revenue, constitutional limitations on raising and spending, 479–480
Richmond, Va., Board of Education, 456
"Right-to-work" laws, union shop prohibited by, 328
Rights, procedural: defined, 67n.; and legislative investigations, 85–86; review of, 82; Supreme Court reasoning on, 68
Rights, substantive: defined, 67n.; and First Amendment, 75; and Fourteenth Amendment, 68; Supreme Court reasoning on, 68
Riis, Jacob August, 186
Rochdale Weavers, first successful co-operative, 283
Rockhurst College, Mo., wage system of, 254
Rogers Act (1924), 550
Roosevelt, Franklin D.: biography of, 503; foreign policy of, 530; "four freedoms" of, 69–70; meeting with Ibn Saud, 531; Supreme Court reorganization attempt, 427; and Teheran and Yalta conferences, 530
Roosevelt, Theodore: biography of, 502; conservation program of, 348, 349
Rumania, status of after World War II, 530
Rural community: complexity of problems of, 275–277; composition of, 280; declining population in, 274, 275; dependent on elements beyond its control, 276–277; effect of industrial decentralization, 278–279; importance of, 274–275; importance of right attitude toward, 280; importance of school in, 282–283; influence of automobile on, 278; loss of personal and social values in, 279–280; percentage of population in, 256; prosperity of, dependent on farmer's income, 282; role of farmers' co-operatives in, 283–284; results of revolutionary changes in, 279; v. urban, 256–257; weakened by migration to city, 285;
Rural mentality, defined, 256
Rusk, Dr. Howard A., on problem of rehabilitative medicine, 230–231
Russia: Communist revolution in, 112; defeat of empire, 528. *For events after 1919, see* U.S.S.R.
Rutledge, Wiley B., on state support of religion, 51

Sabotage, existing legislation on, 98
Safety: an important responsibility of city, 265–266; restrictions on strikes endangering, 327
St. Lawrence River, U.S. interest in development of, 517–518
St. Lawrence Seaway, 518
St. Louis, Mo.: metropolitan area of, 260; tax on incomes earned in, 272
St. Michael's High School (Ariz.), first Navajo graduates of, 199
Salk, Dr. Jonas E., 224
Sanford, Edward, and Gitlow case, 68
Sanitation: problem of in crowded cities, 22; responsibility of city, 266; and slum problem, 263
Schall, Rev. James V., on use of civil power, 365
Schenck v. *United States,* 67
Schmiedeler, Rev. Edgar, advocates family allowance plan, 252
Schools: compulsory attendance laws, 128; expenditures per pupil (1852), 130; a factor in cultural

Truman, Harry S.: (*cont.*)
government as civil-rights protector, 72; defends veto of McCarran-Walter Act, 188; loyalty program of, 94–96; on needed revision of foreign trade policies, 554; Point Four policy of, 565; and policy of UN co-operation, 595; at Potsdam conference, *531;* on practical concern for successful family life, 243; on UMT, 606
Truman Doctrine, aimed against U.S.S.R., 531
Trust, a form of monopoly, 306
Trusteeship Council (UN), function of, 585–586
Tuberculosis, decreased death rate from, 225
Turkey, U.S. military aid to, 531
Twelfth Amendment, governs procedure of presidential elections, 418

Un-American Activities Committee, defines "subversive activity," 90; purpose of, 94
Unemployment, compensation under Social Security Act, 494–495
Unionization: effect of depression on, 319; mobility of workers an early deterrent to, 319
Unions, labor: aims of, 322–323; bargaining methods of, 323–324; collective bargaining a reason for existence of, 323–324; development of in Civil Service, 477; development of in U.S., 318–319; in Europe, 318; factors influencing composition of, 321; and "fringe benefits," 323; growth of, *317;* half-truths concerning, 328–329; increase in membership after Wagner Act, 326; industrialization a factor in, 319–320; legislation unfriendly toward, 328; and management, 330; necessity of, 316; opinions on worker's duty to join, 316–317; place of worker in, 329–330; political participation of, *386;* present-day membership in, 321–322; prospects of, 329–330; under Taft-Hartley Act, 327–328; rise of, 36
Union shop: a kind of union security, 323; prohibited under "right-to-work" laws, 328
United Automobile Workers, guaranteed annual wage a goal of, 322
United Auto Workers, affiliated with CIO, 321
United Mine Workers of America: aim of, 318; an independent union, 322; present membership in, 321
United Nations: aerial view, *583, 584;* agencies of, *584,* 587; Charter, provisions of, 593; Charter reforms advocated, 593–594; Economic and Social Council, function of, 585; General Assembly, function of, 582; inspired by "four freedoms," 70; as instrument for maintaining peace, 588–590; International Court of Justice, function of, 587; map, *586;* membership expanded, 590; and national sovereignty of U.S., 595; objectives of, 582; and question of China, 590–591; recognition of need for, 581–582; role of in Korean War, 589–590; Secretariat, function of, 587; Security Council, function of, 582–583, 585; social and economic activity of, 587–588; structure of, 582; Trusteeship Council, function of, 585–587; U.S. criticism of, 591–592; value of to U.S., 594–595
United Nations Educational and Scientific Commission (UNESCO), criticism of, 588
United Nations International Children's Fund (UNICF), accomplishments of, 587
United Nations Relief for Palestine Refugees, accomplishments of, 588
United States: budget receipts and expenditures, *488;* commitments to Formosa, 537; Communist party established in, 105; compared with U.S.S.R., *110, 601;* countermeasures against Soviet aggression,

United States: (*cont.*)
531, 533; defense problems of, 605–607; foreign affairs, conduct of, 512–516; foreign policy of, 511–512; foreign trade policy of, 552; Good Neighbor Policy of, 519; growing dependence on imported raw materials, 568–570; interests of in Africa, 522; interests of in Asia, 522–524; interests of in Caribbean area, 518–519; interests of in Europe, 520–521; interests of in Middle East, 521–522, interests of in North America, 517–519; interests of in South America, 519–520; military and economic aid to Europe, *520,* 563–564; military alliances of during World War II, 530; neutrality policy of during beginning of World War II, 529; objective of Communist revolutionary activity, 107; opposes UN membership for Communist China, 590–591; policy of concerning Korean conflict, 535; post-war foreign aid expenditures, 561, 563; production of, *606;* relations with U.S.S.R. during World War II, 530; a religious nation, 29; role of in European recovery, 560–566; sovereignty not violated by UN membership, 595; technical assistance to underdeveloped areas, 564–566; value of UN to, 594–595; widening international interests, *20*
United States Chamber of Commerce, business interests represented by, 386
United States Customs Court, jurisdiction of, 551
United States Tariff Commission, function of, 550
Urban community: advantage of decentralization on, 271; functions of, 265–268; haphazard growth of, 257, 259; modern problems of, 271–272; need for adequate planning, 262–263; slum problem of, 263–265; percentage of population in, 256; v. rural, 256–257; shift of population to, *275;* sources of revenue a pressing problem, 271–272
Urbanization: adverse effects of on family, 245; defined, 256; a factor in population trends, 173
U.S. v. *Tarble,* 393
U.S.S. *Coral Sea,* 480
U.S.S.R. (Union of Soviet Socialist Republics): ambiguity of foreign policy, 529; aggression of after World War II, 530–531; changes in policy after NATO, 534; cold war brought on by, 530–531; compared with U.S., *110, 601;* compulsory voting in, 374; diplomatic defeat of, 538; emerges as world power, 528; "peaceful co-existence" propaganda of, 539; post-war exploitation in Europe, 560–561; a threat to western European freedom, 521; a threat to Asia, 523–524; and use of veto in UN, 584, 589, 590
U.S. *Toledo,* 522

Value, surplus theory of, 110–111
Vermont: general store in, *276;* town meeting in, *32*
Veterans, assistance to by federal government, 129, 497
Veterans of Foreign Wars, in favor of UMT, 606
Veto: President's power of, 421; in UN, 583, 585, 588–589
Vinson, Fred, on necessity of reasonable limits on speech and press, 77
Virginia, denounces Supreme Court ruling on desegregation, 150
Virginia Bill of Rights, on freedom of religion, 28
Vote, right to, regulated by states, 80
Voting: age requirements for, 373; automatic machines for, *385;* compulsory, non-compatibility of, 374; constitutional provisions for, 399–400; percentage in 1952 election, 374; reasons for non-participation in, 374; requirements set by states, 372; resident and citizen qualifications for, 373